Praise for *OpenGL® Shading Language*

"The author has done an excellent job at setting the stage for shader development, what the purpose is, how to do it, and how it all fits together. He then develops on the advanced topics covering a great breadth in the appropriate level of detail. Truly a necessary book to own for any graphics developer!"

—Jeffery Galinovsky
Strategic Software Program Manager, Intel Corporation

"*OpenGL® Shading Language* provides a timely, thorough, and entertaining introduction to the only OpenGL ARB-approved high-level shading language in existence. Whether an expert or a novice, there are gems to be discovered throughout the book, and the reference pages will be your constant companion as you dig into the depths of the shading APIs. From algorithms to APIs, this book has you covered."

—Bob Kuehne
CEO, Blue Newt Software

"Computer graphics and rendering technologies just took a giant leap forward with hardware vendors rapidly adopting the new OpenGL Shading Language. This book presents a detailed treatment of these exciting technologies in a way that is extremely helpful for visualization and game developers."

—Andy McGovern
Founder, Virtual Geographics, Inc.

"The OpenGL Shading Language is at the epicenter of the programmable graphics revolution, and Randi Rost has been at the center of the development of this significant new industry standard. If you need the inside track on how to use the OpenGL Shading Language to unleash new visual effects, and unlock the supercomputer hiding inside the new generation of graphics hardware, then this is the book for you."

—Neil Trevett
Senior Vice President Market Development, 3Dlabs

OpenGL®
Shading Language

OpenGL® Shading Language

Randi J. Rost

with Contributions by
John M. Kessenich
and Barthold Lichtenbelt

★Addison-Wesley

Boston • San Francisco • New York • Toronto • Montreal
London • Munich • Paris • Madrid
Capetown • Sydney • Tokyo • Singapore • Mexico City

Many of the designations used by manufacturers and sellers to distinguish their products are claimed as trademarks. Where those designations appear in this book, and Addison-Wesley was aware of a trademark claim, the designations have been printed with initial capital letters or in all capitals.

The author and publisher have taken care in the preparation of this book, but make no expressed or implied warranty of any kind and assume no responsibility for errors or omissions. No liability is assumed for incidental or consequential damages in connection with or arising out of the use of the information or programs contained herein.

Hewlett-Packard Company makes no warranty as to the accuracy or completeness of the material included in this text and hereby disclaims any responsibility therefore.

The publisher offers discounts on this book when ordered in quantity for bulk purchases and special sales. For more information, please contact:

U.S. Corporate and Government Sales
(800) 382-3419
corpsales@pearsontechgroup.com

For sales outside of the U.S., please contact:

International Sales
(317) 581-3793
international@pearsontechgroup.com

Visit Addison-Wesley on the Web: www.awprofessional.com

Library of Congress Cataloging-in-Publication Data
Rost, Randi J., 1960-
  Open GL. shading language / Randi Rost ; with contributions by John
M. Kessenich and Barthold Lichtenbelt.
    p. cm.
  ISBN 0-321-19789-5 (acid-free paper)
  1. Computer graphics. 2. OpenGL. I. Kessenich, John M. II.
Lichtenbelt, Barthold. III. Title.
  T385.R665 2004
  006.6'86—dc22

                                                2003022926

ISBN: 0-321-19789-5

Text printed on recycled paper

1 2 3 4 5 6 7 8 9 10—CRS—0807060504

First printing, February 2004

To Baby Cakes, Baby Doll, Love Bug, and Baby Z—
thanks for your love and support

To Mom and Pop—my first and best teachers

Contents

Foreword

This book is an amazing measure of how far and how fast interactive shading has advanced. Not too many years ago, procedural shading was something done only in offline production rendering, creating some of the great results we all know from the movies, but were not anywhere close to interactive. Then a few research projects appeared, allowing a slightly modified but largely intact type of procedural shading to run in real-time. Finally, in a rush, widely accessible commercial systems started to support shading. Today, we've come to the point where a real-time shading language developed by a cross-vendor group of OpenGL participants has achieved official designation as an OpenGL Architecture Review Board approved extension. This book, written by one of those most responsible for spearheading the development and acceptance of the OpenGL shading language, is your guide to that language and the extensions to OpenGL that let you use it.

I came to my interest in procedural shading from a strange direction. In 1990, I started graduate school at the University of North Carolina in Chapel Hill because it seemed like a good place for someone whose primary interest was interactive 3D graphics. There, I started working on the Pixel-Planes project. This project had produced a new graphics machine with several interesting features beyond its performance at rendering large numbers of polygons per second. One feature in particular had an enormous impact on the research directions I've followed for the past 13 years. Pixel-Planes 5 had programmable pixel processors—lots of them. Programming these processors was similar in many ways to the assembly-language fragment programs that have burst onto the graphics scene in the past few years.

Programming them was exhilarating, yet also thoroughly exasperating.

I was far from the only person to notice both the power and pain of writing low-level code to execute per-pixel. Another group within the Pixel-Planes team built an assembler for shading code to make it a little easier to write, although it was still both difficult to write a good shader and ever-so-rewarding once you had it working. The shaders produced will be familiar to anyone who has seen demos of any of the latest graphics products, and not surprisingly you'll find versions of many of them in this book: wood, clouds, brick, rock, reflective wavy water, and (of course) the Mandelbrot fractal set.

The rewards and difficulties presented by Pixel-Planes 5 shaders guided many of the design decisions behind the next machine, PixelFlow. PixelFlow was designed and built by a university/industry partnership with industrial participation first by Division, then by Hewlett-Packard. The result was the first interactive system capable of running procedural shaders compiled from a high-level shading language. PixelFlow was demonstrated at the SIGGRAPH conference in 1997. For a few years thereafter, if you were fortunate enough to be at UNC-Chapel Hill, you could write procedural shaders and run them in real-time when no one else could. And, of course, the only way to see them in action was to go there.

I left UNC for a shading project at SGI, with the hopes of providing a commercially supported shading language that could be used on more than just one machine at one site. Meanwhile, a shading language research project started up at Stanford, with some important results for shading on PC-level graphics hardware. PC graphics vendors across the board started to add low-level shading capabilities to their hardware. Soon, people everywhere could write shading code similar in many ways to that that had so inspired me on the Pixel Planes 5 machine. And, not surprisingly, soon people everywhere also knew that we were going to need a higher-level language for interactive shading.

Research continues into the use, improvement, and abuse of these languages at my lab at University of Maryland, Baltimore County; and at many, many others. However, the mere existence of real-time high-level shading languages is no longer the subject of that research. Interactive shading languages have moved from the research phase to wide availability. There are a number of options for anyone wanting to develop an application using the shading capabilities of modern graphics hardware. The principal choices are Cg, HLSL, and the OpenGL Shading Language. The last of which has the distinction of being the only one that has been through a rigorous multivendor review process. I participated in that process, as did over two dozen representatives from a dozen companies and universities.

This brings us back full circle to this book. If you are holding this book now, you are most likely interested in some of the same ideals that drove the creation of the OpenGL Shading Language, the desire for a cross-OS, cross-platform, robust and standardized shading language. You want to learn how to use all of that? Open up and start reading. Then get shading!

—Marc Olano
University of Maryland, Baltimore County, MD
September 2003

Preface

For just about as long as there has been graphics hardware, there has been programmable graphics hardware. Over the years, building flexibility into graphics hardware designs has been a necessary way of life for hardware developers. Graphics APIs continue to evolve, and because a hardware design can take two years or more from start to finish, the only way to guarantee a hardware product that can support the then-current graphics APIs at its release is to build in some degree of programmability from the very beginning.

Until recently, the realm of programming graphics hardware belonged to just a few people, mainly researchers and graphics hardware driver developers. Research into programmable graphics hardware has been taking place for many years, but the point of this research has not been to produce viable hardware and software for application developers and end users. The graphics hardware driver developers have focused on the immediate task of providing support for the important graphics APIs of the time: PHIGS, PEX, Iris GL, OpenGL, Direct3D, and so on. Until recently, none of these APIs exposed the programmability of the underlying hardware, so application developers have been forced into using the fixed functionality provided by traditional graphics APIs.

Hardware companies have not exposed the programmable underpinnings of their products because there is a high cost of educating and supporting customers to use low-level, device-specific interfaces and because these interfaces typically change quite radically with each new generation of graphics hardware. Application developers who use such a device-specific interface to a piece of graphics hardware face the daunting task of updating their software for each new generation of hardware that comes along. And forget about supporting the application on hardware from multiple vendors!

As we move into the 21st century, some of these fundamental tenets about graphics hardware are being challenged. Application developers are pushing the envelope as never before and demanding a variety of new features in hardware in order to create more and more sophisticated onscreen effects. As a result, new graphics hardware designs are more programmable than ever before. Standard graphics APIs have been challenged to keep up with the pace of hardware innovation. For OpenGL, the result has been a spate of extensions to the core API as hardware vendors struggle to support a range of interesting new features that their customers are demanding.

So we are standing today at a crossroads for the graphics industry. A paradigm shift is occurring, one that is taking us from the world of rigid, fixed functionality graphics hardware and graphics APIs to a brave new world where the visual processing unit, or VPU (i.e., graphics hardware), is as important as the central processing unit, or CPU. The VPU will be optimized for processing dynamic media such as 3D graphics and video. Highly parallel processing of floating point data will be the primary task for VPUs, and the flexibility of the VPU will mean that it can also be used to process data other than a stream of traditional graphics commands. Applications can take advantage of the capabilities of both the CPU and the VPU, utilizing the strengths of each to perform the task at hand optimally.

This book describes how graphics hardware programmability is exposed through a high-level language in the leading cross-platform 3D graphics API: OpenGL. This language, the OpenGL Shading Language, allows applications to take total control over the most important stages of the graphics processing pipeline. No longer restricted to the graphics rendering algorithms and formulas chosen by hardware designers and frozen in silicon, software developers are beginning to use this programmability to create stunning effects in real-time.

Intended Audience

The primary audience for this book is application programmers that are interested in writing shaders. This book is intended to be used as both a tutorial and a reference book by people interested in learning to write shaders with the OpenGL Shading Language. Some will use the book in one fashion and some in the other. It is hoped that the organization will be amenable to both uses. It is not expected that most people will read the book in sequential order from back to front.

Readers do not need previous knowledge of OpenGL in order to absorb the material in this book, but it is very helpful. A brief review of OpenGL is included, but this book does not attempt to be a tutorial or reference book for OpenGL. Anyone attempting to develop an OpenGL application that uses shaders should be armed with OpenGL programming documentation in addition to this book.

Computer graphics has a mathematical basis, therefore some knowledge of algebra and trigonometry will help readers understand and appreciate some of the details presented. With the advent of programmable graphics hardware, key parts of the graphics processing pipeline are once again under the control of software developers. In order to develop shaders successfully in this environment, it is imperative that developers understand the mathematical basis of computer graphics.

About This Book

This book has three main parts. Chapters 1 through 8 are aimed at teaching the reader about the OpenGL Shading Language and how to use it. This part of the book covers details of the language and details of the OpenGL commands that are used to create and manipulate shaders. In order to provide the reader with a basis for writing shaders, Chapters 9 through 16 contain a gallery of shader examples and some explanation of the underlying algorithms. This part of the book is intended to be used as a basis for the reader's shader development and as a springboard to inspire new ideas. Finally, Chapter 17 contains a comparison with other notable commercial shading languages, and Appendices A and B contain reference material for the language and the API entry points that support it.

The chapters are arranged to suit the needs of the reader who is least familiar with OpenGL and shading languages. Certain chapters can be skipped by readers who are more familiar with both topics. People don't necessarily read technical books from front to back, and this book is designed to have somewhat compartmentalized chapters in order to allow such usage.

- Chapter 1 contains a review of the fundamentals of the OpenGL API. Readers already familiar with OpenGL may skip to Chapter 2.

- Chapter 2 provides an introduction to the OpenGL Shading Language and the OpenGL entry points that have been added to support it. If you want to know what the OpenGL Shading Language is all about and you have time to read only one chapter of this book, this is the one to read.

- Chapter 3 thoroughly describes the OpenGL Shading Language. This material is organized to present the details of a programming language. This section will be useful as a reference section after readers have developed a general understanding of the language.

- Chapter 4 discusses how the newly defined programmable parts of the rendering pipeline interact with each other and with OpenGL's fixed functionality. This discussion includes descriptions of the built-in variables defined in the OpenGL Shading Language.

- Chapter 5 describes the built-in functions that are part of the OpenGL Shading Language. This section will also be useful as a reference section after readers have developed an understanding of the language.

- Chapter 6 presents and discusses a fairly simple shader example. People who learn best by diving in and studying a real example will benefit from the discussion in this chapter.

- Chapter 7 describes the entry points that have been added to OpenGL to support the creation and manipulation of shaders. This material will need to be understood by application programmers who want to use shaders in their application.

- Chapter 8 presents some general advice on shader development and describes the shader development process. It also describes tools that are currently available to aid the shader development process.

- Chapter 9 begins a series of chapters that present and discuss shaders with a common characteristic. In this chapter, shaders that duplicate some of the fixed functionality of the OpenGL pipeline are presented.

- Chapter 10 presents a few shaders that are based on the capability to store data in and retrieve data from texture maps.

- Chapter 11 is devoted to shaders that are procedural in nature (effects are computed algorithmically rather than being based on information stored in textures).

- Chapter 12 describes noise and the effects that can be achieved by using it properly.

- Chapter 13 contains examples of how shaders can be used to create rendering effects that vary over time.

- Chapter 14 contains a discussion of the aliasing problem and how shaders can be written to reduce the effects of aliasing.

- Chapter 15 illustrates shaders that are used to achieve effects other than photorealism. Such effects include technical illustration, sketching or hatching effects, and other stylized rendering.

- Chapter 16 presents several shaders that are used to modify images as they are being drawn with OpenGL.

- Chapter 17 compares the OpenGL Shading Language with other notable commercial shading languages.

- Appendix A contains the language grammar that more clearly specifies the OpenGL Shading Language.

- Appendix B contains reference pages for the API entry points that are related to the OpenGL Shading Language.

About the Shader Examples

The shaders contained in this book are primarily short programs designed to illustrate the capabilities of the OpenGL Shading Language. None of the example shaders should be presumed to illustrate the "best" way of achieving a particular effect. (Indeed, the "best" way to implement certain effects may have yet to be discovered through the power and flexibility of programmable graphics hardware.) Performance improvements for each shader are possible for any given hardware target. For most of the shaders, image quality may be improved by taking greater care to reduce or eliminate causes of aliasing.

The source code for these shaders is written in a way that I believe represents a reasonable trade-off between source code clarity, portability, and performance. Use them to learn the OpenGL Shading Language, and improve upon them for use in your own projects.

With the exception of the images produced for the toy ball shader (which were produced by ATI Research, Inc. on ATI hardware), all of the images produced for this book were done on the first graphics accelerator to provide support for the OpenGL Shading Language, the 3Dlabs Wildcat VP. This implementation has a variety of limitations, so in a number of cases the image was generated with a shader that could run on this hardware but contained hardware- or driver-dependent idiosyncrasies. A cleaned up version of such shaders is then presented and discussed in this book. I have taken as much care as possible to present shaders that are done "the right way" for the OpenGL Shading Language rather than those with idiosyncrasies due to being developed on the very first implementation. I also have tried to be as careful as I could be during the translation to cleaned up versions of the shaders. The latest and greatest versions of these shaders will be available through a link at this book's Web site at http://3dshaders.com.

The development of this book occurred while OpenGL Shading Language implementations were still very much in their infancy. In choosing shader examples to include and discuss, my goal was to provide *working* shaders, not shaders that *should work* after implementations became capable of supporting the whole breadth of the OpenGL Shading Language specification. Longer, more complex shader examples are prime candidates for inclusion in the second edition of this book, as are shaders that utilize features that are not yet available in any implementation.

Errata

I know that this book contains some errors, but I've done my best to keep them to a minimum. If you find any errors, please report them to me (randi@3dshaders.com) and I will keep a running list on this book's Web site at http://3dshaders.com.

Typographical Conventions

This book contains a number of typographical conventions that are intended to enhance readability and understanding.

- SMALL CAPS are used for the first occurrence of defined terms.

- *Italics* are used for emphasis, document titles, and coordinate values such as x, y, and z.

- **Bold serif** is used for language keywords.

- Sans serif is used for macros and symbolic constants that appear in the text.

- **Bold sans serif** is used for function names.

- *Italic sans serif* is used for variables, parameter names, spatial dimensions, and matrix components.

- Fixed width is used for code examples.

About the Author

Randi Rost is currently the manager of 3Dlabs' Fort Collins, Colorado graphics software team. This group is driving the definition of the OpenGL 2.0 standard and implementing OpenGL drivers for 3Dlabs' graphics products. Prior to joining 3Dlabs, Randi was a graphics software architect for Hewlett-Packard's Graphics Software Lab and the chief architect for graphics software at Kubota Graphics Corporation.

Randi has been involved in the graphics industry for more than 25 years and has participated in emerging graphics standards efforts for over 15 years. He has been involved with the design and evolution of OpenGL since before version 1.0 was released in 1992. He is one of the few people credited as a contributor for each major revision of OpenGL, up through and including OpenGL 1.5. He was one of the chief architects and the specification author for PEX, and he was a member of the Graphics Performance Characterization (GPC) Committee during the development of the Picture-Level Benchmark (PLB). He served as 3Dlabs' representative to the Khronos Group from the time the group started in 1999 until the OpenML 1.0 specification was released, and he chaired the graphics subcommittee of that organization during this time. He received the National Computer Graphics Association (NCGA) 1993 Achievement Award for the Advancement of Graphics Standards.

Randi has participated in or organized numerous graphics tutorials at SIGGRAPH, Eurographics, and the Game Developer's conference since 1990. He has given tutorials on the OpenGL Shading Language at SIGGRAPH 2002 and SIGGRAPH 2003 and made presentations on this topic at the Game Developer's Conference in 2002 and 2003.

Randi received his B.S. degree in computer science and math from Minnesota State University, Mankato, in 1981 and his M.S. in computing science from the University of California, Davis, in 1983.

On a dreary winter day, you might find Randi in a desolate region of southern Wyoming, following a road less traveled.

About the Contributors

Barthold Lichtenbelt received his master's degree in electrical engineering in 1994 from the University of Twente in the Netherlands. From 1994 to 1998, he worked on volume rendering techniques at Hewlett-Packard Company, first at Hewlett-Packard Laboratories in Palo Alto, California, and later at Hewlett Packard's graphics software lab in Fort Collins, Colorado. During that time, he coauthored the book, *Introduction to Volume Rendering*, and wrote several papers on the subject as well. He was awarded four patents in the field of volume rendering. In 1998, Barthold joined Dynamic Pictures, which 3Dlabs subsequently acquired. There, he worked on both Direct3D and OpenGL drivers for professional graphics accelerators. The last several years he has been heavily involved in efforts to extend the OpenGL API and is the author of the three ARB extensions that support the OpenGL Shading Language. Barthold also led the implementation of 3Dlabs' first drivers that use these extensions.

John Kessenich, a Colorado native, has worked in Fort Collins as a software architect in a variety of fields including CAD applications, operating system kernels, and 3D graphics. He received a patent for using Web browsers to navigate through huge collections of source code and another for processor architecture. John studied mathematics and its application to computer graphics, computer languages, and compilers at Colorado State University, receiving a bachelor's degree in applied mathematics in 1985. Later, while working at Hewlett-Packard, he got his master's degree in applied mathematics in 1988. John has been working on OpenGL drivers now for four years at 3Dlabs. During this time, he took the leading role in completing the development of the OpenGL Shading Language. John authored the specification of the OpenGL Shading Language and is currently part of the team that is writing an optimizing compiler for it.

Acknowledgments

John Kessenich of 3Dlabs was the primary author of the OpenGL Shading Language specification document and the author of Chapter 3 of this book. Some of the material from the OpenGL Shading Language specification document was modified and included in Chapter 3, Chapter 4, and Chapter 5, and the OpenGL Shading Language grammar written by John for the specification is included in its entirety in Appendix A. John worked tirelessly throughout the standardization effort discussing, resolving, and documenting language and API issues; updating the specification through numerous revisions; and providing insight and education to many of the other participants in the effort. John also did some of the early shader development, including the very first versions of the wood, bump map, and environment mapping shaders discussed in this book.

Barthold Lichtenbelt of 3Dlabs was the primary author and document editor of the OpenGL extension specifications that defined the OpenGL Shading Language API. Some material from those specifications has been adapted and included in Chapter 7. Barthold worked tirelessly updating the specifications; discussing, resolving, and documenting issues; and guiding the participants of the ARB-GL2 working group to consensus. Barthold is also the coauthor of Chapter 4 of this book.

The industry-wide initiative to define a high-level shading effort for OpenGL was ignited by a white paper, called *The OpenGL 2.0 Shading Language*, written by Dave Baldwin (2002) of 3Dlabs. Dave's ideas provided the basic framework from which the OpenGL Shading Language has evolved.

Publication of this white paper occurred almost a year before any publication of information on competing, commercially viable, high-level shading languages. In this respect, Dave deserves credit as the trailblazer for a standard high-level shading language. Dave continued to be heavily involved in the design of the language and the API during its formative months. His original white paper also included code for a variety of shaders. This code served as the starting point for several of the shaders in this book: notably the brick shaders presented in Chapter 6 and Chapter 14, the traditional shaders presented in Chapter 9, the antialiased checkerboard shader in Chapter 14, and the Mandelbrot shader in Chapter 15. Steve Koren of 3Dlabs was responsible for getting the aliased brick shader and the Mandelbrot shader working on real hardware for the first time.

Bert Freudenberg of the University of Magdeburg developed the hatching shader described in Chapter 15. As part of this effort, Bert also explored some of the issues involved with analytic antialiasing with programmable graphics hardware. I have incorporated some of Bert's diagrams and results in Chapter 14. Bill Licea-Kane of ATI Research developed the toy ball shader presented in Chapter 11 and provided me with its "theory of operation." The stripe shader included in Chapter 11 was implemented by LightWork Design, Ltd. Antonio Tejada of 3Dlabs conceived and implemented the wobble shader presented in Chapter 13.

I would like to thank my colleagues at 3Dlabs for their assistance with the OpenGL 2.0 effort in general and for help in developing this book. Specifically, John Kessenich, Barthold Lichtenbelt, and Steve Koren have been doing amazing work implementing the OpenGL Shading Language compiler, linker, and object support in the 3Dlabs OpenGL implementation. Dave Houlton and Mike Weiblen have been working on Render Monkey as well as doing shader development. Teri Morrison and Na Li have been implementing and testing the OpenGL extensions. Philip Rideout, Atul, Gupta, and several of our 3Dlabs colleagues at other sites have been diligently implementing a full-blown optimizing compiler for the OpenGL Shading Language. This work has made it possible to create the code and images that appear in this book. This group, which I have been privileged to lead for several years now, has been responsible for producing the publicly available specifications and source code for the OpenGL Shading Language and OpenGL Shading Language API.

Dale Kirkland, Jeremy Morris, Phil Huxley, and Antonio Tejada of 3Dlabs have been involved in many of the OpenGL 2.0 discussions and have provided a wealth of good ideas and encouragement as we have moved forward. Antonio also implemented the first parser for the OpenGL Shading Language. Other members of the 3Dlabs driver development teams in Fort

Collins, Colorado; Egham, U.K.; Madison, Alabama; and Austin, Texas have contributed to the effort as well. The 3Dlabs executive staff should be commended for having the vision to move forward with the OpenGL 2.0 proposal and the courage to allocate resources to its development. Thanks to Osman Kent, Hock Leow, Neil Trevett, Jerry Peterson, and John Schimpf in particular.

Numerous other people have been involved in the OpenGL 2.0 discussions. I would like to thank my colleagues and fellow ARB representatives at ATI, SGI, NVIDIA, Intel, Microsoft, Evans & Sutherland, IBM, Sun Microsystems, Apple, Imagination Technologies, Dell, Compaq, and HP for contributing to discussions and for helping to move the process along. In particular, Bill Licea-Kane of ATI has chaired the ARB-GL2 working group since its creation and has successfully steered the group to a remarkable achievement in a relatively short time. Bill, Evan Hart, Jeremy Sandmel, Benjamin Lipchak, and Glenn Ortner of ATI also provided insightful review and studious comments for both the OpenGL Shading Language and the OpenGL Shading Language API. Steve Glanville and Cass Everitt of NVIDIA were extremely helpful during the design of the OpenGL Shading Language, and Pat Brown of NVIDIA contributed enormously to the development of the OpenGL Shading Language API. Others with notable contributions to the final specifications include Marc Olano of the University of Maryland/Baltimore County; Jon Leech of SGI; Folker Schamel of Spinor; Matt Cruikshank, Steve Demlow, and Karel Zuiderveld of Vital Images; Allen Akin, contributing as an individual; and Kurt Akeley of NVIDIA. Numerous others provided review or commentary that helped improve the specification documents.

I think that special recognition should go to people who were not affiliated with a graphics hardware company and still participated heavily in the ARB-GL2 working group. When representatives from a bunch of competing hardware companies get together in a room and try to reach agreement on an important standard that materially affects each of them, there is often squabbling over details that will cause one company or another extra grief in the short term. Marc Olano and Folker Schamel contributed enormously to the standardization effort as "neutral" third parties. Time and time again, their comments helped lead the group back to a higher ground. Allen Akin and Matt Cruikshank also contributed in this regard. Thanks, gentlemen, for your technical contributions and your valuable but underappreciated work as "referees."

A big thank you goes to the software developers who have taken the time to talk with us, send us e-mail, or answer survey questions on http://opengl.org. Our ultimate aim is to provide you with the best possible API for doing graphics application development, and the time that you have spent telling us what you need has been invaluable. A few ISVs lobbied long and hard for certain features, and they were able to convince us to make some significant changes to the original OpenGL 2.0 proposal. Thanks, all you software developers, and keep telling us what you need!

A debt of gratitude is owed to the designers of the C programming language, the designers of RenderMan, and the designers of OpenGL, the three standards that have provided the strongest influence on our efforts. Hopefully, the OpenGL Shading Language will continue their traditions of success and excellence.

The reviewers of various drafts of this book have helped greatly to increase its quality. Thanks to Marc Olano, Bob Kuehne, Andy McGovern, Jeffrey Galinovsky, Slawek Kilanowski, Brad Ritter, Bert Freudenberg, Steve Cunningham, Mike Weiblen, Barthold Lichtenbelt, John Kessenich, Teri Morrison, Dave Houlton, Na Li, Folker Schamel, Teresa Rost, and two anonymous reviewers for reviewing some or all of the material in this book. Your comments have been greatly appreciated! Mary O'Brien and Brenda Mulligan of Addison-Wesley have provided guidance and assistance as this book has gone from being a pipe dream to a reality. Clark Wolter worked with me on the design of the cover image, and he improved and perfected the original concepts.

Thanks go to my two young daughters, Rachel and Hannah, for giving up some play time with Daddy for awhile, and for the smiles, giggles, hugs, and kisses that helped me get through this project. Little Zachary was competing with the copyediting phase for my attention, and he won. It probably won't be the last schedule that he impacts. Finally, thank you, Teresa, the love of my life, for the support you've given me in writing this book. These have been busy times in our personal lives too, but you have had the patience, strength, and courage to see it through to completion. Thank you for helping me make this book a reality.

Chapter 1

Review of OpenGL Basics

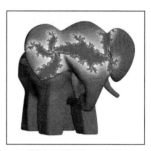

This chapter presents a brief overview of the OpenGL application programming interface (API) in order to lay the foundation for the material in subsequent chapters. It is not intended to be an exhaustive overview. If you are already extremely familiar with OpenGL, you can safely skip ahead to the next chapter. If you are familiar with another 3D graphics API, this chapter should provide enough of an overview that you can become familiar with OpenGL to the extent that you'll be able to begin doing some shader development using the OpenGL Shading Language.

Unless otherwise noted, descriptions of OpenGL functionality are based on the OpenGL 1.5 specification.

1.1 OpenGL History

OpenGL is an industry standard, cross-platform APPLICATION PROGRAMMING INTERFACE (API). The specification for this API was finalized in 1992, and the first implementations appeared in 1993. It was largely compatible with a proprietary API called Iris GL (Graphics Library) that was designed and supported by Silicon Graphics, Inc. In order to establish an industry standard, Silicon Graphics collaborated with various other graphics hardware companies to create an open standard, which was dubbed "OpenGL."

OpenGL shares many of Iris GL's design characteristics. Its intention is to provide access to graphics hardware capabilities at the lowest possible level that still provides hardware independence. It is designed to be the lowest-level interface for accessing graphics hardware. OpenGL has been implemented in a variety of operating environments, including Macs, PCs, and

UNIX-based systems. It has been supported on a variety of hardware architectures, from those that support little in hardware other than the frame buffer itself to those that accelerate virtually everything in hardware.

Since the release of the initial OpenGL specification (version 1.0) in June 1992, there have been five revisions that have added new functionality to the API. The current version of the OpenGL specification is 1.5. The first conformant implementations of OpenGL 1.0 began appearing in 1993. Version 1.1 was finished in 1997 and added support for two important capabilities—vertex arrays and texture objects. The specification for OpenGL 1.2 was released in 1998 and added support for 3D textures and an optional subset of imaging functionality. The OpenGL 1.3 specification was completed in 2001 and added support for cube map textures, compressed textures, multitextures, and other things. OpenGL 1.4 was completed in 2002 and added automatic mipmap generation, additional blending functions, internal texture formats for storing depth values for use in shadow computations, support for drawing multiple vertex arrays with a single command, more control over point rasterization, control over stencil wrapping behavior, and various additions to texturing capabilities. The OpenGL 1.5 specification was approved in July 2003 and published in October 2003. It added support for vertex buffer objects, shadow comparison functions, occlusion queries, and nonpower of two textures. OpenGL 2.0 is expected to be finalized in early 2004, and it will contain programmability for both vertex processing and fragment processing as part of the core OpenGL specification. With this version of OpenGL, applications will gain the capability to implement their own rendering algorithms using a high-level shading language. The addition of programmability to OpenGL represents a fundamental shift in its design, hence the change to version number 2.0 from 1.5. However, the change to the major version number does not represent any loss of compatibility with previous versions of OpenGL. OpenGL 2.0 will be completely backward compatible with OpenGL 1.5—applications that run on OpenGL 1.5 will be able to run unmodified on OpenGL 2.0.

Silicon Graphics created an organization to oversee the evolution of OpenGL and called this body the OpenGL Architecture Review Board, or ARB. This group is governed by a set of by-laws, and its primary task is to guide OpenGL by controlling the specification and conformance tests. The original ARB contained representatives from SGI, Intel, Microsoft, Compaq, Digital Equipment Corporation, Evans & Sutherland, and IBM. The ARB currently has as members 3Dlabs, Apple, ATI, Dell, Evans & Sutherland, Hewlett-Packard, IBM, Intel, Matrox, NVIDIA, SGI, and Sun Microsystems.

1.2 Evolving OpenGL

A great deal of functionality is available in various OpenGL implementations in the form of extensions. OpenGL has a well-defined extension mechanism, and hardware vendors are free to define and implement features that expose new hardware functionality. Because of its fundamental design as a fixed functionality state machine, the only way to modify OpenGL has been to define extensions to it—and only OpenGL implementors can implement extensions. There is no way for applications to extend the functionality of OpenGL beyond what is provided by their OpenGL provider. To date, close to 300 extensions have been defined. Extensions that are supported by only one vendor are identified by a short prefix unique to that vendor (e.g., SGI for extensions developed by Silicon Graphics, Inc.). Extensions that are supported by more than one vendor are denoted by the prefix EXT in the extension name. Extensions that have been thoroughly reviewed by the ARB are designated with an ARB prefix in the extension name to indicate that they have a special status as a recommended way of exposing a certain piece of functionality. The next step after an ARB extension is to be added directly to the OpenGL specification. Published specifications for OpenGL extensions are available at the OpenGL extension registry at http://oss.sgi.com/projects/ogl-sample/registry.

The extensions supported by a particular OpenGL implementation can be determined by passing the symbolic constant GL_EXTENSIONS to the **glGetString** function in OpenGL. The returned string contains a list of all the extensions supported in the implementation, and some vendors currently support close to 100 separate OpenGL extensions. It can be a little bit daunting for an application to try and determine whether the needed extensions are present on a variety of implementations, and what to do if they're not. The proliferation of extensions has been primarily a positive factor for the development of OpenGL, but in a sense, it has become a victim of its own success. It allows hardware vendors to expose new features easily, but it presents application developers with a dizzying array of non-standard options. Like any standards body, the ARB is cautious about promoting functionality from extension status to standard OpenGL.

Since version 1.0 of OpenGL, none of the underlying programmability of graphics hardware has been exposed. The original designers of OpenGL, Mark Segal and Kurt Akeley, stated that, "One reason for this decision is that, for performance reasons, graphics hardware is usually designed to apply certain operations in a specific order; replacing these operations with arbitrary algorithms is usually infeasible." This statement may have been mostly true when it was written in 1994 (there were programmable graphics architectures even then). But today, all of the graphics hardware that is being produced is programmable. Because of the proliferation of OpenGL extensions and the need to support Microsoft's DirectX API, hardware vendors have no choice but to design programmable graphics architectures. (As discussed in the remaining chapters of this book, providing application programmers with access to this programmability is the purpose of the OpenGL Shading Language.)

1.3 Execution Model

The OpenGL API is focused on drawing graphics into frame buffer memory, and, to a lesser extent, in reading back values stored in that frame buffer. It is somewhat unique in that its design includes support for drawing three-dimensional geometry (such as points, lines, and polygons, collectively referred to as PRIMITIVES) as well as for drawing images and bitmaps.

The execution model for OpenGL can be described as client-server. An application program (the client) issues OpenGL commands that are interpreted and processed by an OpenGL implementation (the server). The application program and the OpenGL implementation may be executing on a single computer or on two different computers. Some OpenGL state is stored in the address space of the application (client state), but the majority of it is stored in the address space of the OpenGL implementation (server state).

OpenGL commands are always processed in the order in which they are received by the server, although command completion may be delayed due to intermediate operations that cause OpenGL commands to be buffered. Out-of-order execution of OpenGL commands is not permitted. This means, for example, that a primitive will not be drawn until the previous primitive has been completely drawn. This in-order execution also applies to queries of state and frame buffer read operations. These commands return results that are consistent with complete execution of all previous commands.

Data binding for OpenGL occurs when commands are issued, not when they are executed. Data passed to an OpenGL command is interpreted when the command is issued, and copied into OpenGL memory if needed. Subsequent changes to this data by the application have no effect on the data that is now stored within OpenGL.

1.4 The Frame Buffer

OpenGL is an API for drawing graphics, and so the fundamental purpose for OpenGL is to transform data provided by an application into something that is visible on the display screen. This processing is often referred to as RENDERING. Typically, this processing is accelerated by specially designed hardware, but some or all operations of the OpenGL pipeline can be performed by a software implementation running on the CPU. It is transparent to the user of the OpenGL implementation how this division among the software and hardware is handled. The important thing is that the results of rendering conform to the results defined by the OpenGL specification. The hardware that is dedicated to drawing graphics and maintaining the contents of the display screen is often called the GRAPHICS ACCELERATOR. Graphics accelerators typically have a region of memory that is allocated to maintaining the contents of the display. Every visible picture element (pixel) of the display is represented by one or more bytes of memory on the graphics accelerator. A grayscale display might have a byte of memory to represent the gray level at each pixel. A color display might have a byte of memory for each of red, green, and blue in order to represent the color value for each pixel. This so-called DISPLAY MEMORY is scanned (refreshed) a certain number of times per second in order to maintain a flicker-free representation on the display. Graphics accelerators also typically have a region of memory called OFFSCREEN MEMORY that is not displayable and is used to store things that aren't visible.

OpenGL assumes that allocation of display memory and offscreen memory is handled by the window system. The window system decides which portions of memory may be accessed by OpenGL and how these portions are structured. In each environment in which OpenGL is supported, there is a small set of function calls that tie OpenGL into that particular environment. In the Microsoft Windows environment, this set of routines is called WGL (pronounced "wiggle"). In the X Window System environment, this set of routines is called GLX. In the Macintosh environment, this set of routines is called AGL. In each environment, this set of calls provides support for such things as allocating and deallocating regions of graphics memory, allocating and deallocating data structures called GRAPHICS CONTEXTS that maintain OpenGL state, selecting the current graphics context, selecting the region of graphics memory in which to draw, and synchronizing commands between OpenGL and the window system.

The region of graphics memory that is modified as a result of OpenGL rendering is called the FRAME BUFFER. In a windowing system, the OpenGL notion of a frame buffer corresponds to a window. Facilities are provided in window system-specific OpenGL routines for selecting the frame buffer characteristics for the window. The windowing system will typically also clarify how the OpenGL frame buffer behaves when windows overlap. In a nonwindowed system, the OpenGL frame buffer corresponds to the entire display.

A window that supports OpenGL rendering (i.e., a frame buffer) may consist of some combination of the following:

- Up to four color buffers
- A depth buffer
- A stencil buffer
- An accumulation buffer
- A multisample buffer

Most graphics hardware supports both a front buffer and a back buffer in order to perform DOUBLE BUFFERING. This allows the application to render into the (offscreen) back buffer while displaying the (visible) front buffer. When rendering is complete, the two buffers are swapped so that the completed rendering is now displayed as the front buffer and rendering can begin anew in the back buffer. When double buffering is used, the end user never sees the graphics when they are in the process of being drawn, only the finished image. This technique is used to allow smooth animation at interactive rates.

Stereo viewing is supported by having a color buffer for the left eye and one for the right eye. Double buffering is supported by having both a front and a back buffer. A double-buffered stereo window will therefore have four color buffers: front left, front right, back left, and back right. A normal (non-stereo) double-buffered window will have a front buffer and a back buffer. A single buffered window will have only a front buffer.

If 3D objects are to be drawn with hidden-surface removal, a DEPTH BUFFER is needed. This buffer stores the depth of the displayed object at each pixel. As additional objects are drawn, a depth comparison can be performed at each pixel in order to determine whether the new object is visible or obscured.

A STENCIL BUFFER is used to perform complex masking operations. A complex shape can be stored in the stencil buffer, and subsequent drawing operations can use the contents of the stencil buffer to determine whether to update each pixel.

The ACCUMULATION BUFFER is a color buffer that typically has higher precision components than the color buffers. This allows several images to be accumulated to produce a composite image. One use of this would be to draw several frames of an object in motion into the accumulation buffer. When each pixel of the accumulation buffer is divided by the number of frames, the result will be a final image that shows motion blur for the moving objects. Similar techniques can be used to simulate depth-of-field effects and to perform high-quality full screen antialiasing.

Normally, when objects are drawn, a single decision is made as to whether the graphics primitive affects a pixel on the screen. The MULTISAMPLE BUFFER is a buffer that allows everything that is rendered to be sampled multiple times within each pixel in order to perform high-quality full screen antialiasing without rendering the scene more than once. Each sample within a pixel contains color, depth, and stencil information, and the number of samples per pixel may be queried. When a window includes a multisample buffer, it does not include separate depth or stencil buffers. As objects are rendered, the color samples are combined to produce a single color value, and that color value is passed on to be written into the color buffer. Because they contain multiple samples (often 4, 8, or 16) of color, depth, and stencil for every pixel in the window, multisample buffers can use up large amounts of offscreen graphics memory.

1.5 State

OpenGL was designed as a state machine for updating the contents of a frame buffer. The process of turning geometric primitives, images, and bitmaps into pixels on the screen is controlled by a fairly large number of state settings. These state settings are orthogonal with one another—setting one piece of state does not affect the others. Cumulatively, the state settings define the behavior of the OpenGL rendering pipeline and how primitives are transformed into pixels on the display device.

OpenGL state is collected into a data structure called a graphics context. Window system-specific functions are provided for creating and deleting graphics contexts. Another window system-specific call is provided to designate a graphics context and an OpenGL frame buffer that will be used as the targets for subsequent OpenGL commands.

There are quite a few server-side state values in OpenGL that have just two states: on or off. To turn a mode on, you must pass the appropriate symbolic constant to the OpenGL command **glEnable**. To turn a mode off, you pass the symbolic constant to **glDisable**. Client-side state (such as pointers used to define vertex arrays) can be enabled by calling **glEnableClientState** and disabled by calling **glDisableClientState**.

OpenGL maintains a server-side stack for pushing and popping any or all of the defined state values. This stack can be manipulated by calling **glPushAttrib** and **glPopAttrib**. Similarly, client state can be manipulated on a second stack by calling **glPushClientAttrib** and **glPopClientAttrib**.

glGet is a generic function that can be used to query many of the components of a graphics context. Symbolic constants are defined for simple state items (e.g., GL_CURRENT_COLOR, GL_LINE_WIDTH, etc.), and these values can be passed as arguments to **glGet** in order to retrieve the current value of the indicated component of a graphics context. There are variants of **glGet** for returning the state value as an integer, float, double, or boolean. More complex state values are returned by "get" functions that are specific to that state value, for instance, **glGetClipPlane**, **glGetLight**, **glGetMaterial**, and so on. Error conditions can be detected by calling the **glGetError** function.

1.6 Processing Pipeline

For the purpose of specifying the behavior of OpenGL, the various operations are defined to be applied in a particular order, so we can also think of OpenGL as a GRAPHICS PROCESSING PIPELINE.

Let's start by looking at a block diagram of how OpenGL was defined up through OpenGL 1.5. Figure 1.1 is a diagram of the so-called FIXED FUNCTIONALITY of OpenGL. This diagram shows the fundamentals of how OpenGL has worked since its inception. This is a simplified representation of how OpenGL still works. It attempts to show the main features of the OpenGL pipeline for the purposes of this overview. Some new features have been added to OpenGL in versions 1.1, 1.2, 1.3, 1.4, and 1.5, but the basic architecture of OpenGL has remained unchanged. We use the term *fixed functionality* because every OpenGL implementation is required to have the same functionality and a result that is consistent with the OpenGL specification for a given set of inputs. Both the set of operations and the order in which they occur are defined (fixed) by the OpenGL specification.

It is important to note that OpenGL implementations are not required to match precisely the order of operations shown in Figure 1.1. Implementations are free to modify the order of operations as long as the rendering results are consistent with the OpenGL specification. Many innovative software and hardware architectures have been designed to implement OpenGL, and most block diagrams of those implementations look nothing like Figure 1.1. However, the diagram does help ground our discussion of the way the rendering process *appears* to work in OpenGL, even if the underlying implementation does things a bit differently.

1.7 Drawing Geometry

As you can see from Figure 1.1, data for drawing geometry (points, lines, and polygons) starts off in application controlled memory (1). This memory may be on the host CPU, or, with the help of some recent additions to OpenGL or under-the-covers data caching by the OpenGL implementation, it may actually reside in video memory on the graphics accelerator. Either way, the fact is that it is memory that contains geometry data that the application can cause to be drawn.

1.7.1 Specifying Geometry

The geometric primitives supported in OpenGL are points, lines, line strips, line loops, polygons, triangles, triangle strips, triangle fans,

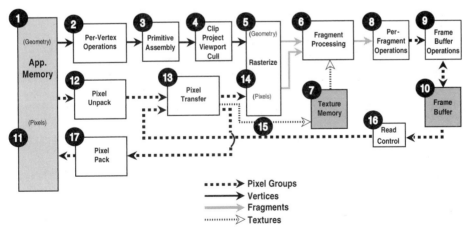

Figure 1.1   Overview of OpenGL operation

quadrilaterals, and quadrilateral strips. There are three main ways to send geometry data to OpenGL. The first is the vertex at a time method, which uses a call to **glBegin** to start a primitive and a call to **glEnd** to end it. In between are commands that set specific VERTEX ATTRIBUTES such as vertex position, color, normal, texture coordinates, secondary color, edge flags, and fog coordinates, using calls such as **glVertex**, **glColor**, **glNormal**, and **glTexCoord**. (There are a number of variants of these function calls to allow the application to pass these values with various data types as well as to pass them by value or by reference.) Up through and including version 1.5 of OpenGL, there was no way to send arbitrary (user-defined) per-vertex data. The only per-vertex attributes allowed were those specifically defined in the OpenGL specification.

When the vertex-at-a-time method is used, the call to **glVertex** signals the end of the data definition for a single vertex, and it may also define the completion of a primitive. After calling **glBegin** and specifying a primitive type, a graphics primitive is completed whenever **glVertex** is called enough times to specify completely a primitive of the indicated type. For independent triangles, a triangle will be completed every third time **glVertex** is called. For triangle strips, a triangle will be completed when **glVertex** is called for the third time, and an additional connecting triangle will be completed for each subsequent call to **glVertex**.

The second method of drawing primitives is to use vertex arrays. With this method, applications store vertex attributes in user-defined arrays, set up pointers to the arrays, and use **glDrawArrays**, **glMultiDrawArrays**, **glDrawElements**, **glMultiDrawElements**, **glDrawRangeElements**, or **glInterleavedArrays** to draw a large number of primitives at once. Because these entry points are capable of efficiently passing large amounts of geometry data to OpenGL, applications are encouraged to use them for portions of code that are extremely performance critical. The **glBegin/glEnd** method requires a function call for each attribute of each vertex, so the function call overhead can become substantial when drawing objects with thousands of vertices. In contrast, vertex arrays can be used to draw a large number of primitives with a single function call after the vertex data is organized into arrays. Processing the array data in this fashion can be faster because it is often more efficient for the OpenGL implementation to deal with data organized in this way. The current array of color values is specified by calling **glColorPointer**, the current array of vertex positions is specified by calling **glVertexPointer**, the current array of normal vectors is specified by calling **glNormalPointer**, and so on. The function **glInterleavedArrays** can be used to specify and enable several interleaved arrays simultaneously (e.g., each vertex might be defined with three floating-point values representing a normal followed by three floating-point values representing a vertex position.)

The preceding two methods are referred to as drawing in IMMEDIATE MODE because primitives are rendered as soon as they have been specified. The third method involves storing either the vertex-at-a-time function calls or the vertex array calls in a DISPLAY LIST (an OpenGL-managed data structure that stores commands for execution at a later time). Display lists can include commands to set state as well as commands to draw geometry. Display lists are stored on the server side and can be processed at a later time by calling **glCallList** or **glCallLists**. This is not illustrated in Figure 1.1, but it is another way that data can be provided to the OpenGL processing pipeline. The definition of a display list is initiated by calling **glNewList**, and display list definition is completed by calling **glEndList**. All of the commands issued between those two calls will become part of the display list (however, certain OpenGL commands are not allowed within display lists). Depending on the implementation, DISPLAY LIST MODE can provide a performance advantage over immediate mode. Storing commands in a display list gives the OpenGL implementation an opportunity to optimize the commands in the display list for the underlying hardware. It also gives the implementation the chance to store the commands in a location that enables better drawing performance, perhaps even in memory on the graphics accelerator. Of course, some extra computation or data movement is usually required to implement these optimizations, so applications will typically only see a performance benefit if the display list is executed more than once.

Vertex array data can be stored in server-side memory using new API calls added to OpenGL in version 1.5. This will typically provide the highest performance rendering because the data can be stored in memory on the graphics accelerator and need not be transferred over the I/O bus each time it is rendered. The API also supports the concept of efficiently streaming data from client to server. The **glBindBuffer** command is used to create a buffer object, and **glBufferData** and **glBufferSubData** can be used to specify the data values in such a buffer. It is also possible to use **glMapBuffer** to map a buffer object into the client's address space and to obtain a pointer to this memory that can be used to specify the data values directly. The command **glUnmapBuffer** must be called before the values in the buffer are accessed by subsequent GL rendering commands. **glBindBuffer** is also used to make a particular buffer object part of current state. If buffer object 0 is bound when calls are made to vertex array pointer commands such as **glColorPointer**, **glNormalPointer**, **glVertexPointer**, and so on, the pointer parameter to these calls is understood to be a pointer to client-side memory. When a buffer object other than 0 is bound, the pointer parameter is understood to be an offset into the currently bound buffer object. Subsequent calls to one of the vertex array drawing commands (e.g., **glMultiDrawArrays**) can thus obtain their vertex data from either client- or server-side memory or a combination thereof.

OpenGL provides support for rendering curves and surfaces with evaluators. Evaluators use a polynomial mapping to produce vertex attributes such as color, normal, and position that are sent to the vertex processing stage just as if they had been provided by the client. See the OpenGL specification for a complete description of this functionality.

1.7.2 Per-Vertex Operations

No matter which of these methods is used, the net result is that geometry data is transferred into the first stage of processing in OpenGL, VERTEX PROCESSING (2). At this point, vertex positions are transformed by the modelview and projection matrices, normals are transformed by the inverse transpose of the upper leftmost 3×3 matrix taken from the modelview matrix, texture coordinates are transformed by the texture matrices, lighting calculations are applied to modify the base color, texture coordinates may be automatically generated, color material state is applied, and point sizes are computed. All of these things are rigidly defined by the OpenGL specification. They are performed in a specific order, using specific formulas, with specific items of OpenGL state controlling the process.

Because the most important things that occur in this stage are transformation and lighting, the vertex processing stage is sometimes called TRANSFORMATION AND LIGHTING or, more familiarly, T&L. There is no application control to this process other than modifying OpenGL state values (e.g., turning lighting on or off with **glEnable/glDisable**, changing lighting attributes with **glLight** and **glLightModel**, changing material properties with **glMaterial**, modifying the modelview matrix by calling matrix manipulation functions such as **glMatrixMode**, **glLoadMatrix**, **glMultMatrix**, **glRotate**, **glScale**, **glTranslate**, etc.). At this stage of processing, each vertex is treated independently. The vertex position computed by the transformation stage is used in subsequent clipping operations. This process is discussed in Section 1.9.

Lighting effects in OpenGL are controlled by manipulating the attributes of one or more of the simulated light sources defined in OpenGL. There is a specific limit to the number of light sources supported by an OpenGL implementation (GL_MAX_LIGHTS). This value can be queried by calling

glGet and must be at least 8. Each simulated light source in OpenGL has attributes that cause it to behave as either a directional light source, a point light source, or a spotlight. Light attributes that may be adjusted by an application include the color of the emitted light (defined as ambient, diffuse, and specular RGBA intensity values); the light source position; attenuation factors that define how rapidly the intensity drops off as a function of distance; and direction, exponent, and cutoff factors for spotlights. These attributes can be modified for any light by calling **glLight**. Individual lights can be turned on or off by calling **glEnable/glDisable** with a symbolic constant that specifies the affected light source. Lighting produces a primary and secondary color for each vertex. Lighting can be turned on or off by calling **glEnable/glDisable** with the symbolic constant GL_LIGHTING. If lighting is disabled, the values of the primary and secondary color are taken from the last color and secondary color value set with the **glColor** and **glSecondaryColor** commands.

The effects from enabled light sources are used in conjunction with surface material properties to determine the lit color at a particular vertex. Materials are characterized by the color of light they emit; the color of ambient, diffuse, and specular light they reflect; and their shininess. Material properties can be defined separately for front-facing surfaces and for back-facing surfaces and are specified by calling **glMaterial**.

Global lighting parameters are controlled by calling **glLightModel**. This function can be used to set a value used as a global ambient lighting value for the entire scene, whether the lighting calculations assume a local viewer or one positioned at infinity (this affects the computation of specular reflection angles), whether one- or two-sided lighting calculations are performed on polygons (if one-sided, only front material properties are used in lighting calculations, otherwise normals are reversed on back-facing polygons and back material properties are used to perform the lighting computation), and whether a separate specular color component is computed. This specular component is later added to the result of the texturing stage to provide specular highlights. The entire process of lighting can be enabled by calling **glEnable** and disabled by calling **glDisable**.

1.7.3 Primitive Assembly

After vertex processing, all of the attributes associated with each vertex are completely determined. The vertex data is then sent on to a stage called PRIMITIVE ASSEMBLY (3). It is at this point that the vertex data is collected into complete primitives. Points require a single vertex, lines require two, triangles require three, quadrilaterals require four, and general polygons can have an arbitrary number of vertices. For the vertex-at-a-time API, an argument to **glBegin** specifies the primitive type, and for vertex arrays, the primitive type is passed as an argument to the function that draws the vertex array. The primitive assembly stage effectively collects up enough vertices to construct a single primitive, and then this primitive is passed on to the next stage of processing. The reason this stage is needed is that at the very next stage, operations are performed on a set of vertices, and the operations are dependent on the type of primitive. In particular, clipping is done differently depending on whether the primitive is a point, line, or polygon.

1.7.4 Primitive Processing

The next stage of processing (4), actually consists of several distinct steps that have been combined into a single box in Figure 1.1 just to simplify the diagram. The first step that occurs is clipping, and this operation compares each primitive to any user-defined clipping planes set by calling **glClipPlane** as well as to the VIEW VOLUME established by the modelview and projection matrices. If the primitive is completely within the view volume and the user-defined clipping planes, it is passed on for subsequent processing. If it is completely outside the view volume or the user-defined clipping planes, the primitive is rejected, and no further processing is required. If the primitive is partially in and partially out, it is divided (CLIPPED) in such a way that only the portion within the clip volume and the user-defined clipping planes is passed on for further processing.

Another operation that occurs at this stage is perspective projection. If the current view is a perspective view, each vertex will have its x, y, and z components divided by its homogeneous coordinate w. Following this, each vertex will be transformed by the current viewport transformation (set by calling **glDepthRange** and **glViewport**) in order to generate window coordinates. Certain OpenGL states can be set to cause an operation called CULLING to be performed on polygon primitives at this stage. Using the computed window coordinates, each polygon primitive is tested to see whether it is facing away from the current viewing position. The culling state can be enabled by calling **glEnable**, and **glCullFace** can be called to specify that back-facing polygons will be discarded (culled), front-facing polygons will be discarded, or both will be discarded.

1.7.5 Rasterization

Geometric primitives that are passed through the OpenGL pipeline contain a set of data at each of the vertices of the primitive. At the next stage (5), primitives (points, lines, or polygons) are decomposed into smaller units corresponding to pixels in the destination frame buffer. This process is called RASTERIZATION. Each of these smaller units generated by rasterization is referred to as a FRAGMENT. For instance, a line might cover five pixels on the screen, and the process of rasterization converts the line (defined by two vertices) into five fragments. A fragment is comprised of a window coordinate and depth and of other associated attributes such as color, texture coordinates, and so on. The values for each of these attributes is determined by interpolating between the values specified (or computed) at the vertices of the primitive. At the time they are rasterized, vertices have a primary color and a secondary color. The **glShadeModel** function can be called to specify whether these color values are interpolated between the vertices (SMOOTH SHADING) or whether the color values for the last vertex of the primitive are used for the entire primitive (FLAT SHADING).

There are different rasterization rules and a different OpenGL state for each type of primitive. Points have a width controlled by calling **glPointSize** and other rendering attributes that are defined by calling **glPointParameter**. Lines have a width that is controlled by calling **glLineWidth** and a stipple pattern that is set by calling **glLineStipple**. Polygons have a stipple pattern that is set by calling **glPolygonStipple**. Polygons can be drawn as filled, outline, or vertex points depending only on the value set by calling **glPolygonMode**. The depth values for each fragment in a polygon can be modified by a value that is computed using state set with **glPolygonOffset**. The orientation of polygons that are to be considered front facing can be set by calling **glFrontFace**. The process of smoothing the jagged appearance of a primitive is called ANTIALIASING, and primitive antialiasing can be enabled by calling **glEnable** with the appropriate symbolic constant (GL_POINT_SMOOTH, GL_LINE_SMOOTH, or GL_POLYGON_SMOOTH).

1.7.6 Fragment Processing

After fragments have been generated by rasterization, a number of operations occurs on fragments. Collectively, these operations are called FRAGMENT PROCESSING (6). Perhaps the most important operation that occurs at this point is called TEXTURING. In this operation, the texture coordinates associated with the fragment are used to access a region of graphics memory called TEXTURE MEMORY (7). OpenGL defines a lot of states that affect how textures are accessed as well as how the retrieved values are applied to the current fragment. Many extensions have been defined to this area that is rather complex to begin with. We will spend some time talking about texturing operations in Section 1.10.

Other operations that occur at this point are FOG (modifying the color of the fragment depending on its distance from the view point) and COLOR SUM (combining the values of the fragment's primary color and secondary color). Fog parameters are set by calling **glFog**, and secondary colors are vertex attributes that can be passed in using the vertex attribute command **glSecondaryColor** or computed by the lighting stage.

1.7.7   Per-Fragment Operations

After fragment processing, fragments are submitted to a set of fairly simple operations called PER-FRAGMENT OPERATIONS (8). This includes things like the PIXEL OWNERSHIP TEST (determining whether the destination pixel is visible or obscured by an overlapping window), the SCISSOR TEST (fragments are clipped against a rectangular region established by calling **glScissor**), the ALPHA TEST (using the fragment's alpha value and the function established by calling **glAlphaFunc** to decide whether to discard the fragment), the STENCIL TEST (using a comparison established by calling **glStencilFunc** and **glStencilOp** to compare the value in the stencil buffer with a reference value in order to decide the fate of the fragment), the DEPTH TEST (deciding whether to draw the fragment by using the function established by calling **glDepthFunc** to compare the depth of the incoming fragment to the depth stored in the frame buffer), blending (using the fragment's color, the color stored in the frame buffer, and the blending state set up by calling **glBlendFunc**, **glBlendColor**, and **glBlendEquation** to determine the color to be written into the frame buffer), dithering, and the logical operation (combining the final fragment value with the value in the frame buffer using the logical operation established by calling **glLogicOp**).

Each of these operations is conceptually simple and nowadays can be implemented very efficiently and inexpensively in hardware. Some of these operations also involve reading values from the frame buffer (i.e., color, depth, or stencil). With today's hardware, all of these back-end rendering operations can be performed at millions of pixels per second, even those that require reading from the frame buffer.

1.7.8 Frame Buffer Operations

Things that control or affect the whole frame buffer are called FRAME BUFFER OPERATIONS (9). Certain OpenGL state is used to control the region of the frame buffer into which primitives are drawn. OpenGL supports display of stereo images as well as double-buffering, so there are a number of choices for the destination of rendering. Regions of the frame buffer are called BUFFERS and are referred to as the front, back, left, right, front left, front right, back left, back right, and front and back. Any of these buffers can be set as the destination for subsequent rendering operations by calling **glDrawBuffer**. Regions within the draw buffer(s) can be write protected. The **glColorMask** function determines whether writing is allowed to the red, green, blue, or alpha components of the destination buffer. The **glDepthMask** function determines whether the depth components of the destination buffer can be modified. The **glStencilMask** function controls the writing of particular bits in the stencil components of the destination buffer. Values in the frame buffer can be initialized by calling **glClear**. Values that will be used to initialize the color components, depth components, stencil components, and accumulation buffer components are set by calling **glClearColor**, **glClearDepth**, **glClearStencil**, and **glClearAccum**, respectively. The accumulation buffer operation can be specified by calling **glAccum**.

For performance reasons, OpenGL implementations often employ a variety of buffering schemes in order to send larger batches of graphics primitives to the 3D graphics hardware. To make sure that all graphics primitives for a specific rendering context are making progress toward completion, an application should call **glFlush**. To make sure that all graphics primitives for a particular rendering context have finished rendering, an application should call **glFinish**. This command blocks until the effects of all previous commands have been completed. This can be costly in terms of performance, so it should be used sparingly.

The overall effect of these stages is that graphics primitives defined by the application are converted into pixels in the frame buffer for subsequent display. But so far, we have discussed only geometric primitives such as points, lines, and polygons. OpenGL also has facilities for rendering bitmap and image data.

1.8 Drawing Images

As mentioned previously, OpenGL has a great deal of support for drawing images in addition to its support for drawing 3D geometry. In OpenGL parlance, images are called PIXEL RECTANGLES. The values that define a pixel rectangle start out in application-controlled memory as shown in Figure 1.1 (11). Color or grayscale pixel rectangles are rendered into the frame buffer by calling **glDrawPixels**, and bitmaps are rendered into the frame buffer by calling **glBitmap**. Images that are destined for texture memory are specified by calling **glTexImage** or **glTexSubImage**. Up to a point, the same basic processing is applied to the image data supplied with each of these commands.

1.8.1 Pixel Unpacking

OpenGL is capable of reading image data provided by the application in a variety of formats. Parameters that define how the image data is stored in memory (length of each pixel row, number of rows to skip before the first one, number of pixels to skip before the first one in each row, etc.) can be specified by calling **glPixelStore**. In order to allow operations on pixel data to be defined more precisely, pixels read from application memory are converted into a coherent stream of pixels by an operation referred to as PIXEL UNPACKING (12). When a pixel rectangle is transferred to OpenGL via a call like **glDrawPixels**, this operation applies the current set of pixel unpacking parameters to determine how the image data should be read and interpreted. As each pixel is read from memory, it is converted to a PIXEL GROUP that contains either a color, a depth, or a stencil value. If the pixel group consists of a color, the image data is destined for the color buffer in the frame buffer. If the pixel group consists of a depth value, the image data is destined for the depth buffer. If the pixel group consists of a stencil value, the image data is destined for the stencil buffer. Color values are made up of a red, a green, a blue, and an alpha component (i.e., RGBA) and are constructed from the input image data according to a set of rules defined by OpenGL. The result is a stream of RGBA values that are sent to OpenGL for further processing.

1.8.2 Pixel Transfer

After a coherent stream of image pixels is created, pixel rectangles undergo a series of operations called PIXEL TRANSFER (13). These operations are applied whenever pixel rectangles are transferred from the application to OpenGL (**glDrawPixels, glTexImage, glTexSubImage**) or from OpenGL back to the application (**glReadPixels**) or when they are copied within OpenGL (**glCopyPixels, glCopyTexImage, glCopyTexSubImage**).

The behavior of the pixel transfer stage is modified by calling **glPixelTransfer**. This command sets state that controls whether red, green, blue, alpha, and depth values are scaled and biased. It can also be used to set state that determines whether incoming color or stencil values are mapped to different color or stencil values through the use of a lookup table. The lookup tables used for these operations are specified using the **glPixelMap** command.

Some additional operations that occur at this stage are part of the OpenGL IMAGING SUBSET, which is an optional part of OpenGL. Hardware vendors that find it important to support advanced imaging capabilities will support the imaging subset in their OpenGL implementations, and other vendors will not support it. To determine whether the imaging subset is supported, applications need to call **glGetString** with the symbolic constant GL_EXTENSIONS. This returns a list of extensions supported by the implementation, and the application should check for the presence of the string "ARB_imaging" within the returned extension string.

The pixel transfer operations that are defined to be part of the imaging subset are convolution, color matrix, histogram, min/max, and additional color lookup tables. Together, this functionality can be used to perform powerful image processing and color correction operations on image data as it is being transferred to, from, or within OpenGL.

1.8.3 Rasterization and Back-End Processing

Following the pixel transfer stage, fragments are generated through the process of rasterizating pixel rectangles in much the same way as they are generated from 3D geometry (14). This process, along with the current OpenGL state, determines where the image will be drawn in the frame buffer. Rasterization takes into account the current RASTER POSITION (which can be set by calling **glRasterPos** or **glWindowPos**) and the current zoom factor (which can be set by calling **glPixelZoom** and causes an image to be magnified or reduced in size as it is drawn).

After fragments have generated from pixel rectangles, they undergo the same set of fragment processing operations as geometric primitives (6) and then go on to the remainder of the OpenGL pipeline in exactly the same manner as geometric primitives, all the way until pixels are deposited in the frame buffer (8, 9, 10).

Pixel values provided through a call to **glTexImage** or **glTexSubImage** do not go through rasterization or the subsequent fragment processing but are used directly to update the appropriate portion of texture memory (15).

1.8.4 Read Control

Pixel rectangles are read from the frame buffer and returned to application memory by calling **glReadPixels**. They can also be read from the frame buffer and written to another portion of the frame buffer by calling **glCopyPixels**, or they can be read from the frame buffer and written into texture memory by calling **glCopyTexImage** or **glCopyTexSubImage**. In all of these cases, the portion of the frame buffer that is to be read is controlled by the READ CONTROL stage of OpenGL and set using the **glReadBuffer** command (16).

The values read from the frame buffer are sent through the pixel transfer stage (13) where various image processing operations may be performed. For copy operations, the resulting pixels are sent to texture memory or back into the frame buffer, depending on the command that initiated the transfer. For read operations, the pixels are formatted for storage in application memory under the control of the PIXEL PACKING stage (17). This stage is the mirror of the pixel unpacking stage (12), in that parameters that define how the image data is to be stored in memory (length of each pixel row, number of rows to skip before the first one, number of pixels to skip before the first one in each row, etc.) can be specified by calling **glPixelStore**. This gives applications a lot of flexibility in determining how the image data is returned from OpenGL into application memory.

1.9 Coordinate Transforms

The purpose of the OpenGL graphics processing pipeline is to convert three-dimensional descriptions of objects into a two-dimensional image that can be displayed. In many ways, this process is similar to using a camera to convert a real-world scene into a two-dimensional print. To accomplish the transformation from three dimensions to two, OpenGL defines several coordinate spaces and transformations between those spaces. Each coordinate space has some properties that make it useful for some part of the rendering process. The transformations defined by OpenGL provide applications a great deal of flexibility in defining the 3D-to-2D mapping. In order to be successful at writing shaders using the OpenGL Shading Language, it is important to understand the various transformations and coordinate spaces used by OpenGL.

In computer graphics, MODELING is the process of defining a numerical representation of an object that is to be rendered. For OpenGL, this usually means creating a polygonal representation of an object in order that it can be drawn using the polygon primitives built into OpenGL. At a minimum, a polygonal representation of an object needs to include the coordinates of each vertex in each polygon and the connectivity information that defines the polygons. Additional data might include the color of each vertex, the surface normal at each vertex, one or more texture coordinates at each vertex, and so on.

In the past, modeling an object was a painstaking effort, requiring precise physical measurement and data entry. (This is one of the reasons the Utah teapot, modeled by Martin Newell in 1975, has been used in so many graphics images. It is an interesting object, and the numerical data is freely available. Several of the shaders presented in this book are illustrated with this object; see for example Color Plate 20.) More recently, a variety of modeling tools has become available, both hardware and software, and this has made it relatively easy to create numerical representations of three-dimensional objects that are to be rendered.

Three-dimensional object attributes, such as vertex positions and surface normals, are defined in OBJECT SPACE. This coordinate space is one that is convenient for describing the object that is being modeled. Coordinates are specified in units that are convenient to that particular object. Microscopic objects may be modeled using units of angstroms, everyday objects may be modeled using inches or centimeters, buildings might be modeled using feet or meters, planets could be modeled using miles or kilometers, and galaxies might be modeled using light years or parsecs. The origin of this coordinate system (i.e., the point (0, 0, 0)) is also something that is convenient for the object being modeled. For some objects, the origin might be placed at one corner of the object's three-dimensional bounding box. For other objects, it might be more convenient to define the origin at the centroid of the object. Because of its intimate connection with the task of modeling, this coordinate space is also often referred to as MODEL SPACE or the MODELING COORDINATE SYSTEM. Coordinates are referred to equivalently as object coordinates or modeling coordinates.

In order to compose a scene that contains a variety of three-dimensional objects, each of which might be defined in its own unique object space, we need a common coordinate system. This common coordinate system is called WORLD SPACE or the WORLD COORDINATE SYSTEM, and it will provide a common frame of reference for all objects in the scene. By transforming all of the objects in the scene into a single coordinate system, the spatial relationships between all the objects, the light sources, and the viewer will be known. The units of this coordinate system are chosen in a way that is convenient for describing a scene. You might choose feet or meters if you are composing a scene that represents one of the rooms in your house, but you might choose city blocks as your units if you are composing a scene that represents a city skyline. The choice for the origin of this coordinate system is also arbitrary. You might define a three-dimensional bounding box for your scene and set the origin at the corner of the bounding box such that all of the other coordinates of the bounding box have positive values. Or you may want to pick an important point in your scene (the corner of a building, the location of a key character, etc.) and make that the origin.

After world space is defined, all of the objects in the scene must be transformed from their own unique object coordinates into world coordinates. The transformation that takes coordinates from object space to world space is called the MODELING TRANSFORMATION. If the object's modeling coordinates are in feet, but the world coordinate system is defined in terms of inches, it will be necessary to scale the object coordinates by a factor of 12 to produce world coordinates. If the object is defined to be facing forward but in the scene it needs to be facing backwards, a rotation needs to be applied to the object coordinates. A translation will also typically be required to position the object at its desired location in world coordinates. All of these individual transformations can be put together into a single matrix, the MODEL TRANSFORMATION MATRIX, that represents the transformation from object coordinates to world coordinates.

After the scene has been composed, it is necessary to specify the viewing parameters. One aspect of this is to define the vantage point (i.e., the eye or camera position) from which the scene will be viewed. Viewing parameters also include the focus point (also called the lookat point or the direction in which the camera is pointed) and the up direction (e.g., the camera may be held upside down).

The viewing parameters collectively define the VIEWING TRANSFORMATION, and they can be combined into a matrix called the VIEWING MATRIX. When multiplied by this matrix, a coordinate is transformed from world space into EYE SPACE. By definition, the origin of this coordinate system is at the viewing (or eye) position. Coordinates in this space are called EYE COORDINATES. The spatial relationships in the scene remain unchanged, but orienting the coordinate system in this way makes it easy to determine the distance from the viewpoint to various objects in the scene.

Although some 3D graphics APIs allow applications to specify the modeling matrix and the viewing matrix separately, OpenGL combines them into a single matrix called the MODELVIEW MATRIX. This matrix is defined to transform coordinates from object space into eye space (see Figure 1.2). There are a number of matrices that can be manipulated in OpenGL. The **glMatrixMode** function can be called to select the modelview matrix or one of OpenGL's other matrices. The current matrix can be loaded with the identity matrix by calling **glLoadIdentity**, or it can be replaced by an arbitrary matrix by calling **glLoadMatrix** (make sure you know what you're doing if you specify an arbitrary matrix—the transformation might give you a completely incomprehensible image!). You can also multiply the current matrix by an arbitrary matrix by calling **glMultMatrix**.

Often times, applications will start by setting the current modelview matrix to the view matrix and then add on the necessary modeling matrices. The modelview matrix can be set to a reasonable viewing transformation using the **gluLookAt** function. (This function is not part of OpenGL proper but is part of the OpenGL utility library that is provided with every OpenGL implementation.) OpenGL actually supports a stack of modelview matrices, and the top-most matrix can be duplicated and copied onto the top of the stack by calling **glPushMatrix**. When this is done, other transformations can be concatenated to the top-most matrix using the functions **glScale**, **glTranslate**, and **glRotate** in order to define the modeling transformation for a particular three-dimensional object in the scene. Then, this top-most matrix can be popped off the stack by calling

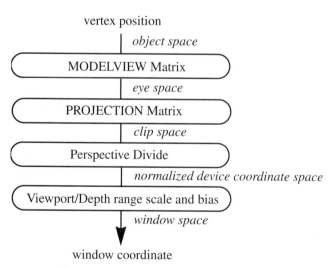

Figure 1.2 Coordinate spaces and transforms in OpenGL

glPopMatrix to get back to the original view transformation matrix. This process can be repeated for each object in the scene.

At the time light source positions are specified using the **glLight** function, they are transformed by the current modelview matrix. Therefore, light positions are stored within OpenGL as eye coordinates. The modelview matrix must be set up to perform the proper transformation before light positions are specified, or you won't get the lighting effects that you expect. The lighting calculations that occur in OpenGL are defined to happen on a per-vertex basis in the eye coordinate system. In order to do the necessary reflection computations, light positions and surface normals must be in the same coordinate system. OpenGL implementations will often choose to do lighting calculations in eye space; therefore the incoming surface normals have to be transformed into eye space as well. This is accomplished by transforming surface normals by the inverse transpose of the modelview matrix. At that point, the per-vertex lighting formulas defined by OpenGL can be applied to determine the lit color at each vertex.

After coordinates have been transformed into eye space, the next thing is to define a viewing volume. This is the region of the three-dimensional scene that will be visible in the final image. The transformation that takes the objects in the viewing volume into CLIP SPACE (a coordinate space that is suitable for clipping) is called the PROJECTION TRANSFORMATION. In OpenGL, the projection transformation is established by calling **glMatrixMode** to select the projection matrix and then setting this matrix appropriately. Parameters that may go into creating an appropriate projection matrix are the field of view (how much of the scene is visible), the aspect ratio (the horizontal field of view may differ from the vertical field of view), and near and far clipping planes to eliminate things that are too far away or too close (for perspective projections, weirdness will occur if you try to draw things that are at or behind the viewing position). Three utility functions that are provided for setting the projection matrix are **glOrtho**, **glFrustum**, and **gluPerspective**. The difference between these functions is that **glOrtho** defines a parallel projection (i.e., parallel lines in the scene are projected to parallel lines in the final two-dimensional image), whereas **glFrustum** and **gluPerspective** define perspective projections (parallel lines in the scene are foreshortened to produce a vanishing point in the image, such as railroad tracks converging to a point in the distance).

FRUSTUM CLIPPING is the process of eliminating any graphics primitives that lie outside of an axis-aligned cube in clip space. This cube is defined such that the x, y, and z components of the clip space coordinate are less than or equal to the w component for the coordinate, and greater than or equal to $-w$ (i.e., $-w \leq x \leq w$, $-w \leq y \leq w$, and $-w \leq z \leq w$). Graphics primitives (or portions thereof) that lie outside this cube will be discarded. Frustum clipping is always performed on all incoming primitives in OpenGL. USER CLIPPING, on the other hand, is a feature that can be enabled or disabled by the application. Applications can call **glClipPlane** to specify one or more clipping planes that further restrict the size of the viewing volume, and each clipping plane can be individually enabled by calling **glEnable**. When specified, user clipping planes are transformed into eye space by OpenGL using the inverse of the current modelview matrix. Each plane specified in this manner defines a half-space, and only the portions of primitives that lie within the intersection of the view volume and all of the enabled half-spaces defined by user clipping planes will be drawn.

The next step in the transformation of vertex positions is the perspective divide. This operation divides each component of the clip space coordinate by the homogeneous coordinate w. The resulting x, y, and z components will range from [–1,1], and the resulting w coordinate will always be 1, so it is no longer needed. In other words, all of the visible graphics primitives will be transformed into a cubic region between the point (–1, –1, –1) and the point (1, 1, 1). This is the NORMALIZED DEVICE COORDINATE SPACE, which is an intermediate space that allows the viewing area to be properly mapped onto a viewport of arbitrary size and depth.

Pixels within a window on the display device aren't referred to using floating-point coordinates from –1 to 1; they are usually referred to using WINDOW COORDINATES, where x values range from 0 to the width of the window minus 1, and y values range from 0 to the height of the window minus 1. Therefore, one more transformation step is required. The VIEWPORT TRANSFORMATION is used to specify the mapping from normalized device coordinates into window coordinates, and this mapping can be specified by calling the OpenGL functions **glViewport** (which specifies the mapping of the x and y coordinates) and **glDepthRange** (which specifies the mapping of the z coordinate). Rasterization of graphics primitives occurs using window coordinates.

1.10 Texturing

The area of texture mapping is one of the more complex areas of the OpenGL API. It has been extended more often than most of the other areas of OpenGL primarily because this was the area of graphics for which hardware was the least mature when OpenGL was defined in the early 1990s. The programmability added through the OpenGL Shading Language makes this area much more straightforward, but the existing OpenGL APIs are still used to create, modify, and define the behavior of textures. This section describes the texturing functionality that exists for OpenGL 1.5. Some significant changes have been made to this model, particularly to the concept of texture units, by the OpenGL extensions that define support for the OpenGL Shading Language and are described later in this book.

OpenGL currently supports four basic types of texture maps: one-dimensional, two-dimensional, three-dimensional, and cube maps. (Only one- and two-dimensional textures were supported in OpenGL 1.0.) A 1D TEXTURE is an array containing *width* pixel values, a 2D TEXTURE is an array containing *width × height* pixel values, and a 3D TEXTURE is an array containing *width × height × depth* pixel values. A CUBE MAP TEXTURE contains six two-dimensional textures: one for each major axis direction (i.e., ±*x*, ±*y*, and ±*z*).

OpenGL has the notion of a TEXTURE UNIT. A texture unit corresponds to the underlying piece of graphics hardware that performs the various texturing operations. With OpenGL 1.3, support was added for multiple texture units. Each texture unit maintains the following state for performing texturing operations:

- Whether the texture unit is currently enabled or disabled

- A texture matrix stack that is used to transform incoming texture coordinates

- State used for automatic texture coordinate generation

- Texture environment state

- A current 1D texture

- A current 2D texture

- A current 3D texture

- A current cube map texture

Commands to set the state in the preceding list operate on the ACTIVE TEXTURE UNIT. Texture units are numbered from 0 to GL_MAX_TEXTURE_UNITS–1 (a value that can be queried by calling **glGet**), and the active texture unit can be set by calling **glActiveTexture** with a symbolic constant indicating the desired texture unit. Subsequent commands to set state in the preceding list operate on only the active texture unit. A texture unit can be enabled for 1D, 2D, 3D, or cube map texturing by calling **glEnable** with the appropriate symbolic constant.

The active texture unit specifies the texture unit accessed by commands involving texture coordinate processing. Such commands include those accessing the current texture matrix stack (if GL_MATRIX_MODE is GL_TEXTURE), **glTexGen**, **glEnable/glDisable** (if any texture coordinate generation enum is selected), as well as queries of the current texture coordinates and current raster texture coordinates. The active texture unit selector also selects the texture unit accessed by commands involving texture image processing. Such commands include all variants of **glTexEnv**, **glTexParameter**, and **glTexImage** commands; **glBindTexture**; **glEnable/glDisable** for any texture target (e.g., GL_TEXTURE_2D); and queries of all such state.

A TEXTURE OBJECT can be created by calling **glBindTexture** and providing a texture target (a symbolic constant that indicates whether the texture will be a 1D, 2D, 3D, or cube map texture) and a previously unused texture name (an integer other than zero) that can be used to refer to the newly created texture object. The newly created texture object also becomes active and will be used in subsequent texturing operations. If **glBindTexture** is called with a texture name that has already been used, that previously created texture becomes active. In this way, an application can create any number of textures and switch between them easily.

After a texture object has been created, the pixel values that define the texture can be provided. Pixel values for a 3D texture can be supplied by calling **glTexImage3D**, pixel values for 2D or cube map textures can be provided by calling **glTexImage2D**, and pixel values for a 1D texture can be specified by calling **glTexImage1D**. When using any of these three commands, each dimension of the texture map must be a size that is a power of two (including the border width). These functions all work in the same way as **glDrawPixels**, except that the pixels comprising a texture are deposited into texture memory prior to rasterization. If only a portion of a texture needs to be respecified, the **glTexSubImage1D/2D/3D** functions can be used. When using any of these three commands, there is no power-of-two restriction on the texture size. Textures can be created or modified with values copied from frame buffer memory by calling **glCopyTexImage1D/2D/3D** or **glCopyTexSubImage1D/2D/3D**.

Provisions have also been made for specifying textures using compressed image formats. Applications can use the commands **glCompressedTexImage1D/2D/3D** and **glCompressedTexSubImage1D/2D/3D** to create and store compressed textures in texture memory. Compressed textures may use significantly less memory on the graphics accelerator and thereby enhance an application's functionality or performance. Standard

OpenGL does not define any particular compressed image formats, so applications need to query the extension string in order to determine the compressed texture formats supported by a particular implementation.

Each of the preceding texture creation commands includes a LEVEL-OF-DETAIL argument that supports the creation of MIPMAP TEXTURES. A mipmap texture is an ordered set of arrays representing the same image. Each array has a resolution that is half the previous one in each dimension. The idea behind mipmaps is that more pleasing final images will result if the texture to be used has roughly the same resolution as the object being drawn on the display. If a mipmap texture is supplied, OpenGL can automatically choose the appropriately sized texture (i.e., MIPMAP LEVEL) for use in drawing the object on the display. Interpolation between the TEXELS (pixels that comprise a texture) of two mipmap levels can also be performed. Objects that are textured using mipmap textures can therefore be rendered with high quality, no matter how they change size on the display.

After a texture object has been defined and bound to a texture unit, properties other than the pixels that define the texture can be modified using the command **glTexParameter**. This command sets parameters that control how the texture object is treated when it is specified, changed, or accessed. Texture object parameters include

- The wrapping behavior in each dimension (i.e., whether the texture repeats, clamps, or is mirrored when texture coordinates go outside of the range [0,1])

- The minification filter (i.e., how the texture is to be sampled if the mapping from texture space to window space causes the texture image to be made smaller in order to map it onto the surface)

- The magnification filter (i.e., how the texture is to be sampled if the mapping from texture space to window space causes the texture image to be made larger in order to map it onto the surface)

- The border color to be used if the wrapping behavior indicates clamping to a border color

- The priority to be assigned to the texture (a value from [0,1] that tells OpenGL the importance of performance for this texture)

- Values for clamping and biasing the level-of-detail value that is automatically computed by OpenGL

- The level that is defined as the base (highest resolution) level for a mipmap texture

- The level that is defined as the maximum (lowest resolution) level for a mipmap texture

- Values that indicate whether a comparison operation should be performed when the texture is accessed, what type of comparison operation should be performed, and how to treat the result of the comparison (this is used with depth textures to implement shadowing)

- A value that indicates whether mipmap levels are to be computed automatically by OpenGL whenever the base level is specified or modified

The manner in which a texture value is applied to a graphics primitive is controlled by the parameters of the texture environment, which are set with the **glTexEnv** function. The set of fixed formulas for replacing an object color with a value computed through texture access is rather lengthy. Suffice it to say that texture functions include replacement, modulation, decal application, blending, adding, and even more complex combining of red, green, blue, and alpha components. A wide variety of texturing effects can be achieved using the flexibility provided by the **glTexEnv** function. This function can also be used to specify an additional per-texture-unit level-of-detail bias that is added to the per-texture-object level-of-detail bias described in the preceding paragraph.

OpenGL supports the concept of multitexturing, where the results of more than one texture access are combined to determine the value of the fragment. Each texture unit has a texture environment function. Texture units are connected in a serial fashion. A fragment value is computed by the first texture unit using the texture value that it reads from texture memory and its texture environment function, and the result is passed on to be used as the input fragment value for the second texture unit. This fragment value is used together with the texture environment function for the second texture unit and the texture value read from texture memory by the second texture unit to provide the input fragment value for the third texture unit. This process is repeated for all enabled texture units.

After texture objects have been defined and one or more texture units have been properly set up and enabled, texturing is performed on all subsequent graphics primitives. Texture coordinates are supplied at each vertex by calling **glTexCoord** or **glMultiTexCoord** (using the vertex-at-a-time entry points) or as an array indicated by **glTexCoordPointer** (for use with vertex array commands). The **glMultiTexCoord** command is provided to specify texture coordinates that are to be operated on by a specific texture unit. This command specifies the texture unit as well as the texture coordinates to be used. The command **glTexCoord** is equivalent to the command **glMultiTexCoord** with its texture parameter set to GL_TEXTURE0. For vertex arrays, it is necessary to call **glClientActiveTexture** between each call to **glTexCoordPointer** in order to specify different texture coordinate arrays for different texture units.

Texture coordinates can also be generated automatically by OpenGL. Parameters for controlling automatic texture coordinate generation are set on a per-texture unit basis using the **glTexGen** command. This function lets the application select a texture generation function and supply coefficients for that function for the currently active texture unit. Supported texture generation functions are object linear (useful for automatically generating texture coordinates for terrain models), eye linear (useful for producing dynamic contour lines on moving objects), and sphere map (useful for a type of environment mapping that requires just one texture).

When texture coordinates have been sent to OpenGL or generated by the texture unit's texture generation function, they are transformed by the texture unit's current texture transformation matrix. The **glMatrixMode** command is used to select the texture matrix stack for modification, and subsequent matrix commands will modify the texture matrix stack of the currently active texture unit. This provides the capability to translate the texture across the object, rotate it, stretch it, shrink it, and so on. Both texture generation and texture transformation are defined by OpenGL to occur as part of vertex processing (i.e., they are performed once per-vertex prior to rasterization).

After rasterization of the graphics primitive (and interpolation of the transformed texture coordinates), TEXTURE ACCESS, the process by which the texture coordinates are used by a texture unit to access the enabled texture for that unit, occurs. The texture access is performed according to the bound texture object's parameters for filtering, wrapping, computed level-of-detail, and so on.

After a texture value has been retrieved, it is combined with the incoming color value according to the texture function established by calling **glTexEnv**. This operation is called TEXTURE APPLICATION. This computation produces a new fragment color value that is used for all subsequent processing of the fragment. Both texture access and texture application are defined to occur on every fragment that results from the rasterization process.

1.11 Summary

This chapter has attempted to provide a short review of the fundamentals of the OpenGL API. In it, we've touched on the vast majority of the important OpenGL function calls. If you haven't used OpenGL for quite some time, the hope is that this review chapter has been enough to orient you properly for the task of writing shaders using the OpenGL Shading Language. If you have been using another 3D graphics programming API, the hope is that this short overview is enough to get you started using OpenGL and writing your own shaders. If not, the next section lists a number of resources for learning more about OpenGL.

1.12 Further Information

The Web site http://opengl.org has the latest information for the OpenGL community, forums for developers, and links to a variety of demos and technical information. OpenGL developers should have this site book-marked and visit it often.

Although now slightly out-of-date, the standard reference books for the OpenGL API are the *OpenGL Programming Guide, Third Edition* (1999) and the *OpenGL Reference Manual, Third Edition* (1999), both by the OpenGL Architecture Review Board. These books are currently being updated with the fourth edition of the former expected in 2003 and the fourth edition of the latter expected in 2004. Another useful OpenGL book is *OpenGL SuperBible, Second Edition,* by Richard S. Wright, Jr. and Michael Sweet (1999). This book is also currently undergoing a revision.

A good overview of OpenGL is provided in the technical paper *The Design of the OpenGL Graphics Interface* by Mark Segal and Kurt Akeley (1994). Of course, the definitive document on OpenGL is the specification itself, *The OpenGL Graphics System: A Specification, (Version 1.5),* by Mark Segal and Kurt Akeley, edited by Chris Frazier and Jon Leech (2002).

The OpenGL.org Web site, http://opengl.org, is also a good source for finding source code for OpenGL example programs. Another useful site is Tom Nuyden's site at http://delphi3d.net. The hardware vendors that support OpenGL typically provide lots of example programs, especially for newer OpenGL functionality and extensions. The SGI, NVIDIA, and ATI Web sites are particularly good in this regard.

[1] *ATI developer Web site.* http://www.ati.com/na/pages/resource_
centre/dev_rel/devrel.html

[2] *Delphi3D Web site.* http://delphi3d.net

[3] *NVIDIA developer Web site.* http://developer.nvidia.com

[4] OpenGL Architecture Review Board, J. Neider, T. Davis, and M. Woo,
*OpenGL Programming Guide, Third Edition: The Official Guide to
Learning OpenGL, Version 1.2*, Addison-Wesley, Reading,
Massachusetts, 1999.

[5] OpenGL Architecture Review Board, *OpenGL Reference Manual, Third
Edition: The Official Reference to OpenGL, Version 1.2*, Addison-
Wesley, Reading, Massachusetts, 1999.

[6] OpenGL, official Web site. http://opengl.org

[7] Segal, Mark, and Kurt Akeley, *The OpenGL Graphics System: A
Specification (Version 1.5)*, Editor (v1.1): Chris Frazier, Editor
(v1.2–1.5): Jon Leech, July 2003. http://opengl.org

[8] Segal, Mark, and Kurt Akeley, *The Design of the OpenGL Graphics
Interface*, Silicon Graphics Inc., 1994. http://opengl.org

[9] *SGI OpenGL Web site.* http://www.sgi.com/software/opengl

[10] Wright, Richard, and Michael Sweet, *OpenGL SuperBible,
Second Edition*, Waite Group Press, Corte Madera, California,
1999. http://www.starstonesoftware.com/OpenGL/opengl_
superbbile.htm

Chapter 2

Basics

This chapter introduces the OpenGL Shading Language to get you started writing your own shaders as quickly as possible. When you finish reading this chapter, you should understand how programmability has been added to OpenGL and be ready to tackle the details of the shading language description in the next three chapters and the simple example in Chapter 6. After that, you can learn more details about the API that supports the shading language or explore the examples contained in the later chapters.

2.1 Introduction to the OpenGL Shading Language

This book is aimed at helping you learn and use a high-level graphics programming language formally called the OPENGL SHADING LANGUAGE. This language and the OpenGL extensions that support it were approved as ARB extensions in June 2003. It is expected that they will be added to the OpenGL core for the next revision of OpenGL, which will be called OpenGL 2.0.

The recent trend in graphics hardware has been to replace fixed functionality with programmability in areas that have grown exceedingly complex. Two such areas are vertex processing and fragment processing. Vertex processing involves the operations that occur at each vertex, most notably transformation and lighting. Fragments are per-pixel data structures that are created by the rasterization of graphics primitives. A fragment contains all of the data necessary to update a single location in the frame buffer. Fragment processing consists of the operations that occur on a per-fragment basis, most notably reading from texture memory and applying the texture value(s) at each fragment. With the OpenGL Shading Language, the fixed functionality stages for vertex processing and fragment processing have been augmented with programmable stages that can do everything the fixed functionality stages can do—and a whole lot more. The OpenGL Shading Language has been designed to allow application programmers to express the processing that occurs at those programmable points of the OpenGL pipeline.

The OpenGL Shading Language code that is intended for execution on one of the OpenGL programmable processors is called a SHADER. The term OPENGL SHADER is sometimes used to differentiate a shader written in the OpenGL Shading Language from a shader written in another shading language such as RenderMan. Because two programmable processors are defined in OpenGL, there are two types of shaders: VERTEX SHADERS and FRAGMENT SHADERS. OpenGL provides mechanisms for compiling shaders and linking them together to form executable code called a program. A program contains one or more EXECUTABLES that can run on the programmable processing units.

The OpenGL Shading Language has its roots in C and has features similar to RenderMan and other shading languages. The language has a rich set of types, including vector and matrix types to make code more concise for typical 3D graphics operations. A special set of type qualifiers manages the unique forms of input and output needed by shaders. Some mechanisms from C++, such as function overloading based on argument types, and the capability to declare variables where they are first needed instead of at the beginning of blocks, have also been borrowed. The language includes support for loops, subroutine calls, and conditional expressions. An extensive set of built-in functions provides many of the capabilities needed for implementing shading algorithms. In brief

- The OpenGL Shading Language is a high-level procedural language.

- The same language, with a small set of differences, is used for both vertex and fragment shaders.

- It is based on C and C++ syntax and flow control.

- It natively supports vector and matrix operations, as these are inherent to many graphics algorithms.

- It is stricter with types than C and C++, and functions are called by value-return.

- It uses type qualifiers rather than reads and writes to manage input and output.

- There are no practical limits to a shader's length, nor is there a need to query it.

The following sections contain some of the key concepts that you will need to understand in order to use the OpenGL Shading Language effectively. The concepts will be covered in much more detail later in the book, but this introductory chapter should help you understand the big picture.

2.2 Why Write Shaders?

Until recently, OpenGL has presented application programmers with a flexible but static interface for putting graphics on the display device. As described in Chapter 1, you could think of OpenGL as a sequence of operations that occurred on geometry or image data as it was sent through the graphics hardware to be displayed on the screen. Various parameters of these pipeline stages could be altered in order to select variations on the processing that occurred for that pipeline stage. But neither the fundamental operation of the OpenGL graphics pipeline nor the order of operations could be changed through the OpenGL API.

By exposing support for traditional rendering mechanisms, OpenGL has evolved to serve the needs of a fairly broad set of applications. If your particular application was well served by the traditional rendering model presented by OpenGL, you may never have the need to write shaders. But if you have ever been frustrated by the fact that OpenGL does not allow you to define area lights or the fact that lighting calculations are performed per-vertex rather than per-fragment or if you have run into any of the many limitations of the traditional OpenGL rendering model, you may need to write your own OpenGL shader.

The purpose of the OpenGL Shading Language and its supporting OpenGL API entry points is to allow *applications* to define the processing that occurs at key points in the OpenGL processing pipeline using a high-level programming language specifically designed for this purpose. These key points in the pipeline are defined to be programmable in order to give applications complete freedom to define the processing that occurs. This gives applications the capability to utilize the underlying graphics hardware to achieve a much wider range of rendering effects.

To get an idea of the range of effects possible with OpenGL shaders, take a minute now and browse through the color images that are included in this book. This book presents a variety of shaders that only begin to scratch the surface of what is possible. With each new generation of graphics hardware, more complex rendering techniques can be implemented as OpenGL shaders and can be used in real-time rendering applications. Here's a brief list of what's possible using OpenGL shaders:

- Increasingly realistic materials—metals, stone, wood, paints, and so on

- Increasingly realistic lighting effects—area lights, soft shadows, and so on

- Natural phenomena—fire, smoke, water, clouds, and so on

- Non-photorealistic materials—painterly effects, pen-and-ink drawings, simulation of illustration techniques, and so on

- New uses for texture memory—textures can be used to store normals, gloss values, polynomial coefficients, and so on

- Fewer texture accesses—textures can be created procedurally instead of accessing texture maps stored in texture memory

- Image processing—convolution, unsharp masking, complex blending, and so on

- Animation effects—key frame interpolation, particle systems, procedurally defined motion

- User programmable antialiasing methods

Many of these techniques have been available before now only through software implementations. If at all possible through OpenGL, they were possible only in a limited way. The fact that these techniques can now be implemented with hardware acceleration provided by dedicated graphics hardware means that rendering performance can be increased dramatically and at the same time the CPU can be off-loaded so that it can perform other tasks.

2.3 OpenGL Programmable Processors

The biggest change to OpenGL since its inception and the reason a high-level shading language is needed are the introduction of programmable vertex and fragment processors. In Chapter 1, we discussed the OpenGL pipeline and the fixed functionality that implements vertex processing and fragment processing. With the introduction of programmability, the fixed functionality vertex processing and fixed functionality fragment processing are disabled when an OpenGL Shading Language program is made current (i.e., made part of the current rendering state).

Figure 2.1 shows the OpenGL processing pipeline when the programmable processors are active. In this case, the fixed functionality vertex and the fragment processing shown in Figure 1.1 are replaced by programmable vertex and fragment processors as shown in Figure 2.1. All other parts of the OpenGL processing remain the same.

This diagram illustrates the stream processing nature of OpenGL via the programmable processors that are defined as part of the OpenGL Shading Language. Data flows from the application to the vertex processor, on to the fragment processor, and ultimately to the frame buffer.

2.3.1 Vertex Processor

The VERTEX PROCESSOR is a programmable unit that operates on incoming vertex values and their associated data. The vertex processor is intended to perform traditional graphics operations such as the following:

- Vertex transformation

- Normal transformation and normalization

- Texture coordinate generation

- Texture coordinate transformation

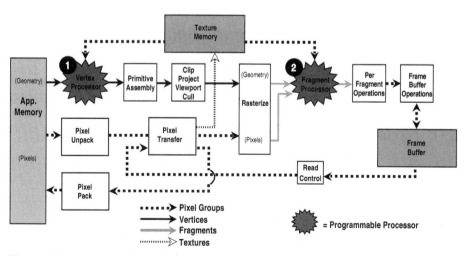

Figure 2.1   OpenGL logical diagram showing programmable processors for vertex and fragment shaders rather than fixed functionality

- Lighting
- Color material application

Because of its general purpose programmability, this processor can also be used to perform a variety of other computations. Shaders that are intended to run on this processor are called vertex shaders. Vertex shaders can be used to specify a completely general sequence of operations to be applied to each vertex and its associated data. Vertex shaders that perform some of the computations in the preceding list are responsible for writing the code for all desired functionality from the preceding list. For instance, it is not possible to use the existing fixed functionality to perform the vertex and normal transformation but to have a vertex shader perform a specialized lighting function. The vertex shader must be written to perform all three functions.

The vertex processor does not replace graphics operations that require knowledge of several vertices at a time or that require topological knowledge. OpenGL operations that remain as fixed functionality in between the vertex processor and the fragment processor include perspective divide and viewport mapping, primitive assembly, frustum and user clipping, backface culling, two-sided lighting selection, polygon mode, polygon offset, selection of flat or smooth shading, and depth range.

Figure 2.2 shows the data values that are used as inputs to the vertex processor and the data values that are produced by the vertex processor. Vertex shaders are used to express the algorithm that executes on the vertex processor to produce output values based on the provided input values. Type qualifiers that are defined as part of the OpenGL Shading Language are used to manage the input to the vertex processor and the output from it.

Variables defined in a vertex shader may be qualified as ATTRIBUTE VARIABLES. These represent values that are passed from the application to the vertex processor on a very frequent basis. Because this type of variable is used only for data from the application that defines vertices, it is permitted only as part of a vertex shader. Applications can provide attribute values between calls to **glBegin** and **glEnd** or via vertex array calls, so they can change as often as every vertex.

There are two types of attribute variables: built-in and user-defined. Standard attribute variables in OpenGL include things like color, surface normal, texture coordinates, and vertex position. The OpenGL calls **glColor**, **glNormal**, **glVertex**, and so on, and the OpenGL vertex array drawing commands can be used to send standard OpenGL vertex attributes to the vertex processor.

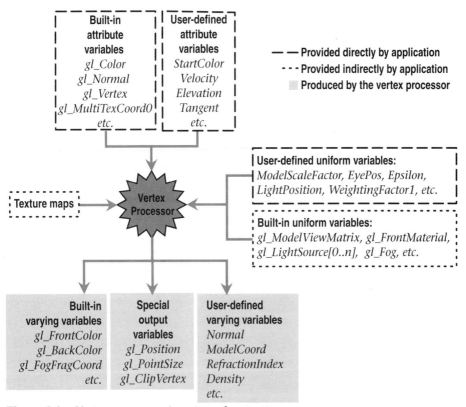

Figure 2.2 Vertex processor inputs and outputs

When a vertex shader is executing, it can access these data values through built-in attribute variables named *gl_Color*, *gl_Normal*, *gl_Vertex*, and so on.

Because this method restricts vertex attributes to the set that is already defined by OpenGL, a new interface has been added to allow applications to pass arbitrary per-vertex data. Within the OpenGL API, generic vertex attributes are defined and referenced by numbers from 0 up to some implementation-dependent maximum value. The command **glVertexAttribARB** sends generic vertex attributes to OpenGL by specifying the index of the generic attribute to be modified and the value for that generic attribute.

Vertex shaders are allowed to access these generic vertex attributes through user-defined attribute variables. Another new command, **glBindAttribLocationARB**, has been added to OpenGL to allow an application to tie together the index of a generic vertex attribute and the name with which to associate that attribute in a vertex shader.

UNIFORM VARIABLES are used for passing data values from the application to either the vertex processor or the fragment processor. Uniform variables are typically used to provide values that change relatively infrequently. A shader can be written so that it is parameterized using uniform variables. The application can provide initial values for these uniform variables, and the end user can be allowed to manipulate them through a graphical user interface to achieve a variety of effects with a single shader. But they cannot be specified between calls to **glBegin** and **glEnd**, so they can change at most once per primitive.

The OpenGL Shading Language supports both built-in and user-defined uniform variables. Vertex shaders and fragment shaders can access current OpenGL state through built-in uniform variables containing the reserved prefix "gl_". User-defined uniform variables can be used by the application to make arbitrary data values available directly to a shader. **glGetUniformLocationARB** can be used to obtain the location of a user-defined uniform variable that has been defined as part of a shader. Data can be loaded into this location using another new OpenGL command, **glUniformARB**. There are a number of variations of this command in order to facilitate loading of floating-point, integer, Boolean, and matrix values, as well as arrays of these.

Another new feature is that vertex processors have also been given the capability to read from texture memory. This allows vertex shaders to implement displacement mapping algorithms, among other things. (However, the minimum number of vertex texture image units required by an implementation is 0, so texture map access from the vertex processor still may not be possible on all implementations that support the OpenGL Shading Language.) For accessing mipmap textures, level of detail can be specified directly in the shader. Existing OpenGL parameters for texture maps define the behavior of the filtering operation, borders, and wrapping.

Conceptually, the vertex processor operates on one vertex at a time (but an implementation may have multiple vertex processors that operate in parallel). The vertex shader is executed once for each vertex passed to OpenGL. The design of the vertex processor is focused on the functionality needed to transform and light a single vertex. Output from the vertex shader is accomplished partly by using special output variables. Vertex shaders must compute the homogeneous position of the coordinate in clip space and store the result in the special output variable *gl_Position*. Values to be used during user clipping and point rasterization can be stored in the special output variables *gl_ClipVertex* and *gl_PointSize*.

Variables that define data that is passed from the vertex processor to the fragment processor are called VARYING VARIABLES. Both built-in and user-defined varying variables are supported. They are called varying variables because the values will be potentially different at each vertex and perspective-correct interpolation will be performed to provide a value at each fragment for use by the fragment shader. Built-in varying variables include those defined for the standard OpenGL color and texture coordinate values. A vertex shader can use a user-defined varying variable to pass anything along that needs to be interpolated: colors, normals (useful for per-fragment lighting computations), texture coordinates, model coordinates, and other arbitrary values.

There is actually no harm (other than a possible loss of performance) in having a vertex shader calculate more varying variables than are needed by the fragment shader. A warning may be generated if the fragment shader consumes fewer varying variables than the vertex shader produces. But you may have good reasons to use a somewhat generic vertex shader with a variety of fragment shaders. The fragment shaders can be written to use a subset of the varying variables produced by the vertex shader. Applications that manage a large number of shaders may find that reducing the costs of shader development and maintenance is more important than squeezing out an additional percent of performance.

The vertex processor output (special output variables and user-defined and built-in varying variables) is sent on to subsequent stages of processing that are defined exactly the same as they are for OpenGL 1.5: primitive assembly, user clipping, frustum clipping, perspective divide, viewport mapping, polygon offset, polygon mode, shade mode, and culling.

2.3.2 Fragment Processor

The FRAGMENT PROCESSOR is a programmable unit that operates on fragment values and their associated data. The fragment processor is intended to perform traditional graphics operations such as the following:

- Operations on interpolated values
- Texture access
- Texture application
- Fog
- Color sum

A wide variety of other computations can be performed on this processor. Shaders that are intended to run on this processor are called fragment shaders. Fragment shaders are used to express the algorithm that executes on the fragment processor and produces output values based on the input values that are provided. A fragment shader cannot change a fragment's x/y position. Fragment shaders that perform some of the computations from the preceding list must perform all desired functionality from the preceding list. For instance, it is not possible to use the existing fixed functionality to compute fog but have a fragment shader perform specialized texture access and texture application. The fragment shader must be written to perform all three functions.

The fragment processor does not replace graphics operations that require knowledge of several fragments at a time. To support parallelism at the fragment processing level, fragment shaders are written in a way that expresses the computation required for a single fragment, and access to neighboring fragments is not allowed. An implementation may have multiple fragment processors that operate in parallel.

The fragment processor can be used to perform operations on each fragment that is generated by the rasterization of points, lines, polygons, pixel rectangles, and bitmaps. If images are first downloaded into texture memory, the fragment processor can also be used for pixel processing that requires access to a pixel and its neighbors. A rectangle can be drawn with texturing enabled, and the fragment processor can read the image from texture memory and apply it to the rectangle while performing traditional operations such as the following:

- Pixel zoom

- Scale and bias

- Color table lookup

- Convolution

- Color matrix

The fragment processor does not replace the fixed functionality graphics operations that occur at the back end of the OpenGL pixel processing pipeline such as coverage, pixel ownership test, scissor, stipple, alpha test, depth test, stencil test, alpha blending, logical operations, dithering, and plane masking.

Figure 2.3 shows the values that are used to provide input to the fragment processor and the data values that are produced by the fragment processor.

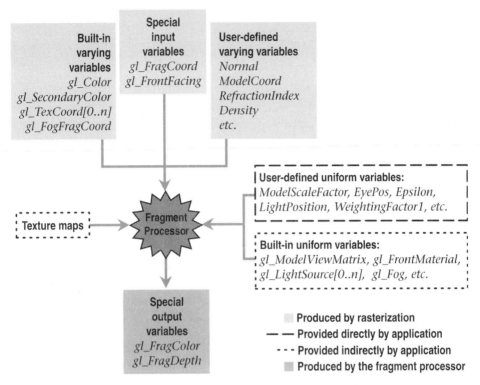

Figure 2.3 Fragment processor inputs and outputs

The primary inputs to the fragment processor are the interpolated varying variables (both built-in and user-defined) that are the results of rasterization. User-defined varying variables must be defined in a fragment shader, and their types must match those defined in the vertex shader.

Values computed by fixed functionality between the vertex processor and the fragment processor are made available through special input variables. The window coordinate position of the fragment and whether the fragment was generated by rasterizing a front-facing primitive are communicated through the special input variables *gl_FragCoord* and *gl_FrontFacing*.

Just as in the vertex shader, existing OpenGL state is accessible to a fragment shader through built-in uniform variables. All of the OpenGL state that is available through built-in uniform variables is available to both vertex and fragment shaders. This makes it possible to implement traditional vertex operations such as lighting in the fragment shader using standard OpenGL state management.

User-defined uniform variables are used to allow the application to pass relatively infrequently changing values to a fragment shader. The same uniform variable can be accessed by both a vertex shader and a fragment shader if it is declared by both shaders using the same data type.

One of the biggest advantages of the fragment processor is that it can access texture memory an arbitrary number of times and combine the values that it reads in arbitrary ways. A fragment shader is free to read multiple values from a single texture or multiple values from multiple textures. The result of one texture access can be used as the basis for performing another texture access (a DEPENDENT TEXTURE READ). There is no inherent limitation on the number of such dependent reads that are possible, so ray-casting algorithms can be implemented in a fragment shader.

The OpenGL parameters for texture maps continue to define the behavior of the filtering operation, borders, wrapping, and texture comparison modes. These operations are applied when a texture is accessed from within a shader. The shader is free to use the resulting value however it chooses. It is possible for a shader to read multiple values from a texture and perform a custom filtering operation. It is also possible to use a texture to perform a lookup table operation.

The fragment processor defines almost all of the capabilities necessary to implement the pixel transfer operations defined in OpenGL 1.5, including those in the imaging subset. This means that advanced pixel processing is supported with the fragment processor. Lookup table operations can be done with 1D texture accesses, allowing applications to have full control over their size and format. Scale and bias operations are easily expressed through the programming language. The color matrix can be accessed through a built-in uniform variable. Convolution and pixel zoom are supported by accessing a texture multiple times to compute the proper result. Histogram and minimum/maximum operations are left to be defined as extensions because these prove to be quite difficult to support at the fragment level with high degrees of parallelism.

For each fragment, the fragment shader may compute color and depth (writing these values into the special output variables *gl_FragColor* and *gl_FragDepth*) or completely discard the fragment. The results of the fragment shader are then sent on for further processing. The remainder of the OpenGL pipeline remains as defined in OpenGL 1.5. Fragments are submitted to coverage application, pixel ownership testing, scissor testing, alpha testing, stencil testing, depth testing, blending, dithering, logical operations, and masking before ultimately being written into the frame buffer. The back end of the processing pipeline remains as fixed functionality because it is easy to implement in nonprogrammable hardware. Making these functions programmable is more complex because read/modify/write operations can introduce significant instruction scheduling issues and pipeline stalls. Most of these fixed functionality operations can be disabled, and alternate operations can be performed within a fragment shader if desired (albeit with possibly lower performance).

2.4 Language Overview

Because of its success as a standard, OpenGL has been the target of our efforts to define an industry standard high-level shading language. The shading language that has been defined as a result of the efforts of OpenGL ARB members is called the OpenGL Shading Language. This language has been designed to be forward looking and eventually to support programmability in other areas as well.

This section provides a brief overview of the OpenGL Shading Language. For a complete discussion of the language, see Chapter 3, Chapter 4, and Chapter 5.

2.4.1 Language Design Considerations

In the past few years, semiconductor technology has progressed to the point where the levels of computation that can be done per vertex or per fragment have gone beyond what is feasible to describe by the traditional OpenGL mechanisms of setting state to influence the action of fixed pipeline stages. A natural way of taming this complexity and the proliferation of OpenGL extensions is to allow parts of the pipeline to be replaced by user programmable stages. This has been done in some recent OpenGL extensions but the programming is done in assembly language. By definition, assembly languages are hardware-specific, so going down this path would lead software developers to create code that is hardware- or vendor-specific and that might not even run on future generations of graphics hardware.

The ideal solution to these issues was to define a forward looking hardware-independent high-level language that would be easy to use, powerful enough to stand the test of time, and drastically reduce the need for extensions. These desires were tempered by the need for fast implementations within a generation or two of hardware.

The following design goals were fundamental to the design of the OpenGL Shading Language.

Define a language that works well with OpenGL—The OpenGL Shading Language is designed specifically for use within the OpenGL environment. It is intended to provide programmable alternatives to certain parts of the fixed functionality of OpenGL. Therefore, the language itself and the programmable processors it defines were required to have at least as much functionality as they were replacing. Furthermore, by design, it is quite easy to refer to existing OpenGL state from within a shader. By design, it is also quite easy to use fixed functionality in one part of the OpenGL processing pipeline and programmable processing in another.

Expose the flexibility of near-future hardware—Graphics hardware has been changing rapidly to a model that allows general programmability for vertex and fragment processing. To expose this programmability, the shading language was designed to be high-level and with appropriate abstractions for the graphics problem domain. The language includes a rich set of built-in functions that allow expression of operations on vectors as easily as on scalars. Exposing hardware capabilities through a high-level programming language was also intended to obviate the need for OpenGL extensions that define small changes to the fixed functionality behavior. By exposing an abstraction that is independent of the actual underlying hardware, there is no need to continue a proliferation of piecemeal extensions to OpenGL.

Provide hardware independence—As previously mentioned, the first attempts at exposing the programmability of graphics hardware focused on assembly language interfaces. This was a dangerous direction for software developers to take because it causes software to be inherently nonportable. The goal of a high-level shading language is that the abstraction level should be high enough that applications can be written in a portable way and hardware vendors have plenty of room to provide innovative hardware architectures and compiler technology.

Performance is important—It is an established fact nowadays that compiler technology can be used to generate extremely high-performance executable code. With the complexity of today's CPUs, it is difficult to generate by hand code that can surpass the performance of code generated by a compiler. It is the intent that the object code generated for a shader be independent of other OpenGL state, so that recompiles or managing multiple copies of object code are not necessary.

Define a language that is easy to use—One of the considerations here is that writing shaders should be simple and easy. Since most graphics application programmers are familiar with C and C++, this led us to adopt the salient features of these languages as the basis for the OpenGL Shading Language. We also felt that compilers, not application programmers, should perform difficult tasks. We concluded that a single language (with very minor variations) should be the basis for programming all of the programmable processors that we were defining, as well as those we envisioned adding in future versions of OpenGL. This allows application programmers to become familiar with the basic shading language constructs and apply them to all programming tasks involving the programmable processors in OpenGL.

Define a language that will stand the test of time—This design consideration also led us to base the design of the OpenGL Shading Language on previously successful programming languages such as C and RenderMan. Our hope is that programs written when the OpenGL Shading Language was first defined will still be valid in 10 years. Longevity also requires standardization of some sort, so a great deal of effort has gone into both making all the hardware vendors happy with the final language specification and pushing the specification through the approval process of OpenGL's governing body, the OpenGL Architecture Review Board (ARB).

Don't preclude higher levels of parallel processing—Newer graphics hardware architectures are providing more and more parallelism at both the vertex and the fragment processing levels. Great care has been taken in the definition of the OpenGL Shading Language to allow for even higher levels of parallel processing. This consideration has shaped the definition of the language in some subtle but important ways.

Ease of Implementation—Some features of C have made implementing optimizing compilers difficult. Some OpenGL Shading Language features have been chosen to address this. For example, C allows hidden aliasing of memory by using pointers and passing pointers as function arguments, which may give multiple names to the same memory. These potential aliases handicap the optimizer, leading to complexity and/or less optimized code. The OpenGL Shading language does not allow pointers and uses call by value-return to prevent such aliasing. In general, aliasing is disallowed, simplifying the job of the optimizer.

2.4.2 C Basis

As stated previously, the OpenGL Shading Language is based on the syntax of the ANSI C programming language, and at first glance, programs written in this language look very much like C programs. This is intentional, and it is designed to make the language easier to use for those most likely to be using it, namely those developing graphics applications using C and/or C++.

The basic structure of programs written in the OpenGL Shading Language is the same as it is for programs written in C. The entry point of a set of shaders is the function **void main()**, and the body of this function is delimited by curly braces. Constants, identifiers, operators, expressions, and statements are basically the same for the OpenGL Shading Language as they are for C. Control flow for looping, if-then-else, and function calls are virtually identical to C.

2.4.3 Additions to C

The OpenGL Shading Language has a number of language features that have been added because of its special-purpose nature as a language for encoding graphics algorithms. Here are some of the main things that have been added to the OpenGL Shading Language that are different from ANSI C.

Vector types are supported for floating-point, integer, and Boolean values. For floating-point values, these vector types are referred to as **vec2** (two floats), **vec3** (three floats), and **vec4** (four floats). Operators work as readily on vector types as they do on scalars. To add vectors *v1* and *v2* together, you simply would say *v1* + *v2*. Individual components of a vector can be accessed either using array syntax or as fields of a structure. Color values can be accessed by adding .r to the name of a vector variable to access the first component, .g to access the second component, .b to access the third, and .a to access the fourth. Position values can be accessed with .x, .y, .z, and .w, and texture values can be accessed with .s, .t, .p, and .q. Multiple components can be selected by specifying multiple names, like .xy.

Floating-point matrix types are also supported as basic types. The data type **mat2** refers to a 2×2 matrix of floating-point values, **mat3** refers to a 3×3 matrix, and **mat4** refers to a 4×4 matrix. This is a convenient type for expressing the linear transformations common in 3D graphics. Columns of a matrix can be selected using array syntax, yielding a vector whose components can be accessed as just described.

A set of basic types called samplers has also been added to create the mechanism used by shaders to access texture memory. Samplers are a special type of opaque variable used to access a particular texture map. A variable of type **sampler1D** can be used to access a 1D texture map, a variable of type **sampler2D** can be used to access a 2D texture map, and so on. Shadow and cube map textures are also supported through this mechanism.

Qualifiers have been added to manage the input and output of shaders. The **attribute**, **uniform**, and **varying** qualifiers specify what type of input or output a variable serves. Attribute variables communicate frequently changing values from the application to a vertex shader, uniform variables communicate infrequently changing values from the application to any shader, and varying variables communicate interpolated values from a vertex shader to a fragment shader.

Shaders written in the OpenGL Shading Language can use built-in variables that begin with the reserved prefix "gl_" in order to access existing OpenGL state and to communicate with the fixed functionality of OpenGL. For instance, both vertex and fragment shaders can access built-in uniform variables that contain state values that are readily available within the current rendering context. Some examples are *gl_ModelViewMatrix* for obtaining the current modelview matrix, *gl_LightSource[i]* for obtaining the current parameters of the *i*th light source, and *gl_Fog.color* for accessing the current fog color. The vertex shader must write the special variable *gl_Position* in order to provide necessary information to the fixed functionality stages between vertex processing and fragment processing, namely, primitive assembly, clipping, culling, and rasterization. A fragment shader will typically write into one or both of the special variables *gl_FragColor* or *gl_FragDepth*. These values represent the computed fragment color and computed fragment depth. These values will be submitted to the back-end fixed functionality fragment operations such as alpha testing, stencil testing, and depth testing, before reaching their ultimate destination, the frame buffer.

A variety of built-in functions is also provided in the OpenGL Shading Language in order to make coding easier and to take advantage of possible hardware acceleration for certain operations. The language defines built-in functions for a variety of trigonometric operations (sine, cosine, tangent, etc.), exponential operations (power, exponential, logarithm, square root, and inverse square root), common math operations (absolute value, floor, ceiling, fractional part, modulus, etc.), geometric operations (length, distance, dot product, cross product, normalization, etc.), relational operations based on vectors (component-wise greater than, less than, equal to, etc.), specialized fragment shader functions for computing derivatives and estimating filter widths for antialiasing, functions for accessing values in texture memory, and functions that return noise values for procedural texturing effects.

2.4.4 Additions from C++

The OpenGL Shading Language also includes a few notable language features from C++. In particular, function overloading is supported in order to make it easy to define functions that differ only in the type or number of arguments being passed. This feature is heavily used by the built-in functions. For instance, the dot product function is overloaded to deal with arguments that are types **float**, **vec2**, **vec3**, and **vec4**.

The concept of constructors also comes from C++. Initializers are done only with constructors in the OpenGL shading language. Using constructors allows for more than one way of initializing variables.

Another feature borrowed from C++ is that variables can be declared when they are needed; they do not have to be declared at the beginning of a basic block. The basic type **bool** is supported as in C++.

Like C++, functions must be declared before being used. This can be accomplished by either providing the function's definition (its body) or just with a prototype.

2.4.5 C Features Not Supported

Unlike ANSI C, there is no automatic promotion of data types. Compiler errors will be generated if variables used in an expression are of different types. For instance, an error will be generated for the statement `float f = 0`; but not for the statement `float f = 0.0;`. This might seem like a bit of a nuisance, but it simplifies the language by making it unnecessary to specify type promotion rules. This also removes a class of confusing mistakes when selecting which of a set of overloaded functions is being called based on argument type.

The OpenGL Shading Language does not contain support for pointers, strings or characters, or for any operations based on these. It is fundamentally a language for processing numerical data, not for processing character or string data, so there is no need for these features to complicate the language. In order to keep the implementation burden lower (both for the compiler and for the graphics hardware), there is no support for double-precision floats; byte, short, or long integers; or unsigned variants of these.

A few other C language features that were eliminated from consideration in order to simplify the OpenGL Shading Language (or because there was no compelling need for them at the time) are unions, enumerated types, bit-fields in structures, and bit-wise operators. Finally, the language is not file based, so you won't see any **#include** directives or other references to file names.

2.4.6 Other Differences

There are a few areas where the OpenGL Shading Language provides the same functionality as C but does so in a different way. One of these is that constructors are used for data type conversion rather than for type casts and for variable initialization rather than for C-style initializers. There is no support at all for type casting without conversion, so constructors keep the language type safe. Constructors use the syntax of a function call, where the function name is the name of the desired type and the arguments are the values that will be used to construct the desired value.

Constructors allow a much richer set of operations than simple type casts or C-style initializers, and the flexibility that this provides comes in quite handy when dealing with vector and matrix data types. In addition to converting from one scalar type to another, constructors can be used to create a larger type out of a smaller type, or to reduce a larger type to a smaller type. For instance the constructor vec3(1.0, 2.0, 3.0) will construct a **vec3** data type out of three scalar values, and the constructor vec3(myVec4) will strip the fourth component from *myVec4* to create a **vec3** value.

The other area of difference is that, unlike the call by value calling convention used by C, the OpenGL Shading Language uses CALL BY VALUE-RETURN. Input parameters are copied into the function at call time, and output parameters are copied back to the caller before the function exits. Because the function deals only with copies of the function parameters, there are no issues regarding aliasing of variables within a function. Function parameters are identified as input parameters with the qualifier **in**, they are identified as output parameters with the qualifier **out**, and they are identified as both input and output parameters with the qualifier **inout** (if no qualifier is present, they are identified as input parameters).

2.5 System Overview

We have already described briefly some of the pieces that provide applications with access to the programmability of underlying graphics hardware. This section gives an overview of how these pieces go together in a working system.

2.5.1 Driver Model

A piece of software that controls a piece of hardware and manages shared access to that piece of hardware is commonly called a DRIVER. No matter what the environment in which it is implemented, OpenGL will fall into this category because OpenGL manages shared access to the underlying graphics hardware. Some of its tasks must also be coordinated with, or supervised by, facilities in the operating system.

Figure 2.4 illustrates how OpenGL shaders are handled in the execution environment of OpenGL. Applications communicate with OpenGL by calling functions that are part of the OpenGL API. A new OpenGL function, **glCreateShaderObjectARB**, has been created to allow applications to allocate within the OpenGL driver, the data structures that are necessary for storing an OpenGL shader. These data structures are called SHADER OBJECTS. After a shader object has been created, the application can provide the source code for the shader by calling **glShaderSourceARB**. This command is used to provide to OpenGL the character strings containing the shader source code.

As you can see from Figure 2.4, the compiler for the OpenGL Shading Language is actually part of the OpenGL driver environment. This is one of the key differences between the OpenGL Shading Language and other shading language designs, such as the Stanford Shading Language, High-Level Shader Language (HLSL) from Microsoft, or Cg from NVIDIA. In these other languages, the high-level shading language compiler sits above the graphics API and translates the high-level shading language into something that can be consumed by the underlying graphics API. (See Chapter 17 for more details.) With the OpenGL Shading Language, the source code for shaders is passed to the OpenGL driver, and in that environment, the shaders will be compiled to the native machine code as efficiently as possible.

After source code for a shader has been loaded into a shader object in the OpenGL driver environment, it can be compiled by calling **glCompileShaderARB**. A PROGRAM OBJECT is an OpenGL-managed data structure that acts as a container for shader objects. Applications are required to attach shader objects to a program object by using the command **glAttachObjectARB**.

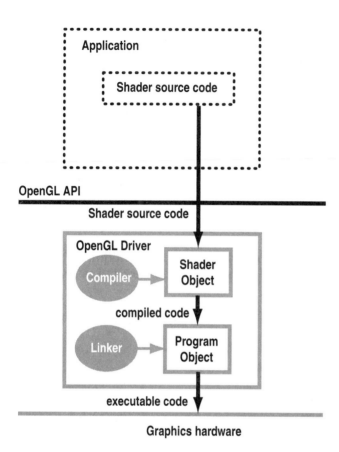

Figure 2.4 Execution model for OpenGL shaders

When attached to a program object, the compiled shader objects can be linked together by calling **glLinkProgramARB**. Support for multiple shader objects (and the subsequent need for a linker built into OpenGL) is a key difference between the OpenGL Shading Language and assembly-level APIs such as those provided by the OpenGL extensions *ARB_vertex_program* and *ARB_fragment_program*. For more complex shading tasks, separately compiled shader objects are a much more attractive alternative than a single, monolithic block of assembly-level code.

The link step will resolve external references between the shaders, check the compatibility between the vertex shader and the fragment shader, assign memory locations to uniform variables, and so on. The result is one or more executables that can be installed as part of OpenGL's current state by calling **glUseProgramObjectARB**. This command installs the executables on the vertex processor and/or the fragment processor where they will be used to render all subsequent graphics primitives.

2.5.2 OpenGL Shading Language Compiler/Linker

The source for a single shader is an array of strings of characters, and a single shader is made from the concatenation of these strings. Each string can contain multiple lines, separated by new-lines. No new-lines need be present in a string; a single line can be formed from multiple strings. No new-lines or other characters are inserted by the OpenGL implementation when it concatenates the strings to form a single shader. It is entirely up to the application programmer to provide shader source code to OpenGL with new-lines between each line of source code.

Diagnostic messages returned from compiling a shader must identify both the line number within a string and the source string to which the diagnostic message applies. Source strings are counted sequentially with the first string counted as string 0. When parsing source code, the current line number is one more than the number of new-lines that have been processed.

The front end of the OpenGL Shading Language compiler has been released as open source by 3Dlabs and can be used by anyone interested in writing his or her own compiler. This publicly available front end is capable of doing lexical analysis of OpenGL Shading Language source code to produce a token stream and then performing syntactic and semantic analysis of this token stream to produce a binary, high-level representation of the language. This front end is intended to act as a reference implementation of the OpenGL Shading Language, and therefore it goes hand-in-hand with the language specification in order to define the language clearly. Another advantage to using this publicly available front end in an OpenGL Shading Language compiler implementation is that the syntax and semantics for shaders will be checked consistently by all implementations that use this front end. More conistency among compiler implementations makes it easier for developers to write shaders that work as intended across a variety of implementations.

It is assumed that the back end of the OpenGL Shading Language compiler will be implemented differently on different platforms. Each implementation will need to take the high-level representation produced by the publicly available front end and produce optimized machine code for a particular hardware target. This is an area where individual hardware vendors will add value to their shading language implementation by figuring out ways to map the high-level representation onto the actual machine instructions found in their hardware. Likewise, the linking stage will also be highly hardware dependent because it involves operations like assigning variables to actual memory locations in the hardware.

The net result of this is that graphics hardware vendors will be implementing the majority of the OpenGL Shading Language compiler and linker. Along with the OpenGL driver itself, this software will typically be included as part of the graphics driver installation package that is provided by a graphics hardware vendor.

2.5.3 OpenGL API Extensions

Currently, support for the OpenGL Shading Language is not available as part of standard OpenGL, but it is available as a set of extensions that are supported by a number of graphics hardware vendors. It is expected that these extensions will fairly quickly be adopted as part of the OpenGL standard. When this happens, there is expected to be no change, except for dropping the ARB suffix on the function names, constants, and data types that are defined by these extensions. For now, the way to get to this functionality is through these commonly supported extensions.

The extension that provides the framework for the shader and program objects and the functionality that is common to all the programmable processors is called *ARB_shader_objects*. This extension provides the following basic capabilities:

- **glCreateShaderObjectARB**—Create a shader object

- **glCreateProgramObjectARB**—Create a program object

- **glDeleteObjectARB**—Delete a shader object or a program object

- **glShaderSourceARB**—Load source code strings into a shader object

- **glCompileShaderARB**—Compile a shader

- **glAttachObjectARB**—Attach a shader object to a program object

- **glDetachObjectARB**—Detach a shader object from a program object

- **glLinkProgramARB**—Link a program object to create executable code

- **glUseProgramObjectARB**—Install a program object's executable code as part of current state

- **glValidateProgramARB**—Return validation information for a program object

- **glUniformARB**—Set the value of a uniform variable

- **glGetActiveUniformARB**—Obtain the name, size, and type of an active uniform variable for a program object

- **glGetAttachedObjectsARB**—Get the list of shader objects attached to a program object

- **glGetHandleARB**—Obtain the handle for the program object currently in use

- **glGetObjectParameterARB**—Query one of the parameters of an object

- **glGetShaderSourceARB**—Get the source code for a specific shader object

- **glGetUniformARB**—Query the current value of a uniform variable

- **glGetUniformLocationARB**—Query the location assigned to a uniform variable by the linker

- **glGetInfoLogARB**—Obtain the information log for a shader object or a program object

The extension *ARB_vertex_shader* addresses the capabilities of the newly defined programmable vertex processor. This extension defines how the programmable vertex processor fits into the OpenGL processing pipeline, and it provides API entry points for features that are unique to the vertex processor. Functionality defined by this extension includes

- How vertex shaders are created

- How vertex shaders are enabled/disabled

- Which OpenGL fixed functionality is disabled when a vertex shader is active

- How values passed to standard OpenGL vertex entry points are passed into a vertex shader

- How generic vertex attributes are handled

- How a vertex shader interfaces with OpenGL fixed functionality that follows vertex processing, including primitive assembly, clipping, and rasterization

New entry points defined by the *ARB_vertex_shader* extension are

- **glVertexAttribARB**—Send generic vertex attributes to OpenGL a vertex at a time

- **glVertexAttribPointerARB**—Specify location and organization of generic vertex attributes to be sent to OpenGL using vertex arrays

- **glBindAttribLocationARB**—Specify the generic vertex attribute index to be used for a particular user-defined attribute variable in a vertex shader

- **glEnableVertexAttribArrayARB**—Enable a generic vertex attribute to be sent to OpenGL using vertex arrays

- **glDisableVertexAttribArrayARB**—Disable a generic vertex attribute from being sent to OpenGL using vertex arrays

- **glGetVertexAttribARB**—Returns current state for the specified generic vertex attribute

- **glGetVertexAttribLocationARB**—Returns the generic vertex attribute index that is bound to a specified user-defined attribute variable

- **glGetVertexAttribPointerARB**—Returns the vertex array pointer value for the specified generic vertex attribute

- **glGetActiveAttribARB**—Obtains the name, size, and type of an active attribute for a program object

The third and final extension that provides support for the OpenGL Shading Language is called *ARB_fragment_shader*. This extension is similar to the *ARB_vertex_shader* extension, except that it defines the capabilities of the newly defined programmable fragment processor and how the programmable fragment processor fits into the OpenGL processing pipeline. There are actually no new API entry points defined by this extension because it builds on the generic capabilities defined in the *ARB_shader_objects* extension. It does provide new functionality, however, including

- How fragment shaders are created

- How fragment shaders are enabled/disabled

- Which OpenGL fixed functionality is disabled when a fragment shader is active

- How values produced by OpenGL rasterization are passed into a fragment shader

- How values produced by a fragment shader are provided to OpenGL's fixed functionality back-end processing

These new entry points are all discussed in more detail in Chapter 7. Reference pages for all of the API entry points defined by these extensions are included in Appendix B at the back of this book.

2.6 Key Benefits

The following key benefits are derived from the choices that were made during the design of the OpenGL Shading Language.

Tight integration with OpenGL—The OpenGL Shading Language was designed for use in OpenGL. It is designed in such a way that an existing, working OpenGL application can be easily modified to take advantage of the capabilities of programmable graphics hardware. Built-in access to existing OpenGL state, reuse of API entry points that are already familiar to application developers, and a close coupling with the existing architecture of OpenGL are all key benefits to using the OpenGL Shading Language for shader development.

Compilation occurs at runtime—Source code stays as source code, in its easiest-to-maintain form, for as long as possible. An application passes source code to any conforming OpenGL implementation that supports the OpenGL Shading Language, and it will be compiled and executed properly. There is no need for a multitude of binaries for a multitude of different platforms.[1]

No reliance on cross-vendor assembly language—Both DirectX and OpenGL have widespread support for assembly language interfaces to graphics programmability. High-level shading languages could be (and have been) built on top of these assembly language interfaces, and such high-level languages can be translated into these assembly language interfaces completely outside the environment of OpenGL or DirectX. This does have some advantages, but relying on an assembly language interface as the primary interface to hardware programmability restricts innovation by graphics hardware designers. Hardware designers have many more choices

---

[1] At the time of this writing, the OpenGL ARB is still considering the need for an API that allows shaders to be specified in a form other than source code. The primary issues are the protection of intellectual property that may be embedded in string-based shader source code and the performance that would be gained by allowing shaders to be at least partially precompiled. When such an API is defined, shader portability may be reduced, but application developers will have the option of getting better code security and/or better performance.

for acceleration of an expressive high-level language than they do for a restrictive assembly language. It is much too early in the development of programmable graphics hardware technology to establish an assembly language standard for graphics programmability. C, on the other hand, was developed long before any CPU assembly languages that are in existence today, and it is still a viable choice for application development.

Unconstrained opportunities for compiler optimization will lead to optimal performance on a wider range of hardware—As we've learned through experience with CPUs, compilers are much better at quickly generating efficient code than humans are. By allowing high-level source code to be compiled within OpenGL, rather than outside of OpenGL, individual hardware vendors have the best possible opportunity to deliver optimal performance on their graphics hardware. In fact, compiler improvements can be made with each and every OpenGL driver release, and the applications won't need to change any application source code, recompile the application, or even relink it. Furthermore, the current crop of assembly language interfaces is string based, so using these as an interface requires that string-based high-level source be translated into string-based assembly language, and then that string-based assembly language must be passed to OpenGL and translated from string-based assembly language to machine code.

A truly open, cross-platform standard—No other high-level graphics shading language has been approved as part of an open, multivendor standard. Like OpenGL itself, the OpenGL Shading Language will be implemented by a variety of different vendors for a variety of different environments.

One high-level language for all programmable graphics processing—The OpenGL Shading Language is used to write shaders for both the vertex processor and the fragment processor in OpenGL, with very small differences in the language for the two types of shaders. In the future, it is intended that the OpenGL Shading Language will be used to bring programmability to other areas of OpenGL as well. Areas that have already received some discussion include programmability for packing/unpacking arbitrary image formats and support for programmable tessellation of higher order surfaces in the graphics hardware.

Support for modular programming—By defining compilation and linking as two separate steps, shader writers have a lot more flexibility in how they choose to implement complex shading algorithms. Rather than implement a complex algorithm as a single, monolithic shader, developers are free to implement it as a collection of shaders that can be independently compiled and attached to a program object. Shaders can be designed with common interfaces so that they are interchangeable, and a link operation is used to join them to create a program.

No additional libraries or executables—The OpenGL Shading Language and the compiler and linker that support it are defined as part of OpenGL. Applications need not worry about linking against any additional runtime libraries. Compiler improvements are delivered as part of OpenGL driver updates.

2.7 Summary

Here are the key points to understand about how all the pieces fit together at execution time.

- When installed as part of current state, the executable created for the vertex processor will be executed once for every vertex provided to OpenGL.

- When installed as part of current state, the executable created for the fragment processor will be executed once for every fragment that is produced by rasterization.

- There are two ways for an application to communicate directly with a vertex shader: by using attribute variables and by using uniform variables.

- Attribute variables are expected to change very frequently and may be supplied by the application as often as every vertex.

- Applications can pass arbitrary vertex data to a vertex shader using user-defined attribute variables.

- Applications can pass standard vertex attributes (color, normal, texture coordinates, position, etc.) to a vertex shader using built-in attribute variables.

- An application communicates directly with a fragment shader using uniform variables.

- Uniform variables are expected to change relatively infrequently (at a minimum, they are constant for an entire graphics primitive).

- The compiler and linker for the language are contained within OpenGL (but tools for compiling, linking, and debugging shaders can exist outside of OpenGL as well).

To summarize, the following are the most important points about the language.

- The language is based on the syntax of C.

- Basic structure and many keywords are the same as in C.

- Vectors and matrices are included in the language as basic types.

- Type qualifiers **attribute**, **uniform**, and **varying** are added to describe variables that manage shader I/O.

  - Variables of type **attribute** allow the communication of frequently changing values from the application to the vertex shader.

  - Variables of type **varying** are the output from a vertex shader and the input to a fragment shader.

  - Variables of type **uniform** allow the application to provide relatively infrequently changing values to both vertex shaders and fragment shaders.

- The data type **sampler** is added for accessing textures.

- Built-in variable names can be used to access standard OpenGL state and to communicate with OpenGL fixed functionality.

- A variety of built-in functions are included for performing common graphics operations.

- Function declarations are required, and overloading based on number and type of arguments is supported as in C++.

- Variables can be declared when needed.

To install and use OpenGL shaders, you need to do the following:

1. Create one or more (empty) shader objects using **glCreateShaderObjectARB**.

2. Provide source code for these shaders by calling **glShaderSourceARB**.

3. Compile each of the shaders by calling **glCompileShaderARB**.

4. Create a program object by calling **glCreateProgramObjectARB**.

5. Attach all the shader objects to the program object by calling **glAttachObjectARB**.

6. Link the program object by calling **glLinkProgramARB**.

7. Install the executable program as part of OpenGL's current state by calling **glUseProgramObjectARB**.

After these steps, subsequent graphics primitives will be drawn using the shaders you've provided rather than with OpenGL's defined fixed functionality pipeline.

2.8 Further Information

Just keep reading this book, and you'll get to all of the really good stuff! If you really must go and get more technical details, here are pointers to the official specification documents. The 3Dlabs Web site also has additional material, including slide presentations, demos, example shaders, and source code.

[1] *3Dlabs developer Web site.* http://www.3dlabs.com/support/developer

[2] Kessenich, John, Dave Baldwin, and Randi Rost, *The OpenGL Shading Language, Version 1.051*, 3Dlabs, February 2003. http://www.3dlabs.com/support/developer/ogl2

[3] OpenGL Architecture Review Board, *ARB_vertex_shader Extension Specification*, OpenGL Extension Registry. http://oss.sgi.com/projects/ogl-sample/registry

[4] OpenGL Architecture Review Board, *ARB_fragment_shader Extension Specification*, OpenGL Extension Registry. http://oss.sgi.com/projects/ogl-sample/registry

[5] OpenGL Architecture Review Board, *ARB_shader_objects Extension Specification*, OpenGL Extension Registry. http://oss.sgi.com/projects/ogl-sample/registry

Chapter 3

Language Definition

by John Kessenich

In this chapter, we'll present all the language features of the OpenGL Shading Language. We'll start with a simple example of a working pair of vertex and fragment shaders to show their basic structure and interfaces. Each aspect of the language will then be discussed in turn.

The OpenGL Shading Language syntax comes from the C family of programming languages. Tokens, identifiers, semicolons, nesting with curly braces, control-flow, and many keywords look like C. Both comment styles // ... and /* ... */ are accepted. Much is also different though, and all important differences from C will be discussed.

Each shader example is presented as it might appear in a file or onscreen. However, as explained in Chapter 7, the OpenGL API passes shaders as strings, not files, as OpenGL does not consider shaders file based.

3.1 Example Shader Pair

A program will typically contain two shaders: one vertex shader and one fragment shader. More than one shader of each type can be present, but there must be exactly one function **main** between all the fragment shaders and exactly one function **main** between all the vertex shaders. Frequently, it's easiest to just have one shader of each type.

The following is a simple pair of vertex and fragment shaders that can smoothly express a surface's temperature with color. The range of temperatures and their colors are parameterized. First, we'll show the vertex shader. It will be executed once for each vertex.

```
// uniform qualified variables are changed at most once per primitive
uniform float CoolestTemp;
uniform float TempRange;

// attribute qualified variables are typically changed per vertex
attribute float VertexTemp;

// varying qualified variables communicate from the vertex shader to
// the fragment shader
varying float Temperature;

void main()
{
    // compute a temperature to be interpolated per fragment,
    // in the range [0.0, 1.0]
    Temperature = (VertexTemp - CoolestTemp) /  TempRange;

    /*
       The vertex position written in the application using
       glVertex() can be read from the built-in variable
       gl_Vertex. Use this value and the current model
       view transformation matrix to tell the rasterizer where
       this vertex is.
    */
    gl_Position = gl_ModelViewProjectionMatrix * gl_Vertex;
}
```

That's it for the vertex shader. Primitive assembly will follow the preceding vertex processing, providing the rasterizer with enough information to create fragments. The rasterizer interpolates the *Temperature* values written per vertex to create values per fragment. Each fragment is then delivered to a single execution of the fragment shader, as follows:

```
// uniform qualified variables are changed at most once per primitive
// by the application, and vec3 declares a vector of three
// floating-point numbers
uniform vec3 CoolestColor;
uniform vec3 HottestColor;

// Temperature contains the now interpolated per-fragment
// value of temperature set by the vertex shader
varying float Temperature;

void main()
{
    // get a color between coolest and hottest colors, using
    // the mix() built-in function
    vec3 color = mix(CoolestColor, HottestColor, Temperature);
```

```
      // make a vector of 4 floating-point numbers by appending an
      // alpha of 1.0, and set this fragment's color
      gl_FragColor = vec4(color, 1.0);
}
```

Both shaders receive user-defined state from the application through the declared **uniform** qualified variables. The vertex shader gets information associated with each vertex through the **attribute** qualified variable. Information is passed from the vertex shader to the fragment shader through **varying** qualified variables, whose declarations must match between the vertex and fragment shaders. The fixed functionality located between the vertex and fragment processors will interpolate the per-vertex values written to this varying variable. When the fragment shader reads this same varying variable, it reads the value interpolated for the fragment being processed.

Shaders interact with the fixed functionality OpenGL pipeline by writing built-in variables. OpenGL prefixes built-in variables with "gl_". In the preceding examples, writing to *gl_Position* tells the OpenGL pipeline where the transformed vertices are located, and writing to *gl_FragColor* tells the OpenGL pipeline what color to attach to a fragment.

Execution of the preceding shaders occurs multiple times to process a single primitive, once per vertex for the vertex shader and once per fragment for the fragment shader. Many such executions of the same shader can happen in parallel. In general, there is no direct tie or ordering between shader executions. Information can be communicated neither from vertex to vertex, nor from fragment to fragment.

3.2 Data Types

We saw vectors of floating-point numbers in the example in the previous section. Many other built-in data types are available to ease the expression of graphical procedures. Booleans, integers, matrices, vectors of other types, structures, and arrays are all included. Each is discussed in the following sections. Notably missing are string and character types, as there is little use for them in processing vertex and fragment data.

3.2.1 Scalars

The scalar types available are

float	declares a single floating-point number
int	declares a single integer number
bool	declares a single Boolean number

These are used to declare variables, as is familiar from C/C++.

```
float f;
float g, h = 2.4;
int NumTextures = 4;
bool skipProcessing;
```

Unlike the original C, you must provide the type name, as there are no default types. As in C++, declarations may typically appear when needed, not just after an open curly brace ({).

Literal floating-point numbers are also specified as in C, except there are no suffixes to specify precision, as there is only one floating-point type.

```
3.14159
3.
0.2
.609
1.5e10
0.4E-4
etc.
```

In general, floating-point values and operations act as they do in C.

Integers are not the same as in C. There is no requirement that they appear to be backed in hardware by a fixed-width integer register. Consequently, wrapping behavior, when arithmetic would overflow or underflow a fixed-width integer register, is undefined. Bit-wise operations like left-shift (**<<**) and bit-wise and (**&**) are also not supported.

What can be said about integers? They are guaranteed to have at least 16 bits of precision; they can be positive, negative, or zero; and integer arithmetic that stays within this range will give the expected results. Note that the precision truly is 16 bits plus the sign of the value—that is, a full range of [-65535, 65535] or greater.

Literal integers can be given as decimal values, octal values, or hexadecimal values, as in C.

```
42    // a literal decimal integer
052   // a literal octal integer
0x2A  // a literal hexadecimal integer
```

Again, there are no suffixes to specify precision, as there is only one integer type. Integers are useful as sizes of structures or arrays and as loop counters. Graphical types, such as color or position, are best expressed in floating-point variables within a shader.

Boolean variables are as **bool** in C++. They can have only one of two values: true or false. Literal Boolean constants **true** and **false** are provided. Relational operators like less-than (<) and logical operators like logical-and (**&&**) always result in Boolean type. Flow-control constructs like **if-else** will accept only Boolean-typed expressions. In these regards, the OpenGL Shading Language is more restrictive than C++.

3.2.2 Vectors

Vectors of **float, int,** or **bool** are built-in basic types. They can have two, three, or four components and are named as follows:

vec2	Vector of two floating-point numbers
vec3	Vector of three floating-point numbers
vec4	Vector of four floating-point numbers
ivec2	Vector of two integers
ivec3	Vector of three integers
ivec4	Vector of four integers
bvec2	Vector of two Booleans
bvec3	Vector of three Booleans
bvec4	Vector of four Booleans

Built-in vectors are quite useful. They conveniently store and manipulate colors, positions, texture coordinates, and so on. Built-in variables and built-in functions make heavy use of these types. Also, special operations are supported. Finally, hardware is likely to have vector-processing capabilities that mirror vector expressions in shaders.

Note that the language does not distinguish between a color vector and a position vector or other uses of a floating-point vector. These are all just floating-point vectors from the language's perspective.

Special features of vectors include component access that can be done either through field selection (as with structures) or as array accesses. For example, if *position* is a **vec3**, it can be considered as the vector (x, y, z), and *position.x* will select the first component of the vector.

In all, the following names are available for selecting components of vectors:

x, y, z, w   Treat a vector as a position or direction

r, g, b, a   Treat a vector as a color

s, t, p, q   Treat a vector as a texture coordinate

There is no explicit way of stating a vector is a color, a position, a coordinate, and so on. Rather, these component selection names are provided simply for readability in a shader. The only compile-time checking done is that the vector is large enough to provide a specified component. Also, if multiple components are selected (swizzling, discussed in Section 3.7.2), all the components are from the same family.

Vectors can also be indexed as a zero-based array to obtain components. For instance, *position[2]* returns the third component of *position*. Variable indices are allowed, making it possible to loop over the components of a vector. Multiplication takes on special meaning when operating on a vector, as linear algebraic multiplies with matrices are understood. Swizzling, indexing, and other operations are discussed in detail in section Section 3.7.

3.2.3 Matrices

Built-in types are available for matrices of floating-point numbers. There are 2×2, 3×3, and 4×4 sizes.

mat2 2×2 matrix of floating-point numbers

mat3 3×3 matrix of floating-point numbers

mat4 4×4 matrix of floating-point numbers

These are useful for storing linear transforms or other data. They are treated semantically as matrices, particularly when a vector and a matrix are multiplied together, in which case the proper linear-algebraic computation is performed. When relevant, matrices are organized in column-major order, as is the tradition in OpenGL.

You may access a matrix as an array of column vectors—that is, if *transform* is a **mat4**, *transform[2]* is the third column of *transform*. The resulting type of *transform[2]* is **vec4**. Column 0 is the first column. Because *transform[2]* is a vector and you can also treat vectors as arrays, *transform[3][1]* is the second component of the vector forming the fourth column of *transform*. Hence, it ends up looking as if *transform* is a two-dimensional array. Just remember that the first index selects the column, not the row, and the second index selects the row.

3.2.4 Samplers

Texture lookups require some indication as to what texture and/or texture unit will do the lookup. The OpenGL Shading Language doesn't really care about the underlying implementation of texture units or other forms of organizing texture lookup hardware. Hence, it provides a simple opaque handle to encapsulate what to look up. These handles are called SAMPLERS. The sampler types available are

sampler1D	Accesses a one-dimensional texture
sampler2D	Accesses a two-dimensional texture
sampler3D	Accesses a three-dimensional texture
samplerCube	Accesses a cube-mapped texture
sampler1DShadow	Accesses a one-dimensional depth texture with comparison
sampler2DShadow	Accesses a two-dimensional depth texture with comparison

When the application initializes a sampler, the OpenGL implementation stores into it whatever information is needed to communicate what texture is being looked up. Shaders cannot themselves initialize samplers. They can only receive them from the application, through a **uniform** qualified sampler, or pass them on to user or built-in functions. As a function parameter, a sampler cannot be modified, so shaders cannot change a sampler's value.

For example, a sampler could be declared as

```
uniform sampler2D Grass;
```

(Uniform qualifiers are talked about in more detail in Section 3.5.)

This variable can then be passed into a corresponding texture lookup function to access a texture:

```
vec4 color = texture2D(Grass, coord);
```

coord is a **vec2** holding the two-dimensional position to index the grass texture with, and *color* is the result of doing the texture lookup. Together, the compiler and the OpenGL API will validate that *Grass* really encapsulates a two-dimensional texture and that *Grass* is only passed into two-dimensional texture lookups.

Shaders may not manipulate sampler values. For example, the expression `Grass + 1` is not allowed. If a shader wants to combine multiple textures procedurally, an array of samplers can be used as shown here:

```
const int NumTextures = 4;
uniform sampler2D textures[NumTextures];
```

These can be processed in a loop:

```
for (int i = 0; i < NumTextures; ++i)
    … = texture2D(textures[i], …);
```

The idiom `Grass + 1` could then become something like textures `[GrassIndex + 1]`, which is a valid way of manipulating what sampler to use.

3.2.5 Structures

The OpenGL Shading Language provides user-defined structures similar to C. For example,

```
struct light
{
    vec3 position;
    vec3 color;
};
```

As in C++, the name of the structure is the name of this new user-defined type. No **typedef** is needed. In fact, the **typedef** keyword is still reserved, as there is not yet a need for it. A variable of type *light* from the preceding example is simply declared as

```
light ceilingLight;
```

Most other aspects of structures mirror C. They can be embedded and nested. Embedded structure type names have the same scope as the structure they are declared in. However, embedded structures cannot be anonymous. Structure members can be arrays. Finally, each level of structure has its own name space for its member's names, as is familiar.

Bit-fields, the capability to declare an integer with a specified number of bits, are not supported.

Currently, structures are the only user-definable type. The keywords **union**, **enum**, and **class** are reserved for possible future use.

3.2.6 Arrays

Arrays of any type can be created. The declaration

```
vec4 points[10];
```

creates an array of ten **vec4**, indexed starting with zero. There are no pointers; the only way to declare an array is with square brackets.

Arrays do not have to be declared with a size. A declaration like

```
vec4 points[];
```

is allowed, as long as *either* of the following two cases is true:

1. Before the array is referenced, it is declared again with a size, with the same type as the first declaration. For example,

```
vec4 points[];     // points is an array of unknown size
vec4 points[10];   // points is now an array of size 10
```

This cannot be followed by another declaration:

```
vec4 points[];     // points is an array of unknown size
vec4 points[10];   // points is now an array of size 10
vec4 points[20];   // this is illegal
vec4 points[];     // this is also illegal
```

2. All indices that statically reference the array are compile-time constants. In this case, the compiler will make the array large enough to hold the largest index it sees used. For example,

```
vec4 points[];          // points is an array of unknown size
points[2] = vec4(1.0); // points is now an array of size 3
points[7] = vec4(2.0); // points is now an array of size 8
```

In this case, at runtime the array will only have one size, determined by the largest index the compiler sees.

This feature is quite useful for handling the built-in array of texture coordinates. Internally, this array is declared as

```
varying vec4 gl_TexCoord[];
```

If a program uses only compile-time constant indices of 0 and 1, the array will be implicitly sized as *gl_TexCoord[2]*. If a shader uses a nonconstant variable to index the array, that shader will have to explicitly declare the array with the desired size. Of course, keeping the size to a minimum is important, especially for varying variables, as they are likely a limited hardware resource.

Multiple shaders sharing the same array can each declare it with a different size. The linker will size the array to the maximum size appearing in all the shaders being linked together.

3.2.7 Void

The type **void** is provided for declaring a function that returns no value. For example, the function **main** returns no value and must be declared as type **void**.

```
void main()
{
    . . .
}
```

Other than for functions that return nothing, the **void** type is not useful.

3.2.8 Declarations and Scope

Variables are declared quite similarly to C++. They can be declared where needed and have scope as in C++. For example,

```
float f;

f = 3.0;

vec4 u, v;

for (int i = 0; i < 10; ++i)
    v = f * u + v;
```

The scope of a variable declared in a **for** statement ends at the end of the loop's substatement. However, variables may not be declared in an **if** statement, simplifying implementation of scoping across the **else** substatement, with little practical cost.

As in C, variable names are case sensitive must start with a letter or underscore (_) and contain only letters, numbers, and underscore (_). User defined variables cannot start with the string "gl_", as those names are reserved for future use by OpenGL. Names containing consecutive under-scores (__) are also reserved.

3.2.9 Type Matching and Promotion

The OpenGL Shading Language is strict with type matching. In general, types being assigned must match, argument types passed into functions must match formal parameter declarations, and types being operated on must match the requirements of the operator. There are no automatic promotions from one type to another. This may occasionally make a shader have an extra explicit conversion. However, it also simplifies the language, preventing some forms of obfuscated code and some classes of defects. For example, there are no ambiguities in which overloaded function should be chosen for a given function call.

3.3 Initializers and Constructors

A shader variable may be initialized when it is declared. As is familiar from C, the following example initializes *b* at declaration time and leaves *a* and *c* undefined:

```
float a, b = 3.0, c;
```

Constant qualified variables have to be initialized.

```
const int Size = 4;   // initializer is required
```

Attribute, uniform, and varying variables *cannot* be initialized when declared.

```
attribute float Temperature;  // no initializer allowed,
                              // the vertex API sets this

uniform int Size;             // no initializer allowed,
                              // the uniform setting API sets this

varying float density;        // no initializer allowed, the vertex
                              // shader must programmatically set this
```

To initialize aggregate types, at either declaration time or elsewhere, CONSTRUCTORS are used. There is no initializer using the brace syntax "{...}" from C, only constructors. Syntactically, constructors look like function calls that have a type name where the function name would go—for example, to initialize a **vec4** to the value (1.0, 2.0, 3.0, 4.0).

```
vec4 v = vec4(1.0, 2.0, 3.0, 4.0);
```

Or, because constructor syntax is the same whether it's in an initializer or not,

```
vec4 v;
v = vec4(1.0, 2.0, 3.0, 4.0);
```

There are constructors for all the built-in types (except samplers) as well as for structures. Some examples:

```
vec4 v = vec4(1.0, 2.0, 3.0, 4.0);
ivec2 c = ivec2(3, 4);
vec3 color = vec3(0.2, 0.5, 0.8);
mat2 m = mat2(1.0, 2.0, 3.0, 4.0);
struct light
{
    vec4 position;
    struct lightColor
    {
        vec3 color;
        float intensity;
    }
} light1 = light(v, lightColor(color, 0.9));
```

For matrices, the components are filled in using column-major order. The variable *m* from the previous example is the matrix

$$\begin{bmatrix} 1.0 & 3.0 \\ 2.0 & 4.0 \end{bmatrix}$$

So far, we've shown only constructors taking one argument for each component being constructed. Built-in constructors for vectors can also take a single argument, which is replicated into each component.

```
vec3 v = vec3(0.6);
```

is equivalent to

```
vec3 v = vec3(0.6, 0.6, 0.6);
```

This is true only for vectors. Structures must get one argument per member being constructed. Matrix constructors also have a single argument form, but in this case it initializes just the diagonal of the matrix. The remaining components are initialized to 0.0.

```
mat2 m = mat2(1.0);  // makes a 2x2 identity matrix
```

is equivalent to

```
mat2 m = mat2(1.0, 0.0, 0.0, 1.0);      // makes a 2x2 identity matrix
```

Constructors can also have vectors and matrices as arguments. The only rule is that there have to be enough components present to initialize all members of the object being constructed.

```
vec4 v = vec4(1.0);
vec2 u = vec2(v);   // the first two components of v initialize u
mat2 m = mat2(v);
vec2 t = vec2(1.0, 2.0, 3.0);   // allowed; the 3.0 is ignored
```

Matrix components will be read out of arguments in column major order and filled-in in column major order. Extra components or arguments to a constructor are silently ignored. Normally, this is useful for shrinking a value, like eliminating *alpha* from a color or *w* from a position.

3.4 Type Conversions

Explicit type conversions are also done using constructors. For example,

```
float f = 2.3;
bool b = bool(f);
```

will set b to **true**. This is useful for flow-control constructs, like **if**, which require Boolean values. Boolean constructors convert non-zero numeric values to **true** and zero numeric values to false.

The OpenGL Shading Language does not provide C-style typecast syntax, which can be ambiguous as to whether a value is converted to a different type or simply reinterpreted as a different type. In fact, there is no way of reinterpreting a value as a different type. There are no pointers, no type unions, no implicit type changes, and no reinterpret casts. Instead, use constructors to perform conversions. The arguments to a constructor are converted to the type they are constructing. Hence, the following are allowed:

```
float f = float(3);   // convert integer 3 to floating-point 3.0
float g = float(b);   // convert Boolean b to floating point
vec4 v = vec4(2);     // all components of v are set to 2.0
```

When converting from a Boolean, **true** is converted to 1 or 1.0, and **false** is converted to a zero.

3.5 Qualifiers and Interface to a Shader

Qualifiers prefix both variables and formal function parameters. The qualifiers used to modify formal function parameters (**const, in, out,** and **inout**) are discussed in Section 3.6.2. This section will focus on the other qualifiers, most of which form the interfaces of the shaders. The following is the complete list of qualifiers used outside of formal function parameters.

attribute	For frequently changing information, from the application to a vertex shader
uniform	For infrequently changing information, for vertex and fragment shaders
varying	For interpolated information passed from a vertex shader to a fragment shader
const	To declare nonwritable, compile time constant variables, as in C

Getting information into and out of a shader is quite different from more typical programming environments. Information is transferred to and from a shader by reading and writing built-in variables and user-defined **attribute**, **uniform,** and **varying** variables. The most common built-in variables were shown in the example at the beginning of this chapter. They are *gl_Position* for output of the homogeneous coordinates of the vertex position and *gl_FragColor* for output of the fragment's color from a fragment shader. The complete set of built-in variables is provided in Chapter 4. The **attribute**, **uniform,** and **varying** variables have been seen briefly in the opening example for getting other information into and out of shaders. Each is discussed in this section.

Variables qualified as **attribute, uniform**, or **varying** must be declared at global scope. This is sensible as they are visible outside of shaders and, for a single program, they all share a single name space.

Qualifiers are always specified before the type of a variable, and because there is no default type, the form of a qualified variable declaration will always include a type.

```
attribute float Temperature;
const int NumLights = 3;
uniform vec4 LightPosition[NumLights];
varying float LightIntensity;
```

3.5.1 Attribute Qualifiers

Attribute qualified variables (or attributes) are provided for an application to pass frequently modified data into a vertex shader. They can be changed as often as once per vertex, either directly or indirectly by the application. There are built-in attributes, like *gl_Vertex* and *gl_Normal*, for reading traditional OpenGL state, and there are user-defined attributes, which the coder can name.

Attributes are limited to floating-point scalars, floating-point vectors, and matrices. There are no integer, Boolean, structures, or arrays of attributes. This is, in part, a result of encouraging high-performance frequent changing of attributes in implementations of the OpenGL system. Attributes cannot be modified by a shader.

Attributes cannot be declared in fragment shaders.

3.5.2 Uniform Qualifiers

Uniform qualified variables (or uniforms), like attributes, are set only outside a shader and are intended for data that changes less frequently. They can be changed at most once per primitive. All data types and arrays of all data types are supported for uniform qualified variables. All the vertex and fragment shaders forming a single program share a single global name space for uniforms. Hence, uniforms of the same name in a vertex and fragment program will be the same uniform variable.

Uniforms cannot be written to in a shader. This is sensible because an array of processors may be sharing the same resources to hold uniforms and other language semantics break down if uniforms could be modified.

Recall that unless a sampler (e.g., **sampler2D**) is a function parameter, the **uniform** qualifier must be used when declaring it. This is because samplers are opaque, and making them uniforms allows the system to validate that the application initializes a sampler with a texture and texture unit consistent with its use in the shader.

3.5.3 Varying Qualifiers

Varying qualified variables (or varyings) are the only way a vertex shader can communicate results to a fragment shader. Such variables form the dynamic interface between vertex and fragment shaders. The intention is that for a particular attribute of a drawing primitive, each vertex might have a different value and that these values need to be interpolated across the fragments in the primitive. The vertex shader writes the per-vertex values into a varying variable, and when the fragment shader reads from this variable, it gets back a value interpolated between the vertices. If some attribute were to be the same across a large primitive, not requiring interpolation, the vertex shader need not communicate it to the fragment shader at all. Instead, the application could pass this value directly to the fragment shader through a uniform qualified variable.

The exception to using varying variables only for interpolated values is for any value the application will change often, either per triangle or per some small set of triangles or vertices. These values may be faster to pass as **attribute** variables and forwarded on as **varying** variables because changing **uniform** values frequently may impact performance.

The automatic interpolation of **varying** qualified variables is done in a perspective correct manner. This is necessary no matter what type of data is being interpolated. Otherwise, such values would not change smoothly across edges introduced for surface subdivision. The interpolated result would be continuous, but its derivative would not be.

A **varying** qualified variable is typically written in a vertex shader and read in a fragment shader. It is illegal for a fragment shader to write to a varying variable. However, the vertex shader may read a varying variable, getting back what it has just written. Reading a varying qualified variable before writing it returns an undefined value.

3.5.4 Constant Qualifiers

Variables qualified as **const** (except for formal function parameters) are compile-time constants and not visible outside the shader that declares them. There is also support for nonscalar constants.

```
const int numIterations = 10;
const float pi = 3.14159;
const vec2 v = vec2(1.0, 2.0);
const vec3 u = vec3(v, pi);
const struct light
{
    vec3 position;
    vec3 color;
} fixedLight = light(vec3(1.0, 0.5, 0.5), vec3(0.8, 0.8, 0.5));
```

All the preceding variables are compile-time constants. The compiler may propagate and fold constants at compile time, using the precision of the processor executing the compiler, and need not allocate any runtime resources to **const** qualified variables.

3.5.5 Absent Qualifier

If no qualifier is specified when declaring a variable (not a function parameter), the variable can be both read and written by the shader. Nonqualified variables declared at global scope can be shared between shaders of the same type that are linked in the same program. Vertex shaders and fragment shaders each have their own global name space for nonqualified globals. However, nonqualified user-defined variables are not visible outside of a program. That privilege is reserved for variables qualified as **attribute** or **uniform** and for built-in variables representing OpenGL state.

Unqualified variables have a lifetime limited to a single run of a shader. There is also no concept corresponding to a **static** variable in a C function that would allow a variable to be set to a value and have its shader retain that value from one execution to the next. This is made more difficult by the parallel processing nature of the execution environment, where multiple instantiations run in parallel, sharing much of the same memory. In general, writable variables must have unique instances per processor executing a shader and therefore cannot be shared.

Because unqualified global variables have a different name space for vertex shaders than for fragment shaders, it is not possible to share information through such variables between vertex and fragment shaders. Read-only variables can be shared if declared as **uniform**, and variables written by a vertex shader can be read by the fragment shader only through the **varying** mechanism.

3.6 Flow Control

Flow control is very much like C++. The entry point into a shader is the function **main**. A program containing both vertex and fragment shaders will have two functions named **main**, one for entering a vertex shader to process each vertex, and one to enter a fragment shader to process each fragment. Before **main** is entered, any initializers for global variable declarations will be executed.

Looping can be done with **for**, **while**, and **do-while**, just as in C++. Variables can be declared in **for** and **while** statements, and their scope lasts until the end of their substatements. The keywords **break** and **continue** also exist and behave as in C.

Selection can be done with **if** and **if-else**, just as in C++, with the exception that a variable cannot be declared in the **if** statement. Selection using the selection operator (**?:**) is also available, with the extra constraint that the second and third operands have exactly the same type.

The type of the expression provided to an **if** statement or a **while** statement, or to terminate a **for** statement, must be a scalar Boolean. As in C, the right-hand operand to logical-and (**&&**) is not evaluated if the left-hand operand evaluates to false, and the right-hand operand to logical-or (**||**) is not evaluated if the left-hand operand evaluates to true. Similarly, only one of the second or third operands in the selection operator (**:?**) will be evaluated. A logical exclusive or (**^^**) is also provided, for which both sides are always evaluated.

A special branch, **discard**, can prevent a fragment from updating the frame buffer. When flow control goes through this keyword, the fragment being processed is marked to be discarded. An implementation might or might not continue executing the shader, but it is guaranteed that there will be no effect on the frame buffer.

A **goto** keyword or equivalent is not available, nor are labels. Switching with **switch** is also not provided.

3.6.1 Functions

Function calls operate much as in C++. Function names can be overloaded by parameter type but not solely by return type. Either a function definition (body) or declaration must be in scope before calling a function. Parameter types are always checked. This means an empty parameter list (**)** in a function declaration is not ambiguous but rather explicitly means the function accepts no arguments. Also, parameters have to have exact matches as no automatic promotions are done, so selection of overloaded functions is quite straightforward.

Exiting from a function with **return** operates the same as in C++. Functions returning nonvoid types must return values, whose type must exactly match the return type of the function.

Functions may not be called recursively, either directly or indirectly.

3.6.2 Calling Conventions

The OpenGL Shading Language uses call by value-return as its calling convention. The call by value part is familiar from C: Parameters qualified as input parameters will be copied into the function and not passed as a reference. Because there are no pointers, this means a function need not worry about its parameters being aliases of the same memory. The call by the return part of call by value-return means parameters qualified as output parameters will be returned to the caller by being copied back out from the called function to the caller when the function returns.

To say which parameters are copied when, prefix them with the qualifier keywords **in, out**, or **inout**. For something that is just copied into the function but not returned, use **in**. The **in** qualifier is also implied when no qualifiers are specified. To say a parameter is not to be copied in but is to be set and copied back on return, use the qualifier **out**. To say a parameter is copied both in and out, use the qualifier **inout**.

in	Copy in but don't copy back out; still writable within the function
out	Only copy out; readable, but undefined at entry to function
inout	Copy in and copy out

The **const** qualifier can also be applied to function parameters. Here, it does not mean the variable is a compile-time constant, but rather that the function is not allowed to write it. Note that an ordinary, nonqualified input-only parameter can be written to, it just won't be copied back to the caller. Hence, there is a distinction between a parameter qualified as **const in** and one qualified only as **in** (or with no qualifier). Of course, **out** and **inout** parameters cannot be declared as **const**.

Some examples:

```
void ComputeCoord(in vec3 normal,   // Parameter 'normal' is copied in,
                                     // can be written to, but will not be
                                     // copied back out.
                  vec3 tangent,      // Same behavior as if "in" was used.
                  inout vec3 coord)// Copied in and copied back out.
```

Or,

```
vec3 ComputeCoord(const vec3 normal,// normal cannot be written to
                  vec3 tangent,
                  in vec3 coord)     //the function will return the result
```

The following are not legal:

```
void ComputeCoord(const out vec3 normal, //not legal; can't write normal
                  const inout vec3 tang, //not legal; can't write tang
                  in out vec3 coord)     //not legal; use inout
```

Functions can either return a value or return nothing. If a function returns nothing, it must be declared as type **void**. If a function returns a value, the type can be any type except an array. However, structures can be returned, and structures can contain arrays.

3.6.3 Built-in Functions

There is a large set of built-in functions available. These are documented in full in Chapter 5.

A shader can override these functions, providing its own definition. To override a function, provide a prototype or definition that is in scope at the time of call time. The compiler or linker then looks for a user-defined version of the function to resolve that call. For example, one of the built-in sine functions is declared as

```
float sin(float x);
```

If a shader wants to experiment with performance/accuracy trade-offs in a sine function or specialize it for a particular domain, it can override them and do so.

```
float sin(float x)
{
    return <.. some function of x..>
}

void main()
{
    // call the sin function above, not the built-in sin function
    float s = sin(x);
}
```

This is similar to the standard language linking techniques of using libraries of functions and to having more locally scoped function definitions satisfy references before the library is checked. If the definition is in a different shader, just make sure a prototype is visible before calling the function. Otherwise, the built-in version will be used.

3.7 Operations

Table 3.1 includes the operators, in order of precedence, available in the OpenGL Shading Language. The precedence and associativity is consistent with C.

Table 3.1   Operators, in order of precedence

Operator	Description
[ ]	Index
.	Member selection and swizzle
++ --	Postfix increment/decrement
++ --	Prefix increment/decrement
- !	Unary negation and logical not
* /	Multiply and divide
+ -	Add and subtract
< > <= >=	Relational
== !=	Equality
&&	Logical and
^^	Logical exclusive or
||	Logical inclusive or
?:	Selection
= += -= *= /=	Assignment
,	Sequence

3.7.1 Indexing

Vectors, matrices, and arrays can be indexed using the index operator ([ ]). All indexing is zero based; the first element is at index 0. Indexing an array operates just as in C.

Indexing a vector returns scalar components. This allows giving components numerical names of 0, 1, ..., and also provides variable selection of vector components, should that be needed. For example,

```
vec4 v = vec4(1.0, 2.0, 3.0, 4.0);
float f = v[2];  // f takes the value 3.0
```

Here, *v[2]* will be the floating-point scalar 3.0, which is then assigned into *f*.

Indexing a matrix returns columns of the matrix as vectors. For example,

```
mat4 m = mat4(3.0);  // initializes the diagonal to all 3.0
vec4 v;
v = m[1];    // places the vector (0.0, 3.0, 0.0, 0.0) into v
```

Here, the second column of *m, m[1]* is treated as a vector that is copied into *v.*

Behavior is undefined if an array, vector, or matrix is accessed with an index that's less than zero or greater than or equal to the size of the object.

3.7.2 Swizzling

The normal structure-member selector (**.**) is also used to SWIZZLE components of a vector—that is, components can be selected and/or rearranged by listing their names after the swizzle operator (**.**). Examples:

```
vec4 v4;
v4.rgba;   // is a vec4 and the same as just using v4,
v4.rgb;    // is a vec3,
v4.b;      // is a float,
v4.xy;     // is a vec2,
v4.xgba;   // is illegal - the component names do not come from
           // the same set.
```

The component names can be out of order to rearrange the components or replicated to duplicate them:

```
vec4 pos = vec4(1.0, 2.0, 3.0, 4.0);
vec4 swiz = pos.wzyx; // swiz = (4.0, 3.0, 2.0, 1.0)
vec4 dup = pos.xxyy;  // dup = (1.0, 1.0, 2.0, 2.0)
```

At most, four component names can be listed in a swizzle; otherwise, they would result in a nonexistent type. The rules for swizzling are slightly different for R-VALUES (expressions that are read from) and L-VALUES (expressions that say where to write to). R-values can have any combination and repetition of components. L-values must not have any repetition. For example:

```
vec4 pos = vec4(1.0, 2.0, 3.0, 4.0);
pos.xw = vec2(5.0, 6.0); // pos = (5.0, 2.0, 3.0, 6.0)
pos.wx = vec2(7.0, 8.0); // pos = (8.0, 2.0, 3.0, 7.0)
pos.xx = vec2(3.0, 4.0); // illegal - 'x' used twice
```

For R-values, this syntax can be used on any expression whose resultant type is a vector. For example, getting a two-component vector from a texture lookup can be done as

```
vec2 v = texture1D(sampler, coord).xy;
```

where the built-in function **texture1D** returns a **vec4**.

3.7.3 Component-wise Operation

With a few important exceptions, when an operator is applied to a vector, it behaves as if it were applied to each component of the vector, independently.

For example,

```
vec3 v, u;
float f;
v = u + f;
```

will be equivalent to

```
v.x = u.x + f;
v.y = u.y + f;
v.z = u.z + f;
```

And

```
vec3 v, u, w;
w = v + u;
```

will be equivalent to

```
w.x = v.x + u.x;
w.y = v.y + u.y;
w.z = v.z + u.z;
```

If a binary operation operates on a vector and a scalar, the scalar is applied to each component of the vector. If two vectors are operated on, their sizes must match.

Exceptions are multiplication of a vector times a matrix and a matrix times a matrix, which perform standard linear-algebraic multiplies, not component-wise multiplies.

Increment and decrement operators (**++** and **--**) and unary negation (**-**) behave as in C. When applied to a vector or matrix, they increment or decrement each component. They operate on integer and floating-point-based types.

Arithmetic operators of addition (**+**), subtraction (**-**), multiplication (*****), and division (**/**) behave as in C, or component-wise, with the previously described exception of using linear-algebraic multiplication on vectors and matrices:

```
vec4 v, u;
mat4 m;
v * u;   // This is a component-wise multiply
v * m;   // This is a linear-algebraic row-vector times matrix multiply
m * v;   // This is a linear-algebraic matrix times column-vector multiply
m * m;   // This is a linear-algebraic matrix times matrix multiply
```

All other operations are performed component by component.

Logical not (**!**), logical and (**&&**), logical or (**||**), and logical inclusive or (**^^**) operate only on expressions that are typed as scalar Booleans, and they result in a Boolean. These cannot operate on vectors. There is a built-in function, **not**, to compute the component-wise logical not of a vector of Booleans.

Relational operations (**<**, **>**, **<=**, and **>=**) operate only on floating-point and integer scalars and result in a scalar Boolean. There are built-in functions, for instance **lessThanEqual,** to compute a Boolean vector result of component-wise comparisons of two vectors.

The equality operators (**==** and **!=**) operate on all types except arrays. They compare every component or structure member across the operands. This results in a scalar Boolean, indicating whether the two operands were equal. For two operands to be equal, their types must match, and each of their components or members must be equal. To get a component-wise vector result, call the built-in functions **equal** and **notEqual**.

Scalar Booleans are produced by the operators equal (**==**), not equal (**!=**), relational (**<**, **>**, **<=**, and **>=**), and logical not (**!**) because flow-control constructs (**if**, **for,** etc.) expect a scalar Boolean. If built-in functions like **equal** are called to compute a vector of Booleans, such a vector can be turned into a scalar Boolean using the built-in functions **any** and **all**. For example, to do something if any component of a vector is less than the corresponding component of another vector, say

```
vec4 u, v;
...
```

```
if (any(lessThan(u, v)))
    ...
```

Assignment (=) requires exact type match between the left- and right-hand side. Any type, except for arrays, can be assigned. Other assignment operators (+=, -=, *=, and /=) are similar to C but must make semantic sense when expanded out

```
a *= b    ⇒    a = a * b
```

where the expression *a * b* must be semantically valid, and the type of the expression *a * b* must be the same as the type of *a*. The other assignment operators behave similarly.

The ternary selection operator (?:) operates on three expressions *(exp1 ? exp2 : exp3)*. This operator evaluates the first expression, which must result in a scalar Boolean. If the result is true, it selects to evaluate the second expression; otherwise, it selects to evaluate the third expression. Only one of the second and third expressions is evaluated. The second and third expressions must be the same type, but they can be of any type other than an array. The resulting type is the same as the type of the second and third expressions.

The sequence operator (,) operates on expressions by returning the type and value of the right-most expression in a comma-separated list of expressions. All expressions are evaluated, in order, from left to right.

3.8 Preprocessor

The preprocessor is much like that in C. Support for

> **#define**
> **#undef**
> **#if**
> **#ifdef**
> **#ifndef**
> **#else**
> **#elif**
> **#endif**

as well as the **defined** operator are exactly as in standard C. This includes macros with arguments and macro expansion. Built-in macros are

```
__LINE__
__FILE__
__VERSION__
```

__LINE__ substitutes a decimal integer constant that is one more than the number of preceding new-lines in the current source string.

__FILE__ substitutes a decimal integer constant that says which source string number is currently being processed.

__VERSION__ substitutes a decimal integer reflecting the version number of the OpenGL Shading Language. The version of the shading language described in this document will have __VERSION__ substitute the decimal integer 100.

There is also the usual support for

> **#error** message
>
> **#line**
>
> **#pragma**

#error puts *message* into the shader's information log. The compiler then proceeds as if a semantic error has been encountered.

#pragma is implementation dependent. If an implementation does not recognize the subsequent tokens, it should be ignored. However, the following pragmas are portable.

Use the optimize pragma

> **#pragma** optimize(on)
>
> **#pragma** optimize(off)

to turn optimizations on or off as an aid in developing and debugging shaders. It can occur only outside function definitions. By default, optimization is turned on for all shaders.

The debug pragma

> **#pragma** debug(on)
>
> **#pragma** debug(off)

enables compiling and annotating a shader with debug information so it can be used with a debugger. The debug pragma can occur only outside function definitions. By default, debug is set to off.

#line must have, after macro substitution, one of the following two forms:

> **#line** line
> **#line** line source-string-number

where *line* and *source-string-number* are constant integer expressions. After processing this directive (including its new-line), the implementation will behave as if it is compiling at line number *line+1* and source string number *source-string-number*. Subsequent source strings will be numbered sequentially until another **#line** directive overrides that numbering.

3.9 Preprocessor Expressions

Preprocessor expressions can contain the following operators as shown in Table 3.2.

Table 3.2   Preprocessor operators

Operator	Description
+ - ~ ! defined	unary
* / %	multiplicative
+ -	additive
<< >>	bit-wise shift
< > <= >=	relational
== !=	equality
& ^ |	bit-wise
&& ||	logical

They have precedence and behavior matching the standard C preprocessor.

The most important thing to keep in mind with preprocessor expressions is they may execute on the processor running the compiler and not on the graphics processor that will execute the shader. Precision is allowed to be this host processor's precision and hence will likely be different from the precision available when executing expressions in the core language.

As with the core language, string types and operations are not provided. None of the hash-based operators (#, ##, etc.) is provided, nor is a preprocessor **sizeof** operator.

3.10 Error Handling

Compilers accept some ill-formed programs because it is impossible to detect all ill-formed programs. For example, completely accurate detection of usage of an uninitialized variable is not possible. Such ill-formed shaders may execute differently on different platforms. Therefore, the OpenGL Shading Language specification states that portability is ensured only for well-formed programs.

OpenGL Shading Language compilers are encouraged to detect ill-formed programs and issue diagnostic messages, but are not required to do so for all cases. Compilers are required to return messages regarding shaders that are lexically, grammatically, or semantically incorrect. Shaders that generate such error messages cannot be executed. The OpenGL entry points for obtaining any diagnostic messages are discussed in Section 7.5.

3.11 Summary

The OpenGL Shading Language is a high-level procedural language designed specifically for the OpenGL environment. This language allows applications to specify the behavior of programmable, highly parallel graphics hardware. It contains constructs that allow succinct expression of graphics shading algorithms in a way that is natural for programmers experienced in C and C++.

The OpenGL Shading Language includes support for scalar, vector, and matrix types; structures and arrays; sampler types that are used to access textures; data type qualifiers that are used to define shader input and output; constructors for initialization and type conversion; and operators and flow control statements like those in C/C++.

3.12 Further Information

The OpenGL Shading Language is defined in the document *The OpenGL Shading Language, Version 1.051*, by Kessenich, Baldwin, and Rost (2003).

The grammar for the OpenGL Shading Language is included in its entirety in Appendix A. These two documents can be consulted for additional details about the language itself. Additional tutorials, slides, and white papers are available at the 3Dlabs Web site.

The functionality of the OpenGL Shading Language is augmented by the OpenGL extensions that were designed to support it. The specifications for these extensions and the OpenGL specification itself should be read to gain further clarity on the behavior of a system that supports the OpenGL Shading Language. The OpenGL books referenced at the conclusion of Chapter 1 can also be consulted for a better overall understanding of OpenGL.

The standard reference for the C programming language is *The C Programming Language* by the designers of the language, Brian Kernighan and Dennis Ritchie (1988). Likewise, the standard for the C++ programming language is *The C++ Programming Language*, written by the designer of C++, Bjarne Stroustrup (2000). Numerous other books on both languages are available.

[1] *3Dlabs developer Web site.* http://www.3dlabs.com/support/developer

[2] Kernighan, Brian, and Dennis Ritchie, *The C Programming Language, Second Edition*, Prentice Hall, Englewood Cliffs, New Jersey, 1988.

[3] Kessenich, John, Dave Baldwin, and Randi Rost, *The OpenGL Shading Language, Version 1.051*, 3Dlabs, February 2003. http://www.3dlabs.com/support/developer/ogl2

[4] OpenGL Architecture Review Board, *ARB_vertex_shader Extension Specification*, OpenGL Extension Registry. http://oss.sgi.com/projects/ogl-sample/registry

[5] OpenGL Architecture Review Board, *ARB_fragment_shader Extension Specification*, OpenGL Extension Registry. http://oss.sgi.com/projects/ogl-sample/registry

[6] OpenGL Architecture Review Board, *ARB_shader_objects Extension Specification*, OpenGL Extension Registry. http://oss.sgi.com/projects/ogl-sample/registry

[7] Segal, Mark, and Kurt Akeley, *The OpenGL Graphics System: A Specification (Version 1.5)*, Editor (v1.1): Chris Frazier, Editor (v1.2–1.5): Jon Leech, July 2003. http://opengl.org

[8] Stroustrup, Bjarne, *The C++ Programming Language (Special 3rd Edition)*, Addison-Wesley, Reading, Massachusetts, 2000.

Chapter 4

The OpenGL Programmable Pipeline

With contributions by Barthold Lichtenbelt

The OpenGL Shading Language is designed specifically for use with OpenGL. Vertex shader and fragment shader input and output are tied into the standard OpenGL pipeline in a well-defined manner. The basics of how the programmable processors fit into the OpenGL pipeline were covered in Section 2.3. This chapter discusses the details of that integration and the language mechanisms used to achieve it.

Applications can provide data to shaders using user-defined attribute variables and user-defined uniform variables. The OpenGL Shading Language also provides built-in variables that are used to communicate between the programmable processors and the surrounding fixed functionality in the following ways.

- Standard OpenGL attributes can be accessed from within a vertex shader using built-in attribute variable names.

- A variety of OpenGL state is accessible from either vertex shaders or fragment shaders using built-in uniform variables.

- Vertex shaders communicate to subsequent processing in OpenGL through the use of special built-in vertex shader output variables and built-in varying variables.

- Fragment shaders obtain the results from the preceding processing through special built-in fragment shader input variables and built-in varying variables.

- Fragment shaders communicate results to subsequent processing stages of OpenGL through special fragment shader output variables.

- Built-in constants are accessible from within both types of shaders and define some of the same implementation-dependent constants that are accessible with OpenGL's **glGet** function.

All of the built-in identifiers begin with the reserved prefix "gl_" to set them apart.

4.1   The Vertex Processor

The vertex processor executes a vertex shader and replaces the following fixed functionality OpenGL per-vertex operations. A vertex shader has no knowledge of the primitive type for the vertex it is working on.

- The modelview matrix is not applied to vertex coordinates.

- The projection matrix is not applied to vertex coordinates.

- The texture matrices are not applied to texture coordinates.

- Normals are not transformed to eye coordinates.

- Normals are not rescaled or normalized.

- Normalization of GL_AUTO_NORMAL evaluated normals is not performed.

- Texture coordinates are not generated automatically.

- Per-vertex lighting is not performed.

- Color material computations are not performed.

- Color index lighting is not performed.

- Point size distance attenuation is not performed.

- All of the preceding applies when setting the current raster position.

The following fixed functionality operations are applied to vertex values that are the result of executing the vertex shader:

- Color clamping or masking (for built-in varying variables that deal with color but not for user-defined varying variables)

- Perspective division on clip coordinates

- Viewport mapping

- Depth range

- Clipping, including user clipping

- Front face determination

- Flat-shading

- Color, texture coordinate, fog, point-size and user-defined varying clipping

- Final color processing

The basic operation of the vertex processor was discussed in Section 2.3.1. As shown in Figure 2.2, data can come into the vertex shader via attribute variables (built in or user defined), uniform variables (built in or user defined), or texture maps (a vertex processing capability that is new with the OpenGL Shading Language). Data exits the vertex processor through built-in varying variables, user-defined varying variables, and special vertex shader output variables. Built-in constants (described in Section 4.4) are also accessible from within a vertex shader.

OpenGL has a mode that causes color index values to be produced rather than RGBA values. However, this mode is not supported in conjunction with vertex shaders. If the frame buffer is configured as a color index buffer, behavior is undefined when using a vertex shader.

4.1.1 Vertex Attributes

In order to draw things with OpenGL, applications must provide vertex information such as normal, color, texture coordinates, and so on. These attributes can be specified a vertex at a time using OpenGL functions such as **glNormal**, **glColor**, and **glTexCoord**. When set using these function calls, the attributes become part of OpenGL's current state.

Geometry can also be drawn using vertex arrays. With this method, applications arrange vertex attributes in separate arrays containing positions, normals, colors, texture coordinates, and so on. By calling **glDrawArrays**, a large number of vertex attributes can be sent to OpenGL in a single function call. Vertex buffer objects (i.e., server-side storage for vertex arrays) were added in OpenGL 1.5 to provide better performance for drawing vertex arrays.

Vertex attributes come in two flavors: standard and generic. The standard attributes are the attributes as defined by OpenGL; these are color, secondary color, normal, vertex position, texture coordinates, and the fog coordinate.

The index attribute, used for setting the current color index, and the edge flag attribute are not available to a vertex shader (but the application is allowed to send the edge flags to OpenGL while using a vertex shader). A vertex shader accesses the standard attributes using the following built-in names. A compiler error will be generated if these names are used in a fragment shader.

```
//
// Vertex Attributes
//
attribute vec4  gl_Color;
attribute vec4  gl_SecondaryColor;
attribute vec3  gl_Normal;
attribute vec4  gl_Vertex;
attribute vec4  gl_MultiTexCoord0;
attribute vec4  gl_MultiTexCoord1;
attribute vec4  gl_MultiTexCoord2;
// ... up to gl_MultiTexCoordN-1 where N = gl_MaxTextureCoords
attribute float gl_FogCoord;
```

Details on providing generic vertex attributes to a vertex shader through the OpenGL Shading Language API are provided in Section 7.6.

Both standard attributes and generic attributes are part of the current OpenGL state. That means that they retain their values, once set. An application is free to set values for all generic and all standard attributes and count on OpenGL to store them (except for vertex position, see Section 7.6). However, there is a limit on the number of attributes a vertex shader can use. Typically, this limit will be smaller than the sum of all the standard and generic attributes. This limit is implementation specific and can be queried by calling **glGet** with the symbolic constant GL_MAX_VERTEX_ATTRIBS_ARB. Every OpenGL implementation is required to support at least 16 vertex attributes in a vertex shader.

To signal the end of one vertex, either the conventional vertex attribute *gl_Vertex* can be set by the application or the generic vertex attribute with index zero can be set. The *gl_Vertex* attribute is set with the **glVertex** command or one of the vertex array commands, and the generic attribute with index zero is set by calling **glVertexAttribARB** with an index of zero. These two commands are equivalent, and either one will signal the end of a vertex.

4.1.2   Uniform Variables

Shaders can access current OpenGL state through built-in uniform variables containing the reserved prefix "gl_". For instance, the current modelview matrix can be accessed with the built-in variable name *gl_ModelViewMatrix*. Various properties of a light source can be accessed through the array containing light parameters as in *gl_LightSource[2].spotDirection*. Any OpenGL state used by the shader is automatically tracked and made available to the shader. This automatic state tracking mechanism allows the application to use existing OpenGL state commands for state management and have the current values of such state automatically available for use in the shader.

OpenGL state is accessible to both vertex shaders and fragment shaders using the built-in uniform variables defined in Section 4.3.

Applications can also define their own uniform variables in a vertex shader and use OpenGL API calls to set their values (see Section 7.7 for a complete description). There is an implementation-dependent limit on the amount of storage allowed for uniform variables in a vertex shader. The limit refers to the storage for the combination of built-in uniform variables and user-defined uniform variables that are actually used in a vertex shader. It is defined in terms of components, where a component is the size of a **float**. Thus a **vec2** takes up two components, a **vec3** takes three, and so on. This value can be queried by calling **glGet** with the symbolic constant GL_MAX_VERTEX_UNIFORM_COMPONENTS_ARB.

4.1.3   Special Output Variables

Earlier we learned that results from the vertex shader are sent on for additional processing by fixed functionality within OpenGL, including primitive assembly and rasterization. Several built-in variables are defined as part of the OpenGL Shading Language in order to allow the vertex shader to pass information on to these subsequent processing stages. The built-in variables discussed in this section are available only from within a vertex shader.

The variable *gl_Position* is intended for writing the vertex position in clipping coordinates after it has been computed in a vertex shader. Every execution of a well-formed vertex shader must write a value into this variable. Compilers may generate an error message if they detect *gl_Position* is not written or read before being written, but not all such cases are detectable. Results are undefined if a vertex shader is executed and it does not store a value into *gl_Position*.

The built-in variable *gl_PointSize* is intended for writing the size (diameter) of a point primitive. It is measured in pixels. This allows a vertex shader to compute a screen size that is related to the distance to the point, for instance. Section 4.5.2 provides more details on using *gl_PointSize*.

If user clipping is enabled, it will occur as a fixed functionality operation after the vertex shader has been executed. In order for user clipping to function properly in conjunction with the use of a vertex shader, the vertex shader must compute a vertex position that is relative to the user-defined clipping planes. This value must then be stored in the built-in variable *gl_ClipVertex*. It is up to the application to ensure that the clip vertex value computed by the vertex shader and the user clipping planes are defined in the same coordinate space. User clip planes work properly only under linear transform. More details on using *gl_ClipVertex* are contained in Section 4.5.3.

These variables each have global scope. They can be written to at any time during the execution of the vertex shader, and they can be read back after they have been written. Reading them before writing them results in undefined behavior. If they are written more than once, the last value written will be the one that is consumed by the subsequent operations.

These variables can be referenced only from within a vertex shader and are intrinsically declared with the following types:

```
vec4  gl_Position;   // must be written to
float gl_PointSize;  // may be written to
vec4  gl_ClipVertex; // may be written to
```

4.1.4 Built-in Varying Variables

As explained previously, varying variables are used to describe attributes that vary across a primitive. The vertex shader is responsible for writing values that need to be interpolated into varying variables. The fragment shader reads the interpolated results from varying variables and operates on them to produce a resulting value for each fragment. For each user-defined varying variable actually used by the fragment shader, there must be a matching varying variable declared in the vertex shader; otherwise, a link error will occur.

In order to properly communicate with the fixed functionality of OpenGL, the OpenGL Shading Language defines a number of built-in varying variables. A vertex shader can write certain varying variables that are not accessible from the fragment shader, and a fragment shader has the capability to read certain varying variables that were not accessible from the vertex shader.

The following built-in varying variables can be written in a vertex shader. The vertex shader should write to those that are required for the desired fixed functionality fragment processing (if no fragment shader is to be used), or to those required by the corresponding fragment shader.

```
varying vec4  gl_FrontColor;
varying vec4  gl_BackColor;
varying vec4  gl_FrontSecondaryColor;
varying vec4  gl_BackSecondaryColor;
varying vec4  gl_TexCoord[gl_MaxTextureCoords];
varying float gl_FogFragCoord;
```

Values written to *gl_FrontColor*, *gl_BackColor*, *gl_FrontSecondaryColor*, and *gl_BackSecondaryColor* will be clamped to the range [0,1] by fixed functionality when they exit the vertex shader. These four values are used together with fixed functionality to determine whether the primitive is front facing or back facing in order to compute the two varying variables *gl_Color* and *gl_SecondaryColor* that are available in the fragment shader.

One or more sets of texture coordinates can be passed from a vertex shader using the *gl_TexCoord* array. This makes them available for fixed functionality processing if no fragment shader is present. Alternatively, they can be accessed from within a fragment shader using the *gl_TexCoord* varying variable.

For *gl_FogFragCoord*, the value written should be the one required by the current fog coordinate source as set by a previous call to **glFog**. If the fog coordinate source is set to GL_FRAGMENT_DEPTH, the value written into *gl_FogFragCoord* should be the distance from the eye to the vertex in eye coordinates (where the eye position is assumed to be (0, 0, 0, 1)). If the fog coordinate source is set to GL_FOG_COORDINATE, the value written into *gl_FogFragCoord* should be the fog coordinate value that is to be interpolated across the primitive (i.e., the built-in attribute variable *gl_FogCoord*).

4.1.5 User-Defined Varying Variables

Vertex shaders can also define varying variables in order to pass arbitrary values on to the fragment shader. Such values are not clamped, but they are subjected to subsequent fixed functionality processing such as clipping and interpolation. There is an implementation-dependent limit to the number of floating-point values that can be interpolated. This limit can be queried by calling **glGet** with the symbolic constant GL_MAX_VARYING_FLOATS_ARB.

4.2 The Fragment Processor

The fragment processor executes a fragment shader and replaces the texturing, color sum, and fog fragment operations. Specifically, it replaces the following per-fragment operations:

- The texture environments and texture functions are not applied.
- Texture application is not applied.
- Color sum is not applied.
- Fog is not applied.

The behavior of the following operations does not change:

- Texture image specification.
- Alternate texture image specification.
- Compressed texture image specification.
- Texture parameters behave as specified even when a texture is accessed from within a fragment shader.
- Texture state and proxy state.
- Texture object specification.
- Texture comparison modes.

The basic operation of the fragment processor was discussed in Section 2.3.2. As shown in Figure 2.3, data can come into the fragment shader via varying variables (built in or user defined), uniform variables (built in or user defined), special input variables, or texture maps. Data exits the fragment processor through special fragment shader output variables. Built-in constants (described in Section 4.4) are also accessible from within a fragment shader.

Like vertex shaders, the behavior of a fragment shader is undefined when the frame buffer is configured as a color index buffer rather than an RGBA buffer (i.e., OpenGL is in color index mode).

4.2.1 Varying Variables

The following built-in varying variables can be read in a fragment shader. The *gl_Color* and *gl_SecondaryColor* names are the same as built-in attribute variable names available in the vertex shader. However, there is no name conflict because attributes are visible only in vertex shaders and the following are only visible in fragment shaders:

```
varying vec4  gl_Color;
varying vec4  gl_SecondaryColor;
varying vec4  gl_TexCoord[gl_MaxTextureCoords];
varying float gl_FogFragCoord;
```

The values in *gl_Color* and *gl_SecondaryColor* will be derived automatically from *gl_FrontColor, gl_BackColor, gl_FrontSecondaryColor,* and *gl_BackSecondaryColor* as part of fixed functionality processing that determines whether the fragment belongs to a front facing or a back facing primitive (see Section 4.5.1). If fixed functionality is used for vertex processing, *gl_FogFragCoord* will be either the *z*-coordinate of the fragment in eye space or the interpolated value of the fog coordinate, depending on whether the fog coordinate source is currently set to GL_FRAGMENT_DEPTH or GL_FOG_COORDINATE. The *gl_TexCoord[]* array will contain either the values of the interpolated *gl_TexCoord[]* values from a vertex shader or the texture coordinates from the fixed functionality vertex processing. No automatic division of texture coordinates by their *q*-component is performed.

When the fragment shader is processing fragments resulting from the rasterization of a pixel rectangle or bitmap, results are undefined if the fragment shader uses a varying variable that is not a built-in varying variable. In this case, the values for the built-in varying variables are supplied by the current raster position because a vertex shader is not executed.

Fragment shaders also obtain input data from user-defined varying variables. Both built-in and user-defined varying variables contain the result of perspective-correct interpolation of values that are defined at each vertex.

4.2.2 Uniform Variables

As described in Section 4.1.2, OpenGL state is available to both vertex shaders and fragment shaders through built-in uniform variables that begin with the reserved prefix "gl_". The list of uniform variables that can be used to access OpenGL state is provided in Section 4.3.

User-defined uniform variables can be defined and used within fragment shaders in the same manner as for vertex shaders. OpenGL API calls are provided to set their values (see Section 7.7 for complete details).

The implementation-dependent limit that defines the amount of storage available for uniform variables in a fragment shader can be queried by calling **glGet** with the symbolic constant GL_MAX_FRAGMENT_UNIFORM_ COMPONENTS_ARB. This limit refers to the storage for the combination of built-in uniform variables and user-defined uniform variables that are actually used in a fragment shader.

4.2.3 Special Input Variables

The variable *gl_FragCoord* is available as a read-only variable from within fragment shaders, and it holds the window relative coordinates *x*, *y*, *z*, and 1/*w* for the fragment. This window position value is the result of the fixed functionality that interpolates primitives after vertex processing to generate fragments. The *z* component will contain the depth value as modified by the polygon offset calculation. This built-in variable is available to allow implementation of window position-dependent operations such as screen-door transparency (e.g., use **discard** on any fragment for which *gl_FragCoord.x* is odd or *gl_FragCoord.y* is odd, but not both).

The fragment shader also has access to the read-only built-in variable *gl_FrontFacing* whose value is true if the fragment belongs to a front-facing primitive, and false otherwise. This value can be used to select between two colors calculated by the vertex shader in order to emulate two-sided lighting, or it can be used to apply completely different shading effects to front and back surfaces. A fragment derives its facing direction from the primitive that generates the fragment. All fragments generated by primitives other than polygons, triangles, or quadrilaterals are considered to be front facing. For all other fragments (including ones resulting from point-and line-mode polygons), the determination is made by examining the sign of the area of the primitive in window coordinates. This sign can possibly be reversed, depending on the last call to **glFrontFace**. If the sign is positive, the fragments are front facing; otherwise, they are back facing.

These special input variables have global scope and can be referenced only from within a fragment shader. They are intrinsically declared with the following types:

```
vec4  gl_FragCoord;
bool  gl_FrontFacing;
```

4.2.4 Special Output Variables

The primary purpose of a fragment shader is to compute values that will ultimately be written into the frame buffer. The output of the fragment shader goes on to be processed by the fixed function operations at the back end of the OpenGL pipeline. Fragment shaders send their results on to the back end of the OpenGL pipeline using the built-in variables *gl_FragColor* and *gl_FragDepth*. These built-in fragment shader variables have global scope, and they may be written more than once by a fragment shader. If they are written more than once, the last value assigned will be the one used in the subsequent operations.

The color value that is to be written into the frame buffer (assuming that is passes through the various back-end fragment processing stages unscathed) is computed by the fragment shader and stored in the built-in variable *gl_FragColor*. Most shaders will compute a value for *gl_FragColor*, but it is not required that this value be computed by all fragment shaders. It is perfectly legal for a shader to compute only *gl_FragDepth*. It is also possible that the shader will use the **discard** keyword to mark the fragment to be discarded rather than used to update the frame buffer. It should be noted that if subsequent fixed functionality consumes fragment color and an execution of a fragment shader does not write a value to *gl_FragColor*, the behavior is undefined.

If depth buffering is enabled and a shader does not write *gl_FragDepth*, the fixed function value for depth will be used as the fragment's depth value. Otherwise, writing to *gl_FragDepth* will establish the depth value for the fragment being processed. As it exits the fragment processor, this value will be clamped to the range [0,1] and converted to fixed point with at least as many bits as there are in the frame buffer. Fragment shaders that write to *gl_FragDepth* should take care to write to it for every execution path through the shader. If it is written in one branch of a conditional statement but not the other, the depth value will be undefined for some execution paths.

There is also no guarantee that a shader can compute the same depth value as the fixed functionality value. The value produced by a shader may not exactly equal the value produced by fixed functionality even when the fragment's depth value is assigned by copying *gl_FragCoord.z* into *gl_FragDepth*. The only depth invariance guarantee is that fragment shaders that either conditionally or unconditionally assign *gl_FragCoord.z* to *gl_FragDepth* will be depth invariant with respect to one another.

The values written to *gl_FragColor* and *gl_FragDepth* do not need to be clamped within a shader. The fixed functionality pipeline following the fragment processor will clamp these values, if needed, to the range required by the buffer into which the fragment will be written.

If a shader executes the **discard** keyword, the fragment is discarded, and the values of *gl_FragDepth* and *gl_FragColor* become irrelevant.

The fragment shader output variables have global scope, can be referenced only from within a fragment shader, and are intrinsically declared with the following types:

```
vec4  gl_FragColor;
float gl_FragDepth;
```

4.3 Built-in Uniform Variables

OpenGL was designed as a state machine. It has a variety of state that can be set. As graphics primitives are provided to OpenGL for rendering, the current state settings affect how the graphics primitives are treated and ultimately how they are rendered into the frame buffer.

Some applications heavily utilize this aspect of OpenGL. Large amounts of application code might be dedicated to manipulating OpenGL state and providing an interface to allow the end user to change state to produce different rendering effects.

The OpenGL Shading Language was designed to make it easy for these types of applications to take advantage of programmable graphics technology. It contains a variety of built-in uniform variables that allow a shader to access current OpenGL state. In this way, an application can continue to use OpenGL as a state management machine and still provide shaders that combine that state in ways that aren't possible using the OpenGL fixed functionality path. Because they are defined as uniform variables, shaders are allowed to read from these built-in variables but not to write to them.

The built-in uniform variables in Listing 4.1 are provided to allow shaders to access current OpenGL state. They can be accessed from within either vertex shaders or fragment shaders. If an OpenGL state value has not been modified by an application, it will contain the default value as defined by OpenGL, and the corresponding built-in uniform variable will also be equal to that value.

Listing 4.1   Built-in uniform variables

```
//
// Matrix state
//
uniform mat4  gl_ModelViewMatrix;
uniform mat4  gl_ProjectionMatrix;
uniform mat4  gl_ModelViewProjectionMatrix;
uniform mat3  gl_NormalMatrix;      // derived
uniform mat4  gl_TextureMatrix[gl_MaxTextureCoords];

//
// Normal scaling
//
uniform float gl_NormalScale;

//
// Depth range in window coordinates
//
struct gl_DepthRangeParameters
{
    float near;         // n
    float far;          // f
    float diff;         // f - n
};
uniform gl_DepthRangeParameters gl_DepthRange;

//
// Clip planes
//
uniform vec4  gl_ClipPlane[gl_MaxClipPlanes];

//
// Point Size
//
struct gl_PointParameters
{
    float size;
    float sizeMin;
    float sizeMax;
```

```
       float fadeThresholdSize;
       float distanceConstantAttenuation;
       float distanceLinearAttenuation;
       float distanceQuadraticAttenuation;
};

uniform gl_PointParameters gl_Point;

//
// Material State
//
struct gl_MaterialParameters
{
    vec4  emission;      // Ecm
    vec4  ambient;       // Acm
    vec4  diffuse;       // Dcm
    vec4  specular;      // Scm
    float shininess;     // Srm
};
uniform gl_MaterialParameters  gl_FrontMaterial;
uniform gl_MaterialParameters  gl_BackMaterial;

//
// Light State
//

struct gl_LightSourceParameters
{
    vec4  ambient;             // Acli
    vec4  diffuse;             // Dcli
    vec4  specular;            // Scli
    vec4  position;            // Ppli
    vec4  halfVector;          // Derived: Hi
    vec3  spotDirection;       // Sdli
    float spotExponent;        // Srli
    float spotCutoff;          // Crli
                               // (range: [0.0,90.0], 180.0)
    float spotCosCutoff;       // Derived: cos(Crli)
                               // (range: [1.0,0.0],-1.0)
    float constantAttenuation; // K0
    float linearAttenuation;   // K1
    float quadraticAttenuation;// K2
};

uniform gl_LightSourceParameters  gl_LightSource[gl_MaxLights];

struct gl_LightModelParameters
{
    vec4  ambient;       // Acs
};
```

```
uniform gl_LightModelParameters  gl_LightModel;

//
// Derived state from products of light and material.
//

struct gl_LightModelProducts
{
    vec4   sceneColor;      // Derived. Ecm + Acm * Acs
};

uniform gl_LightModelProducts gl_FrontLightModelProduct;
uniform gl_LightModelProducts gl_BackLightModelProduct;

struct gl_LightProducts
{
    vec4   ambient;        // Acm * Acli
    vec4   diffuse;        // Dcm * Dcli
    vec4   specular;       // Scm * Scli
};

uniform gl_LightProducts gl_FrontLightProduct[gl_MaxLights];
uniform gl_LightProducts gl_BackLightProduct[gl_MaxLights];

//
// Texture Environment and Generation
//
uniform vec4  gl_TextureEnvColor[gl_MaxTextureImageUnits];
uniform vec4  gl_EyePlaneS[gl_MaxTextureCoords];
uniform vec4  gl_EyePlaneT[gl_MaxTextureCoords];
uniform vec4  gl_EyePlaneR[gl_MaxTextureCoords];
uniform vec4  gl_EyePlaneQ[gl_MaxTextureCoords];
uniform vec4  gl_ObjectPlaneS[gl_MaxTextureCoords];
uniform vec4  gl_ObjectPlaneT[gl_MaxTextureCoords];
uniform vec4  gl_ObjectPlaneR[gl_MaxTextureCoords];
uniform vec4  gl_ObjectPlaneQ[gl_MaxTextureCoords];

//
// Fog
//
struct gl_FogParameters
{
    vec4 color;
    float density;
    float start;
    float end;
    float scale;   //  1 / (gl_Fog.end - gl_Fog.start)
};

uniform gl_FogParameters gl_Fog;
```

As you can see, these built-in uniform variables have been defined in such a way as to take advantage of the language features whenever possible. Structures are used as containers to group a collection of parameters such as depth range parameters, material parameters, light source parameters, and fog parameters. Arrays are used to define clip planes and light sources. Defining these uniform variables in this way improves code readability and allows shaders to take advantage of language capabilities like looping.

The list of built-in uniform variables also includes some derived state. These state values are things that aren't passed in directly by the application but are derived by the OpenGL implementation from values that are passed. For various reasons, it's convenient to have the OpenGL implementation compute these derived values and allow shaders to access them. The normal matrix (*gl_NormalMatrix*) is an example of this. It is simply the inverse transpose of the upper-left 3 × 3 subset of the modelview matrix. Because it is used so often, it wouldn't make sense to require shaders to compute this from the modelview matrix whenever it is needed. Instead, the OpenGL implementation is responsible for computing this whenever it is needed, and it is accessible to shaders through a built-in uniform variable.

Here are some examples of how these built-in uniform variables might be used. A vertex shader can transform the incoming vertex position (*gl_Vertex*) by OpenGL's current modelview-projection matrix (*gl_Model-ViewProjectionMatrix*) with the following line of code:

```
gl_Position = gl_ModelViewProjectionMatrix * gl_Vertex;
```

Similarly, if a normal is needed, it will be transformed by the current normal matrix:

```
tnorm = gl_NormalMatrix * gl_Normal;
```

(The transformed normal would typically also need to be normalized in order to use it in lighting computations. This can be done using the built-in function **normalize** that will be discussed in Section 5.4.)

Here are some other examples of accessing built-in OpenGL state:

```
gl_FrontMaterial.emission   // emission value for front material
gl_LightSource[0].ambient   // ambient term of light source #0
gl_ClipPlane[3][0]          // first component of user clip plane #3
gl_Fog.color.rgb            // r, g, and b components of fog color
gl_TextureMatrix[1][2][3]   // 3rd column, 4th component of 2nd
                            // texture matrix
```

The mapping of OpenGL state values to these built-in variables should be straightforward, but if more details are needed, see the *OpenGL Shading Language Specification* document.

4.4 Built-in Constants

The OpenGL Shading Language defines a number of built-in constants. These values can be accessed from within either vertex or fragment shaders. Values for lights, clip planes, and texture units are values that are equivalent to those that would be returned by OpenGL's **glGet** function for the underlying implementation. Implementation-dependent values that are new with the OpenGL Shading Language are the number of floating-point values that could be stored as uniform values accessible by the vertex shader and by the fragment shader, the number of floating-point values that could be defined as varying variables, the number of texture image units that are accessible by the vertex processor and by the fragment processor, the total number of texture image units available to the vetex processor and the fragment processor combined, and the number of texture coordinates sets that are supported. All of these new implementation-dependent constants can also be obtained in application code by calling the OpenGL **glGet** function (see Section 7.10).

OpenGL defines minimum values for each implementation-dependent constant. The minimum value informs application writers of the lowest value that is permissible for a conforming OpenGL implementation. The minimum value for each of the built-in constants is shown here.

```
//
// Implementation dependent constants.  The values below
// are the minimum values allowed for these constants.
//
const int  gl_MaxLights = 8;
const int  gl_MaxClipPlanes = 6;
const int  gl_MaxTextureUnits = 2;
const int  gl_MaxTextureCoords = 2;
const int  gl_MaxVertexAttribs = 16;
const int  gl_MaxVertexUniformComponents = 512;
const int  gl_MaxVaryingFloats = 32;
const int  gl_MaxVertexTextureImageUnits = 0;
const int  gl_MaxTextureImageUnits = 2;
const int  gl_MaxFragmentUniformComponents = 64;
const int  gl_MaxCombinedTextureImageUnits = 2;
```

These values can occasionally be useful within a shader. For instance, a shader might include a general-purpose lighting function that loops through the available OpenGL lights and adds contributions from each enabled light source. The loop can easily be set up using the built-in constant gl_MaxLights. More likely, however, is that an application will use OpenGL's **glGet** function to obtain these implementation-dependent constants and decide whether to even load a shader based on those values (see Section 7.10).

4.5 Interaction with OpenGL Fixed Functionality

This section contains a little more detail for programmers that are intimately familiar with OpenGL operations and need to know precisely how the programmable capabilities introduced by the OpenGL Shading Language interact with the rest of the OpenGL pipeline. It is more suitable for seasoned OpenGL programmers than for OpenGL novices.

4.5.1 Two-Sided Color Mode

Vertex shaders can operate in two-sided color mode. Front and back colors can be computed by the vertex shader and written to the *gl_FrontColor*, *gl_BackColor*, *gl_FrontSecondaryColor*, and *gl_BackSecondaryColor* output variables. If two-sided color mode is enabled after vertex processing, OpenGL fixed functionality will choose which of the front or back colors to forward to the rest of the pipeline. Which side OpenGL picks depends on the primitive type being rendered and the sign of the area of the primitive in window coordinates (see the OpenGL specification for details). If two-sided color mode is disabled, OpenGL will always select the front color outputs. Two-sided color mode is enabled and disabled by calling **glEnable** or **glDisable** with the symbolic value GL_VERTEX_PROGRAM_TWO_SIDE_ ARB.

The colors resulting from this front/back facing selection step are clamped to the range [0, 1] and converted to a fixed-point representation before being interpolated across the primitive that is being rendered. This is normal OpenGL behavior. When higher precision and dynamic range colors are required, the application should use its own user-defined varying variables instead of the four built-in *gl_Color* ones. The front/back facing selection step will then be skipped. However, there is a built-in variable available in the fragment shader (*gl_FrontFacing*) that indicates if the current fragment is the result of rasterizing a front or back facing primitive.

4.5.2 Point Size Mode

Vertex shaders can also operate in point size mode. A vertex shader can compute a point size in pixels and assign it to the built-in variable *gl_PointSize*. If point size mode is enabled, the point size is taken from this variable and used in the rasterization stage; otherwise, it is taken from the value set with the **glPointSize** command. If *gl_PointSize* is not written while vertex shader point size mode is enabled, the point size used in the rasterization stage is undefined. Vertex shader point size mode is enabled and disabled by calling **glEnable** or **glDisable** with the symbolic value GL_VERTEX_PROGRAM_POINT_SIZE_ARB.

This point size enable is convenient for the majority of applications that do not change the point size within a vertex shader. By default, this mode is disabled, so most vertex shaders that don't care about point size don't need to worry about writing a value to *gl_PointSize*. The value set by calls to **glPointSize** will always be used by the rasterization stage.

If the primitive is clipped and vertex shader point size mode is enabled, the point size values are also clipped in a manner analogous to color clipping. The potentially clipped point size is used by the fixed functionality part of the pipeline as the derived point size (the distance attenuated point size). Thus, if the application wants points further away to be smaller, it should compute some kind of distance attenuation in the vertex shader and scale the point size accordingly. If vertex shader point size mode is disabled, the derived point size is taken directly from the value set with the **glPointSize** command, and no distance attenuation is performed. The derived point size is then used, as usual, optionally to alpha-fade the point when multi-sampling is also enabled. Again, see the OpenGL specification for details.

Distance attenuation should be computed in a vertex shader and cannot be left to the fixed functionality distance attenuation algorithm. This fixed functionality algorithm computes distance attenuation as a function of the distance between the eye at (0, 0, 0, 1) and the vertex position, in eye coordinates. However, the vertex position computed in a vertex shader might not have anything to do with locations in eye coordinates. Therefore, when a vertex shader is active, this fixed functionality algorithm is skipped. A point's alpha-fade, on the other hand, can be computed correctly only with the knowledge of the primitive type. That information is not available to a vertex shader because it executes before primitive assembly. Consider the case of rendering a triangle and having the back polygon mode set to GL_POINT and the front polygon mode to GL_FILL. The vertex shader should fade only the alpha if the vertex belongs to a back-facing triangle. But it cannot do that because it does not know the primitive type.

4.5.3 Clipping

User clipping can be used in conjunction with a vertex shader. The user clip planes are specified as usual using the **glClipPlane** command. When specified, these clip planes will be transformed by the inverse of the current modelview matrix. The vertices resulting from the execution of a vertex shader are evaluated against these transformed clip planes. The vertex shader must provide the position of the vertex in the same space as the user-defined clip planes (typically eye space). It does that by writing this location to the output variable *gl_ClipVertex*. If *gl_ClipVertex* is not specified and user clipping is enabled, the results are undefined.

When using a vertex shader that mimics OpenGL's fixed functionality, the vertex shader should compute the eye coordinate position of the vertex and store it in *gl_ClipVertex*. For example,

```
gl_ClipVertex = gl_ModelViewMatrix * gl_Vertex;
```

When it is desired to do object space clipping instead, keep in mind that the clip planes are transformed with the inverse of the modelview matrix. In order to get correct object clipping, the modelview matrix needs to be set to the identity matrix.

After user clipping, vertices are clipped against the view volume, as usual. In this operation, the value specified by *gl_Position* (i.e., the homogeneous vertex position in clip space) is evaluated against the view volume.

4.5.4 Raster Position

A vertex shader processes the coordinates provided with the **glRasterPos** command just as if these coordinates were specified with a **glVertex** command. The vertex shader is responsible for outputting the values necessary to compute the current raster position data.

The data making up the current raster position consists of the following seven items:

1. Window coordinates computed from the value written to *gl_Position*. These coordinates are treated as if they belong to a point and passed to the clipping stage and then projected to window coordinates.

2. A valid bit indicating if this point was culled.

3. The raster distance, which is set to the vertex shader varying variable *gl_FogFragCoord*.

4. The raster color, which is set to either the vertex shader varying variable *gl_FrontColor* or *gl_BackColor*, depending on the front/back facing selection process.

5. The raster secondary color, which is set to either the vertex shader varying variable *gl_FrontSecondaryColor* or *gl_BackSecondaryColor*, depending on the front/back facing selection process.

6. One or more raster texture coordinates. These are set to the vertex shader varying variable array *gl_TexCoord[]*.

7. The raster color index. Because the result of a vertex shader is undefined in color index mode, the raster color index will always be set to 1.

If any of the outputs necessary to compute the first six items are not provided, the value(s) for the associated item will be undefined.

4.5.5 Position Invariance

For multipass rendering, where some passes are performed with a vertex shader and other passes use the fixed functionality pipeline, positional invariance is important. This means that both the vertex shader and fixed functionality will compute the exact same vertex position in clip coordinates, given the same vertex position in object coordinates and the same modelview and projection matrices. Positional invariance can be achieved by using the built-in function **ftransform** in a vertex shader as follows:

```
gl_Position = ftransform();
```

In general, the vertex shader code

```
gl_Position = gl_ModelViewProjectMatrix * gl_Vertex
```

will not result in positional invariance because of possible compiler optimizations and potential underlying hardware differences.

4.5.6 Texturing

One of the major improvements to OpenGL made by the OpenGL Shading Language is in the area of texturing. For one thing, texturing operations can be performed in a vertex shader. But the fragment side of the pipeline has improved as well. A fragment shader can potentially have access to more texture image units than the fixed functionality pipeline does. This means that more texture lookups can be performed in a single rendering pass. And with programmability, the results of all those texture lookups can be combined in any way the shader writer sees fit.

The changes to the pipeline have resulted in some clarification to the language used to describe texturing capabilities in OpenGL. The term "texture unit" in OpenGL was formerly used to specify more than one thing. It was used to specify the number of texture coordinates that can be attached to a vertex (now called texture coordinate sets) as well as the number of hardware units that can be used simultaneously for accessing texture maps (now called texture image units). A texture coordinate set encompasses vertex texture coordinate attributes, as well as the texture matrix stack and texture generation state. The symbolic constant GL_MAX_TEXTURE_UNITS can be queried by calling **glGet** to obtain a single number that indicates the quantity of both of these items.

For the implementations that support the OpenGL Shading Language, these two things might actually have different values, so the number of available texture coordinate sets is now decoupled from the maximum number of texture image units. Typically, the number of available texture coordinate sets will be less than the available texture image units. This is fine because new texture coordinates can be derived, for example, from the texture coordinate attributes passed in or stored in a texture map.

There are a total of five different limits related to texture mapping to take into account.

1. For a vertex shader, the maximum number of available texture image units is given by GL_MAX_VERTEX_TEXTURE_IMAGE_UNITS_ARB.

2. For a fragment shader, the maximum number of available texture image units is given by GL_MAX_TEXTURE_IMAGE_UNITS_ARB.

3. The combined number of texture image units used in the vertex and the fragment processing parts of OpenGL (either a fragment shader or fixed function) cannot exceed the limit GL_MAX_COMBINED_TEXTURE_IMAGE_UNITS_ARB. If a vertex shader and the fragment processing part of OpenGL both use the same texture image unit, that counts as two units against this limit. This rule is there because an OpenGL implementation might have only GL_MAX_COMBINED_TEXTURE_IMAGE_UNITS_ARB actual texture image units implemented, and it might share those units between the vertex and fragment processing parts of OpenGL.

4. When a fragment shader is not active, OpenGL can still perform multitexturing. In this case, the maximum available multitexture stages are given by the state variable GL_MAX_TEXTURE_UNITS.

5. The number of supported texture coordinate sets is given by GL_MAX_ TEXTURE_COORDS_ARB. This limit applies regardless of using a vertex shader or fixed-function OpenGL to perform vertex processing.

The fixed-function hierarchy of texture enables (GL_TEXTURE_CUBE_MAP, GL_TEXTURE_3D, GL_TEXTURE_2D, and GL_TEXTURE_1D) is ignored by shaders. For example, even if the texture target GL_TEXTURE_1D is enabled for a texture image unit, it is possible to use a sampler to access the GL_TEXTURE_2D target for that texture image unit.

Samplers of type **sampler1DShadow** or **sampler2DShadow** need to be used to access depth textures (textures with a base internal format of GL_DEPTH_COMPONENT). The texture comparison mode requires the shader to use one of the variants of the **shadow1D** or **shadow2D** built-in functions for accessing the texture (see Section 5.7). If these built-in functions are used to access a texture with a base internal format other than GL_DEPTH_ COMPONENT, the result will be undefined. Similarly, if a texture access function other than one of the shadow variants is used to access a depth texture, the result will be undefined.

If a shader uses a sampler to reference a texture object that is not complete (e.g., one of the textures in a mipmap has a different internal format or border width than the others, see the OpenGL specification for a complete list), the texture image unit will return (R, G, B, A) = (0, 0, 0, 1).

4.6 Summary

Two new programmable units have been added to OpenGL: the vertex processor and the fragment processor. The same language, with minor differences, is used to express algorithms intended to run on either processor. The vertex processor replaces the fixed functionality vertex processing of OpenGL, and a shader intended for execution on this processor is called a vertex shader. When installed as part of current state, the vertex shader will be executed once for each vertex that is processed by OpenGL. The fragment processor replaces the fixed functionality fragment processing of OpenGL, and a shader that is intended for execution on this processor is called a fragment shader. When installed as part of current state, the fragment shader will be executed once for each fragment that arises from rasterization.

Great care has been taken to define the interfaces between the program-mable stages of OpenGL and the intervening fixed functionality. As a result, rendering is permitted with programmable vertex processing and fixed functionality fragment processing, or vice versa. Built-in variables allow access to standard OpenGL attributes, implementation-dependent constants, and a variety of current state. They also allow a shader to communicate with the preceding and following fixed functionality stages of the graphics-processing pipeline.

4.7 Further Information

The built-in variables defined in this chapter will be used in various examples throughout this book. The OpenGL Shading Language specification and the OpenGL specification can be consulted for additional details. The OpenGL books referenced at the conclusion of Chapter 1 can also be consulted for a better understanding of the OpenGL state that is referenced through built-in variables. Parts of the paper *Integrating the OpenGL Shading Language* by Barthold Lichtenbelt have been adapted for inclusion in this book. The full text of this paper should be available from the 3Dlabs Web site by the time this book is published.

[1] Kessenich, John, Dave Baldwin, and Randi Rost, *The OpenGL Shading Language, Version 1.051*, 3Dlabs, February 2003. http://www.3dlabs.com/support/developer/ogl2

[2] Lichtenbelt, Barthold, *Integrating the OpenGL Shading Language*, 3Dlabs internal white paper, July 2003.

[3] Segal, Mark, and Kurt Akeley, *The OpenGL Graphics System: A Specification (Version 1.5)*, Editor (v1.1): Chris Frazier, Editor (v1.2–1.5): Jon Leech, July 2003. http://opengl.org

Chapter 5

Built-in Functions

This chapter provides the details of the functions that are defined as part of the OpenGL Shading Language. Feel free to skip ahead to the next chapter if you want to get down to the nitty-gritty of writing your own shaders. This chapter can be useful as a reference after you are well on your way to writing OpenGL shaders for your own application.

The OpenGL Shading Language defines an assortment of built-in convenience functions for scalar and vector operations. The built-in functions basically fall into three categories.

1. They expose some necessary hardware functionality in a convenient way such as accessing a texture map. There is no way in the language for these functions to be emulated by a shader.

2. They represent a trivial operation (clamp, mix, etc.) that is very simple for the user to write, but they are very common and may have direct hardware support. It is a problem for the compiler to map expressions to complex assembler instructions.

3. They represent an operation that graphics hardware is likely to accelerate at some point. The trigonometry functions fall into this category.

Many of the functions are similar to the same named ones in common C libraries, but they support vector input as well as the more traditional scalar input. Because the OpenGL Shading Language supports function overloading, the built-in functions usually have several variants, all with the same name. The difference in the functions is in the type of arguments and the type of the value returned. Quite a few of the built-in functions have four variants: one that takes **float** parameters and returns a **float**, one that takes **vec2** parameters and returns a **vec2**, one that takes **vec3** parameters and returns a **vec3**, and one that takes **vec4** parameters and returns a **vec4**.

Whenever possible, you should use the built-in functions rather than do the equivalent computations in your own shader code. It is expected that the built-in functions will be implemented in an optimal way, perhaps even supported directly in hardware. Almost all of the built-in functions can be used in either a vertex shader or a fragment shader, but a few are available only for a specific type of shader. You can write a shader to replace a built-in function with your own code simply by redeclaring and defining the same name and argument list.

Graphical representations of some of the functions will be shown in order to illustrate them clearly. The functions are generally simple ones, and most readers would have no trouble constructing such diagrams themselves. But as we will see in later chapters, many of the built-in functions can be used in unconventional ways to achieve interesting effects in shaders. When developing a shader, it is often helpful to draw a simple function diagram to clearly envision the value of a variable at a particular spot in a shader. By seeing a pictorial representation of some of these functions, it may be easier for you to draw such diagrams yourself and to gain some insight for how they may be put to use in procedural shaders. Some common uses for these functions will be pointed out along the way, and some are illustrated by shader examples in the later chapters of this book.

5.1 Angle and Trigonometry Functions

Trigonometry functions can be used within either vertex shaders or fragment shaders. Function parameters specified as *angle* are assumed to be in units of radians. In no case will any of these functions result in a divide by zero error. If the divisor of a ratio is 0, results will be undefined.

These functions all operate component-wise (see Table 5.1).

Table 5.1 Angle and Trigonometry Functions

Syntax	Description
float **radians** (float *degrees*) vec2 **radians** (vec2 *degrees*) vec3 **radians** (vec3 *degrees*) vec4 **radians** (vec4 *degrees*)	Converts *degrees* to radians and returns the result, i.e., result = $\pi/180 \cdot degrees$.
float **degrees** (float *radians*) vec2 **degrees** (vec2 *radians*) vec3 **degrees** (vec3 *radians*) vec4 **degrees** (vec4 *radians*)	Converts *radians* to degrees and returns the result, i.e., result = $180/\pi \cdot radians$.
float **sin** (float *radians*) vec2 **sin** (vec2 *radians*) vec3 **sin** (vec3 *radians*) vec4 **sin** (vec4 *radians*)	The standard trigonometric sine function. The values returned by this function will range from [–1,1].
float **cos** (float *radians*) vec2 **cos** (vec2 *radians*) vec3 **cos** (vec3 *radians*) vec4 **cos** (vec4 *radians*)	The standard trigonometric cosine function. The values returned by this function will range from [–1,1].
float **tan** (float *radians*) vec2 **tan** (vec2 *radians*) vec3 **tan** (vec3 *radians*) vec4 **tan** (vec4 *radians*)	The standard trigonometric tangent function.
float **asin** (float *x*) vec2 **asin** (vec2 *x*) vec3 **asin** (vec3 *x*) vec4 **asin** (vec4 *x*)	Arc sine. Returns an angle whose sine is *x*. The range of values returned by this function is [$-\pi/2$, $\pi/2$]. Results are undefined if $|x| > 1$.
float **acos** (float *x*) vec2 **acos** (vec2 *x*) vec3 **acos** (vec3 *x*) vec4 **acos** (vec4 *x*)	Arc cosine. Returns an angle whose cosine is *x*. The range of values returned by this function is [0, π]. Results are undefined if $|x| > 1$.

Table 5.1 Angle and Trigonometry Functions, continued

Syntax	Description
float **atan** (float *y*, float *x*) vec2 **atan** (vec2 *y*, vec2 *x*) vec3 **atan** (vec3 *y*, vec3 *x*) vec4 **atan** (vec4 *y*, vec4 *x*)	Arc tangent. Returns an angle whose tangent is *y/x*. The signs of *x* and *y* are used to determine what quadrant the angle is in. The range of values returned by this function is $[-\pi, \pi]$. Results are undefined if *x* and *y* are both 0.
float **atan** (float *y_over_x*) vec2 **atan** (vec2 *y_over_x*) vec3 **atan** (vec3 *y_over_x*) vec4 **atan** (vec4 *y_over_x*)	Arc tangent. Returns an angle whose tangent is *y_over_x*. The range of values returned by this function is $[-\pi/2, \pi/2]$.

In addition to their usefulness as trigonometric functions, **sin** and **cos** can be used in a variety of ways as the basis for a smoothly varying function with no cusps or discontinuities (see Figure 5.1). Such a function can be used to model waves on the surface of an object, to change periodically between two materials, to introduce a rocking motion to an object, or for many other things.

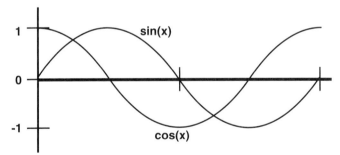

Figure 5.1 The **sin** and **cos** functions

5.2 Exponential Functions

Exponential functions can be used within either vertex shaders or fragment shaders. These all operate component-wise (see Table 5.2).

Table 5.2 Exponential Functions

Syntax	Description
float **pow** (float *x*, float *y*) vec2 **pow** (vec2 *x*, vec2 *y*) vec3 **pow** (vec3 *x*, vec3 *y*) vec4 **pow** (vec4 *x*, vec4 *y*)	Returns *x* raised to the *y* power, i.e., x^y.
float **exp2** (float *x*) vec2 **exp2** (vec2 *x*) vec3 **exp2** (vec3 *x*) vec4 **exp2** (vec4 *x*)	Returns 2 raised to the *x* power, i.e., 2^x.
float **log2** (float *x*) vec2 **log2** (vec2 *x*) vec3 **log2** (vec3 *x*) vec4 **log2** (vec4 *x*)	Returns the base 2 log of *x*, i.e., returns the value *y*, which satisfies the equation $x = 2^y$.
float **sqrt** (float *x*) vec2 **sqrt** (vec2 *x*) vec3 **sqrt** (vec3 *x*) vec4 **sqrt** (vec4 *x*)	Returns the positive square root of *x*.
float **inversesqrt** (float *x*) vec2 **inversesqrt** (vec2 *x*) vec3 **inversesqrt** (vec3 *x*) vec4 **inversesqrt** (vec4 *x*)	Returns the reciprocal of the positive square root of *x*.

5.3 Common Functions

Common functions can be used within either vertex shaders or fragment shaders. These functions all operate in a component-wise fashion (see Table 5.3).

Table 5.3 Common Functions

Syntax	Description
float **abs** (float x) vec2 **abs** (vec2 x) vec3 **abs** (vec3 x) vec4 **abs** (vec4 x)	Returns x if $x >= 0$; otherwise, it returns $-x$.
float **sign** (float x) vec2 **sign** (vec2 x) vec3 **sign** (vec3 x) vec4 **sign** (vec4 x)	Returns 1.0 if $x > 0$, 0.0 if $x = 0$, or -1.0 if $x < 0$.
float **floor** (float x) vec2 **floor** (vec2 x) vec3 **floor** (vec3 x) vec4 **floor** (vec4 x)	Returns a value equal to the nearest integer that is less than or equal to x.
float **ceil** (float x) vec2 **ceil** (vec2 x) vec3 **ceil** (vec3 x) vec4 **ceil** (vec4 x)	Returns a value equal to the nearest integer that is greater than or equal to x.
float **fract** (float x) vec2 **fract** (vec2 x) vec3 **fract** (vec3 x) vec4 **fract** (vec4 x)	Returns $x -$ **floor** (x).
float **mod** (float x, float y) vec2 **mod** (vec2 x, float y) vec3 **mod** (vec3 x, float y) vec4 **mod** (vec4 x, float y)	Modulus. Returns $x - y *$ **floor** (x/y) for each component in x using the floating-point value y.
vec2 **mod** (vec2 x, vec2 y) vec3 **mod** (vec3 x, vec3 y) vec4 **mod** (vec4 x, vec4 y)	Modulus. Returns $x - y *$ **floor** (x/y) for each component in x using the corresponding component of y.

Table 5.3   Common Functions, continued

Syntax	Description
float **min** (float x, float y) vec2 **min** (vec2 x, vec2 y) vec3 **min** (vec3 x, vec3 y) vec4 **min** (vec4 x, vec4 y)	Returns y if $y < x$; otherwise, it returns x.
vec2 **min** (vec2 x, float y) vec3 **min** (vec3 x, float y) vec4 **min** (vec4 x, float y)	Returns minimum of each component of x compared with the floating-point value y.
float **max** (float x, float y) vec2 **max** (vec2 x, vec2 y) vec3 **max** (vec3 x, vec3 y) vec4 **max** (vec4 x, vec4 y)	Returns y if $x < y$; otherwise, it returns x.
vec2 **max** (vec2 x, float y) vec3 **max** (vec3 x, float y) vec4 **max** (vec4 x, float y)	Returns maximum of each component of x compared with the floating-point value y.

float **clamp** (float x, float $minVal$,
        float $maxVal$)
vec2 **clamp** (vec2 x, float $minVal$,
        float $maxVal$)
vec3 **clamp** (vec3 x, float $minVal$,
        float $maxVal$)
vec4 **clamp** (vec4 x, float $minVal$,
        float $maxVal$)
	Returns **min** (**max** (x, $minVal$), $maxVal$) for each component in x using the floating-point values $minVal$ and $maxVal$.

vec2 **clamp** (vec2 x, vec2 $minVal$,
        vec2 $maxVal$)
vec3 **clamp** (vec3 x, vec3 $minVal$,
        vec3 $maxVal$)
vec4 **clamp** (vec4 x, vec4 $minVal$,
        vec4 $maxVal$)
	Returns the component-wise result of **min** (**max** (x, $minVal$), $maxVal$).

Table 5.3 Common Functions, continued

Syntax	Description
float **mix** (float *x*, float *y*, float *a*) vec2 **mix** (vec2 *x*, vec2 *y*, float *a*) vec3 **mix** (vec3 *x*, vec3 *y*, float *a*) vec4 **mix** (vec4 *x*, vec4 *y*, float *a*)	Returns $x * (1.0 - a) + y * a$, i.e., the linear blend of *x* and *y* using the floating-point value *a*. The value for *a* is not restricted to the range [0,1].
vec2 **mix** (vec2 *x*, vec2 *y*, vec2 *a*) vec3 **mix** (vec3 *x*, vec3 *y*, vec3 *a*) vec4 **mix** (vec4 *x*, vec4 *y*, vec4 *a*)	Returns the component-wise result of $x * (1.0 - a) + y * a$, i.e., the linear blend of vectors *x* and *y* using the vector *a*. The value for *a* is not restricted to the range [0,1].
float **step** (float *edge*, float *x*) vec2 **step** (vec2 *edge*, vec2 *x*) vec3 **step** (vec3 *edge*, vec3 *x*) vec4 **step** (vec4 *edge*, vec4 *x*)	Returns 0 if $x <= edge$; otherwise, it returns 1.0.

float **smoothstep** (float *edge0*,
    float *edge1*, float *x*)
vec2 **smoothstep** (vec2 *edge0*,
    vec2 *edge1*, vec2 *x*)
vec3 **smoothstep** (vec3 *edge0*,
    vec3 *edge1*, vec3 *x*)
vec4 **smoothstep** (vec4 *edge0*,
    vec4 *edge1*, vec4 *x*)
	Returns 0 if $x <= edge0$ and 1.0 if $x >= edge1$ and performs smooth Hermite interpolation between 0 and 1 when $edge0 < x < edge1$.

Aside from their general usefulness as math functions, many of these functions are useful in creating interesting shaders as we shall see in subsequent chapters. The **abs** function can be used to ensure that a particular function never produces negative values. It can also be used to introduce a discontinuity in an otherwise smooth function. As we shall see in Section 12.5, this property of the **abs** function will be used to introduce discontinuities in a noise function to produce an effect that looks like turbulence. A graphical representation of the **abs** function is shown in Figure 5.2.

The **sign** function simply maps the incoming value to –1, 0, or 1, depending on its sign. This results in a discontinuous function as shown in Figure 5.3.

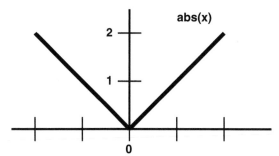

Figure 5.2   The **abs** function

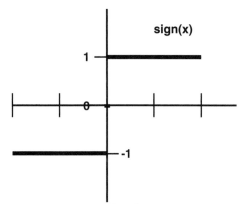

Figure 5.3   The **sign** function

The **floor** function produces a discontinuous stair-step pattern as shown in Figure 5.4. The fractional part of each incoming value is dropped, so the output value is always the integer value that is closest but less than or equal to the input value.

The **ceil** function is almost the same as the **floor** function, except that value returned is always the integer value that is closest but greater than or equal to the input value. This function is shown in Figure 5.5. As you can see, this function looks the same as Figure 5.4 except the output values are shifted up by one. (Although **ceil** and **floor** always produce integer values, the functions are defined to return floating-point data types.)

The **fract** function produces a discontinuous function where each segment has a slope of 1.0 (see Figure 5.6).

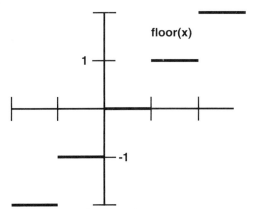

Figure 5.4   The **floor** function

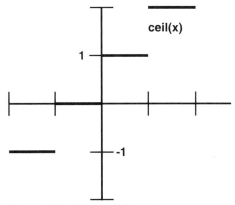

Figure 5.5   The **ceil** function

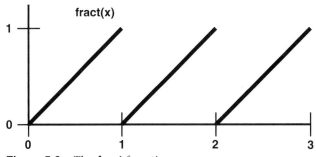

Figure 5.6   The **fract** function

The **mod** function is very similar to **fract**. In fact, if we divide the result of **mod**(x, y) by y, the result is very nearly the same. The only difference is the period of the discontinuous segments (see Figure 5.7).

The **clamp** function is very useful for making sure that a value is within a particular range. A very common operation is

```
clamp(x, 0.0, 1.0);
```

which will clamp the variable x to the range [0,1]. Because two comparisons are necessary for this function, you should use it only when there is a chance that the tested value could be outside either end of the specified range. For the **min** and **max** functions, only one comparison is necessary. If you know a value will not be less than 0, using

```
min(x, 1.0);
```

will likely be faster and may use fewer machine instructions than

```
clamp(x, 0.0, 1.0);
```

because there is no point in testing to see whether the final value is less than 0. Keep in mind that there is no need to clamp the final color and depth values computed by a fragment shader because they will be clamped automatically by the back-end fixed functionality processing.

The **min**, **max**, and **clamp** functions are shown in Figure 5.8, Figure 5.9, and Figure 5.10. The **min**(x, y) function has a slope of 1 where x is less than y, and a slope of 0 where x is greater than y. This function is often used to put an upper bound on a value, for instance, to make sure the computed result never exceeds 1.0.

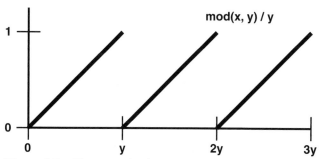

Figure 5.7   The periodic function **mod**(x, y) / y

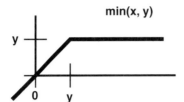

Figure 5.8   The **min** function

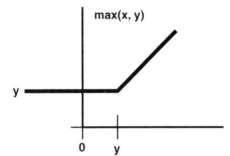

Figure 5.9   The **max** function

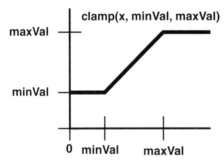

Figure 5.10   The **clamp** function

The **max**(x, y) function has a slope of 0 where x is less than y, and a slope of 1 where x is greater than y. This function is often used to put a lower bound on a value, for instance, to make sure the computed result never goes below 0.

The **clamp**(x, minVal, maxVal) function has a slope of 0 where x is less than minVal and where x is greater than maxVal, and it has a slope of 1 in between where x is greater than minVal and less than maxVal. It is functionally equivalent to the expression **min**(**max**(x, minVal), maxVal).

The **step** function can be used to create a discontinuous jump at an arbitrary point (see Figure 5.11). We will see how this function can be used to create a simple procedural brick shader in Chapter 6.

The **smoothstep** function (see Figure 5.12) is useful in cases where you want a threshold function with a smooth transition. For the case where *t* is a **float**, this is equivalent to

```
float t;
t = clamp ((x - edge0) / (edge1 - edge0), 0.0, 1.0);
return t * t * (3.0 - 2.0 * t);
```

The cases for **vec2**, **vec3**, and **vec4** differ from the preceding example only in the data type used to declare *t*.

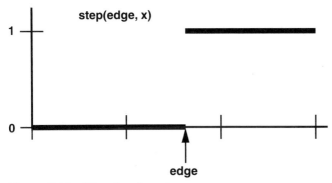

Figure 5.11   The **step** function

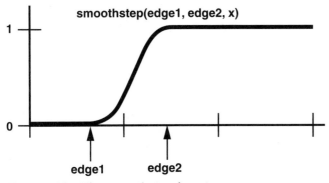

Figure 5.12   The **smoothstep** function

5.4 Geometric Functions

Except for **ftransform**, geometric functions can be used within either vertex shaders or fragment shaders. These functions operate on vectors as vectors, not in a component-wise fashion (see Table 5.4).

Table 5.4 Geometric Functions

Syntax	Description
float **length** (float x) float **length** (vec2 x) float **length** (vec3 x) float **length** (vec4 x)	Returns the length of vector x, i.e., **sqrt** $(x[0] * x[0] + x[1] * x[1] + ...)$.
float **distance** (float $p0$, float $p1$) float **distance** (vec2 $p0$, vec2 $p1$) float **distance** (vec3 $p0$, vec3 $p1$) float **distance** (vec4 $p0$, vec4 $p1$)	Returns the distance between $p0$ and $p1$, i.e., **length** $(p0 - p1)$.
float **dot** (float x, float y) float **dot** (vec2 x, vec2 y) float **dot** (vec3 x, vec3 y) float **dot** (vec4 x, vec4 y)	Returns the dot product of x and y, i.e., result = $x[0] * y[0] + x[1] * y[1] + ...$
vec3 **cross** (vec3 x, vec3 y)	Returns the cross product of x and y, i.e., result[0] = $x[1] * y[2] - y[1] * x[2]$ result[1] = $x[2] * y[0] - y[2] * x[0]$ result[2] = $x[0] * y[1] - y[0] * x[1]$
float **normalize** (float x) vec2 **normalize** (vec2 x) vec3 **normalize** (vec3 x) vec4 **normalize** (vec4 x)	Returns a vector in the same direction as x but with a length of 1.
vec4 **ftransform**()	For vertex shaders only. This function will ensure that the incoming vertex position will be transformed in a way that produces exactly the same result as would be produced by OpenGL's fixed functionality transform. This function is intended to be used to compute the value for *gl_Position*.

Table 5.4 Geometric Functions, continued

Syntax	Description
float **faceforward** (float *N*, float *I*, float *Nref*) vec2 **faceforward** (vec2 *N*, vec2 *I*, vec2 *Nref*) vec3 **faceforward** (vec3 *N*, vec3 *I*, vec3 *Nref*) vec4 **faceforward** (vec4 *N*, vec4 *I*, vec4 *Nref*)	If **dot** (*Nref*, *I*) < 0.0, return *N*; otherwise, return −*N*.
float **reflect** (float *I*, float *N*) vec2 **reflect** (vec2 *I*, vec2 *N*) vec3 **reflect** (vec3 *I*, vec3 *N*) vec4 **reflect** (vec4 *I*, vec4 *N*)	For the incident vector *I* and surface orientation *N*, returns the reflection direction: result = *I* − 2.0 ∗ **dot** (*N*, *I*) ∗ *N* *N* should be normalized to achieve the desired result.

The **float** version of the **distance** function may not seem terribly useful (it's the same as the absolute value of the difference), but the vector forms compute the Euclidean distance between two points. Similarly, the **float** version of **normalize** will always return 1, and the **float** version of **length** will always return the absolute value of the input argument as the result. These scalar forms are useful in that the data type of the argument can be changed without changing the code that calls the built-in function.

The **ftransform** function is intended to be used to compute *gl_Position*, e.g.,

```
gl_Position = ftransform()
```

It transforms the value of *gl_Vertex* by the current modelview-projection matrix to produce a value for *gl_Position* that is identical to what would have been computed by the fixed functionality pipeline. This function should be used, for example, when an application is rendering the same geometry in separate passes, where one pass uses the fixed functionality path to render and another pass uses the programmable processors.

5.5 Matrix Functions

Matrix functions can be used within either vertex shaders or fragment shaders (see Table 5.5).

These functions produce the component-wise multiplication of two matrices. For instance, the result of calling **matrixcompmult** using two 3D matrices *x* and *y* will look like this:

```
mat3 x, y, newmat;
.  .  .
newmat = matrixcompmult(x, y);
```

$$
\begin{bmatrix} x_{00} & x_{01} & x_{02} \\ x_{10} & x_{11} & x_{12} \\ x_{20} & x_{21} & x_{22} \end{bmatrix}
\begin{bmatrix} y_{00} & y_{01} & y_{02} \\ y_{10} & y_{11} & y_{12} \\ y_{20} & y_{21} & y_{22} \end{bmatrix}
=
\begin{bmatrix} x_{00}y_{00} & x_{01}y_{01} & x_{02}y_{02} \\ x_{10}y_{10} & x_{11}y_{11} & x_{12}y_{12} \\ x_{20}y_{20} & x_{21}y_{21} & x_{22}y_{22} \end{bmatrix}
$$

This is not usually what you want if you are using matrices to represent transformation steps. In this case, you would want to use the multiply operator (*****) to perform the linear algebraic matrix multiplication:

```
mat3 x, y, newmat;
.  .  .
newmat = x * y;
```

which performs the following operation:

$$
\begin{bmatrix} x_{00} & x_{01} & x_{02} \\ x_{10} & x_{11} & x_{12} \\ x_{20} & x_{21} & x_{22} \end{bmatrix}
\begin{bmatrix} y_{00} & y_{01} & y_{02} \\ y_{10} & y_{11} & y_{12} \\ y_{20} & y_{21} & y_{22} \end{bmatrix}
=
$$

$$
\begin{bmatrix} x_{00}y_{00} + x_{01}y_{10} + x_{02}y_{20} & x_{00}y_{01} + x_{01}y_{11} + x_{02}y_{21} & x_{00}y_{02} + x_{01}y_{12} + x_{02}y_{22} \\ x_{10}y_{00} + x_{11}y_{10} + x_{12}y_{20} & x_{10}y_{01} + x_{11}y_{11} + x_{12}y_{21} & x_{10}y_{02} + x_{11}y_{12} + x_{12}y_{22} \\ x_{20}y_{00} + x_{21}y_{10} + x_{22}y_{20} & x_{20}y_{01} + x_{21}y_{11} + x_{22}y_{21} & x_{20}y_{02} + x_{21}y_{12} + x_{22}y_{22} \end{bmatrix}
$$

Table 5.5 Matrix Functions

Syntax	Description
mat2 **matrixcompmult** (mat2 *x*, mat2 *y*) mat3 **matrixcompmult** (mat3 *x*, mat3 *y*) mat4 **matrixcompmult** (mat4 *x*, mat4 *y*)	Multiply matrix *x* by matrix *y* component-wise, i.e., *result*[i][j] is the scalar product of *x*[i][j] and *y*[i][j]. Note: To get linear algebraic matrix multiplication, use the multiply operator (*****).

5.6 Vector Relational Functions

Relational and equality operators (**<, <=, >, >=, ==, !=**) are defined to produce scalar. Boolean results and can be used within either vertex shaders or fragment shaders. For vector results, use the following built-in functions (see Table 5.6).

Table 5.6 Vector Relational Functions

Syntax	Description
bvec2 **lessThan**(vec2 *x*, vec2 *y*) bvec3 **lessThan**(vec3 *x*, vec3 *y*) bvec4 **lessThan**(vec4 *x*, vec4 *y*) bvec2 **lessThan**(ivec2 *x*, ivec2 *y*) bvec3 **lessThan**(ivec3 *x*, ivec3 *y*) bvec4 **lessThan**(ivec4 *x*, ivec4 *y*)	Returns the component-wise compare of *x* < *y*.
bvec2 **lessThanEqual**(vec2 *x*, vec2 *y*) bvec3 **lessThanEqual**(vec3 *x*, vec3 *y*) bvec4 **lessThanEqual**(vec4 *x*, vec4 *y*) bvec2 **lessThanEqual**(ivec2 *x*, ivec2 *y*) bvec3 **lessThanEqual**(ivec3 *x*, ivec3 *y*) bvec4 **lessThanEqual**(ivec4 *x*, ivec4 *y*)	Returns the component-wise compare of *x* <= *y*.
bvec2 **greaterThan**(vec2 *x*, vec2 *y*) bvec3 **greaterThan**(vec3 *x*, vec3 *y*) bvec4 **greaterThan**(vec4 *x*, vec4 *y*) bvec2 **greaterThan**(ivec2 *x*, ivec2 *y*) bvec3 **greaterThan**(ivec3 *x*, ivec3 *y*) bvec4 **greaterThan**(ivec4 *x*, ivec4 *y*)	Returns the component-wise compare of *x* > *y*.

Table 5.6   Vector Relational Functions, continued

Syntax	Description
bvec2 **greaterThanEqual**(vec2 *x*, vec2 *y*) bvec3 **greaterThanEqual**(vec3 *x*, vec3 *y*) bvec4 **greaterThanEqual**(vec4 *x*, vec4 *y*) bvec2 **greaterThanEqual**(ivec2 *x*, ivec2 *y*) bvec3 **greaterThanEqual**(ivec3 *x*, ivec3 *y*) bvec4 **greaterThanEqual**(ivec4 *x*, ivec4 *y*)	Returns the component-wise compare of $x >= y$.
bvec2 **equal**(vec2 *x*, vec2 *y*) bvec3 **equal**(vec3 *x*, vec3 *y*) bvec4 **equal**(vec4 *x*, vec4 *y*) bvec2 **equal**(ivec2 *x*, ivec2 *y*) bvec3 **equal**(ivec3 *x*, ivec3 *y*) bvec4 **equal**(ivec4 *x*, ivec4 *y*) bvec2 **equal**(bvec2 *x*, bvec2 *y*) bvec3 **equal**(bvec3 *x*, bvec3 *y*) bvec4 **equal**(bvec4 *x*, bvec4 *y*)	Returns the component-wise compare of $x == y$.
bvec2 **notEqual**(vec2 *x*, vec2 *y*) bvec3 **notEqual**(vec3 *x*, vec3 *y*) bvec4 **notEqual**(vec4 *x*, vec4 *y*) bvec2 **notEqual**(ivec2 *x*, ivec2 *y*) bvec3 **notEqual**(ivec3 *x*, ivec3 *y*) bvec4 **notEqual**(ivec4 *x*, ivec4 *y*) bvec2 **notEqual**(bvec2 *x*, bvec2 *y*) bvec3 **notEqual**(bvec3 *x*, bvec3 *y*) bvec4 **notEqual**(bvec4 *x*, bvec4 *y*)	Returns the component-wise compare of $x != y$.
bool **any**(bvec2 *x*) bool **any**(bvec3 *x*) bool **any**(bvec4 *x*)	Returns true if any component of *x* is **true**.
bool **all**(bvec2 *x*) bool **all**(bvec3 *x*) bool **all**(bvec4 *x*)	Returns true only if all components of *x* are **true**.

Table 5.6   Vector Relational Functions, continued

Syntax	Description
bvec2 **not**(bvec2 *x*) bvec3 **not**(bvec3 *x*) bvec4 **not**(bvec4 *x*)	Returns the component-wise logical complement of *x*.

5.7   Texture Access Functions

Texture access functions are available to both vertex and fragment shaders. Each of these functions takes as its first argument a variable of type **sampler**. If a variable qualified by **sampler1D** is used, the texture access operation will read from the 1D texture that has been previously associated with that sampler by the application. (It is an error for the application to associate a non-1D texture with a **sampler1D** variable.) Similarly, a **sampler2D** variable is used to access a 2D texture, and so on. The texture precedence rules for OpenGL fixed functionality will be ignored. It is up to the application to set up texture state before the shader executes in order to get the expected results (see Section 7.8).

The texture access functions can be used to obtain texture values from either mipmapped or non-mipmapped textures. However, level-of-detail is not computed by fixed functionality for vertex shaders, so there are some differences in operation between vertex and fragment texture access functions. Texture properties such as size, pixel format, number of dimensions, filtering method, number of mipmap levels, depth comparison, and so on are also defined by OpenGL API calls. Such properties are taken into account as the texture is accessed via the built-in functions defined in this section.

In all functions that follow, the *bias* parameter is optional for fragment shaders. The *bias* parameter is not accepted in a vertex shader. For a fragment shader, if *bias* is present, it is added to the calculated level of detail prior to performing the texture access operation. If the *bias* parameter is not provided, the implementation automatically selects level-of-detail. For a texture that is not mipmapped, the texture is used directly. If a mipmap texture is accessed from a fragment shader, the level-of-detail computed by the implementation is used to do the texture lookup. If a mipmapped texture is accessed from a vertex shader, the base texture is used.

The built-in functions suffixed with "**Lod**" are allowed only in a vertex shader. For the "**Lod**" functions, *lod* is directly used as the level of detail. The built-in functions suffixed with "**Proj**" can be used to perform projective texturing. This allows a texture to be projected onto an object in much the same way that a slide projector projects an image onto a surface. This can be used to compute shadow maps for rendering shadows, among other things.

A number of examples in later sections will illustrate the use of these functions. With the programmability available with the OpenGL Shading Language, texture memory can be used as storage for much more than just image data. These texture access functions provide fast, flexible access to such data in order to achieve a wide variety of effects (see Table 5.7).

Table 5.7 Texture Access Functions

Syntax	Description

vec4 **texture1D** (sampler1D *sampler*,
        float *coord* [, float *bias*])
vec4 **texture1DProj** (sampler1D *sampler*,
        vec2 *coord* [, float *bias*])
vec4 **texture1DProj** (sampler1D *sampler*,
        vec4 *coord* [, float *bias*])
vec4 **texture1DLod** (sampler1D *sampler*,
        float *coord*, float *lod*)
vec4 **texture1DProjLod** (sampler1D *sampler*,
        vec2 *coord*, float *lod*)
vec4 **texture1DProjLod** (sampler1D *sampler*,
        vec4 *coord*, float *lod*)
	Use the texture coordinate *coord* to do a texture lookup in the 1D texture currently specified by *sampler*. For the projective ("**Proj**") versions, the texture coordinate *coord.s* is divided by the last component of *coord*. The second and third components of *coord* are ignored for the **vec4** *coord* variant.

vec4 **texture2D** (sampler2D *sampler*,
        vec2 *coord* [, float *bias*])
vec4 **texture2DProj** (sampler2D *sampler*,
        vec3 *coord* [, float *bias*])
vec4 **texture2DProj** (sampler2D *sampler*,
        vec4 *coord* [, float *bias*])
vec4 **texture2DLod** (sampler2D *sampler*,
        vec2 *coord*, float *lod*)
vec4 **texture2DProjLod** (sampler2D *sampler*,
        vec3 *coord*, float *lod*)
vec4 **texture2DProjLod** (sampler2D *sampler*,
        vec4 *coord*, float *lod*)
	Use the texture coordinate *coord* to do a texture lookup in the 2D texture currently specified by *sampler*. For the projective ("**Proj**") versions, the texture coordinate (*coord.s*, *coord.t*) is divided by the last component of *coord*. The third component of *coord* is ignored for the **vec4** *coord* variant.

Table 5.7 Texture Access Functions, continued

Syntax	Description

vec4 **texture3D** (sampler3D *sampler,*
         vec3 *coord* [, float *bias*])
vec4 **texture3DProj** (sampler3D *sampler,*
         vec4 *coord* [, float *bias*])
vec4 **texture3DLod** (sampler3D *sampler,*
         vec3 *coord,* float *lod*)
vec4 **texture3DProjLod** (sampler3D *sampler,*
         vec4 *coord,* float *lod*)
	Use the texture coordinate *coord* to do a texture lookup in the 3D texture currently specified by *sampler.* For the projective ("**Proj**") versions, the texture coordinate is divided by *coord.q.*

vec4 **textureCube** (samplerCube *sampler,*
         vec3 *coord* [, float *bias*])
vec4 **textureCubeLod** (samplerCube *sampler,*
         vec3 *coord,* float *lod*)
	Use the texture coordinate *coord* to do a texture lookup in the cube map texture currently specified by *sampler.* The direction of *coord* is used to select the face in which to do a two-dimensional texture lookup.

vec4 **shadow1D** (sampler1DShadow *sampler,*
         vec3 *coord* [, float *bias*])
vec4 **shadow2D** (sampler2DShadow *sampler,*
         vec3 *coord* [, float *bias*])
vec4 **shadow1DProj** (sampler1DShadow *sampler,*
         vec4 *coord* [, float *bias*])
vec4 **shadow2DProj** (sampler2DShadow *sampler,*
         vec4 *coord* [, float *bias*])
vec4 **shadow1DLod** (sampler1DShadow *sampler,*
         vec3 *coord,* float *lod*)
vec4 **shadow2DLod** (sampler2DShadow *sampler,*
         vec3 *coord,* float *lod*)
vec4 **shadow1DProjLod** (sampler1DShadow *sampler,*
         vec4 *coord,* float *lod*)
vec4 **shadow2DProjLod** (sampler2DShadow *sampler,*
         vec4 *coord,* float *lod*)
	Use texture coordinate *coord* to do a depth comparison lookup on the depth texture specified by *sampler.* The third component of *coord* (*coord.p*) is compared to the value read from the depth texture. The texture bound to *sampler* must be a depth texture, or results are undefined. For the projective ("**Proj**") version of each built-in, the texture coordinate is divided by *coord.q,* giving a depth value of *coord.p/coord.q.* The second component of *coord* is ignored for the "**1D**" variants.

If a nonshadow texture function is called with a sampler whose texture has depth comparisons enabled, the results are undefined. If a shadow texture call is made to a sampler whose texture does not have depth comparisons enabled, the results are also undefined.

5.8 Fragment Processing Functions

Fragment processing functions are only available in shaders intended for use on the fragment processor. There are three built-in functions in this category, two that are used to obtain derivatives and one that is commonly used to estimate the filter width used to antialias procedural textures.

The derivative functions, **dFdx** and **dFdy**, are used to determine the rate of change of an expression. The function **dFdx**(p) evaluates the derivative of the expression p in the x direction in window coordinates, and the function **dFdy**(p) evaluates the derivative of the expression p in the y direction in window coordinates. These values indicate how fast the expression is changing in window space, and this information can be used to take steps to prevent aliasing. For instance, if texture coordinates are changing rapidly, it may be better to set the resulting color to the average color for the texture in order to avoid aliasing.

It only makes sense to apply these functions to expressions that vary from one fragment to the next. Because the value of a uniform variable does not change from one pixel to the next, its derivative in x and in y will always be 0. See Table 5.8.

Table 5.8 Fragment Processing Functions

Syntax	Description
float **dFdx** (float p) vec2 **dFdx** (vec2 p) vec3 **dFdx** (vec3 p) vec4 **dFdx** (vec4 p)	Returns the derivative in x for the input argument p.
float **dFdy** (float p) vec2 **dFdy** (vec2 p) vec3 **dFdy** (vec3 p) vec4 **dFdy** (vec4 p)	Returns the derivative in y for the input argument p.

Table 5.8 Fragment Processing Functions, continued

Syntax	Description
float **fwidth** (float p) vec2 **fwidth** (vec2 p) vec3 **fwidth** (vec3 p) vec4 **fwidth** (vec4 p)	Returns the sum of the absolute derivative in x and y for the input argument p, i.e., return = **abs** (**dFdx** (p)) + **abs** (**dFdy** (p));

5.9   Noise Functions

Noise functions (see Table 5.9) are available to both fragment and vertex shaders. They are stochastic functions first described by Ken Perlin that can be used to increase visual complexity. Values returned by the following noise functions give the appearance of randomness, but they are not truly random. A more complete description of and motivation for the noise function can be found in Chapter 12.

The built-in noise functions are defined to have the following characteristics:

- The return value(s) are always in the range [–1,1].

- The return value(s) have an overall average of 0.

- They are repeatable, in that a particular input value will always produce the same return value.

- They are statistically invariant under rotation (i.e., no matter how the domain is rotated, it has the same statistical character).

- They have a statistical invariance under translation (i.e., no matter how the domain is translated, it has the same statistical character).

- They typically give different results under translation.

- They have a narrow bandpass limit in frequency (i.e., it has no visible features larger or smaller than a certain narrow size range).

- They are C^1 continuous everywhere (i.e., the first derivative is continuous).

Table 5.9 Noise Functions

Syntax	Description
float **noise1** (float *x*) float **noise1** (vec2 *x*) float **noise1** (vec3 *x*) float **noise1** (vec4 *x*)	Returns a 1D noise value based on the input value *x*.
vec2 **noise2** (float *x*) vec2 **noise2** (vec2 *x*) vec2 **noise2** (vec3 *x*) vec2 **noise2** (vec4 *x*)	Returns a 2D noise value based on the input value *x*.
vec3 **noise3** (float *x*) vec3 **noise3** (vec2 *x*) vec3 **noise3** (vec3 *x*) vec3 **noise3** (vec4 *x*)	Returns a 3D noise value based on the input value *x*.
vec4 **noise4** (float *x*) vec4 **noise4** (vec2 *x*) vec4 **noise4** (vec3 *x*) vec4 **noise4** (vec4 *x*)	Returns a 4D noise value based on the input value *x*.

5.10 Summary

The OpenGL Shading Language contains a rich set of built-in functions. Some of these functions are similar to those found in C/C++, and others are similar to those found in RenderMan. These functions are aimed at exposing hardware functionality (e.g., texture access) or providing support for common operations (e.g., square root, clamp, etc.), or they represent operations likely to be accelerated in future generations of graphics hardware (trigonometry functions, noise, etc.).

Function overloading is used extensively, as many of these functions operate on either vectors or scalars. Vendors that support the OpenGL Shading Language are expected to provide optimal implementations of these functions, so they should be used whenever possible.

The built-in mathematical functions can be used in some unique and perhaps unexpected ways to create procedural textures. Shader examples throughout the rest of this book will illustrate this. Visualizing the function needed to achieve a particular effect can be a vital part of the shader development process.

5.11 Further Information

Many of the built-in functions described in this chapter will be used in example shaders in the remainder of this book. All you need to do is keep reading to see them in action.

Some additional detail on the built-in functions can be found in the *The OpenGL Shading Language, Version 1.051,* by John Kessenich, Dave Baldwin, and Randi Rost (2003).

Various OpenGL Shading Language built-in functions, including the derivative and filter width functions, were inspired by similar functions in RenderMan. Motivation for some of these functions is discussed in *The RenderMan Companion: A Programmer's Guide to Realistic Computer Graphics* by Steve Upstill (1990) and *Advanced RenderMan: Creating CGI for Motion Pictures* by Tony Apodaca and Larry Gritz (1999). For additional details on noise functions, see the papers by Perlin and the additional references provided at the end of Chapter 12.

[1] Apodaca, Anthony A., and Larry Gritz, *Advanced RenderMan: Creating CGI for Motion Pictures*, Morgan Kaufmann Publishers, San Francisco, 1999. http://www.bmrt.org/arman/materials.html

[2] Kessenich, John, Dave Baldwin, and Randi Rost, *The OpenGL Shading Language, Version 1.051*, 3Dlabs, February 2003. http://www.3dlabs.com/support/developer/ogl2

[3] Perlin, Ken, *An Image Synthesizer*, Computer Graphics (SIGGRAPH '85 Proceedings), pp. 287–296, July 1985.

[4] Perlin, Ken, *Improving Noise*, Computer Graphics (SIGGRAPH 2002 Proceedings), pp. 681–682, July 2002. http://mrl.nyu.edu/perlin/paper445.pdf

[5] Pixar, *The RenderMan Interface Specification*, Version 3.2, Pixar, July 2000. https://renderman.pixar.com/products/rispec/index.htm

[6] Segal, Mark, and Kurt Akeley, *The OpenGL Graphics System: A Specification (Version 1.5)*, Editor (v1.1): Chris Frazier, Editor (v1.2–1.5): Jon Leech, July 2003. http://opengl.org

[7] Upstill, Steve, *The RenderMan Companion: A Programmer's Guide to Realistic Computer Graphics*, Addison-Wesley, Reading, Massachusetts, 1990.

[8] Zwillinger, Dan, *CRC Standard Mathematical Tables and Formulas*, 30th Edition, CRC Press, 1995.
    http://geom.math.uiuc.edu/docs/ reference/CRC-formulas

Chapter 6

Simple Shading Example

Now that we've described the OpenGL Shading Language, let's look at a simple example. In this example, we'll be applying a brick pattern to an object. The brick pattern will be calculated entirely within a fragment shader. If you'd prefer to skip ahead to the next chapter for a more in-depth discussion of the API that allows shaders to be defined and manipulated, feel free to do so.

In this example, and in most of the others in this book, there are three essential components: the source code for the vertex shader, the source code for the fragment shader, and the application code that is used to initialize and use these shaders. This chapter focuses on the vertex and fragment shaders. The application code for using these shaders will be discussed in Section 7.11, after the details of the OpenGL Shading Language API have been discussed.

With this first example, we'll take a little more time discussing the details in order to give you a better grasp of what's going on. In examples later in the book, we'll focus mostly on the details that differ from previous examples.

6.1 Brick Shader Overview

One approach to writing shaders is to come up with a description of the effect that you're trying to achieve and then decide which parts of the shader need to be implemented in the vertex shader, which need to be implemented in the fragment shader, and how the application will tie everything together.

In this example, we'll develop a shader that applies a computed brick pattern to all objects that are drawn. We're not going to attempt the most realistic looking brick shader, but rather a fairly simple one that illustrates many of the concepts we introduced in the previous chapters. We won't be using textures for this brick pattern; the pattern itself will be generated algorithmically. We can build a lot of flexibility into this shader by parameterizing the different aspects of our brick algorithm.

Let's first come up with a description of the overall effect we're after:

- A single light source

- Diffuse and specular reflection characteristics

- A brick pattern that is based on the position in modeling coordinates of the object being rendered—where the *x* coordinate will be related to the brick horizontal position and the *y* coordinate will be related to the brick vertical position

- Alternate rows of bricks will be offset by one-half the width of a single brick

- Parameters that control the brick color, mortar color, brick-to-brick horizontal distance, brick-to-brick vertical distance, brick width fraction (ratio of the width of a brick to the overall horizontal distance between two adjacent bricks), and brick height fraction (ratio of the height of a brick to the overall vertical distance between two adjacent bricks)

The brick geometry parameters that we'll be using are illustrated in Figure 6.1. Brick size and brick percentage parameters will both be stored in user-defined uniform variables of type **vec2**. The horizontal distance between two bricks, including the width of the mortar, will be provided by *BrickSize.x*. The vertical distance between two rows of bricks, including the height of the mortar, will be provided by *BrickSize.y*. These two values will be given in units of modeling coordinates. The fraction of *BrickSize.x* represented by the brick only will be provided by *BrickPct.x*. The fraction of *BrickSize.y* represented by the brick only will be provided by *BrickPct.y*. These two values will be in the range [0,1]. Finally, the brick color and the mortar color will be represented by the variables *BrickColor* and *MortarColor*.

Now that we're armed with a firm grasp of our desired outcome, we'll design our vertex shader, then our fragment shader, and then the application code that will tie it all together.

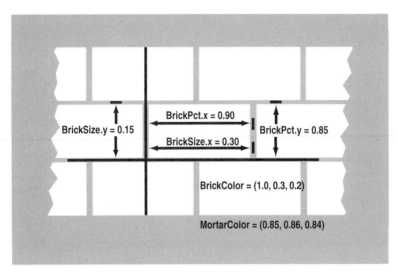

Figure 6.1   Parameters for defining brick

6.2 Vertex Shader

The vertex shader embodies the operations that will occur on each vertex that is provided to OpenGL. To define our vertex shader, we need to answer three questions.

1. What data must be passed to the vertex shader for every vertex (i.e., attribute variables)?

2. What global state is required by the vertex shader (i.e., uniform variables)?

3. What values are computed by the vertex shader (i.e., varying variables)?

Let's look at these questions one at a time.

We can't draw any geometry at all without specifying a value for each vertex position. Furthermore, we can't do any lighting unless we have a surface normal for each location for which we want to apply a lighting computation. So at the very least, we'll need a vertex position and a normal for every incoming vertex. These attributes are already defined as part of OpenGL, and the OpenGL Shading Language provides built-in variables to refer to them (*gl_Vertex* and *gl_Normal*). If we use the standard OpenGL entry points for passing vertex positions and normals, we don't need any user-defined attribute variables in our vertex shader. We can access the current values for vertex position and normal simply by referring to *gl_Vertex* and *gl_Normal*.

We need access to several pieces of OpenGL state for our brick algorithm. These are available to our shader as built-in uniform variables. We'll need to access the current modelview-projection matrix (*gl_ModelView-ProjectionMatrix*) in order to transform our vertex position into the clipping coordinate system. We'll need to access the current modelview matrix (*gl_ModelViewMatrix*) in order to transform the vertex position into eye coordinates for use in the lighting computation. And we'll also need to transform our incoming normals into eye coordinates using OpenGL's normal transformation matrix (*gl_NormalMatrix*, which is just the inverse transpose of the upper-left 3×3 subset of *gl_ModelViewMatrix*).

In addition, we'll need the position of a single light source. We could use the OpenGL lighting state and reference that state within our vertex shader, but in order to illustrate the use of uniform variables, we'll define the light source position as a uniform variable like this:[1]

```
uniform vec3   LightPosition;
```

We also need values for the lighting calculation to represent the contribution due to specular reflection and the contribution due to diffuse reflection. We could define these as uniform variables so that they could be changed dynamically by the application, but in order to illustrate some additional features of the language, we'll define them as constants like this:

```
const float SpecularContribution = 0.3;
const float DiffuseContribution  = 1.0 - SpecularContribution;
```

Finally, we need to define the values that will be passed on to the fragment shader. Every vertex shader must compute the homogeneous vertex position and store its value in the standard variable *gl_Position*, so we know that our brick vertex shader will need to do likewise. We're going to compute the brick pattern on-the-fly in the fragment shader as a function of the incoming geometry's *x* and *y* values in modeling coordinates, so we'll define a varying variable called *MCposition* for this purpose. In order to apply the lighting effect on top of our brick, we'll need to do part of the lighting

---

[1] The shaders in this book use the convention of capitalizing the first letter of user-specified uniform, varying, and attribute variable names in order to set them apart from local and (nonqualified) global variables.

computation in the fragment shader and apply the final lighting effect after the brick/mortar color has been computed in the fragment shader. We'll do most of the lighting computation in the vertex shader and simply pass the computed light intensity to the fragment shader in a varying variable called *LightIntensity.* These two varying variables are defined like this:

```
varying float LightIntensity;
varying vec2  MCposition;
```

We're now ready to get to the meat of our brick vertex shader. We begin by declaring a main function for our vertex shader and computing the vertex position in eye coordinates:

```
void main(void)
{
    vec3 ecPosition = vec3 (gl_ModelViewMatrix * gl_Vertex);
```

In this first line of code, our vertex shader defines a variable called *ecPosition* to hold the eye coordinate position of the incoming vertex. The eye coordinate position is computed by transforming the vertex position (*gl_Vertex*) by the current modelview matrix (*gl_ModelViewMatrix*). Because one of the operands is a matrix and the other is a vector, the * operator performs a matrix multiplication operation rather than a component-wise multiplication.

The result of the matrix multiplication will be a **vec4**, but *ecPosition* is defined as a **vec3**. There is no automatic conversion between variables of different types in the OpenGL Shading Language so we convert the result to a **vec3** using a constructor. This causes the fourth component of the result to be dropped so that the two operands have compatible types. (Constructors provide an operation that is similar to type casting, but it is much more flexible, as discussed in Section 3.3). As we'll see, the eye coordinate position will be used a couple of times in our lighting calculation.

The lighting computation that we'll perform is a very simple one. Some light from the light source will be reflected in a diffuse fashion (i.e., in all directions). Where the viewing direction is very nearly the same as the reflection direction from the light source, we'll see a specular reflection. To compute the diffuse reflection, we'll need to compute the angle between the incoming light and the surface normal. To compute the specular reflection, we'll need to compute the angle between the reflection direction and the viewing direction. First, we'll transform the incoming normal:

```
    vec3 tnorm      = normalize(gl_NormalMatrix * gl_Normal);
```

This line defines a new variable called *tnorm* for storing the transformed normal (remember, in the OpenGL Shading Language, variables can be declared when needed). The incoming surface normal (*gl_Normal*, a built-in

variable for accessing the normal value supplied through the standard
OpenGL entry points) is transformed by the current OpenGL normal transformation matrix (*gl_NormalMatrix*). The resulting vector is normalized
(converted to a vector of unit length) by calling the built-in function
normalize, and the result is stored in *tnorm*.

Next, we need to compute a vector from the current point on the surface of
the three-dimensional object we're rendering to the light source position.
Both of these should be in eye coordinates (which means that the value for
our uniform variable *LightPosition* must be provided by the application in
eye coordinates). The light direction vector is computed as follows:

```
vec3 lightVec   = normalize(LightPosition - ecPosition);
```

The object position in eye coordinates was previously computed and stored
in *ecPosition*. To compute the light direction vector, we need to subtract the
object position from the light position. The resulting light direction vector
is also normalized and stored in the newly defined local variable *lightVec*.

The calculations we've done so far have set things up almost perfectly to call
the built-in function **reflect**. Using our transformed surface normal and the
computed incident light vector, we can now compute a reflection vector at
the surface of the object; however, **reflect** requires the incident vector (the
direction from the light to the surface), and we've computed the direction
to the light source. Negating *lightVec* gives us the proper vector:

```
vec3 reflectVec = reflect(-lightVec, tnorm);
```

Because both vectors used in this computation were unit vectors, the
resulting vector is a unit vector as well. To complete our lighting calculation, one more vector is needed—a unit vector in the direction of the
viewing position. Because, by definition, the viewing position is at the
origin (i.e., (0,0,0)) in the eye coordinate system, we simply need to negate
and normalize the computed eye coordinate position, *ecPosition:*

```
vec3 viewVec    = normalize(-ecPosition);
```

With these four vectors, we can perform a per-vertex lighting computation.
The relationship of these vectors is shown in Figure 6.2.

Diffuse reflection is modeled by assuming that the incident light is scattered
in all directions according to a cosine distribution function. The reflection
of light will be strongest when the light direction vector and the surface
normal are coincident. As the difference between the two angles increases
to 90°, the diffuse reflection will drop off to zero. Because both vectors have
been normalized to produce unit vectors, the cosine of the angle between

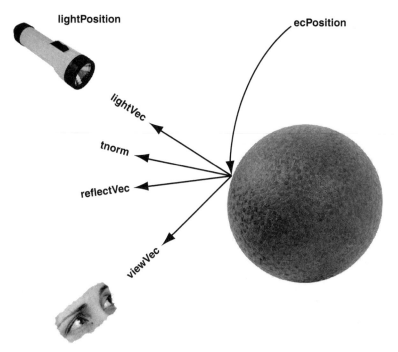

Figure 6.2 Vectors involved in the lighting computation for the brick vertex shader

lightVec and *tnorm* can be determined by performing a dot product operation between them. We want the diffuse contribution to be 0 if the angle between the light and the surface normal is greater than 90° (there should be no diffuse contribution if the light is behind the object), and the **max** function is used to accomplish this:

```
float diffuse = max(dot(lightVec, tnorm), 0.0);
```

The specular component of the light intensity for this vertex is computed by

```
float spec = 0.0;
if (diffuse > 0.0)
{
    spec = max(dot(reflectVec, viewVec), 0.0);
    spec = pow(spec, 16.0);
}
```

The variable for the specular reflection value is defined and initialized to 0. We'll compute only a specular value other than 0 if the angle between the light direction vector and the surface normal is less than 90° (i.e., the diffuse value is greater than 0) because we don't want any specular high-lights if the light source is behind the object. Because both *reflectVec* and *viewVec* are normalized, computing the dot product of these two vectors gives us the cosine of the angle between them. If the angle is near zero (i.e., the reflection vector and the viewing vector are almost the same), the resulting value will be near 1.0. By raising the result to the 16th power in the subsequent line of code, we're effectively "sharpening" the highlight, ensuring that we'll have a specular highlight only in the region where the reflection vector and the view vector are almost the same. The choice of 16 for the exponent value is arbitrary. Higher values will produce more concentrated specular highlights, and lower values will produce less concentrated highlights. This value could also be passed in as a uniform variable in order to allow it to be easily modified by the end user.

All that remains is to multiply the computed diffuse and specular reflection values by the *diffuseContribution* and *specularContribution* constants and add the two values together:

```
LightIntensity = DiffuseContribution * diffuse +
                 SpecularContribution * spec;
```

This is the value that will be assigned to the varying variable *LightIntensity* and interpolated between vertices. We also have one other varying variable to compute, and it is done quite easily:

```
MCposition = gl_Vertex.xy;
```

When the brick pattern is applied to a geometric object, we want the brick pattern to remain constant with respect to the surface of the object, no matter how the object is moved. We also want the brick pattern to remain constant with respect to the surface of the object, no matter what the viewing position. In order to generate the brick pattern algorithmically in the fragment shader, we need to provide a value at each fragment that represents a location on the surface. For this example, we will provide the modeling coordinate at each vertex by setting our varying variable *MCposition* to the same value as our incoming vertex position (which is, by definition, in modeling coordinates).

We're not going to need the *z* or *w* coordinate in the fragment shader, so we need a way to select the *x* and *y* components of *gl_Vertex*. We could have used a constructor here (e.g., **vec2** (*gl_Vertex*)), but to show off another language feature, we'll use the component selector **.xy** to select the first two components of *gl_Vertex* and store them in our varying variable *MCposition*.

The only thing that remains to be done is the thing that must be done by all vertex shaders: computing the homogeneous vertex position. We do this by transforming the incoming vertex value by the current modelview-projection matrix using the built-in function **ftransform**:

```
    gl_Position = ftransform();
}
```

For clarity, the code for our vertex shader is provided in its entirety in Listing 6.1.

Listing 6.1   Source code for brick vertex shader

```
uniform vec3 LightPosition;

const float SpecularContribution = 0.3;
const float DiffuseContribution  = 1.0 - SpecularContribution;

varying float LightIntensity;
varying vec2  MCposition;

void main(void)
{
    vec3 ecPosition = vec3 (gl_ModelViewMatrix * gl_Vertex);
    vec3 tnorm      = normalize(gl_NormalMatrix * gl_Normal);
    vec3 lightVec   = normalize(LightPosition - ecPosition);
    vec3 reflectVec = reflect(-lightVec, tnorm);
    vec3 viewVec    = normalize(-ecPosition);
    float diffuse   = max(dot(lightVec, tnorm), 0.0);
    float spec      = 0.0;

    if (diffuse > 0.0)
    {
        spec = max(dot(reflectVec, viewVec), 0.0);
        spec = pow(spec, 16.0);
    }

    LightIntensity  = DiffuseContribution * diffuse +
                      SpecularContribution * spec;

    MCposition      = gl_Vertex.xy;
    gl_Position     = ftransform();
}
```

6.3 Fragment Shader

The purpose of a fragment shader is to compute the color to be applied to a fragment or to compute the depth value for the fragment or both. In this case (and indeed with most fragment shaders), we're concerned only about the color of the fragment. We're perfectly happy using the depth value that's been computed by the OpenGL rasterization stage. Therefore, the entire purpose of this shader is to compute the color of the current fragment.

Our brick fragment shader starts off by defining a few more uniform variables than did the vertex shader. The brick pattern that will be rendered on our geometry is parameterized in order to make it easier to modify. The parameters that are constant across an entire primitive can be stored as uniform variables and initialized (and later modified) by the application. This makes it easy to expose these controls to the end user for modification through user interface elements such as sliders and color pickers. The brick fragment shader uses the parameters that are illustrated in Figure 6.1. These are defined as uniform variables as follows:

```
uniform vec3  BrickColor, MortarColor;
uniform vec2  BrickSize;
uniform vec2  BrickPct;
```

We want our brick pattern to be applied in a consistent way to our geometry in order to have the object look the same no matter where it is placed in the scene or how it is rotated. The key to determining the placement of the brick pattern is the modeling coordinate position that is computed by the vertex shader and passed in the varying variable *MCposition*:

```
varying vec2  MCposition;
```

This variable was computed at each vertex by the vertex shader in the previous section, and it is interpolated across the primitive and made available to the fragment shader at each fragment location. Our fragment shader can use this information to determine where the fragment location is in relation to the algorithmically defined brick pattern. The other varying variable that is provided as input to the fragment shader is defined as follows:

```
varying float LightIntensity;
```

This varying variable contains the interpolated value for the light intensity that we computed at each vertex in our vertex shader. Note that both of the varying variables we defined in our fragment shader are defined with the same type that was used to define them in our vertex shader. A link error would be generated if this were not the case.

With our uniform and varying variables defined, we can begin with the actual code for the brick fragment shader:

```
void main (void)
{
    vec3  color;
    vec2  position, useBrick;
```

In this shader, we'll do things more like we would in C and define all our local variables before they're used at the beginning of our **main** function. In some cases, this can make the code a little cleaner or easier to read, but it is mostly a matter of personal preference and coding style. The first actual lines of code in our brick fragment shader will compute values for the local **vec2** variable *position*:

```
position = MCposition / BrickSize;
```

This statement divides the fragment's x position in modeling coordinates by the column width and the y position in modeling coordinates by the row height. This gives us a "brick row number" (*position.y*) and a "brick number" within that row (*position.x*). Keep in mind that these are signed, floating-point values, so it is perfectly reasonable to have negative row and brick numbers as a result of this computation. Next, we'll use a conditional to determine whether the fragment is in a row of bricks that is offset:

```
if (fract(position.y * 0.5) > 0.5)
    position.x += 0.5;
```

The "brick row number" (*position.y*) is multiplied by 0.5, and the result is compared against 0.5. Half the time (or every other row) this comparison will be true, and the "brick number" value (*position.x*) is incremented by 0.5 to offset the entire row by half the width of a brick. Following this, we need to compute the fragment's location within the current brick:

```
position = fract(position);
```

This computation provides us with the vertical and horizontal position within a single brick. This will be used as the basis for determining whether to use the brick color or the mortar color.

Next we need a function that gives us a value of 1.0 when the brick color should be used and 0 when the mortar color should be used. If we can achieve this, we'll end up with a simple way to choose the appropriate color. We know that we're working with a horizontal component of the brick texture function and a vertical component. If we can create the desired function for the horizontal component and the desired function for the vertical component, we can just multiply the two values together to get our final answer. If the result of either of the individual functions is 0 (mortar color), the multiplication will cause the final answer to be 0; otherwise, it will be 1.0, and the brick color will be used.

The **step** function can be used to achieve the desired effect. It takes two arguments, an edge (or threshold) and a parameter, to test against that edge. If the value of the parameter to be tested is less than or equal to the edge value, the function returns 0; otherwise, it returns 1.0. (Refer to Figure 5.11

for a graph of this function). In typical use, the **step** function is used to produce a pattern of pulses (i.e., a square wave) where the function starts off at 0 and rises to 1 when the threshold is reached. We can get a function that starts off at 1.0 and drops to 0 just by reversing the order of the two arguments provided to this function:

```
useBrick = step(position, BrickPct);
```

In these two lines, we compute two values that tell us whether we are in the brick or in the mortar in the horizontal direction (*useBrick.x*) and in the vertical direction (*useBrick.y*). The built-in function **step** will produce a value of 0 when *BrickPct.x* <= *position.x* and a value of 1.0 when *BrickPct.x* > *position.x*. Because of the **fract** function, we know that *position.x* will vary from [0,1). The variable *BrickPct* is a uniform variable, so its value will be constant across the primitive. This means that the value of *useBrick.x* will be 1.0 when the brick color should be used and 0 when the mortar color should be used as we move horizontally. The same thing is done in the vertical direction using *position.y* and *BrickPct.y* to compute the value for *useBrick.y*. By multiplying *useBrick.x* and *useBrick.y* together, we can get a value of 0 or 1.0 that will let us select the appropriate color for the fragment. The periodic step function for the horizontal component of the brick pattern is illustrated in Figure 6.3.

The values of *BrickPct.x* and *BrickPct.y* can be computed by the application to give a uniform mortar width in both directions based on the ratio of column width to row height, or they can be chosen arbitrarily to give a mortar appearance that looks right.

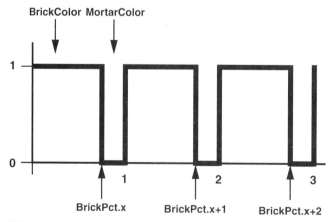

Figure 6.3   The periodic step function that produces the horizontal component of the procedural brick pattern

All that remains is to compute our final color value and store it in the special variable *gl_FragColor:*

```
color = mix(MortarColor, BrickColor, useBrick.x * useBrick.y);
color *= LightIntensity;
gl_FragColor = vec4 (color, 1.0);
}
```

Here we compute the color of the fragment and store it in the local variable *color.* The built-in function **mix** is used to choose the brick color or the mortar color, depending on the value of *useBrick.x * useBrick.y.* Because *useBrick.x* and *useBrick.y* can have values of only 0 (mortar) or 1.0 (brick), we will choose the brick color only if both values are 1.0; otherwise, we will choose the mortar color.

The resulting value is then multiplied by the light intensity, and that result is stored in the local variable *color.* This local variable is a **vec3**, and *gl_FragColor* is defined as a **vec4**, so we create our final color value by using a constructor to add a fourth component (alpha) equal to 1.0 and assign the result to the built-in variable *gl_FragColor.*

The source code for the complete fragment shader is shown in Listing 6.2.

Listing 6.2 Source code for brick fragment shader

```
uniform vec3  BrickColor, MortarColor;
uniform vec2  BrickSize;
uniform vec2  BrickPct;

varying vec2  MCposition;
varying float LightIntensity;

void main(void)
{
    vec3  color;
    vec2  position, useBrick;

    position = MCposition / BrickSize;

    if (fract(position.y * 0.5) > 0.5)
        position.x += 0.5;

    position = fract(position);

    useBrick = step(position, BrickPct);

    color = mix(MortarColor, BrickColor, useBrick.x * useBrick.y);
    color *= LightIntensity;
    gl_FragColor = vec4 (color, 1.0);
}
```

When comparing this shader to the vertex shader in the previous example, we notice one of the key features of the OpenGL Shading Language, namely that the language used to write these two shaders is almost identical. Both shaders have a main function, some uniform variables, and some local variables; expressions are the same; built-in functions are called in the same way; constructors are used in the same way; and so on. The only perceptible differences exhibited by these two shaders are (A) the vertex shader accesses built-in attributes, such as *gl_Vertex* and *gl_Normal*, (B) the vertex shader writes to the built-in variable *gl_Position*, whereas the fragment shader writes to the built-in variable *gl_FragColor*, and (C) the varying variables are written by the vertex shader and are read by the fragment shader.

The application code to create and use these shaders will be shown in Section 7.11, after the OpenGL Shading Language API has been presented. The result of rendering some simple objects with these shaders is shown in Figure 6.4. A color version of the result is shown in Color Plate 25.

6.4 Observations

There are a couple of problems with our shader that make it unfit for anything but the simplest cases. Because the brick pattern is computed by using the modeling coordinates of the incoming object, the apparent size of the bricks depends on the size of the object in modeling coordinates. The brick pattern might look fine with some objects, but the bricks may turn out much too small or much too large on other objects. At the very least, we should probably have a uniform variable that could be used in the vertex shader to scale the modeling coordinates. The application could allow the end user to adjust the scale factor to make the brick pattern look good on the object being rendered.

Figure 6.4   A flat polygon, a sphere, and a torus rendered with the brick shaders

Another issue stems from the fact that we've chosen to base the brick pattern on the object's x and y coordinates in the modeling space. This can result in some unrealistic looking effects on objects that aren't as regular as the objects shown in Figure 6.4. By using only the x and y coordinates of the object, we end up modeling bricks that are infinitely deep. The brick pattern looks fine when viewed from the front of the object, but when you look at it from the side, you'll be able to see how the brick extends in depth. To get a truly three-dimensional brick shader, we'd need to add a third dimension to our procedural texture calculation and use the z component of the position in modeling coordinates to determine whether we were in brick or mortar in the z dimension as well (see if you can modify the shaders to do this).

If we look closely at our brick pattern, we'll also notice that there are aliasing artifacts (jaggies) along the transition from brick color to mortar color. These artifacts are due to the **step** function causing an instantaneous change from 0 to 1.0 (or from 1.0 to 0) when we cross the transition point between brick color and mortar color. Our shader has no alternative but to pick one color or the other for each fragment, and, because we cannot sample at a high enough frequency to represent this instantaneous change at the brick/mortar border, aliasing artifacts occur. Instead of using the **step** function, we could have used the built-in **smoothstep** function. This function is like the **step** function, except that it defines two edges and a smooth interpolation between 0 and 1.0 between those two edges. This would have the effect of blurring the transition between the brick color and the mortar color, thus making the aliasing artifacts much less noticeable. A method for analytically antialiasing the procedural brick texture is described in Section 14.4.5.

Despite these shortcomings, our brick shaders are perfectly good examples of a working OpenGL shader. Together, our brick vertex and fragment shaders illustrate a number of the interesting features of the OpenGL Shading Language.

6.5 Summary

This chapter has applied the language concepts from previous chapters in order to create working shaders that create a procedurally defined brick pattern. The vertex shader is responsible for transforming the vertex position, passing along the modeling coordinate position of the vertex, and computing a light intensity value at each vertex using a single simulated light source. The fragment shader is responsible for determining whether each fragment should be brick color or mortar color. Once this determination is made, the light intensity value is applied to the chosen color, and the final color value is passed from the fragment shader so that it might ultimately be written in the frame buffer. The source code for these two shaders was discussed line by line in order to explain clearly how they work. This pair of shaders illustrates many of the features of the OpenGL Shading Language and can be used as a springboard for doing bigger and better things with the language.

6.6 Further Information

The brick shader presented in this chapter is similar to the RenderMan brick shader written by Darwyn Peachey (2002) and presented in the book, *Texturing and Modeling: A Procedural Approach, Third Edition*. This shader and others are available from the 3Dlabs developer Web site. Source code for getting started with OpenGL shaders is also available.

[1] *3Dlabs developer Web site.* http://www.3dlabs.com/support/developer

[2] Ebert, David S., John Hart, Bill Mark, F. Kenton Musgrave, Darwyn Peachey, Ken Perlin, and Steven Worley, *Texturing and Modeling: A Procedural Approach, Third Edition*, Morgan Kaufmann Publishers, San Francisco, 2002. http://www.texturingandmodeling.com

[3] Kessenich, John, Dave Baldwin, and Randi Rost, *The OpenGL Shading Language, Version 1.051*, 3Dlabs, February 2003. http://www.3dlabs.com/support/developer/ogl2

[4] OpenGL Architecture Review Board, *ARB_vertex_shader Extension Specification*, OpenGL Extension Registry. http://oss.sgi.com/projects/ogl-sample/registry

[5] OpenGL Architecture Review Board, *ARB_fragment_shader Extension Specification*, OpenGL Extension Registry. http://oss.sgi.com/projects/ogl-sample/registry

[6] OpenGL Architecture Review Board, *ARB_shader_objects Extension Specification*, OpenGL Extension Registry. http://oss.sgi.com/projects/ogl-sample/registry

Chapter 7

OpenGL Shading
Language API

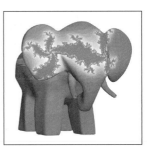

The *ARB_shader_objects*, *ARB_vertex_shader*, and *ARB_fragment_shader* extensions introduce new API calls and capabilities to support shaders written in the OpenGL Shading Language. This set of API calls is referred to throughout this book as the OPENGL SHADING LANGUAGE API. To determine if an OpenGL implementation supports the OpenGL Shading Language API, you can call **glGetString** with the symbolic constant GL_EXTENSIONS and see whether the returned string contains the extension names "GL_ARB_shader_objects", "GL_ARB_vertex_shader", and "GL_ARB_fragment_shader". This mechanism can also be used to determine the version of the OpenGL Shading Language that is supported. If the returned extension string contains the string "GL_ARB_shading_language_100", version 1.00 of the OpenGL Shading Language is supported.

In this chapter, we'll look at the OpenGL entry points that have been added to create, load, compile, and link shaders, as well as the entry points that have been added for passing generic vertex attributes and uniform variables to shaders. Reference pages for all of the shader entry points are found in Appendix B.

At the end of this chapter, we'll discuss the application code that is needed to create and use the brick shader presented in Chapter 6. If you just can't wait, go ahead and sneak a peek at Section 7.11, and then come back here to learn the details of the API.

Here is an overview of creating and using OpenGL shaders:

*   Create one or more (empty) shader objects using **glCreateShaderObjectARB**.

- Provide source code for these shaders by calling **glShaderSourceARB**.

- Compile each of the shaders by calling **glCompileShaderARB**.

- Create a program object by calling **glCreateProgramObjectARB**.

- Attach all the shader objects to the program object by calling **glAttachObjectARB**.

- Link the program object by calling **glLinkProgramARB**.

- Install the executable program as part of OpenGL's current state by calling **glUseProgramObjectARB**.

- If the shaders utilize uniform variables, their locations should be queried by calling **glGetUniformLocationARB** after **glLinkProgramARB** has been called. The values for uniform variables can then be set by calling **glUniformARB**.

- If the vertex shader uses user-defined attribute variables, the index of the generic vertex attribute to be used can either be assigned by the application by calling **glBindAttribLocationARB** prior to linking or be assigned by OpenGL automatically during linking and queried by calling **glGetAttribLocationARB**. Generic vertex attributes can then be passed to a vertex shader by calling **glVertexAttribARB** or by using **glVertexAttribPointerARB** and **glEnableVertexArrayPointer** in conjunction with standard OpenGL commands to draw vertex arrays.

7.1 Creating Shader Objects

The design of the OpenGL Shading Language API is intended to mimic the process of developing a C or C++ application. The first step is to create the source code source code must then be compiled, the various compiled modules must be linked together, and finally the resulting code can be executed by the target processor.

To support the concept of a high-level shading language within OpenGL, something must be done to provide storage for source code, compiled code, and executable code. The solution to this problem is to define two new OpenGL-managed data structures, or objects. These objects provide the storage necessary, and operations on these objects have been defined in order to provide functionality for specifying source code and then compiling, linking, and executing the resulting code. When one of these objects is created, OpenGL returns a handle to it. This handle can be used to manipulate the object itself and to set or query the parameters of the object.

The first step toward utilizing programmable graphics hardware is to create a shader object. This will create an OpenGL-managed data structure that can be used to store the shader's source code. A shader is created using

---

GLhandleARB **glCreateShaderObjectARB**(GLenum *shaderType*)

Creates an empty shader object and returns its handle. A shader object is used to maintain the source code strings that define a shader. *shaderType* indicates the type of shader to be created. Two types of shaders are supported. A shader of type GL_VERTEX_SHADER_ARB is a shader that is intended to run on the programmable vertex processor and replace the fixed functionality vertex processing in OpenGL. A shader of type GL_FRAGMENT_SHADER_ARB is a shader that is intended to run on the programmable fragment processor and replace the fixed functionality fragment processing in OpenGL.

When created, a shader object's GL_OBJECT_TYPE_ARB parameter is set to GL_SHADER_OBJECT_ARB, and its GL_OBJECT_SUBTYPE_ARB parameter is set to either GL_VERTEX_SHADER_ARB or GL_FRAGMENT_SHADER_ARB, depending on the value of *shaderType*.

After a shader object is created, strings that define the shader's source code must be provided. The source code for a shader is provided as an array of strings. The command for defining a shader's source code is

---

void **glShaderSourceARB**(GLhandleARB *shader*,
　　　　　　　　　　GLuint *nstrings*,
　　　　　　　　　　const GLcharARB ***strings*,
　　　　　　　　　　GLint **lengths*)

Sets the source code in *shader* to the source code in the array of strings specified by *strings*. Any source code previously stored in the shader object is completely replaced. The number of strings in the array is specified by *nstrings*. If *lengths* is NULL, then each string is assumed to be null terminated. If *lengths* is a value other than NULL, it points to an array containing a string length for each of the corresponding elements of *strings*. Each element in the *lengths* array may contain the length of the corresponding string (the null character is not counted as part of the string length) or a value less than 0 to indicate that the string is null terminated. The source code strings are not scanned or parsed at this time; they are simply copied into the specified shader object. An application can modify or free its copy of the source code strings immediately after the function returns.

The multiple strings interface provides a number of benefits including:

- A way to organize common pieces of source code

- A way to share prefix strings (analogous to header files) between shaders

- A way of sharing #define values to control the compilation process

- A way for including user-defined or third-party library functions

7.2 Compiling Shader Objects

After the source code strings have been loaded into a shader object, the source code must be compiled to check its validity. The result of compilation will remain as part of the shader object until another compilation operation occurs, or until the shader object itself is deleted. The command to compile a shader object is

---

void **glCompileShaderARB**(GLhandleARB *shader*)

Compiles the source code strings that have been stored in the shader object specified by *shader*.

The compilation status will be stored as part of the shader object's state. This value will be set to GL_TRUE if the shader was compiled without errors and is ready for use, and GL_FALSE otherwise. It can be queried by calling **glGetObjectParameterARB** with arguments *shader* and GL_OBJECT_COMPILE_STATUS_ARB.

A shader will fail to compile if it is lexically, grammatically, or semantically incorrect. Whether or not the compilation was successful, information about the compilation can be obtained from the shader object's information log by calling **glGetInfoLogARB**.

The OpenGL Shading Language has compilation rules that are slightly different depending on the type of shader being compiled, and so the compilation will take into consideration whether the shader is a vertex shader or a fragment shader.

Information about the compile operation can be obtained by calling **glGetInfoLogARB** (described in Section 7.5) with *shader*, but the information log should not be used as an indication of whether the compilation was successful. If the shader object was compiled successfully, either the information log will be an empty string, or it will contain information about the compile operation. If the shader object was not compiled successfully, the information log will contain information about any lexical, grammatical, or semantic errors that occurred, along with warning messages and any other information the compiler deems pertinent.

glCompileShaderARB is not required to wait until the compilation operation is completed before returning control back to the application. Any subsequent command that depends on the completion of the compilation (e.g., **glLinkProgramARB**) will block until the compilation is completed. If you need to ensure that the compilation has completed successfully before continuing, you should call **glGetObjectParameterARB** to query for successful compilation. This query will block until the compilation is complete and the status is available.

7.3   Linking and Using Shaders

Each shader object is compiled independently. In order to create a program, there needs to be a mechanism for applications to specify a list of shader objects to be linked together. This is accomplished by creating a program object and attaching to it all of the shader objects that are needed to create the program.

To create a program object, use the following command:

GLhandleARB **glCreateProgramObjectARB**(void)

Creates an empty program object and returns its handle. A program object is an object to which shader objects can be attached. This provides a way to specify the shader objects that will be linked to create a program. It also provides a means for checking the compatibility between shaders that will be used to create a program (for instance, checking the compatibility between a vertex shader and a fragment shader). When no longer needed as part of a program object, shader objects can be detached.

After the program object has been defined, shader objects can be attached to it. Attaching simply means creating a reference to the shader object so that it will be included when attempting to link a program object. This is the application's way of describing the recipe for creating a program. Shader objects are attached to a program object with the command

---

void **glAttachObjectARB**(GLhandleARB *program,*
GLhandleARB *shader)*

Attaches the shader object specified by *shader* to the program object specified by *program*. This indicates that *shader* will be included in link operations that are performed on *program.*

There is no inherent limit on the number of shader objects that can be attached to a program object. All operations that can be performed on a shader object are valid whether or not the shader object is attached to a program object. It is permissible to attach a shader object to a program object before source code has been loaded into the shader object or before the shader object has been compiled. It is also permissible to attach a shader object to more than one program object. In other words, **glAttachObjectARB** is simply used to specify the set of shader objects to be linked.

In order to create a valid program, all of the shader objects attached to a program object must be compiled, and the program object itself must be linked. The link operation will assign locations for uniform variables, resolve references between independently compiled shader objects, and check to make sure the vertex and fragment shaders are compatible with one another. To link a program object, use the command

---

void **glLinkProgramARB**(GLhandleARB *program)*

Links the program object specified by *program.* If any shader objects of subtype GL_VERTEX_SHADER_ARB are attached to *program,* they will be used to create an executable that will run on the programmable vertex processor. If any shader objects of subtype GL_FRAGMENT_SHADER_ARB are attached to *program,* they will be used to create an executable that will run on the programmable fragment processor.

The status of the link operation will be stored as part of the program object's state. This value will be set to GL_TRUE if the program object was linked without errors and is ready for use and set to GL_FALSE otherwise. It can be queried by calling **glGetObjectParameterARB** with arguments *program* and GL_OBJECT_LINK_STATUS_ARB.

glLinkProgramARB will also install the generated executables as part of the current rendering state if the link operation was successful and the specified program object is already currently in use as a result of a previous call to **glUseProgramObjectARB**.

As a result of a successful link operation, all active user-defined uniform variables (see Section 7.7) belonging to *program* will be initialized to 0, and each of the program object's active uniform variables will be assigned a location that can be queried by calling **glGetUniformLocationARB**. Also, any active user-defined attribute variables (see Section 7.6) that have not been bound to a generic vertex attribute index will be bound to one at this time.

If *program* contains shader objects of type GL_VERTEX_SHADER_ARB but it does not contain shader objects of type GL_FRAGMENT_SHADER_ARB, the vertex shader will be linked against the implicit interface for fixed functionality fragment processing. Similarly, if *program* contains shader objects of type GL_FRAGMENT_SHADER_ARB but it does not contain shader objects of type GL_VERTEX_SHADER_ARB, the fragment shader will be linked against the implicit interface for fixed functionality vertex processing.

Linking of a program object can fail for a number of reasons.

- The number of active attribute variables supported by the implementation has been exceeded.

- The number of active uniform variables supported by the implementation has been exceeded.

- The **main** function is missing for the vertex shader or the fragment shader.

- A varying variable actually used in the fragment shader is not declared with the same type (or is not declared at all) in the vertex shader.

- A reference to a function or variable name is unresolved.

- A shared global is declared with two different types or two different initial values.

- One or more of the attached shader objects has not been successfully compiled.

If the link operation is successful, a program is generated. It may contain an executable for the vertex processor, an executable for the fragment processor, or both. Whether the link operation succeeds or fails, the information and executables from the previous link operation will be lost. After the link operation, applications are free to modify attached shader objects, compile attached shader objects, detach shader objects, and attach additional shader objects. None of these operations affects the information log or the program that is part of the program object until the next link operation on the program object.

Information about the link operation can be obtained by calling
glGetInfoLogARB (described in Section 7.5) with *program*. If the program
object was linked successfully, the information log either will be an empty
string or will contain information about the link operation. If the program
object was not linked successfully, the information log will contain information about any link errors that occurred, along with warning messages and
any other information the linker chooses to provide.

glLinkProgramARB is not required to wait until the link operation is completed before returning control back to the application. Any subsequent
command that depends on the result of linking will block until the link operation is complete. If you need to ensure that the link operation has completed
successfully before continuing, you should call **glGetObjectParameterARB** to
query for successful linking. This query will block until the link operation is
complete and the status is available.

When the link operation has completed successfully, the executables it
contains may be installed as part of the current rendering state. To do this,
use the command

---

void **glUseProgramObjectARB**(GLhandleARB *program*)

Installs the program object specified by *program* as part of current rendering
state.

A program object will contain an executable that will run on the vertex
processor if it contains one or more shader objects of subtype GL_VERTEX_
SHADER_ARB that have been successfully compiled and linked. Similarly,
a program object will contain an executable that will run on the fragment
processor if it contains one or more shader objects of subtype GL_
FRAGMENT_SHADER_ARB that have been successfully compiled and
linked.

If *program* contains shader objects of type GL_VERTEX_SHADER_ARB but
it does not contain shader objects of type GL_FRAGMENT_SHADER_ARB,
an executable will be installed on the vertex processor but fixed functionality will be used for fragment processing. Similarly, if *program* contains
shader objects of type GL_FRAGMENT_SHADER_ARB but it does not contain shader objects of type GL_VERTEX_SHADER_ARB, an executable will
be installed on the fragment processor but fixed functionality will be used
for vertex processing. If *program* is 0, the programmable processors will be
disabled, and fixed functionality will be used for both vertex and fragment
processing.

Successfully installing an executable on a programmable processor will cause the corresponding fixed functionality of OpenGL to be disabled. Specifically, if an executable is installed on the vertex processor, the OpenGL fixed functionality will be disabled as described in Section 4.1. Similarly, if an executable is installed on the fragment processor, the OpenGL fixed functionality will be disabled as described in Section 4.2.

While a program object is in use, applications are free to modify attached shader objects, compile attached shader objects, attach additional shader objects, detach shader objects, delete any shader objects attached, or delete the program object itself. None of these operations will affect the executables that are part of the current state. However, relinking the program object that is currently in use will install the program as part of the current rendering state if the link operation was successful. While a program object is in use, the state that controls the disabled fixed functionality may also be updated using the normal OpenGL calls.

7.4 Cleaning Up

Objects should be deleted when they are no longer needed, and this can be accomplished with the command

---

void **glDeleteObjectARB**(GLhandleARB *object*)

Frees the memory and invalidates the handle associated with the OpenGL-managed object specified by *object*. This command effectively undoes the effects of a call to **glCreateShaderObjectARB** or **glCreateProgramObjectARB**.

If a shader object to be deleted is attached to a program object, it will be flagged for deletion, but it will not be deleted until it is no longer attached to any program object for any rendering context (i.e., it must be detached from wherever it was attached before it will be deleted). If a program object is in use as part of a current rendering state, it will be flagged for deletion, but it will not be deleted until it is no longer part of current state for any rendering context. If a program object to be deleted has shader objects attached to it, those shader objects will be automatically detached but not deleted unless they have already been flagged for deletion by a previous call to **glDeleteObjectARB**.

To determine whether an object has been flagged for deletion, call **glGetObjectParameterARB** with arguments *object* and GL_OBJECT_DELETE_STATUS_ARB.

When a shader object no longer needs to be attached to a program object, it can be detached with the command

---

void **glDetachObjectARB**(GLhandleARB *program*, GLhandleARB *shader*)

Detaches the shader object specified by *shader* from the program object specified by *program*. This command can be used to undo the effect of the command **glAttachObjectARB.**

A programming tip that might be useful in keeping things orderly is to delete shader objects as soon as they have been attached to a program object. They won't be deleted at this time, but they will be flagged for deletion when they are no longer referenced. To clean up later, the application only needs to delete the program object. All the attached shader objects will be automatically detached, and, because they are flagged for deletion, they will be automatically deleted at that time as well.

7.5 Query Functions

The OpenGL Shading Language API contains several functions for querying object state. To obtain the object type, object subtype, status of an operation on an object, number of attached objects, number of active attributes (see Section 7.6), number of active uniform variables (see Section 7.7), or the length of any of the strings maintained by an object, use one of the following commands:

---

void **glGetObjectParameterfvARB** (GLhandleARB *object*,

GLenum *pname*,

GLfloat **params*)

void **glGetObjectParameterivARB** (GLhandleARB *object*,

GLenum *pname*,

GLint **params*)

Returns in *params* the value of an object parameter. This function can be used to return information about an object. In Table 7.1, the value for *pname* is shown on the left, and the operation performed is shown on the right.

Table 7.1 Queriable Object Parameters

Parameter	Operation
GL_OBJECT_TYPE_ARB	*params* returns a value of either GL_PROGRAM_OBJECT_ARB or GL_SHADER_OBJECT_ARB, depending on whether *object* is the handle of a program object or a shader object.
GL_OBJECT_SUBTYPE_ARB	*params* returns a value of either GL_VERTEX_SHADER_ARB or GL_FRAGMENT_SHADER_ARB, depending on whether *object* is the handle of a vertex shader object or a fragment shader object.
GL_OBJECT_DELETE_STATUS_ARB	*params* returns 1 or 1.0f if the object is currently flagged for deletion, and 0 or 0.0f otherwise.
GL_OBJECT_COMPILE_STATUS_ARB	*params* returns 1 or 1.0f, if the last compile operation on the specified shader object was successful, and 0 or 0.0f otherwise.
GL_OBJECT_LINK_STATUS_ARB	*params* returns 1 or 1.0f, if the last link operation on the specified program object was successful, and 0 or 0.0f otherwise.
GL_OBJECT_VALIDATE_STATUS_ARB	*params* returns 1 or 1.0f, if the last validation operation on the specified program object was successful, and 0 or 0.0f otherwise.
GL_OBJECT_INFO_LOG_LENGTH_ARB	*params* returns the number of characters in the information log for the specified object, including the null termination character. If the object has no information log, a value of 0 or 0.0f is returned.
GL_OBJECT_ATTACHED_OBJECTS_ARB	*params* returns the number of objects attached to the specified program object.
GL_OBJECT_ACTIVE_ATTRIBUTES_ARB	*params* returns the number of active attribute variables for the specified program object.

Table 7.1   Queriable Object Parameters, continued

Parameter	Operation
GL_OBJECT_ACTIVE_ ATTRIBUTE_MAX_LENGTH_ ARB	*params* returns the length of the longest active attribute variable name for the specified program object, including the null termination character. If no active uniform variables exist, 0 or 0.0f is returned.
GL_OBJECT_ACTIVE_ UNIFORMS_ARB	*params* returns the number of active uniform variables for the specified program object.
GL_OBJECT_ACTIVE_ UNIFORM_MAX_LENGTH_ARB	*params* returns the length of the longest active uniform variable name for the specified program object, including the null termination character. If no active uniform variables exist, 0 or 0.0f is returned.
GL_OBJECT_SHADER_ SOURCE_LENGTH_ARB	*params* returns the length of the concatenation of the source strings that make up the shader source for the specified shader object, including the null termination character. If no source code exists, 0 or 0.0f is returned.

The current shader string can be obtained from a shader object by calling the following function:

> void **glGetShaderSourceARB**(GLhandleARB *shader*
>
> GLsizei *maxLength*,
>
> GLsizei **length*,
>
> GLcharARB **source*)

Returns a concatenation of the source code strings from the shader object specified by *shader*. The source code strings for a shader object are the result of a previous call to **glShaderSourceARB**. The string returned by the function will be null terminated.

glGetShaderSourceARB returns in *source* as much of the source code string as it can, up to a maximum of *maxLength* characters. The number of characters actually returned, excluding the null termination character, is specified by *count*. If the length of the returned string is not required, a value of NULL can be passed in the *length* argument. The size of the buffer required to store the returned source code string can be obtained by calling **glGetObjectParameterARB** with the value GL_OBJECT_SHADER_ SOURCE_LENGTH_ARB.

Information about the compilation operation will be stored in the information log for a shader object. Similarly, information about the link and validation operations will be stored in the information log for a program object. The information log is a string that will contain diagnostic messages and warnings. The information log may contain information useful during application development even if the compilation or link operation was successful. The information log is typically only useful during application development, and an application should not expect different OpenGL implementations to produce identical descriptions of error. To obtain the information log for a shader object or a program object, call

---

void **glGetInfoLogARB**(GLhandleARB *object*,

GLsizei *maxLength*,

GLsizei **length*,

GLcharARB **infoLog*)

Returns the information log for the specified OpenGL-managed object. The information log for a shader object is modified when the shader is compiled, and the information log for a program object is modified when the program object is linked or validated. The string that is returned will be null terminated.

glGetInfoLogARB returns in *infoLog* as much of the information log as it can, up to a maximum of *maxLength* characters. The number of characters actually returned, excluding the null termination character, is specified by *length*. If the length of the returned string is not required, a value of NULL can be passed in the *length* argument. The size of the buffer required to store the returned information log can be obtained by calling **glGetObjectParameterARB** with the value GL_OBJECT_INFO_ LOG_LENGTH_ARB.

The information log is a string that may contain diagnostic messages, warning messages, and other information about the last compile operation (for shader objects) or the last link or validate operation (for program objects). When a shader object or a program object is created, its information log will be a string of length 0.

The way the API is set up, you first need to perform a query to find out the length of the the information log (number of characters in the string). After allocating a buffer of the approprate size, you can call **glGetInfoLogARB** to put the information log string into the allocated buffer. You can then print it out if you want to do so. Listing 7.1 shows a C function that does just that.

Listing 7.1   C function to print the information log for an object

```
void printInfoLog(GLhandleARB obj)
{
    int infologLength = 0;
    int charsWritten  = 0;
    GLcharARB *infoLog;

    printOpenGLError();  // Check for OpenGL errors

    glGetObjectParameterivARB(obj, GL_OBJECT_INFO_LOG_LENGTH_ARB,
                                     &infologLength);
    printOpenGLError();  // Check for OpenGL errors

    if (infologLength > 0)
    {
        infoLog = (GLcharARB*)malloc(infologLength);
        if (infoLog == NULL)
        {
            printf("ERROR: Could not allocate InfoLog buffer\n");
            exit(1);
        }
        glGetInfoLogARB(obj, infologLength, &charsWritten, infoLog);
        printf("InfoLog:\n%s\n\n", infoLog);
        free(infoLog);
    }
    printOpenGLError();  // Check for OpenGL errors
}
```

The program object that is currently in use can be obtained by calling

---

GLhandleARB **glGetHandleARB**(GLenum *pname*)

Returns the handle to an object that is in use as part of current state. The argument *pname* specifies the state value to be queried. The value GL_PROGRAM_OBJECT_ARB is passed to obtain the handle of the program object that is currently in use as part of current state.

Finally, the list of shader objects attached to a particular program object can also be queried using this command:

---

void **glGetAttachedObjectsARB**(GLhandleARB *program,*

GLsizei *maxCount,*

GLsizei **count,*

GLhandleARB **objects*)

Returns the handles of the shader objects attached to *program.* It returns in *objects* as many of the handles of these shader objects as it can, up to a maximum of *maxCount.* The number of handles actually returned is specified by *count.* If the number of handles actually returned is not required (for instance, if it has just been obtained by calling **glGetObjectParameterARB**), a value of NULL may be passed for *count.* If no shader objects are attached to *program,* a value of 0 will be returned in *count.* The actual number of attached shaders can be obtained by calling **glGetObjectParameterARB** with the value GL_OBJECT_ATTACHED_ OBJECTS_ARB.

7.6 Specifying Vertex Attributes

One way vertex data is passed to OpenGL is by calling **glBegin**, followed by some sequence of **glColor**/**glNormal**/**glVertex**/etc. A call to **glEnd** terminates this method of specifying vertex data.

These calls continue to work in the OpenGL programmable environment. As before, a call to **glVertex** indicates that the data for an individual vertex is complete and should be processed. However, if a valid vertex shader has been installed by calling **glUseProgramObjectARB**, the vertex data will be processed by that vertex shader instead of by the usual fixed functionality of OpenGL. A vertex shader can access the standard types of vertex data passed to OpenGL using the following built-in variables:

```
attribute vec4 gl_Color;
attribute vec4 gl_SecondaryColor;
attribute vec3 gl_Normal;
attribute vec4 gl_Vertex;
attribute vec4 gl_MultiTexCoord0;
attribute vec4 gl_MultiTexCoord1;
attribute vec4 gl_MultiTexCoord2;
 . . .
attribute vec4 gl_FogCoord;
```

OpenGL's vertex-at-a-time interface is simple and powerful, but on today's systems it is definitely not the highest performance way of transferring vertex data to the graphics accelerator. Whenever possible, applications should use the vertex array interface instead. This interface allows you to store vertex data in arrays and set pointers to those arrays. Instead of sending a vertex at a time to OpenGL, you can send a whole set of primitives at a time. With vertex buffer objects, it is even possible that vertex arrays are stored in memory on the graphics board to allow for maximum performance.

The vertex array interface also works the same way in the OpenGL programmable environment as it did previously. When a vertex array is sent to OpenGL, the vertex data in the vertex array is processed one vertex at a time, just like the vertex-at-a-time interface. If a vertex shader is active, each vertex will be processed by the vertex shader rather than by the fixed functionality of OpenGL.

However, the brave new world of programmability means that applications no longer need to be limited to the standard attributes defined by OpenGL. There are many additional per-vertex attributes that applications might like to pass into a vertex shader. It is easy to imagine that applications will want to specify per-vertex data such as tangents, temperature, pressure, and who knows what else. How do we allow applications to pass nontraditional attributes to OpenGL and operate on them in vertex shaders?

The answer is that OpenGL provides a small number of generic locations for passing in vertex attributes. Each location is numbered and has room to store up to four floating-point components (i.e., it is a **vec4**). An implementation that supports 16 attribute locations will have them numbered from 0 to 15. An application can pass a vertex attribute into any of the numbered slots using one of the following functions:

---

void **glVertexAttrib{1|2|3|4}{s|f|d}ARB**(GLuint *index*, *TYPE v*)

void **glVertexAttrib{1|2|3}{s|f|d}vARB**(GLuint *index*, const *TYPE *v*)

void **glVertexAttrib4{b|s|i|f|d|ub|us|ui}vARB**(GLuint *index*, const *TYPE *v*)

Sets the generic vertex attribute specified by *index* to the value specified by *v*. This command can have up to three suffixes that differentiate variations of the parameters accepted. The first suffix can be 1, 2, 3, or 4 to indicate whether *v* contains 1, 2, 3, or 4 components. If the second and third components are not provided, they are assumed to be 0, and if the fourth component is not provided, it is assumed to be 1. The second suffix indicates the data type of *v* and may indicate byte (**b**), short (**s**), int (**i**), float (**f**), double (**d**), unsigned byte (**ub**), unsigned short (**us**), or unsigned int (**ui**). The third suffix is an optional **v** which indicates that *v* is a pointer to an array of values of the specified data type.

This set of commands has a certain set of rules for converting data to the floating-point internal representation specified by OpenGL. Floats and doubles are mapped into OpenGL internal floating-point values as you would expect, and integer values are converted to floats by adding a decimal point to the right of the value provided. Thus a value of 27 for a byte, int, short, unsigned byte, unsigned int, or unsigned short will become a value of 27.0 for the purpose of computation within OpenGL.

Another set of entry points adds support for passing normalized values as generic vertex attributes:

---

void **glVertexAttrib4NubARB**(GLuint *index*, *TYPE v*)

void **glVertexAttrib4N{b|s|i|f|d|ub|us|ui}vARB**(GLuint *index*, const *TYPE *v*)

Sets the generic vertex attribute specified by *index* to the normalized value specified by *v*. In addition to **N** (to indicate normalized values), this command can have two suffixes that differentiate variations of the parameters accepted. The first suffix indicates the data type of *v* and may indicate byte (**b**), short (**s**), int (**i**), float (**f**), double (**d**), unsigned byte (**ub**), unsigned short (**us**), or unsigned int (**ui**). The second suffix is an optional **v**, which indicates that *v* is a pointer to an array of values of the specified data type.

The commands containing **N** indicate that, for data types other than float or double, the arguments will be linearly mapped to a normalized range in the same way as data provided to the integer variants of **glColor** or **glNormal**—that is, for signed integer variants of the functions, the most positive, representable value maps to 1.0, and the most negative representable value maps to –1.0. For the unsigned integer variants, the largest representable value maps to 1.0, and the smallest representable value maps to 0.

Attribute variables are allowed to be of type **mat2**, **mat3**, or **mat4**. Attributes of these types may be loaded using the **glVertexAttribARB** entry points. Matrices must be loaded into successive generic attribute slots in column major order, with one column of the matrix in each generic attribute slot. Thus, to load a **mat4** attribute, you would load the first column in generic attribute slot *i*, the second in slot *i* + 1, the third in slot *i* + 2, and the fourth in slot *i* + 3.

With one exception, generic vertex attributes are just that—generic. They may be used to pass additional color values, tangents, binormals, depth values, or anything. The exception is that the generic vertex attribute with index 0 is used to indicate the completion of a vertex just like a call to

glVertex. A **glVertex2**, **glVertex3**, or **glVertex4** command is completely equivalent to the corresponding **glVertexAttribARB** command with an index argument of 0. There are no current values for generic vertex attribute 0 (an error will be generated if you attempt to query its current value). This is the only generic vertex attribute with this property; calls to set other standard vertex attributes can be freely mixed with calls to set any of the other generic vertex attributes. You are also free to mix calls to **glVertex** and **glVertexAttribARB** with *index* 0.

The vertex array API has been extended in a similar fashion in order to allow generic vertex attributes to be specified as vertex arrays. The following call will establish the vertex array pointer for a generic vertex attribute:

void **glVertexAttribPointerARB**(GLuint *index*,

GLint *size*,

GLenum *type*,

GLboolean *normalized*,

GLsizei *stride*,

const GLvoid **pointer*)

Specifies the location and data format of an array of generic vertex attribute values to use when rendering. The generic vertex attribute array to be specified is indicated by *index*. *size* specifies the number of components per attribute and must be 1, 2, 3, or 4. *type* specifies the data type of each component (GL_BYTE, GL_UNSIGNED_BYTE, GL_SHORT, GL_UNSIGNED_SHORT, GL_INT, GL_UNSIGNED_INT, GL_FLOAT, or GL_DOUBLE). *stride* specifies the byte stride from one attribute to the next, allowing attribute values to be intermixed with other attribute values or stored in a separate array. If set to GL_TRUE, *normalize* indicates that values stored in an integer format are to be mapped to the range [–1.0, 1.0] (for signed values) or [0.0, 1.0] (for unsigned values) when they are accessed and converted to floating point. Otherwise, values will be converted to floats directly without normalization. *pointer* is the memory address of the first generic vertex attribute in the vertex array.

After the vertex array information has been specified for a generic vertex attribute array, the array needs to be enabled. When enabled, the generic vertex attribute data in the specified array is provided along with other enabled vertex array data when vertex array drawing commands such as **glDrawArrays** are called. To enable or disable a generic vertex attribute array, use the commands:

---

void **glEnableVertexAttribArrayARB**(GLuint *index*)

void **glDisableVertexAttribArrayARB**(GLuint *index*)

Enable or disable the generic vertex attribute array specified by *index*. By default, all client-side capabilities are disabled, including all generic vertex attribute arrays. If enabled, the values in the generic vertex attribute array will be accessed and used for rendering when calls are made to vertex array commands such as **glArrayElement, glDrawArrays, glDrawElements, glDrawRangeElements, glMultiDrawArrays,** or **glMultiDrawElements.**

This solves the question of how generic vertex data is passed into OpenGL, but how do we access that data from within a vertex shader? We don't want to refer to these numbered locations in our shader because this is not very descriptive and is prone to errors. The OpenGL Shading Language API provides two ways for associating generic vertex indices with vertex shader attribute variables.

The first way is to let the linker assign the bindings automatically. In this case, the application would need to query OpenGL after linking to determine the generic vertex indices that were assigned and then to use these indices when passing the attributes to OpenGL.

The second way is for the application to choose the generic vertex attribute index value to be used and explicitly bind it to a specific attribute variable in the vertex shader by using the following function before linking occurs:

---

void **glBindAttribLocationARB**(GLhandleARB *program,*

GLuint *index,*

const GLcharARB **name*)

Associates a user-defined attribute variable in the program object specified by *program* with a generic vertex attribute index. The name of the user-defined attribute variable is passed as a null-terminated string in *name*. If *name* was bound previously, that information is lost. Thus you cannot bind one user-defined attribute variable to multiple indices, but you can bind multiple user-defined attribute variables to the same index. The generic vertex attribute index to be bound to this variable is specified by *index*. When *program* is made part of current state, values provided via the generic vertex attribute *index* will modify the value of the user-defined attribute variable specified by *name*.

If *name* refers to a matrix attribute variable, *index* refers to the first column of the matrix. Other matrix columns are then automatically bound to locations *index+1* for a matrix of type **mat2**; *index+1* and *index+2* for a matrix of type **mat3**; and *index+1*, *index+2*, and *index+3* for a matrix of type **mat4**.

Applications are not allowed to bind any of the standard OpenGL vertex attributes using this command, as they are bound automatically when needed. Any attribute binding that occurs after the program object has been linked will not take effect until the next time the program object is linked.

glBindAttribLocationARB can be called before any vertex shader objects are attached to the specified program object. It is also permissible to bind an attribute variable name that is never used in a vertex shader to a generic attribute index.

Applications are allowed to bind more than one vertex shader attribute name to the same generic vertex attribute index. This is called ATTRIBUTE ALIASING, and it is allowed only if just one of the aliased attributes is active in the executable program or if no path through the shader consumes more than one attribute of a set of attributes aliased to the same location. Another way of saying this is that more than one attribute name may be bound to a generic attribute index if, in the end, only one name is used to access the generic attribute in the vertex shader. The compiler and linker are allowed to assume that no aliasing is done and are free to employ optimizations that work only in the absence of aliasing. OpenGL implementations are not required to do error checking to detect attribute aliasing. Because there is no way to bind standard attributes, it is not possible to alias generic attributes with conventional ones.

Attribute variable name-to-generic attribute index bindings can be specified at any time by calling **glBindAttribLocationARB**. Attribute bindings do not go into effect until **glLinkProgramARB** is called, so any attribute variables that need to be bound explicitly for a particular use of a shader should be bound before the link operation occurs. After a program object has been linked successfully, the index values for attribute variables remain fixed (and their values can be queried) until the next link command occurs. To query the attribute binding for a named vertex shader attribute variable, use the following function:

GLint **glGetAttribLocationARB**(GLhandleARB *program*,
const GLcharARB **name*)

Queries the previously linked program object specified by *program* for the attribute variable specified by *name* and returns the index of the generic vertex attribute that is bound to that attribute variable. If *name* is a matrix attribute variable, the index of the first column of the matrix is returned. If the named attribute variable is not an active attribute in the specified program object or if *name* starts with the reserved prefix *gl_*, a value of –1 is returned.

glGetAttribLocationARB returns the binding that actually went into effect the last time **glLinkProgramARB** was called for the specified program object. Attribute bindings that have been specified since the last link operation are not returned by **glGetAttribLocationARB**. Using these functions, we can create a vertex shader that contains a user-defined attribute variable named *Opacity* that is used directly in the lighting calculations. We can decide that we want to pass per-vertex opacity values in generic attribute location 1 and set up the proper binding with the following line of code:

```
glBindAttribLocationARB(myProgram, 1, "Opacity");
```

Subsequently, we can call **glVertexAttribARB** to pass an opacity value at every vertex in the following manner:

```
glVertexAttrib1fARB(1, opacity);
```

The **glVertexAttribARB** calls are all designed for use between **glBegin** and **glEnd**. As such, they offer replacements for the standard OpenGL calls such as **glColor**, **glNormal**, and so on. But as we have already pointed out, vertex arrays should be used if graphics performance is a concern.

The jargon in this section can get a little confusing, so let's look at a diagram to make sure we have things straight. Figure 7.1 illustrates how commands to set standard vertex attributes can be used to modify the values of built-in attribute variables defined by the OpenGL Shading Language. The mappings between commands to set standard attributes (color, normal, vertex, etc.) and the built-in attribute variables (*gl_Color*, *gl_Normal*, *gl_Vertex*, etc.) are done automatically, and they are done in a way that doesn't conflict with the use of any generic attribute location that will be used. Each of these calls except **glVertex** also sets the current state for that attribute. (The value provided in a call to **glVertex** is never saved as

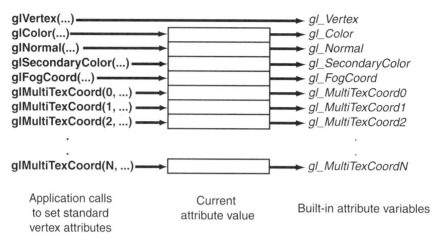

Figure 7.1   Mapping of standard vertex attribute commands to built-in attribute variables

part of current state.) The value for a built-in attribute variable is automatically updated when a call is made to set the value of the corresponding standard vertex attribute.

Now let's look at the case of generic vertex attributes as illustrated in Figure 7.2. A user-defined attribute variable must be bound to a generic

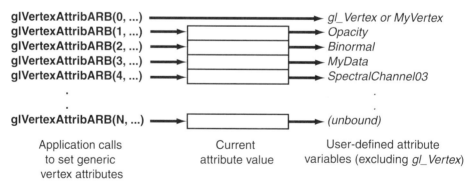

Figure 7.2   Mapping of generic vertex attribute commands to user-defined attribute variables

vertex attribute index. This binding can be done explicitly by calling **glBindAttribLocationARB**, or it can happen implicitly at link time.

Let's assume we have a vertex shader that uses three user-defined attribute variables: *Opacity*, *Binormal*, and *MyData*. These are shown on the right side of Figure 7.2. These user-defined attribute variables can each be bound to a generic vertex attribute index as follows:

```
glBindAttribLocationARB(myProgram, 1, "Opacity");
glBindAttribLocationARB(myProgram, 2, "Binormal");
glBindAttribLocationARB(myProgram, 3, "MyData");
```

This sets up the mapping so that values written into generic vertex attribute locations 1, 2, and 3 will modify the values of the attribute variables *Opacity*, *Binormal*, and *MyData* in the vertex shader. Generic vertex attribute 0 can be bound to a user-defined attribute variable, or its value can be obtained through the built-in attribute variable *gl_Vertex*. The diagram shows that generic vertex attribute index *N* is not currently bound to any user-defined attribute variable.

As mentioned, each of the generic attribute locations has enough room for four floating-point components. Applications are permitted to store 1, 2, 3, or 4 components in each location. A vertex shader may access a single location using a user-defined attribute variable that is a **float**, a **vec2**, a **vec3**, or a **vec4**. It may access two consecutive locations using a user-defined attribute variable that is a **mat2**, three using a **mat3**, and four using a **mat4**.

The generic attribute index to user-defined attribute variable bindings (i.e., the arrows on the right side of Figure 7.2) are part of the state maintained within a program object, whereas the contents of the attribute array itself is considered current attribute state (except for the generic vertex attribute with index 0). The application can provide a different program object and specify different names and mappings for attribute variables in the vertex shader, and if no calls have been made to update the attribute values in the interim, the attribute variables in the new vertex shader will get the values left behind by the previous one.

Attribute variables that may be accessed when a vertex shader is executed are called ACTIVE ATTRIBUTES. To obtain information about an active attribute, use the following command:

void **glGetActiveAttribARB**(GLhandleARB *program*,
GLuint *index*,
GLsizei *maxLength*,
GLsizei **length*,
GLint **size*,
GLenum **type*,
GLcharARB **name*)

Returns information about an active attribute variable in the program object specified by *program*. The size of a character buffer allocated by the application is specified by *maxLength*, and a pointer to this character buffer is passed in *name*. An attribute variable (either built-in or user-defined) is considered active if it is determined during the link operation that it may be accessed during program execution. Therefore, *program* should have previously been the target of a call to **glLinkProgramARB**, but it is not necessary for it to have been linked successfully.

glGetActiveAttribARB returns the name of the attribute variable indicated by *index*, storing it in the character buffer specified by *name*. The string returned will be null terminated. The actual number of characters written into this buffer is returned in *length*, and this count does not include the null termination character. If the length of the returned string is not required, a value of NULL can be passed in the *length* argument.

The number of active attributes in a program object can be obtained by calling **glGetObjectParameterARB** with the value GL_OBJECT_ACTIVE_ ATTRIBUTES_ARB. A value of 0 for *index* will cause information about the first active attribute variable to be returned, and a value of GL_OBJECT_ ACTIVE_ATTRIBUTES_ARB – 1 for *index* will cause information about the last active attribute variable to be returned. The length of the longest attribute variable name in *program* can be obtained by calling **glGetObjectParameterARB** with the value GL_OBJECT_ACTIVE_ ATTRIBUTE_MAX_LENGTH_ARB.

The *type* argument will return a pointer to the attribute variable's data type. The symbolic constants GL_FLOAT, GL_FLOAT_VEC2_ARB, GL_FLOAT_ VEC3_ARB, GL_FLOAT_VEC4_ARB, GL_FLOAT_MAT2_ARB, GL_FLOAT_ MAT3_ARB, and GL_FLOAT_MAT4_ARB may be returned. The *size* argument will return the size of the attribute in units of the type returned in *type*.

This function will return as much information as it can about the specified active attribute variable. If no information is available, *length* will be 0 and *name* will be an empty string. This situation could occur if this function is called after a link operation that failed.

This command can be useful in an environment where shader development occurs separately from application development. If some attribute naming conventions are agreed to between the shader writers and the application developers, it would be possible for the application developers to query the program object at runtime in order to determine the attributes that are actually needed and to pass those down. This approach can provide more flexibility in the shader development process.

To query the state of a particular generic vertex attribute, call one of the following commands:

void **glGetVertexAttribfvARB**(GLuint *index*,

GLenum *pname*,

GLfloat **params*)

void **glGetVertexAttribivARB**(GLuint *index*,

GLenum *pname*,

GLint **params*)

void **glGetVertexAttribdvARB**(GLuint *index*,

GLenum *pname*,

GLdouble **params*)

Returns in *params* the value of a generic vertex attribute parameter. The generic vertex attribute to be queried is specified by *index*, and the parameter to be queried is specified by *pname*. Parameters and return values are summarized in Table 7.2. All of the parameters except GL_CURRENT_VERTEX_ATTRIB_ARB represent client-side state.

Table 7.2   Generic Vertex Attribute Parameters

Parameter	Operation
GL_VERTEX_ATTRIB_ ARRAY_ENABLED_ARB	*params* returns a single value that is non-zero (true) if the vertex attribute array for *index* is enabled and 0 (false) if it is disabled. The initial value is GL_FALSE.
GL_VERTEX_ATTRIB_ ARRAY_SIZE_ARB	*params* returns a single value, the size of the vertex attribute array for *index*. The size is the number of values for each element of the vertex attribute array, and it will be 1, 2, 3, or 4. The initial value is 4.

Table 7.2   Generic Vertex Attribute Parameters, continued

Parameter	Operation
GL_VERTEX_ATTRIB_ ARRAY_STRIDE_ARB	*params* returns a single value, the array stride for (number of bytes between successive elements in) the vertex attribute array for *index*. A value of 0 indicates that the array elements are stored sequentially in memory. The initial value is 0.
GL_VERTEX_ATTRIB_ ARRAY_TYPE_ARB	*params* returns a single value, a symbolic constant indicating the array type for the vertex attribute array for *index*. Possible values are GL_ BYTE, GL_UNSIGNED_BYTE, GL_SHORT, GL_ UNSIGNED_SHORT, GL_INT, GL_UNSIGNED_ INT, GL_FLOAT, and GL_DOUBLE. The initial value is GL_FLOAT.
GL_VERTEX_ATTRIB_ ARRAY_NORMALIZED_ ARB	*params* returns a single value that is non-zero (true) if fixed-point data types for the vertex attribute array indicated by *index* are normalized when they are converted to floating point and 0 (false) otherwise. The initial value is GL_FALSE.
GL_CURRENT_VERTEX_ ATTRIB_ARB	*params* returns four values that represent the current value for the generic vertex attribute specified by *index*. Generic vertex attribute 0 is unique in that it has no current state, so an error will be generated if *index* is 0. The initial value for all other generic vertex attributes is (0, 0, 0, 1).

void **glGetVertexAttribPointervARB**(GLuint *index*,

GLenum *pname*,

GLvoid ****pointer*)

Returns pointer information. *index* is the generic vertex attribute to be queried, *pname* is a symbolic constant indicating the pointer to be returned, and *params* is a pointer to a location in which to place the returned data. The only accepted value for *pname* is GL_VERTEX_ATTRIB_ ARRAY_POINTER_ARB. This causes *params* to return a single value that is a pointer to the vertex attribute array for the generic vertex attribute specified by *index*.

7.7 Specifying Uniform Variables

As described in the previous section, attribute variables are used to provide frequently modified data to the vertex shader. Less frequently changing data can be specified using uniform variables. Uniform variables are declared within a shader and can be loaded directly by the application. This gives applications the capability to provide any type of arbitrary data to a shader. Applications can modify these values as often as every primitive in order to modify the behavior of the shader (although performance may suffer if this is done). Typically, uniform variables are used to supply state that stays constant for many primitives.

The OpenGL Shading Language also defines a number of built-in variables that track OpenGL state. Applications can continue using OpenGL to manage state through existing OpenGL calls and can use these built-in uniform variables in custom shaders. Of course, if you want something that isn't already supported directly by OpenGL, it is a simple matter to define your own uniform variable and supply the value to your shader.

When a program object is made current, built-in uniform variables that track OpenGL state are initialized to the current value of that OpenGL state. Subsequent calls that modify an OpenGL state value will cause the built-in uniform variable that tracks that state value to be updated as well.

The basic model for specifying uniform variables is different from the model for specifying attribute variables. As discussed in the preceding section, for attribute variables, the application can specify the attribute location before linking occurs. The locations of uniform variables are determined by OpenGL at link time. As a result, applications always need to query the uniform location after linking occurs.

To update the value of a user-defined uniform variable, an application needs to determine its location and then specify its value. The locations of uniform variables are assigned at link time and will not change until the next link operation occurs. Each time linking occurs, the locations of uniform variables may change, and so the application must query them again before setting them. The locations of the user-defined uniform variables in a program object can be queried with the following command:

GLint **glGetUniformLocationARB**(GLhandleARB *program*,

const GLcharARB **name*)

Returns an integer that represents the location of a specific uniform variable. The name of the uniform variable to be queried is specified in the null-terminated string indicated by *name*. The array element operator "[]" and the structure field operator "." may be used in *name* in order to select elements within an array or fields within a structure, but no white space is allowed. The location of the first element of an array can be retrieved by using the name of the array or by using the name appended by "[0]". The result of using these operators is not allowed to be another structure, an array of structures, or a subcomponent of a vector or matrix. If the named uniform variable is not found in the specified program object or if *name* starts with the reserved prefix "gl_", a value of –1 is returned.

The locations assigned to uniform variables are not known until the program object is linked. After linking has occurred, this command can be used to obtain the location of a uniform variable. This location value can then be passed to **glUniformARB** to set the value of a uniform variable or to **glGetUniformARB** in order to query the current value of the uniform variable. After a program object has been linked successfully, the locations for uniform variables remain fixed (and their values can be queried) until the next link command occurs.

Loading of user-defined uniform values is only possible for the program object that is currently in use. All user-defined uniform variables are initialized to 0 when a program object is successfully linked. User-defined uniform values are part of the state of a program object. Their values can be modified only when the program object is part of current rendering state, but the values of uniform variables will be preserved as the program object is swapped in and out of current state. The following commands are used to load uniform variables into the program object that is currently in use:

void **glUniform{1|2|3|4}{f|i}ARB**(GLint *location*, *TYPE v*)

Sets the user-defined uniform variable or uniform variable array specified by *location* to the value specified by *v.* The suffix **1**, **2**, **3**, or **4** indicates whether *v* contains 1, 2, 3, or 4 components. This value should match the number of components in the data type of the specified uniform variable (e.g., **1** for **float**, **int**, **bool**; **2** for **vec2**, **ivec2**, **bvec2**, etc.). The suffix **f** indicates that floating-point values are being passed and the suffix **i** indicates that integer values are being passed; this type should also match the data type of the specified uniform variable. The **i** variants of this function should be used to provide values for uniform variables defined as **int**, **ivec2**, **ivec3**, and **ivec4**, or arrays of these. The **f** variants should be used to provide values for uniform variables of type **float**, **vec2**, **vec3**, or **vec4**, or arrays of these. Either the **i** or the **f** variants may be used to provide values for uniform variables of type **bool**, **bvec2**, **bvec3**, and **bvec4** or arrays of these. The uniform variable will be set to **false** if the input value is 0 or 0.0f, and it will be set to **true** otherwise.

void **glUniform{1|2|3|4}{f|i}vARB**(GLint *location*,

GLuint *count*,

const *TYPE v*)

Sets the user-defined uniform variable or uniform variable array specified by *location* to the values specified by *v.* These commands pass a count and a pointer to the values to be loaded into a uniform variable or a uniform variable array. A count of 1 should be used if modifying the value of a single uniform variable, and a count of 1 or greater can be used to modify an array. The number specified in the name of the command indicates the number of components for each element in *v,* and it should match the number of components in the data type of the specified uniform variable (e.g., **1** for **float**, **int**, **bool**; **2** for **vec2**, **ivec2**, **bvec2**, etc.). The **v** in the command name indicates that a pointer to a vector of values is being passed. The **f** and **i** suffixes are defined in the same way as for the nonvector variants of **glUniform**.

For uniform variable arrays, each element of the array is considered to be of the type indicated in the name of the command (e.g., **glUniform3f** or **glUniform3fv** can be used to load a uniform variable array of type **vec3**). The number of elements of the uniform variable array to be modified is specified by *count.*

---

void **glUniformMatrix{2|3|4}fvARB**(GLint *location*,

GLuint *count*,

GLboolean *transpose*,

const GLfloat **v*)

Sets the user-defined uniform matrix variable or uniform matrix array variable specified by *location* to the values specified by *v*. The number in the command name is interpreted as the dimensionality of the matrix. The number **2** indicates a 2×2 matrix (i.e., 4 values), the number **3** indicates a 3×3 matrix (i.e., 9 values), and the number **4** indicates a 4×4 matrix (i.e., 16 values). If *transpose* is GL_FALSE, each matrix is assumed to be supplied in column major order. If transpose is GL_TRUE, each matrix is assumed to be supplied in row major order. The *count* argument indicates the number of matrices to be passed. A count of 1 should be used if modifying the value of a single matrix, and a count greater than 1 can be used to modify an array of matrices.

glUniform1iARB and **glUniform1ivARB** are the only two functions that may be used to load uniform variables defined as sampler types (see Section 7.8). Attempting to load a sampler with any other function will result in an error.

Errors can also be generated by **glUniformARB** for any of the following reasons:

• If there is no current program object

• If *location* is an invalid uniform variable location for the current program object

• If the number of values specified by *count* would exceed the declared extent of the indicated uniform variable or uniform variable array

• Other than the preceding exceptions noted, if the type and size of the uniform variable as defined in the shader do not match the type and size specified in the name of the command used to load its value

In all of these cases, the indicated uniform variable will not be modified.

The location of a uniform variable cannot be used for anything other than specifying or querying that particular uniform variable. Say you declare a uniform variable as a structure that has three fields in succession that are defined as floats. If you call **glGetUniformLocationARB** to determine that the first of those three floats is at location *n*, do not assume that the next one is at location *n* + 1. It is possible to query the location of the *i*th element in an array. That value can then be passed to **glUniformARB** to load one or more values into the array, starting at the *i*th element of the array. It is not possible to take *i* and add an integer *N* and use the result to try and modify element $i + N$ in the array. The location of array element $i + N$ should be queried specifically prior to any attempt to set its value. These location values do not necessarily represent real memory locations. Applications that assume otherwise will not work.

For example, consider the following structure defined within a shader:

```
struct
{
    struct
    {
        float a;
        float b[10];
    } c[2];
    vec2 d;
} uniform e;
```

and consider the API calls that attempt to determine locations within that structure:

```
loc1 = glGetUniformLocationARB(progObj, "e.d");         // is valid
loc2 = glGetUniformLocationARB(progObj, "e.c[0]");      // is not valid
loc3 = glGetUniformLocationARB(progObj, "e.c[0].b") ;   // is valid
loc4 = glGetUniformLocationARB(progObj, "e.c[0].b[2]"); // is valid
```

The location *loc2* cannot be retrieved because *e.c[0]* references a structure.

Now consider the commands to set parts of the uniform variable:

```
glUniform2fARB(loc1, 1.0f, 2.0f);      // is valid
glUniform2iARB(loc1, 1, 2);            // is not valid
glUniform1fARB(loc1, 1.0f);            // is not valid
glUniform1fvARB(loc3, 10, floatPtr);   // is valid
glUniform1fvARB(loc4, 10, floatPtr);   // is not valid
glUniform1fvARB(loc4, 8, floatPtr);    // is valid
```

The second command in the preceding list is invalid because *loc1* references a uniform variable of type **vec2**, not **ivec2**. The third command is invalid because *loc1* references a **vec2**, not a **float**. The fifth command in the preceding list is invalid because it attempts to set values that will exceed the length of the array.

Uniform variables that may be accessed when a shader is executed (either built-in or user-defined) are called ACTIVE UNIFORM VARIABLES. You can think of this as though the compiler and/or the linker is actually smart enough to deactivate uniform variables that are declared but never used. This provides more flexibility in coding style—modular code can define lots of uniform variables, and those that can be determined to be unused will typically be optimized away.

To obtain the list of active uniform variables from a program object, use **glGetActiveUniformARB**. This command can be used by an application to query the uniform variables in a program object and set up user interface elements to allow direct manipulation of all of the user-defined uniform values.

---

void **glGetActiveUniformARB**(GLhandleARB *program,*

GLuint *index,*

GLsizei *maxLength,*

GLsizei **length,*

GLint **size,*

GLenum **type,*

GLcharARB **name*)

Returns information about the uniform variable specified by *index*. The program object to be queried is specified by *program*. The size of a character buffer allocated by the application is specified by *maxLength*, and a pointer to that character buffer is passed in *name*. A uniform variable (either built-in or user-defined) is considered active in a shader if it is determined during the link operation that it may be accessed when the shader is executed. Therefore, *program* should have previously been the target of a call to **glLinkProgramARB**, but it is not necessary for it to have been linked successfully. The list of active uniform variables may include both built-in uniform variables (which begin with the prefix "gl_") as well as user-defined uniform variable names.

glGetActiveUniformARB returns the name of the uniform variable indicated by *index*, storing it in the character buffer specified by *name*. The string returned will be null terminated. The actual number of characters written into this buffer is returned in *length*, and this count does not include the null termination character. If the length of the returned string is not required, a value of NULL can be passed in the *length* argument.

The number of active uniform variables can be obtained by calling **glGetObjectParameterARB** with the value GL_OBJECT_ACTIVE_ UNIFORMS_ARB. A value of 0 for *index* will cause information about the first active uniform variable to be returned, and a value of GL_OBJECT_ ACTIVE_UNIFORMS_ARB – 1 for *index* selects the last active uniform variable. The size of the character buffer required to store the longest uniform variable name in *program* can be obtained by calling **glGetObjectParameterARB** with the value GL_OBJECT_ACTIVE_ UNIFORM_MAX_LENGTH_ARB.

The *type* argument will return a pointer to the uniform variable's data type. The symbolic constants GL_FLOAT, GL_FLOAT_VEC2_ARB, GL_FLOAT_VEC3_ARB, GL_FLOAT_VEC4_ARB, GL_INT, GL_INT_VEC2_ARB, GL_INT_VEC3_ARB, GL_INT_VEC4_ARB, GL_BOOL_ARB, GL_BOOL_VEC2_ARB, GL_BOOL_VEC3_ARB, GL_BOOL_VEC4_ARB, GL_FLOAT_MAT2_ARB, GL_FLOAT_MAT3_ARB, and GL_FLOAT_MAT4_ARB may be returned.

Uniform variables that are declared as structures or arrays of structures will not be returned directly by this function. Instead, each of these uniform variables will be reduced to its fundamental components using the "." and "[]" operators in its name such that each of the names returned will be a data type in the preceding list. Each of these reduced uniform variables is counted as one active uniform variable and is assigned an index. If an active uniform variable reduces to an element of an array, all elements in the array are considered to be active.

The size of the uniform variable will be returned in *size*. Uniform variables other than arrays will have a size of 1, and uniform variable arrays will return the size of the array. Structures and arrays of structures will be reduced as described previously, such that each of the names returned will be a data type in the preceding list. If this reduction results in an array, the size returned will be the size of this array; otherwise, the size returned will be 1.

This function will return as much information as it can about the specified active uniform variable. If no information is available, *length* will be 0 and *name* will be an empty string. This situation could occur if this function is called after a link operation that failed.

Using **glGetActiveUniformARB**, the application developer can programmatically query the uniform variables actually used in a shader and automatically create a user interface that allows the end user to modify those uniform variables. If among the shader writers there were some convention concerning the names of uniform variables, the user interface could be even more specific. For instance, any uniform variable name that ended with "Color" would be edited with the color selection tool. This function can also be useful when mixing and matching a set of vertex and fragment shaders designed to play well with each other, using a subset of known uniform variables. It can be much safer and less tedious to programmatically determine which uniform variables to send down than to hardcode all the combinations.

7.8 Samplers

glUniform1iARB and **glUniform1ivARB** are used to load uniform variables defined as sampler types (i.e., uniform variables of type **sampler1D**, **sampler2D**, **sample3D**, **samplerCube**, **sampler1DShadow**, or **sampler2DShadow**). They may be declared within either vertex shaders or fragment shaders.

The value contained in a sampler is used within a shader to access a particular texture map. The value loaded into the sampler by the application should be the number of the texture unit to be used to access the texture. For vertex shaders, this value should be less than the implementation-dependent constant GL_MAX_VERTEX_TEXTURE_IMAGE_UNITS_ARB, which can be queried by calling **glGet**. For fragment shaders, this value should be less than the implementation-dependent constant GL_MAX_TEXTURE_IMAGE_UNITS_ARB.

The suffix on the sampler type indicates the texture type to be accessed: 1D, 2D, 3D, cube map, 1D shadow, or 2D shadow. In OpenGL, a texture object of each of the first four texture types can be bound to a single texture unit, and this suffix allows the desired texture object to be chosen. A 1D shadow sampler is used to access the 1D texture when depth comparisons are enabled, and a 2D shadow sampler is used to access the 2D texture when depth comparisons are enabled. If two uniform variables of different sampler types contain the same value, an error will be generated when the next rendering command is issued. Attempting to load a sampler with any command other than **glUniform1iARB** or **glUniform1ivARB** will result in an error being generated.

From within a shader, samplers should be considered an opaque data type. The current API provides a way of specifying an integer representing the texture image unit to be used. In the future, the API may be extended to allow a sampler to refer directly to a texture object.

Samplers that may be accessed when a program is executed are called ACTIVE SAMPLERS. The link operation will fail if it determines that the number of active samplers exceeds the maximum allowable limits. The number of active samplers permitted on the vertex processor is indicated by GL_MAX_VERTEX_TEXTURE_IMAGE_UNITS_ARB, the number of active samplers permitted on the fragment processor is indicated by GL_MAX_TEXTURE_IMAGE_UNITS_ARB, and the number of active samplers permitted on both processors combined is GL_COMBINED_TEXTURE_IMAGE_UNITS_ARB.

More detail on using samplers within a shader is provided in Section 10.1.

7.9   Development Aids

A situation that can be difficult to diagnose is that a program may fail to execute because of the value of a sampler variable. These variables can be changed anytime between linking and program execution. To ensure robust behavior, OpenGL implementations must do some runtime checking just before the shader is executed (i.e., when a rendering operation is about to occur). At this point, the only way to report an error is to set the OpenGL error flag, and this is not usually something that applications will check at this performance-critical juncture.

To provide more information when these situations occur, the OpenGL Shading Language API defines a new function that can be called to perform this runtime check explicitly and provide diagnostic information.

---

void **glValidateProgramARB**(GLhandleARB *program*)

Checks to see whether the executables contained in *program* can execute given the current OpenGL state. The information generated by the validation process will be stored in *program*'s information log. The validation information may consist of an empty string, or it may be a string containing information about how the current program object interacts with the rest of current OpenGL state. This provides a way for OpenGL implementors to convey more information about why the current program is inefficient, suboptimal, failing to execute, and so on.

The status of the validation operation will be stored as part of the program object's state. This value will be set to GL_TRUE if the validation succeeded and GL_FALSE otherwise. It can be queried by calling **glGetObjectParameterARB** with arguments *program* and GL_OBJECT_VALIDATE_STATUS_ARB.

This function is typically useful only during application development. The informational string stored in the information log is completely implementation-dependent therefore; an application should not expect different OpenGL implementations to produce identical information strings.

Because the operations described in this section can severely hinder performance, they should be utilized only during application development and removed prior to shipment of the production version of the application.

7.10   Implementation-Dependent API Values

Some of the features we've described in previous sections have implementation-dependent limits. All of the implementation-dependent values in the OpenGL Shading Language API are defined in the list that follows, and all of them can be queried using **glGet**.

GL_MAX_VERTEX_ATTRIBS_ARB—Defines the number of active vertex attributes that are available. The minimum legal value is 16.

GL_MAX_VERTEX_UNIFORM_COMPONENTS_ARB—Defines the number of components (i.e., floating-point values) that are available for vertex shader uniform variables. The minimum legal value is 512.

GL_MAX_VARYING_FLOATS_ARB—Defines the number of floating-point variables avalable for varying variables. The minimum legal value is 32.

GL_MAX_VERTEX_TEXTURE_IMAGE_UNITS_ARB—Defines the number of hardware units that can be used to access texture maps from the vertex processor. The minimum legal value is 0.

GL_MAX_COMBINED_TEXTURE_IMAGE_UNITS_ARB—Defines the total number of hardware units that can be used to access texture maps from the vertex processor and the fragment processor combined. The minimum legal value is 2.

GL_MAX_TEXTURE_IMAGE_UNITS_ARB—Defines the total number of hardware units that can be used to access texture maps from the fragment processor. The minimum legal value is 2.

GL_MAX_TEXTURE_COORDS_ARB—Defines the number of texture coordinate sets that are available. The minimum legal value is 2.

GL_MAX_FRAGMENT_UNIFORM_COMPONENTS_ARB—Defines the number of components (i.e., floating-point values) that are available for fragment shader uniform variables. The minimum legal value is 64.

7.11   Application Code for Brick Shaders

Each shader is going to be a little bit different. Each vertex shader may use a different set of attributes or different uniform variables, and attributes may be bound to different locations, and so on. One of the demo programs whose source code is available for download from the 3Dlabs Web site is called **ogl2example**. In this program, there is an "install" function for each set of shaders that we want to install and use. We'll do something similar (but simpler) here and define an install function for our brick shaders. This function will install the brick shaders that were presented in Chapter 6. But first, we'll define a simple function that will make it a little easier to set the values of uniform variables.

```
GLint getUniLoc(GLhandleARB program, const GLcharARB *name)
{
    GLint loc;

    loc = glGetUniformLocationARB(program, name);

    if (loc == -1)
        printf("No such uniform named \"%s\"\n", name);

    printOpenGLError();  // Check for OpenGL errors
    return loc;
}
```

Shaders are passed to OpenGL as strings. For our shader installation function, we'll assume that each of the shaders has been defined as a single string, and pointers to those strings are passed to the following function. This function will do all the work to load, compile, link, and install our brick shaders. The function definition and local variables for this function are declared as follows:

```
int installBrickShaders(GLcharARB *brickVertex,
                        GLcharARB *brickFragment)
{
    GLhandleARB brickVS, brickFS, brickProg;   // handles to objects
    GLint       vertCompiled, fragCompiled;    // status values
    GLint       linked;
```

The argument *brickVertex* contains a pointer to the string containing the source code for the brick vertex shader, and the argument *brickFragment* contains a pointer to the source code for the brick fragment shader. Next, we declare variables for the handles of three OpenGL objects: a shader object that will be used to store and compile the brick vertex shader, a second shader object that will be used to store and compile the brick fragment shader, and a program object to which the shader objects will be attached. Flags to indicate the status of the compile and link operations are defined next.

The first step is to create two empty shader objects, one for the vertex shader and one for the fragment shader:

```
    brickVS = glCreateShaderObjectARB(GL_VERTEX_SHADER_ARB);
    brickFS = glCreateShaderObjectARB(GL_FRAGMENT_SHADER_ARB);
```

Source code can be loaded into the shader objects after they have been created. The shader objects are empty, and we have a single null-terminated string containing the source code for each shader, so we can call **glShaderSourceARB** as follows:

```
glShaderSourceARB(brickVS, 1, &brickVertex, NULL);
glShaderSourceARB(brickFS, 1, &brickFragment, NULL);
```

The shaders are now ready to be compiled. For each shader, we call **glCompileShaderARB** and then call **glGetObjectParameterARB** in order to see what transpired. **glCompileShaderARB** will set the shader object's GL_OBJECT_COMPILE_STATUS_ARB parameter to GL_TRUE if it succeeded and GL_FALSE otherwise. Regardless of whether the compilation succeeded or failed, we print out the information log for the shader. If the compilation was unsuccessful, this log will have information about the compilation errors. If the compilation was successful, this log may still have useful information that would help us improve the shader in some way. You would typically only check the info log during application development or if you're running a shader for the first time on a new platform. We're going to exit if the compilation of either shader fails.

```
glCompileShaderARB(brickVS);
printOpenGLError();  // Check for OpenGL errors
glGetObjectParameterivARB(brickVS,
        GL_OBJECT_COMPILE_STATUS_ARB, &vertCompiled);
printInfoLog(brickVS);

glCompileShaderARB(brickFS);
printOpenGLError();  // Check for OpenGL errors
glGetObjectParameterivARB(brickFS,
        GL_OBJECT_COMPILE_STATUS_ARB, &fragCompiled);
printInfoLog(brickFS);

if (!vertCompiled || !fragCompiled)
    return 0;
```

This section of code uses the **printInfoLog** function that we defined previously.

At this point, the shaders have been compiled successfully, and we're almost ready to try them out. First, the shader objects need to be attached to a program object so that they can be linked.

```
brickProg = glCreateProgramObjectARB();
glAttachObjectARB(brickProg, brickVS);
glAttachObjectARB(brickProg, brickFS);
```

Our program object must be linked by calling **glLinkProgramARB**. Again, we'll look at the information log of the program object regardless of whether the link succeeded or failed. There may be useful information for us if we've never tried this shader before.

```
glLinkProgramARB(brickProg);
printOpenGLError();  // Check for OpenGL errors
glGetObjectParameterivARB(brickProg,
            GL_OBJECT_LINK_STATUS_ARB, &linked);
printInfoLog(brickProg);

if (!linked)
    return 0;
```

If we make it to the end of this code, we have a valid program that can be made part of current state simply by calling **glUseProgramObjectARB:**

```
glUseProgramObjectARB(brickProg);
```

Before returning from this function, we also want to initialize the values of the uniform variables used in the two shaders. To obtain the location that was assigned by the linker, we query the uniform variable by name using the **getUniLoc** function defined previously. Then we use that location to immediately set the initial value of the uniform variable .

```
glUniform3fARB(getUniLoc(brickProg, "BrickColor"), 1.0, 0.3, 0.2);
glUniform3fARB(getUniLoc(brickProg, "MortarColor"), 0.85, 0.86, 0.84);
glUniform2fARB(getUniLoc(brickProg, "BrickSize"), 0.30, 0.15);
glUniform2fARB(getUniLoc(brickProg, "BrickPct"), 0.90, 0.85);
glUniform3fARB(getUniLoc(brickProg, "LightPosition"), 0.0, 0.0, 4.0);

return 1;
}
```

When this function returns, the application is ready to draw geometry that will be rendered with our brick shaders. The result of rendering some simple objects with this application code and the shaders described in Chapter 6 is shown in Figure 6.4. The complete C function is shown in Listing 7.2.

Listing 7.2 C function for installing brick shaders

```
int installBrickShaders(GLcharARB *brickVertex,
                        GLcharARB *brickFragment)
{

    GLhandleARB brickVS, brickFS, brickProg;  // handles to objects
    GLint       vertCompiled, fragCompiled;   // status values
    GLint       linked;

    // Create a vertex shader object and a fragment shader object

    brickVS = glCreateShaderObjectARB(GL_VERTEX_SHADER_ARB);
    brickFS = glCreateShaderObjectARB(GL_FRAGMENT_SHADER_ARB);
```

```
// Load source code strings into shaders

glShaderSourceARB(brickVS, 1, &brickVertex, NULL);
glShaderSourceARB(brickFS, 1, &brickFragment, NULL);

// Compile the brick vertex shader and print out
// the compiler log file.

glCompileShaderARB(brickVS);
printOpenGLError();  // Check for OpenGL errors
glGetObjectParameterivARB(brickVS,
          GL_OBJECT_COMPILE_STATUS_ARB, &vertCompiled);
printInfoLog(brickVS);

// Compile the brick vertex shader and print out
// the compiler log file.

glCompileShaderARB(brickFS);
printOpenGLError();  // Check for OpenGL errors
glGetObjectParameterivARB(brickFS,
          GL_OBJECT_COMPILE_STATUS_ARB, &fragCompiled);
printInfoLog(brickFS);

if (!vertCompiled || !fragCompiled)
    return 0;

// Create a program object and attach the two compiled shaders

brickProg = glCreateProgramObjectARB();
glAttachObjectARB(brickProg, brickVS);
glAttachObjectARB(brickProg, brickFS);

// Link the program object and print out the info log

glLinkProgramARB(brickProg);
printOpenGLError();  // Check for OpenGL errors
glGetObjectParameterivARB(brickProg,
          GL_OBJECT_LINK_STATUS_ARB, &linked);
printInfoLog(brickProg);

if (!linked)
    return 0;

// Install program object as part of current state

glUseProgramObjectARB(brickProg);

// Set up initial uniform values

glUniform3fARB(getUniLoc(brickProg, "BrickColor"), 1.0, 0.3, 0.2);
glUniform3fARB(getUniLoc(brickProg, "MortarColor"), 0.85, 0.86, 0.84);
```

```
glUniform2fARB(getUniLoc(brickProg, "BrickSize"), 0.30, 0.15);
glUniform2fARB(getUniLoc(brickProg, "BrickPct"), 0.90, 0.85);
glUniform3fARB(getUniLoc(brickProg, "LightPosition"), 0.0, 0.0, 4.0);

    return 1;
}
```

7.12 Summary

The set of function calls added to OpenGL to create and manipulate shaders is actually quite small. The interface is intended to mimic the software development process followed by a C/C++ programmer. To install and use OpenGL shaders, you need to do the following:

1. Create one or more (empty) shader objects using **glCreateShaderObjectARB**.

2. Provide source code for these shaders by calling **glShaderSourceARB**.

3. Compile each of the shaders by calling **glCompileShaderARB**.

4. Create a program object by calling **glCreateProgramObjectARB**.

5. Attach all the shader objects to the program object by calling **glAttachObjectARB**.

6. Link the program object by calling **glLinkProgramARB**.

7. Install the executable program as part of OpenGL's current state by calling **glUseProgramObjectARB**.

The locations of user-defined uniform variables can be queried after linking has occurred by calling **glGetUniformLocationARB**, and values can then be stored in these locations by calling one of the variants of **glUniformARB**.

User-defined attribute variables can be explicitly associated with a generic vertex attribute index by calling **glBindAttribLocationARB**, or such associations can be assigned implicitly at link time and queried with **glGetAttribLocationARB**. Generic vertex attribute values can then be supplied by the application a vertex at a time by using one of the variants of **glVertexAttribARB** or as part of a vertex array by calling **glEnableVertexAttribArrayARB** and **glVertexAttribPointerARB**.

A number of query functions are provided for obtaining information about shader and program objects.

7.13 Further Information

Reference pages for the OpenGL functions that deal with shaders can be found in Appendix B. Source code similar to that presented in this chapter, along with various example shaders, can be found at the 3Dlabs developers Web site.

[1] *3Dlabs developer Web site.* http://www.3dlabs.com/support/developer.

[2] Ebert, David S., John Hart, Bill Mark, F. Kenton Musgrave, Darwyn Peachey, Ken Perlin, and Steven Worley, *Texturing and Modeling: A Procedural Approach, Third Edition*, Morgan Kaufmann Publishers, San Francisco, 2002. http://www.texturingandmodeling.com

[3] Kessenich, John, Dave Baldwin, and Randi Rost, *The OpenGL Shading Language, Version 1.051*, 3Dlabs, February 2003. http://www.3dlabs.com/support/developer/ogl2

[4] OpenGL Architecture Review Board, J. Neider, T. Davis, and M. Woo, *OpenGL Programming Guide, Third Edition: The Official Guide to Learning OpenGL, Version 1.2*, Addison-Wesley, Reading, Massachusetts, 1999.

[5] OpenGL Architecture Review Board, *OpenGL Reference Manual, Third Edition: The Official Reference Document to OpenGL, Version 1.2*, Addison-Wesley, Reading, Massachusetts, 1999.

[6] OpenGL Architecture Review Board, *ARB_vertex_shader Extension Specification*, OpenGL Extension Registry. http://oss.sgi.com/projects/ogl-sample/registry

[7] OpenGL Architecture Review Board, *ARB_fragment_shader Extension Specification*, OpenGL Extension Registry. http://oss.sgi.com/projects/ogl-sample/registry

[8] OpenGL Architecture Review Board, *ARB_shader_objects Extension Specification*, OpenGL Extension Registry. http://oss.sgi.com/projects/ogl-sample/registry

[9] Segal, Mark, and Kurt Akeley, *The OpenGL Graphics System: A Specification (Version 1.5)*, Editor (v1.1): Chris Frazier, Editor (v1.2–1.5): Jon Leech, July 2003. http://opengl.org

Chapter 8

Shader Development

At the time of this writing, shader development tools for the OpenGL Shading Language are in their infancy. Although some tools for shader development do exist (notably, ATI's RenderMonkey), there are no existing tools for debugging or profiling shaders. This situation is expected to improve rapidly as hardware and software companies develop tools for use in shader development.

This chapter provides some ideas on the shader development process and describes the tools that are currently available. Both general software development techniques and techniques that are unique to shader development will be discussed. In all likelihood, we will soon see software developers step in to the void with products to assist shader development, and a whole ecosystem of tools for shader development will eventually arise.

8.1 General Principles

Shader development can be thought of as another form of software engineering; therefore, existing software engineering principles and practices should be brought into play when developing shaders. Some time should be spent designing the shader before any code is written. The design should aim to keep things as simple as possible while still getting the job done. If the shader is part of a larger shader development effort, care should be taken to design the shader for reliability and reuse.

In short, you should treat shader development the same as you would any other software development tasks, allocating appropriate amounts of time for design, implementation, testing, and documentation.

Here are a few more useful thoughts for developing shaders. Consider these to be friendly advice and not mandates. There will be some situations where some of these shader development suggestions make sense and others where they do not.

8.1.1 Understand the Problem

This seems fairly obvious, but it is worth reminding yourself periodically that you will be most successful at developing shaders if you understand the problem before you write any of the shader code.

The very first step to take is to make sure you understand the rendering algorithm you plan on implementing. If your aim is to develop a shader for doing bump-mapping, make sure you understand the necessary mathematics before plunging into coding. It is usually easier to think things through with a pencil and paper and get the details straight in your mind before you begin to write code.

Because the tools for developing shaders are currently less powerful than those for developing code intended to run on the CPU, you might consider implementing a simulation of your algorithm on the CPU prior to coding it up in the OpenGL Shading Language. Doing this will let you use the powerful debugging tools available for typical software development, single-step through source code, set breakpoints, and really watch your code in action. Of course, tools should soon be available to let you do these things directly on the graphics hardware as well.

8.1.2 Add Complexity Progressively

Many shaders depend on a combination of details to achieve the desired effect. Develop your shader in such a way that you implement and test the largest and most important details first and add progressive complexity after the basic shader is working. For instance, you may want to develop a shader that combines effects from noise with values read from several texture maps and then performs some unique lighting effects. You can approach this task in a couple of different ways. One way would be to get your unique lighting effects working first using a simple shading model. After testing this part of the shader, you can add the effects from, reading the texture maps and thoroughly test again. After this, you can add the noise effects, again, testing as you proceed.

In this way, you have reduced a large development task into several smaller ones. After a task has been successfully completed and tested, you can move on to the next task.

8.1.3 Test and Iterate

There will be times when it is impossible to visualize ahead of time the effect a shader will have. This is particularly true when dealing with mathematical functions that are complex or hard to visualize, such as noise. In this case, you may want to parameterize your algorithm and modify the parameters systematically. You can take notes as you modify the parameters and observe the effect. These observations would be useful comments in the shader source code for someone who might come along later and want to tweak the shader in a different direction.

After you have found a set of parameters that gives you the desired effect, you can consider simplifying the shader by removing some of the "tweakable" parameters and replacing them with constants. This may make your shader less flexible, but it may make it easier to understand for someone coming along later.

8.1.4 Strive for Simplicity

There's a lot to be said for simplicity. Simple shaders are easier to understand and easier to maintain. There's often more than one algorithm for achieving the effect you want. Have you chosen the simplest one? There's often more than one way to implement a particular algorithm. Have you chosen the language features that let you express the algorithm in the simplest way possible?

8.1.5 Modularity

The OpenGL Shading Language and its API support modular shaders, so take advantage of this capability. Use the principle of "divide and conquer" to develop small, simple modules that are designed to work together. Your lighting modules might all be interchangeable and offer support for standard light source types as well as custom lighting modules. You may also have fog modules that offer a variety of fog effects. If you do things right, you can mix and match any of your lighting modules with any of your fog modules. This principle can be applied to other aspects of shader computation, both for vertex shaders and for fragment shaders.

8.2 Performance Considerations

After doing all the right things from a software engineering standpoint, your shader may or may not have acceptable performance. Here are some ideas for eking out better performance from your carefully crafted shader.

8.2.1 Consider Computational Frequency

There are three areas where shading computations can occur: on the CPU, on the vertex processor, and on the fragment processor. It is tempting to put most of your shader computation in the fragment shader because this will be executed for every pixel that is drawn and you will, therefore, get the highest quality image. But if performance is a concern, you may be able to find computations that can be done with acceptable quality per vertex instead of per fragment. By moving the computation to the vertex shader, you can make your fragment shader faster. In some cases, there may be no visible difference between doing the computation in the vertex shader versus doing it in the fragment shader. This can be the case with fog computations, for example.

One way to think about the problem is to implement rapidly changing characteristics in the fragment shader and to implement characteristics that don't change as rapidly in the vertex shader. For instance, diffuse lighting effects change slowly over a surface and so can usually be computed with sufficient quality in the vertex shader. Specular lighting effects might need to be implemented in the fragment shader in order to achieve high quality. If a particular value changes linearly across an object's surface, you will get the same result by computing the value per vertex and using a varying variable to interpolate it as you would by computing the value at each fragment. In this case, you may as well have the vertex shader do the computation. Unless you are rendering very small triangles, your fragment shader will execute far more times than your vertex shader will, so it will be more efficient to do the computation in the vertex shader.

Similarly, you may be able to find computations that can be done once on the CPU and remain constant for a great many executions of your vertex shader or fragment shader. You can often save shader instruction space or improve shader performance (or both) by precomputing values in your application code and passing them to your shader as uniform variables. Sometimes you can spot these things by analyzing your shader code. If you pass *length* in as a uniform variable and your shader always computes **sqrt**(*length*), you're better off doing the computation once on the host CPU and passing that value to your shader rather than computing the value for every execution of your shader. If your shader needs both *length* and **sqrt**(*length*), you can pass both values in as uniform variables.

Deciding where to perform computation also involves knowing where the computational bottleneck occurs for a particular rendering operation. You only need speed up the slowest part of the system to see an improvement in performance. Conversely, you shouldn't spend your time improving the performance of something that isn't the bottleneck because you won't see the gain in performance anyway.

8.2.2 Analyze Your Algorithm

Often you can make your shader more efficient just by understanding the math it uses. For instance, you might want to limit the range of the variable *finalcolor* to [0,1]. But if you know that you are only adding values to compute this variable and the values that you're adding are always positive, there's really no need to check the result against 0. An instruction like **min**(*finalcolor*, 1.0) will clamp the result at 1.0, and this instruction will likely be higher performance than an instruction like **clamp**(*finalcolor*, 0.0, 1.0) because it needs only to compare values against one number instead of two. If you define the valid range of all the variables in your shader, it will be easier to see the boundary conditions that need to be handled.

8.2.3 Use the Built-in Functions

Whenever possible, use the built-in functions to implement the effect that you're trying to achieve. Built-in functions are intended to be implemented in an optimal way by the graphics hardware vendor. If your shader hand-codes the same effect as a built-in function, there's little chance that it will be faster than the built-in function but a good chance that it will be slower.

8.2.4   Use Vectors

The OpenGL Shading Language lets you express vector computations in a very natural way, and underlying graphics hardware is often built to operate on a vector of values simultaneously. Therefore, you should take advantage of this and use vectors for calculations whenever possible. On the other hand, you shouldn't use vectors that are bigger than the computations require. This can waste registers, hardware interpolants (in the case of varying variables), processing bandwidth, or memory bandwidth.

8.2.5   Use Textures to Encode Complex Functions

Because fragment processing is now programmable, textures can be used for a lot more than just image data. You might want to consider storing a complex function in a texture and doing a single lookup rather than a complex computation within the fragment shader. This is illustrated in Chapter 12 where a noise function is encoded as a 3D texture. This approach takes advantage of the specialized high-performance hardware that performs texture access, and it can also take advantage of texture filtering hardware to do interpolation between values encoded in the texture.

8.2.6   Review the Information Logs

One of the main ways that an OpenGL implementation will be able to provide feedback to an application developer is through the shader object and program object information logs (see Section 7.5). During shader development, you should review the messages in the information logs for compiler and linker errors, but you should also review them to see if they include any performance or functionality warnings or other descriptive messages. These information logs will be one of the primary ways for OpenGL implementations to convey implementation-dependent information about performance, resource limitations, and so on.

8.3   Shader Debugging

Shader development tools are in their infancy, so debugging shaders can be a difficult task. Here are a few practical tips that may be helpful as you try to debug your shaders.

8.3.1 Use the Vertex Shader Output

In order to see whether vertex shader code is behaving as expected, you can use conditionals to test intermediate values to see if the value is something unexpected. If it is, you can modify one of the shader's output values so that a visually distinct change occurs. For instance, if you think that the value *foo* should never be greater than 5.0, you can set the color values that are being passed on to the fragment shader to black or pink or neon green if the value of *foo* exceeds 5.0. If that's not distinctive enough and you've already computed the transformed homogeneous position, you can do something like this:

```
if (foo > 5.0)
    gl_Position += 1.0;
```

This will add 1 to each component of the transformed position for which *foo* was greater than 5. When it is executed, you should see the object shift on the screen. With this approach, you can systematically check your assumptions about the intermediate values being generated by the vertex shader.

8.3.2 Use the Fragment Shader Output

The only possible outcomes for a fragment shader are that it will output a fragment color, a fragment depth, or both a color and a depth or that the framebuffer will not be updated because the **discard** keyword was encountered. The depth value may not be helpful during debugging, but you can either color-code your fragment colors or use the **discard** keyword to discard fragments with certain qualities. This will provide you with some visual feedback about what's going on within the shader.

For instance, if you're not quite sure if your 2D texture coordinates span the whole range from 0 to 1.0, you might want to put an **if** test in the shader and discard fragments with certain qualities. You can discard all the fragments for which both *s* and *t* texture coordinates are greater than 0.5 or if either coordinate is greater than 0.99, and so on. The model will be drawn with "missing" pixels where fragments were discarded. The **discard** keyword is quite useful because it can appear anywhere in a fragment shader. You can put the discard statement near the beginning of a complex fragment shader and gradually move it down in the code as you verify that things are working properly.

Similarly, you can assign values to *gl_FragColor* that convey debugging information. If you have a mathematical function in your shader that is expected to range from [0,1] and average 0.5, you can assign solid green to *gl_FragColor* if the value is less than 0, solid red if it is between 0 and 0.5, solid blue if it is between 0.5 and 1.0, and solid white if it is greater than 1.0. This kind of debugging information can quickly tell you whether a certain computation is going astray.

8.3.3 Use Simple Geometry

For debugging texture computations, it may be useful to render a single large rectangle with identity matrices for the modeling, viewing, and projection matrices and to look carefully at what is occurring. Use a distinct texture image, for example, color bars or a gray scale ramp, so that you can visually verify that the texturing operation is occurring as you expect it to.

8.4 Shader Development Tools

In coming years, we should see some exciting advances in the area of tools for shader development. This section describes shader development tools available at the time of this writing.

8.4.1 RenderMonkey

As the era of programmable graphics hardware has unfolded, we've learned that there is more to developing shaders than just developing the code for the shaders themselves. Shaders can be highly customized to the point that they may work as intended only on a single model. Shader source code, textures, geometry, and initial values for uniform variables are all important parts of a production-quality shader. To aid developers, it is necessary to provide tools that capture all the essential elements of a shader and allow these elements to easily be modified and maintained.

Another factor in shader development is that the person writing the shader is not necessarily the same person that is developing the application code that deploys the shader. Oftentimes, an artist will be employed to design textures and to contribute to or even to control the shader development process. The collaboration between the artist and programmer is an important one for entertainment-based applications and must be supported by shader development tools.

An integrated development environment (IDE) allows programmers and artists to develop and experiment with shaders outside the environment of the application. This reduces the complexity of the shader development task and encourages rapid prototyping and experimentation. Finished shaders are a form of intellectual property, and maintenance, portability, and easy deployment to a variety of platforms are essential to maximizing the benefit of this type of company asset. The idea behind an IDE is that all of the essential elements of the finished shader can be encapsulated, managed, shared, and exported for use in the final application.

ATI first released an IDE called RenderMonkey in 2002. In its initial release, RenderMonkey supported shader development for DirectX vertex shaders and pixel shaders. However, RenderMonkey was architected in such a way that it could easily be extended to support other shader programming languages. In early 2004, ATI and 3Dlabs collaborated to produce a version of RenderMonkey that contains support for high-level shader development in OpenGL with the OpenGL Shading Language in addition to the support that it contains for DirectX shader development. The RenderMonkey IDE is currently available for free from both companies' Web sites (http://www.3dlabs.com and http://www.ati.com).

RenderMonkey was designed for extensibility. At its core is a flexible framework that allows easy incorporation of shading languages. It is intended to be an environment that is language agnostic, allowing any high-level shading language to be supported via plug-ins. It currently supports the pixel shaders and vertex shaders defined in Microsoft's DirectX 8.1 and 9.0, the High-Level Shader Language (HLSL) defined in DirectX 9.0, and the OpenGL Shading Language.

The encapsulation of all of the information necessary to recreate a shading effect is called an effect workspace. An effect workspace consists of effects group nodes, variable nodes, and stream mapping nodes. Each effects group is made up of one or more effect nodes, and each effect node is made up of one or more rendering passes. Each rendering pass may contain rendering state, source code for a vertex shader and a fragment shader, geometry, and textures. All of the effect data is organized into a tree hierarchy that is visible in the workspace viewer.

Effects group nodes are used to group related effects into a single container. This is sometimes handy for taming the complexity of dealing with lots of different effects. You might also use an effects group as a container for several similar effects with different performance characteristics (for instance, "best quality," "fast," and "fastest"). The criteria for grouping things within effects groups is entirely up to you.

Effect nodes encompass all the information needed to implement a real-time visual effect. The effect may be composed of multiple passes. Starting state is inherited from a default effect in order to provide a known starting state for all effects. The default effect can be used to store effect data that is common to all shading effects.

Pass nodes define a drawing operation. Each pass will inherit data from previous passes within the effect, and the first pass inherits from the default effect. A typical pass contains a vertex shader and fragment shader pair, a render state block, textures, geometry, and nodes of other types (e.g., variable nodes). Different geometry can be used in each pass to render things like fur.

Variable nodes define the parameters that are available from within a shader. For the purposes of the OpenGL Shading Language, variable nodes are the mechanisms for defining uniform variables. Intuitive names and types can be assigned to variable nodes, and the contents of a variable node can be manipulated with a GUI widget.

RenderMonkey is built completely out of plug-ins. Source code for some plug-ins is available, and you are encouraged to write your own plug-ins to perform tasks necessary for your work flow or to support importing and exporting your data using proprietary formats. Existing RenderMonkey modules are listed here.

• Shader editors—Modeled on the interface of Microsoft's Visual Studio in order to provide an intuitive interface; supports editing of vertex and fragment shaders; supports syntax coloring; supports creation of OpenGL, HLSL, and assembly language shaders.

• Variable editors—Shader parameters can be edited using GUI widgets that utilize knowledge of the underlying data type for editing; editors exist for colors, vectors, matrices, scalars; custom widgets can be created.

• Artist editor—Shader parameters relevant to the art designer can be presented in an artist-friendly fashion, allowing them to be viewed and modified; programmers can select which parameters are artist-editable; changes can be seen in real-time.

• Previewers—Allows real-time viewing of the shading effect; changes to the shader source code or its parameters are immediately reflected in the preview window; customizable view settings; preset views (front, back, side, etc.); support for DirectX 9.0 and OpenGL Shading Language/OpenGL previews.

- Exporter—Everything required to recreate a shading effect is encapsulated and written into a single XML file.

- Importer—Everything required to recreate a shading effect is read back from an XML file.

The XML file format was chosen as the basis for encapsulating shader information in RenderMonkey because it is an industry standard, it has a user-readable file format, it is user extensible, and there are lots of free parsers available for people to use. It is relatively easy to adapt an existing XML parser for your own use or to write a new one. The XML file that encapsulates a shader effect contains all shader source code, all render states, all models, and all texture information. This makes it straightforward to create, manage, and share shader assets.

8.4.2 OpenGL Shading Language Compiler Front End

In June 2003, 3Dlabs released an open source version of its lexical analyzer, parser, and semantic checker (i.e., an OpenGL Shading Language COMPILER FRONT END). This code is capable of reading an OpenGL shader and turning it into a token stream. This process is called LEXICAL ANALYSIS. The token stream is then processed to ensure that the program is comprised of valid statements. This process is referred to as SYNTACTIC ANALYSIS, or parsing. SEMANTIC ANALYSIS is then performed in order to determine whether the shader conforms to the semantic rules defined or implied by the OpenGL Shading Language specification. The result of this processing is turned into a high-level representation of the original source code. This high-level intermediate language (HIL) is a binary representation of the original source code that can be further processed by a target-specific back end to provide machine code for a particular type of graphics hardware.

It is anticipated that individual hardware vendors will implement the back end needed for their particular hardware. The compiler back end will typically include intellectual property and hardware-specific information that is proprietary to the graphics hardware vendor. It is not anticipated that 3Dlabs or other hardware vendors will make the source code for their compiler back ends public.

Still, the compiler front end provided by 3Dlabs has been, and will continue to be, a useful tool for the development of the OpenGL Shading Language, and it will be useful for other organizations that want to develop an OpenGL Shading Language compiler. As the language specification was nearing completion, the compiler front end was being developed. Except for the preprocessor (which was derived from another open source preprocessor), it was implemented from scratch using the publicly available system utilities *flex* and *bison*. It was not derived from existing code. This made it a clean way to double-check the specification and discover language flaws before the specification was released. Indeed, a number of such flaws were discovered through this effort, and, as a result, the specification was improved before its release.

Because of its clean implementation, the OpenGL Shading Language compiler front end also serves as additional technical documentation about the language. The specification should be your first stop, but if you really want to know the details of what's allowed in the language and what's not, studying the compiler front end will provide a definitive answer.

OpenGL implementors that base their compiler on the compiler front end from 3Dlabs will also be doing a big favor to their end users: the semantics of the OpenGL Shading Language will be checked in the same way for all implementations that use this front end. This will be a benefit to developers as they encounter consistent error-checking between different implementations.

Although few readers of this book will likely end up developing an OpenGL Shading Language compiler, this resource is nevertheless a useful one to know about. The source code for the compiler front end is available for download at the 3Dlabs Web site (http://www.3dlabs.com).

8.5 Summary

Writing shaders is similar in many ways to other software engineering tasks. A good dose of common sense can go a long way. Software engineering principles should be applied just like any other software engineering task. This is especially true in these early generations of programmable graphics hardware. Because early OpenGL Shading Language implementations might be incomplete in some ways, compilers will be immature, performance characteristics may differ widely between vendors, and tools to aid shader development are in their infancy. RenderMonkey is one shader development tool that is available now; hopefully others will rapidly follow.

On the other hand, writing shaders for programmable graphics hardware presents some unique challenges. Good decisions need to be made about how to split the computation between the CPU, the vertex processor, and the fragment processor. It is useful to have a solid foundation in mathematics and computer graphics before attempting to write shaders. Thorough knowledge of how OpenGL works is also a key asset, and having some understanding of the underlying graphics hardware can be helpful. It often pays to develop a shader together with an artist. This can help the shader implementor develop a shader that is parameterized in such a way that it can be put to a variety of uses in the final application.

8.6 Further Information

There are numerous books that describe sound software engineering principles and practices. Two that describe tactics specific to developing shaders are *Texturing and Modeling: A Procedural Approach* by Ebert, et. al. (2002) and *Advanced RenderMan: Creating CGI for Motion Pictures* by Apodaca and Gritz (1999). Some of the shader development discussion in these books is specific to RenderMan, but many of the principles are also relevant to developing shaders with the OpenGL Shading Language.

For performance tuning, the best advice I have right now is to become good friends with the developer relations staff at your favorite graphics hardware company (or companies). These are the people that can provide you with additional insight or information about the underlying graphics hardware architecture and the relative performance of various aspects of the hardware. Until we go through another generation or two of programmable graphics hardware development (and perhaps even longer), there will be lots of performance differences between various hardware architectures depending on the trade-offs made by the hardware architects and the driver developers. Scour the Web sites of these companies, attend their presentations at trade shows, and ask lots of questions.

The ATI developer Web site contains a number of presentations on Render-Monkey. The RenderMonkey IDE and documentation can be downloaded from either the ATI Web site or the 3Dlabs Web site.

[1] *3Dlabs developer Web site*. http://www.3dlabs.com/support/developer

[2] Apodaca, Anthony A., and Larry Gritz, *Advanced RenderMan: Creating CGI for Motion Pictures*, Morgan Kaufmann Publishers, San Francisco, 1999. http://www.bmrt.org/arman/materials.html

[3] *ATI developer Web site.* http://www.ati.com/na/pages/resource_
       centre/dev_rel/devrel.html

[4] Ebert, David S., John Hart, Bill Mark, F. Kenton Musgrave, Darwyn
       Peachey, Ken Perlin, and Steven Worley, *Texturing and Modeling:
       A Procedural Approach, Third Edition*, Morgan Kaufmann Publishers,
       San Francisco, 2002. http://www.texturingandmodeling.com

[5] *NVIDIA developer Web site.* http://developer.nvidia.com

Chapter 9

Traditional Shaders

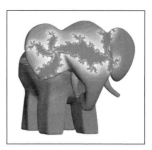

The programmability of OpenGL opens up many new possibilities for never before seen rendering effects. Still, it can be instructive to examine how some of OpenGL's fixed functionality rendering steps could be implemented with OpenGL shaders. While simplistic, these code snippets may be useful as stepping stones to bigger and better things.

This chapter describes OpenGL shader code that mimics the behavior of the OpenGL fixed functionality vertex and fragment processing. The goal of the shader code in this chapter is faithful representation of OpenGL 1.5 fixed functionality. The code examples in this chapter reference existing OpenGL state wherever possible through built-in variables. In your own shaders, feel free to provide these values as user-defined uniform variables rather than accessing existing OpenGL state. By doing this, you will be prepared to throw off the shackles of the OpenGL state machine and extend your shaders in exciting and different new ways.

9.1 Transformation

The features of the OpenGL Shading Language make it very easy to express transformations between the coordinate spaces defined by OpenGL. We've already seen the transformation that will be used by almost every vertex shader. The incoming vertex position must be transformed into clipping coordinates for use by the fixed functionality stages that occur after vertex processing. This is done in one of two ways, either this:

```
// Transform vertex to clip space
gl_Position = gl_ModelViewProjectionMatrix * gl_Vertex;
```

or this:

```
gl_Position = ftransform();
```

The only difference between these two methods is that the second case is guaranteed to compute the transformed position in exactly the same way as the fixed functionality method. Some implementations may have different hardware paths that result in small differences between the transformed position as computed by the first method and as computed by fixed functionality. This can cause problems in rendering if a multipass algorithm is used to render the same geometry more than once. In this case, the second method is preferred because it will produce the same transformed position as the fixed functionality.

OpenGL specifies that light positions are transformed by the modelview matrix when they are provided to OpenGL. This means that they are stored in eye coordinates. It is often convenient to perform lighting computations in eye space, so it will often be necessary to transform the incoming vertex position into eye coordinates as shown in Listing 9.1.

Listing 9.1   Computation of eye coordinate position

```
vec4 ecPosition;
vec3 ecPosition3;      // in 3 space

// Transform vertex to eye coordinates
if (NeedEyePosition)
{
    ecPosition  = gl_ModelViewMatrix * gl_Vertex;
    ecPosition3 = (vec3 (ecPosition)) / ecPosition.w;
}
```

This snippet of code computes the homogeneous point in eye space (a **vec4**) as well as the nonhomogeneous point (a **vec3**). Both values will be useful as we shall see.

To perform lighting calculations in eye space, incoming surface normals must also be transformed. A built-in uniform variable is available to access the normal transformation matrix, as shown in Listing 9.2.

Listing 9.2   Transformation of normal

```
normal = gl_NormalMatrix * gl_Normal;
```

In many cases, the application may not know anything about the characteristics of the surface normals that are being provided. In order to ensure that the lighting computations work correctly, it is necessary to normalize each incoming normal so that it is unit length. For OpenGL fixed functionality, normalization is a mode in OpenGL that can be controlled by providing the symbolic constant GL_NORMALIZE to **glEnable** or **glDisable**. In an OpenGL shader, if normalization is required, we do it as shown in Listing 9.3.

Listing 9.3   Normalization of normal

```
normal = normalize(normal);
```

Sometimes the application knows that it will always be sending normals that are unit length and that the modelview matrix is one that does uniform scaling. In this case, rescaling can be used to avoid the possibly expensive square root operation. The rescaling coefficients must be supplied by the application, and the normal can be scaled as shown in Listing 9.4.

Listing 9.4   Normal rescaling

```
normal = normal * gl_NormalScale;
```

The rescaling factors are stored as state within OpenGL and can be accessed from within a shader using the built-in uniform variable *gl_NormalScale*.

Texture coordinates can also be transformed. A texture matrix is defined for each texture unit in OpenGL and can be accessed with the built-in uniform matrix array variable *gl_TextureMatrix*. Incoming texture coordinates can be transformed in the same manner as vertex positions, as shown in Listing 9.5.

Listing 9.5   Texture coordinate transformation

```
gl_TexCoord[0] = gl_TextureMatrix[0] * gl_MultiTexCoord0;
```

9.2   Light Sources

The lighting computations defined by OpenGL are somewhat involved. Let's start by defining a function for each of the types of light sources defined by OpenGL: directional lights, point lights, and spotlights. We'll pass in variables that will store the total ambient, diffuse, and specular contributions from all light sources. These must be initialized to 0 before any of the light source computation routines are called.

9.2.1   Directional Lights

A directional light is a light that is assumed to be at an infinite distance from the objects being lit. As a result of this assumption, all light rays from the light source are parallel when they reach the scene. A single light direction vector can be used for every point in the scene. This assumption simplifies the math, so the code to implement a directional light source is simpler and will typically run faster than other types of lights. Because the light source is assumed to be infinitely far away, the direction of maximum highlights is the same for every point in the scene. This direction vector can be computed ahead of time for each light source *i* and stored in *gl_LightSource[i].halfVector*. This type of light source is useful for mimicking the effects of a light source like the sun.

The directional light function shown in Listing 9.6 computes the cosine of the angle between the surface normal and the light direction, as well as the cosine of the angle between the surface normal and the half angle between the light direction and the viewing direction. The former value is multiplied by the light's diffuse color to compute the diffuse component from the light. The latter value is raised to the power indicated by *gl_FrontMaterial.shininess* before being multiplied by the light's specular color.

The only way either a diffuse reflection component or a specular reflection component can be present is if the angle between the light source direction and the surface normal is in the range $[-90^\circ, 90^\circ]$. This is determined by examining *nDotVP*. This value is set to the greater of 0 and the cosine of the angle between the light source direction and the surface normal. If this value ends up being 0, the value that determines the amount of specular reflection is set to 0 as well. Our directional light function assumes that the vectors of interest are normalized, so the dot product between two vectors results in the cosine of the angle between them.

Listing 9.6 Directional light source computation

```
void DirectionalLight(in int i,
                      in vec3 normal,
                      inout vec4 ambient,
                      inout vec4 diffuse,
                      inout vec4 specular)
{
    float nDotVP;         // normal . light direction
    float nDotHV;         // normal . light half vector
    float pf;             // power factor

    nDotVP = max(0.0, dot(normal, vec3 (gl_LightSource[i].position)));
    nDotHV = max(0.0, dot(normal, vec3 (gl_LightSource[i].halfVector)));

    if (nDotVP == 0.0)
        pf = 0.0;
    else
        pf = pow(nDotHV, gl_FrontMaterial.shininess);
```

```
    ambient  += gl_LightSource[i].ambient;
    diffuse  += gl_LightSource[i].diffuse * nDotVP;
    specular += gl_LightSource[i].specular * pf;
}
```

9.2.2 Point Lights

Point lights are intended to mimic lights that are near the scene or within the scene such as lamps or ceiling lights or street lights. There are two main differences between point lights and directional lights. First, with this type of light source, the direction of maximum highlights must be computed at each vertex rather than using the precomputed value from *gl_LightSource[i].halfVector*. Second, light received at the surface is expected to decrease as the light source gets further and further away. This is called ATTENUATION. Each light source has constant, linear, and quadratic attenuation factors that are taken into account when computing the lighting contribution from a point light.

These differences show up in the first few lines of the point light function (see Listing 9.7). The first step is to compute the vector from the surface to the light position. This distance is computed using the length function. Next, *VP* is normalized so that it can be used in a dot product operation to compute a proper cosine value. The attenuation factor and the direction of maximum highlights are then computed as required. The remaining code is the same as for our directional light function, except that the diffuse and specular terms are multiplied by the attenuation factor.

One optimization that could be made is to have two point light functions, one that computes the attenuation factor and one that does not. If the values for the constant, linear, and quadratic attenuation factors are (1, 0, 0) (the default values), you can use the function that does not compute attenuation and get better performance.

Listing 9.7 Point light source computation

```
void PointLight(in int i,
                in vec3 eye,
                in vec3 ecPosition3,
                in vec3 normal,
                inout vec4 ambient,
                inout vec4 diffuse,
                inout vec4 specular)
{
    float nDotVP;          // normal . light direction
    float nDotHV;          // normal . light half vector
```

```
float pf;              // power factor
float attenuation;     // computed attenuation factor
float d;               // distance from surface to light source
vec3  VP;              // direction from surface to light position
vec3  halfVector;      // direction of maximum highlights

// Compute vector from surface to light position
VP = vec3 (gl_LightSource[i].position) - ecPosition3;

// Compute distance between surface and light position
d = length(VP);

// Normalize the vector from surface to light position
VP = normalize(VP);

// Compute attenuation
attenuation = 1.0 / (gl_LightSource[i].constantAttenuation +
                gl_LightSource[i].linearAttenuation * d +
                gl_LightSource[i].quadraticAttenuation * d * d);

halfVector = normalize(VP + eye);

nDotVP = max(0.0, dot(normal, VP));
nDotHV = max(0.0, dot(normal, halfVector));

if (nDotVP == 0.0)
    pf = 0.0;
else
    pf = pow(nDotHV, gl_FrontMaterial.shininess);

ambient  += gl_LightSource[i].ambient;
diffuse  += gl_LightSource[i].diffuse * nDotVP * attenuation;
specular += gl_LightSource[i].specular * pf * attenuation;
}
```

9.2.3 Spotlights

In stage and cinema, spotlights provide a strong beam of light that produces illumination in a well-defined area. The illuminated area can be further shaped through the use of flaps or shutters on the sides of the light. OpenGL includes light attributes that are used to simulate a simple type of spotlight. Whereas point lights are modeled as sending light equally in all directions, OpenGL models spotlights as light sources that are restricted to producing a cone of light in a particular direction.

The first and last parts of our spotlight function (see Listing 9.8) look the same as our point light function (see Listing 9.7). The differences occur in the middle of the function. A spotlight has a focus direction

(*gl_LightSource[i].spotDirection*), and this direction is dotted with
the vector from the light position to the surface (−*VP*). The resulting
cosine value is compared to the precomputed cosine cutoff value
(*gl_LightSource[i].spotCosCutoff*) in order to determine whether the position on the surface is inside or outside of the spotlight's cone of illumination. If it is outside, the spotlight attenuation is set to 0; otherwise, this
value is raised to a power specified by *gl_LightSource[i].spotExponent*. The
resulting spotlight attenuation factor is multiplied by the previously
computed attenuation factor to get the overall attenuation factor. The
remaining lines of code are the same as they were for point lights.

Listing 9.8 Spotlight computation

```
void SpotLight(in int i,
               in vec3 eye,
               in vec3 ecPosition3,
               in vec3 normal,
               inout vec4 ambient,
               inout vec4 diffuse,
               inout vec4 specular)
{
    float nDotVP;           // normal . light direction
    float nDotHV;           // normal . light half vector
    float pf;               // power factor
    float spotDot;          // cosine of angle between spotlight
    float spotAttenuation;  // spotlight attenuation factor
    float attenuation;      // computed attenuation factor
    float d;                // distance from surface to light source
    vec3 VP;                // direction from surface to light position
    vec3 halfVector;        // direction of maximum highlights

    // Compute vector from surface to light position
    VP = vec3 (gl_LightSource[i].position) - ecPosition3;

    // Compute distance between surface and light position
    d = length(VP);

    // Normalize the vector from surface to light position
    VP = normalize(VP);

    // Compute attenuation
    attenuation = 1.0 / (gl_LightSource[i].constantAttenuation +
                         gl_LightSource[i].linearAttenuation * d +
                         gl_LightSource[i].quadraticAttenuation * d * d);

    // See if point on surface is inside cone of illumination
    spotDot = dot(-VP, gl_LightSource[i].spotDirection);
```

```
    if (spotDot < gl_LightSource[i].spotCosCutoff)
        spotAttenuation = 0.0; // light adds no contribution
    else
        spotAttenuation = pow(spotDot, gl_LightSource[i].spotExponent);

    // Combine the spotlight and distance attenuation.
    attenuation *= spotAttenuation;

    halfVector = normalize(VP + eye);

    nDotVP = max(0.0, dot(normal, VP));
    nDotHV = max(0.0, dot(normal, halfVector));

    if (nDotVP == 0.0)
        pf = 0.0;
    else
        pf = pow(nDotHV, gl_FrontMaterial.shininess);

    ambient  += gl_LightSource[i].ambient;
    diffuse  += gl_LightSource[i].diffuse * nDotVP * attenuation;
    specular += gl_LightSource[i].specular * pf * attenuation;
}
```

9.3 Material Properties and Lighting

OpenGL lighting calculations require knowing the viewing direction in the eye coordinate system in order to compute specular reflection terms. By default, the view direction is assumed to be parallel to and in the direction of the $-z$ axis. OpenGL also has a mode that requires the viewing direction to be computed from the origin of the eye coordinate system (local viewer). To compute this, we can transform the incoming vertex into eye space using the current modelview matrix. The x, y, and z coordinates of this point are divided by the homogeneous coordinate w in order to get a **vec3** value that can be used directly in the lighting calculations. The computation of this eye coordinate position (*ecPosition3*) was illustrated in Section 9.1. To get a unit vector corresponding to the viewing direction, the eye space position is normalized and negated. Shader code to implement these computations is shown in Listing 9.9.

Listing 9.9 Local viewer computation

```
if (LocalViewer)
    eye = -normalize(ecPosition3);
else
    eye = vec3 (0.0, 0.0, 1.0);
```

With the viewing direction calculated, we can initialize the variables that will be used to accumulate the ambient, diffuse, and specular lighting contributions from all of the light sources in the scene. Then we can call the functions defined in the previous section to compute the contributions from each light source. In the code in Listing 9.10, we assume that all lights with an index less than the constant NumEnabledLights are enabled. Directional lights are distinguished by having a position parameter with a homogeneous (w) coordinate equal to 0 at the time they were provided to OpenGL. (These positions are transformed by the modelview matrix when the light is specified, so the w coordinate will remain 0 after transformation if the last column of the modelview matrix is the typical (0 0 0 1)). Point lights are distinguished by having a spotlight cutoff angle equal to 180.

Listing 9.10 Loop to compute contributions from all enabled light sources

```
// Clear the light intensity accumulators
amb  = vec4 (0.0);
diff = vec4 (0.0);
spec = vec4 (0.0);

// Loop through enabled lights, compute contribution from each
for (i = 0; i < NumEnabledLights; i++)
{
    if (gl_LightSource[i].position.w == 0.0)
        DirectionalLight(i, normal, amb, diff, spec);
    else if (gl_LightSource[i].spotCutoff == 180.0)
        PointLight(i, eye, ecPosition3, normal, amb, diff, spec);
    else
        SpotLight(i, eye, ecPosition3, normal, amb, diff, spec);
}
```

One of the changes made to OpenGL in version 1.2 was to add functionality to compute the color at a vertex in two parts: a primary color that contains the combination of the emissive, ambient, and diffuse terms as computed by the usual lighting equations, and a secondary color that contains just the specular term as computed by the usual lighting equations. If this mode is not enabled (the default case), the primary color is computed with the combination of emissive, ambient, diffuse, and specular terms.

Computing the specular contribution separately allows specular highlights to be applied after texturing has occurred. The specular value is added to the computed color after texturing has occurred to allow the specular highlights to be the color of the light source rather than the color of the surface.

Listing 9.11 shows how to compute the surface color (according to OpenGL rules) with everything but the specular contribution:

Listing 9.11   Surface color computation, omitting the specular contribution

```
color = gl_FrontLightModelProduct.sceneColor +
            amb  * gl_FrontMaterial.ambient +
            diff * gl_FrontMaterial.diffuse;
```

The OpenGL Shading Language conveniently provides us a built-in variable (*gl_FrontLightModelProduct.sceneColor*) that contains the emissive material property for front facing surfaces plus the product of the ambient material property for front facing surfaces and the global ambient light for the scene (i.e., *gl_FrontMaterial.emission + gl_FrontMaterial.ambient * gl_LightModel.ambient*). We can add this together with the intensity of reflected ambient light and the intensity of reflected diffuse light. Next, we can do the appropriate computations, depending on whether the separate specular color mode is indicated, as shown in Listing 9.12.

Listing 9.12   Final surface color computation

```
if (SeparateSpecular)
    gl_FrontSecondaryColor = vec4 (spec *
                                    gl_FrontMaterial.specular, 1.0);
else
    color += spec * gl_FrontMaterial.specular;

gl_FrontColor = color;
```

There is no need to perform clamping on the values assigned to *gl_FrontSecondaryColor* and *gl_FrontColor* because these will be clamped automatically by definition.

9.4 Two-Sided Lighting

To mimic OpenGL's two-sided lighting behavior, you need to invert the surface normal and perform the same computations as defined in the preceding section using the back-facing material properties. You can probably do it more cleverly than this, but it might look like Listing 9.13.

Listing 9.13   Two-sided lighting computation

```
normal = -normal;

// Clear the light intensity accumulators
```

```
amb  = vec4 (0.0);
diff = vec4 (0.0);
spec = vec4 (0.0);

// Loop through enabled lights, compute contribution from each
for (i = 0; i < NumEnabledLights; i++)
{
    if (gl_LightSource[i].position.w == 0.0)
        DirectionalLight(i, normal, amb, diff, spec);
    else if (gl_LightSource[i].spotCutoff == 180.0)
        PointLight(i, eye, ecPosition3, normal, amb, diff, spec);
    else
        SpotLight(i, eye, ecPosition3, normal, amb, diff, spec);
}

color = gl_BackLightModelProduct.sceneColor +
        amb * gl_BackMaterial.ambient +
        diff * gl_BackMaterial.diffuse;

if (SeparateSpecular)
    gl_BackSecondaryColor = vec4 (spec *
                                  gl_BackMaterial.specular, 1.0);
else
    color += spec * gl_BackMaterial.specular;

gl_BackColor = color;
```

There is no need to perform clamping on the values assigned to *gl_BackSecondaryColor* and *gl_BackColor* because these will be clamped automatically by definition.

9.5 No Lighting

If there are no enabled lights in the scene, it is a simple matter to pass the per-vertex color and secondary color on for further processing with the following commands shown in Listing 9.14.

Listing 9.14 Setting final color values with no lighting

```
if (SecondaryColor)
    gl_FrontSecondaryColor = gl_SecondaryColor;

// gl_FrontColor will be clamped automatically by OpenGL
gl_FrontColor = gl_Color;
```

9.6 Fog

In OpenGL, DEPTH-CUING and fog effects are controlled by fog parameters. A fog factor is computed using one of three equations, and this fog factor is used to perform a linear blend between the fog color and the computed color for the fragment. The depth value to be used in the fog equation can be either the fog coordinate passed in as a standard vertex attribute (*gl_FogCoord*) or the eye-coordinate distance from the eye. In the latter case it is usually sufficient to approximate the depth value using the absolute value of the *z*-coordinate in eye space (i.e., **abs**(*ecPosition.z*)). When there is a wide angle of view, this approximation may cause a noticeable artifact (too little fog) near the edges. If this is the case, you could compute *z* as the true distance from the eye to the fragment with **length**(*ecPosition*). (This method involves a square root computation, so the code may run slower as a result.) The choice of which depth value to use would normally be done in the vertex shader as follows:

```
if (UseFogCoordinate)
    gl_FogFragCoord = gl_FogCoord;
else
    gl_FogFragCoord = abs(ecPosition.z);
```

A linear computation (which corresponds to the traditional computer graphics operation of depth-cuing) can be selected in OpenGL with the symbolic constant GL_LINEAR. For this case, the fog factor *f* is computed using the following equation:

$$f = \frac{end - z}{end - start}$$

start, *end*, and *z* are all distances in eye coordinates. *start* is the distance to where the fog effect starts, *end* is the distance to where the effect ends, and *z* is the value stored in *gl_FogFragCoord*. The start and end positions can be provided explicitly as uniform variables, or we can access the current values in OpenGL state by using the built-in variables *gl_Fog.start* and *gl_Fog.end*. The shader code to compute the fog factor in this fashion using the built-in variables for accessing OpenGL state is shown in Listing 9.15.

Listing 9.15 GL_LINEAR fog computation

```
fog = (gl_Fog.end - gl_FogFragCoord)) * gl_Fog.scale;
```

Because $1.0 / (gl\_Fog.end - gl\_Fog.start)$ doesn't depend on any per-vertex or per-fragment state, this value is precomputed and made available as the built-in variable *gl_Fog.scale*.

A more realistic fog effect may be achieved with an exponential function. By using a negative exponent value, the exponential function will model the diminishing of the original color as a function of distance. A simple exponential fog function can be selected in OpenGL with the symbolic constant GL_EXP. The formula corresponding to this fog function is

$$f = e^{-(density \cdot z)}$$

The z value is computed as described for the previous function, and *density* is a value that represents the density of the fog. *density* can be provided as a uniform variable, or the built-in variable *gl_Fog.density* can be used to obtain the current value from OpenGL state. The larger this value becomes, the "thicker" the fog becomes. For this function to work as intended, *density* must be greater than or equal to 0.

The OpenGL Shading Language does not have a built-in **exp** (base *e*) function, but it does have a base 2 exponential function, **exp2**. We can get the result we're after by remembering that $\mathbf{exp}(x) = \mathbf{exp2}(x / \mathbf{log}(2))$. We compute the reciprocal of the natural log of 2 and get the constant 1.442695. Our OpenGL shader code to compute the preceding equation is shown in Listing 9.16.

Listing 9.16 GL_EXP fog computation

```
const float LOG2E = 1.442695;     // = 1 / log(2)
fog = exp2(-gl_Fog.density * gl_FogFragCoord * LOG2E);
```

This code is illustrating the formula defined for OpenGL 1.5 fixed functionality. If you decide to use this formula for fog, you can improve the code by multiplying the constant LOG2E by *−gl_Fog.density* in the application and passing the result as a user-defined uniform. This will save a multiply operation in the previous expression.

The final fog function defined by OpenGL is selected with the symbolic constant GL_EXP2 and is defined as

$$f = e^{-(density \cdot z)^2}$$

This function changes the slope of the exponential decay function by squaring the exponent. The OpenGL shader code to implement it looks very similar to the previous function (see Listing 9.17).

Listing 9.17 GL_EXP2 fog computation

```
const float LOG2E = 1.442695;    // = 1 / log(2)
fog = exp2(-gl_Fog.density * gl_Fog.density *
           gl_FogFragCoord * gl_FogFragCoord * LOG2E);
```

The performance of this code would be improved by passing in a single user-defined uniform that contains the value of *–gl_Fog.density* * *gl_Fog.density* * LOG2E.

OpenGL also requires the final value for the fog factor to be limited to the range [0, 1]. We can accomplish this with the statement in Listing 9.18.

Listing 9.18 Clamping the fog factor

```
fog = clamp(fog, 0.0, 1.0);
```

Any of these three fog functions can be computed in either a vertex shader or a fragment shader. Unless you have very large polygons in your scene, you probably won't see any difference if the fog factor is computed in the vertex shader and passed to the fragment shader as a **varying** variable. This will probably also give you better performance overall, so it's generally the preferred approach. In the fragment shader, when the (almost) final color is computed, the fog factor can be used to compute a linear blend between the fog color and the (almost) final fragment color. The OpenGL shader code in Listing 9.19 does the trick using the fog color saved as part of current OpenGL state.

Listing 9.19 Applying fog to compute final color value

```
color = mix(vec3 (gl_Fog.color), color, fog);
```

The code presented in this section can be used to achieve the same results as OpenGL's fixed functionality. But with programmability, you are free to use a completely different approach to compute fog effects.

9.7 Texture Coordinate Generation

OpenGL can be set up to compute texture coordinates automatically based only on the incoming vertex positions. There are five methods that are defined, and each can be useful for certain purposes. The texture generation mode specified by GL_OBJECT_LINEAR is useful for cases where a texture is intended to remain fixed to a geometric model, such as in a terrain modeling application. GL_EYE_LINEAR is useful for producing dynamic contour lines on an object. Examples of this usage include a scientist studying isosurfaces or a geologist interpreting seismic data. GL_SPHERE_ MAP can be used to generate texture coordinates that can be used for simple environment mapping. GL_REFLECTION_MAP and GL_NORMAL_MAP can be used in conjunction with cube map textures. GL_REFLECTION_MAP passes the reflection vector as the texture coordinate. GL_NORMAL_MAP simply passes the computed eye space normal as the texture coordinate.

A function that can be used to generate sphere map coordinates according to the OpenGL specification is shown in Listing 9.20.

Listing 9.20 GL_SPHERE_MAP computation

```
vec2 SphereMap(in vec3 ecPosition3, in vec3 normal)
{
    float m;
    vec3 r, u;
    u = normalize(ecPosition3);
    r = reflect(u, normal);
    m = 2.0 * sqrt(r.x * r.x + r.y * r.y + (r.z + 1.0) * (r.z + 1.0));
    return vec2 (r.x / m + 0.5, r.y / m + 0.5);
}
```

A function that can be used to generate reflection map coordinates according to the OpenGL specification looks almost identical to the function shown in Listing 9.20. The difference is that it returns the reflection vector as its result (see Listing 9.21).

Listing 9.21 GL_REFLECTION_MAP computation

```
vec3 ReflectionMap(in vec3 ecPosition3, in vec3 normal)
{
    float NdotU, m;
    vec3 u;
    u = normalize(ecPosition3);
    return (reflect(u, normal));
}
```

Selecting between the five texture generation methods and computing the appropriate texture coordinate values can be accomplished with the code shown in Listing 9.22.

Listing 9.22 Texture coordinate generation computation

```
// Compute sphere map coordinates if needed
if (TexGenSphere)
    sphereMap = SphereMap(ecposition3, normal);

// Compute reflection map coordinates if needed
if (TexGenReflection)
    reflection = ReflectionMap(ecposition3, normal);

// Compute texture coordinate for each enabled texture unit
for (i = 0; i < NumEnabledTextureUnits; i++)
{
    if (TexGenObject)
    {
        gl_TexCoord[i].s = dot(gl_Vertex, gl_ObjectPlaneS[i]);
        gl_TexCoord[i].t = dot(gl_Vertex, gl_ObjectPlaneT[i]);
        gl_TexCoord[i].p = dot(gl_Vertex, gl_ObjectPlaneR[i]);
        gl_TexCoord[i].q = dot(gl_Vertex, gl_ObjectPlaneQ[i]);
    }

    if (TexGenEye)
    {
        gl_TexCoord[i].s = dot(ecPosition, gl_EyePlaneS[i]);
        gl_TexCoord[i].t = dot(ecPosition, gl_EyePlaneT[i]);
        gl_TexCoord[i].p = dot(ecPosition, gl_EyePlaneR[i]);
        gl_TexCoord[i].q = dot(ecPosition, gl_EyePlaneQ[i]);
    }

    if (TexGenSphere)
        gl_TexCoord[i] = vec4(sphereMap, 0.0, 1.0);

    if (TexGenReflection)
        gl_TexCoord[i] = vec4(reflection, 1.0);

    if (TexGenNormal)
        gl_TexCoord[i] = vec4(normal, 1.0);
}
```

In this code, we assume that each texture unit less than NumEnabledTextureUnits is enabled. If this value is 0, the whole loop will be skipped. Otherwise, each texture coordinate that is needed will be computed in the loop.

Because the sphere map and reflection computations do not depend on any of the texture unit state, they can be performed once, and the result is used for all texture units. For the GL_OBJECT_LINEAR and GL_EYE_LINEAR methods, there is a plane equation for each component of each set of texture coordinates. For the former case, the components of *gl_TexCoord[0]* are generated by multiplying the plane equation coefficients for the specified component by the incoming vertex position. For the latter case, the components of *gl_TexCoord[0]* are computed by multiplying the plane equation coefficients by the eye coordinate position of the vertex. Depending on what type of texture access is done during fragment processing, it may not be necessary to compute the t, p,[1] or q texture component, so these computations could be eliminated.

9.8 User Clipping

To take advantage of OpenGL's user clipping (which remains as fixed functionality in between vertex processing and fragment processing in programmable OpenGL), a vertex shader must transform the incoming vertex position into the same coordinate space as that in which the user clip planes are stored. The usual case is that the user clip planes are stored in eye space coordinates, so the OpenGL shader code shown in Listing 9.23 can be used to provide the transformed vertex position.

Listing 9.23 User-clipping computation

```
gl_ClipVertex = gl_ModelViewMatrix * gl_Vertex;
```

9.9 Texture Application

The built-in texture functions are used to read values from texture memory. The values read from texture memory can be used in a variety of ways. OpenGL fixed functionality includes support for texture application formulas enabled with the symbolic constants GL_REPLACE, GL_MODU-LATE, GL_DECAL, GL_BLEND, and GL_ADD. These modes operate differently, depending on the format of the texture being accessed. The following code illustrates the case where an RGBA texture is accessed using the sampler *tex0*. The variable *color* is initialized to be *gl_Color* and then modified as needed so that it contains the color value that results from texture application.

---

[1] For historical reasons, the OpenGL texture coordinate components are named s, t, r, and q. Because of the desire to have single letter component selection names in the OpenGL Shading Language, components for textures are named s, t, p, and q. This avoids using r, which is needed for selecting color components as r, g, b, and a.

GL_REPLACE is the simplest texture application mode of all. It simply replaces the current fragment color with the value read from texture memory. See Listing 9.24.

Listing 9.24 GL_REPLACE computation

```
color = texture2D(tex0, gl_TexCoord[0].xy);
```

GL_MODULATE causes the incoming fragment color to be multiplied by the value retrieved from texture memory. This is a good texture function to use if lighting is computed before texturing (e.g., the vertex shader performs the lighting computation, and the fragment shader does the texturing). White can be used as the base color for an object rendered with this technique, and the texture then provides the diffuse color. This technique is illustrated with the following OpenGL shader code in Listing 9.25.

Listing 9.25 GL_MODULATE computation

```
color *= texture2D(tex0, gl_TexCoord[0].xy);
```

GL_DECAL is useful for applying an opaque image to a portion of an object. For instance, you might want to apply a number and company logos to the surfaces of a race car or tattoos to the skin of a character in a game. When an RGBA texture is accessed, the alpha value at each texel is used to linearly interpolate between the incoming fragment's RGB value and the texture's RGB value. The incoming fragment's alpha value is used as is. The code for implementing this mode is in Listing 9.26.

Listing 9.26 GL_DECAL computation

```
vec4 texture = texture2D(tex0, gl_TexCoord[0].xy);
vec3 col = mix(color.rgb, texture.rgb, texture.a);
color = vec4 (col, color.a);
```

GL_BLEND is the only texture application mode that takes the current texture environment color into effect. The RGB values read from the texture are used to linearly interpolate between the RGB values of the incoming fragment and the texture environment color. The new alpha value is computed by multiplying the alpha of the incoming fragment by the alpha read from the texture. The OpenGL shader code is shown in Listing 9.27.

Listing 9.27 GL_BLEND computation

```
vec4 texture = texture2D(tex0, gl_TexCoord[0].xy);
vec3 col = mix(color.rgb, gl_TextureEnvColor[0].rgb, texture.rgb);
color = vec4 (col, color.a * texture.a);
```

GL_ADD computes the sum of the incoming fragment color and the value read from the texture. The two alpha values are multiplied together to compute the new alpha value. This is the only traditional texture application mode for which the resulting values can exceed the range [0,1], so we clamp the final result (see Listing 9.28).

Listing 9.28 GL_ADD computation

```
vec4 texture = texture2D(tex0, gl_TexCoord[0].xy);
color.rgb += texture.rgb;
color.a   *= texture.a;
color = clamp (color, 0.0, 1.0);
```

The texture combine environment mode that was added in OpenGL 1.3 and extended in OpenGL 1.4 defines a large number of additional simple ways to perform texture application A variety of new formulas, source values, and operands were defined. The mapping of these additional modes into OpenGL shader code is straightforward but tiresome, so it is omitted here.

9.10 Summary

The rendering formulas specified by OpenGL have been reasonable ones to implement in fixed functionality hardware for the past decade or so, but they are not necessarily the best ones to use in your shaders. Still, it can be instructive to see how these formulas can be expressed in shaders written in the OpenGL Shading Language. The shader examples presented in this chapter demonstrate the expression of these fixed functionality rendering formulas, but they should not be considered optimal implementations. Take the ideas and the shading code illustrated in this chapter and adapt them to your own needs.

9.11 Further Information

Complete, working shaders that contain the code described in this chapter can be downloaded from this book's Web site at http://www.3dshaders.com.

The *OpenGL Programming Guide, Third Edition*, by the OpenGL Architecture Review Board, Woo, Neider, Davis, and Shreiner (1999), contains more complete descriptions of the various formulas presented in this chapter. The functionality is defined in the OpenGL specification, *The OpenGL Graphics System: A Specification, (Version 1.4)*, by Mark Segal and Kurt Akeley, edited by

Chris Frazier and Jon Leech (2002). Basic graphics concepts like transformation, lighting, fog, and texturing are also covered in standard graphics texts such as *Introduction to Computer Graphics* by Foley, van Dam, et. al., (1994). *Real-Time Rendering*, by Akenine-Möller and Haines (2002), also contains good descriptions of these basic topics.

[1] *3Dlabs developer Web site.* http://www.3dlabs.com/support/developer

[2] Akenine-Möller, Tomas, E. Haines, *Real-Time Rendering, Second Edition*, A K Peters, Ltd., Natick, Massachusetts, 2002. http://www.realtimerendering.com

[3] Foley, J.D., A. van Dam, S.K. Feiner, J.H. Hughes, and R.L. Philips, *Introduction to Computer Graphics*, Addison-Wesley, Reading, Massachusetts, 1994.

[4] Foley, J.D., A. van Dam, S.K. Feiner, and J.H. Hughes, *Computer Graphics: Principles and Practice, Second Edition in C, Second Edition*, Addison-Wesley, Reading, Massachusetts, 1996.

[5] OpenGL Architecture Review Board, J. Neider, T. Davis, and M. Woo, *OpenGL Programming Guide, Third Edition: The Official Guide to Learning OpenGL, Version 1.2.*, Addison-Wesley, Reading, Massachusetts, 1999.

[6] OpenGL Architecture Review Board, *OpenGL Reference Manual, Third Edition: The Official Document to OpenGL, Version 1.2.*, Addison-Wesley, Reading, Massachusetts, 1999.

[7] Segal, Mark, and Kurt Akeley, *The OpenGL Graphics System: A Specification (Version 1.5)*, Editor (v1.1): Chris Frazier, Editor (v1.2–1.5): Jon Leech, July 2003. http://opengl.org

Chapter 10

Stored Texture Shaders

Texture mapping is a very powerful mechanism built into OpenGL. At the time OpenGL was initially defined (1992), texture mapping hardware was just starting to be available on commercial products. Nowadays, texture mapping is available on graphics hardware at all price points, even entry-level consumer graphics boards.

When OpenGL 1.0 was defined, texture mapping had a fairly narrow definition. It was simply a way to apply an image to the surface of an object. Since then, hardware has become capable of doing much more in this area, and researchers have come up with a lot of interesting things to do with textures other than just plastering images on surfaces. The scope of texture mapping has also been extended in OpenGL. Texture objects were one of the key additions in OpenGL 1.1. Three-dimensional textures were made part of the standard in OpenGL 1.2. The capability of hardware to access two or more textures simultaneously was exposed in OpenGL 1.3, along with cube map textures and a framework for supporting compressed textures formats. OpenGL 1.4 added support for depth textures and shadows, automatic mipmap generation, and another texture wrap mode (mirrored repeat). If you need a quick review of how texturing works in OpenGL, refer to Section 1.10.

The programmability introduced with the OpenGL Shading Language allows for a much broader definition of texture mapping. With programmable shaders, an application can read values from any number of textures and use them in any way that makes sense. This includes supporting sophisticated algorithms that use the results of one texture access to define the parameters of another texture access. Textures can also be used to store intermediate rendering results; they can be used as lookup tables for complex functions; they can be used for storing normals, normal perturbation factors,

235

gloss values, visibility information, and polynomial coefficients; and many other things. These things could not be done nearly as easily, if at all, in unextended OpenGL, and this flexibility means that texture maps are coming closer to being general purpose memory that can be used for arbitrary purposes. (Filtering and wrapping behavior still differentiate texture map access from normal memory access operations.)

This chapter describes several shaders that, at their core, rely on looking up values in texture memory and using those values to achieve interesting effects. We'll start by talking a little bit about how textures are accessed from within a shader, and then we'll look at several examples of shaders that access texture memory for various purposes other than just the straightforward application of an image to the surface of a 3D object.

10.1   Accessing Texture Maps from a Shader

Applications are required to set up and initialize texturing state properly before executing a shader that accesses texture memory. An application needs to perform the following steps in order to set up a texture for use within a shader:

1. Select a specific texture unit, and make it active by calling **glActiveTexture**.

2. Create a texture object, and bind it to the active texture unit by calling **glBindTexture**.

3. Set various parameters (wrapping, filtering, etc.) of the texture object by calling **glTexParameter**.

4. Define the texture using **glTexImage**.

Two additional steps are required if using fixed functionality but not if using an OpenGL shader—enabling the desired texture on the texture unit by calling **glEnable** and setting the texture function for the texture unit (modulate, decal, replace, etc.) by calling **glTexEnv**. (These steps are not required when using an OpenGL shader because the fixed functionality hierarchy of texture enables is ignored and the texture function is expressed within the shader code.) When these steps have been completed, the texture is ready for use by an OpenGL shader.

It is quite straightforward to access textures from within a shader after texture state has been set up properly by the application. The OpenGL

Shading Language has built-in data types (see Section 3.2.4) and built-in functions (see Section 5.7) to accomplish this task.

A uniform variable of type **sampler** must be used to access a texture from within a shader. Within a shader, a sampler is considered an opaque data type containing a value that can be used to access a particular texture. The shader is responsible for declaring such a uniform variable for each texture that it wants to access. The application must provide a value for the sampler prior to execution of the shader as described in Section 7.8.

The type of the sampler indicates the type of texture that is to be accessed. A variable of type **sampler1D** is used to access a 1D texture; a variable of type **sampler2D** is used to access a 2D texture; a variable of type **sampler3D** is used to access a 3D texture; a variable of type **samplerCube** is used to access a cube map texture; and variables of type **samplerShadow1D** and **samplerShadow2D** are used to access 1D and 2D depth textures. For instance, if the application intends to use texture unit 4 to store a 2D texture, the shader must declare a uniform variable of type **sampler2D**, and the application must load a value of 4 into this variable prior to the execution of the shader.

The built-in functions **texture1D, texture2D, texture3D, textureCube, shadow1D**, and so on, perform texture access within a shader. The first argument in each of these built-in functions is a sampler, and the type of the sampler must correspond to the name of the function. For instance, a sampler of type **sampler1D** must be the first argument to **texture1D**, a sampler of type **sampler2D** must be the first argument to **texture2D**, and so on. Mismatches will cause a compiler error to occur.

Each of these built-in texture access functions also takes a texture coordinate as an argument. This texture coordinate is used by the hardware to determine which locations in the texture map are to be accessed. A 1D texture will be accessed using a single floating-point texture coordinate. A 2D texture will be accessed with a **vec2**, and a 3D texture will be accessed with a **vec3**. Projective versions of the texture access functions are also provided. In these functions, the individual components of the texture coordinate are divided by the last component of the texture coordinate and the result is used in the texture access operation.

There are some differences between accessing a texture from a vertex shader and accessing a texture from a fragment shader (the OpenGL Shading Language allows both). The level of detail to be used when accessing a mipmap texture is calculated by fixed functionality in between the vertex processor and the fragment processor. Therefore, this value is known within the fragment processor but not within the vertex processor. For this reason, the OpenGL Shading Language includes special built-in functions that can be used only in a vertex shader that allows the level of detail to be expressed directly as a function argument. The OpenGL Shading Language also includes built-in functions that can only be used in a fragment shader that allows a level-of-detail bias to be passed in. This bias value is added to the mechanically computed level-of-detail value. In this way, a shader writer can add a little extra sharpness or blurriness to the texture mapping function, depending on the situation. If any of these functions is used with a texture that is not a mipmap texture, the level-of-detail bias value will be ignored.

The built-in functions to access cube maps (**textureCube** and **textureCubeLod**) operate in the same way as defined for fixed functionality. The texture coordinate that is provided is treated as a direction vector that emanates from the center of a cube. This value is used to select one of the cube map's 2D textures based on the coordinate with the largest magnitude. The other two coordinates are divided by the absolute value of this coordinate and scaled and biased in order to calculate a 2D coordinate that will be used to access the chosen face of the cube map.

The built-in functions to access depth textures (**shadow1D**, **shadow2D**, etc.) also operate in the same way as defined for fixed functionality. The texture accessed by one of these functions must have a base internal format of GL_DEPTH_COMPONENT. The value that is returned when accessing this type of texture depends on the texture comparison mode, the texture comparison function, and the depth texture mode. Each of these values can be set by calling **glTexParameter**.

The built-in texture access functions operate according to the current state of the texture unit that is being accessed and according to the parameters of the texture object that is bound to that texture unit. In other words, the value returned by the built-in texture access functions will take into consideration the texturing state that has already been established for the texture unit and the texture object, including wrap mode, minification filter, magnification filter, border color, minimum/maximum level of detail, texture comparison mode, and so on.

10.2   Simple Texturing Example

With these built-in functions for accessing textures, it's easy to write a simple shader that does texture mapping.

To achieve good results, it helps to start with excellent textures. Color Plate 2 shows an example of a two-dimensional texture map, a cylindrical projection of the earth's surface, including clouds. This image, and other images in this section, were obtained from the NASA Web site and were created by Reto Stöckli of the NASA/Goddard Space Flight Center. These images of Earth are part of a series of consistently processed data sets (land, sea ice, and clouds) from NASA's remote sensing satellite, the Moderate Resolution Imaging Spectroradiometer, or MODIS. Data from this satellite was combined with other related data sets (topography, land cover, and city lights), all at 1 kilometer resolution. The resulting series of images is extremely high resolution (43200×21600 pixels). For our purposes, we can get by with a much smaller texture, so we'll use versions that have been sampled down to 2048×1024.

10.2.1 Application Setup

We'll assume that the image data has been read into our application and that the image width, image height, a pointer to the image data, and a texture name generated by OpenGL can be passed to our texture initialization function:

```
init2DTexture(GLint texName, GLint texWidth,
            GLint texHeight, GLubyte *texPtr)
{
    glBindTexture(GL_TEXTURE_2D, texName);
    glTexParameteri(GL_TEXTURE_2D, GL_TEXTURE_WRAP_S, GL_REPEAT);
    glTexParameteri(GL_TEXTURE_2D, GL_TEXTURE_WRAP_T, GL_REPEAT);
    glTexParameteri(GL_TEXTURE_2D, GL_TEXTURE_MAG_FILTER, GL_LINEAR);
    glTexParameteri(GL_TEXTURE_2D, GL_TEXTURE_MIN_FILTER, GL_LINEAR);
    glTexImage2D(GL_TEXTURE_2D, 0, GL_RGB, texWidth, texHeight, 0,
                GL_RGB, GL_UNSIGNED_BYTE, texPtr);
}
```

This creates a texture object named *texName*. Calls to **glTexParameter** set the wrapping behavior and filtering modes. We've chosen to use repeat as our wrapping behavior and to do linear filtering. The data for the texture is specified by calling **glTexImage2D** (the values passed to this function will depend on how the image data has been stored in memory).

When we're ready to use this texture, we can use the following OpenGL calls:

```
glActiveTexture(GL_TEXTURE0);
glBindTexture(GL_TEXTURE_2D, earthTexName);
```

This sequence of calls will set the active texture unit to texture unit 0, bind our earth texture to this texture unit, and make it active. We will need to provide the values for two uniform variables. The vertex shader will need to know the light position, and the fragment shader will need to know the texture unit that is to be accessed. The light position will be defined as a **vec3** in the vertex shader named *lightPosition*, and the texture unit will be defined as a **sampler2D** in the fragment shader named *EarthTexture*. Our application code needs to determine the location of these uniform variables and then provide appropriate values. We assume that our shaders have been compiled, linked using a program object whose handle is *programObj*, and installed as part of current state. We can make the following calls to initialize the uniform variables:

```
lightLoc = glGetUniformLocationARB(programObj, "LightPosition");
glUniform3fARB(lightLoc, 0.0, 0.0, 4.0);
texLoc   = glGetUniformLocationARB(programObj, "EarthTexture");
glUniform1iARB(texLoc, 0);
```

The light source position is set to a point right in front of the object along the viewing axis. We plan to use texture unit 0 for our earth texture, so that is the value that is loaded into our sampler variable.

The application can now make appropriate OpenGL calls to draw a sphere, and the earth texture will be applied. A surface normal, a 2D texture coordinate, and a vertex position must be specified for each vertex.

10.2.2 Vertex Shader

The vertex shader for our simple texturing example is pretty similar to the simple brick vertex shader described in Section 6.2. The main difference is that a texture coordinate is passed in as a vertex attribute, and it is passed on as a varying variable using the built-in variable name *gl_TexCoord[0]* (see Listing 10.1).

Listing 10.1 Vertex shader for simple texturing

```
varying float LightIntensity;
uniform vec3 LightPosition;

const float specularContribution = 0.1;
const float diffuseContribution  = 1.0 - specularContribution;

void main(void)
{
    vec3 ecPosition = vec3 (gl_ModelViewMatrix * gl_Vertex);
    vec3 tnorm      = normalize(gl_NormalMatrix * gl_Normal);
    vec3 lightVec   = normalize(LightPosition - ecPosition);
    vec3 reflectVec = reflect(-lightVec, tnorm);
    vec3 viewVec    = normalize(-ecPosition);
```

```
float spec       = clamp(dot(reflectVec, viewVec), 0.0, 1.0);
spec             = pow(spec, 16.0);

LightIntensity  = diffuseContribution * max(dot(lightVec, tnorm), 0.0)
                   + specularContribution * spec;

gl_TexCoord[0]  = gl_MultiTexCoord0;
gl_Position     = ftransform();
}
```

10.2.3 Fragment Shader

The fragment shader shown in Listing 10.2 will apply the earth texture to the incoming geometry. So, for instance, if we define a sphere where the s texture coordinates are related to longitude (e.g., 0° longitude is $s = 0$, and 360° longitude is $s = 1.0$) and t texture coordinates are related to latitude (90° south latitude is $t = 0.0$ and 90° north latitude is $t = 1.0$), we can apply the texture map to the sphere's geometry as shown in Color Plate 3.

In the following fragment shader, the incoming s and t texture coordinate values (part of the built-in varying variable *gl_TexCoord0*) are used to look up a value from the texture currently bound to texture unit 0. The resulting value is multiplied by the light intensity computed by the vertex shader and passed as a varying variable. The color is then clamped, and an alpha value of 1.0 is added to create the final fragment color, which is sent on for further processing, including depth testing. The resulting image as mapped onto a sphere is shown in Color Plate 3.

Listing 10.2 Fragment shader for simple texture mapping example

```
varying float LightIntensity;
uniform sampler2D EarthTexture;

void main (void)
{
    vec3 lightColor = vec3 (texture2D(EarthTexture, gl_TexCoord[0].st));
    gl_FragColor    = vec4 (lightColor * LightIntensity, 1.0);
}
```

10.3 Multitexturing Example

The resulting image looks pretty good, but with a little more effort, we can get it looking even better. For one thing, we know that there are lots of man-made lights on our planet, so when it's nighttime, major towns and cities can be seen as specks of light, even from space. We'll use the angle between the light direction and the normal at each surface location to determine whether that location is in "daytime" or "nighttime." For points that are in daytime, we'll access the texture map that contains daylight colors and do an appropriate lighting calculation. For points in the nighttime region of the planet, we'll do no lighting and access a texture that shows the earth as illuminated at night. The daytime and nighttime textures are shown in Color Plate 5.

Another somewhat unrealistic aspect to our simple approach is the reflection of sunlight off the surface of oceans and large lakes. Water is a very good reflective surface, and when our viewpoint is nearly the same as the reflection angle for the light source, we should see a specular reflection. But we know that desert, grass, and trees don't have this same kind of reflective property, so how can we get a nice specular highlight on the water but not on the land?

The answer is a technique called a GLOSS MAP. We'll make a single channel (i.e., grayscale) version of our original texture and assign values of 1.0 for areas that represent water and 0 for everything else. At each fragment, we'll read this gloss texture and multiply its value by the specular illumination portion of our lighting equation. It's fairly simple to create the gloss map in an image editing program. The easiest way to do this is by editing the red channel of the cloudless daytime image. In this channel, all the water areas will appear black or nearly black because they contain very little red information. You can use a selection tool to select all of the black (water) areas. When selected, fill the selected area (water regions) with white. Invert the selection and fill the land areas with black. The result is a texture that will contain a value of 1.0 (white) for areas in which we want a specular highlight, and a value of 0 (black) for areas in which we don't. This "gloss" value will be used as a multiplier in our specular reflection calculation, so areas that represent water will include a specular reflection term, and areas that represent land won't. Our gloss map is shown in Figure 10.1.

As you saw in Color Plate 5, our daytime and nighttime textures no longer include cloud cover. We'll store our cloud texture as a single channel (i.e., grayscale) texture as shown in Figure 10.2. By doing this, we'll have more flexibility about how we combine the cloud image with the images of the Earth's surface. For daytime views, we want the clouds to have diffuse reflection but no specular reflection. Furthermore, clouds obscure the surface so a value of 1.0 for the cloud cover indicates that the earth's surface at that location is completely obscured by clouds. For nighttime views, we don't want any light reflecting from the clouds, but we do want them to obscure

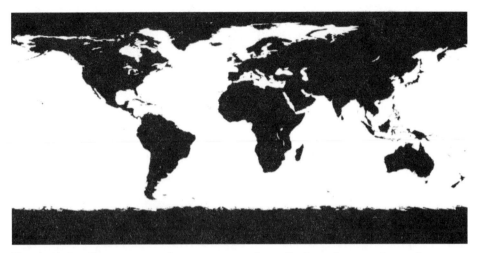

Figure 10.1   Gloss map used to create specular reflections from water surfaces

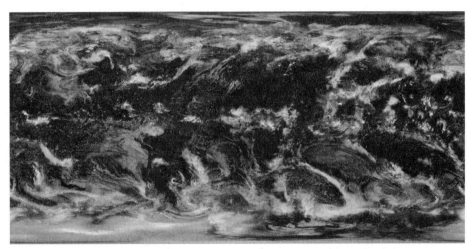

Figure 10.2   Texture map showing cloud cover (Blue Marble image by Reto Stöckli, NASA Goddard Space Flight Center)

the surface below. For convenience, we've stored our single channel cloud image into the red channel of an RGB texture, and we've stored our gloss map as the green channel. The blue channel will be unused. (Another choice would be to store the gloss map as the alpha channel for our daytime image and the cloud texture as the alpha channel in our nighttime image.)

10.3.1 Application Setup

The setup required for multitexturing is about the same as it was for the simple texturing example, except that we need to set up three textures instead of one. We can call the **init2Dtexture** function described in Section 10.2.1 three times, once each for the daytime earth texture, the nighttime earth texture, and the cloud/gloss texture. We can activate these textures with the following OpenGL calls:

```
glActiveTexture(GL_TEXTURE0);
glBindTexture(GL_TEXTURE_2D, earthDayTexName);

glActiveTexture(GL_TEXTURE1);
glBindTexture(GL_TEXTURE_2D, earthNightTexName);

glActiveTexture(GL_TEXTURE2);
glBindTexture(GL_TEXTURE_2D, earthCloudsTexName);
```

The necessary uniform variables can be initialized as follows:

```
lightLoc = glGetUniformLocationARB(programObj, "LightPosition");
glUniform3fARB(lightLoc, 0.0, 0.0, 4.0);
texLoc   = glGetUniformLocationARB(programObj, "EarthDay");
glUniform1iARB(texLoc, 0);
texLoc   = glGetUniformLocationARB(programObj, "EarthNight");
glUniform1iARB(texLoc, 1);
texLoc   = glGetUniformLocationARB(programObj, "EarthCloudGloss");
glUniform1iARB(texLoc, 2);
```

The application can now make appropriate OpenGL calls to draw a sphere. A surface normal, a 2D texture coordinate, and a vertex position must be specified for each vertex.

10.3.2 Vertex Shader

The vertex shader for this multitexturing example is pretty similar to the one described for the simple texturing example in Section 10.2.2, except that the diffuse and specular factors are computed by the vertex shader and passed as separate varying variables to the fragment shader. The computed specular value is multiplied by the constant vector (1.0, 0.941, 0.898) to approximate the color of sunlight (see Listing 10.3).

Listing 10.3 Vertex shader for multitexturing

```
varying float Diffuse;
varying vec3  Specular;
varying vec2  TexCoord;
```

```
uniform vec3 LightPosition;

void main(void)
{
    vec3 ecPosition  = vec3 (gl_ModelViewMatrix * gl_Vertex);
    vec3 tnorm       = normalize(gl_NormalMatrix * gl_Normal);
    vec3 lightVec    = normalize(LightPosition - ecPosition);
    vec3 reflectVec  = reflect(-lightVec, tnorm);
    vec3 viewVec     = normalize(-ecPosition);

    float spec       = clamp(dot(reflectVec, viewVec), 0.0, 1.0);
    spec             = pow(spec, 8.0);
    Specular         = vec3 (spec) * vec3 (1.0, 0.941, 0.898) * 0.3;

    Diffuse          = max(dot(lightVec, tnorm), 0.0);

    TexCoord         = gl_MultiTexCoord0.st;
    gl_Position      = ftransform();
}
```

10.3.3 Fragment Shader

The fragment shader that performs the desired multitexturing is shown in Listing 10.4. The application has loaded the daytime texture in the texture unit specified by *EarthDay*, the nighttime texture into the texture unit specified by *EarthNight*, and the cloud/gloss texture into the texture unit specified by *EarthCloudGloss*. The lighting computation is done in a vertex shader that computes diffuse and specular reflection factors and passes them to the fragment shader independently. The texture coordinates supplied by the application are also passed on to the fragment shader and form the basis of our texture lookup operation.

In our fragment shader, the first thing we do is access our cloud/gloss texture because its values will be used in the computations that follow. Next, we look up the value from our daytime texture, multiply it by our diffuse lighting factor, and add to it the specular lighting factor multiplied by the gloss value. If the fragment is unobscured by clouds, this gives us the desired effect of diffuse lighting over the whole surface of the Earth with specular highlights from water surfaces. This value is multiplied by 1.0 minus the cloudiness factor. Finally, we add the cloud effect by multiplying our cloudiness factor by the diffuse lighting value and adding this to our previous result.

The nighttime calculation is simpler. Here we will just look up the value from our nighttime texture and multiply that result by 1.0 minus the cloudiness factor. Because this fragment will be in shadow, the diffuse and specular components are not used.

With these values computed, we can determine the value to be used for each fragment. The key will be our diffuse lighting factor, which will be greater than zero for areas in sunlight, less than zero for areas in shadow, and near zero for areas near the terminator. We use conditional statements to use the computed *daytime* value in the sunlit areas, the computed *nighttime* value in the areas in shadow, and we'll do a mix of the two values to make a gradual transition near the terminator.

An alpha value of 1.0 is added to produce our final fragment color. Several views from the final shader are shown in Color Plate 6. You can see the nice specular highlight off the Gulf of Mexico in the first image. If you look closely at the third (nighttime) image, you can see the clouds obscuring the central part of the east coast of the United States and the northwestern part of Brazil.

It is worth pointing out that this shader should not be considered a general purpose shader because it has some built-in assumptions about the type of geometry that will be drawn. It will only look "right" when used with a sphere with proper texture coordinates. There is more that can be done to make the shader even more realistic. The color of the atmosphere actually varies, depending on the viewing position and the position of the sun. It is redder when near the shadow boundary, a fact that we often notice near sunrise and sunset. See the references at the end of the chapter for more information about achieving realistic effects such as Rayleigh scattering.

Listing 10.4 "As the world turns" fragment shader

```
uniform sampler2D EarthDay;
uniform sampler2D EarthNight;
uniform sampler2D EarthCloudGloss;

varying float Diffuse;
varying vec3  Specular;
varying vec2  TexCoord;

void main (void)
{
    // Monochrome cloud cover value will be in clouds.r
    // Gloss value will be in clouds.g
    // clouds.b will be unused

    vec3 clouds    = texture2D(EarthCloudGloss, TexCoord).stp;
    vec3 daytime   = (texture2D(EarthDay, TexCoord).stp * Diffuse +
                        Specular * clouds.g) * (1.0 - clouds.r) +
                        clouds.r * Diffuse;
    vec3 nighttime = texture2D(EarthNight, TexCoord).stp *
                        (1.0 - clouds.r);
```

```
    vec3 color = daytime;
    if (Diffuse < -0.1)
        color = nighttime;
    if (abs(Diffuse) < 0.1)
        color = mix(nighttime, daytime, (Diffuse + 0.1) * 5.0);

    gl_FragColor = vec4 (color, 1.0);
}
```

10.4 Environment Mapping Example

A technique that is used to model reflections in a complex environment without resorting to ray-tracing is called ENVIRONMENT MAPPING. In this technique, one or more texture maps are used to simulate the reflections in the environment that are being rendered. It is best used when rendering objects that have mirror-like qualities. There are several ways to do environment mapping, including SPHERE MAPPING and CUBE MAPPING, both of which are supported in standard OpenGL.

If the desired effect doesn't require perfection, a simple way to do environment mapping is to use a single equirectangular texture map. This type of texture can be obtained from a real-world environment using photography techniques, or it can be created to represent a synthetic environment. An example is shown in Color Plate 7.

Whatever means is used to obtain an image, the result is a single image that spans 360° horizontally and 180° vertically. The image is also distorted as you move up or down from the center of the image. This distortion is done deliberately so that you will see a reasonable representation of the environment if you "shrink-wrap" this texture around the object that you're rendering.

The fundamental idea behind environment mapping is that we will use the reflection vector from the surface of an object to look up the reflection color from our "environment" that is stored in a texture map. If done properly, it looks as if the object being rendered is shiny and is reflecting its environment.

The key to using an equirectangular texture as the environment map is to produce a pair of angles that are used to index into the texture. An altitude angle is computed by determining the angle between the reflection direction and the *XZ* plane. This altitude angle will vary from 180° (reflection is straight up) to –180° (reflection is straight down). The sine of this angle will vary from 1.0 to –1.0, and we'll be able to use this fact to get a texture coordinate in the range of [0,1].

An azimuth angle is determined by projecting the reflection direction onto the *XZ* plane. The azimuth angle will vary from 0° to 360°, and this will give us the key to get a second texture coordinate in the range of [0,1].

The following OpenGL shaders will work together to perform environment mapping on an object. The altitude and azimuth angles are computed to determine *s* and *t* values for indexing into our environment textures. The object is assumed to have an underlying layer that acts as a diffuse reflector. The result from the diffuse portion is combined with the environment reflection to produce a final value at each pixel.

10.4.1 Application Setup

The application needs to do very little to set up this shader. A very simple lighting model is used, so the only lighting state that we need to pass in is a single light source position. In this example, the environment map will be set up in texture unit 4. We will set its wrapping behavior to wrap in both *s* and *t*. (This is necessary to support a little trick that we'll be doing in the fragment shader.) The color of the diffuse underlayer of our object will be defined by *baseColor*, and the ratio of base color to environment map reflection will be set by *mixRatio*. Here are the definitions for the uniform variables that will be used:

```
LightPos     0.0,  0.0,  4.0
BaseColor    0.4,  0.4,  1.0
MixRatio     0.8
EnvMap       4
```

After the shaders have been installed and the uniform variables have been provided, the application is expected to send a normal and the vertex position for each vertex that is to be drawn. The current values for the modelview matrix, the modelview-projection matrix, and the normal matrix will all be accessed from within the vertex shader.

10.4.2 Vertex Shader

Listing 10.5 comprises the vertex shader that is used to do environment mapping.

Listing 10.5 Vertex shader used for environment mapping

```
varying vec3  Normal;
varying vec3  EyeDir;
varying float LightIntensity;

uniform vec3  LightPos;

void main(void)
{
    gl_Position    = ftransform();
    Normal         = normalize(gl_NormalMatrix * gl_Normal);
    vec4 pos       = gl_ModelViewMatrix * gl_Vertex;
    EyeDir         = pos.xyz;
    LightIntensity = max(dot(normalize(LightPos - EyeDir), Normal), 0.0);
}
```

The goal of this vertex shader is to produce three values that will be inter-polated across each primitive: a diffuse lighting value, a surface normal, and an eye direction. These latter two values will allow us to compute an accu-rate reflection direction at each fragment, and from the reflection direction, we will be able to compute the necessary altitude and azimuth angles.

The transformed position of the vertex is computed in the first line of the program in the usual way. We transform and normalize the incoming normal, and then we compute the eye direction based on the current modelview matrix and the incoming vertex value. We will use these two values in the fragment shader to determine the reflection direction vector. Finally, we compute a diffuse lighting value in the same manner that we've done in previous examples.

10.4.3 Fragment Shader

Listing 10.6 contains the fragment shader that is used to do environment mapping.

Listing 10.6 Fragment shader for doing environment mapping

```
const vec3 Xunitvec = vec3 (1.0, 0.0, 0.0);
const vec3 Yunitvec = vec3 (0.0, 1.0, 0.0);

uniform vec3  BaseColor;
uniform float MixRatio;

uniform sampler2D EnvMap;  // = 4

varying vec3  Normal;
varying vec3  EyeDir;
varying float LightIntensity;
```

```
void main (void)
{
    // Compute reflection vector

    vec3 reflectDir = reflect(EyeDir, Normal);

    // Compute altitude and azimuth angles

    vec2 index;

    index.y = dot(normalize(reflectDir), Yunitvec);
    reflectDir.y = 0.0;
    index.x = dot(normalize(reflectDir), Xunitvec) * 0.5;

    // Translate index values into proper range

    if (reflectDir.z >= 0.0)
        index = (index + 1.0) * 0.5;
    else
    {
        index.t = (index.t + 1.0) * 0.5;
        index.s = (-index.s) * 0.5 + 1.0;
    }

    // if reflectDir.z >= 0.0, s will go from 0.25 to 0.75
    // if reflectDir.z <  0.0, s will go from 0.75 to 1.25, and
    // that's OK, because we've set the texture to wrap.

    // Do a lookup into the environment map.

    vec3 envColor = vec3 (texture2D(EnvMap, index));

    // Add lighting to base color and mix

    vec3 base = LightIntensity * BaseColor;
    envColor = mix(envColor, base, MixRatio);

    gl_FragColor = vec4 (envColor, 1.0);
}
```

The varying variables *Normal* and *EyeDir* are the values generated by the vertex shader and then interpolated across the primitive. To get truly precise results, these values should be normalized again in the fragment shader. Skipping the normalization gives us a little better performance, and the quality is acceptable for certain objects.

The constants *Xunitvec* and *Yunitvec* have been set up with the proper values for computing our altitude and azimuth angles. First, we compute our altitude angle by normalizing the *reflectionDir* vector and performing a dot product with the *Yunitvec*. Because both vectors are unit vectors, this gives us a cosine value for the desired angle that ranges from [–1,1]. Setting the *y* component of our reflection vector to 0 causes it to be projected onto the *XZ* plane. We normalize this new vector to get the cosine of our azimuth angle. Again, this value will range from [–1,1]. Because the horizontal direction of our environment texture spans 360°, we multiply by 0.5 so that we get a value that maps into half of our environment map. Then we need to do a little more work to determine which half this is.

If the *z* portion of our reflection direction is positive, it indicates that the reflection direction is "toward the front," and we'll use the computed texture map indices directly. The index values are scaled and biased so that when we access the environment map texture, we'll get *s* values that range from [0.25,0.75] and *t* values that range from [0,1].

If *z* is negative, we do our calculations a little differently. The *t* value is still computed the same way, but the *s* value is scaled and biased so that it ranges from [0.75,1.25]. We'll be able to use these values directly because we've set our texture wrap modes to GL_REPEAT. *s* values between 1.0 and 1.25 will map to *s* values from 0 to 0.25 in our actual texture (the "trick" alluded to earlier). In this way, we'll be able to properly access the entire environment texture, depending on the reflection direction. We could compare *s* to 1.0 and subtract 1.0 if its value is greater than 1.0, but this would end up requiring additional instructions in the machine code and hence the performance would be reduced. By using the repeat mode trick, the hardware will take care of this for free.

With our index values set, all we need to do is look up the value in the texture map. A diffusely lit base color value is computed by multiplying our incoming light intensity by *BaseColor*. This value is mixed with our environment map value to create a ceramic effect. We then create a **vec4** by adding an alpha value of 1.0 and send the final fragment color on for further processing. The final result is shown in Color Plate 8. You can see the branches from the tree in the environment on the back and rear of the triceratops. For this example, I've used a color of (0.4, 0.4, 1.0) (i.e., light blue) and a mix ratio of 0.8 (i.e., 80% diffuse color, 20% environment map value).

An example of environment mapping that assumes a mirror-like surface and adds procedural bumps is shown in Color Plate 9.

10.5   Polynomial Texture Mapping with BRDF Data

In order to model more physically realistic surfaces, we must go beyond the simplistic lighting/reflection model that is built into OpenGL and assumes that all surfaces have mirror-like reflection properties. For some time, computer graphics researchers have been rendering images with a more realistic reflection model called the BIDIRECTIONAL REFLECTANCE DISTRIBUTION FUNCTION, or BRDF. This model for computing the reflection from a surface takes into account the input direction of incoming light and the outgoing direction of reflected light. The elevation and azimuth angles of these direction vectors are used to compute the relative amount of light reflected in the outgoing direction (the fixed functionality OpenGL model uses only the elevation angle). This model can be used to render surfaces with ANISOTROPIC reflection properties (i.e., surfaces that are not rotationally invariant in their surface reflection properties). Instruments have been developed to measure the BRDF of real materials. These BRDF measurements can be sampled to produce texture maps that can be used to reconstruct the BRDF function at runtime. A variety of different sampling and reconstruction methods have been devised for rendering BRDF materials.

This section describes the OpenGL Shading Language BRDF shaders that use the Polynomial Texture Mapping technique developed by Hewlett-Packard. The shaders presented are courtesy of Brad Ritter, Hewlett-Packard. The BRDF data is from Cornell University. It was obtained by measuring reflections from several types of automotive paints that were supplied by Ford Motor Co.

One of the reasons this type of rendering is important is to achieve realistic rendering of materials whose reflection characteristics vary as a function of view angle and light direction. Such is the case with these automotive paints. To a car designer, it is extremely important to be able to visualize the final "look" of the car, even when it is painted with a material whose reflection characteristics vary as a function of view angle and light direction. One of the paint samples tested by Cornell, Mystique Lacquer, has the peculiar property that the color of its specular highlight color changes as a function of viewing angle. This material cannot be adequately rendered using only conventional texture mapping techniques.

The textures that are used in this example are called POLYNOMIAL TEXTURE MAPS, or PTMs. PTMs are essentially light-dependent texture maps and are described in a SIGGRAPH paper by Malzbender, Gelb, and Wolters (2001). PTMs can be used to reconstruct the color of a surface under varying lighting conditions. When a surface is rendered using a PTM, it takes on different illumination characteristics depending on the direction of the light source. Like bump mapping, this helps viewers by providing perceptual clues about the surface geometry. But PTMs are capable of going beyond bump maps in that they are capable of capturing surface variations due to self-shadowing and interreflections. PTMs are generated from real materials and are intended to preserve the visual characteristics of the actual materials. Polynomial texture mapping is an image-based technique that does not require bump maps or the modeling of complex geometry.

The image in Color Plate 10 shows two triangles from a PTM demo developed by Hewlett-Packard. The triangle on the upper right has been rendered using a polynomial texture map, and the triangle on the lower left has been rendered using a conventional 2D texture map. The objects that were used to construct the texture maps were a metallic bezel with the Hewlett-Packard logo on it and a brushed metal notebook cover with an embossed 3Dlabs logo. As you move the simulated light source in the demo, the conventional texture looks flat and somewhat unrealistic, whereas the PTM texture faithfully reproduces the highlights and surface shadowing that occur on the real-life objects. In the image captured here, the light source is a bit in front and above the two triangles. The PTM shows realistic reflections, but the conventional texture can only reproduce the lighting effect from a single lighting angle (in this case, as if the light were directly in front of the object).

The PTM technique developed by HP requires as input a set of images of the desired object, with the object illuminated by a light source of a different known direction for each image, all captured from the same viewpoint. For each texel of the PTM, these source images are sampled and a least-squares biquadric curve fit is performed to obtain a polynomial that approximates the lighting function for that texel. This part of the process is partly science and partly art (a bit of manual intervention can improve the end results). The biquadric equation generated in this manner will allow runtime reconstruction of the lighting function for the source material. The coefficients stored in the PTM are A, B, C, D, E, and F as shown in this equation:

$$Au^2 + Bv^2 + Cuv + Du + Ev + F$$

One use of PTMs is for representing materials with surface properties that vary spatially across the surface. Things like brushed metal, woven fabric, wood, and stone are all materials that reflect light differently depending on the viewing angle and light source direction. They may also have interreflections and self-shadowing. The PTM technique is capable of capturing these details and reproducing them at runtime. There are two variants for

PTMs: luminance (LRGB) and RGB. An LRGB PTM uses the biquadric polynomials to determine the brightness of each rendered pixel. Because each texel in an LRGB PTM has its own biquadric polynomial function, the luminance or brightness characteristics of each texel can be unique. An RGB PTM uses a separate biquadric polynomial for each of the three colors: red, green, and blue. This allows objects rendered with an RGB PTM to vary in color as the light position shifts. Thus color-shifting materials such as holograms can be accurately reconstructed with an RGB PTM.

The key to creating a PTM for these types of spatially varying materials is to capture images of them as lit from a variety of light source directions. Engineers at Hewlett-Packard have developed an instrument—a dome with multiple light sources and a camera mounted at the top—to do just that. This device can automatically capture 50 images of the source material from a single fixed camera position as illuminated by light sources in different positions. A picture of this picture-taking device is shown in Figure 10.3.

The image data collected with this device is the basis for creating a PTM for the real-world texture of a material (e.g., automobile paints). These types of PTMs have four degrees of freedom. Two of these will be used to represent the spatially varying characteristics of the material. These two degrees of freedom are controlled using the 2D texture coordinates. The remaining

Figure 10.3 A device for capturing images for the creation of polynomial texture maps (© Copyright 2003 Hewlett-Packard Development Company, L.P., Reproduced with Permission)

two degrees of freedom are used to represent the light direction. These are the two independent variables in the biquadric polynomial.

A BRDF PTM is slightly different than a spatially varying PTM. BRDF PTMs are used to model homogeneous materials—that is, they do not vary spatially. BRDF PTMs use two degrees of freedom to represent the light direction, and the remaining two degrees of freedom are used to represent the view direction. The parameterized light direction (Lu, Lv) is used for the independent variables of the biquadric polynomial, and the parameterized view direction (Vu, Vv) is used as the 2D texture coordinate.

There is no single parameterization that works well for all BRDF materials. A further refinement to enhance quality for BRDF PTMs for the materials we are trying to reproduce is to reparameterize the light and view vectors as half angle and difference vectors (Hu, Hv) and (Du, Dv). In the BRDF PTM shaders discussed in the next section, Hu and Hv are used as the independent variables of the biquadric polynomial, and (Du, Dv) is used as the 2D texture coordinate. A large part of the function of the vertex shader is to calculate (Hu, Hv) and (Du, Dv).

BRDF PTMs can be created as either LRGB or RGB PTMs. The upcoming example shows how an RGB BRDF PTM is rendered with OpenGL shaders. RGBA textures with 8 bits per component are used because the PTM file format and tools developed by HP are based on this format.

10.5.1 Application Setup

To render BRDF surfaces using the following shaders, the application needs to set up a few uniform variables. The vertex shader must be provided with values for uniform variables that describe the eye direction (i.e., an infinite viewer) and the position of a single light source (i.e., a point light source). The fragment shader requires the application to provide values for scaling and biasing the six polynomial coefficients. (These values were prescaled when the PTM was created in order to preserve precision, and they must be rescaled using the scale and bias factors that are specific to that PTM.)

The application is expected to provide four attributes for every vertex. Two of them are standard OpenGL attributes and need not be defined by our vertex program: *gl_Vertex* (position) and *gl_Normal* (normal). The other two attributes are a tangent vector and a binormal vector, which will be computed by the application. These two attributes should be provided to OpenGL using either the **glVertexAttribARB** function or a generic vertex array. The location to be used for these generic attributes can be bound to the appropriate attribute in our vertex shader by calling **glBindAttribLocationARB**.

For instance, if we choose to pass the tangent values in at vertex attribute location 3 and the binormal values in at vertex attribute location 4, we would set up the binding using these lines of code:

```
glBindAttribLocationARB(programObj, 3, "Tangent");
glBindAttribLocationARB(programObj, 4, "Binormal");
```

If the variable *tangent* is defined to be an array of three floats and *binormal* is also defined as an array of three floats, these generic vertex attributes can be passed in using the following calls:

```
glVertexAttrib3fvARB(3, tangent);
glVertexAttrib3fvARB(4, binormal);
```

Alternatively, these values could be passed to OpenGL using generic vertex arrays.

Prior to rendering, the application should also set up seven texture maps: three 2D texture maps will hold the A, B, and C coefficients for red, green, and blue components of the PTM; three 2D texture maps will hold the D, E, and F coefficients for red, green, and blue components of the PTM; and a 1D texture will hold a lighting function.

This last texture is set up by the application whenever the lighting state is changed. The light factor texture is solving four problems:

1. Front facing/back facing discrimination. This texture is indexed with *LdotN*, which is positive for front facing vertices and negative for back facing vertices. As a first level of complexity, the light texture can solve the front facing/back facing problem by being 1.0 for positive index values and 0.0 for back facing values.

2. We'd like to be able to light BRDF PTM shaded objects with colored lights. As a second level of complexity, the light texture (which has three channels, R, G, and B) will use a light color instead of 1.0 for positive index values.

3. An abrupt transition from front facing to back facing will look awkward and unrealistic on rendered images. As a third level of complexity, we apply a gradual transition in the light texture values from 0 to 1.0. A sine or cosine curve can be used to determine these gradual texture values.

4. There is no concept of ambient light for PTM rendering. It can look very unrealistic to render back facing pixels as (0,0,0). Instead of using 0 values for negative indices, values such as 0.1 are used.

10.5.2 Vertex Shader

The BRDF PTM vertex shader is shown in Listing 10.7. The purpose of this shader is to produce five varying values:

1. *gl_Position*, as required by every vertex shader

2. *TexCoord*, which will be used to access our texture maps to get the two sets of polynomial coefficients

3. *Du*, a float that contains the cosine of the angle between the light direction and the tangent vector

4. *Dv*, a float that contains the cosine of the angle between the light direction and the binormal vector

5. *LdotN*, a float that contains the cosine of the angle between the incoming surface normal and the light direction.

The shader assumes a viewer at infinity and one point light source.

Listing 10.7 Vertex shader for rendering BRDF-based polynomial texture maps

```
//
// PTM vertex shader by Brad Ritter, Hewlett-Packard
// and Randi Rost, 3Dlabs.
//
// © Copyright 2003 3Dlabs, Inc., and
// Hewlett-Packard Development Company, L.P.,
// Reproduced with Permission
//
uniform vec3 LightPos;
uniform vec3 EyeDir;

attribute vec3 Tangent;
attribute vec3 Binormal;

varying float Du;
varying float Dv;
varying float LdotN;
varying vec2  TexCoord;

void main(void)
{
    vec3 lightTemp;
    vec3 halfAngleTemp;
    vec3 tPrime;
    vec3 bPrime;
```

```
// Transform vertex
gl_Position = ftransform();
lightTemp = normalize(LightPos - gl_Vertex.xyz);

// Calculate the Half Angle vector
halfAngleTemp = normalize(EyeDir + lightTemp);

// Calculate T' and B'
//      T' = |T - (T.H)H|
tPrime = Tangent - (halfAngleTemp * dot(Tangent, halfAngleTemp));
tPrime = normalize(tPrime);

//      B' = H x T'
bPrime = cross(halfAngleTemp, tPrime);

Du = dot(lightTemp, tPrime);
Dv = dot(lightTemp, bPrime);

// Multiply the Half Angle vector by NOISE_FACTOR
// to avoid noisy BRDF data
halfAngleTemp = halfAngleTemp * 0.9;

// Hu = Dot(HalfAngle, T)
// Hv = Dot(HalfAngle, B)
// Remap [-1.0..1.0] to [0.0..1.0]
TexCoord.s = dot(Tangent,  halfAngleTemp) * 0.5 + 0.5;
TexCoord.t = dot(Binormal, halfAngleTemp) * 0.5 + 0.5;

// "S" Text Coord3: Dot(Light, Normal);
LdotN = dot(lightTemp, gl_Normal) * 0.5 + 0.5;
}
```

The light source position and eye direction are passed in as uniform variables by the application. In addition to the standard OpenGL vertex and normal vertex attributes, the application is expected to pass in a tangent and a binormal per vertex as described in the previous section. These two generic attributes are defined with appropriate names in our vertex shader.

The first line of the vertex shader transforms the incoming vertex value by the current modelview-projection matrix. The next line computes the light source direction for our positional light source by subtracting the vertex position from the light position. Because *LightPos* is defined as a **vec3** and the built-in attribute *gl_Vertex* is defined as a **vec4**, we must use the **.xyz** component selector to obtain the first three elements of *gl_Vertex* prior to doing the vector subtraction operation. The result of the vector subtraction is then normalized and stored as our light direction.

The following line of code computes the half angle by adding together the eye direction vector and the light direction vector and normalizing the result.

The next few lines of code compute the 2D parameterization of our half angle and difference vector. The goal here is to compute values for *u* (*Du*) and *v* (*Dv*) that can be plugged into the biquadric equation in our fragment shader. The technique used here is called Gram-Schmidt orthonormalization. *H* (half angle), *T'*, and *B'* are the orthogonal axes of a coordinate system. *T'* and *B'* maintain a general alignment with the original *T* (tangent) and *B* (binormal) vectors. Where *T* and *B* lie in the plane of the triangle being rendered, *T'* and *B'* are in a plane perpendicular to the half angle vector. More details on the reasons for choosing *H*, *T'*, and *B'* to define the coordinate system are available in the paper *Interactive Rendering with Arbitrary BRDFs Using Separable Approximations*, by Jan Kautz and Michael McCool (1999).

BRDF data often has noisy data values for extremely large incidence angles (i.e., close to 180°), so in the next line of code, we avoid the noisy data in a somewhat unscientific manner by applying a scale factor to the half angle. This will effectively cause these values to be ignored.

Our vertex shader code then computes values for *Hu* and *Hv* and places them in the varying variable *TexCoord*. These will be plugged into our biquadric equation in the fragment shader as the *u* and *v* values. These values hold our parameterized difference vector and will be used to look up the required polynomial coefficients from the texture maps, so they are mapped into the range [0,1].

Finally, we compute a value that will be used to apply the lighting effect. This value is simply the cosine of the angle between the surface normal and the light direction. It is also mapped into the range [0,1] because it will be used as the texture coordinate for accessing a 1D texture to obtain the lighting factor that will be used.

10.5.3 Fragment Shader

The fragment shader for our BRDF PTM surface rendering is shown in Listing 10.8.

Listing 10.8 Fragment shader for rendering BRDF-based polynomial texture maps

```
//
// PTM fragment shader by Brad Ritter, Hewlett-Packard
// and Randi Rost, 3Dlabs.
//
// © Copyright 2003 3Dlabs, Inc., and
// Hewlett-Packard Development Company, L.P.,
// Reproduced with Permission
//
uniform sampler2D ABCred;          // = 0
uniform sampler2D DEFred;          // = 1
uniform sampler2D ABCgrn;          // = 2
uniform sampler2D DEFgrn;          // = 3
uniform sampler2D ABCblu;          // = 4
uniform sampler2D DEFblu;          // = 5
uniform sampler1D Lighttexture;    // = 6

uniform vec3 ABCscale, ABCbias;
uniform vec3 DEFscale, DEFbias;

varying float Du;        // passes the computed L*tPrime value
varying float Dv;        // passes the computed L*bPrime value
varying float LdotN;     // passes the computed L*Normal value
varying vec2  TexCoord;  // passes s, t, texture coords

void main(void)
{
    vec3    ABCcoef, DEFcoef;
    vec3    ptvec;

    // Read coefficient values for red and apply scale and bias factors
    ABCcoef = (texture2D(ABCred, TexCoord).rgb - ABCbias) * ABCscale;
    DEFcoef = (texture2D(DEFred, TexCoord).rgb - DEFbias) * DEFscale;

    // Compute red polynomial
    ptvec.r = ABCcoef[0] * Du * Du +
              ABCcoef[1] * Dv * Dv +
              ABCcoef[2] * Du * Dv +
              DEFcoef[0] * Du +
              DEFcoef[1] * Dv +
              DEFcoef[2];

    // Read coefficient values for green and apply scale and bias factors
    ABCcoef = (texture2D(ABCgrn, TexCoord).rgb - ABCbias) * ABCscale;
    DEFcoef = (texture2D(DEFgrn, TexCoord).rgb - DEFbias) * DEFscale;

    // Compute green polynomial
    ptvec.g = ABCcoef[0] * Du * Du +
              ABCcoef[1] * Dv * Dv +
              ABCcoef[2] * Du * Dv +
```

```
            DEFcoef[0] * Du +
            DEFcoef[1] * Dv +
            DEFcoef[2];

    // Read coefficient values for blue and apply scale and bias factors
    ABCcoef = (texture2D(ABCblu, TexCoord).rgb - ABCbias) * ABCscale;
    DEFcoef = (texture2D(DEFblu, TexCoord).rgb - DEFbias) * DEFscale;

    // Compute blue polynomial
    ptvec.b = ABCcoef[0] * Du * Du +
              ABCcoef[1] * Dv * Dv +
              ABCcoef[2] * Du * Dv +
              DEFcoef[0] * Du +
              DEFcoef[1] * Dv +
              DEFcoef[2];

    // Multiply result * light factor
    ptvec *= texture1D(Lighttexture, LdotN).rgb;

    // Assign result to gl_FragColor
    gl_FragColor = vec4 (ptvec, 1.0);
}
```

This shader is relatively straightforward if you've digested the information in the previous three sections. The values in the *s* and *t* components of *TexCoord* hold a 2D parameterization of the difference vector. This is used to index into each of our coefficient textures and retrieve the values for the A, B, C, D, E, and F coefficients. The BRDF PTMs are stored as mipmap textures, and, because we're not providing a *bias* argument, the computed level-of-detail bias will just be used directly. Using vector operations, the six coefficients are scaled and biased by values passed from the application via uniform variables.

These scaled, biased coefficient values are then used together with our parameterized half angle (*Du* and *Dv*) in the biquadric polynomial to compute the red value for the surface. This process is repeated to compute the green and blue values as well. The lighting factor is computed by accessing the 1D light texture using the cosine of the angle between the light direction and the surface normal. This lighting factor is multiplied by our polynomial vector, and an alpha value of 1.0 is provided to produce the final fragment color.

The image in Color Plate 11 shows our BRDF PTM shaders rendering a torus with the BRDF PTM created for the Mystique Lacquer automotive paint. The basic color of this paint is black, but, in the orientation captured for the still image, the specular highlight shows up as mostly white with a reddish-brown tinge on one side of the highlight and a bluish tinge on the other. As the object is moved around, or as the light is moved around, our BRDF PTM shaders will properly render the shifting highlight color.

10.6 Summary

This chapter discussed several shaders that rely on information stored in texture maps. The programmability of OpenGL opens up all sorts of new uses for texture memory. In the first example, we used two typical color images as texture maps, and we also used one texture as an opacity map and another as a gloss map. In the second example, we used a typical color image as a texture, but the shader accessed it in a unique manner. In the third example, we used six textures to store the coefficients needed to perform polynomial texture mapping, and a seventh to store a lookup table for the lighting computation.

In examples later in this book, you'll see how textures can be used to store normal maps and noise functions. There is really no end to the possibilities for creating unique effects with stored textures when your mind is free to think of texture memory as storage for things other than color images.

10.7 Further Information

The basics of OpenGL texture mapping are explained in much more detail in the *OpenGL Programming Guide, Third Edition*, by Woo, Neider, Davis, and Shreiner (1999), from Addison-Wesley.

More information about the Earth images used in Section 10.2 can be found at the NASA Web site at http://earthobservatory.nasa.gov/Newsroom/BlueMarble.

Papers regarding the realistic rendering of planets include Jim Blinn's 1982 SIGGRAPH paper *Light Reflection Functions for Simulation of Clouds and Dusty Surfaces*, the 1993 SIGGRAPH paper *Display of the Earth Taking into Account Atmospheric Scattering*, by Nishita, et. al., and the 2002 paper *Physically-based Simulation: A Survey of the Modelling and Rendering of the Earth's Atmosphere* by Jaroslav Sloup.

A good overview of environment mapping techniques is available in the paper, *Environment Maps and Their Applications*, by Wolfgang Heidrich. This paper was part of the course notes for SIGGRAPH 2000 Course 27, entitled *Procedural Shading on Graphics Hardware*. This material, and a thorough treatment of reflectance and lighting models, can be found in the book *Real-Time Shading*, by Marc Olano, et. al. (2002).

The SIGGRAPH 2001 proceedings contain the paper *Polynomial Texture Maps*, by Tom Malzbender, Dan Gelb, and Hans Wolters. Additional information is available at the Hewlett-Packard Laboratories Web site, http://www.hpl.hp.com/ptm/. At this site, you will find example data files, a PTM viewing program, the PTM file format specification, and utilities to assist in creating PTMs.

[1] Blinn, James, *Light Reflection Functions for Simulation of Clouds and Dusty Surfaces*, Computer Graphics (SIGGRAPH '82 Proceedings), pp. 21–29, July 1982.

[2] Heidrich, Wolfgang, and Hans-Peter Seidel, *View-Independent Environment Maps*, ACM SIGGRAPH/Eurographics Workshop on Graphics Hardware, pp. 39–45, August 1998.

[3] Heidrich, Wolfgang, *Environment Maps and Their Applications*, SIGGRAPH 2000, Course 27, course notes. http://www.csee.umbc.edu/~olano/s2000c27/envmap.pdf

[4] Hewlett-Packard, *Polynomial Texture Mapping*, Web site. http://www.hpl.hp.com/ptm

[5] Kautz, Jan, and Michael D. McCool, *Interactive Rendering with Arbitrary BRDFs Using Separable Approximations*, 10th Eurographics Workshop on Rendering, pp. 281–292, June 1999. http://www.mpi-sb.mpg.de/~jnkautz/publications

[6] Malzbender, Tom, Dan Gelb, and Hans Wolters, *Polynomial Texture Maps*, Computer Graphics (SIGGRAPH 2001 Proceedings), pp. 519–528, August 2001.

[7] NASA, *Earth Observatory*, Web site. http://earthobservatory.nasa.gov/Newsroom/BlueMarble

[8] Nishita, Tomoyuki, Takao Sirai, Katsumi Tadamura, and Eihachiro Nakamae, *Display of the Earth Taking Into Account Atmospheric Scattering*, Computer Graphics (SIGGRAPH '93 Proceedings), pp. 175–182, August 1993. http://nis-lab.is.s.u-tokyo.ac.jp/~nis/abs_sig.html#sig93

[9] Olano, Marc, John Hart, Wolfgang Heidrich, and Michael McCool, *Real-Time Shading*, A K Peters, Ltd., Natick, Massachusetts, 2002.

[10] OpenGL Architecture Review Board, J. Neider, T. Davis, and M. Woo, *OpenGL Programming Guide, Third Edition: The Official Guide to Learning OpenGL, Version 1.2*, Addison-Wesley, Reading, Massachusetts, 1999.

[11] Sloup, Jaroslav, *Physically-based Simulation: A Survey of the Modeling and Rendering of the Earth's Atmosphere*, Proceedings of the 18th Spring Conference on Computer Graphics, pp. 141–150, April 2002. http://sgi.felk.cvut.cz/~sloup/html/research/project

Chapter 11

Procedural Texture Shaders

The fact that we have a full-featured, high-level programming language to express the processing at each fragment means that we can algorithmically compute a pattern on an object's surface. This new freedom can be used to create a wide variety of rendering effects that wouldn't be possible otherwise.

In the previous chapter, we discussed shaders that depend on values read from texture memory to achieve their primary effect. This chapter focuses on shaders that do interesting things primarily via an algorithm defined by the shader. The results from such a shader are synthesized according to the algorithm rather than being based primarily on precomputed values such as a digitized painting or photograph. This type of shader is sometimes called a PROCEDURAL TEXTURE SHADER, and the process of applying such a shader is called PROCEDURAL TEXTURING. Often the texture coordinate or the object coordinate position at each point on the object will be the only piece of information needed to shade the object with a shader that is entirely procedural.

In principle, procedural texture shaders can be used to accomplish many of the same tasks as shaders that access stored textures. In practice, there are times when it is more convenient or feasible to use a procedural texture shader and times when it is more convenient or feasible to use a stored texture shader. When deciding whether to write a procedural texture shader or one that uses stored textures, here are some things to keep in mind. The following are some of the main advantages of procedural texture shaders.

- Textures generated procedurally have very low memory requirements compared with stored textures. The only representation of the texture is in the algorithm defined by the code in the procedural texture shader. This representation is extremely compact compared with the size of stored 2D textures. Typically, it is a couple of orders of magnitude smaller (e.g., a few kilobytes for the code in a procedural shader versus a few hundred kilobytes or more for a high-quality 2D texture). This means procedural texture shaders require far less memory on the graphics accelerator. Procedural texture shaders have an even greater advantage when the desire is to have a 3D (solid) texture applied to an object (a few kilobytes versus tens of megabytes or more for a stored 3D texture).

- Textures generated by procedural texture shaders have no fixed area or resolution. They can be applied to objects of any scale with precise results because they are defined algorithmically rather than by using sampled data as in the case of stored textures. There are no decisions to be made about how to map a 2D image onto a 3D surface patch that is larger or smaller than the texture, and there are no seams or unwanted replication. As your viewpoint gets closer and closer to a surface rendered with a procedural texture shader, you won't see reduced detail or sampling artifacts like you might with a shader that uses a stored texture.

- Procedural texture shaders can be written to parameterize key aspects of the algorithm. These parameters can be easily changed, allowing a single shader to produce an interesting variety of effects. There is very little that can be done to alter the effect from a stored texture after it has been created.

Some of the disadvantages of using procedural shaders rather than stored textures are as follows.

- Procedural texture shaders require the algorithm to be encoded in a program. Not everyone has the technical skills needed to write such a program, whereas it is fairly straightforward to create a 2D or 3D texture with limited technical skills.

- Performing the algorithm embodied by a procedural texture shader at each location on an object can be a lot slower than accessing a stored texture.

- Procedural texture shaders can have serious aliasing artifacts that can be difficult to overcome. Today's graphics hardware has built-in capabilities for antialiasing stored textures (e.g., filtering methods and mipmaps).

- Because of differences in arithmetic precision and differences in implementations of built-in functions such as **noise**, it is possible that procedural texture shaders can produce somewhat different results on different platforms.

The ultimate choice of whether to use a procedural shader or a stored texture shader should be made in a pragmatic way. Things that would be artwork in the real world (paintings, billboards, anything with writing, etc.) are good candidates for rendering with stored textures. Objects that are extremely important to the final "look" of the image (character faces, costumes, important props) may also be rendered using stored textures because this presents the easiest route for an artist to be involved. Things that are relatively unimportant to the final image and yet cover a lot of area are good candidates for rendering with a procedural shader (walls, floors, ground).

Oftentimes, a hybrid approach will be the right answer. A golf ball might be rendered with a base color, a hand-painted texture that contains scuff marks, a logo, and a procedurally generated dimple pattern. Stored textures may also be used to control or constrain procedural effects. If our golf ball needs grass stains on certain parts of its surface and it is important to achieve and reproduce just the right look, an artist could paint a gray scale map that would direct the shader where grass smudges should be applied on the surface (for instance, black portions of the gray scale map) and where they should not be applied (white portions of the gray scale map). The shader can read this CONTROL TEXTURE and use it to blend between a grass-smudged representation of the surface and a pristine surface.

Having said all of this, let's turn our attention to a few examples of shaders that are entirely procedural.

11.1 Regular Patterns

In Chapter 6, we examined a procedural shader for rendering bricks. Our first example in this chapter is another simple one. We'll try to construct a shader that renders stripes on an object. A variety of man-made objects can be rendered with such a shader: children's toys, wallpaper, wrapping paper, flags, fabrics, and so on.

The object in Color Plate 13 is a partial torus rendered with a stripe shader. The stripe shader and the application in which it is shown were both developed in 2002 by LightWork Design, a company that develops software to provide photorealistic views of objects created with commercial CAD/CAM packages. The application developed by LightWork Design contains a graphical user interface that allows the user to modify the shader's parameters interactively. The various shaders that are available are accessible on the upper-right portion of the user interface, and the modifiable parameters for the current shader are accessible in the lower-right portion of the user interface. In this case, you can see that the parameters for the stripe shader include the stripe color (blue), the background color (orange), the stripe scale (how many stripes there will be), and the stripe width (the ratio of stripe to background; in this case it is 0.5 to make blue and orange stripes of equal width). A screen shot containing a variety of objects rendered with OpenGL procedural shaders is shown in Color Plate 12.

For our stripe shader to work properly, the application needs to send down only the geometry (vertex values) and the texture coordinate at each vertex. The key to drawing the stripe color or the background color will be the *t* texture coordinate at each fragment (the *s* texture coordinate will not be used at all). The application must also supply values that will be used by the vertex shader to perform a lighting computation. And the aforementioned stripe color, background color, scale, and stripe width must be passed to the fragment shader so that our procedural stripe computation can be performed at each fragment.

11.1.1 Stripes Vertex Shader

The vertex shader for our stripe effect is shown in Listing 11.1.

Listing 11.1 Vertex shader for drawing stripes

```
uniform vec3   LightPosition;
uniform vec3   LightColor;
uniform vec3   EyePosition;
uniform vec3   Specular;
uniform vec3   Ambient;
uniform float  Kd;

varying vec3   DiffuseColor;
varying vec3   SpecularColor;

void main(void)
{
    vec3 ecPosition = vec3 (gl_ModelViewMatrix * gl_Vertex);
    vec3 tnorm      = normalize(gl_NormalMatrix * gl_Normal);
    vec3 lightVec   = normalize(LightPosition - ecPosition);
    vec3 viewVec    = normalize(EyePosition - ecPosition);
    vec3 hvec       = normalize(viewVec + lightVec);

    float spec = clamp(dot(hvec, tnorm), 0.0, 1.0);
```

```
    spec = pow(spec, 16.0);

    DiffuseColor    = LightColor * vec3 (Kd * dot(lightVec, tnorm));
    DiffuseColor    = clamp(Ambient + DiffuseColor, 0.0, 1.0);
    SpecularColor   = clamp((LightColor * Specular * spec), 0.0, 1.0);

    gl_TexCoord[0]  = gl_MultiTexCoord0;
    gl_Position     = ftransform();
}
```

There are some nice features to this particular shader. There is really nothing in it that makes it specific to drawing stripes. It provides a good example of how we might do the lighting calculation in a general way that would be compatible with a variety of fragment shaders.

As we mentioned, the values for doing the lighting computation (*LightPosition, LightColor, EyePosition, Specular, Ambient,* and *Kd*) are all passed in by the application as uniform variables. The purpose of this shader is to compute *DiffuseColor* and *SpecularColor,* two varying variables that will be interpolated across each primitive and made available to the fragment shader at each fragment location. These values are computed in the typical way. A small optimization is that *Ambient* is added to the value computed for the diffuse reflection in order to send one less value to the fragment shader as a varying variable. The incoming texture coordinate is passed down to the fragment shader as the built-in varying variable *gl_TexCoord[0],* and the vertex position is transformed in the usual way.

11.1.2 Stripes Fragment Shader

The fragment shader contains the algorithm for drawing procedural stripes. It is shown in Listing 11.2.

Listing 11.2 Fragment shader for drawing stripes

```
uniform vec3   StripeColor;
uniform vec3   BackColor;
uniform float  Width;
uniform float  Fuzz;
uniform float  Scale;

varying vec3   DiffuseColor;
varying vec3   SpecularColor;

void main(void)
{
    float scaledT = fract(gl_TexCoord[0].t * Scale);
```

```
        float frac1 = clamp(scaledT / Fuzz, 0.0, 1.0);
        float frac2 = clamp((scaledT - Width) / Fuzz, 0.0, 1.0);

        frac1 = frac1 * (1.0 - frac2);
        frac1 = frac1 * frac1 * (3.0 - (2.0 * frac1));

        vec3 finalColor = mix(BackColor, StripeColor, frac1);
        finalColor = finalColor * DiffuseColor + SpecularColor;

        gl_FragColor = vec4 (finalColor, 1.0);
    }
```

The only uniform variable provided by the application that we haven't already mentioned is called *Fuzz*. This value will be used to provide smooth transitions (i.e., antialiasing) between stripe color and background color. With a *Scale* value of 10.0, a reasonable value for *Fuzz* is 0.1. It can be adjusted as the object changes size in order to prevent excessive blurriness at high magnification levels. It shouldn't really be set to a value higher than 0.5 (maximum blurriness of stripe edges).

The first step in this shader is to multiply the incoming *t* texture coordinate by the stripe scale factor and take the fractional part. This computation provides the position of the fragment within the stripe pattern. The larger the value of *Scale*, the more stripes we will have as a result of this calculation. The resulting value for the local variable *scaledT* will range from [0,1).

We'd like to have nicely antialiased transitions between the stripe colors. One way to do this would be to use **smoothstep** in the transition from *StripeColor* to *BackColor*, and use it again in the transition from *BackColor* to *StripeColor*. But this shader uses the fact that these transitions are symmetric to combine the two transitions into one.

To accomplish this, *scaledT* is used to compute two other values, *frac1* and *frac2*. These two values tell us where we are in relation to the two transitions between *BackColor* and *StripeColor*. For *frac1*, if *scaledT/Fuzz* is greater than 1, it indicates that this point is not in the transition zone, and the value is clamped to 1. If *scaledT* is less than *Fuzz*, *scaledT/Fuzz* indicates the fragment's relative distance into the transition zone for one side of the stripe. A similar value is computed for the other edge of the stripe by subtracting *Width* from *scaledT*, dividing by *Fuzz*, clamping the result, and storing it in *frac2*.

These values represent the amount of fuzz (blurriness) to be applied. At one edge of the stripe, *frac2* will be 0, and *frac1* will be the relative distance into the transition zone. At the other edge of the stripe, *frac1* will be 1 and *frac2* will be the relative distance into the transition zone. Our next line of code (*frac1* = *frac1* * (1.0 - *frac2*)) produces a value that can be used to do a proper linear blend between *BackColor* and *StripeColor*. But we'd actually like to perform a transition that is smoother than a linear blend. The next line of code performs a Hermite interpolation in the same way as the **smoothstep** function. The final value for *frac1* is used to perform the blend between *BackColor* and *StripeColor*.

The result of this is a smoothly "fuzzed" boundary in the transition region between the stripe colors. Without this fuzzing effect, we'd have abrupt transitions between the stripe colors that would flash and pop as the object is moved on the screen. The fuzzing of the transition region eliminates those artifacts. A close up view of the fuzzed boundary is shown in Color Plate 14. (More information about antialiasing procedural shaders can be found in Chapter 14.)

Now all that remains to be done is to apply the diffuse and specular lighting effects computed by the vertex shader and supply an alpha value of 1.0 to produce our final fragment color. By modifying the five basic parameters of our fragment shader, we can create a fairly interesting number of variations of our stripe pattern using the exact same shader.

11.2 Toy Ball

Programmability is the key to procedurally defining all sorts of texture patterns. This next shader takes things a bit further by shading a sphere with a procedurally defined star pattern and a procedurally defined stripe. The author of this shader, Bill Licea-Kane of ATI Research, Inc., was inspired to create a ball like the one featured in one of Pixar's early short animations, *Luxo Jr.* This shader is quite specialized. As Bill will tell you, "It shades any surface as long as it's a sphere." The reason for this is that the fragment shader exploits the property of the sphere that the surface normal for any point on the surface points in the same direction as the vector from the center of the sphere to that point on the surface. This property will be used to analytically compute the surface normal used in the shading calculations within the fragment shader.

The key to this shader is that the star pattern is defined by the coefficients for five half-spaces that define the star shape. These coefficients were chosen to make the star pattern an appropriate size for the ball. Points on the sphere are classified as "in" or "out," relative to each half space. Locations in the very center of the star pattern will be "in" with respect to all five half-spaces. Locations in the points of the star will be "in" with respect to four of the five half-spaces. All other locations will be "in" with respect to three or fewer half-spaces.

Fragments that are in the stripe pattern are simpler to compute. After we have classified each location on the surface as "star," "stripe," or "other," we can color each fragment appropriately. The color computations are applied in an order that ensures a reasonable result even if the ball is viewed from far away. A surface normal is calculated analytically (i.e., exactly) within the fragment shader. A lighting computation that includes a specular highlight calculation is also applied at every fragment.

11.2.1 Application Setup

The application only needs to provide vertex positions for this shader to work properly. Both colors and normals will be computed algorithmically in the fragment shader. The only catch is that in order for this shader to work properly, the vertices must define a sphere. The sphere can be of arbitrary size because the fragment shader will do all the necessary computations based on the known geometry of a sphere.

A number of parameters to this shader are specified using uniform variables. The values used to produce the images shown in the remainder of this section are summarized in Listing 11.3.

Listing 11.3 Values for uniform variables used by the toy ball shader

LightDir	0.57735, 0.57735, 0.57735, 0.0
HVector	0.32506, 0.32506, 0.88808, 0.0
BallCenter	0.0, 0.0, 0.0, 1.0
SpecularColor	0.4, 0.4, 0.4, 60.0
Red	0.6, 0.0, 0.0, 1.0
Blue	0.0, 0.3, 0.6, 1.0
Yellow	0.6, 0.5, 0.0, 1.0
HalfSpace0	1.0, 0.0, 0.0, 0.2
HalfSpace1	0.309016994, 0.951056516, 0.0, 0.2
HalfSpace2	−0.809016994, 0.587785252, 0.0, 0.2
HalfSpace3	−0.809016994, −0.587785252, 0.0, 0.2
HalfSpace4	0.309016994, −0.951056516, 0.0, 0.2
InOrOutInit	−3.0
StripeWidth	0.3
FWidth	0.005

11.2.2 Vertex Shader

The fragment shader will be the workhorse for this shader duo, so the vertex shader needs only to compute the ball's center position in eye coordinates, the eye coordinate position of the vertex, and the clip space position at each vertex. The application could provide the ball's center position in eye coordinates, but our vertex shader doesn't have much to do, and doing it this way means the application doesn't have to keep track of the modelview matrix. This value could easily be computed in the fragment shader, but the fragment shader will likely have a little better performance if we leave the computation in the vertex shader and pass the result as a varying variable (see Listing 11.4).

Listing 11.4 Vertex shader for drawing a toy ball

```
varying vec4 ECposition;   // surface position in eye coordinates
varying vec4 ECballCenter; // ball center in eye coordinates
uniform vec4 BallCenter;   // ball center in modeling coordinates

void main(void)
{
    ECposition  = gl_ModelViewMatrix * gl_Vertex;
    ECballCenter = gl_ModelViewMatrix * BallCenter;
    gl_Position = ftransform();
}
```

11.2.3 Fragment Shader

The toy ball fragment shader is a little bit longer than some of the previous examples, so we'll build it up a few lines of code at a time and provide some illustrations of intermediate results. Here are the definitions for the local variables that will be used in the toy ball fragment shader:

```
vec4   normal;        // Analytically computed normal
vec4   p;             // Point in shader space
vec4   surfColor;     // Computed color of the surface
float intensity;     // Computed light intensity
vec4   distance;      // Computed distance values
float inorout;       // Counter for computing star pattern
```

The first thing we'll do is turn the surface location that we're shading into a point on a sphere with a radius of 1.0. We can do this using the **normalize** function:

```
p.xyz = normalize(ECposition.xyz - ECballCenter.xyz);
p.w   = 1.0;
```

We don't want to include the *w* coordinate in the computation, so we use the component selector **.xyz** to select the first three components of *ECposition* and *ECballCenter*. This normalized vector is stored in the first three components of *p*. With this computation, p represents a point on the sphere with radius 1, so all three components of *p* will be in the range [–1,1]. The *w* coordinate isn't really pertinent to our computations at this point, but to make subsequent calculations work properly, we initialize it to a value of 1.0.

Next, we need to perform our half-space computations. A counter called *inorout* will be initialized to a value of –3. The counter will be incremented each time the surface location is "in" with respect to a half-space. Because there are five half-spaces defined, the final counter value will be in the range [–3,2]. Values of 1 or 2 will indicate that the fragment is within the star pattern. Values of 0 or less will indicate that the fragment is outside the star pattern.

```
inorout = InOrOutInit;       // initialize inorout to -3
```

We could have defined the half-spaces as an array of five **vec4** values and done our "in" or "out" computations and stored the results in an array of five **float** values. But we can take a little better advantage of the parallel nature of the underlying graphics hardware if we do things a bit differently. We'll see how in a minute. First, we compute the distance between *p* and the first four half-spaces using the built-in dot product function:

```
distance[0] = dot(p, HalfSpace0);
distance[1] = dot(p, HalfSpace1);
distance[2] = dot(p, HalfSpace2);
distance[3] = dot(p, HalfSpace3);
```

The results of these half-space distance calculations are visualized in (A)–(D) of Figure 11.1. Surface locations that are "in" with respect to the half-space are shaded in gray and points that are "out" are shaded in black.

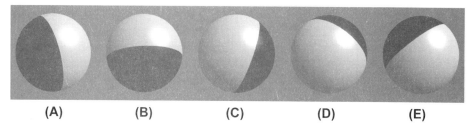

(A)   (B)   (C)   (D)   (E)

Figure 11.1 Visualizing the results of the half-space distance calculations (Courtesy of ATI Research, Inc.)

You may have been wondering why our counter was defined as a **float** instead of an **int**. We're going to use the counter value as the basis for a smoothly antialiased transition between the color of the star pattern and the color of the rest of the ball's surface. To this end, we use the **smoothstep** function to set the distance to 0 if the computed distance is less than *–FWidth*, to 1 if the computed distance is greater than *FWidth*, and to a smoothly interpolated value between 0 and 1 if the computed distance is in between those two values. By defining *distance* as a **vec4**, the smooth step computation can be performed on four values in parallel. **smoothstep** implies a divide operation, and because *FWidth* is a float, only one divide operation is necessary. This makes it all very efficient.

```
distance = smoothstep(-FWidth, FWidth, distance);
```

Now we can quickly add the values in *distance* by performing a dot product between *distance* and a **vec4** containing all 1s:

```
inorout += dot(distance, vec4(1.0));
```

Because we initialized *inorout* to –3, we add the result of the dot product to the previous value of *inorout*. This variable now contains a value in the range [–3,1], and we have one more half-space distance to compute. We'll compute the distance to the fifth half-space, and we'll do the computation to determine whether we're "in" or "out" of the stripe around the ball. We'll call the **smoothstep** function to do the same operation on these two values as was performed on the previous four half-space distances. The *inorout* counter is updated by adding the result from the distance computation with the final half-space. The distance computation with respect to the fifth half-space is illustrated in (E) of Figure 11.1.

```
distance.x = dot(p, HalfSpace4);
distance.y = StripeWidth - abs(p.z);
distance = smoothstep(-FWidth, FWidth, distance);
inorout += distance.x;
```

(In this case, we're performing a smooth step operation on a **vec4**, and we only really care about two of the components. The performance will probably be fine on a graphics device designed to process **vec4** values in parallel, but it might be somewhat inefficient on a graphics device with a scalar architecture. In the latter case, however, the OpenGL Shading Language compiler may very well be smart enough to realize that the results of the third and fourth components were never consumed later in the program, so it might optimize away the instructions for computing those two values.)

The value for *inorout* is now in the range [–3,2]. This intermediate result is illustrated in of Figure 11.2 (A). By clamping the value of *inorout* to the range [0,1], we obtain the result shown in Figure 11.2 (B).

```
inorout = clamp(inorout, 0.0, 1.0);
```

At this point, we can compute the surface color for the fragment. We use the computed value of *inorout* to perform a linear blend between yellow and red to define the star pattern. If we were to stop here, the result would look like Color Plate 16 (A). If we take the results of this calculation and do a linear blend with the color of the stripe, we get the result shown in Color Plate 16 (B). Because we used **smoothstep**, the values of *inorout* and *distance.y* will provide a nicely antialiased edge at the border between colors.

```
surfColor = mix(Yellow, Red, inorout);
surfColor = mix(surfColor, Blue, distance.y);
```

The result at this stage is flat and unrealistic. Performing a lighting calculation will fix this. The first step is to analytically compute the normal for this fragment, which we can do because we know the eye coordinate position of the center of the ball (it's provided in the varying variable *ECballCenter*) and we know the eye coordinate position of the fragment (it's passed in the varying variable *ECposition*). (This approach could have been used with the earth shader discussed in Section 10.2 in order to avoid passing the surface

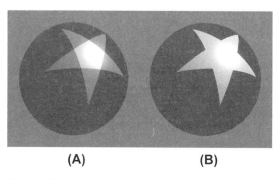

(A)   **(B)**

Figure 11.2   Intermediate results from "in" or "out" computation. Surface points that are "in" with respect to all five half-planes are shown in white, and points that are "in" with respect to four half-planes are shown in gray (A). The value of *inorout* is clamped to the range [0,1] to produce the result shown in (B). (Courtesy of ATI Research, Inc.)

normal as a varying variable and using the interpolated results.) As a matter of fact, we've already computed this value and stored it in *p*:

```
// normal = point on surface for sphere at (0,0,0)
normal = p;
```

The diffuse part of the lighting equation is computed with these three lines of code:

```
intensity  = 0.2; // ambient
intensity += 0.8 * clamp(dot(LightDir, normal), 0.0, 1.0);
surfColor *= intensity;
```

The result of diffuse-only lighting is shown in Color Plate 17 (A). The final step is to add in a specular contribution with these three lines of code:

```
intensity  = clamp(dot(HVector, normal), 0.0, 1.0);
intensity  = pow(intensity, SpecularColor.a);
surfColor += SpecularColor * intensity;
```

Notice in Color Plate 17 (B) that the specular highlight is perfect! Because the surface normal at each fragment is computed exactly, there is no misshapen specular highlight caused by tesselation facets like we're used to seeing. The resulting value is written to *gl_FragColor* and sent on for final processing before ultimately being written into the frame buffer.

```
gl_FragColor = vec4 (surfColor, 1.0);
```

Voila! Your very own toy ball, created completely out of thin air! The complete listing of the toy ball fragment shader is shown in Listing 11.5.

Listing 11.5 Fragment shader for drawing a toy ball

```
varying vec4 ECposition;   // surface position in eye coordinates
varying vec4 ECballCenter; // ball center in eye coordinates

uniform vec4  LightDir;    // light direction, should be normalized
uniform vec4  HVector;     // reflection vector for infinite light

uniform vec4  SpecularColor;
uniform vec4  Red, Yellow, Blue;

uniform vec4  HalfSpace0;   // half-spaces used to define star pattern
uniform vec4  HalfSpace1;
uniform vec4  HalfSpace2;
uniform vec4  HalfSpace3;
uniform vec4  HalfSpace4;
```

```
uniform float InOrOutInit;   // = -3
uniform float StripeWidth;   // = 0.4
uniform float FWidth;        // = TBD

void main(void)
{
    vec4  normal;            // Analytically computed normal
    vec4  p;                 // Point in shader space
    vec4  surfColor;         // Computed color of the surface
    float intensity;         // Computed light intensity
    vec4  distance;          // Computed distance values
    float inorout;           // Counter for computing star pattern

    p.xyz = normalize(ECposition.xyz - ECballCenter.xyz);
    p.w   = 1.0;

    inorout = InOrOutInit;      // initialize inorout to -3

    distance[0] = dot(p, HalfSpace0);
    distance[1] = dot(p, HalfSpace1);
    distance[2] = dot(p, HalfSpace2);
    distance[3] = dot(p, HalfSpace3);

    distance = smoothstep(-FWidth, FWidth, distance);

    inorout += dot(distance, vec4(1.0));

    distance.x = dot(p, HalfSpace4);
    distance.y = StripeWidth - abs(p.z);
    distance = smoothstep(-FWidth, FWidth, distance);
    inorout += distance.x;

    inorout = clamp(inorout, 0.0, 1.0);

    surfColor = mix(Yellow, Red, inorout);
    surfColor = mix(surfColor, Blue, distance.y);

    // normal = point on surface for sphere at (0,0,0)
    normal = p;

    // Per-fragment diffuse lighting
    intensity  = 0.2; // ambient
    intensity += 0.8 * clamp(dot(LightDir, normal), 0.0, 1.0);
    surfColor *= intensity;

    // Per-fragment specular lighting
    intensity  = clamp(dot(HVector, normal), 0.0, 1.0);
    intensity  = pow(intensity, SpecularColor.a);
```

```
    surfColor += SpecularColor * intensity;

    gl_FragColor = vec4 (surfColor, 1.0);
}
```

11.3 Lattice

Here's a little bit of a gimmick. In this example, we'll show how *not* to draw the object procedurally.

In this example, we'll look at how the **discard** command can be used in a fragment shader to achieve some interesting effects. The **discard** command causes fragments to be discarded rather than used to update the frame buffer. We'll use this to draw geometry with "holes." The vertex shader will be the exact same vertex shader used for stripes (Section 11.1.1). The fragment shader is shown in Listing 11.6.

Listing 11.6 Fragment shader for procedurally discarding part of an object

```
varying vec3  DiffuseColor;
varying vec3  SpecularColor;

uniform vec2  Scale;
uniform vec2  Threshold;
uniform vec3  SurfaceColor;

void main (void)
{
    float ss = fract(gl_TexCoord[0].s * Scale.s);
    float tt = fract(gl_TexCoord[0].t * Scale.t);

    if ((ss > Threshold.s) && (tt > Threshold.t)) discard;

    vec3 finalColor = SurfaceColor * DiffuseColor + SpecularColor;
    gl_FragColor = vec4 (finalColor, 1.0);
}
```

The part of the object to be discarded is determined by the values of the *s* and *t* texture coordinates. A scale factor is applied to adjust the frequency of the lattice. The fractional part of this scaled texture coordinate value is computed to provide a number in the range [0,1]. These values are compared against the threshold values that have been provided. If both values exceed the threshold, the fragment is discarded. Otherwise, we do a simple lighting calculation and render the fragment.

In Color Plate 15, the threshold values were both set to 0.13. This means that more than three-quarters of the fragments were being discarded! And that's what I call a "holy cow!"

11.4 Bump Mapping

We have already seen procedural shaders that modified color (*brick, stripes*) and opacity (*lattice*). Another whole class of interesting effects can be applied to a surface using a technique called BUMP MAPPING. Bump mapping involves modulating the surface normal before lighting is applied. The modulation can be done algorithmically to apply a regular pattern, it can be done by adding noise to the components of a normal, or it can be done by looking up a perturbation value in a texture map. Bump mapping has proven to be an effective way of increasing the apparent realism of an object without increasing the geometric complexity. It can be used to simulate surface detail or surface irregularities.

This technique does not truly alter the surface being shaded, it merely "tricks" the lighting calculations. Therefore, the "bumping" will not show up on the silhouette edges of an object. Imagine modeling a planet as a sphere and shading it with a bump map so that it appears to have mountains that are quite large relative to the diameter of the planet. Because nothing has been done to change the underlying geometry, which is perfectly round, the silhouette of the sphere will always appear perfectly round, even if the mountains (bumps) go right up to the silhouette edge. In real life, you would expect the mountains on the silhouette edges to prevent the silhouette from looking perfectly round. For this reason, it is a good idea to use bump mapping to only apply "small" effects to a surface (at least relative to the size of the surface). Wrinkles on an orange, embossed logos, and pitted bricks are all good examples of things that can be successfully bump mapped.

Bump mapping adds apparent geometric complexity during fragment processing, so once again the key to the process will be our fragment shader. This implies that the lighting operation will need to be performed by our fragment shader, instead of by the vertex shader where it is often handled. Again, this points out one of the advantages of the programmability that is available through the OpenGL Shading Language. We are free to perform whatever operations are necessary, in either the vertex shader or the fragment shader. We don't need to be bound to the fixed functionality ideas of where things like lighting are performed.

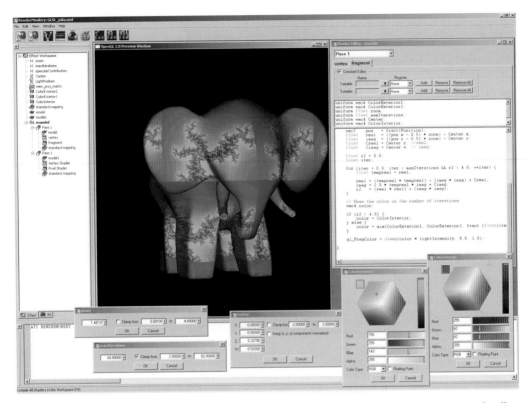

Color Plate 1 Screen shot of the RenderMonkey IDE user interface. The shader that is procedurally generating a Julia set on the surface of the elephant is shown in the source code window. Color selection tools and user interface elements for manipulating user-defined uniform variables are also shown.

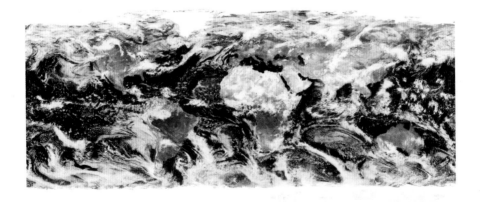

Color Plate 2 A full-color image of Earth that is used as a texture map for the shader discussed in Section 10.2. (Blue Marble image by Reto Stöckli, NASA Goddard Space Flight Center)

Color Plate 3 Earth image texture mapped onto a sphere using the fragment shader described in Section 10.2. (3Dlabs, Inc./Blue Marble image by Reto Stöckli, NASA Goddard Space Flight Center)

Color Plate 4 Screen shot of the SolidWorks 2004 application, showing a jigsaw rendered with OpenGL shaders to simulate a chrome body, galvanized steel housing, and cast iron blade. (Courtesy of SolidWorks Corporation)

Color Plate 5 "Daytime" and "Nighttime" texture maps used in the fragment shader described in Section 10.3. (Blue Marble images by Reto Stöckli, NASA Goddard Space Flight Center)

Color Plate 6 As the world turns—Daytime, dawn, and nighttime views of Earth, rendered by the shaders discussed in Section 10.3 (3Dlabs, Inc./Blue Marble image by Reto Stöckli, NASA Goddard Space Flight Center)

Color Plate 7 An equirectangular texture map of a house exterior. This image is used as the environment map for the shader presented in Section 10.4. (Image courtesy Jerome Dewhurst, jerome@photographica.co.uk, http://www.photographica.co.uk.)

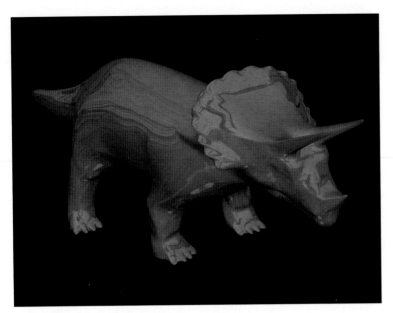

Color Plate 8 Environment mapped shader example. The environment map shown in Color Plate 7 is used together with the environment mapping shaders discussed in Section 10.4. (3Dlabs, Inc.)

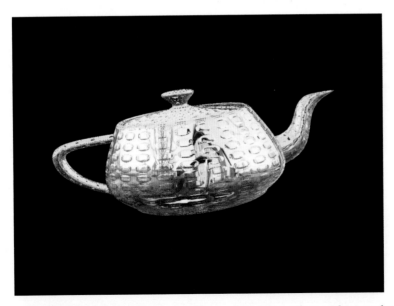

Color Plate 9 Environment mapping a mirror-like surface with procedural bumps using the environment map shown in Color Plate 7. The bumps are applied using the technique described in Section 11.4. (3Dlabs, Inc.)

Color Plate 10 Image showing the difference between a conventional texture map (lower left) and a polynomial texture map (PTM) (upper right). The conventional texture looks flat and unrealistic as the light source is moved, while the PTM faithfully reproduces changing specular highlights and self-shadowing. (© Copyright 2003 Hewlett-Packard Development Company, L.P., Reproduced with Permission)

Color Plate 11 A torus rendered using the BRDF PTM shaders described in Section 10.5. Although the paint is basically black, note the change in the highlight color (from bluish-purple in the back to reddish-brown in the front) as the reflection angle changes. (© Copyright 2003 Hewlett-Packard Development Company, L.P., Reproduced with Permission)

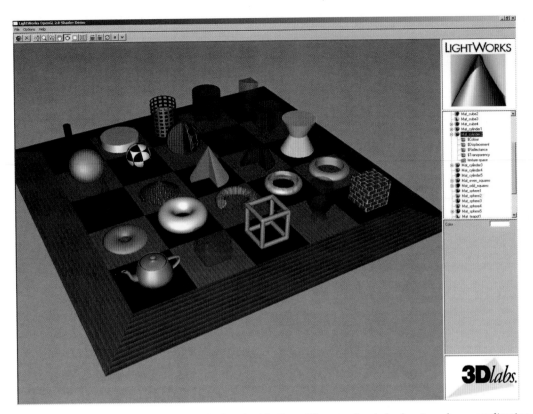

Color Plate 12 A variety of objects rendered with OpenGL procedural shaders in a demo application by LightWork Design. This application shows a graphics user interface designed for interacting with procedural shaders. (Courtesy of LightWorks Design)

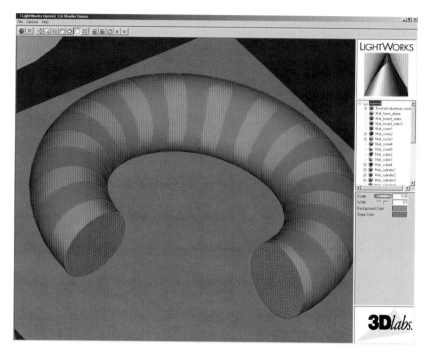

Color Plate 13 Close-up of a partial torus rendered with the stripe shader described in Section 11.1. (Courtesy of LightWork Design)

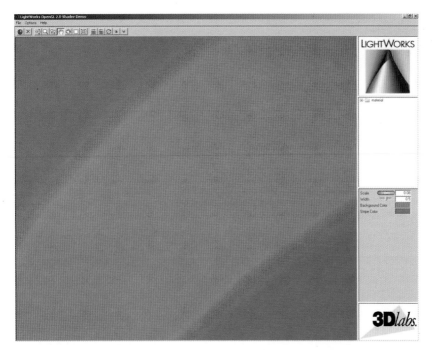

Color Plate 14 Extreme close-up view of one of the stripes that shows the effect of the "fuzz" calculation from the shader described in Section 11.1. (Courtesy of LightWork Design)

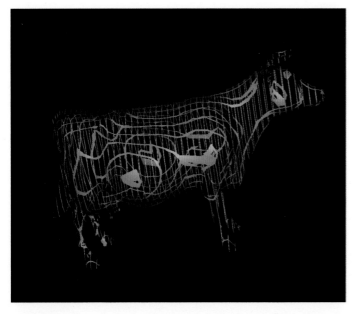

Color Plate 15 The lattice shader presented in Section 11.3 is applied to the cow model. (3Dlabs, Inc.)

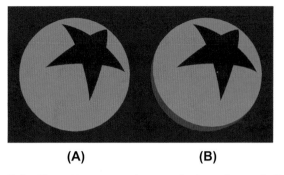

(A)   (B)

Color Plate 16 Intermediate results from the toy ball shader described in Section 11.2. In (A), red is applied to the procedurally defined star pattern and yellow to the rest of the sphere. In (B), the blue stripe is added. (Courtesy of ATI Research, Inc.)

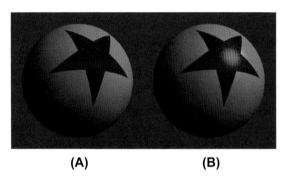

(A)   (B)

Color Plate 17 Lighting is applied to the toy ball shader described in Section 11.2. In (A), diffuse lighting is applied. In (B), the analytically defined normal is used to apply a specular highlight. (Courtesy of ATI Research, Inc.)

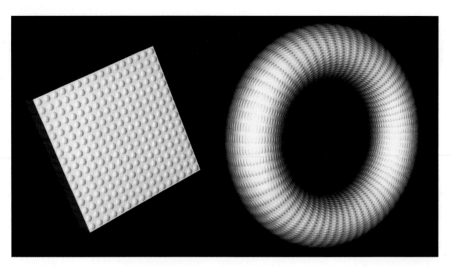

Color Plate 18 A simple box and a torus that have been bump mapped using the procedural method described in Section 11.4. (3Dlabs, Inc.)

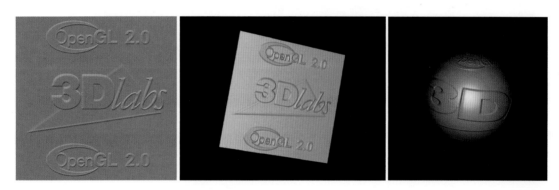

Color Plate 19 A normal map (left) and the rendered result on a simple box and a sphere using the techniques described in Section 11.4.4. (3Dlabs, Inc.)

Color Plate 20 Teapots rendered with noise shaders, as described in Chapter 12. Clockwise from upper left: a cloud shader that sums four octaves of noise and uses a blue-to-white color gradient to code the result; a sun surface shader that uses the absolute value function to introduce discontinuities (turbulence); a granite shader that uses a single high-frequency noise value to modulate between white and black; a marble shader that uses noise to modulate a sine function to produce alternating "veins" of color. (3Dlabs, Inc.)

Color Plate 21 Several frames from the animated sequence produced by the wobble shader described in Section 13.7. (3Dlabs, Inc.)

Color Plate 22 Various objects rendered with the wood shader described in Section 12.7. (3Dlabs, Inc.)

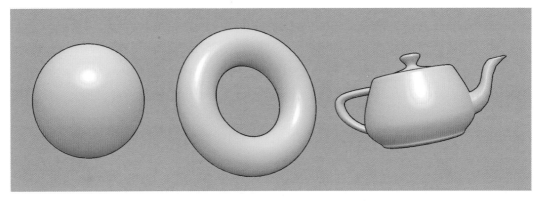

Color Plate 23 Gooch shading applied to three objects (see Section 15.2). Background color (gray), warm color (yellow), and cool color (blue) are chosen in order that they do not impede the clarity of the outline color (black) or highlight color (white). Details are still visible in this rendering that would be lost in shadow using traditional shading. (3Dlabs, Inc.)

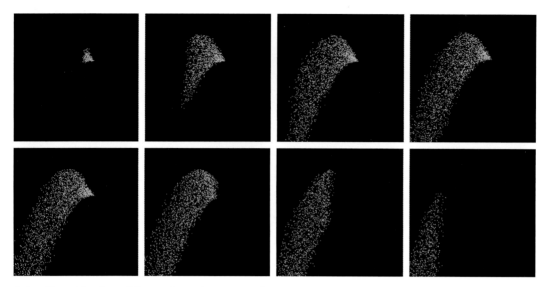

Color Plate 24 Several frames from the animated sequence produced by the particle system shader described in Section 13.6. In this animation, the particle system contains 10,000 points with randomly assigned initial velocities and start times. The position of the particle at each frame is computed entirely in the vertex shader according to a formula that simulates the effects of gravity. (3Dlabs, Inc.)

Color Plate 25 Brick shader with and without antialiasing. On the left, the results of the brick shader presented in Chapter 6. On the right, results of antialiasing by analytic integration using the brick shader described in Section 14.4.5. (3Dlabs, Inc.)

Color Plate 26 Results of the image brightness shader discussed in Section 16.5.1 with *alpha* equal to 0.4, 0.6, 0.8, 1.0, and 1.2 from left to right. The image with *alpha* = 1.0 is the same as the unmodified source image.

Color Plate 27 Results of the image contrast shader discussed in Section 16.5.2 with *alpha* equal to 0.4, 0.6, 0.8, 1.0, and 1.2 from left to right. The image with *alpha* = 1.0 is the same as the unmodified source image.

Color Plate 28 Results of the image saturation shader discussed in Section 16.5.3 with *alpha* equal to 0.0, 0.5, 0.75, 1.0, and 1.25 from left to right. The image with *alpha* = 0.0 is the same as the unmodified target image. The image with *alpha* = 1.0 is the same as the unmodified source image.

Color Plate 29 Results of the image sharpness shader discussed in Section 16.5.4 with *alpha* equal to 0.0, 0.5, 1.0, 1.5, and 2.0 from left to right. The image with *alpha* = 0.0 is the same as the unmodified target image. The image with *alpha* = 1.0 is the same as the unmodified source image.

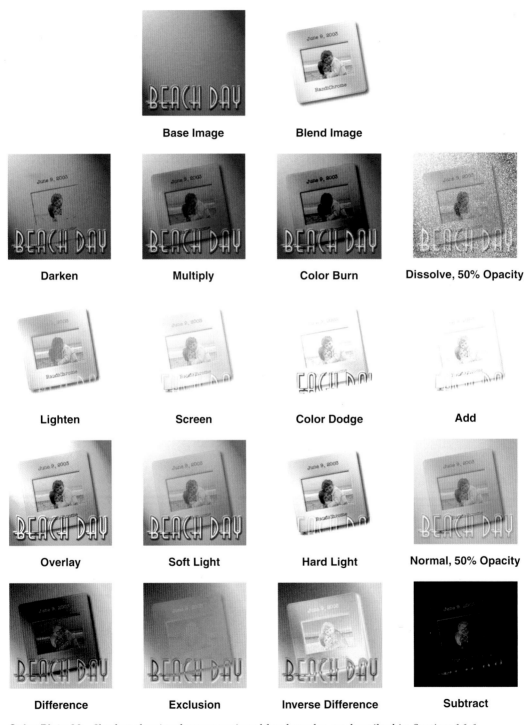

Base Image

Blend Image

Darken

Multiply

Color Burn

Dissolve, 50% Opacity

Lighten

Screen

Color Dodge

Add

Overlay

Soft Light

Hard Light

Normal, 50% Opacity

Difference

Exclusion

Inverse Difference

Subtract

Color Plate 30 Shaders that implement various blend modes, as described in Section 16.6.

The key to bump mapping is that we need a valid surface normal at each fragment location, and we also need a light source and viewing direction vectors. If we have access to all of these values in the fragment shader, we can procedurally perturb the normal prior to the light source calculation in order to produce the appearance of "bumps." In this case, we really will be attempting to produce bumps, or small spherical nodules on the surface being rendered.

The light source computation is typically performed using dot products. In order for the result to have meaning, it must be arranged that all of the components of the light source calculation be defined in the same coordinate space. When the vertex shader is used to perform lighting, we typically use the eye coordinate system to perform lighting. Light source positions or directions are defined in eye coordinates, and incoming normals and vertex values are transformed into this space in order to do the calculation.

However, the eye coordinate system isn't necessarily the best choice for doing lighting in the fragment shader. We could normalize the light direction and surface normal after transforming them to eye space and then pass them to the fragment shader as varying variables. However, the light direction vector would need to be renormalized after interpolation in order to get accurate results. In addition, whatever method is used to compute the perturbation normal, it would need to be transformed into eye space and added to the surface normal; that vector would also need to be normalized. Without renormalization, the lighting artifacts would be quite noticeable. Per-forming these operations at every fragment might be reasonably costly in terms of performance. There is a better way.

Let us look at another coordinate space that is called the SURFACE-LOCAL COORDINATE SPACE. This is a coordinate system that varies over a rendered object, and it assumes that each point is at (0, 0, 0) and that the unperturbed surface normal at each point is (0, 0, 1). This would be a pretty convenient coordinate system in which to do our bump mapping calculations. But, in order to do our lighting computation, we need to make sure that our light direction, viewing direction, and the computed perturbed normal are all defined in the same coordinate system. If our perturbed normal is defined in surface local coordinates, that means we need to transform our light direction and viewing direction into surface-local space as well. How is that accomplished?

What we need is a transformation matrix that will transform each incoming vertex into surface-local coordinates (i.e., incoming vertex (x, y, z) will be transformed to (0, 0, 0)). We'll need to construct this transformation matrix at each vertex. Then, at each vertex, we'll use the surface-local transformation matrix to transform both the light direction and the viewing direction. In this way, the surface local coordinates of the light direction and the viewing direction will be computed at each vertex and interpolated across the primitive. At each fragment, we can utilize these values to perform our lighting calculation with the perturbed normal that we calculate.

But we still haven't answered the real question. How do we create the transformation matrix that will transform from object coordinates to surface-local coordinates? There are an infinite number of transforms that will transform a particular vertex to (0, 0, 0). To transform incoming vertex values, we'll need a way that gives consistent results as we interpolate between them.

The solution is to require the application to send down one more attribute value for each vertex, a tangent value. Furthermore, we'll require the application to send us tangents that are consistently defined across the surface of the object. By definition, this tangent vector will be in the plane of the surface being rendered and perpendicular to the incoming surface normal. If defined consistently across the object, it will serve to orient consistently the coordinate system that we derive. If we perform a cross product between the tangent vector and the surface normal, we'll get a third vector that is perpendicular to the other two. This third vector is called the binormal, and it's something that we can compute in our vertex shader. Together, these three vectors form an orthonormal basis, which is what we need to define the transformation from object coordinates into surface-local coordinates. Because this particular surface-local coordinate system is defined with a tangent vector as one of the basis vectors, this coordinate system is sometimes referred to as TANGENT SPACE.

The transformation to go from object space to surface-local space is shown in Figure 11.3. The object space vector (O_x, O_y, O_z) is transformed into surface-local space by multiplying it by a matrix that contains the tangent vector (T_x, T_y, T_z) in the first row, the binormal vector (B_x, B_y, B_z) in the second row, and the surface normal (N_x, N_y, N_z) in the third row. We can use

$$\begin{bmatrix} S_x \\ S_y \\ S_z \end{bmatrix} = \begin{bmatrix} T_x & T_y & T_z \\ B_x & B_y & B_z \\ N_x & N_y & N_z \end{bmatrix} \begin{bmatrix} O_x \\ O_y \\ O_z \end{bmatrix}$$

Figure 11.3   Transformation from object space to surface-local space

this process to transform both the light direction vector and the viewing direction vector into surface-local coordinates. The transformed vectors will be interpolated across the primitive, and the interpolated vectors will be used in the fragment shader to compute the reflection using the procedurally perturbed normal.

11.4.1 Application Setup

For our procedural bump map shader to work properly, the application must send a vertex position, a surface normal, and a tangent vector in the plane of the surface being rendered. The tangent vector will be passed as a generic vertex attribute, and the index of the generic attribute to be used should be bound to the vertex shader variable *tangent* by calling **glBindAttribLocationARB**. The application is also responsible for providing values for the uniform variables *LightPosition*, *SurfaceColor*, *BumpDensity*, *BumpSize*, and *SpecularFactor*.

Care must be taken to orient the tangent vectors consistently between vertices; otherwise, the transformation into surface-local coordinates will be inconsistent and the lighting computation will yield unpredictable results. Consistent tangents can be computed algorithmically for mathematically defined surfaces. Consistent tangents for polygonal objects can be computed using neighboring vertices and applying a consistent ordering with respect to the object's texture coordinates.

The problem with inconsistently defined normals is illustrated in Figure 11.4. This diagram shows two triangles, one with consistently defined tangents and one with inconsistently defined tangents. The gray arrowheads indicate the tangent and binormal vectors (the surface normal is pointing straight out of the page). The white arrowheads indicate the direction toward the light source (in this case, a directional light source is illustrated).

When we transform vertex 1 to surface-local coordinates, we get the same initial result in both cases. When we transform vertex 2, we get a large difference because the tangent vectors are very different between the two vertices. If tangents were defined consistently, this situation would not occur unless the surface had a high degree of curvature across this polygon. And if that was the case, you would really want to tessellate the geometry further in order to prevent this from happening.

The result is that in case 1, our light direction vector will be smoothly interpolated from the first vertex to the second and all the interpolated vectors

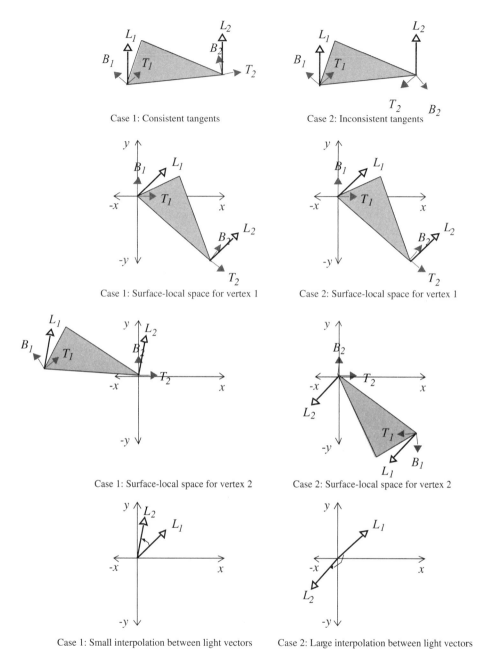

Case 1: Consistent tangents   Case 2: Inconsistent tangents

Case 1: Surface-local space for vertex 1   Case 2: Surface-local space for vertex 1

Case 1: Surface-local space for vertex 2   Case 2: Surface-local space for vertex 2

Case 1: Small interpolation between light vectors   Case 2: Large interpolation between light vectors

Figure 11.4   Inconsistently defined tangents can lead to large lighting errors

will be roughly the same length. If we normalize this light vector at each vertex, the interpolated vectors will be very close to unit length as well.

But in case 2, the interpolation will cause vectors of wildly different lengths to be generated, some of them near zero. This will cause severe artifacts in the lighting calculation.

OpenGL does not have a defined vertex attribute for a tangent vector. The best choice is to use a generic vertex attribute to pass in the tangent value just as we did in the polynomial texture mapping example back in Section 10.5.1. The only difference between the application set up for this shader is that we won't be passing down the binormal; we'll have the vertex shader compute it automatically.

11.4.2 Vertex Shader

The vertex shader for our procedural bump map shader is shown in Listing 11.7. This shader is responsible for computing the surface-local light direction and the surface-local eye direction. In order to do this, it accepts the incoming vertex position, surface normal, and tangent vector, computes the binormal, and transforms the object space light direction and viewing direction using the created surface-local transformation matrix. The texture coordinates are also passed on to the fragment shader, as these will be used to determine the position of our procedural bumps.

Listing 11.7 Vertex shader for doing procedural bump mapping

```
varying vec3 LightDir;
varying vec3 EyeDir;

uniform vec3 LightPosition;

attribute vec3 Tangent;

void main(void)
{
    EyeDir        = vec3 (gl_ModelViewMatrix * gl_Vertex);
    gl_Position   = ftransform();
    gl_TexCoord[0] = gl_MultiTexCoord0;

    vec3 n = normalize(gl_NormalMatrix * gl_Normal);
    vec3 t = normalize(gl_NormalMatrix * Tangent);
    vec3 b = cross(n, t);

    vec3 v;
    v.x = dot(LightPosition, t);
```

```
        v.y = dot(LightPosition, b);
        v.z = dot(LightPosition, n);
        LightDir = normalize(v);

        v.x = dot(EyeDir, t);
        v.y = dot(EyeDir, b);
        v.z = dot(EyeDir, n);
        EyeDir = normalize(v);
}
```

11.4.3 Fragment Shader

The fragment shader for doing procedural bump mapping is shown in
Listing 11.8. A couple of the characteristics of the bump pattern are parameterized by declaring them as uniform variables, namely *BumpDensity* (how
many bumps per unit area) and *BumpSize* (how wide each bump will be).
Two of the general characteristics of the overall surface are also defined as
uniform variables, *SurfaceColor* (base color of the surface) and *SpecularFactor*
(specular reflectance property).

The bumps that we compute are round. Because the texture coordinate will
be used to determine the positioning of the bumps, the first thing we do is
multiply the incoming texture coordinate by the *density* value. This
controls whether we see more or fewer bumps on the surface. Using the
resulting grid, we proceed to compute a bump located in the center of each
grid square. The components of the perturbation vector *p* are computed as
the distance from the center of the bump in the *x* direction and the distance
from the center of the bump in the *y* direction. (We're only going to perturb
the normal in the *x* and *y* directions. The *z* value for our perturbation
normal will always be 1.0.) A "pseudodistance" *d* is computed by squaring
the components of *p* and adding them together. (The real distance could be
computed at the cost of doing another square root, but it's not really necessary if we consider *BumpSize* to be a relative value rather than an absolute
value.)

In order to do a proper reflection calculation later on, we really need to
normalize the perturbation normal. This normal must be a unit vector in
order to allow us to do dot products and get accurate cosine values for use
in the lighting computation. A vector is normalized by multiplying each
component of the normal by $1.0 / \textbf{sqrt}(x^2 + y^2 + z^2)$. Because of our computation for *d*, we've already computed part of what we need (i.e., $x^2 + y^2$).
Furthermore, because we're not perturbing *z* at all, we know that z^2 will
always be 1.0. In order to minimize the computation, we'll just finish
computing our normalization factor at this point in the shader by
computing $1.0 / \textbf{sqrt}(d + 1.0)$.

Next, we compare *d* to *BumpSize* to see if we're in a bump or not. If we're not, we set our perturbation vector to 0 and our normalization factor to 1.0. The lighting computation happens in the next few lines. We compute our normalized perturbation vector by multiplying through with the normalization factor *f*. The diffuse and specular reflection values are computed in the usual way, except that the interpolated surface-local coordinate light and view direction vectors are used. We'll get decent results without normalizing these two vectors as long as we don't have large differences in their values between vertices.

Listing 11.8 Fragment shader for procedural bump mapping

```
varying vec3 LightDir;
varying vec3 EyeDir;

uniform vec3  SurfaceColor;    // = (0.7, 0.6, 0.18)
uniform float BumpDensity;     // = 16.0
uniform float BumpSize;        // = 0.15
uniform float SpecularFactor;  // = 0.5

void main (void)
{
    vec3 litColor;
    vec2 c = BumpDensity * gl_TexCoord[0].st;
    vec2 p = fract(c) - vec2 (0.5);

    float d, f;
    d = p.x * p.x + p.y * p.y;
    f = 1.0 / sqrt(d + 1.0);

    if (d >= BumpSize)
        { p = vec2(0.0); f = 1.0; }

    vec3 normDelta = vec3 (p.x, p.y, 1.0) * f;
    litColor = SurfaceColor * max(dot(normDelta, LightDir), 0.0);
    vec3 reflectDir = reflect(LightDir, normDelta);

    float spec = max(dot(EyeDir, reflectDir), 0.0);
    spec = pow(spec, 6.0);
    spec *= SpecularFactor;
    litColor = min(litColor + spec, vec3 (1.0));

    gl_FragColor = vec4 (litColor, 1.0);
}
```

The results from the procedural bump map shader are shown applied to two objects, a simple box and a torus, in Color Plate 18. The texture coordinates are used as the basis for positioning the bumps, and, because the texture coordinates go from 0.0 to 1.0 four times around the diameter of the torus, the bumps look much closer together on that object.

11.4.4 Normal Maps

It is easy to modify our shader to obtain the normal perturbation values from a texture rather than to generate them procedurally. A texture that contains normal values for the purpose of bump mapping is called a NORMAL MAP.

An example of a normal map and the results applied to our simple box object are shown in Color Plate 19. Individual components for the normals can range from [–1,1]. To encode them into an RGB texture with 8 bits per component, they must be mapped into the range [0,1]. The normal map appears chalk blue because the default perturbation vector of (0,0,1) is encoded in the normal map as (0.5,0.5,1.0). Support for floating-point textures with 16 bits per component is becoming more and more common on graphics accelerators, but it is not yet ubiquitous. If you use a floating-point texture format for storing normals, you will tend to increase your image quality (for instance, reducing banding effects in specular highlights). Of course, textures that are 16 bits per component require twice as much texture memory as 8-bit per component textures, and performance might be reduced.

The vertex program is identical to the one described in Section 11.4.2. The fragment shader is almost the same, except that instead of computing the perturbed normal procedurally, it is obtained from a normal map stored in texture memory.

11.5 Summary

A master magician can make it look like something is created out of thin air. With procedural textures, you, as a shader writer, can express algorithms that turn flat gray surfaces into colorful, patterned, bumpy, or reflective ones. The trick is to come up with an algorithm that expresses the texture you envision. By coding this algorithm as an OpenGL shader, you too can create something out of thin air.

In this chapter, we only scratched the surface of what's possible. We created a stripe shader, but grids and checkerboards and polka dots are no more difficult. We created a toy ball with a star, but we could have created a beach ball with snowflakes. Shaders can be written to procedurally include or exclude geometry or to add bumps or grooves. The next chapter will show how an irregular function (noise) can be used to achieve a wide range of procedural texturing effects. Shaders for generating procedural textures with a more complex mathematical function (the Mandelbrot and Julia sets) and for creating non-photorealistic effects will also be described later in the book.

Procedural textures are mathematically precise, are easy to parameterize, and don't require large amounts of texture memory. The end goal of a vertex shader/fragment shader pair is to produce a color value (and possibly a depth value) that will be written into the frame buffer. Because the OpenGL Shading Language is a procedural programming language, the only limit to this computation is your imagination.

11.6 Further Information

The book *Texturing and Modeling: A Procedural Approach, Third Edition*, by Ebert, et. al. (2002) is entirely devoted to creating images procedurally. This book contains a wealth of information and provides a ton of inspiration regarding the creation and use of procedural models and textures.

The shaders written in the RenderMan Shading Language are often procedural in nature, and *The RenderMan Companion* by Steve Upstill (1990) and *Advanced RenderMan: Creating CGI for Motion Pictures,* by Apodaca and Gritz (1999) contain some notable examples.

Bump mapping was invented by Jim Blinn and described in his 1978 SIGGRAPH paper, *Simulation of Wrinkled Surfaces*. A very good overview of bump mapping techniques can be found in a paper titled *A Practical and Robust Bump-mapping Technique for Today's GPUs* by Mark Kilgard (2000).

A Photoshop plug-in for creating a normal map from an image is available at NVIDIA's developer Web site at http://developer.nvidia.com/view.asp?IO=ps_texture_compression_plugin.

[1] Apodaca, Anthony A., and Larry Gritz, *Advanced RenderMan: Creating CGI for Motion Pictures*, Morgan Kaufmann Publishers, San Francisco, 1999. http://www.bmrt.org/arman/materials.html

[2] Blinn, James, *Simulation of Wrinkled Surfaces*, Computer Graphics (SIGGRAPH '78 Proceedings), pp. 286–292, August 1978.

[3] Ebert, David S., John Hart, Bill Mark, F. Kenton Musgrave, Darwyn Peachey, Ken Perlin, and Steven Worley, *Texturing and Modeling: A Procedural Approach, Third Edition*, Morgan Kaufmann Publishers, San Francisco, 2002. http://www.texturingandmodeling.com

[4] Kilgard, Mark J., *A Practical and Robust Bump-mapping Technique for Today's GPUs*, Game Developers Conference, NVIDIA White Paper, 2000. http://developer.nvidia.com

[5] *NVIDIA developer Web site.* http://developer.nvidia.com

[6] Upstill, Steve, *The RenderMan Companion: A Programmer's Guide to Realistic Computer Graphics*, Addison-Wesley, Reading, Massachusetts, 1990.

Chapter 12

Noise

In computer graphics, it's easy to make things look good. By definition, geometry is drawn and rendered precisely. However, when realism is a goal, perfection isn't always such a good thing. Real world objects have dents and dings and scuffs. They show wear and tear. Computer graphics artists have to work hard to make a perfectly defined bowling pin look like it has been used and abused for 20 years in a bowling alley or to make a space ship that seems a little worse for the wear after many years of galactic travel.

This was the problem that Ken Perlin was trying to solve when he worked for a company called Magi in the early 1980s. Magi was working with Disney on a feature film called *Tron* that was the most ambitious in its use of computer graphics until that time. Perlin recognized the "imperfection" of the perfectly rendered objects in that film, and he resolved to do something about it.

In a seminal paper published in 1985, Perlin described a renderer that he had written that used a technique he called NOISE. His definition of noise was a little different than the everyday definition of noise. Normally, when we refer to noise, we're referring to something like a random pattern of pixels on a television channel with no signal (also called "snow") or static on the radio on a frequency that doesn't have any nearby station broadcasting.

But a truly random function like this isn't that useful for computer graphics. For computer graphics, we need a function that is repeatable, in order that an object can be drawn from different view angles. We also need the ability to draw the object the same way, frame after frame, in an animation. Truly random functions do not depend on any input values, so an object rendered with such a function would look different each time it was drawn. The visual artifacts caused by this type of rendering would look horrible as the object was moved about the screen. What is needed is a function that produces the same output value for a given input value every time and yet gives the appearance of randomness. This function also needs to be continuous at all levels of detail.

Perlin was the first to come up with a function that was used for this purpose. Since then, a variety of similar noise functions have been defined and used in combinations to produce interesting rendering effects such as

- Rendering natural phenomena (clouds, fire, smoke, wind effects, etc.)

- Rendering natural materials (marble, granite, wood, mountains, etc.)

- Rendering man-made materials (stucco, asphalt, cement, etc.)

- Adding imperfections to perfect models (rust, dirt, smudges, dents, etc.)

- Adding imperfections to perfect patterns (wiggles, bumps, color variations, etc.)

- Adding imperfections to time periods (time between blinks, amount of change between successive frames, etc.)

- Adding imperfections to motion (wobbles, jitters, bumps, etc.)

Actually, the list is endless. Today, most rendering libraries include support for Perlin noise or something nearly equivalent. It is a staple of realistic rendering, and it's been heavily used in the generation of computer graphics images for the movie industry. For his groundbreaking work in this area, Perlin was presented with an Academy Award for technical achievement in 1997.

Because noise is such an important technique, it is included as a built-in function in the OpenGL Shading Language. There are several ways to make use of noise within a fragment shader. After laying the groundwork for noise, we'll take a look at several shader examples that depend on noise to achieve an interesting effect.

12.1 Defining Noise

The purpose of this section is not to explain the mathematical underpinnings of noise, but to provide enough of an intuitive feel that readers will be able to grasp the noise-based OpenGL shaders presented in the chapter and then use the OpenGL Shading Language to create additional noise-based effects. For a deeper understanding of noise functions, readers are invited to consult the references listed at the end of this chapter, especially *Texturing and Modeling: A Procedural Approach, Third Edition,* by Ebert, et. al., which contains several significant discussions of noise, including a description by Perlin of his original noise function. In this book, Darwyn Peachey also provides a taxonomy of noise functions called *Making Noises*. The application of different noise functions and combinations of noise functions are discussed by Ken Musgrave in his section on building procedural planets.

As Perlin describes it, you can think of noise as "seasoning" for graphics. It often helps to add a little noise, but noise all by itself isn't all that appealing. A perfect model looks a little less perfect and, therefore, a little more realistic if some subtle noise effects are applied.

The ideal noise function has some important qualities.

- It is a continuous function that gives the appearance of randomness.

- It is a function that is repeatable (i.e., will generate the same value each time it is presented with the same input).

- It has a well-defined range of output values (usually the range is [–1,1] or [0,1]).

- The resulting values should not show obvious regular patterns or periods.

- It is a function whose small scale form is roughly independent of large scale position.

- It is a function that is isotropic (i.e., its statistical character should be rotationally invariant).

- It can be defined for 1, 2, 3, 4, or even more dimensions.

This definition of noise provides an irregular primitive that can be used to add variety or an apparent element of "randomness" to a regular pattern or period. It can be used as part of modeling, rendering, or animation. Its characteristics make it a valuable tool for creating a variety of interesting effects. Algorithms for creating noise functions make various trade-offs in quality and performance, so they meet the preceding criteria with varying degrees of success.

A simple noise function (called VALUE NOISE by Peachey) can be constructed by first assigning a pseudorandom number in the range [–1,1] to each integer value along the x axis as shown in Figure 12.1 and then smoothly interpolating between these points as shown in Figure 12.2. The function is

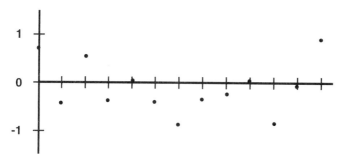

Figure 12.1   A discrete 1D noise function

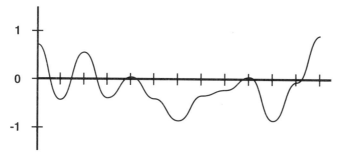

Figure 12.2   A continuous 1D noise function

repeatable in that, for a given input value, it always returns the same output value.

A key choice to be made in this type of noise function is the method used to interpolate between successive points. Linear interpolation is not good enough because the resulting noise pattern will show obvious artifacts. A cubic interpolation method is usually used to produce smooth looking results.

By varying the frequency and the amplitude, you can get a variety of noise functions (see Figure 12.3).

As you can see, the "features" in these functions get smaller and closer together as the frequency increases and the amplitude decreases. When two frequencies are related by a ratio of 2:1, it's called an OCTAVE. Figure 12.3 illustrates five octaves of the 1D noise function. These images of noise don't look all that useful, but by themselves they can provide some interesting characteristics to shaders. If we add the functions at different frequencies (see Figure 12.4), we start to see something that looks even more interesting.

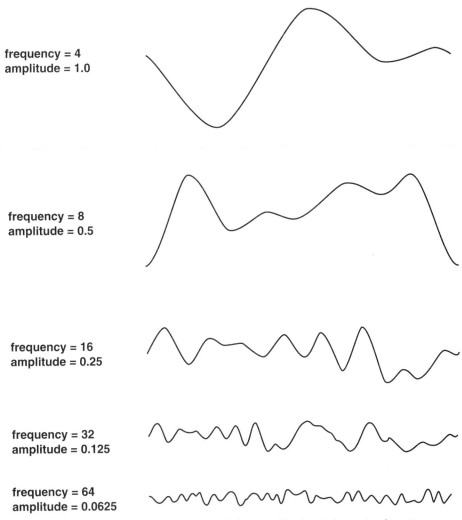

frequency = 4
amplitude = 1.0

frequency = 8
amplitude = 0.5

frequency = 16
amplitude = 0.25

frequency = 32
amplitude = 0.125

frequency = 64
amplitude = 0.0625

Figure 12.3 Varying the frequency and the amplitude of the noise function

The result is a function that contains features of various sizes. The larger bumps from the lower frequency functions provide the overall shape, whereas the smaller bumps from the higher frequency functions provide detail and interest at a smaller scale. The function that results from adding together noise of consecutive octaves, each at half the amplitude of the previous octave, was called 1/f noise by Perlin, but the terms "fractional Brownian motion" or "fBm" are used more commonly today.

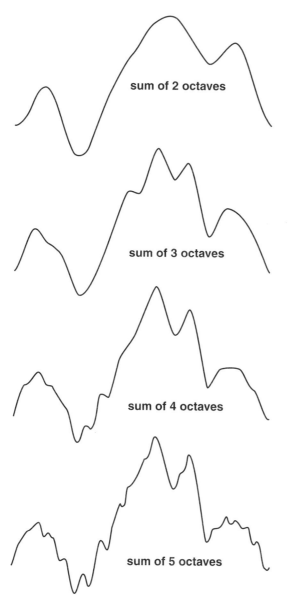

sum of 2 octaves

sum of 3 octaves

sum of 4 octaves

sum of 5 octaves

Figure 12.4   Result of adding together noise functions of different amplitude and frequency

If you are adding together octaves of noise in a procedural shader, there will come a point at which you are beginning to add frequencies that will cause aliasing artifacts. Algorithms for antialiasing noise functions will typically stop adding detail (higher frequency noise) before this occurs. This is another key aspect of the noise function—it can be faded to the average value at the point at which aliasing artifacts would begin to occur.

The noise function defined by Perlin (PERLIN NOISE) is sometimes called gradient noise. It is defined as a function whose value is 0 at each integer input value, and its shape is created by defining a pseudorandom gradient vector for the function at each of these points. The characteristics of this noise function make it a somewhat better choice, in general, for the effects we're after (see Ebert, et. al. (2002) for details). It is used for the implementation of the noise function in RenderMan, and it is also intended to be used for implementations of the **noise** function built into the OpenGL Shading Language.

Lots of other noise functions have been defined. Interesting effects can be achieved by using different noise functions for different situations or by combining noise functions of different types. It's not that easy to visualize in advance the results of calculations that depend on noise values, so varied experience will be a key ally as you try to achieve the effect you're after.

12.1.1 2D Noise

Armed with a basic idea of what the noise function looks like in one dimension, we can take a look at two-dimensional noise. Figure 12.5 contains images of 2D Perlin noise at various frequencies mapped into the range [0,1] and displayed as a grayscale image. Each successive image is twice the frequency of the previous one. In each image, the contrast has been enhanced to make the peaks brighter and the valleys darker. In actual use,

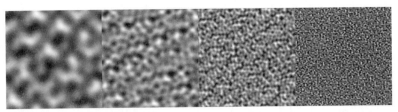

Figure 12.5 Basic 2D noise, at frequencies 4, 8, 16, and 32 (contrast enhanced)

each subsequent image has an average that is half of the previous one and an amplitude that is half the previous one. If we were to print images of the actual values, the images would be much grayer and it would be harder to see what 2D noise really looks like.

As in the 1D case, adding the different frequency functions provides more interesting results (Figure 12.6).

The first image in Figure 12.6 is exactly the same as the first image in Figure 12.5. The second image in Figure 12.6 is the sum of the first image in Figure 12.6 plus half of the second image in Figure 12.5 shifted so that its average intensity value is 0. This causes intensity to be increased in some areas and decreased in others. The third image in Figure 12.6 adds the third octave of noise to the first two, and the fourth image in Figure 12.6 adds the fourth octave. The fourth picture is starting to look a little bit like clouds in the sky.

12.1.2 Higher Dimensions of Noise

3D and 4D noise functions are obvious extensions of the 1D and 2D functions. It's a little hard to generate pictures of 3D noise, but the images in Figure 12.5 can be thought of as 2D slices out of a 3D noise function. Neighboring slices have continuity between them.

Often, a higher dimension of noise is used to control the time aspect of the next lower dimension noise function. For instance, 1D noise can be used to add some wiggle to otherwise straight lines in a drawing. If you have a 2D noise function, one dimension can be used to control the wiggle, and the second dimension can be used to animate the effect (i.e., make the wiggles move in successive frames). Similarly, a 2D noise function can be used to create a 2D cloud pattern, whereas a 3D noise function can generate the 2D cloud pattern and animate it in a realistic way. With a 4D noise function, you can create a 3D object like a planet and use the fourth dimension to watch it evolve in "fits and starts."

Figure 12.6   Summed noise, at 1, 2, 3, and 4 octaves (contrast enhanced)

12.1.3   Using Noise in OpenGL Shaders

There are three ways to include noise in an OpenGL shader:

1.   Use the OpenGL Shading Language built-in noise function

2.   Write your own noise function in the OpenGL Shading Language

3.   Use a texture map to store a previously computed noise function

Unfortunately, at the time of this writing, there is only one available implementation of the OpenGL Shading Language, and it has neither a built-in **noise** function nor the capabilities for implementing user-defined functions. But noise is too important a topic to defer, and some very interesting shaders can be written using a noise texture, so we'll focus on the third approach for the remainder of this chapter.

12.2   Noise Textures

The programmability offered by the OpenGL Shading Language allows us to use values stored in texture memory in new and unique ways. It is possible to precompute a noise function and save it in a 1D, 2D, or 3D texture map. This texture map (or texture maps) can then be accessed from within a shader. Because textures can contain up to four components, we can use a single texture map to store four octaves of noise or four completely separate noise functions.

Listing 12.1 shows a C function that generates a 3D noise texture. This function creates an RGBA texture with the first octave of noise stored in the red texture component, the second octave stored in the green texture component, the third octave stored in the blue component, and the fourth octave stored in the alpha component. Each octave has twice the frequency and half the amplitude as the previous one.

This function assumes the existence of a **noise3** function that can generate 3D noise values in the range [–1,1]. If you want, you can start with Perlin's C implementation (available from http://www.texturingandmodeling.com/ CODE/PERLIN/PERLIN.C). John Kessenich made some small changes to this code (adding a **setNoiseFrequency** function) to allow it to produce noise values that wrap smoothly from one edge of the array to the other. This means we can use the texture with the wrapping mode set to GL_REPEAT, and we won't see any discontinuities in the function when it wraps. The revised version of the code can be downloaded from this book's Web site at http://3dshaders.com.

Listing 12.1   C function to generate a 3D noise texture

```c
int noise3DTexSize = 128;
GLuint noise3DTexName = 0;
GLubyte *noise3DTexPtr;

void make3DNoiseTexture(void)
{
    int f, i, j, k, inc;
    int startFrequency = 4;
    int numOctaves = 4;
    double ni[3];
    double inci, incj, inck;
    int frequency = startFrequency;
    GLubyte *ptr;
    double amp = 0.5;

    if ((noise3DTexPtr = (GLubyte *) malloc(noise3DTexSize *
                                            noise3DTexSize *
                                            noise3DTexSize * 4)) == NULL)
    {
        fprintf(stderr,"ERROR: Could not allocate 3D noise texture\n");
        exit(1);
    }

    for (f = 0, inc = 0; f < numOctaves;
         ++f, frequency *= 2, ++inc, amp *= 0.5)
    {
        setNoiseFrequency(frequency);
        ptr = noise3DTexPtr;
        ni[0] = ni[1] = ni[2] = 0;

        inci = 1.0 / (noise3DTexSize / frequency);
        for (i = 0; i < noise3DTexSize; ++i, ni[0] += inci)
        {
            incj = 1.0 / (noise3DTexSize / frequency);
            for (j = 0; j < noise3DTexSize; ++j, ni[1] += incj)
            {
                inck = 1.0 / (noise3DTexSize / frequency);
                for (k = 0; k < noise3DTexSize; ++k, ni[2] += inck, ptr+= 4)
                {
                    *(ptr+inc) = (GLubyte)(((noise3(ni)+1.0) * amp)*128.0);
                }
            }
        }
    }
}
```

This function will compute noise values for four octaves of noise and store them in a 3D RGBA texture of size $128 \times 128 \times 128$. This code also assumes that each component of the texture is stored as an 8-bit integer value. The first octave has a frequency of 4 and an amplitude of 0.5. In the innermost part of the loop, we call the **noise3** function to generate a noise value based on the current value of *ni*. The **noise3** function returns a value in the range [–1,1], so by adding 1, we end up with a noise value in the range [0,2]. Multiplying by our amplitude value of 0.5 gives a value in the range [0,1]. Finally, we multiply by 128 to give us an integer value in the range [0,128] that can be stored in the red component of a texture. (When accessed from within a shader, the value will be a floating-point value in the range [0,0.5].)

The amplitude value is cut in half and the frequency is doubled in each pass through the loop. The result is that integer values in the range [0,64] will be stored in the green component of the noise texture, integer values in the range [0,32] will be stored in the blue component of the noise texture, and integer values in the range [0,16] will be stored in the alpha component of the texture. The images in Figure 12.5 were generated by looking at each of these channels independently after scaling the values by a constant value that allowed them to span the maximum intensity range (i.e., integer values in the range [0,255] or floating-point values in the range [0,1]).

After the values for the noise texture are computed, it can be provided to the graphics hardware using the code in Listing 12.2. First, we pick a texture unit and bind to it the 3D texture we've created. We set up its wrapping parameters so that the texture will wrap in all three dimensions. This way, we'll always get a valid result for our noise function, no matter what input values are used. We'll still have to be somewhat careful to avoid using the texture in a way that makes obvious repeating patterns. The next two lines set the texture filtering modes to linear because the default is mipmap linear and we're not using mipmap textures here. (Using a mipmap texture might be appropriate in some circumstances, but we'll be controlling the scaling factors from within our noise shaders, so a single texture is sufficient.) When all the parameters are set up, we can download the noise texture to the hardware using the **glTexImage3D** function.

Listing 12.2 A function for activating the 3D noise texture

```
void init3DNoiseTexture()
{
    glGenTextures(1, &noise3DTexName);

    glActiveTexture(GL_TEXTURE6);
    glBindTexture(GL_TEXTURE_3D, noise3DTexName);
    glTexParameterf(GL_TEXTURE_3D, GL_TEXTURE_WRAP_S, GL_REPEAT);
```

```
glTexParameterf(GL_TEXTURE_3D, GL_TEXTURE_WRAP_T, GL_REPEAT);
glTexParameterf(GL_TEXTURE_3D, GL_TEXTURE_WRAP_R, GL_REPEAT);
glTexParameterf(GL_TEXTURE_3D, GL_TEXTURE_MAG_FILTER, GL_LINEAR);
glTexParameterf(GL_TEXTURE_3D, GL_TEXTURE_MIN_FILTER, GL_LINEAR);

glTexImage3D(GL_TEXTURE_3D, 0, GL_RGBA, noise3DTexSize,
             noise3DTexSize, noise3DTexSize, 0, GL_RGBA,
             GL_UNSIGNED_BYTE, noise3DTexPtr);
}
```

This approach is an excellent one if the period of repeatability can be avoided in the final rendering. One way of accomplishing this is to make sure that no texture value is accessed more than once when rendering the target object. For instance, if a $128 \times 128 \times 128$ texture is being used and the position on the object is used as the input to the noise function, the repeatability won't be visible if the entire object fits within the texture.

12.3 Trade-offs

After graphics hardware contains built-in support for the **noise** function and user-defined functions, there will be three methods that can be used to generate noise values in a shader. How do you know which is the best choice for your application? A lot depends on the underlying implementation, but generally speaking, if we assume a hardware computation of noise that does not use texturing, the points favoring usage of the OpenGL Shading Language built-in **noise** function are the following.

- It doesn't consume any texture memory (a $128 \times 128 \times 128$ texture map stored as RGBA with 8 bits per component uses up 8Mb of texture memory).

- It doesn't use a texture unit (this is expensive if the hardware supports only 2 or 4 texture units).

- It is a continuous function rather than a discrete one, so it will not look "pixelated," no matter what the scaling is.

- The repeatability of the function should be undetectable, especially for 2D and 3D noise (but it depends on the hardware implementation).

- Shaders written with the built-in **noise** function aren't dependent on the application to set up appropriate textures.

The advantages of using a texture map to implement the noise function are as follows.

- Because the noise function is computed by the application, the application has total control of this function and can ensure matching behavior on every hardware platform.

- It is possible to store four noise values (i.e., one each for the R, G, B, and A values of the texture) at each texture location. This makes it possible to precompute four octaves of noise, for instance, and retrieve all four values with a single texture access.

- Accessing a texture map may be faster than calling the built-in **noise** function.

User-defined functions can be used to implement noise functions that provide a different appearance than that of the built-in noise function. A user-defined function may also provide matching behavior on every platform whereas the built-in noise function may not (at least not until all graphics hardware developers support the **noise** function in exactly the same way.) But hardware developers will optimize the built-in **noise** function, perhaps accelerating it with special hardware, so it is apt to be faster than user-defined noise functions.

In the long run, using the built-in **noise** function or user-defined noise functions will be the way to go for most applications. This will result in noise that doesn't show a repetitive pattern, has greater numerical precision, and doesn't use up any texture resources. Applications that want full control over the noise function and can live within the constraints of a fixed size noise function can be successful using textures for their noise. With current generation hardware, noise textures may also provide better performance and require fewer instructions in the shader.

12.4 A Simple Noise Shader

Now we will put all of these ideas into some OpenGL shaders that will do some interesting rendering for us. The first shader we'll look at will use noise in a simple way to produce a cloud effect.

12.4.1 Application Setup

Very little needs to be passed to the noise shaders discussed in this section and in Section 12.5 and Section 12.6. The vertex position must be passed in as always, and the surface normal is needed for performing lighting computations. Colors and scale factors are parameterized as uniform variables for the various shaders.

12.4.2 Vertex Shader

The code shown in Listing 12.3 is the vertex shader that we'll use for the four noise fragment shaders that follow. It is fairly simple because it really only needs to accomplish three things.

1. As in all vertex shaders, the incoming vertex value must be transformed and stored in the built-in varying variable *gl_Position*.

2. The incoming normal and the uniform variable *LightPos* are used to compute the light intensity from a single white light source. A scale factor of 1.5 is applied to increase the amount of illumination.

3. The incoming vertex value is stored in the varying variable *MCposition*. This value will be available to us in our fragment shader as the modeling coordinate position of the object at every fragment. It will be an ideal value to use as the input for our 3D texture lookup. No matter how the object is drawn, fragments will always produce the same position values (or very close to them); therefore, the noise value obtained for each point on the surface will also be the same (or very close to it). A uniform variable called *Scale* can be set by the application in order to optimally scale the object in relationship to the size of the noise texture.

Listing 12.3   Cloud vertex shader

```
varying float LightIntensity;
varying vec3  MCposition;

uniform vec3  LightPos;
uniform float Scale;

void main(void)
{
    vec3 ECposition = vec3 (gl_ModelViewMatrix * gl_Vertex);
    MCposition      = vec3 (gl_Vertex) * Scale;
    vec3 tnorm      = normalize(vec3 (gl_NormalMatrix * gl_Normal));
    LightIntensity  = dot(normalize(LightPos - ECposition), tnorm);
    LightIntensity *= 1.5;
    gl_Position     = ftransform();
}
```

12.4.3 Fragment Shader

After we've computed a noise texture and used OpenGL calls to download it to the graphics card, we can use a pretty simple fragment shader together

with the vertex shader described in the previous section to make an interesting "cloudy sky" effect (see Listing 12.4). This shader will result in something that looks like the sky on a mostly cloudy day. You can experiment
with the color values to get a result that is visually pleasing.

This fragment shader receives as input the two varying variables that were
computed by the vertex shader shown in the previous section: *LightIntensity*
and *MCposition*. These values were computed at each vertex by the vertex
shader and then interpolated across the primitive by the rasterization hardware. Here, in our fragment shader, we have access to the interpolated value
of each of these variables at every fragment.

The first line of code in the shader performs a 3D texture lookup on our 3D
noise texture to produce a four-component result. We compute the value of
intensity by summing the four components of our noise texture. This value
is then scaled by 1.5 and used to perform a linear blend between two colors:
white and sky blue. The four channels in our noise texture have mean
values of 0.25, 0.125, 0.0625, and 0.03125. An additional 0.03125 term is
added to account for the average values of all the octaves at higher frequencies. You can think of this as fading to the average values of all the higher
frequency octaves that aren't being included in the calculation as described
earlier in Section 12.1. Scaling the sum by 1.5 will stretch the resulting value
to use up more of the range from [0,1].

The computed color is then scaled by *LightIntensity* value to simulate a
diffuse surface lit by a single light source. Each component of the color is
then clamped to the range [0,1], and the result is assigned to the built-in
variable *gl_FragColor* with an alpha value of 1.0 to produce the color value
that will be used by the remainder of the OpenGL pipeline. An object
rendered with this shader is shown in Color Plate 20. Notice that the texture
on the teapot looks a lot like the final image in Figure 12.6.

Listing 12.4   Fragment shader for cloudy sky effect

```
varying float LightIntensity;
varying vec3  MCposition;

uniform sampler3D Noise;
uniform vec3 SkyColor;      // (0.0, 0.0, 0.8)
uniform vec3 CloudColor;    // (0.8, 0.8, 0.8)

void main (void)
{
    vec4  noisevec  = texture3D(Noise, MCposition);
```

```
float intensity = (noisevec[0] + noisevec[1] +
                   noisevec[2] + noisevec[3] + 0.03125) * 1.5;

vec3 color   = mix(SkyColor, CloudColor, intensity) * LightIntensity;
gl_FragColor = vec4 (color, 1.0);
}
```

12.5 Turbulence

Some additional interesting effects can be obtained by taking the absolute value of the noise function. This introduces a discontinuity of the derivative because the function folds on itself when it reaches 0 (see Figure 5.2 for an illustration of the absolute value function). When this is done to noise functions at several frequencies and the results are added together, the result is cusps or creases in the texture at various scales. Perlin started referring to this type of noise as TURBULENCE because it is reminiscent of turbulent flow. This shows up in a variety of places in nature, so this type of noise can be used to simulate various things, like flames or lava. The two-dimensional appearance of this type of noise is shown in Figure 12.7.

12.5.1 Sun Surface Shader

An effect that looks like a pit of hot molten lava or the surface of the sun can be achieved using the same vertex shader as the cloud shader and a slightly different fragment shader. The main difference is that each of the noise values is scaled and shifted over so that it is centered at 0; then its absolute value is taken. After adding the values together, the result is scaled again to occupy nearly the full range of [0,1]. This value is clamped, and we

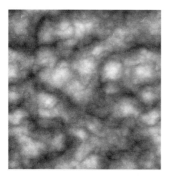

Figure 12.7   Absolute value noise or "turbulence"

use it to mix between yellow and red in order to get the result shown in Color Plate 20 (see Listing 12.5). (In Chapter 13, we'll examine some ways of animating these textures to make them more interesting.)

Listing 12.5 Sun surface fragment shader

```
varying float LightIntensity;
varying vec3  MCposition;

uniform sampler3D Noise;
uniform vec3 Color1;       // (0.8, 0.7, 0.0)
uniform vec3 Color2;       // (0.6, 0.1, 0.0)
uniform float NoiseScale;  // 1.2

void main (void)
{
    vec4 noisevec = texture3D(Noise, MCposition * NoiseScale);


    float intensity = abs(noisevec[0] - 0.25) +
                      abs(noisevec[1] - 0.125) +
                      abs(noisevec[2] - 0.0625) +
                      abs(noisevec[3] - 0.03125);

    intensity    = clamp(intensity * 6.0, 0.0, 1.0);
    vec3 color   = mix(Color1, Color2, intensity) * LightIntensity;
    gl_FragColor = vec4 (color, 1.0);
}
```

12.5.2 Marble

Yet another variation on the noise function is to use it as part of a periodic function such as sine. By adding noise to the input value for the sine function, you will get a "noisy" oscillating function. This can be used to create a look similar to the alternating color veins of some types of marble. Listing 12.6 shows the fragment shader to do it. Again, the same vertex shader can be used. Results of this shader are also shown in Color Plate 20.

Listing 12.6 Fragment shader for marble

```
varying float LightIntensity;
varying vec3  MCposition;

uniform sampler3D Noise;
uniform vec3 MarbleColor;
uniform vec3 VeinColor;

void main (void)
{
```

```
    vec4 noisevec   = texture3D(Noise, MCposition);

    float intensity = abs(noisevec[0] - 0.25) +
                      abs(noisevec[1] - 0.125) +
                      abs(noisevec[2] - 0.0625) +
                      abs(noisevec[3] - 0.03125);

    float sineval = sin(MCposition.y * 6.0 + intensity * 12.0) * 0.5 + 0.5;
    vec3 color    = mix(VeinColor, MarbleColor, sineval) * LightIntensity;
    gl_FragColor  = vec4 (color, 1.0);
}
```

12.6 Granite

With noise, it's also easy just to try and make stuff up. In this example, I wanted to simulate a grayish rocky material with small black specks. To generate a relatively high-frequency noise texture, only the fourth component (the highest frequency one) is used. It is scaled by an arbitrary amount to provide an appropriate intensity level, and this value is then used for each of the red, green, and blue components. The result shown in Listing 12.7 is an appearance similar to granite as shown in Color Plate 20.

Listing 12.7   Granite fragment shader

```
varying float LightIntensity;
varying vec3  MCposition;

uniform sampler3D Noise;
uniform float NoiseScale;

void main(void)
{
    vec4  noisevec = texture3D(Noise, NoiseScale * MCposition);
    float intensity = min(1.0, noisevec[3] * 18.0);
    vec3  color    = vec3 (intensity * LightIntensity);
    gl_FragColor   = vec4 (color, 1.0);
}
```

12.7 Wood

We can do a fair approximation of wood with this approach as well. Here are the basic ideas behind the wood fragment shader shown in Listing 12.8.

- The wood is composed of light and dark areas alternating in concentric cylinders surrounding a central axis.

- Noise is added to warp the cylinders to create a more natural looking pattern.

- The center of the "tree" is taken to be the y-axis.

- Throughout the wood, there is a high-frequency grain pattern to give the appearance of wood that has been sawed, exposing the open grain nature of the wood.

The wood shader will utilize the same vertex shader as the other noise-based shaders discussed in this chapter.

12.7.1 Application Setup

The wood shaders don't require too much from the application. The application is expected to pass in a vertex position and a normal per vertex using the usual OpenGL entry points. In addition, the vertex shader takes a light position and a scale factor that are passed in as uniform variables. The fragment shader takes a number of uniform variables that are used to parameterize the appearance of the wood.

The uniform variables needed for the wood shaders are initialized as follows:

LightPos	`0.0, 0.0, 4.0`
Scale	`2.0`
LightWood	`0.6, 0.3, 0.1`
DarkWood	`0.4, 0.2, 0.07`
RingFreq	`4.0`
LightGrains	`1.0`
DarkGrains	`0.0`
GrainThreshold	`0.5`
NoiseScale	`0.5, 0.1, 0.1`
Noisiness	`3.0`
GrainScale	`27.0`

12.7.2 Fragment Shader

Listing 12.8 shows the fragment shader for procedurally generated wood.

Listing 12.8   Fragment shader for wood

```
varying float LightIntensity;
varying vec3  MCposition;

uniform sampler3D Noise;

uniform vec3  LightWood;
uniform vec3  DarkWood;
uniform float RingFreq;
uniform float LightGrains;
uniform float DarkGrains;
uniform float GrainThreshold;
uniform vec3  NoiseScale;
uniform float Noisiness;
uniform float GrainScale;

void main(void)
{
    vec3 noisevec = vec3 (texture3D(Noise, MCposition * NoiseScale) *
                                                Noisiness);
    vec3 location = MCposition + noisevec;

    float dist = sqrt(location.x * location.x + location.z * location.z);
    dist *= RingFreq;

    float r = fract(dist + noisevec[0] + noisevec[1] + noisevec[2]) * 2.0;

    if (r > 1.0)
        r = 2.0 - r;

    vec3 color = mix(LightWood, DarkWood, r);

    r = fract((MCposition.x + MCposition.z) * GrainScale + 0.5);
    noisevec[2] *= r;
    if (r < GrainThreshold)
        color += LightWood * LightGrains * noisevec[2];
    else
        color -= LightWood * DarkGrains * noisevec[2];

    color *= LightIntensity;
    gl_FragColor = vec4 (color, 1.0);
}
```

As you can see, we've parameterized quite a bit of this shader through the use of uniform variables in order to make it easy to manipulate through the application's user interface. As in many procedural shaders, the object position is used as the basis for computing the procedural texture. In this case, the object position is multiplied by *NoiseScale* (a **vec3** that allows us to scale the noise independently in the *x*, *y*, and *z* directions), and the computed value is used as the index into our 3D noise texture. The noise values obtained from the texture are scaled by the value *Noisiness*, which allows us to increase or decrease the contribution of the noise.

Our tree is assumed to be a series of concentric rings of alternating light wood and dark wood. In order to give some interest to our grain pattern, we'll add the noise vector to our object position. This has the effect of adding our low frequency (first octave) noise to the *x* coordinate of the position and the third octave noise to the *z* coordinate (the *y* coordinate won't be used). The result will be rings that are still relatively circular but have some variation in width and distance from the center of the tree.

To compute where we are in relation to the center of the tree, we square the *x* and *z* components and take the square root of the result. This gives us the distance from the center of the tree. The distance is multiplied by *RingFreq*, a scale factor that can be used to give the wood pattern more rings or fewer rings.

Following this, we attempt to create a function that goes from 0 up to 1.0 and then back down to 0. Three octaves of noise are added to the distance value to give more interest to the wood grain pattern. We could compute different noise values here, but the ones we've already obtained will do just fine. Taking the fractional part of the resulting value gives us a function that will range from [0,1). Multiplying this value by 2.0 gives us a function that ranges from [0,2). And finally, by subtracting 1.0 from values that are greater than 1.0, we get our desired function that varies from 0 to 1.0 and back to 0.

This "triangle" function will be used to compute the basic color for the fragment using the built-in **mix** function. The **mix** function will do a linear blend of *LightWood* and *DarkWood* based on our computed value *r*.

At this point, we would have a pretty nice result for our wood function, but we attempt to make it a little better by adding a subtle effect to simulate the look of open-grain wood that has been sawed. (You may not be able to see this effect on the objects shown in Color Plate 22.)

Our desire is to produce streaks that are roughly parallel to the y-axis. This is done by adding the *x* and *z* coordinates, multiplying by the *GrainScale* factor (another uniform variable that can be adjusted to change the frequency of this effect), adding 0.5, and taking the fractional part of the result. Again, this gives us a function that varies from [0,1), but for the default values for *GrainScale* (27.0) and *RingFreq* (4.0), this function for *r* will go from 0 to 1.0 much more often than our previous function for *r*.

We could just make our "grains" go from light to dark in a linear fashion, but we'll try to do something a little more subtle. The value of *r* is multiplied by our third octave noise value to produce a value that increases in a non-linear fashion. Finally, we compare our value of *r* to the *GrainThreshold* value (default is 0.5). If the value of *r* is less than *GrainThreshold*, we modify our current color by adding to it a value computed by multiplying the *Light-Wood* color, the *LightGrains* color, and our modified noise value. Conversely, if the value of *r* is greater than *GrainThreshold*, we modify our current color by subtracting from it a value computed by multiplying the *DarkWood* color, the *DarkGrains* color, and our modified noise value. (By default, the value of *LightGrains* is 1.0, and the value of *DarkGrains* is 0, so we don't actually see any change if *r* is greater than *GrainThreshold*.)

You can play around with this effect and see if it really does help the appearance. It seemed to me that it added to the effect of the wood texture for the default settings I've chosen, but there probably is a way to achieve a better effect in a simpler way.

With our final color computed, all that remains is to multiply the color by the interpolated diffuse lighting factor and add an alpha value of 1.0 to produce our final fragment value. The results of our shader are applied to three different objects in Color Plate 22.

12.8 Summary

This chapter provided an introduction to noise, an incredibly useful function for adding irregularity to procedural shaders. After a brief description of the mathematical definition of this function, we used it as the basis for shaders that simulated clouds, turbulent flow, marble, granite, and wood. The noise function is available as a built-in function in the OpenGL Shading Language. Noise functions can also be created with user-defined shader functions or textures. However it is implemented, noise can be used to increase the apparent realism of an image or an animation by adding imperfections, complexity, and an element of apparent randomness.

12.9 Further Information

Ken Perlin has a tutorial and history of the noise function as well as a recent reference implementation in Java at his Web site (http://www.noisema-chine.com). A lot of other interesting things are available on Ken's home page at NYU (http://mrl.nyu.edu/~perlin). His paper, *An Image Synthesizer*, appeared in the 1985 SIGGRAPH proceedings, and his improvements to the original algorithm were published in the paper *Improving Noise* as part of SIGGRAPH 2002.

The book, *Texturing & Modeling: A Procedural Approach, Third Edition*, by David S. Ebert, et. al. (2000) contains several excellent discussions on noise, and the book's Web site, http://www.texturingandmodeling.com contains C source code for a variety of noise functions that appear in the book, including Perlin's original noise function. Perlin has written a chapter for this book that provides more depth on his noise algorithm, and Ken Musgrave explores breathtakingly beautiful mathematical worlds based on a variety of noise functions. Planet-building software built on these ideas is available from Musgrave's company, Pandromeda, at http://www.pandromeda.com. In Chapter 2 of this book, Darwyn Peachey describes a variety of noise functions, and in Chapter 7, David Ebert describes an approach similar to the 3D texturing approach described previously. *Advanced RenderMan: Creating CGI for Motion Pictures,* by Tony Apodaca and Larry Gritz (1999), also contains a discussion of noise and presents some excellent noise-based RenderMan shaders.

[1] Apodaca, Anthony A., and Larry Gritz, *Advanced RenderMan: Creating CGI for Motion Pictures*, Morgan Kaufmann Publishers, San Francisco, 1999. http://www.bmrt.org/arman/materials.html

[2] Ebert, David S., John Hart, Bill Mark, F. Kenton Musgrave, Darwyn Peachey, Ken Perlin, and Steven Worley, *Texturing and Modeling: A Procedural Approach, Third Edition*, Morgan Kaufmann Publishers, San Francisco, 2002. http://www.texturingandmodeling.com

[3] Hart, John C., *Perlin Noise Pixel Shaders*, ACM SIGGRAPH/Eurographics Workshop on Graphics Hardware, pp. 87–94, August 2001. http://graphics.cs.uiuc.edu/~jch/papers/pixelnoise.pdf

[4] Perlin, Ken, *An Image Synthesizer*, Computer Graphics (SIGGRAPH '85 Proceedings), pp. 287–296, July 1985.

[5] Perlin, Ken, *Improving Noise*, Computer Graphics (SIGGRAPH 2002 Proceedings), pp. 681–682, July 2002. http://mrl.nyu.edu/perlin/paper445.pdf

[6] Perlin, Ken, personal Web site. http://www.noisemachine.com

[7] Perlin, Ken, personal Web site. http://mrl.nyu.edu/~perlin

Chapter 13

Animated Shaders

Animation can explain whatever the mind of man can conceive. This facility makes it the most versatile and explicit means of communication yet devised for quick mass appreciation.

— *Walt Disney*

As Walt Disney noted, animation is largely about explanation. Rotating an object provides information about shape and form. Doing a simulated walk-through of a building gives a sense of how it would feel to be inside the building. Watching a character's facial expressions provides insight into the emotions it is feeling.

With the latest graphics hardware and the OpenGL Shading Language, we have the ability to do even more realistic rendering in real-time on low-cost graphics hardware. I was somewhat surprised when I found out how easy it was to animate programmable shaders. By developing shaders that modify their behavior over time, even more of the rendering task can be turned over to the graphics hardware.

This chapter describes how a shader can be written to produce an animation effect. Typically, the animation effect is controlled by one or more uniform variables that convey an application's sense of time. This can be done by passing a frame count, an elapsed time value, or some other value that can be used as the basis for chronology. If there are multiple objects in a scene and they are expected to animate in different ways, each object will be

315

rendered with its own unique shader. If objects have identical characteristics other than the animation effect, the source code for each of the shaders can be the same except for the portion that defines the animation effect.

A shader can be written to behave differently depending on these control values, and so, if they are updated each frame, the scene will be drawn slightly differently in each frame to produce the animation effect. To avoid discontinuities in cyclical motion, the effect can be designed with a smooth overlap where the end of the cycle wraps back to the beginning. By controlling the animation effect in an OpenGL shader, the application need not perform any complex computations to achieve this motion. All it needs to do is update the control value(s) of each frame and redraw the object. However, the application can perform animation computations in addition to the animation effects built into a shader in order to produce extremely interesting effects.

Interesting animation effects can be created using stored textures, procedural textures, noise, and other mechanisms. In this chapter, we describe simple animation effects and discuss shaders for modifying the shape and position of an object and for simulating an oscillating motion.

13.1 On/Off

Suppose you have an object in the scene that must be drawn two different ways, such as a neon restaurant sign saying "OPEN" that repeatedly flashes on and off. It would certainly be possible to write two different shaders for rendering this object, one for when the sign is "on" and one for when the sign is "off." However, in a situation like this, it may actually be easier to write a single shader that takes a control variable indicating whether the object is to be drawn as on or off. The shader can be written to render one way if the control variable is on and another way if it is off.

To do this, the application would set up a uniform variable that indicates the on/off state. This variable would be updated as needed by the application. To achieve a sequence of 3 seconds on and 1 second off, the application would write the variable with the value for on, update the value to off 3 seconds later, update the value to on 1 second later, and repeat this sequence. In the interim, the application just continually rederaws the geometry each frame. The decoupling of the rendering from the animation effect might make the application a little simpler and a little more maintainable as a result.

13.2 Threshold

An improvement to the "on/off" animation is to have the application pass the shader one or more values that will be tested against one or more threshold values within the shader. One control value and two threshold values would allow you to write a shader with three behaviors: one for when the the control value is less than the first threshold value, one for when the control value is between the two threshold values, and one for when the control value is greater than the second threshold value.

In the case just described, you actually may have a transition period where the neon light is warming up to full brightness or dissipating to its off condition. This type of transition helps to "soften" the change between two states so that the transition appears more natural. The **smoothstep** function is handy for calculating such a transition.

13.3 Translation

A very simple animation effect for stored textures or procedural textures can be achieved simply by adding an offset to the texture access calculation. For instance, if you want to have procedural clouds that drift slowly across the sky, you can make a very simple change to the cloud shader that we discussed in Section 12.4. Instead of using the object position as the index into our 3D noise texture, we add an offset value. The offset is defined as a uniform variable and can be updated by the application each frame. If we want the clouds to drift slowly from left to right, we just subtract a small amount from the *x* component of this uniform variable each frame. If we want the clouds to move rapidly from bottom to top, we just subtract a larger amount from the *y* component of this value. To achieve a more complex effect, all three coordinates might be modified each frame. A noise function can be used in computing this offset to make the motion more natural and less like a scrolling effect.

The cloud shader as modified so as to be animatable is shown in Listing 13.1.

Listing 13.1   Animatable fragment shader for cloudy sky effect

```
varying float LightIntensity;
varying vec3  MCposition;

uniform sampler3D Noise;
uniform vec3 SkyColor;     // (0.0, 0.0, 0.8)
```

```
uniform vec3 CloudColor;    // (0.8, 0.8, 0.8)
uniform vec3 Offset;        // updated each frame by the application

void main (void)
{
    vec4   noisevec  = texture3D(Noise, MCposition + Offset);

    float intensity = (noisevec[0] + noisevec[1] +
                       noisevec[2] + noisevec[3]) * 1.5;

    vec3 color = mix(SkyColor, CloudColor, intensity) * LightIntensity;
    gl_FragColor = vec4 (color, 1.0);
}
```

13.4 Key-Frame Interpolation

Another cool animation effect is to gradually blend between two things. This could be used to mix two effects over a sequence of frames. Instead of the application doing complex calculations to determine the proper way to render the "in between" object or effect, it can all be done automatically within the shader.

You can blend between the geometry of two objects to create a tweened (in between) version or do a linear blend between two colors, two textures, two procedural patterns, and so on. All it takes is a shader that uses a control value updated each frame by the application that indicates the ratio of the two items being blended. In some cases, a linear blend will be sufficient. For an oscillating effect, you'll probably want to have the application compute the interpolation factor using a spline function in order to avoid jarring discontinuities in the animation. (You could have the shader compute the interpolation value, but it's better to have the application compute it once per frame rather than have the vertex shader compute it once per vertex or have the fragment shader compute it needlessly at every fragment.)

For instance, using generic vertex attributes, you can actually pass the geometry for two objects at a time. The geometry for the first object would be passed through the usual OpenGL calls (**glVertex**, **glColor**, **glNormal**, etc.). A second set of vertex information can be passed using generic vertex attributes 0, 1, 2, etc. The application can provide a blending factor through a uniform variable, and the vertex shader can use this blending factor to do a weighted average of the two sets of vertex data. The tweened vertex position is the one that actually gets transformed, the tweened normal is the one actually used for lighting calculations, and so on.

In order to animate a character realistically, you need to choose the right number of key frames as well as the proper number of inbetweens to use. In their classic book, *Disney Animation—The Illusion of Life*, Frank Thomas and Ollie Johnston (1995, pp. 64–65) describe this concept as "Timing," and explain it in the following way:

> *Just two drawings of a head, the first showing it leaning toward the right shoulder and second with it over on the left and its chin slightly raised, can be made to communicate a multitude of ideas, depending entirely on the Timing used. Each inbetween drawing added between these two "extremes" gives a new meaning to the action.*

No inbetweens	*The character has been hit by a tremendous force. His head is nearly snapped off.*
One inbetween	*. . . has been hit by a brick, rolling pin, frying pan.*
Two inbetweens	*. . . has a nervous tic, a muscle spasm, an uncontrollable twitch.*
Three inbetweens	*. . . is dodging the brick, rolling pin, frying pan.*
Four inbetweens	*. . . is giving a crisp order, "Get going!" "Move it!"*
Five inbetweens	*. . . is more friendly, "Over here." "Come on—hurry!"*
Six inbetweens	*. . . sees a good-looking girl, or the sports car he has always wanted.*
Seven inbetweens	*. . . tries to get a better look at something.*
Eight inbetweens	*. . . searches for the peanut butter on the kitchen shelf.*
Nine inbetweens	*. . . appraises, considering thoughtfully.*
Ten inbetweens	*. . . stretches a sore muscle.*

13.4.1 Key-Frame Interpolation Vertex Shader

This vertex shader in Listing 13.2 is very similar to ones presented previously except for two things: (A) a second set of vertex data (vertex position and surface normal) is passed in via attribute variables, and (B) a linear blend is performed between the two sets of vertex data in order to compute the vertex data that is actually used in the transformation and lighting calculations that follow.

Listing 13.2   Vertex shader for interpolating between two objects

```
varying float LightIntensity;
varying vec2  TexCoord;

uniform vec3  LightPosition;
uniform float SpecularContribution;
uniform float DiffuseContribution;
uniform float Weight;    // updated each frame by the application

attribute vec4 VertexB;
attribute vec3 NormalB;

void main(void)
{
    vec4 vert       = mix(gl_Vertex, VertexB, Weight);
    vec3 ecPosition = vec3 (gl_ModelViewMatrix * vert);
    vec3 tnorm      = mix(gl_Normal, NormalB, Weight);
         tnorm      = normalize(gl_NormalMatrix * tnorm);
    vec3 lightVec   = normalize(LightPosition - ecPosition);
    vec3 reflectVec = reflect(-lightVec, tnorm);
    vec3 viewVec    = normalize(-ecPosition);

    float spec      = max(dot(reflectVec, viewVec), 0.0);
    spec            = pow(spec, 16.0);

    LightIntensity  = DiffuseContribution * max(dot(lightVec, tnorm), 0.0)
                    + SpecularContribution * spec;

    TexCoord        = gl_MultiTexCoord0.st;
    gl_Position     = gl_ModelViewProjectionMatrix * vert;
}
```

13.5 Other Blending Effects

Another blending effect is to gradually cause an object to disappear over a sequence of frames. The control value could be used as the alpha value to cause the object to be drawn totally opaque (alpha is 1.0), totally invisible (alpha is 0), or partially visible (alpha is between 0 and 1.0).

You can also fade something in or out using the **discard** keyword. The lattice shader described in Section 11.3 discards a specific percentage of pixels in the object each time it is drawn. This percentage could be varied from 0 to 1.0 to make the object appear, or varied from 1.0 to 0 to make it disappear. Alternatively, a noise function can be evaluated at each location on the surface, and the comparison can be done with this value instead. In this way, an object can be made to erode or rust away over time.

13.6 Particle Systems

A new type of rendering primitive was invented by Bill Reeves and his colleagues at Lucasfilm in the early 1980s as they struggled to come up with a way to animate the fire sequence called "The Genesis Demo" in the motion picture *Star Trek II: The Wrath of Khan*. Traditional rendering methods were more suitable for rendering smooth, well-defined surfaces.What Reeves was after was a way to render a class of objects he called "fuzzy"—things like fire, smoke, liquid spray, comet tails, fireworks, and other natural phenomena. These things are fuzzy because none of them has a well-defined boundary and the components typically change over time.

The technique that Reeves invented to solve this problem was described in the 1983 paper, *Particle Systems—A Technique for Modeling a Class of Fuzzy Objects*. PARTICLE SYSTEMS had been used in rendering before, but Reeves realized that he could get the particles to behave the way he wanted them to by giving each particle its own set of initial conditions and by establishing a set of probabilistic rules that governed how particles would change over time.

There are three main differences between particle systems and traditional surface-based rendering techniques. First, an object is represented by a cloud of primitive particles that define its volume rather than defining it with polygons or curved surfaces. Second, the object is considered dynamic rather than static. The constituent particles come into existence, evolve, and then die. During their lifetime, they can change position and form. Finally, objects defined in this manner are not completely specified. A set of initial conditions are specified, along with rules for birth, death, and evolution. Stochastic processes are used to influence all three stages, so the shape and appearance of the object is nondeterministic.

Some assumptions are usually made in order to simplify the rendering of particle systems, among them,

- Particles do not collide with other particles.

- Particles do not reflect light; they emit light.

- Particles do not cast shadows on other particles.

Particle attibutes often include position, color, transparency, velocity, size, shape, and lifetime. In rendering a particle system, each particle's attributes are used along with certain global parameters in order to update its position and appearance at each frame. Each particle's position might be updated based on the initial velocity vector and the effects from gravity, wind, friction, and other global factors. Each particle's color (including transparency), size, and shape may be modified as a function of global time, the age of the particle, its height, its speed, or any other parameter that can be calculated.

What are the benefits of using particle systems as a rendering technique? For one thing, complex systems can be created with little human effort. For another, the complexity can easily be adjusted. And as Reeves says in his 1983 paper, "The most important thing about particle systems is that they move: good dynamics are quite often the key to making things look real."

13.6.1 Application Setup

For this shader, my goal was to produce a shader that acted like a "confetti cannon"—something that spews out a large quantity of small, brightly colored pieces of paper. They don't come out all at once, but they come out in a steady stream until there are none left. Initial velocities are somewhat random, but there is a general direction that points up and away from the origin. Gravity will influence these particles and eventually bring them back to earth.

The code in Listing 13.3 shows the C subroutine that I used to create the initial values for my particle system. To accomplish the look I was after, I decided that for each particle I needed its initial position, a randomly generated color, a randomly generated initial velocity (with some constraints), and a randomly generated start time.

The subroutine **createPoints** will let you create an arbitrary size, two-dimensional grid of points for the particle system. There's no reason that this needs to be thought of as a two-dimensional grid, but I was interested in seeing the effect of particles "popping off the grid" like pieces of popcorn. It would be even easier to define the particle system as a 1D array, and all of the vertex positions could have exactly the same initial value (for instance (0,0,0)).

But I set it up as a 2D array, and so you can pass in a width and height to define the number of particles that will be created. After the memory for the arrays is allocated, a nested loop computes the values for each of the particle attributes at each grid location. Each vertex position has a y-coordinate value of 0, and the x and z coordinates vary across the grid. Each color value is assigned a random number in the range [0.5,1.0]. This was done so that mostly bright pastel colors would be used. The velocity vectors are assigned random numbers that are given a strong bias upwards by multiplying the y coordinate by 10. The general direction of the particles is aimed away from the origin by adding 3 to both the x- and the z- coordinates. Finally, each particle is provided a start time value in the range [0,10].

Listing 13.3 C subroutine to create vertex data for particles

```c
static GLint arrayWidth, arrayHeight;
static GLfloat *verts = NULL;
static GLfloat *colors = NULL;
static GLfloat *velocities = NULL;
static GLfloat *startTimes = NULL;

void createPoints(GLint w, GLint h)
{
    GLfloat *vptr, *cptr, *velptr, *stptr;
    GLfloat i, j;

    if (verts != NULL)
        free(verts);

    verts  = malloc(w * h * 3 * sizeof(float));
    colors = malloc(w * h * 3 * sizeof(float));
    velocities = malloc(w * h * 3 * sizeof(float));
    startTimes = malloc(w * h * sizeof(float));

    vptr = verts;
    cptr = colors;
    velptr = velocities;
    stptr  = startTimes;

    for (i = 0.5 / w - 0.5; i < 0.5; i = i + 1.0/w)
        for (j = 0.5 / h - 0.5; j < 0.5; j = j + 1.0/h)
        {
            *vptr       = i;
            *(vptr + 1) = 0.0;
            *(vptr + 2) = j;
            vptr += 3;

            *cptr       = ((float) rand() / RAND_MAX) * 0.5 + 0.5;
            *(cptr + 1) = ((float) rand() / RAND_MAX) * 0.5 + 0.5;
            *(cptr + 2) = ((float) rand() / RAND_MAX) * 0.5 + 0.5;
            cptr += 3;

            *velptr       = (((float) rand() / RAND_MAX)) + 3.0;
            *(velptr + 1) =  ((float) rand() / RAND_MAX) * 10.0;
            *(velptr + 2) = (((float) rand() / RAND_MAX)) + 3.0;
            velptr += 3;

            *stptr = ((float) rand() / RAND_MAX) * 10.0;
            stptr++;
        }

    arrayWidth  = w;
    arrayHeight = h;
}
```

OpenGL has built-in attributes for vertex position, which we'll use to pass the initial particle position, and for color, which we'll use to pass the particle's color. We'll need to use generic vertex attributes to specify the particle's initial velocity and start time. Let's pick indices 3 and 4 and define the necessary constants:

```
#define VELOCITY_ARRAY 3
#define START_TIME_ARRAY 4
```

After we have created a program object, we can bind a generic vertex attribute index to a vertex shader attribute variable name. (We can do this even before the vertex shader is attached to the program object.) These bindings will be checked and go into effect at the time **glLinkProgramARB** is called. To bind the generic vertex attribute index to a vertex shader variable name, we do the following:

```
glBindAttribLocationARB(ProgramObject, VELOCITY_ARRAY, "Velocity");
glBindAttribLocationARB(ProgramObject, START_TIME_ARRAY, "StartTime");
```

After the shaders are compiled, attached to the program object, and linked, we're ready to draw the particle system. All we need to do is call the **drawPoints** function shown in Listing 13.4. In this function, we set the point size to 2 in order to render somewhat larger points. The next four lines of code set up pointers to the vertex arrays that we're using. In this case, we'll have four: one for vertex positions (i.e., initial particle position), one for particle color, one for initial velocity, and one for the particle's start time (i.e., birth). After that, we enable the arrays for drawing by making calls to **glEnableClientState** for the standard vertex attributes and **glEnableVertexAttribArrayARB** for the generic vertex attributes. Next we call **glDrawArrays** to render the points, and finally, we clean up by disabling each of the enabled vertex arrays.

Listing 13.4   C subroutine to draw particles as points

```
void drawPoints()
{

    glPointSize(2.0);

    glVertexPointer(3, GL_FLOAT, 0, verts);
    glColorPointer (3, GL_FLOAT, 0, colors);
    glVertexAttribPointerARB(VELOCITY_ARRAY,   3, GL_FLOAT,
                             GL_FALSE, 0, velocities);
    glVertexAttribPointerARB(START_TIME_ARRAY, 1, GL_FLOAT,
                             GL_FALSE, 0, startTimes);

    glEnableClientState(GL_VERTEX_ARRAY);
    glEnableClientState(GL_COLOR_ARRAY);
    glEnableVertexAttribArrayARB(VELOCITY_ARRAY);
```

```
    glEnableVertexAttribArrayARB(START_TIME_ARRAY);

    glDrawArrays(GL_POINTS, 0, arrayWidth * arrayHeight);

    glDisableClientState(GL_VERTEX_ARRAY);
    glDisableClientState(GL_COLOR_ARRAY);
    glDisableVertexAttribArrayARB(VELOCITY_ARRAY);
    glDisableVertexAttribArrayARB(START_TIME_ARRAY);
}
```

In order to achieve the animation effect, the application must communicate its notion of time to the vertex shader, as shown in Listing 13.5. Here, the variable *ParticleTime* is incremented once each frame and loaded into the uniform variable *Time*. This allows the vertex shader to perform computations that vary (animate) over time.

Listing 13.5   C code snippet to update the time variable each frame

```
if (DoingParticles)
{
    location = glGetUniformLocationARB(ProgramObject, "Time");
    ParticleTime += 0.001f;
    glUniform1fARB(location, ParticleTime);
    CheckOglError();
}
```

13.6.2 Confetti Cannon Vertex Shader

The vertex shader (see Listing 13.6) is the key to this example of particle system rendering. Instead of simply transforming the incoming vertex, we will use it as the initial position to compute a new position based on a computation involving the uniform variable *Time*. It is this newly computed position that will actually be transformed and rendered.

This vertex shader defines the attribute variables *Velocity* and *StartTime*. In the previous section, we saw how generic vertex attribute arrays were defined and bound to these vertex shader attribute variables. As a result of this, each vertex will have an updated value for the attribute variables *Velocity* and *StartTime*, as well as for the standard vertex attributes specified by *gl_Vertex* and *gl_Color*.

The vertex shader starts by computing the age of the particle. If this value is less than zero, the particle has not yet been born. In this case, the particle is just assigned the color provided through the uniform variable *Background*. (If you actually want to see the grid of yet-to-be-born particles, you could provide a color value other than the background color. And if you want to be a bit more clever, you could pass the value *t* as a varying variable to the fragment shader and let it discard fragments for which *t* is less than zero. For my purposes, this wasn't necessary.)

If a particle's start time is less than the current time, the following kinematic equation is used to determine its current position:

$$P = P_i + vt + \frac{1}{2}at^2$$

In this equation P_i represents the initial position of the particle, *v* represents the initial velocity, *t* represents the elapsed time, *a* represents the acceleration, and *P* represents the final computed position. For acceleration, we'll use the value of acceleration due to gravity on Earth, which is 9.8 meters per second. In our simplistic model, we'll assume that gravity affects only the particle's height (*y* coordinate) and that the acceleration is negative (i.e., the particle is slowing down and falling back to the ground). The coefficient for the t^2 term in the preceding equation therefore appears in our code as the constant –4.9, and it is applied only to *vert.y*.

After this, all that remains is to transform the computed vertex and store the result in *gl_Position*.

Listing 13.6   Confetti cannon (particle system) vertex shader

```
uniform float Time;            // updated each frame by the application
uniform vec4  Background;      // constant color equal to background

attribute vec3  Velocity;      // initial velocity
attribute float StartTime;     // time at which particle is activated

varying vec4 Color;

void main(void)
{
    vec4  vert;
    float t = Time - StartTime;

    if (t >= 0.0)
    {
        vert    = gl_Vertex + vec4 (Velocity * t, 0.0);
        vert.y -= 4.9 * t * t;
        Color   = gl_Color;
    }
    else
    {
```

```
    vert  = gl_Vertex;      // Initial position
    Color = Background;      // "pre-birth" color
    }

    gl_Position = gl_ModelViewProjectionMatrix * vert;
}
```

13.6.3 Confetti Cannon Fragment Shader

The fragment shader used to generate the images in Color Plate 24 defies description (see Listing 13.7). Gaining thorough comprehension of this shader will be left as an exercise to the reader.

Listing 13.7 Confetti cannon (particle system) fragment shader

```
varying vec4 Color;

void main (void)
{
    gl_FragColor = Color;
}
```

13.6.4 Further Enhancements

There's a lot that can be done to make this shader more interesting. You might pass the *t* value from the vertex shader to the fragment shader as suggested earlier and make the color of the particle change over time. For instance, you could make the color change from yellow to red to black in order to simulate an explosion. The alpha value could be reduced over time to make the particle fade out. You might also provide a "time of death" and extinguish the particle completely at a certain time or when it reaches a certain distance from the origin. Instead of drawing the particles as points, you might draw them as short lines. This would permit you to do a motion blur effect with each particle. The size of the point (or line) can also be varied over time to create particles that grow or shrink. The physics model can be made a lot more sophisticated than the one illustrated. To make the particles look better, they could be rendered as textured quadrilaterals that always face the viewer (i.e., billboards). (An extension for doing this by drawing a single point rather than a quadrilateral is an official ARB extension that is supported by several hardware vendors—the point sprite extension.)

The real beauty in doing particle systems within a shader is that the computation is done completely in graphics hardware rather than on the host CPU. If the particle system data is stored in a vertex buffer object, there's a good chance that it will be stored in the on-board memory of the graphics hardware, so you won't even be using up any I/O bus bandwidth as you render the particle system each frame. With the OpenGL Shading Language, the equation for updating each particle can be arbitrarily complex. And, because the particle system is rendered like any other 3D object, you can rotate it around and view it from any angle while it is animating. There's really no end to the effects (and the fun!) that you can have with particle systems.

13.7 Wobble

The previous two examples discussed animating the geometry of an object, and used the vertex processor to achieve this (because the geometry of an object cannot be modified by the fragment processor). The fragment processor can also be used to create animation effects. The main purpose of most fragment shaders is to compute the fragment color, and any of the factors that affect this computation can be varied over time. In this section, we'll take a look at a shader that perturbs the texture coordinates in a time-varying way in order to achieve an oscillating or wobbling effect. With the right texture, this effect can make it very simple to produce an animated effect to simulate a gelatinous surface or a "dancing" logo.

This shader was developed to mimic the wobbly 2D effects demonstrated in some of the real-time graphics demos that are available on the Web (see http://www.scene.org for some examples). Its author, Antonio Tejada of 3Dlabs, wanted to create a similar effect using the OpenGL Shading Language.

The central premise of the shader is that a sine function is used in the fragment shader to perturb the texture coordinates prior to the texture lookup operation. The amount and frequency of the perturbation can be controlled through uniform variables sent by the application. Because the goal of the shader was to produce an effect that looked good, the accuracy of the sine computation was not critical. For this reason, and because the sine function had not been implemented at the time he wrote this shader, Antonio chose to approximate the sine value using the first two terms of the Taylor series for sine. The fragment shader would have been simpler if the built-in **sin** function had been used, but this approach demonstrates that numerical methods can be used as needed within a shader. (As to whether using two terms of the Taylor series would result in better performance than using the built-in **sin** function, it's hard to say. It will probably vary from one graphics hardware vendor to the next, depending on how the **sin** function is implemented.)

For this shader to work properly, the application will be required to provide the frequency and amplitude of the wobbles, as well as a light position. In addition, the application will increment a uniform variable called *StartRad* each frame. This value will be used as the basis for the perturbation calculation in the fragment shader. By incrementing it each frame, the wobble effect can be animated. The application must provide the vertex position, the surface normal, and the texture coordinate at each vertex of the object to be rendered.

The vertex shader for the wobble effect will be responsible for a simple lighting computation based on the surface normal and the light position provided by the application. It will pass along the texture coordinate without modification. This is exactly the same as the functionality of the Earth vertex shader described in Section 10.2.2, so we can simply use that vertex shader.

The fragment shader to achieve the wobbling effect is shown in Listing 13.8. It receives as input the varying variable *LightIntensity* as computed by the vertex shader. This variable will be used at the very end to apply a lighting effect to the fragment. The uniform variable *StartRad* provides the starting point for the perturbation computation in radians, and it is incremented by the application at each frame in order to animate the wobble effect. The wobble effect can be made to go faster by using a larger increment value, and it can be made to go slower by using a smaller increment amount. We found that an increment value of about 1° gave visually pleasing results.

The frequency and amplitude of the wobbles can be adjusted by the application with the uniform variables *Freq* and *Amplitude*. These are defined as **vec2** variables so that the *x* and *y* components can be adjusted independently. The final uniform variable defined by this fragment shader is *WobbleTex*, which is used to indicate the texture unit to be used for accessing the 2D texture that will be wobbled.

In order for the Taylor series approximation for sine to give more precise results, it is necessary to ensure that the value for which sine is computed is in the range $[-\pi/2, \pi/2]$. The constants C_PI (π), C_2PI (2π), C_2PI_I ($1/2\pi$), and C_PI_2 ($\pi/2$) are defined to assist in this process.

The first half of the fragment shader computes a perturbation factor for the *x* direction. We want to end up with a perturbation factor that is dependent on both the *s* and the *t* components of the texture coordinate. To this end, the local variable *rad* is computed as a linear function of the *s* and *t* values of the texture coordinate. (A similar but different expression will be used to compute the *y* perturbation factor in the second half of the shader.) The current value of *StartRad* is added. Finally, the *x* component of *Freq* is used to scale the result.

The value for *rad* will increase as the value for *StartRad* increases. As the scaling factor *Freq.x* increases, the frequency of the wobbles will also increase. The scaling factor should be increased as the size of the texture increases on the screen in order to keep the apparent frequency of the wobbles the same at different scales. You can think of the *Freq* uniform variable as the Richter scale for wobbles. A value of 0 will result in no wobbles whatsoever. A value of 1.0 will result in gentle rocking, a value of 2.0 will cause jiggling, a value of 4.0 will result in wobbling, and a value of 8.0 will result in magnitude 8.0 earthquake-like effects.

The next seven lines of the shader bring the value of *rad* into the range $[-\pi/2, \pi/2]$. When this is accomplished, we can compute **sin**(*rad*) using the first two terms of the Taylor series for sine, which is just $x - x^3/3!$ The result of this computation is multiplied by the *x* component of *Amplitude*. The value for the computed sine value will be in the range $[-1,1]$. If we just add this value to the texture coordinate as the perturbation factor, it will *really* perturb the texture coordinate. We want a wobble, not an explosion! Multiplying the computed sine value by a value of 0.05 will result in reasonable size wobbles. Increasing this scale factor will make the wobbles bigger, and decreasing it will make them smaller. You can think of this as how far the texture coordinate is stretched from its original value. Using a value of 0.05 means that the perturbation will alter the orginal texture coordinate by no more than ±0.05. A value of 0.5 means that the perturbation will alter the orginal texture coordinate by no more than ±0.5.

With the *x* perturbation factor computed, the whole process is repeated to compute the *y* perturbation factor. This computation is also based on a linear function of the *s* and *t* texture coordinate values, but it is different than what was used for the *x* perturbation factor. Computing the *y* perturbation value differently avoids symmetries between the *x* and *y* perturbation factors in the final wobbling effect, which doesn't look as good when animated.

With the perturbation factors computed, we can finally do our (perturbed) texture access. The color value that is retrieved from the texture map is multiplied by *LightIntensity* to compute the final color value for the fragment. Several frames from the animation produced by this shader are shown in Color Plate 21. These frames show the shader applied to a logo in order to illustrate the perturbation effects more clearly in static images. But the animation effect is also quite striking when the texture used looks like the surface of water, lava, slime, or even animal/monster skin.

Listing 13.8 Fragment shader for wobble effect

```
// Constants
const float C_PI    = 3.1415;
const float C_2PI   = 2.0 * C_PI;
const float C_2PI_I = 1.0 / (2.0 * C_PI);
const float C_PI_2  = C_PI / 2.0;

varying float LightIntensity;

uniform float StartRad;
uniform vec2  Freq;
uniform vec2  Amplitude;

uniform sampler2D WobbleTex;

void main (void)
{
    vec2  perturb;
    float rad;
    vec3  color;

    // Compute a perturbation factor for the x-direction
    rad = (gl_TexCoord[0].s + gl_TexCoord[0].t - 1.0 + StartRad) * Freq.x;

    // Wrap to -2.0*PI, 2*PI
    rad = rad * C_2PI_I;
    rad = fract(rad);
    rad = rad * C_2PI;

    // Center in -PI, PI
    if (rad >  C_PI) rad = rad - C_2PI;
    if (rad < -C_PI) rad = rad + C_2PI;

    // Center in -PI/2, PI/2
    if (rad >  C_PI_2) rad =  C_PI - rad;
    if (rad < -C_PI_2) rad = -C_PI - rad;

    perturb.x  = (rad - (rad * rad * rad / 6.0)) * Amplitude.x;

    // Now compute a perturbation factor for the y-direction
    rad = (gl_TexCoord[0].s - gl_TexCoord[0].t + StartRad) * Freq.y;

    // Wrap to -2*PI, 2*PI
    rad = rad * C_2PI_I;
    rad = fract(rad);
    rad = rad * C_2PI;

    // Center in -PI, PI
    if (rad >  C_PI) rad = rad - C_2PI;
    if (rad < -C_PI) rad = rad + C_2PI;
```

```
    // Center in -PI/2, PI/2
    if (rad >  C_PI_2) rad =  C_PI - rad;
    if (rad < -C_PI_2) rad = -C_PI - rad;

    perturb.y  = (rad - (rad * rad * rad / 6.0)) * Amplitude.y;

    color = vec3 (texture2D(WobbleTex, perturb + gl_TexCoord[0].st));

    gl_FragColor = vec4 (color * LightIntensity, 1.0);
}
```

13.8 Summary

With the fixed functionality in previous versions of OpenGL, animation effects were strictly in the domain of the application and had to be computed on the host CPU. With programmability, it has become easy to specify animation effects within a shader and let the graphics hardware do this work. Just about any aspect of a shader can be varied based on a global definition of current time: position, shape, color, texture coordinates, and lighting to name just a few.

When you develop a shader for an object that will be in motion, you should also consider how much of the animation effect can be encoded within the shader. Encoding animation effects within a shader can offload the CPU and simplify the code in the application. This chapter described some simple ways for doing this. On and off, scrolling, and threshold effects are quite easy to do within a shader. Key-frame interpolation can be supported in a very simple way through the power of programmability. Particles can be animated, including their position, color, velocity, and any other important attributes. Objects and textures can be made to oscillate, move, grow, or change based on mathematical expressions.

Animation is a powerful tool for conveying information, and the OpenGL Shading Language provides another avenue for expressing animation effects.

13.9 Further Information

If you're serious about animated effects, you really should read *Disney Animation: The Illusion of Life*, by two of the "Nine Old Men" of Disney animation fame, Frank Thomas and Ollie Johnston (1981). This book is loaded with color images and insight into the development of the animation art form at Disney Studios. It contains several decades worth of information about making great animated films. If you can, try to find a used copy of the original printing from Abbeville Press rather than the reprint by Hyperion. A softcover version was also printed by Abbeville, but this version eliminates much of the history of Disney Studios. A brief encapsulation of some of the material in this book can be found in the 1987 SIGGRAPH paper, *Principles of Traditional Animation Applied to 3D Computer Animation*, by John Lasseter.

Rick Parent's 2001 book, *Computer Animation: Algorithms and Techniques*, contains descriptions of a variety of algorithms for computer animation. The book *Game Programming Gems*, edited by Mark DeLoura (2000), also has several pertinent sections on animation.

Particle systems were first described by Bill Reeves in his 1983 SIGGRAPH paper, *Particle Systems—A Technique for Modeling a Class of Fuzzy Objects*. Jeff Lander wrote an easy-to-follow description of particle systems in his column for *Game Developer Magazine* in 1998, "The Ocean Spray in Your Face." He also made source code available for a simple OpenGL-based particle system demonstration program that he wrote.

[1] DeLoura, Mark, ed., *Game Programming Gems*, Charles River Media, Hingham, Massachusetts, 2000.

[2] Lander, Jeff, *The Ocean Spray in Your Face, Game Developer Magazine*, vol. 5, no. 7, pp. 13–19, July 1998.
http://www.darwin3d.com/gdm1998.htm

[3] Lasseter, John, *Principles of Traditional Animation Applied to 3D Computer Animation*, Computer Graphics, (SIGGRAPH '87 Proceedings), pp. 35–44, July 1987.

[4] Parent, Rick, *Computer Animation: Algorithms and Techniques*, Morgan Kaufmann Publishers, San Francisco, 2001.
http://www.cis.ohio-state.edu/~parent/book/outline.html

[5] Reeves, William T., *Particle Systems—A Technique for Modeling a Class of Fuzzy Objects*, ACM Transactions on Graphics, vol. 2, no. 2, pp. 91–108, April 1983.

[6] Reeves, William T., and Ricki Blau, *Approximate and Probabilistic Algorithms for Shading and Rendering Structured Particle Systems*, Computer Graphics (SIGGRAPH '85 Proceedings), pp. 313–322, July 1985.

[7] Thomas, Frank, and Ollie Johnston, *Disney Animation—The Illusion of Life*, Abbeville Press, New York, 1981.

[8] Thomas, Frank, and Ollie Johnston, *The Illusion of Life—Disney Animation, Revised Edition*, Hyperion, 1995.

[9] Watt, Alan H., and Mark Watt, *Advanced Animation and Rendering Techniques: Theory and Practice*, Addison-Wesley, Reading, Massachusetts, 1992.

Chapter 14

Antialiasing Procedural
Textures

Jaggies, popping, sparkling, stair steps, strobing, and marching ants. They're all names used to describe the anathema of computer graphics—ALIASING. Anyone who has used a computer has seen it. For still images, it's not always that noticeable or objectionable. But as soon as you put an object in motion, the movement of the jagged edges catches your eye and distracts you. From the early days of computer graphics, the fight to eliminate these nasty artifacts has been called ANTIALIASING.

This chapter does not contain a thorough description of the causes of aliasing, nor the methods used to combat it. But it does attempt to provide an introduction as to how the problem occurs and the facilities within the OpenGL Shading Language that can be used for antialiasing. Armed with this knowledge, you should be well on your way to fighting the jaggies in your own shaders.

14.1 Sources of Aliasing

The human eye is extremely good at noticing edges. This is how we comprehend shape and form and how we recognize letters and words. Our eye is naturally good at it, and we spend our whole lives practicing it, so naturally it is something we do very, very well.

A computer display is limited in its capability to present an image. It is made up of a finite number of discrete elements called pixels. At a given time, each pixel is capable of producing only one color. This makes it impossible for a computer display to accurately represent detail that is smaller than one pixel in screen space, such as an edge.

When you combine these two things, the human eye's ability to discern edges and the computer graphics display's limitations in replicating them, you have a problem, and this problem is known as aliasing. In a nutshell, aliasing occurs when we try to reproduce a signal with an insufficient sampling frequency. With a computer graphics display, we'll always have a fixed number of samples (pixels) with which to reconstruct our image, and this will always be insufficient to provide adequate sampling, so we will always have aliasing. We can reduce it to the point that it's not noticeable, or we can transform it into some other problem that is less objectionable, like blurriness or noise.

The problem is illustrated in Figure 14.1. In this diagram, we show the results of trying to draw a gray object. The intended shape is shown in Figure 14.1 (A). The computer graphics display limits us to a discrete sampling grid. If we choose only one location within each grid square (usually the center) and determine the color to be used by sampling the desired image at that point, we will see some apparent artifacts. This is called POINT SAMPLING and is illustrated in Figure 14.1 (B). The result is ugly aliasing artifacts for edges that don't line up naturally with the sampling grid (see Figure 14.1 (C)). (The drawing is idealized because pixels on a standard CRT do not produce light in the shape of a square, but the artifacts are obvious even when the sampled points are reconstructed as overlapping circles on the computer display.)

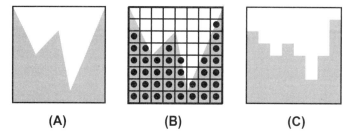

(A)   **(B)**   **(C)**

Figure 14.1   Aliasing artifacts caused by point sampling. The gray region represents the shape of the object to be rendered (A). The computer graphics display presents us with a limited sampling grid (B). The result of choosing to draw gray or not at each pixel results in jaggies, or aliasing artifacts (C).

Aliasing takes on other forms as well. If you are developing a sequence of images for an animation and you don't properly sample objects that are in motion, you might notice TEMPORAL ALIASING. This is caused by objects that are moving too rapidly for the sampling frequency being used. Objects may appear to stutter as they move or blink on and off. The classic example of temporal aliasing is the moving vehicle (car, truck, or covered wagon) in the movies that is going forward, but the spokes of the wheels appear to be rotating backwards. This is caused when the sampling rate (movie frames per second) is too low relative to the motion of the wheel spokes. In reality, the wheel may be rotating two- and three-quarter revolutions per frame, but on film it looks like it's rotating one-quarter revolution *backwards* each frame.

To render images that look truly realistic rather than computer generated, we need to develop techniques for overcoming the inherent limitations of the graphics display.

14.2 Avoiding Aliasing

One way to achieve good results without aliasing is to avoid situations where aliasing occurs.

For instance, if you know that a particular object will always be a certain size in the final rendered image, you can design a shader that looks good while rendering that object at that size. This is the assumption behind some of the shaders presented previously in this book. The **smoothstep**, **mix**, and **clamp** functions are handy functions to use to avoid sharp transitions and make a procedural texture look good at a particular scale.

Aliasing is often a problem when rendering an object at different sizes. Mipmap textures were designed to address this very issue, and you can do something similar with shaders. If you know that a particular object must appear at different sizes in the final rendering, you can design a shader for each different size. Each of these shaders would provide appropriate level of detail and avoid aliasing for an object of that size. For this to work, the application must determine the approximate size of the final rendered object before it is drawn and then install the appropriate shader. In addition, if a continuous zoom (in or out) is applied to a single object, there will be some "popping" that occurs when the level of detail changes.

You can avoid aliasing in some situations by using a texture instead of computing something procedurally. This lets you take advantage of the filtering (i.e., antialiasing) support that is built into the texture mapping hardware. However, there are issues with using stored textures as opposed to doing things procedurally as discussed in Chapter 11.

14.3 Increasing Resolution

The effects of aliasing can be reduced through a brute force method called SUPERSAMPLING that performs sampling at several locations within a pixel and averages the result of those samples. This is exactly the approach supported in today's graphics hardware with the multisample buffer. This method of antialiasing replaces a single point sampling operation with several, so it doesn't actually eliminate aliasing, but it can reduce aliasing to the point that it is no longer objectionable. You may be able to ignore the issue of aliasing if your shaders will always be used in conjunction with a multisample buffer.

But this approach does use up hardware resources (graphics board memory for storing the multisample buffer), and even with hardware acceleration, it still may be slower than performing the antialiasing as part of the procedural texture generation algorithm. And, because it doesn't eliminate aliasing, your texture is still apt to exhibit signs of aliasing, albeit at a higher frequency than before.

This is illustrated in Figure 14.2. Each of the pixels is rendered by sampling at four locations rather than at one. The average of the four samples is used as the value for the pixel. This provides a better result, but it is not sufficient to eliminate aliasing because high frequency components can still be misrepresented.

Supersampling can also be implemented within a fragment shader. The code that is used to produce the fragment color can be contstructed as a function, and this function can be called several times from within the main function of the fragment shader to sample the function at several discrete locations. The returned values can be averaged together to create the final value for the fragment. Results are improved if the sample positions are varied stochastically rather than spaced on a regular grid. Supersampling within a fragment shader has the obvious downside of requiring N times as much processing per fragment, where N is the number of samples computed at each fragment.

There will be times when aliasing is unavoidable and supersampling is infeasible. If you want to perform procedural texturing and you want a

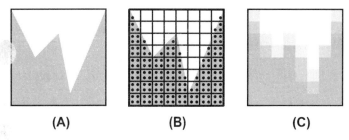

(A)   **(B)**   **(C)**

Figure 14.2   Supersampling with four samples per pixel yields a better result, but aliasing artifacts are still present. The shape of the object to be rendered is shown in (A). Sampling occurs at four locations within each pixel as shown in (B). The results are averaged to produce the final pixel value as shown in (C). Some samples that are ~~most half covered were sampled with just one supersample point instead of two, one pixel contains image data that was missed entirely, even with ~~rsampling.

single shader that is useful at a variety of scales, there's little choice but to address the aliasing issue and take steps to counteract aliasing in your shaders.

14.4   Antialiased Stripe Example

Aliasing does not occur until we attempt to represent a continuous image in screen space. This conversion occurs during rasterization; therefore, our attempts to mitigate its effects will always occur in the fragment shader. The OpenGL Shading Language has several functions for this purpose that are available only to fragment shaders. In order to provide motivation for some of the language facilities for filter estimation, we'll develop a "worst-case" scenario—alternating black and white stripes drawn on a sphere. Developing a fragment shader that performs antialiasing will enable us to further illustrate the aliasing problem and the methods for reducing aliasing artifacts.

14.4.1   Generating Stripes

The antialiasing fragment shader will determine whether each fragment is to be drawn as white or black in order to create lines on the surface of an object. The first step is to determine the method to be used for drawing lines. A single parameter will be used as the basis for our stripe pattern. For purposes of illustration, let's assume it's the *s* coordinate of the object's texture coordinate. We will have the vertex shader pass this value to us as a floating-point varying variable named *V*. This will end up giving us a method for creating vertical stripes on a sphere. Figure 14.3 (A) shows the result of using the *s* texture coordinate directly as the intensity (grayscale) value on the surface of the sphere. The viewing position is slightly above the sphere, so we are looking down at the "north pole." The *s* texture coordinate starts off at 0 (black) and increases to 1 (white) as it goes around the sphere. The edge where black meets white can be seen at the pole, and it runs down the back side of the sphere. The front side of the sphere looks mostly gray, but increases from left to right.

A sawtooth wave is created by multiplying the *s* texture coordinate by 16 and taking the fractional part (see Figure 14.3 (B)). This causes the intensity value to start at 0, rise quickly to 1, and then drop back down to 0. (To get a feel for what a sawtooth wave looks like, see the illustrations for the built-in functions **fract** (refer to Figure 5.6) and **mod** (refer to Figure 5.7)). This sequence is repeated 16 times. The OpenGL shader code to implement this is

```
float sawtooth = fract(V * 16.0);
```

This isn't quite the stripe pattern we're after. To get closer, we employ the absolute value function (see Figure 14.3 (C)). By multiplying the value of *sawtooth* by 2 and subtracting 1, we get a function that varies from [–1,1]. Taking the absolute value of this function results in a function that goes from 1 down to 0 and then back to 1 (i.e., a triangle wave). The line of code to do this is

```
float triangle = abs(2.0 * sawtooth - 1.0);
```

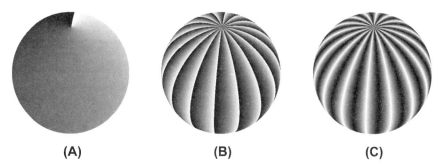

(A)   **(B)**   **(C)**

Figure 14.3   Using the *s* texture coordinate to create stripes on a sphere. In (A), the *s* texture coordinate is used directly as the intensity (gray) value. In (B), a modulus function is used to create a sawtooth function. In (C), the absolute value function is used to turn the sawtooth function into a triangle function. (Courtesy of Bert Freudenberg, University of Magdeburg, 2002)

A stripe pattern is starting to appear, but either it's too blurry or our glasses need adjustment. The stripes are made pure black and white by using the **step** function. If we compare our triangle variable to 0.5, this function will return 0 whenever *triangle* is less than or equal to 0.5, and 1 whenever *triangle* is greater than 0.5. This could be written as

```
float square = step(0.5, triangle);
```

This effectively produces a square wave and the result is illustrated in Figure 14.4 (A). The relative size of the alternating stripes can be modified by adjusting the threshold value provided in the **step** function.

14.4.2 Analytic Prefiltering

In Figure 14.4 (A), we see that the stripes are now distinct, but aliasing has reared its ugly head. The **step** function returns values that are either 0 or 1, with nothing in between, so the jagged edges in the transitions between white and black are easy to spot. They will not go away if we increase the resolution of the image; they'll just be smaller. The problem is caused by the fact that the **step** function introduced an immediate transition from white to black or an edge with infinite frequency (see Figure 5.11). There is no way to sample this transition at a high enough frequency to eliminate the aliasing artifacts. To get good results, we need to take steps within our shader to remove such high frequencies.

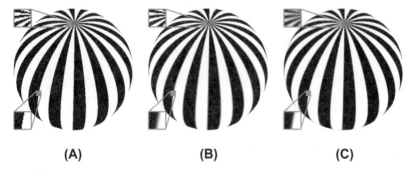

| (A) | (B) | (C) |

Figure 14.4 Antialiasing the stripe pattern. We can see that the square wave produced by the **step** function produces aliasing artifacts (A). The **smoothstep** function with a fixed width filter produces too much blurring near the equator but not enough at the pole (B). An adaptive approach provides reasonable antialiasing in both regions (C). (Courtesy of Bert Freudenberg, University of Magdeburg, 2002)

A variety of antialiasing techniques rely on eliminating extremely high frequencies prior to sampling. This is called LOW-PASS FILTERING because low frequencies are passed through unmodified, whereas high frequencies are eliminated. The visual effect of low-pass filtering is that the resulting image is blurred.

To eliminate the high frequencies from the stripe pattern, we'll use the **smoothstep** function. We know that this function will produce a smooth transition between white and black. It requires that we specify two edges, and a smooth transition will occur between those two edges. Figure 14.4 (B) illustrates the result from the following line of code:

```
float square = smoothstep(0.4, 0.6, triangle);
```

14.4.3 Adaptive Analytic Prefiltering

This produces acceptable results in some regions of the sphere but not in others. The size of the smoothing filter (0.2) is defined in parameter space. But the parameter does not vary at a constant rate in screen space. In this case, the *s* texture coordinate varies quite rapidly in screen space near the poles and less rapidly at the equator. Our fixed width filter produces blurring across several pixels at the equator and very little effect at the poles. What we need is a way to determine the size of the smoothing filter adaptively so that transition can be appropriate at all scales in screen space. This requires a measurement of how rapidly the function we're interested in is changing at a particular position in screen space.

Fortunately, the OpenGL Shading Language provides a built-in function that can give us the rate of change (derivative) of any parameter in screen space. The function **dFdx** provides the rate of change in screen coordinates in the *x* direction, and **dFdy** provides the rate of change in the *y* direction. Because these functions deal with screen space, they are available only in a fragment shader. These two functions can provide the information needed to compute a GRADIENT VECTOR for the position of interest.

Given a function $f(x,y)$, the gradient of f at the position (x, y) is defined as the vector:

$$G[f(x, y)] = \begin{bmatrix} \dfrac{\partial f}{\partial x} \\ \dfrac{\partial f}{\partial y} \end{bmatrix}$$

In English, the gradient vector is comprised of the partial derivative of function f with respect to x (i.e., the measure of how rapidly f is changing in the x direction) and the partial derivative of the function f with respect to y (i.e., the measure of how rapidly f is changing in the y direction). The important properties of the gradient vector are that it points in the direction of the maximum rate of increase of the function $f(x,y)$ (the gradient direction) and that the magnitude of this vector equals the maximum rate of increase of $f(x,y)$ in the gradient direction. (These properties are useful for image processing too, as we will see later.) The built-in functions **dFdx** and **dFdy** give us exactly what we need to define the gradient vector for functions utilized in fragment shaders.

The magnitude of the gradient vector for the function $f(x,y)$ is commonly called the GRADIENT of the function $f(x,y)$. It is defined as

$$\mathbf{mag}[G[f(x, y)]] = \mathbf{sqrt}((\partial f / \partial x)^2 + (\partial f / \partial y)^2)$$

In practice, it is not always necessary to perform the (possibly costly) square root operation. The gradient can be approximated using absolute values:

$$\mathbf{mag}[G[f(x, y)]] \cong \mathbf{abs}(f(x, y) - f(x + 1, y)) + \mathbf{abs}(f(x, y) - f(x, y + 1))$$

This is exactly what is returned by the built-in function **fwidth**. The sum of the absolute values is an upper bound on the width of the sampling filter needed to eliminate aliasing. If it is too large, the resulting image will look somewhat more blurry than it should, but this is usually acceptable.

The two methods of computing the gradient are compared in Figure 14.5. As you can see, there is little visible difference. Because the value of the gradient was quite small for the function being evaluated on this object, the values were scaled so they would be visible.

To compute the actual gradient for a varying variable V within a fragment shader, we use

```
float width = length(vec2 (dFdx(V), dFdy(V)));
```

To approximate it, we use the potentially higher performance calculation:

```
float width = fwidth(V);
```

The filter width can then be used within our call to **smoothstep** as follows:

```
float edge    = width * 32.0;
float square  = smoothstep(0.5 - edge, 0.5 + edge, triangle);
```

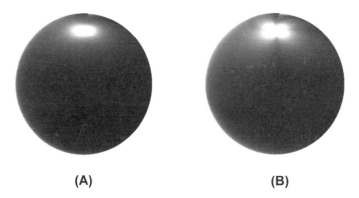

(A)   **(B)**

Figure 14.5 Visualizing the gradient. In (A), the magnitude of the gradient vector is used as the intensity (gray) value. In (B), the gradient is approximated with absolute values. (Actual gradient values are scaled for visualization purposes.) (Courtesy of Bert Freudenberg, University of Magdeburg, 2002)

If we put this all together in a fragment shader, we get Listing 14.1.

Listing 14.1 Fragment shader for adaptive analytic antialiasing

```
varying float V;                    // generic varying
varying float LightIntensity;

uniform float Frequency;            // Stripe frequency = 6

void main (void)
{
    float sawtooth = fract(V * Frequency);
    float triangle = abs(2.0 * sawtooth - 1.0);
    float dp = length(vec2 (dFdx(V), dFdy(V)));
    float edge = dp * Frequency * 2.0;
    float square = smoothstep(0.5 - edge, 0.5 + edge, triangle);
    gl_FragColor = vec4 (vec3 (square), 1.0);
}
```

If we scale the frequency of our texture, we must also increase the filter width accordingly. After the value of the function is computed, it is replicated across the red, green, and blue components of a **vec3** and used as the color of the fragment. The results of this adaptive antialiasing approach are shown in Figure 14.4 (C). The results are much more consistent across the surface of the sphere. A simple lighting computation is added, and the resulting shader is applied to the teapot in Figure 14.6.

Figure 14.6   Effect of adaptive analytical antialiasing on teapots of different sizes. On top, the teapots are drawn with no antialiasing. On the bottom, the adaptive antialiasing shader is used. Antialiasing of the stripe pattern looks good at both scales. However, aliasing artifacts are still visible along the silhouette edges of the object.

This approach to antialiasing works well until the filter width gets larger than the frequency. This is the situation that occurs at the north pole of the sphere. The stripes very close to the pole are much thinner than one pixel, so no step function will produce the correct gray value here. In such regions, you need to switch to integration or frequency clamping, both of which are discussed in subsequent sections.

14.4.4 Analytic Integration

The weighted average of a function over a specified interval is called a CONVOLUTION. The values that are used to do the weighting are called the CONVOLUTION KERNEL or the CONVOLUTION FILTER. In some cases, it is possible to determine the convolution of a function ahead of time and then sample the convolved function rather than the original function in order to reduce or eliminate aliasing. The convolution can be performed over a fixed interval in a computation that is equivalent to convolving the input function with a box filter. A box filter is far from ideal, but it is simple and easy to compute and often good enough.

This corresponds to the notion of antialiasing by AREA SAMPLING. This method is different from point sampling or super sampling in that we attempt to calculate the area of the object being rendered relative to the sampling region. Referring back to Figure 14.2, if we used an area sampling technique, we'd get more accurate values for each of the pixels, and we wouldn't miss that pixel that just had a sliver of coverage.

In *Advanced RenderMan: Creating CGI for Motion Pictures*, Apodaca and Gritz (1999) explain how to perform analytic antialiasing of a periodic step function, sometimes called a PULSE TRAIN. We'll use this technique to analytically antialias the procedural brick shader we described back in Chapter 6. If you recall, the simple brick example used the **step** function to produce the periodic brick pattern. The function that creates the brick pattern in the horizontal direction is illustrated in Figure 14.7. From 0 to *BrickPct.x* (the brick width fraction), the function is 1.0. At the value of *BrickPct.x*, there is an edge with infinite slope as the function drops to 0. At the value 1, the function jumps back up to 1.0, and the process is repeated for the next brick.

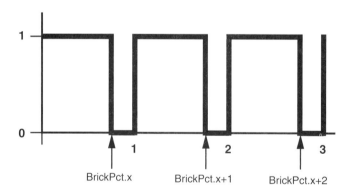

Figure 14.7 The periodic step function, or pulse train, that was used to define the horizontal component of the procedural brick texture

The key to antialiasing this function will be to compute its integral, or accumulated, value. We have to consider the possibility that, in areas of high complexity, the filter width that is computed by **fwidth** will cover several of these pulses. By sampling the integral rather than the function itself, we'll get a properly weighted average and avoid the high frequencies caused by point sampling that would produce aliasing artifacts.

So what is the integral of this function? It is illustrated in Figure 14.8. From 0 to *BrickPct.x*, the function value is 1, so the integral increases with a slope of 1. From *BrickPct.x* to 1.0, the function has a value of 0, so the integral stays constant in this region. At 1, the function jumps back to 1.0, so the integral increases until the function reaches *BrickPct.x* + 1. At this point, the integral changes to a slope of 0 again, and this pattern of ramps and plateaus continues.

Antialiasing can be performed by determining the value of the integral over the area of the filter. This is accomplished by evaluating the integral at the edges of the filter and subtracting the two values. The integral for this function consists of two parts: the sum of the area for all the pulses that have been fully completed prior to the edge we are considering, and the area of the possibly partially completed pulse for the edge we are considering.

For our procedural brick shader, the variable *position.x* was used as the basis for generating the pulse function in the horizontal direction. So the number

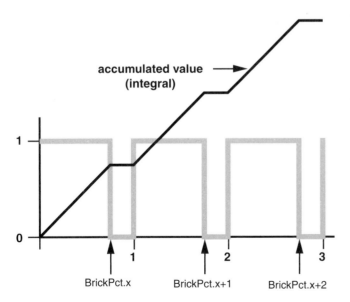

Figure 14.8 Periodic step function (pulse train) and its integral

of fully completed pulses will just be **floor**(*position.x*). Because the height of each pulse is 1.0, the area of each fully completed pulse is just *BrickPct.x*. Multiplying these two values together provides the area for all the fully completed pulses. The edge that we're considering may be in the part of the function that is equal to 0, or it may be in the part of the function that is equal to 1. We can find out by computing **fract**(*position.x*) – (1.0 – *BrickPct.x*). If the result of this subtraction is less than 0, we were in the part of the function that returns 0, so nothing more needs to be done. But if the value is greater than zero, we are part way into a region of the function that is equal to 1. Because the height of the pulse is 1, the area of this partial pulse is **fract**(*position.x*) – (1.0 – *BrickPct.x*). Therefore, the second part of our integral is the expression **max**(**fract**(*position.x*) – (1.0 – *BrickPct.x*), 0.0).

We can use this integral for both the horizontal and vertical components of our procedural brick pattern. Because the application knows the brick width and height fractions (*BrickPct.x* and *BrickPct.y*), it can easily compute 1.0 – *BrickPct.x* and 1.0 – *BrickPct.y* and provide them to our fragment shader as well. This keeps us from computing these values unnecessarily several times for every fragment that is rendered. We'll call these values the mortar percentage. Because we will evaluate this expression twice with different arguments, it will be convenient to define it as a macro or a function:

```
#define Integral(x, p, notp) ((floor(x)*(p)) + max(fract(x)-(notp), 0.0))
```

The parameter *p* indicates the value that is part of the pulse (i.e., when the function is 1.0), and *notp* indicates the value that is not part of the pulse (i.e., when the function is 0). Using this macro, we can write the code to compute the value of the integral over the width of the filter as follows:

```
vec2 fw, useBrick;

fw = fwidth(position);

useBrick = (Integral(position + fw, BrickPct, MortarPct) -
            Integral(position, BrickPct, MortarPct)) / fw;
```

The result is divided by the area of the filter (a box filter is assumed in this case) in order to obtain the average value for the function in the selected interval.

14.4.5 Antialiased Brick Fragment Shader

Now we can put all this to work to build better bricks. The simple point sampling technique used in the example in Chapter 6 is replaced with analytic integration. The resulting shader is shown in Listing 14.2. The difference between the aliased and antialiased brick shaders is shown in Color Plate 25.

Listing 14.2   Source code for an antialiased brick fragment shader

```
uniform vec3  BrickColor, MortarColor;
uniform vec2  BrickSize;
uniform vec2  BrickPct;
uniform vec2  MortarPct;

varying vec2  MCposition;
varying float LightIntensity;

#define Integral(x, p, notp) ((floor(x)*(p)) + max(fract(x)-(notp), 0.0))

void main(void)
{
    vec2 position, fw, useBrick;
    vec3 color;

    // Determine position within the brick pattern
    position = MCposition / BrickSize;

    // Adjust every other row by an offset of half a brick
    if (fract(position.y * 0.5) > 0.5)
        position.x += 0.5;

    // Calculate filter size
    fw = fwidth(position);

    // Perform filtering by integrating the 2D pulse made by the
    // brick pattern over the filter width and height
    useBrick = (Integral(position + fw, BrickPct, MortarPct) -
                Integral(position, BrickPct, MortarPct)) / fw;

    // Determine final color
    color  = mix(MortarColor, BrickColor, useBrick.x * useBrick.y);
    color *= LightIntensity;
    gl_FragColor = vec4 (color, 1.0);
}
```

14.5 Frequency Clamping

Certain functions do not have an analytic solution, or they are just too difficult to solve. If this is the case, you might try a technique called frequency clamping. In this technique, the average value of the function is used to replace the actual value of the function when the filter width is too large. This is convenient for functions whose average is known, such as sine and noise.

14.5.1 Antialiased Checkerboard Fragment Shader

The checkerboard pattern is the standard measure of the quality of an anti-aliasing technique (see Figure 14.9). Listing 14.3 shows a fragment shader that produces a procedurally generated, antialiased checkerboard pattern. The vertex shader transforms the vertex position and passes along the texture coordinate, nothing more. The application provides values for the two colors of the checkerboard pattern, the average of these two colors (the application can compute this and provide it via a uniform, rather than having the fragment shader compute it for every fragment), and the frequency of the checkerboard pattern.

The fragment shader computes the appropriate size of the filter and uses it to perform smooth interpolation between adjoining checkerboard squares. If the filter is too wide (i.e., the varying parameter is changing too quickly to do proper filtering), the average color is substituted. Even though this fragment shader uses a conditional statement, care is taken to avoid aliasing. In the transition zone between the **if** clause and the **else** clause, a smooth interpolation is performed between the computed color and the average color.

Listing 14.3   Source code for an antialiased checkerboard fragment shader

```
uniform vec3   Color1;
uniform vec3   Color2;
uniform vec3   AvgColor;
uniform float Frequency;

varying vec2   TexCoord;

void main(void)
{
    vec3 color;

    // Determine the width of the projection of one pixel into s-t space
    vec2 fw = fwidth(TexCoord);

    // Determine the amount of fuzziness
    vec2 fuzz = fw * Frequency * 2.0;

    float fuzzMax = max(fuzz.s, fuzz.t);

    // Determine the position in the checkerboard pattern
    vec2 checkPos = fract(TexCoord * Frequency);

    if (fuzzMax < 0.5)
    {
```

```
    // If the filter width is small enough, compute the pattern color
    vec2 p = smoothstep(vec2 (0.5), fuzz + vec2 (0.5), checkPos) +
             (1.0 - smoothstep(vec2(0.0), fuzz, checkPos));

    color = mix(Color1, Color2, p.x * p.y + (1.0 - p.x) * (1.0 - p.y));

    // Fade in the average color when we get close to the limit
    color = mix(color, AvgColor, smoothstep(0.125, 0.5, FuzzMax));
}
else
{
    // Otherwise, use only the average color
    color = AvgColor;
}

gl_FragColor = vec4(color, 1.0);
}
```

Figure 14.9 Checkerboard pattern rendered with the antialiased checkerboard shader. On the left, the filter width is set to 0, so aliasing occurs. On the right, the filter width is computed using the **fwidth** function.

14.6 Summary

With increased freedom comes increased responsibility. The OpenGL Shading Language permits the computation of procedural textures without restriction. It is quite easy to write a shader that exhibits unsightly aliasing artifacts (using a conditional or a step function is all it takes), and it can be difficult to eliminate these artifacts. After describing the aliasing problem in general terms, this chapter explored several options for antialiasing procedural textures. Facilities in the language, such as the built-in functions for smooth interpolation (**smoothstep**), for determining derivatives in screen space (**dFdx**, **dFdy**), and for estimating filter width (**fwidth**) can assist in the fight against jaggies. These functions were fundamental components of shaders that were presented to perform antialiasing by prefiltering, adaptive prefiltering, integration, and frequency clamping.

14.7 Further Information

Most signal processing and image processing books contain a discussion of the concepts of sampling, reconstruction, and aliasing. Books by Glassner, Wolberg, and Gonzalez and Woods can be consulted for additional information on these topics. Technical memos by Alvy Ray Smith address the issues of aliasing in computer graphics directly.

The book *Advanced RenderMan: Creating CGI for Motion Pictures* by Tony Apodaca and Larry Gritz (1999) contains a chapter that describes shader antialiasing in terms of the RenderMan shading language, and much of the discussion is germane to the OpenGL Shading Language as well. Darwyn Peachey has a similar discussion in *Texturing & Modeling: A Procedural Approach, Third Edition* by David Ebert, et. al. (2002).

Bert Freudenberg developed an OpenGL shader to do adaptive antialiasing and presented this work at the SIGGRAPH 2002 in San Antonio, Texas. In this chapter, I've recreated the images Bert used in his talk, but he deserves the credit for originally developing the images and the shaders to illustrate some of the topics I've covered. This subject is also covered in his Ph.D. thesis, *Real-Time Stroke-based Halftoning.*

[1] *3Dlabs developer Web site.* http://www.3dlabs.com/support/developer

[2] Apodaca, Anthony A., and Larry Gritz, *Advanced RenderMan: Creating CGI for Motion Pictures*, Morgan Kaufmann Publishers, San Francisco, 1999. http://www.bmrt.org/arman/materials.html

[3] Cook, Robert L., *Stochastic Sampling in Computer Graphics*, ACM Transactions on Graphics, vol. 5, no. 1, pp. 51–72, January 1986.

[4] Crow, Franklin C., *The Aliasing Problem in Computer-Generated Shaded Images*, Communications of the ACM, 20(11), pp. 799–805, November 1977.

[5] Crow, Franklin C., *Summed-Area Tables for Texture Mapping*, Computer Graphics (SIGGRAPH '84 Proceedings), pp. 207–212, July 1984.

[6] Dippé, Mark A. Z., and Erling Henry Wold, *Antialiasing Through Stochastic Sampling*, Computer Graphics (SIGGRAPH '85 Proceedings), pp. 69–78, July 1985.

[7] Ebert, David S., John Hart, Bill Mark, F. Kenton Musgrave, Darwyn Peachey, Ken Perlin, and Steven Worley, *Texturing and Modeling: A Procedural Approach, Third Edition*, Morgan Kaufmann Publishers, San Francisco, 2002. http://www.texturingandmodeling.com

[8] Freudenberg, Bert, *A Non-Photorealistic Fragment Shader in OpenGL 2.0*, Presented at the SIGGRAPH 2002 Exhibition in San Antonio, July 2002. http://isgwww.cs.uni-magdeburg.de/~bert/publications

[9] Freudenberg, Bert, *Real-Time Stroke-based Halftoning*, Ph.D. thesis, University of Magdeburg, submitted in 2003.

[10] Glassner, Andrew S., *Principles of Digital Image Synthesis*, Vol. 1, Morgan Kaufmann Publishers, San Francisco, 1995.

[11] Glassner, Andrew S., *Principles of Digital Image Synthesis*, Vol. 2, Morgan Kaufmann Publishers, San Francisco, 1995.

[12] Gonzalez, Rafael C., and Richard E. Woods, *Digital Image Processing, Second Edition*, Prentice Hall, Upper Saddle River, New Jersey, 2002.

[13] Smith, Alvy Ray, *Digital Filtering Tutorial for Computer Graphics*, Lucasfilm Technical Memo 27, revised March 1983. http://www.alvyray.com/Memos/default.htm

[14] Smith, Alvy Ray, *Digital Filtering Tutorial, Part II*, Lucasfilm Technical Memo 27, revised March 1983. http://www.alvyray.com/Memos/default.htm

[15] Smith, Alvy Ray, *A Pixel Is Not a Little Square, a Pixel Is Not a Little Square, a Pixel Is Not a Little Square! (And a Voxel Is Not a Little Cube)*, Technical Memo 6, Microsoft Research, July 1995. http://www.alvyray.com/memos/default.htm

[16] Wolberg, George, *Digital Image Warping*, Wiley-IEEE Press, 2002.

Chapter 15

Non-Photorealistic Shaders

A significant amount of computer graphics research has been aimed at achieving more and more realistic renditions of synthetic scenes. A long-time goal has been to render a scene so perfectly that it is indistinguishable from a photograph of the real scene, hence the term PHOTOREALISM. With the latest graphics hardware, some photorealistic effects are becoming possible in real-time rendering.

This quest for realism is also reflected in graphics APIs such as OpenGL. The OpenGL specification defines specific formulas for calculating effects such as illumination from light sources, material properties, and fog. These formulas attempt to define effects as realistically as possible while remaining relatively easy to implement in hardware and have duly been cast into silicon by intrepid graphics hardware designers.

But the collection of human art and literature shows us that photorealism is not the only important style for creating images. The availability of low-cost programmable graphics hardware has sparked the growth of an area called NON-PHOTOREALISTIC RENDERING, or NPR. Researchers and practitioners in this field are attempting to use computer graphics to produce a wide range of artistic effects other than photorealism. In this chapter, we'll look at a few examples of shaders whose main focus is something other than generating results that are as realistic as possible.

15.1 Hatching Example

Bert Freudenberg of the University of Magdeburg in Germany was one of the first people outside of 3Dlabs to come up with a unique OpenGL shader. His area of research has been to use programmable hardware to produce real-time NPR effects such as hatching and half-toning. He experimented with a prototype implementation of the OpenGL Shading Language in the summer of 2002 and produced a hatching shader that he agreed to share with us for this book.

This shader has a few unique features, and the steps involved in designing this shader are described in Bert's Ph.D. thesis, *Real-Time Stroke-based Half-toning* (2003). Bert's hatching shader is based on a woodblock printing shader by Scott Johnston that is discussed in *Advanced RenderMan: Creating CGI for Motion Pictures* by Tony Apodaca and Larry Gritz (1999).

The goal in a hatching shader is to render an object in a way that makes it look hand-drawn, for instance with strokes that look like they may have been drawn with pen and ink. Each stroke contributes to the viewer's ability to comprehend the tone, texture, and shape of the object being viewed. The effect being sought in this shader is that of a woodcut printing. In a woodcut, a wooden block etched with small grooves is covered with ink and pressed onto a surface. The image left on the surface is the mirror image of the image carved into the wood block. No ink is left where the grooves are cut, only where the wood is left uncut. Lighting is simulated by varying the width of the grooves according to light intensity.

There are a number of challenges to overcome to develop a shader that simulates the look of a woodcut printing. The first thing that's needed is a way of generating stripes that can be used to define the tone and texture of the object. Alternating white and black lines provides the highest contrast edges and thus represents a worst-case scenario for aliasing artifacts; thus antialiasing will be a prime consideration. We also want our lines to "stay put" on the object so that the object can be used in an animation sequence. Finally, the lines in a woodcut print are not always perfectly straight and uniform as though they were drawn by a computer. They are cut into the wood by a human artist, so they have some character. We'd like the lines that our shader generates to have some character as well.

15.1.1 Application Setup

The application needs to send vertex positions, normals, and a single set of texture coordinates to the hatching shader. The normals will be used in a simple lighting formula, and the texture coordinates will be used as the base for procedurally defining the hatching pattern. The light position will be passed in as a uniform variable, and the application will also update the value of the *Time* uniform variable each frame so that the behavior of the shader can be modified slightly each frame. What do you suppose will be used to give our lines some character? You guessed it—the noise function. In this case, we're going to have the application generate the noise values that are needed and store the results in a 3D texture. For this reason, the value for a uniform variable of type **sampler3D** will be provided by the application in order to inform the fragment shader which texture unit should be accessed to obtain the noise values.

15.1.2 Vertex Shader

The hatch vertex shader is shown in Listing 15.1. The first line is the only line that looks different than things we've discussed previously. The varying variable *ObjPos* will be used as the basis for our hatching stroke computation in the fragment shader. In order to animate the wiggle of the lines, the vertex shader adds the uniform variable *Time* to the z coordinate of the incoming vertex position. This will make it appear as though the wiggles are "flowing" along the z-axis. A scaling value is also used to make the hatching strokes match the scale of the object being rendered. (To accommodate a variety of objects, this value should probably be replaced with a uniform variable.) The remainder of the vertex shader performs a simple diffuse lighting equation, copies the t coordinate of the incoming texture coordinate into the varying variable *V*, and computes the value of the built-in variable *gl_Position*.

Listing 15.1   Vertex shader for hatching

```
uniform vec3   LightPosition;
uniform float  Time;

varying vec3   ObjPos;
varying float  V;
varying float  LightIntensity;

void main(void)
{
    ObjPos          = (vec3 (gl_Vertex) + vec3 (0.0, 0.0, Time)) * 0.2;

    vec3 pos        = vec3 (gl_ModelViewMatrix * gl_Vertex);
    vec3 tnorm      = normalize(gl_NormalMatrix * gl_Normal);
    vec3 lightVec   = normalize(LightPosition - pos);
```

```
LightIntensity   = max(dot(lightVec, tnorm), 0.0);

V = gl_MultiTexCoord0.t;  // try .s for vertical stripes

gl_Position = ftransform();
}
```

15.1.3   Generating Hatching Strokes

The goal of our fragment shader is to determine whether each fragment is to be drawn as white or black in order to create lines on the surface of the object. As we mentioned, there will be some challenges along the way. To prepare for the full-blown hatching shader, we'll develop some of the techniques we need and illustrate them on a simple object: a sphere.

We'll start with the same code that was presented in Section 14.4.1 for generating vertical stripes, namely

```
float sawtooth = fract(V * 16.0);
float triangle = abs(2.0 * sawtooth - 1.0);
float square = step(0.5, triangle);
```

Recall that V was a varying variable passed from the vertex shader and it was equal to the s texture coordinate, if we wanted to generate vertical stripes, and equal to the t texture coordinate, if we wanted to generate horizontal stripes. The number 16 is chosen to give us 16 white stripes and 16 black stripes. The result of this code is illustrated in Figure 15.1. The relative size of the white and black stripes can be modified by adjusting the threshold value provided in the **step** function.

Figure 15.1   A sphere with a stripe pattern generated procedurally based on the s texture coordinate (Courtesy of Bert Freudenberg, University of Magdeburg, 2002)

15.1.4 Obtaining Uniform Line Density

We now have reasonable looking stripes, but they aren't of uniform width. They appear fatter along the equator and pinched in at the pole. We'd like to end up with lines that are of roughly equal width in screen space. This requires the use of the **dFdx** and **dFdy** functions:

```
float dp = length(vec2 (dFdx(V), dFdy(V)));
```

As we learned in Section 14.4.3, this computation provides us with the gradient (i.e., how rapidly *V* is changing at this point on the surface). We can use this value to adjust the density of lines in screen space. (The approximation to the gradient mentioned in Section 14.4.3 isn't quite good enough for our purposes here. We're not using this value to estimate the filter width for antialiasing; we're using it to compute the stripe frequency. This computation needs to be rotationally invariant so that we don't get stripes jumping around just because we rotate the object. For this reason, we need to compute the actual length of the gradient vector, not just the sum of the absolute values of the two components of the gradient vector.) The base 2 logarithm of this value (shown applied to the sphere in Figure 15.2 (A)) is used to adjust the density in discrete steps—each time *dp* doubles, the number of lines will double unless we do something about it. The stripes will get too thin and too dense if this occurs. To counteract this (because we are interested in getting a constant line density in screen space), we have to decrease the number of stripes when the density gets too high. This is accomplished by negating the logarithm.

```
float logdp      = -log2(dp);
float ilogdp     = floor(logdp);
float frequency  = exp2(ilogdp);
float sawtooth   = fract(V * 16.0 * frequency);
```

A sphere with a higher stripe frequency is shown in Figure 15.2 (B). As you can see, the lines look reasonable in the lower part of the sphere, but there are too many at the pole. By applying the stripe frequency adjustment, we end up with stripes of roughly equal width across the sphere (see Figure 15.2 (C)). Notice the correlation between Figure 15.2 (A) and Figure 15.2 (C).

The next issue to address is the abrupt changes that occur as we jump from one stroke frequency to the next. Our eyes detect a distinct edge along these transitions, and we need to take steps to soften this edge so that it isn't as distracting. We can accomplish this by using the fractional part of *logdp* to do a smooth blend between two frequencies of the triangle wave. This value will be 0 at the start of one frequency, and it will increase to 1.0 at the point where the jump to the next frequency occurs.

```
float transition = logdp - ilogdp;
```

As we saw earlier, a triangle wave with frequency double that of a triangle wave with frequency *t* can be generated by taking **abs**(2.0 * *t* – 1.0). We can use the value of *transition* to perform a linear interpolation between *t* and **abs**(2.0 * *t* – 1.0) by computing (1.0 – *transition*) * *t* + *transition* * **abs**(2.0 * *t* – 1.0). This is exactly the same as if we did **mix**(**abs**(2.0 * *t* – 1.0), *t, transition*). But instead of using **mix**, we note that this is equivalent to **abs**((1.0 – *transition*) * *t* - *transition*). Using the previously computed value for our base frequency (*triangle*), we end up with the following code:

```
triangle = abs((1.0 - transition) * triangle - transition);
```

The result of drawing the sphere with uniform stripe density and tapered ends is shown in Figure 15.2 (D).

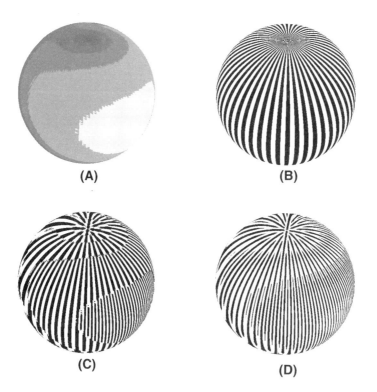

(A)   (B)

(C)   (D)

Figure 15.2   Adjusting the stripe frequency. The integer part of the logarithm of the gradient (A) is used as the basis for determining stripe frequency. First, the sphere is shown with a higher frequency of stripes (B). The integer part of the logarithm is then used to adjust the stripe frequency in (C), and the effect of tapering the ends is shown in (D). (Courtesy of Bert Freudenberg, University of Magdeburg, 2002)

15.1.5 Lighting

To simulate the effect of lighting, we'd like to make the dark stripes more prominent in regions that are in shadow and the white stripes more prominent in regions that are lit. We can do this by using the computed light intensity to modify the threshold value used in the **step** function. In regions that are lit, the threshold value is decreased so that black stripes get thinner. In regions that are in shadow, the threshold value is increased so that the black stripes get wider.

```
const float edgew = 0.2;            // width of smooth step

float edge0  = clamp(LightIntensity - edgew, 0.0, 1.0);
float edge1  = clamp(LightIntensity, 0.0, 1.0);
float square = 1.0 - smoothstep(edge0, edge1, triangle);
```

Once again, we utilize the smoothstep function to antialias the transition. Because our stripe pattern is a (roughly) constant width in screen space, we can use a constant filter width rather than an adaptive one. The results of the lighting effect can be seen in Figure 15.3.

15.1.6 Adding Character

If a woodcut block is made by a human artist and not by a machine, the cuts in the wood will not be perfect in thickness and spacing. How do we

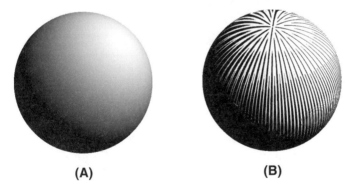

(A) **(B)**

Figure 15.3 Applying lighting to the sphere. In (A), the sphere is lit with a simple lighting model and no stripes. In (B), the light intensity is used to modulate the width of the stripes to simulate the effect of lighting. (Courtesy of Bert Freudenberg, University of Magdeburg, 2002)

add some imperfections into our mathematically perfect description of hatching lines? With noise, as we discussed in Chapter 12. For this shader, we don't need anything fancy; we just want to add some "wiggle" to our otherwise perfect lines or perhaps some "patchiness" to our simple lighting equation. A tileable 3D texture containing Perlin noise can be used in the same way for this shader as for the shaders in Chapter 12.

To add wiggle to our lines, we can modify the sawtooth generation function:

```
float sawtooth = fract((V + noise * 0.1) * frequency * stripes);
```

The result of adding noise to our stripe pattern is illustrated in Figure 15.4.

15.1.7 Hatching Fragment Shader

The pieces described in the preceding sections are put together in the general purpose hatching shader shown in Listing 15.2. It bases its hatching stroke computation on the *t* texture coordinate, so the result is horizontal stripes rather than vertical ones. The results of applying this shader to the teapot model are shown in Figure 15.5

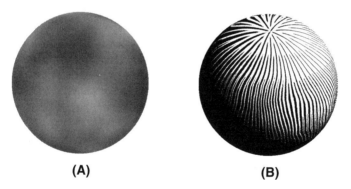

(A)   **(B)**

Figure 15.4   Adding noise to the hatching algorithm. In (A), the Perlin noise function is applied directly to the sphere's surface. In (B), it is used to modulate the parameter used to define the frequency of the hatching strokes. (Courtesy of Bert Freudenberg, University of Magdeburg, 2002)

Figure 15.5   Woodcut-style teapot rendered with the hatching shader (Courtesy of Bert Freudenberg, University of Magdeburg, 2002)

Listing 15.2   Fragment shader for woodcut-style rendering

```
const float frequency = 1.0;

varying vec3  ObjPos;            // object space coord (noisy)
varying float V;                 // generic varying
varying float LightIntensity;

uniform sampler3D Noise;         // value of Noise = 3;

void main (void)
{
    float dp       = length(vec2 (dFdx(V), dFdy(V)));
    float logdp    = -log2(dp * 8.0);
    float ilogdp   = floor(logdp);
    float stripes  = exp2(ilogdp);

    float noise    = texture3D(Noise, ObjPos).x;

    float sawtooth = fract((V + noise * 0.1) * frequency * stripes);
    float triangle = abs(2.0 * sawtooth - 1.0);

    // adjust line width
    float transition = logdp - ilogdp;
```

```
    // taper ends
    triangle = abs((1.0 + transition) * triangle - transition);

    const float edgew = 0.3;              // width of smooth step

    float edge0  = clamp(LightIntensity - edgew, 0.0, 1.0);
    float edge1  = clamp(LightIntensity, 0.0, 1.0);
    float square = 1.0 - smoothstep(edge0, edge1, triangle);

    gl_FragColor = vec4 (vec3 (square), 1.0);
}
```

15.2 Technical Illustration Example

Pick up just about any instruction manual, technical book, or encyclopedia, and you will see a variety of illustrations other than photographs or photo-realistic graphics. Technical illustrators have learned various techniques over the years to convey relevant information as simply and as clearly as possible. Details that do not contribute to understanding are omitted, and details that are crucial to understanding are clear and straightforward. This style of illustration differs from mainstream computer graphics where an enormous amount of detail may be presented in an image in order to make it look more realistic. The effort to convey information as succinctly as possible in a technical illustration is summed up by a strategy referred to by Edward Tufte (1997) as "the smallest effective difference." In his book, *Visual Explanations*, Tufte says, "Make all visual distinctions as subtle as possible, but still clear and effective."

Various NPR practitioners are attempting to develop algorithms to create technical illustrations. The goal is to simplify or even automate the task of creating high-quality technical illustrations according to time-honored illustration techniques. Much of our comprehension about an object's shape comes from lighting. Yet the traditional lighting equation is deficient at conveying shape information in areas that are not lit directly because these areas appear flat. The only lighting in these areas comes from the ambient term, which is constant. Technical illustrations also highlight important edges in black so that they are distinct and clearly convey the shape of the object. If a small ambient term is used in the traditional lighting model, black edge highlights will typically be indistinguishable from unlit regions of the object, which will also be very near black.

In 1998, Bruce and Amy Gooch, Peter Shirley, and Elaine Cohen did a survey of illustrations and came up with a list of common characteristics for color illustrations done with airbrush and pen.

- Surface boundaries, silhouette edges, and discontinuities in the surface of an object are usually drawn with black curves.

- A single light source is used, and it produces a white highlight on objects.

- The light source is usually positioned above the object so that the diffuse reflection term varies from [0,1] across the visible portion of the object.

- Effects that add complexity (realism) such as shadows, reflections, and multiple light sources are not shown.

- Matte objects are shaded with intensities far from white and black so as to be clearly distinct from (black) edges and (white) highlights.

- The warmth or coolness of the color indicates the surface normal (and hence the curvature of the surface).

These characteristics were incorporated into a "low dynamic range artistic tone algorithm" that we now refer to as GOOCH SHADING.

One of the important aspects of Gooch shading is the generation of black curves that represent important edges. There are a number of techniques for rendering such edges. Perhaps the best method is to have them identified during the modeling process by the person designing the model. In this case, the edges can be rendered as antialiased black lines that are drawn on top of the object itself (i.e., in a second rendering pass that draws the edges after the objects in the scene have been completely rendered).

If important edges have not been identified during the modeling process, there are several methods for generating them automatically. Quality of results will vary depending on the method used and the characteristics of the objects in the scene. Interior boundary or crease edges should also be identified, and these are sometimes critical to comprehension. A technique that identifies boundary or crease edges as well as silhouette edges involves using vertex and fragment shaders to write world space normals and depth values into the frame buffer. The result is stored as a texture, and a subsequent rendering pass with different vertex and fragment shaders can use an edge detection algorithm on this "image" in order to detect discontinuities (i.e., edges) in the scene (Jason Mitchell (2002)).

A technique for drawing silhouette edges for simple objects, described by Jeff Lander (2000) in *Under the Shade of the Rendering Tree*, requires drawing the geometry twice. First, just the front-facing polygons are drawn using filled polygons and the depth comparison mode set to GL_LESS. The Gooch shaders will be active when we do this. Then, the back-facing polygons are drawn as lines with the depth comparison mode set to GL_LEQUAL. This has the effect of drawing lines where a front-facing polygon shares an edge with a back-facing polygon. These lines will be drawn in black using fixed functionality OpenGL with polygon mode set so that back-facing polygons are drawn as lines. The OpenGL calls to do this are shown in Listing 15.3.

Listing 15.3 C code for drawing silhouette edges on simple objects

```
// Enable culling
glEnable(GL_CULL_FACE);

// Draw front-facing polygons as filled using the Gooch shader
glPolygonMode(GL_FRONT, GL_FILL);
glDepthFunc(GL_LESS);
glCullFace(GL_BACK);
glUseProgramObjectARB(ProgramObject);
drawSphere(0.6f, 64);

// Draw back-facing polygons as black lines using standard OpenGL
glLineWidth(5.0);
glPolygonMode(GL_BACK, GL_LINE);
glDepthFunc(GL_LEQUAL);
glCullFace(GL_FRONT);
glColor3f(0.0, 0.0, 0.0);
glUseProgramObjectARB(0);
drawSphere(0.6f, 64);
```

A second aspect of Gooch shading is that specular highlights are computed using the exponential specular term of the Phong lighting model and are rendered in white. Highlights convey information about the curvature of the surface, and choosing white as the highlight color will ensure that highlights are distinct from edges (which are black) and the colors used to shade the object (which are chosen to be visually distinct from white or black).

A third aspect of the algorithm is that a limited range of luminance values are used to convey information about the curvature of the surfaces that are being rendered. This part of the shading is performed using the color of the object, which is typically chosen to be an intermediate value that doesn't interfere visually with white or black.

Because the range of luminance values is limited, a warm-to-cool color gradient is also added in order to convey more information about the object's surface. Artists use "warm" colors (yellow, red, and orange) and "cool" colors (blue, violet, and green) to communicate a sense of depth. Warm colors, which appear to advance, are used to indicate objects that are closer. Cool colors, which appear to recede, are used to indicate objects that are farther away.

The actual shading of the object depends on two factors. The diffuse reflection factor is used to generate luminance values in a limited range to provide one part of the shading. A color ramp that blends between two colors provides the other part of the shading. One of the two colors is chosen to be a cool (recessive) color, such as blue, to indicate surfaces that are angled away from the light source. The other color is chosen to be a warm (advancing) color, such as yellow, to indicate surfaces facing toward the light source. The blue-to-yellow ramp will provide an undertone that will ensure a cool-to-warm transition regardless of the diffuse object color that is chosen.

The formulas used to compute the colors used for Gooch shading are as follows:

$$k_{cool} = k_{blue} + \alpha k_{diffuse}$$

$$k_{warm} = k_{yellow} + \beta k_{diffuse}$$

$$k_{final} = \left(\frac{1 + N \cdot L}{2}\right)k_{cool} + \left(1 - \frac{1 + N \cdot L}{2}\right)k_{warm}$$

k_{cool} is the color for the areas that are not illuminated by the light source. This value is computed by adding the blue undertone color and the diffuse color of the object, $k_{diffuse}$. The value α is a variable that defines how much of the object's diffuse color will be added to the blue undertone color. k_{warm} is the color for the areas that are fully illuminated by the light source. This value is computed as the sum of the yellow undertone color and the object's diffuse color multiplied by a scale factor, β.

The final color is just a linear blend between the colors k_{cool} and k_{warm} based on the diffuse reflection term $N \cdot L$, where N is the normalized surface normal and L is the unit vector in the direction of the light source. Since $N \cdot L$ can vary from $[-1,1]$, we add 1 and divide the result by 2 in order to get a value in the range $[0,1]$. This value is used to determine the ratio of k_{cool} and k_{warm} to produce the final color value.

15.2.1 Application Setup

The way we will implement this shading algorithm is in two passes (i.e., we will draw the geometry twice). We'll use the Lander technique to render silhouette edges in black. In the first pass, we'll cull back-facing polygons and render the front-facing polygons with the Gooch shader. In the second pass, we'll cull all the front-facing polygons and use OpenGL fixed functionality to render the edges of the back-facing polygons in black. We'll draw the edges with a line width greater than one pixel so that they can be seen outside of the object. For this shader to work properly, only vertex positions and normals need to be passed to the vertex shader.

15.2.2 Vertex Shader

The goal of the Gooch vertex shader is to produce a value for the $(1 + N \cdot L) / 2$ term in the previous equations, and to pass on the reflection vector and the view vector so that the specular reflection can be computed in the fragment shader (see Listing 15.4). Other elements of the shader are identical to shaders discussed earlier.

Listing 15.4   Vertex shader for Gooch matte shading

```
uniform vec3  LightPosition;  // (0.0, 10.0, 4.0)

varying float NdotL;
varying vec3  ReflectVec;
varying vec3  ViewVec;

void main(void)
{
    vec3 ecPos      = vec3 (gl_ModelViewMatrix * gl_Vertex);
    vec3 tnorm      = normalize(gl_NormalMatrix * gl_Normal);
    vec3 lightVec   = normalize(LightPosition - ecPos);
    ReflectVec      = normalize(reflect(-lightVec, tnorm));
    ViewVec         = normalize(-ecPos);
    NdotL           = (dot(lightVec, tnorm) + 1.0) * 0.5;
    gl_Position     = ftransform();
}
```

15.2.3 Fragment Shader

The fragment shader implements the tone-based shading portion of the Gooch shading algorithm and adds the specular reflection component (see Listing 15.5). The colors and ratios are defined as uniform variables so that they can be easily modified by the application. The reflection and view vectors are normalized in the fragment shader because interpolation may have caused them to have a length other than 1.0. The result of rendering with the Gooch shader and the silhouette edge algorithm described by Lander is shown in Color Plate 23.

Listing 15.5 Fragment shader for Gooch matte shading

```
uniform vec3  SurfaceColor; // (0.75, 0.75, 0.75)
uniform vec3  WarmColor;    // (0.6, 0.6, 0.0)
uniform vec3  CoolColor;    // (0.0, 0.0, 0.6)
uniform float DiffuseWarm;  // 0.45
uniform float DiffuseCool;  // 0.45

varying float NdotL;
varying vec3  ReflectVec;
varying vec3  ViewVec;

void main (void)
{
    vec3 kcool    = min(CoolColor + DiffuseCool * SurfaceColor, 1.0);
    vec3 kwarm    = min(WarmColor + DiffuseWarm * SurfaceColor, 1.0);
    vec3 kfinal   = mix(kcool, kwarm, NdotL);

    vec3 nreflect = normalize(ReflectVec);
    vec3 nview    = normalize(ViewVec);

    float spec    = max(dot(nreflect, nview), 0.0);
    spec          = pow(spec, 32.0);

    gl_FragColor = vec4 (min(kfinal + spec, 1.0), 1.0);
}
```

15.3 Mandelbrot Example

C'mon, now, what kind of a book on graphics programming would this be without an example of drawing the Mandelbrot set?

Our last shader of the chapter doesn't fall into the category of attempting to achieve an artistic or painterly effect, but it's an example of performing a type of general purpose computation on the graphics hardware for the purpose of scientific visualization. In this case, the graphics hardware enables us to do real-time exploration of a famous mathematical function that computes the Mandelbrot set.

The point of including this shader is to emphasize the fact that with the OpenGL Shading Language, computations that were previously possible only in the realm of the CPU can now be executed on the graphics hardware. Performing the computations completely on the graphics hardware is a big performance win because the computations can be carried out on many pixels in parallel. Visualization of a complex mathematical function such as the Mandelbrot set is only the tip of the iceberg for using programmable shader technology for scientific visualization.

15.3.1 About the Mandelbrot Set

To understand the Mandelbrot set, we must first recall a few things from our high school mathematics days. There is a number, called the imaginary number, and denoted i, defined to be equal to the square root of -1.

With it, the square root of any negative number can be easily described. For instance, $3i$ squared is -9, and conversely the square root of -9 is $3i$.

Numbers that consist of a real number and an imaginary number, such as $6 + 4i$, are called complex numbers. Arithmetic operations can be performed on complex numbers just like real numbers. The result of multiplying two complex numbers together is as follows:

$$x = a + bi$$

$$y = c + di$$

$$xy = ac + adi + cbi - bd$$

$$= (ac - bd) + (ad + bc)i$$

Because complex numbers contain two parts, the set of complex numbers is two dimensional. They can be plotted on the complex number plane, which uses the horizontal axis to represent the real part and the vertical axis to represent the imaginary part (see Figure 15.6).

In Figure 15.6, we see three symbols plotted on the complex number plane. A small square is plotted at the complex number $2 + i$, a small circle is plotted at $-1 + 2i$, and a triangle is plotted at $-1.5 - 0.5i$.

With the assistance of 1970s computer technology (quite inferior by today's consumer PC standards), a mathematician named Benoit Mandelbrot began studying a recursive function involving complex numbers:

$$Z_0 = 0 + 0i$$

$$Z_{n+1} = Z_n^2 + c$$

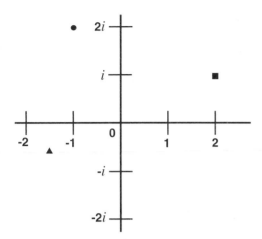

Figure 15.6   A portion of the complex number plane

In this function, the value of Z starts off at $0 + 0i$. For each iteration, the value of Z is squared and added to the constant complex number c to determine a new value for Z. This amazingly simple iterative formula produces what has been called the most complex object in mathematics, and perhaps the most complex structure ever seen!

It turns out that for some values of c, the function will eventually approach infinity, and for other values it will not. Quite simply, values of c that go off to infinity are not part of the Mandelbrot set, and the rest are. If we use a computer (or an OpenGL Shading Language-capable graphics accelerator!) to test thousands of points on the complex number plane and assign a gray level to those that go off to infinity and black to those that don't, we see the following familiar cardioid/prickly pear shape start to appear (see Figure 15.7).

How exactly do we test whether these values go off to infinity? Well, Mandelbrot helped us out a bit here. He showed that if the magnitude of Z (its distance from the origin) was greater than 2, the value of the function would go to infinity. To encode this function in a programming language, all we need to do is stop iterating when the magnitude of Z surpasses 2. Even easier, because we're always dealing with Z^2, we can simply check to see if Z^2 is greater than 4.

The values inside the black region of Figure 15.7 do not go off to infinity in any reasonable number of iterations. How do we deal with these? In order to prevent our computer or graphics hardware from locking up in an

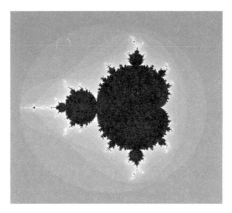

Figure 15.7   Simple plot of the Mandelbrot set

infinite loop, we need to decide on the maximum number of iterations to allow before we give up and assume the point is inside the Mandelbrot set. With these two exit criteria, we can write a simple loop that computes the Mandelbrot set.

The beauty of the Mandelbrot set can be enhanced if we color code the number of iterations needed to determine whether a particular point is inside the set. Values determined to be outside the set on the first iteration are given one color value, values determined to be outside the set on the second iteration are given another color value, and so on. In Figure 15.7, I've used gray levels to indicate the number of iterations. The medium gray on the outside represents values that are identified as outside of the Mandelbrot set on the very first iteration. Values in white along the edge took 20 iterations to be identified as being outside the Mandelbrot set.

The edges of the Mandelbrot set hold an infinite amount of self-similar variety. By continuing to zoom in on the edge detail, you will find complex numbers whose magnitude stayed below 2 for hundreds or even thousands of iterations of the function before finally exceeding the threshold and zooming off to infinity.

Here are a few other deep thoughts that you can use to amaze and amuse your friends:

- The length of the border for the Mandelbrot set is infinite.

- All of the regions inside the Mandelbrot set (i.e., the black regions) are connected.

- There is exactly one band surrounding the Mandelbrot set for each iteration value (e.g., a band that exceeded the threshold on the first iteration, a band that exceeded on the second iteration, and so on). The iteration bands go completely around the Mandelbrot set, do not break, and do not cross each other. When you've zoomed in to explore an edge region with amazing complexity, this is pretty astonishing.

- There is an infinite number of "mini-Mandelbrots" (regions that look like warped or transformed versions of the full Mandelbrot set) within the original.

15.3.2 Vertex Shader

The vertex shader for the Mandelbrot set (see Listing 15.6) is almost exactly the same as the vertex shader for the simple brick example that was described in Section 6.2. The only difference is that we assume texture coordinates will be provided in the range of [0,1] for both s and t, and we map these values into the range [-2.5, 2.5] and store the result into a varying variable named *Position*. This gives the fragment shader the capability to plot values directly onto a coordinate system that is just the right size for plotting the Mandelbrot set, and it has the point (0,0) in the middle. If the application draws a single polygon that's a screen-aligned square and has texture coordinate (0,0) in the lower-left corner and (1,1) in the upper right, the result will be a standard representation of the Mandelbrot set. Of course, with our OpenGL Mandelbrot shader, the Mandelbrot set can be "textured" onto any geometry, and we'll even apply a simple lighting model as an added bonus.

Listing 15.6 Vertex shader for drawing the Mandelbrot set

```
uniform vec3 LightPosition;
uniform float SpecularContribution;
uniform float DiffuseContribution;
uniform float Shininess;

varying float LightIntensity;
varying vec3  Position;

void main(void)
{
    vec3 ecPosition = vec3 (gl_ModelViewMatrix * gl_Vertex);
    vec3 tnorm      = normalize(gl_NormalMatrix * gl_Normal);
    vec3 lightVec   = normalize(LightPosition - ecPosition);
    vec3 reflectVec = reflect(-lightVec, tnorm);
    vec3 viewVec    = normalize(-ecPosition);
```

```
    float spec       = max(dot(reflectVec, viewVec), 0.0);
    spec             = pow(spec, Shininess);
    LightIntensity   = DiffuseContribution *
                         max(dot(lightVec, tnorm), 0.0) +
                         SpecularContribution * spec;
    Position         = vec3(gl_MultiTexCoord0 - 0.5) * 5.0;
    gl_Position      = ftransform();
}
```

15.3.3 Fragment Shader

The fragment shader implements the algorithm described in the previous section. Uniform variables are used to establish the maximum number of iterations and the starting point for viewing the Mandelbrot set (center value and zoom factor). The application is given artistic license to use uniform variables to set one color for points inside the set, and two colors to use for points outside the set. For values outside the set, the color gradient from *OuterColor1* to *OuterColor2* will be broken into 20 separate bands, and the cycle will be repeated if the number of iteration goes above 20. It will be repeated again if the number of iterations goes above 40, and so on.

This shader maps the *x* coordinate of the computed position in the complex number plane (i.e., the value in *Position.x*) to the real number in the iterative function, and the *y* coordinate to the imaginary number. After the initial conditions have been established, the shader enters a loop with two exit criteria—if we reach the maximum number of iterations allowed, or if the point is proven to be outside of the set. Within the loop, the function $Z^2 + c$ is computed for use in the next iteration. After the loop is exited, we compute the color of the fragment. If we're inside the set, the inside color is used. If we're on the edge or outside, a blend is done between the edge color and the outer color depending on the number of iterations that have occurred.

The complete fragment shader is shown in Listing 15.7.

Listing 15.7   Fragment shader for computing the Mandelbrot set

```
varying vec3  Position;
varying float LightIntensity;

uniform float MaxIterations;
uniform float Zoom;
uniform float Xcenter;
uniform float Ycenter;
uniform vec3  InnerColor;
```

```
uniform vec3   OuterColor1;
uniform vec3   OuterColor2;

void main(void)
{
    float    real  = Position.x * Zoom + Xcenter;
    float    imag  = Position.y * Zoom + Ycenter;
    float    Creal = real;    // Change this line...
    float    Cimag = imag;    // ...and this one to get a Julia set

    float r2 = 0.0;
    float iter;

    for (iter = 0.0; iter < MaxIterations && r2 < 4.0; ++iter)
    {
        float tempreal = real;

        real = (tempreal * tempreal) - (imag * imag) + Creal;
        imag = 2.0 * tempreal * imag + Cimag;
        r2   = (real * real) + (imag * imag);
    }

    // Base the color on the number of iterations

    vec3 color;

    if (r2 < 4.0)
        color = InnerColor;
    else
        color = mix(OuterColor1, OuterColor2, fract(iter * 0.05));

    color *= LightIntensity;

    gl_FragColor = vec4 (color, 1.0);
}
```

There is obviously room for improvement in this shader. One thing you
might do is improve the color selection algorithm. One possibility would be
to use a 1D texture to store a color lookup table. The number of iterations
could be used to index into this table to obtain the color to be used for
drawing the fragment.

After you've invented a pleasing coloring scheme, you can explore some of
the popular Mandelbrot "tourist locations." Various books and Web sites
have published the coordinates of interesting locations in the Mandelbrot
set, and these shaders are set up so that you can plug those coordinates in
directly and zoom in and see for yourself. Figure 15.8 shows a few that
I explored.

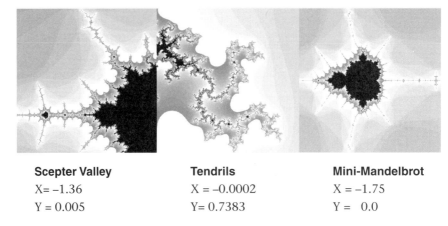

Scepter Valley	Tendrils	Mini-Mandelbrot
X= –1.36	X = –0.0002	X = –1.75
Y = 0.005	Y= 0.7383	Y = 0.0

Figure 15.8   Results from the Mandelbrot shader

15.3.4 Julia Sets

Julia sets are related to the Mandelbrot set. Each point in the Mandelbrot set can be used to generate a Julia set, and these are just as much fun to explore as the Mandelbrot set. The only difference is that the constant c in the equation $Z^2 + c$ is initialized to the value of a point in the Mandelbrot set other than the one currently being plotted. To change the Mandelbrot shader into a fragment shader for doing Julia sets, change the two lines of code that initialize the value of c:

```
float   Creal = -1.36;   // Now we'll see an interesting Julia set
float   Cimag = 0.11;
```

Figure 15.9 shows a few examples of the Julia sets that can be rendered with this shader. You might want to change this shader so that the values for *Creal* and *Cimag* can be passed in as uniform variables when you want to draw a Julia set. The numbers are no longer imaginary. Now we can do real-time exploration of the mathematical universe through the OpenGL Shading Language!

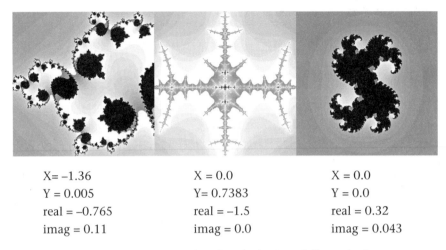

X= –1.36	X = 0.0	X = 0.0
Y = 0.005	Y= 0.7383	Y = 0.0
real = –0.765	real = –1.5	real = 0.32
imag = 0.11	imag = 0.0	imag = 0.043

Figure 15.9 Some Julia sets rendered with the Mandelbrot shader

15.4 Summary

Realism is no longer the goal for all applications of interactive computer graphics. Because of the flexibility of programmable graphics hardware, we no longer have to settle for the classic "look" of computer graphics. A high-level procedural language such as the OpenGL Shading Language allows artists and practitioners to express algorithms for rendering in more artistic styles such as pen-and-ink, woodcut, and paints. A procedural hatching shader was presented and described to illustrate how this can be accomplished. Various styles of technical illustration can be done interactively, as shown by the Gooch shader described in this chapter. It is also possible to write shaders that assist in the visualization of mathematical functions, as demonstrated by the Mandelbrot and Julia set shaders.

The history of human art shows that there is an endless variety of artistic styles. The OpenGL Shading Language can be used to create shaders that emulate some of these styles and perhaps invent new ones.

15.5   Further Information

Books devoted to the topic of non-photorealistic rendering include *Non-Photorealistic Rendering* by Amy and Bruce Gooch (2001) and *Non-Photorealistic Computer Graphics* by Thomas Strothotte and Stefan Schlechtweg (2002).

The Gooch shading algorithm is defined and described in the SIGGRAPH 1998 paper, *A Non-Photorealistic Lighting Model for Automatic Technical Illustration*, by Amy and Bruce Gooch, Peter Shirley, and Elaine Cohen. This paper draws on concepts presented by Edward Tufte in *Visual Explanations* (1997). A short discussion of NPR can be found in *Real-Time Rendering, Second Edition*, by Tomas Akenine-Möller and Eric Haines (2002). I've also included a lot of references to NPR resources in the main bibliography at the end of this book.

The classic text on fractals and the Mandelbrot set is, of course, *The Fractal Geometry of Nature, Updated and Augmented,* by Benoit Mandelbrot (1983). In 1986, Heinz-Otto Peitgen and Peter Richter wrote *The Beauty of Fractals,* another book you can enjoy looking at as well as reading. Peitgen and Dietmer Saupe (1988) edited a book called *The Science of Fractal Images,* which contains numerous examples and algorithms and additional material by Mandelbrot, Richard Voss, and others. A couple of the Mandelbrot "tourist destinations" that I've listed were described by Paul Derbyshire on the now defunct Web site, *PGD's Quick Guide to the Mandelbrot Set.*

[1] Akenine-Möller, Tomas, E. Haines, *Real-Time Rendering, Second Edition*, A K Peters, Ltd., Natick, Massachusetts, 2002. http://www.realtimerendering.com

[2] Derbyshire, Paul, *PGD's Quick Guide to the Mandelbrot Set*, personal Web site. http://www.globalserve.net/~derbyshire/manguide.html

[3] Freudenberg, Bert, Maic Masuch, and Thomas Strothotte, Walk-Through Illustrations: Frame-Coherent Pen-and-Ink Style in a Game Engine, Computer Graphics Forum, Volume 20 (2001), Number 3, Manchester, U.K. http://isgwww.cs.uni-magdeburg.de/~bert/publications

[4] Freudenberg, Bert, Maic Masuch, and Thomas Strothotte, *Real-Time Halftoning: A Primitive For Non-Photorealistic Shading*, Rendering Techniques 2002, Proceedings 13th Eurographics Workshop, pp. 227–231, 2002. http://isgwww.cs.uni-magdeburg.de/~bert/publications

[5] Freudenberg, Bert, and Maic Masuch, *Non-Photorealistic Shading in an Educational Game Engine,* SIGGRAPH and Eurographics Campfire, Snowbird, Utah, June 1–June 4, 2002. http://isgwww.cs.uni-magdeburg.de/ ~bert/publications

[6] Freudenberg, Bert, *Real-Time Stroke-based Halftoning,* Ph.D. thesis, University of Magdeburg, submitted in 2003.

[7] Gooch, Amy, *Interactive Non-Photorealistic Technical Illustration,* Master's thesis, University of Utah, December 1998. http://www.cs.utah.edu/~gooch/publication.html

[8] Gooch, Amy, Bruce Gooch, Peter Shirley, and Elaine Cohen, *A Non-Photorealistic Lighting Model for Automatic Technical Illustration,* Computer Graphics (SIGGRAPH '98 Proceedings), pp. 447–452, July 1998. http://www.cs.utah.edu/~gooch/publication.html

[9] Gooch, Bruce, Peter-Pike J. Sloan, Amy Gooch, Peter Shirley, and Richard Riesenfeld, *Interactive Technical Illustration,* Proceedings 1999 Symposium on Interactive 3D Graphics, pp. 31–38, April 1999. http://www.cs.utah.edu/~gooch/publication.html

[10] Gooch, Bruce, and Amy Gooch, *Non-Photorealistic Rendering,* A K Peters Ltd., Natick, Massachusetts, 2001. http://www.cs.utah.edu/~gooch/book.html

[11] Lander, Jeff, *Under the Shade of the Rendering Tree,* Game Developer Magazine, vol. 7, no. 2, pp. 17–21, Feb. 2000. http://www.darwin3d.com/gdm2000.htm

[12] Mandelbrot, Benoit B., *The Fractal Geometry of Nature, Updated and Augmented,* W. H. Freeman and Company, New York, 1983.

[13] Mitchell, Jason L., *Image Processing with Pixel Shaders in Direct3D,* in Engel, Wolfgang, ed., ShaderX, Wordware, May 2002. http://www.pixelmaven.com/jason

[14] Peitgen, Heinz-Otto, and P. H. Richter, *The Beauty of Fractals, Images of Complex Dynamical Systems,* Springer Verlag, Berlin Heidelberg, 1986.

[15] Peitgen, Heinz-Otto, D. Saupe, M. F. Barnsley, R. L. Devaney, B. B. Mandelbrot, R. F. Voss, *The Science of Fractal Images,* Springer Verlag, New York, 1988.

[16] Strothotte, Thomas, and S. Schlectweg, *Non-Photorealistic Computer Graphics, Modeling, Rendering, and Animation,* Morgan Kaufmann Publishers, San Francisco, 2002.

[17] Tufte, Edward, *Visual Explanations,* Graphics Press, Cheshire, Connecticut, 1997.

Chapter 16

Shaders for Imaging

One of the longtime strengths of OpenGL relative to other graphics APIs is that it has always included facilities for both imaging and 3D rendering operations. Applications can take advantage of both capabilities as needed. For instance, a video effects application might take advantage of OpenGL's imaging capabilities to send a sequence of images (i.e., a video stream) to OpenGL and have the images texture-mapped onto some three-dimensional object. Color space conversion or color correction can be applied to the images as they are sent to OpenGL. Traditional graphics rendering effects such as lighting and fog can also be applied to the object.

The initial release of the OpenGL Shading Language was focused primarily on providing support for 3D rendering operations. Additional imaging capabilities are planned for a future version. Nonetheless, there are still many useful imaging operations that can be done with shaders, as we shall see.

In this chapter, we will be describing shaders whose primary function is to operate on two-dimensional images rather than on three-dimensional geometric primitives.

The rasterization stage in OpenGL can be split into five different units, depending on the primitive type being rasterized. These are point rasterization, line rasterization, polygon rasterization, pixel rectangle rasterization, and bitmap rasterization. The output of each of these five rasterization units can be the input to a fragment shader. This makes it possible to perform programmable operations not only on geometry data, but also on image data, making OpenGL an extremely powerful and flexible rendering engine.

A fragment shader can be used either to process each fragment that is generated as a result of a call to **glBitmap** or **glDrawPixels** or to process texture values read from a texture map. We can divide imaging operations into two broad categories: those that require access to a single pixel at a time, and those that require access to multiple pixels at a time. Imaging operations that require access to only a single pixel at a time can be implemented quite easily in a fragment shader using the OpenGL Shading Language. The varying variable *gl_Color* can be read within a fragment shader to obtain the color value for fragments that were generated as a result of a call to **glBitmap** or **glDrawPixels**. Operations that require access to multiple pixels at a time can also be performed, but the image must first be stored in texture memory. Multiple accesses to the image can then be performed from within a fragment shader to achieve the desired result.

The benefit of using an OpenGL shader to do imaging operations is that it can typically be done much faster on the graphics hardware than it can be done on the CPU due to the highly parallel nature of current graphics hardware. This also frees up the CPU to perform other useful tasks. If the image to be modified is stored as a texture on the graphics accelerator, the user can interact with it in real-time to perform operations such as color correction, noise removal, or image sharpening, and all of the work can be done on the card, with very little traffic on the I/O bus.

16.1 Geometric Image Transforms

As part of its fixed functionality, OpenGL defines only one operation that modifies the geometric properties of an image: pixel zoom. This operation performs scaling on an image as it is sent to the display.

If you want to rotate an image, the traditional response has always been, "Load the image into texture memory, use it to draw a textured rectangle, and transform the rectangle." Although this approach does require an extra read and write of the image within the graphics system (the image must be written into texture memory and then read as the rectangle is drawn), the speed and bandwidth of today's graphics accelerator make this an acceptable approach for all but the most demanding applications. With the OpenGL Shading Language, you can even provide the same rectangle coordinates every time you draw the image and let the vertex shader do the scaling, translation, or rotation of the rectangle. Image warping can be supported by texturing a polygon mesh instead of a single rectangle. Hardware support for texture filtering can produce high-quality results for any of these operations.

16.2 Mathematical Mappings

A common imaging operation that is supported by OpenGL fixed function-ality is scale and bias. In this operation, each incoming color component is multiplied by a scale factor, and a bias value is added. This can be used to map color values from one linear range to another. This is straightforward in the OpenGL Shading Language using the standard math operators. It is also possible to perform more complex mathematical mappings on pixel values using built-in functions such as **pow**, **exp2**, and **log2**.

The built-in dot product function (**dot**) can be used to produce a single intensity value from a color value. To compute a CIE luminance value from linear RGB values defined according to *ITU-R Recommendation BT.709* (the HDTV color standard) use the following:

```
float luminance = dot(vec3 (0.2125, 0.7154, 0.0721), rgbColor);
```

This is the standard used in manufacturing contemporary monitors, and it defines a linear RGB color space. The coefficients 0.299, 0.587, and 0.114 are often used to convert an RGB value to a luminance value. However, these values were established with the inception of the NTSC standard in 1953 to compute luminance for the monitors of that time, and they are used to convert nonlinear RGB values to luminance values. They do not accurately calculate luminance for today's CRT monitors, but it is still appropriate to use them to compute nonlinear video luma from nonlinear RGB input values as follows:

```
float luma = dot(vec3 (0.299, 0.587, 0.114), rgbColor);
```

16.3 Lookup Table Operations

OpenGL defines a number of lookup tables as part of its fixed functionality. Several are defined as part of the imaging subset. Lookup tables are simply a way of mapping an input value to one or more output values. This opera-tion provides a level of indirection that is often useful for processing color information. The fact that we have programmable processors in OpenGL means that the input values can be computed as part of a shader, and the output value can be used as part of further computation within the shader. This opens up a lot of new possibilities for lookup tables.

A flexible and efficient way to perform lookup table operations with an OpenGL shader is to use a 1D texture map. The lookup table can be an arbi-trary size (thus overcoming a common gripe about OpenGL lookup tables often being limited by implementations to 256 entries), and it can be used to map a single input value to a single output value, or it can be used to map a single input value to a two-, three-, or four-component value. If you want the values returned to be discrete values, you can set the 1D texture's filtering modes to GL_NEAREST. If you want interpolation to occur between neighboring lookup table values, use GL_LINEAR.

An intensity value in the range [0,1] can be used as the texture coordinate for a 1D texture access. The built-in texture functions always return an RGBA value. If a texture with a single channel has been bound to the texture unit specified by the sampler, the value of that texture will be contained in each of the red, green, and blue channels, so we can pick any of them:

```
float color = texture1D(lut, intensity).r; // GL_PIXEL_MAP_I_TO_I
```

An intensity-to-RGBA lookup can be performed with a single texture access:

```
vec4 color = texture1D(lut, intensity);    // GL_PIXEL_MAP_I_TO_R,G,B,A
```

An RGBA-to-RGBA lookup operation requires four texture accesses:

```
vec4 colorOut;
colorOut.r = texture1D(lut, colorIn.r).r;   // GL_PIXEL_MAP_R_TO_R
colorOut.g = texture1D(lut, colorIn.g).g;   // GL_PIXEL_MAP_G_TO_G
colorOut.b = texture1D(lut, colorIn.b).b;   // GL_PIXEL_MAP_B_TO_B
colorOut.a = texture1D(lut, colorIn.a).a;   // GL_PIXEL_MAP_A_TO_A
```

16.4 Color Space Conversions

A variety of color space conversions can be implemented in OpenGL shaders. In this section, we'll look at converting CIE colors to RGB, and vice versa. Conversions between other color spaces can be done in a similar way.

The CIE system was defined in 1931 by the Committee Internationale de L'Èclairage (CIE). It defines a device-independent color space based on the characteristics of human color perception. The CIE set up a hypothetical set of primaries, XYZ, that correspond to the way the eye's retina behaves. After experiments based on color matching with human observers, it defined the primaries so that all visible light maps into a positive mixture of X, Y, and Z and that Y correlates approximately to the apparent lightness of a color. The CIE system can be used to precisely define any color. With this as a standard reference, colors can be transformed from the native (device-dependent) color space of one device to the native color space of another device.

A matrix formulation is convenient for performing such conversions. The HDTV standard as defined in ITU-R Recommendation BT.709 (1990) has the following CIE XYZ primaries and uses the D_{65} (natural sunlight) white point:

	R	G	B	white
x	0.640	0.300	0.150	0.3127
y	0.330	0.600	0.060	0.3290
z	0.030	0.100	0.790	0.3582

Listing 16.1 shows the OpenGL shader code that transforms CIE color values to HDTV standard RGB values using the D_{65} white point, and Listing 16.2 shows the reverse transformation. The matrices look like they are transposed compared to the colorimetry literature because in the OpenGL Shading Language, matrix values are provided in column major order.

Listing 16.1 OpenGL shader code to transform CIE values to RGB

```
const mat3 CIEtoRGBmat = mat3 (3.240479, -0.969256,  0.055648,
                              -1.537150,  1.875992, -0.204043,
                              -0.498535,  0.041556,  1.057311);

vec3 rgbColor = cieColor * CIEtoRGBmat;
```

Listing 16.2 OpenGL shader code to transform RGB values to CIE

```
const mat3 RGBtoCIEmat = mat3 (0.412453, 0.212671, 0.019334,
                               0.357580, 0.715160, 0.119193,
                               0.180423, 0.072169, 0.950227);

vec3 cieColor = rgbColor * RGBtoCIEmat;
```

16.5 Image Interpolation and Extrapolation

In 1994, Paul Haeberli and Douglas Voorhies published an interesting paper that described imaging operations that could be performed with interpolation and extrapolation operations. These operations could actually be programmed on the high-end graphics systems of that time; today, they can be done quite easily on consumer graphics hardware using the OpenGL Shading Language.

The technique is quite simple. The idea is to determine a target image that can be used together with the source image to perform interpolation and extrapolation. The equation is set up as a simple linear interpolation that blends two images:

$$Image_{out} = (1 - \alpha) \cdot Image_{target} + \alpha \cdot Image_{source}$$

The target image is actually an image that you want to interpolate or extrapolate away from. Values of *alpha* between 0 and 1 interpolate between the two images, and values greater than 1 perform extrapolation. For instance, to adjust brightness, the target image is one in which every pixel is black. When *alpha* is 1, the result is the source image. When *alpha* is 0, the result is that all pixels are black. When *alpha* is between 0 and 1, the result is a linear blend of the source image and the black image, effectively darkening the image. When *alpha* is greater than 1, the image is brightened.

Such operations can be applied to images (pixel rectangles in OpenGL jargon) with a fragment shader as they are being sent to the display. In cases where a target image is really needed (in many cases, it is not needed, as we shall see), it can be stored in a texture and accessed by the fragment shader. If the source and target images are downloaded into memory on the graphics card (i.e., stored as textures), these operations can be blazingly fast, limited only by the memory speed and the fill rate of the graphics hardware. This should be much faster than performing the same operations on the CPU and downloading the image across the I/O bus every time it's modified.

16.5.1 Brightness

Brightness is the easiest example. Because the target image is composed entirely of black pixels (e.g., pixel values (0,0,0)), the first half of the interpolation equation goes to zero, and the equation reduces to a simple scaling of the source pixel values. This is implemented with Listing 16.3's fragment shader, and the results for several values of *alpha* are shown in Color Plate 26.

```
uniform float Alpha;

void main (void)
{
    gl_FragColor = gl_Color * Alpha;
}
```

Listing 16.3 Fragment shader for adjusting brightness

16.5.2 Contrast

A somewhat more interesting example is contrast (see Listing 16.4). Here the target image is chosen to be a constant gray image with each pixel

containing a value equal to the average luminance of the image. This value
and the *alpha* value are assumed to be computed by the application and sent
to the shader as uniform variables. The results of the contrast shader are
shown in Color Plate 27.

Listing 16.4   Fragment shader for adjusting contrast

```
uniform vec3  AvgLuminance;
uniform float Alpha;

void main (void)
{
    vec3 color     = mix(AvgLuminance, gl_Color, Alpha);
    gl_FragColor   = vec4 (color, 1.0);
}
```

16.5.3   Saturation

The target image for a saturation adjustment is an image containing only
luminance information (i.e., a grayscale version of the source image). This
image can be computed on a pixel-by-pixel basis by extracting the luminance value from each RGB value. The proper computation depends on
knowing the color space in which the RGB values are specified. For RGB
values specified according to the HDTV color standard, you could use the
coefficients shown in the shader in Listing 16.5. Results of this shader are
shown in Color Plate 28. As you can see, extrapolation can provide useful
results for values that are well above 1.0.

Listing 16.5   Fragment shader for adjusting saturation

```
const vec3 lumCoeff = vec3 (0.2125, 0.7154, 0.0721);
uniform float Alpha;

void main (void)
{
    vec3 intensity = vec3 (dot(gl_Color.rgb, lumCoeff));
    vec3 color     = mix(intensity, gl_Color.rgb, Alpha);
    gl_FragColor   = vec4 (color, 1.0);
}
```

16.5.4   Sharpness

Remarkably, this technique also lends itself to adjusting any image convolution operation (see Listing 16.6). For instance, a target image can be
constructed by blurring the original image. Interpolation from the source
image to the blurred image will reduce high frequencies, and extrapolation
(*alpha* greater than 1) will increase them. The result is image sharpening via

UNSHARP MASKING. The results of the sharpness fragment shader are shown in Color Plate 29.

Listing 16.6 Fragment shader for adjusting sharpness

```
uniform sampler2D Blurry;
uniform float Alpha;

void main (void)
{
    vec3 blurred  = vec3 (texture2D(Blurry, gl_TexCoord[0].st));
    vec3 color    = gl_Color.rgb * Alpha + blurred * (1.0 - Alpha);
    gl_FragColor  = vec4 (color, 1.0);
}
```

These examples showed the simple case where the entire image is modified with a single *alpha* value. More complex processing is possible. The *alpha* value could be a function of other variables. A control texture could be used to define a complex shape that indicates the portion of the image that is to be modified. A brush pattern could be used to apply the operation selectively to small regions of the image. The operation could be applied selectively to pixels with a certain luminance range (e.g., shadows, highlights, or midtones).

Fragment shaders can also be used to interpolate between more than two images, and the interpolation does not need to be linear. It is also possible to interpolate along several axes simultaneously with a single target image. A blurry, desaturated version of the source image can be used with the source image to produce a sharpened, saturated version in a single operation.

16.6 Blend Modes

With the expressiveness of a high-level language, it is very easy to combine two images in a variety of ways. Both images can be stored in texture memory, or one can be in texture memory and one can be downloaded by the application by calling **glDrawPixels**. Here are some snippets of OpenGL shader code that perform pixel-by-pixel blending for some of the common blend modes.

- *base* is a **vec4** containing the RGBA color value from the base (original) image.

- *blend* is a **vec4** containing the RGBA color value from the image that is being blended into the base image.

- *result* is a **vec4** containing the RGBA color that results from the blending operation.

- If it's needed in the computation, *white* is a **vec4** containing (1.0, 1.0, 1.0, 1.0).

- If it's needed in the computation, *lumCoeff* is a **vec4** containing (0.2125, 0.7154, 0.0721, 1.0).

- As a final step, *base* and *result* are combined using a floating-point value called *opacity*, which determines the contribution of each.

There is no guarantee that the results of the code snippets provided here will produce results identical to those of your favorite image editing program, but the effects should be very similar. The OpenGL shader code for the various blend modes is based on information published by Jens Gruschel in his article *Blend Modes*, available at http://www.pegtop.net/delphi/blendmodes. Unless otherwise noted, the blend operations are not commutative (you will get different results if you swap the base and blend images).

Results of the blend mode shaders are shown in Color Plate 30.

16.6.1 Normal

This is often used as the default blending mode. The blend image is placed over the base image. The resulting image equals the blend image when the opacity is 1.0 (i.e., the base image is completely covered). For opacities other than 1.0, the result is a linear blend of the two images based on *opacity*.

```
result = blend;
```

16.6.2 Average

This blend mode adds the two images and divides by two. The result is the same as NORMAL when the opacity is set to 0.5. This operation is commutative.

```
result = (base + blend) * 0.5;
```

16.6.3 Dissolve

Either *blend* or *base* is chosen randomly at every pixel. The value of *opacity* is used as a probability factor for choosing the *blend* value. Thus, as the opacity gets closer to 1.0, the *blend* value is more likely to be chosen than the *base* value. If the image is drawn as a texture on a rectangular polygon, the texture coordinate values can be used as the argument to **noise1D** in order to provide a value that can be used to perform the selection in a pseudorandom, but repeatable way. A scale factor can be applied to the texture coordinates in order to obtain noise of a higher frequency and give the appearance of randomness. The value returned by the noise function is in the range [-1,1] so we add one and multiply by 0.5 to get it in the range [0,1].

```
float noise = (noise1(vec2 (gl_TexCoord[0] * noiseScale)) + 1.0) * 0.5;
result = (noise < opacity) ? blend : base;
```

16.6.4 Behind

This mode chooses the *blend* value only where the base image is completely transparent (i.e., *base.a* = 0.0). You can think of the base image as a piece of clear acetate, and the effect of this mode is as if you were painting the blend image on the back of the acetate—only the areas painted behind transparent pixels will be visible.

```
result = (base.a == 0.0) ? blend : base;
```

16.6.5 Clear

The *blend* value is always used, and the alpha value of result is set to 0 (transparent). This blend mode is more apt to be used with drawing tools than on complete images.

```
result.rgb = blend.rgb;
result.a   = 0.0;
```

16.6.6 Darken

The two values are compared, and the minimum value is chosen for each component. This operation will make images darker because the blend image can do nothing except make the base image darker. A blend image that is completely white (RGB = 1.0, 1.0, 1.0) will not alter the base image. Regions of black (0, 0, 0) in either image will cause the result to be black. It is commutative—the result will be the same if the blend image and the base image are swapped.

```
result = min(blend, base);
```

16.6.7 Lighten

This mode can be considered the opposite of DARKEN. Instead of taking the minimum of each component, the maximum is taken. The blend image can therefore never do anything but make the result lighter. A blend image that is completely black (RGB = 0, 0, 0) will not alter the base image. Regions of white (1.0, 1.0, 1.0) in either image will cause the result to be white. It is commutative because swapping the two images does not change the result.

```
result = max(blend, base);
```

16.6.8 Multiply

The two values are multiplied together. This will produce a darker result in all areas where neither image is completely white. White is effectively an identity (or transparency) operator because any color multiplied by white will be the original color. Regions of black (0, 0, 0) in either image will cause the result to be black. The result is similar to the effect of stacking two color transparencies on an overhead projector. This operation is commutative.

```
result = blend * base;
```

16.6.9 Screen

SCREEN can be thought of as the opposite of MULTIPLY because it multiplies together the inverse of the two input values. The result of this multiplication is then inverted to produce the final result. Black is effectively an identity (or transparency) operator because any color multiplied by the inverse of black (i.e., white) will be the original color. This blend mode is commutative.

```
result = white - ((white - blend) * (white - base));
```

16.6.10 Color Burn

COLOR BURN darkens the base color as indicated by the blend color by decreasing luminance. There is no effect if the *blend* value is white. This computation can result in some values less than 0, so truncation may occur when the resulting color is clamped.

```
result = white - (white - base) / blend;
```

16.6.11 Color Dodge

This blend mode brightens the base color as indicated by the blend color by increasing luminance. There is no effect if the *blend* value is black. This computation can result in some values greater than 1, so truncation may occur when the result is clamped.

```
result = base / (white - blend);
```

16.6.12 Overlay

This mode first computes the luminance of the base value. If the luminance value is less than 0.5, the *blend* and *base* values are multiplied together. If the luminance value is greater than 0.5, a screen operation is performed. The effect is that the *base* value is mixed with the *blend* value, rather than being replaced. This allows patterns and colors to overlay the base image, but shadows and highlights in the base image are preserved. A discontinuity occurs where luminance = 0.5. To provide a smooth transition, we actually do a linear blend of the two equations for luminance in the range [0.45,0.55].

```
float luminance = dot(base, lumCoeff);
if (luminance < 0.45)
    result = 2.0 * blend * base;
else if (luminance > 0.55)
    result = white - 2.0 * (white - blend) * (white - base);
else
{
    vec4 result1 = 2.0 * blend * base;
    vec4 result2 = white - 2.0 * (white - blend) * (white - base);
    result = mix(result1, result2, (luminance - 0.45) * 10.0);
}
```

16.6.13 Soft Light

This mode produces an effect similar to a soft (diffuse) light shining through the blend image and onto the base image. The resulting image is essentially a muted combination of the two images.

```
result = 2.0 * base * blend + base * base - 2.0 * base * base * blend;
```

16.6.14 Hard Light

This mode is identical to OVERLAY mode, except that the luminance value is computed using the *blend* value rather than the *base* value. The effect is similar to shining a harsh light through the blend image and onto the base image. Pixels in the blend image with a luminance of 0.5 will have no effect on the base image. This mode is often used to produce embossing effects. The **mix** function is used to provide a linear blend between the two functions for luminance in the range [0.45,0.55].

```
float luminance = dot(blend, lumCoeff);
if (luminance < 0.45)
    result = 2.0 * blend * base;
else if (luminance > 0.55)
    result = white - 2.0 * (white - blend) * (white - base);
else
```

```
{
    vec4 result1 = 2.0 * blend * base;
    vec4 result2 = white - 2.0 * (white - blend) * (white - base);
    result = mix(result1, result2, (luminance - 0.45) * 10.0);
}
```

16.6.15   Add

In this mode, the result is the sum of the blend image and the base image.
Truncation may occur because resulting values can exceed 1.0. The blend
and base images may be swapped, and the result will be the same.

```
result = blend + base;
```

16.6.16   Subtract

This blend mode subtracts the blend image from the base image. Truncation
may occur because resulting values may be less than 0.

```
result = base - blend;
```

16.6.17   Difference

In this mode, the result is the absolute value of the difference between
the *blend* value and the *base* value. A result of black means the two initial
values were equal a result of white means they were opposite. This mode
can be useful for comparing images because identical images will produce a
completely black result. An all-white blend image can be used to invert the
base image. Blending with black produces no change. Because of the absolute value operation, this blend mode is commutative.

```
result = abs(blend - base);
```

16.6.18   Inverse Difference

This mode performs the "opposite" of DIFFERENCE. Blend values of white
and black produce the same results as for DIFFERENCE (white inverts and
black has no effect), but colors in between white and black become lighter
instead of darker. This operation is commutative.

```
result = white - abs(white - base - blend);
```

16.6.19   Exclusion

This blend mode is similar to DIFFERENCE, but it produces an effect that is
lower in contrast (softer). The effect for this mode is in between the effects
of the DIFFERENCE and INVERSE DIFFERENCE modes. Blending with white

inverts the base image, blending with black has no effect, and colors in between become gray. This is also a commutative blend mode.

```
result = base + blend - (2.0 * base * blend);
```

16.6.20 Opacity

An opacity value in the range [0,1] can also be used to specify the relative contribution of the base image and the computed result. The *result* value from any of the preceding formulas can be further modified to compute the effect of the *opacity* value as follows:

```
finalColor = mix(base, result, opacity);
```

16.7 Convolution

CONVOLUTION is a common image processing operation that can be used to filter an image. The filtering is accomplished by computing the sum of products between the source image and a smaller image called the CONVOLUTION KERNEL or the CONVOLUTION FILTER. Depending on the choice of values in the convolution kernel, a convolution operation can perform blurring, sharpening, noise reduction, edge detection, and other useful imaging operations.

Mathematically, the discrete 2D convolution operation is defined as

$$H(x, y) = \sum_{j=0}^{height-1} \sum_{i=0}^{width-1} F(x + i, y + j) \cdot G(i, j)$$

In this equation, the function F represents the base image, and G represents the convolution kernel. The double summation is based on the width and height of the convolution kernel. The value for a particular pixel in the output image is computed by aligning the center of the convolution kernel with the pixel at the same position in the base image, and then multiplying the values of the base image pixels covered by the convolution kernel by the values in the corresponding locations in the convolution kernel, and adding together the results.

The imaging subset of OpenGL 1.5 contains support for a fixed functionality convolution operation, but implementations of this functionality always have limitations in the size of the kernel supported (typical maximum size is 3×3) and in the precision of the intermediate calculations. The flexibility of the OpenGL Shading Language enables convolution operations with arbitrary size kernels and full floating-point precision. Furthermore, the convolution operation can be written in an OpenGL shader such that the minimum number of multiplication operations are actually performed (i.e., kernel values equal to 0 do not need to be stored or used in the convolution computation).

But there are a couple of hurdles to overcome. First, this operation seems naturally suited to implementation as a fragment shader, but the fragment shader is not allowed to access the values of any neighboring fragments. How can we perform a neighborhood operation such as convolution without access to the "neighborhood"?

The answer to this dilemma is to store the base image in texture memory and access it as a texture. A screen-aligned rectangle that's the same size on the screen as the base image can be drawn, and texturing can be enabled to render the image perfectly. We can introduce a fragment shader into this process, and instead of sampling the image just once during the texturing process, we can access each of the values under the convolution kernel and compute the convolution result at every pixel.

A second hurdle is that, although the OpenGL Shading Language supports loops, even nested loops, there is no support for two-dimensional arrays. This is easily overcome by "unrolling" the convolution kernel and storing it as a one-dimensional array. Each location in this array stores an x- and y-offset from the center of the convolution kernel and the value of the convolution kernel at that position. In the fragment shader, we can process this array in a single loop, adding the specified offsets to the current texture location, accessing the base image, and multiplying the retrieved pixel value by the convolution kernel value. Storing the convolution kernel this way means that we can store the values in row major order, column major order, backwards, or all mixed up. We don't even need to include convolution kernel values that are zero because they will have no contribution to the convolved image.

The interesting work for performing convolution will be done using fragment shaders. The vertex shader is required to perform an identity mapping of the input geometry (a screen-aligned rectangle that is the size of the base image), and it is required to pass on texture coordinates. The texture coordinate (0,0) should be assigned to the lower-left corner of the rectangle, and the texture coordinate (1,1) should be assigned to the upper-right corner of the rectangle.

One additional issue with convolution operations is deciding what to do when the convolution kernel extends beyond the edges of the base image.

A convenient side effect of using OpenGL texture operations to perform the convolution is that the texture wrapping modes defined by OpenGL map nicely to the common methods of treating convolution borders. If the application wants the border to behave the same as OpenGL's GL_CONSTANT_BORDER convolution border mode (i.e., use the border color when the convolution kernel extends past the image boundary), the texture containing the base image should have its GL_TEXTURE_WRAP_S and GL_TEXTURE_WRAP_T parameters set to GL_CLAMP_TO_BORDER. If the desired behavior is the same as OpenGL's GL_REPLICATE_BORDER convolution border mode (i.e., use the pixel value at the edge of the image when the convolution kernel extends past the image boundary), the texture containing the base image should have its GL_TEXTURE_WRAP_S and GL_TEXTURE_WRAP_T parameters set to GL_CLAMP_TO_EDGE. If the desired behavior is the GL_REDUCE convolution border mode, the application should draw a rectangle that is smaller than the image to be convolved. For a 3×3 convolution kernel, the rectangle should be smaller by two pixels in *width* and two pixels in *height*. In this case, the texture coordinate of the lower-left corner should be provided as (1/*width*, 1/*height*) and the texture coordinate of the upper-right corner should be provided as (1 – 1/*width*, 1 – 1/*height*). The texture filtering modes should be set to GL_NEAREST to avoid unintended interpolation.

A further complication is that OpenGL requires textures to be stored as images that are powers of 2 in both width and height (which images seldom are these days). This can be handled by creating texture images that are the next largest power of 2 bigger than the base image in width and height and adjusting the texture coordinates of the upper-right hand corner of the rectangle appropriately. This may or may not result in wasting texture memory on the graphics card, depending on whether the underlying graphics hardware supports some form of virtual texturing (i.e., portions of textures are paged to the graphics hardware when needed and texture memory is not wasted). Various vendor specific extensions to solve this problem also exist, and the OpenGL ARB is currently considering a standard solution that will eventually be made part of core OpenGL.

16.7.1 Smoothing

Image smoothing operations are used to attenuate high frequencies in an image. A common image smoothing operation is known as NEIGHBORHOOD AVERAGING. This method uses a convolution kernel that contains a weighting of 1.0 in each location. The final sum is divided by a value equal to the number of locations in the convolution kernel. For instance, a 3×3 neighborhood averaging convolution filter would look like this:

1	1	1
1	1	1
1	1	1

The resulting sum would be divided by 9 (or multiplied by 1/9). Neighborhood averaging, as the name implies, has the effect of averaging together all of the pixels in a region with equal weighting. It effectively smears the value of each pixel to its neighbors, resulting in a blurry version of the original image.

Because all the elements of the convolution kernel are equal to 1, we can write a simplified fragment shader to implement neighborhood averaging (see Listing 16.7). This shader can be used for neighborhood averaging for any kernel size where *width * height* is less than or equal to 25 (i.e., up to 5 × 5). The results of this operation are shown in Figure 16.1 (B).

Listing 16.7 Fragment shader for the neighborhood averaging convolution operation

```
// maximum size supported by this shader
const int MaxKernelSize = 25;

// array of offsets for accessing the base image
uniform vec2 Offset[MaxKernelSize];

// size of kernel (width * height) for this execution
uniform int KernelSize;

// final scaling value
uniform vec4 ScaleFactor;

// image to be convolved
uniform sampler2D BaseImage;

void main(void)
{
    int i;
    vec4 sum = vec4 (0.0);

    for (i = 0; i < KernelSize; i++)
        sum += texture2D(BaseImage, gl_TexCoord[0].st + Offset[i]);

    gl_FragColor = sum * ScaleFactor;
}
```

Image smoothing via convolution is often used to perform noise reduction. This works well in regions of solid color or intensity, but it has the side effect of blurring high frequencies (edges). A convolution filter that applies higher weights to values nearer the center can do a better job of eliminating noise while preserving edge detail. Such a filter is the Gaussian filter, which can be encoded in a convolution kernel as follows:

1/273	4/273	7/273	4/273	1/273
4/273	16/273	26/273	16/273	4/273
7/273	26/273	41/273	26/273	7/273
4/273	16/273	26/273	16/273	4/273
1/273	4/273	7/273	4/273	1/273

Listing 16.8 contains the code for a more general convolution shader. This shader can handle convolution kernels containing up to 25 entries. In this shader, each convolution kernel entry is expected to have been multiplied by the final scale factor so there is no need to scale the final sum.

Listing 16.8   Fragment shader general convolution computation

```
// maximum size supported by this shader
const int MaxKernelSize = 25;

// array of offsets for accessing the base image
uniform vec2 Offset[MaxKernelSize];

// size of kernel (width * height) for this execution
uniform int KernelSize;

// value for each location in the convolution kernel
uniform vec4 KernelValue[MaxKernelSize];

// image to be convolved
uniform sampler2D BaseImage;

void main(void)
{
    int i;
    vec4 sum = vec4 (0.0);

    for (i = 0; i < KernelSize; i++)
    {
        vec4 tmp = texture2D(BaseImage, gl_TexCoord[0].st + Offset[i]);
        sum += tmp * KernelValue[i];
    }

    gl_FragColor = sum;
}
```

The original image in Figure 16.1 (A) has had uniform noise added to it to create the image in Figure 16.1 (C). The Gaussian smoothing filter is then applied to this image to remove noise, and the result is shown in Figure 16.1 (D). Notice in particular that the noise has been significantly reduced in areas of nearly constant intensity.

As the size of the convolution kernel goes up, the number of texture reads that is required increases as the square of the kernel size. For larger kernels, this can become the limiting factor for performance. Some kernels, including the Gaussian kernel just described, are said to be separable because the convolution operation with a *width* × *height* kernel can be performed as two passes, with one-dimensional convolutions of size *width* × 1 and 1 × *height*. With this approach, there is an extra write for each pixel

(A) Original 512 × 512 grayscale image

(B) 5 × 5 neighborhood averaging

(C) Original with noise added

(D) Noise reduction with Gaussian filter

Figure 16.1 Results of various convolution operations.

(the result of the first pass), but the number of texture reads is reduced from *width × height* to *width + height*.

16.7.2 Edge Detection

Another common use for the convolution operation is to perform edge detection. This operation is useful for detecting meaningful discontinuities in intensity level. The resulting image can be used as an aid to image comprehension or used to enhance the image in other ways.

One method for doing edge detection involves the Laplacian operator.

0	1	0
1	−4	1
0	1	0

We can plug the Laplacian convolution kernel into the fragment shader shown in Listing 16.8. This results in the image shown in Figure 16.2.

16.7.3 Sharpening

A common method of image sharpening is to add the results of an edge detection filter back onto the original image. A scaling factor is used to scale the edge image as it is added in order to control the degree of sharpening.

Figure 16.2   Edge detection using the Laplacian convolution kernel. (Image scaled for display purposes.)

One way to do this is with the negative Laplacian operator. This convolution filter is defined as

0	−1	0
−1	4	−1
0	−1	0

The fragment shader that implements image sharpening in this fashion is almost identical to the general convolution shader shown in the previous section (see Listing 16.9). The only difference is that the result of the convolution operation is added to the original image. Before it is added, the convolution result is scaled by a scale factor provided by the application through a uniform variable. The results of unsharp masking are shown in Figure 16.3.

Listing 16.9 Fragment shader for unsharp masking

```
// maximum size supported by this shader
const int MaxKernelSize = 25;

// array of offsets for accessing the base image
uniform vec2 Offset[MaxKernelSize];

// size of kernel (width * height) for this execution
uniform int KernelSize;

// value for each location in the convolution kernel
uniform vec4 KernelValue[MaxKernelSize];

// scaling factor for edge image
uniform vec4 ScaleFactor;

// image to be convolved
uniform sampler2D BaseImage;

void main(void)
{
    int i;
    vec4 sum = vec4 (0.0);

    for (i = 0; i < KernelSize; i++)
    {
        vec4 tmp = texture2D(BaseImage, gl_TexCoord[0].st + Offset[i]);
        sum += tmp * KernelValue[i];
    }

    vec4 baseColor = texture2D(BaseImage, vec2(gl_TexCoord[0]));
    gl_FragColor = ScaleFactor * sum + baseColor;

}
```

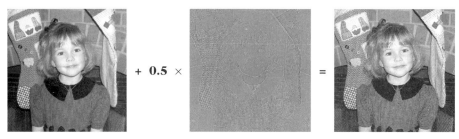

Figure 16.3   Results of the unsharp masking shader. (Laplacian image in center is scaled for display purposes.)

16.8 Summary

In addition to support for rendering 3D geometry, OpenGL also contains a great deal of support for rendering images. The OpenGL Shading Language augments fixed functionality OpenGL imaging capabilities by allowing fully programmable processing of images. With this programmability and the parallel processing nature of the underlying graphics hardware, image processing operations can be performed orders of magnitude faster on the graphics accelerator than on the CPU. This programmability can be used to implement traditional image processing operations such as image blurring, sharpening, and noise removal; high quality color correction; brightness, saturation, and contrast adjustment; geometric transformations such as rotation and warping; blending; and many other image processing operations. Furthermore, applications no longer need to be constrained to manipulating monochrome or color images. Multispectral processing and analysis are also possible.

The world of digital imagery is exploding as a result of the rapid development and acceptance of consumer products for digital photography and digital video. The OpenGL Shading Language will undoubtedly be at the heart of many tools that support this revolution in the future.

16.9 Further Information

The OpenGL literature doesn't always do justice to the imaging capabilities of OpenGL. I wrote a paper in 1996 called *Using OpenGL for Imaging* that attempted to describe and highlight clearly the fixed functionality imaging capabilities of OpenGL, including the capabilities of several pertinent imaging extensions. This paper was published as part of the SPIE Medical Imaging '96 Image Display Conference in Newport Beach, CA, and is available on this book's companion Web site at http://3dshaders.com/pubs. Another good resource for understanding how to use OpenGL for imaging is the course notes for the SIGGRAPH '99 course, *Advanced Graphics Programming Techniques Using OpenGL,* by Tom McReynolds and David Blythe. These can be found online at http://www.opengl.org/developers/code/sig99/advanced99/notes/notes.html.

Charles Poynton (1997) is one of the luminaries (pun intended) of the color technology field, and his *Frequently Asked Questions about Color* and *Frequently Asked Questions about Gamma* are informative and approachable treatments of a variety of topics relating to color and imaging. I found these on the Web on Charles's home page at http://www.poynton.com/Poynton-color.html.

The CIE color system is defined in Publication CIE 17.4 - 1987, *International Lighting Vocabulary,* Vienna, Austria, Central Bureau of the Committee Internationale de L'Èclairage, currently in its fourth edition. The HDTV color standard is defined in *ITU-R BT.709-2 - Parameter Values for the HDTV Standards for Production and International Programme Exchange,* Geneva: ITU, 1990.

The paper *Image Processing by Interpolation and Extrapolation* by Paul Haeberli and Douglas Voorhies appeared in IRIS Universe Magazine in1994. A slightly shorter version of this paper is available online at http://www.sgi.com/grafica/interp/index.html.

A classic textbook on image processing is *Digital Image Processing, Second Edition,* by Rafael C. Gonzalez and Richard E. Woods, Addison-Wesley, 2002. An amazing little book (literally amazing, and literally little) is the *Pocket Handbook of Image Processing Algorithms in C* by Harley Myler and Arthur Weeks (1993).

[1] Gonzalez, Rafael C., and Richard E. Woods, *Digital Image Processing, Second Edition,* Prentice Hall, Upper Saddle River, New Jersey, 2002.

[2] Gruschel, Jens, *Blend Modes,* Pegtop Software Web site. http://www.pegtop.net/delphi/blendmodes

[3] Haeberli, Paul, and Douglas Voorhies, *Image Processing by Interpolation and Extrapolation,* IRIS Universe Magazine No. 28, Silicon Graphics, August, 1994. http:/www.sgi.com/grafica/interp/index.html

[4] Hall, Roy, *Illumination and Color in Computer Generated Imagery,* Springer-Verlag, New York, 1989.

[5] *International Lighting Vocabulary*, Publication CIE No. 17.4, Joint publication IEC (International Electrotechnical Commission) and CIE (Committee Internationale de L'Èclairage), Geneva, 1987. http://www.cie.co.at/framepublications.html

[6] ITU-R Recommendation BT.709, *Basic Parameter Values for the HDTV Standard for the Studio and for International Programme Exchange*, [formerly CCIR Rec. 709], Geneva, ITU, 1990.

[7] Lindbloom, Bruce J., *Accurate Color Reproduction for Computer Graphics Applications*, Computer Graphics (SIGGRAPH '89 Proceedings), pp. 117–126, July 1989.

[8] Lindbloom, Bruce J., personal Web site, 2003. http://www.brucelindbloom.com/

[9] McReynolds, Tom, David Blythe, Brad Grantham, and Scott Nelson, *Advanced Graphics Programming Techniques Using OpenGL*, SIGGRAPH '99 course notes, 1999. http://www.opengl.org/developers/code/sig99/index.html

[10] Myler, Harley R., and Arthur R. Weeks, *The Pocket Handbook of Image Processing Algorithms in C*, Prentice Hall, Upper Saddle River, NJ, 1993.

[11] Poynton, Charles A., *A Technical Introduction to Digital Video*, John Wiley & Sons, New York, 1996.

[12] Poynton, Charles A., *Frequently Asked Questions about Color*, 1997. http://www.poynton.com/Poynton-color.html

[13] Poynton, Charles A., *Frequently Asked Questions about Gamma*, 1997. http://www.poynton.com/Poynton-color.html

[14] Rost, Randi, *Using OpenGL for Imaging*, SPIE Medical Imaging '96 Image Display Conference, February 1996. http://3dshaders.com/pubs

[15] Wolberg, George, *Digital Image Warping*, Wiley-IEEE Press, 2002.

Chapter 17

Language Comparison

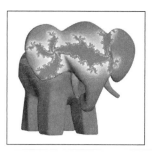

The OpenGL Shading Language is by no means the first graphics shading language ever defined. Here are a few other notable shading languages and a little about how each one compares to the OpenGL Shading Language. The diagrams shown in this chapter should be compared to the OpenGL Shading Language execution model shown in Chapter 2, Figure 2.4.

17.1 Chronology of Shading Languages

Rob Cook and Ken Perlin are usually credited with being the first to develop languages to describe shading calculations. Both of these efforts targeted offline (noninteractive) rendering systems. Perlin's work included the definition of the noise function and the introduction of control constructs. Cook's work on shade trees at Lucasfilm (later Pixar) introduced the classification of shaders as surface shaders, light shaders, atmosphere shaders, and so on, and the ability to describe the operation of each through an expression. This work evolved into the effort to develop a full-featured language for describing shading calculations, which was taken up by Pat Hanrahan and culminated in the 1988 release of the first version of the *RenderMan Interface Specification* by Pixar. Subsequently, RenderMan became the de facto industry standard shading language for offline rendering systems for the entertainment industry. It remains in widespread use today.

The first interactive shading language was demonstrated at UNC on a massively parallel graphics architecture called PixelFlow that was developed over the decade of the 1990s. The shading language used on PixelFlow was capable of rendering scenes with procedural shading at 30 frames per second or more. The shading language component of this system was described by Marc Olano in 1998.

After leaving UNC, Marc Olano joined a team at SGI that was defining and implementing an interactive shading language that would run on top of OpenGL and use multipass rendering methods to execute the shaders. This work culminated in the release in 2000 of a product from SGI called OpenGL Shader, the first commercially available real-time, high-level shading language.

In June 1999, the Computer Graphics Laboratory at Stanford embarked on an effort to define a real-time shading language that could be accelerated by existing consumer graphics hardware. This language was called the Stanford Real-Time Shading Language. Results of this system were demonstrated in 2001.

The OpenGL Shading Language, Microsoft's HLSL, and NVIDIA's Cg are all efforts to define a commercially viable, real-time, high-level shading language. The white paper that first described the shading language that would become the OpenGL Shading Language was published in October 2001, by Dave Baldwin. NVIDIA's Cg specification was published in June of 2002, and Microsoft's HLSL specification was published in November 2002, as part of the beta release of the DirectX 9.0 SDK. Some cross-pollination of ideas occurred among these three efforts because of the interrelationships of the companies involved.

In subsequent sections, we'll compare the OpenGL Shading Language with other commercially available high-level shading languages.

17.2 RenderMan

In 1988, after several years of development, Pixar published the *RenderMan Interface Specification*. This was an interface intended to define the communications protocol between modeling programs and rendering programs aimed at producing images of photorealistic quality. The original target audience for this interface was animation production, and it has proved to be very successful for this market. It has been used as the interface for producing computer graphics special effects for films such as *Jurassic Park*, *Star Wars Episode 1: The Phantom Menace*, *The Lord of the Rings: The Two Towers*, and others. It has also been used for films that have been done entirely with computer graphics such as *Finding Nemo*, *Toy Story*, *A Bug's Life*, and *Monsters, Inc.*

One of the main differences between the OpenGL Shading Language and RenderMan is that RenderMan attempts to define the entire interface between modeling programs and rendering programs. It provides an entire graphics processing pipeline of its own that has no relationship to OpenGL. Although a hardware implementation was envisioned at the time RenderMan was first defined, it was primarily designed as a high-quality realistic rendering interface; therefore, it provides no compromises for interactivity or direct hardware implementation on today's graphics hardware. RenderMan includes support for describing geometric primitives, hierarchical modeling, stacking geometric transformations, camera attributes, shading attributes, and constructive solid geometry. Many of these capabilities are provided for already by OpenGL; therefore, there is no need to address them in the OpenGL Shading Language.

Of particular interest, however, is the portion of RenderMan called the RENDERMAN SHADING LANGUAGE. This language is used to describe completely arbitrary shaders that can be passed to a renderer through the RenderMan interface. This language was also based on C, and as such, it bears some resemblance to the OpenGL Shading Language. In a general way, the RenderMan interface is similar to OpenGL, and the RenderMan Shading Language is similar to the OpenGL Shading Language. The RenderMan interface and OpenGL both let you define the characteristics of a scene (viewing parameters, primitives to be rendered, etc.). The shading languages are both used to compute the color, position, opacity, and other characteristics of a point in the scene.

One of the main differences between the OpenGL Shading Language and the RenderMan Shading Language is in the abstraction of the shading problem. The OpenGL Shading Language is designed to closely map onto today's commercial graphics hardware and has abstracted two types of shaders so far: vertex shaders and fragment shaders. The RenderMan Shading Language has always had uncompromising image quality as its fundamental goal, and it abstracts five shader types: light shaders, displacement shaders, surface shaders, volume shaders, and imager shaders. The RenderMan shader types lend themselves to the implementation of high-quality software rendering implementations, but they do not match up as well with hardware that has been designed to support interactive rendering with OpenGL. As a result, RenderMan implementations have typically been software based, but attempts to accelerate it in hardware have been made (read *Interactive Multi-Pass Programmable Shading* by Peercy, Olano, Airey, and McCool, 2000). The OpenGL Shading Language has been designed from the beginning for acceleration by commodity graphics hardware.

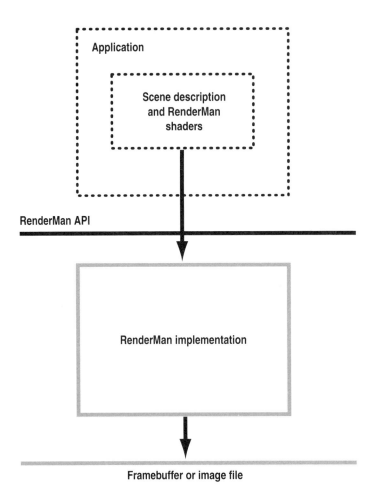

Figure 17.1   RenderMan execution environment

There are some differences in the data types supported by the two languages. RenderMan supports native types that represent colors, points, and normals, whereas the OpenGL Shading Language includes the more generic vectors of 1, 2, 3, or 4 floating-point values that can support any of those. RenderMan goes a bit further in making the language graphics-specific by including built-in support for coordinate spaces named "object," "world," "camera," "NDC," "raster," and "screen."

RenderMan supports a number of predefined surface shader variables, light source variables, volume shader variables, displacement shader variables, and imager shader variables. The OpenGL Shading Language contains built-in variables that are specific to OpenGL state values, some of which are similar to the RenderMan predefined variables. Because it is aimed at producing animation, RenderMan also has built-in variables to represent time. The OpenGL Shading Language does not, but such values can be passed to shaders through uniform variables to accomplish the same thing.

On the other hand, the two languages have much in common. In a very real sense, the OpenGL Shading Language can be thought of as a descendant of the RenderMan Shading Language. The data type qualifiers uniform and varying were invented in RenderMan and have been carried forward to mean the same things in the OpenGL Shading Language. Expressions and precedence of operators in both languages are very much like C. Keywords such as **if**, **else**, **while**, **for**, **break**, and **return** are the same in both languages. The list of built-in math functions for the OpenGL Shading Language is largely similar to the list of built-in math functions for the RenderMan Shading Language.

17.3 OpenGL Shader (ISL)

OpenGL Shader is a software package available as a free download from SGI. Version 3.0 of this package is compatible with IRIX 6.5 or later or RedHat Linux 8.0. OpenGL Shader defines both a shading language (Interactive Shading Language, or ISL) and a set of API calls that can be used to define shaders and use them in the rendering process. This API has also been made part of SGI's OpenGL Performer real-time graphics API scene graph and the SGI OpenGL Volumizer product.

The fundamental premise of OpenGL Shader is that the OpenGL API can be used as an assembly language for executing programmable shaders (see Figure 17.2). Hardware with more features (e.g., multitexture and fragment programmability) is viewed as having a more powerful assembly language. A sequence of statements in an ISL shader may end up being translated into one or more rendering passes. Each pass can be a geometry pass (geometry is drawn in order to use vertex, rasterization, and fragment operations), a copy pass (a region of the framebuffer is copied back into the same place in the framebuffer in order to use pixel, rasterization, and fragment operations), or a copy texture pass (a region of the framebuffer is copied to a texture to use pixel operations). Compiler optimization technology is used to determine the type of pass required to execute a sequence of source code instructions and, if possible, to reduce the number of passes needed overall. The current version of OpenGL Shader is optimized for multiple hardware back ends and will exploit the features exposed on a particular platform in order to reduce the number of passes required.

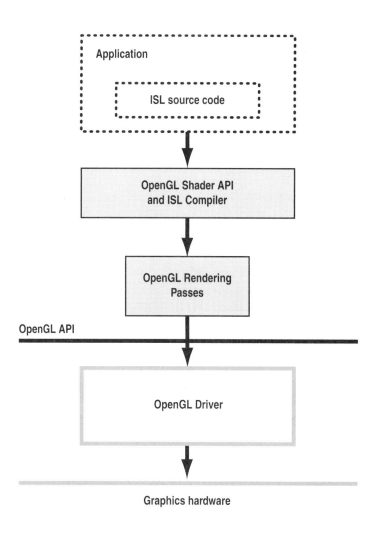

Figure 17.2   OpenGL Shader (ISL) execution environment

Like every other shading language worth its salt, ISL is based on C. However, because of its fundamental premise, ISL shaders end up looking quite different from OpenGL shaders. Many of the instructions in an ISL shader end up looking like directives to perform a rendering pass. For example, consider the following ISL source code:

```
varying color b;
FB  = diffuse();
FB *= color(.5, .2, 0, 1);
b   = FB;
FB  = specular(30.0);
FB += b;
```

The identifier *FB* indicates a result to be stored in the frame buffer. This sequence of operations first calls a subshader that executes a light shader to compute a diffuse color for the geometry being rendered. This value is multiplied by the color value (.5, .2, 0, 1), and then the result is stored in a region of texture memory called *b*. A specular reflection calculation is performed next, and finally the diffuse component and specular components are added together. Although it has the appearance of requiring multiple passes, this sequence of instructions can actually be executed in a single pass on a number of different graphics accelerators.

ISL supports surface and light shaders, which are merged and compiled. In this regard, it is more similar to the RenderMan way of doing things than it is to the OpenGL distinction of vertex and fragment shaders.

Another difference between the OpenGL Shading Language and ISL is that ISL was designed to provide portability for interactive shading using the OpenGL capabilities of both past and current hardware, whereas the OpenGL Shading Language was designed to expose the programmability of current and future hardware. The OpenGL Shading Language is not intended for hardware without a significant degree of programmability, but ISL will execute shaders with the identical visual effect on a variety of hardware, including hardware with little or no explicit support for programmability.

Another difference between ISL and the OpenGL Shading Language is that ISL was designed with the constraints of using the OpenGL API as an assembly language, without requiring any changes in the underlying hardware. The OpenGL Shading Language was designed to define new capabilities for the underlying hardware, and so it supports a more natural syntax for expressing graphics algorithms. The high-level language defined by the OpenGL Shading Language can be translated into the machine code native to the graphics hardware using an optimizing compiler written by the graphics hardware vendor.

17.4 HLSL

HLSL stands for High-Level Shader Language, and it was defined by Microsoft and introduced with DirectX 9 in 2002. In terms of its syntax and functionality, HLSL is much closer to the OpenGL Shading Language than either RenderMan or ISL. HLSL supports the paradigm of programmability at the vertex level and at the fragment level just like the OpenGL Shading Language. An HLSL vertex shader corresponds to an OpenGL vertex shader, and an HLSL pixel shader corresponds to an OpenGL fragment shader.

One of the main differences between the OpenGL Shading Language and HLSL is in the execution environment. HLSL is designed to be a source-code-to-source-code translator (see Figure 17.3). The HLSL compiler is really a translator that lives outside of DirectX in the sense that HLSL programs are never sent directly to the DirectX 9 API for execution. Instead, the HLSL compiler translates HLSL source into assembly-level source programs called vertex shaders and pixel shaders (in Microsoft DirectX parlance). Various levels of functionality have been defined for these assembly level shaders, and they are differentiated by a version number (e.g., Vertex Shader 1.0, 2.0, 3.0; Pixel Shader 1.1, 1.4, 2.0, 3.0).

One advantage of this approach is that HLSL programs can be translated offline, or long before the application is actually executed. However, the translation is done to a string-based representation of assembly code, which must then be parsed and assembled at execution time. This is in contrast to the OpenGL Shading Language model, where the compiler is part of the driver, and the graphics hardware vendor is responsible for writing the compiler. Giving the graphics hardware vendor the responsibility of doing the translation from high-level shading language source to machine code provides the graphics hardware vendors a lot more room for shader optimization and architectural innovation.

HLSL is designed to make it easier for application developers to deal with the various levels of functionality found in these assembly level shaders. Using HLSL and the support environment that has been built around it, applications developers can write shaders in a high-level shading language and be reasonably confident that their shaders will run on hardware with widely varying capabilities.

However, because HLSL is more expressive than the capabilities of graphics hardware that exists today and much more expressive than hardware shipped in the past, HLSL shaders are not guaranteed to run on every plat-form. Shader writers have two choices: They can write their shader for the

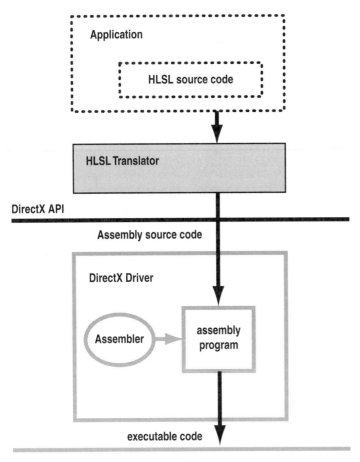

Figure 17.3 Execution environment for Microsoft's HLSL

lowest common denominator (i.e., hardware with very little programma-bility), or they can target their shader at a certain class of hardware using a language feature called profiles. Microsoft provides supporting software called the DirectX Effects Framework to help developers organize and deploy a set of shaders that do the same thing for hardware with differing capabilities.

The fundamental data types in HLSL are the same as those in the OpenGL Shading Language except for slight naming differences. HLSL also includes support for half- and double-precision floats. Like the OpenGL Shading Language, vectors, matrices, structures, and arrays are supported in HLSL. Expressions in HLSL are as in C/C++. User-defined functions and condi-tionals are supported in the same manner as in the OpenGL Shading Language. Looping constructs (**for**, **do**, and **while**) are defined in HLSL, but the current documentation states that they are not yet implemented. HLSL has a longer list of built-in functions than the OpenGL Shading Language, but those that are in both languages are very similar or identical.

One area of difference is the way values are passed between vertex shaders and pixel (HLSL) or fragment (OpenGL Shading Language) shaders. HLSL defines both input semantics and output semantics (annotations that iden-tify data usage) for both vertex shaders and pixel shaders. This provides the same functionality as the OpenGL Shading Language varying and built-in variables. You are allowed to pass arbitrary data into and out of vertex and pixel shaders, but you must do so in named locations such as POSITION, COLOR[i], TEXCOORD[i], and so on. This requirement means that you may have to pass your light direction variable *lightdir* in a semantic slot named TEXCOORD[i], for instance—a curious feature for a high-level language. The OpenGL Shading Language lets you use arbitrary names for passing values between vertex shaders and fragment shaders.

Another obvious difference between HLSL and the OpenGL Shading Language is that HLSL was designed for DirectX, Microsoft's proprietary graphics API, and the OpenGL Shading Language was designed for OpenGL. Microsoft has the capability to add to and change DirectX, whereas OpenGL is an open, cross-platform standard that changes more slowly but retains compatibility with previous versions.

17.5 Cg

Cg is a high-level shading language that is very similar to HLSL. Cg has been defined, implemented, and supported by NVIDIA. Comparing Cg to the OpenGL Shading Language is virtually the same as comparing HLSL to the OpenGL Shading Language. There are a few minor differences between Cg and HLSL (for instance, HLSL has a double data type but Cg does not), but Cg and HLSL were developed by Microsoft and NVIDIA working together, so their resulting products are very similar.

One advantage that Cg has over both HLSL and the OpenGL Shading Language is that the Cg translator can generate either DirectX vertex shader/pixel shader assembly code or OpenGL vertex/fragment program (assembly-level) code. This provides the potential for using Cg shaders in either the DirectX environment or the OpenGL environment (see Figure 17.4). However, it also requires the application to make calls to a library that is provided by NVIDIA that sits in between the application and the underlying graphics API (either OpenGL or DirectX). This library is called the Cg Runtime library. For simple applications, it can be a help in covering up the limitations of the underlying driver (for instance, it can cover up the fact that a DirectX driver supports multiple versions of vertex and pixel shaders and automatically selects the most appropriate version to use). But this intervening layer can also complicate things for more complicated applications because it is covering up details of shader management.

NVIDIA has its own version of the framework that surrounds the shading language. CgFX is a shader specification and interchange format whose file format is the same as that supported by the .fx Effect format for DirectX 9. The CgFX runtime library, like the Cg runtime library, includes support for both OpenGL and DirectX, so in this way the Microsoft and NVIDIA products differ.

Because it is so similar to HLSL, the advantages and disadvantages of Cg with respect to the OpenGL Shading Language are very similar: proprietary versus standard (thus earlier to market), support for less-capable hardware at the cost of hardware dependencies in shader source code, translating from high-level shading language to "standard" assembly interface offline versus embedding the compiler in the driver, more of a complete shader development system but with the requirement of extra runtime libraries, and so on.

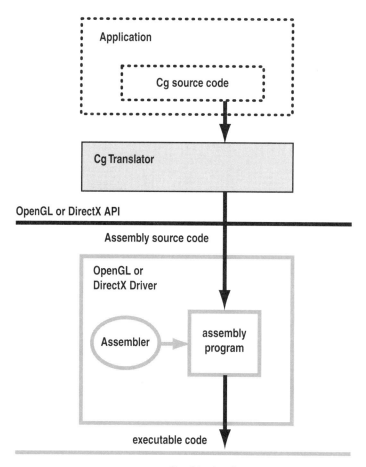

Figure 17.4   The Cg execution environment

17.6 Summary

Shading languages have been around for some time now. The first shading languages were non-real-time and aimed at producing photorealistic imagery. Graphics hardware capable of supporting an interactive shading language showed up in research labs in the 1990s, and today, this type of programmable graphics hardware is available at consumer price points. This has led to the development of several commercially available shading languages, notably, ISL, the OpenGL Shading Language, HLSL, and Cg.

In the spectrum of programming languages, the latter three are extremely similar. Each was designed to provide functionality available in RenderMan using C/C++ as the basis for the language syntax. The result is that all three languages are very similar in terms of syntax and capability. The single biggest technical difference is that HLSL and Cg were designed to sit on top of standard interfaces such as DirectX and OpenGL and perform high-level source code to assembly translation outside of those APIs. The OpenGL Shading Language, on the other hand, was designed to perform high-level source code to machine code translation within the OpenGL driver.

As far as nontechnical differences, the HLSL and CG specifications are controlled by Microsoft and NVIDIA, respectively. The OpenGL Shading Language is controlled by the OpenGL ARB, a standards body made up of representatives from a variety of graphics hardware and computer manufacturers. HLSL is designed for use in Microsoft's DirectX environment, and the OpenGL Shading Language is designed for use with OpenGL in a variety of operating environments. Cg is designed to be used in either DirectX or OpenGL environments.

17.7 Further Information

The RenderMan Shading Language is specified in Pixar's *The RenderMan Interface Specification* (2000), and its use is described in the books *The RenderMan Companion: A Programmer's Guide to Realistic Computer Graphics* (Upstill 1990) and *Advanced RenderMan: Creating CGI for Motion Pictures* (Apodaca and Gritz 1999).

OpenGL Shader and ISL are described in documentation from SGI available on its Web site and in the SIGGRAPH 2000 paper *Interactive Multi-Pass Programmable Shading*. The book, *Real-Time Shading*, by Olano, Hart, Heidrich, and McCool (2002) contains chapters describing various shading languages, including RenderMan, ISL, and shading languages defined and implemented by researchers at UNC, Stanford, and the University of Waterloo.

The Stanford Real-Time Shading Language is described in the SIGGRAPH 2001 paper, *A Real-Time Procedural Shading System for Programmable Graphics Hardware*, and in the course notes for *Real-Time Shading*, Course 24, SIGGRAPH 2001.

There are sure to be books out that describe Microsoft's HLSL, but at the time of this writing, the only documenation I could find is available from Microsoft on the DirectX 9 page of its Web site. http://www.microsoft.com/directx

Cg is described in documentation from NVIDIA, in the book, *The Cg Tutorial: The Definitive Guide to Programmable Real-Time Graphics*, by Fernando and Kilgard (2003), and in the SIGGRAPH 2003 paper, *Cg: A System for Programming Graphics Hardware in a C-like Language*.

The bibliography at the end of this book contains references to other notable noncommercial shading languages.

[1] Apodaca, Anthony A., and Larry Gritz, *Advanced RenderMan: Creating CGI for Motion Pictures*, Morgan Kaufmann Publishers, San Francisco, 1999. http://www.bmrt.org/arman/materials.html

[2] Baldwin, Dave, *OpenGL 2.0 Shading Language White Paper*, Version 1.2, 3Dlabs, February 2002. http://www.3dlabs.com/support/developer/ogl2

[3] Cook, Robert L., *Shade Trees*, Computer Graphics (SIGGRAPH '84 Proceedings), pp. 223–231, July 1984.

[4] Fernando, Randima, and Mark Kilgard, *The Cg Tutorial, the Definitive Guide to Programmable Real-Time Graphics*, Addison-Wesley, Boston, Massachusetts, 2003.

[5] Kessenich, John, Dave Baldwin, and Randi Rost, *The OpenGL Shading Language, Version 1.051*, 3Dlabs, February 2003. http://www.3dlabs.com/support/developer/ogl2

[6] Mark, William R., *Real-Time Shading: Stanford Real-Time Procedural Shading System*, SIGGRAPH 2001, Course 24, course notes, 2001. http://graphics.stanford.edu/projects/shading/pubs/sigcourse2001.pdf

[7] Mark, William R., R. Steven Glanville, Kurt Akeley, and Mark Kilgard, *Cg: A System for Programming Graphics Hardware in a C-like Language*, Computer Graphics (SIGGRAPH 2003 Proceedings), pp. 896–907, July 2003. http://www.cs.utexas.edu/users/billmark/papers/cg

[8] Microsoft, *DirectX 9.0 SDK*, 2003. http://msdn.microsoft.com/directx

[9] NVIDIA Corporation, Cg Toolkit, Release 1.1, software and documentation. http://developer.nvidia.com/Cg

[10] Olano, Marc, and Anselmo Lastra, *A Shading Language on Graphics Hardware: The PixelFlow Shading System*, Computer Graphics (SIGGRAPH '98 Proceedings), pp. 159–168, July 1998. http://www.csee.umbc.edu/~olano/papers

[11] Olano, Marc, John Hart, Wolfgang Heidrich, and Michael McCool, *Real-Time Shading*, A K Peters, Ltd., Natick, Massachusetts, 2002.

[12] Peercy, Mark S., Marc Olano, John Airey, and P. Jeffrey Ungar, *Interactive Multi-Pass Programmable Shading*, Computer Graphics (SIGGRAPH 2000 Proceedings), pp. 425–432, July 2000. http://www.csee.umbc.edu/~olano/papers

[13] Perlin, Ken, *An Image Synthesizer*, Computer Graphics (SIGGRAPH '85 Proceedings), pp. 287–296, July 1985.

[14] Pixar, *The RenderMan Interface Specification*, Version 3.2, Pixar, July 2000. https://renderman.pixar.com/products/rispec/index.htm

[15] Proudfoot, Kekoa, William R. Mark, Svetoslav Tzvetkov, and Pat Hanrahan, *A Real-Time Procedural Shading System for Programmable Graphics Hardware*, Computer Graphics (SIGGRAPH 2001 Proceedings), pp. 159–170, August 2001. http://graphics.stanford.edu/projects/shading/pubs/sig2001

[16] *SGI OpenGL Shader Web site.* http://www.sgi.com/software/shader

[17] Upstill, Steve, *The RenderMan Companion: A Programmer's Guide to Realistic Computer Graphics*, Addison-Wesley, Reading, Massachusetts, 1990.

Language Grammar

The grammar is fed from the output of lexical analysis. The tokens returned from lexical analysis are

```
ATTRIBUTE CONST BOOL FLOAT INT
BREAK CONTINUE DO ELSE FOR IF DISCARD RETURN
BVEC2 BVEC3 BVEC4 IVEC2 IVEC3 IVEC4 VEC2 VEC3 VEC4
MAT2 MAT3 MAT4 IN OUT INOUT UNIFORM VARYING
SAMPLER1D SAMPLER2D SAMPLER3D
SAMPLERCUBE SAMPLER1DSHADOW SAMPLER2DSHADOW
STRUCT VOID WHILE

IDENTIFIER TYPE_NAME FLOATCONSTANT INTCONSTANT BOOLCONSTANT
FIELD_SELECTION
LEFT_OP RIGHT_OP
INC_OP DEC_OP LE_OP GE_OP EQ_OP NE_OP
AND_OP OR_OP XOR_OP MUL_ASSIGN DIV_ASSIGN ADD_ASSIGN
MOD_ASSIGN LEFT_ASSIGN RIGHT_ASSIGN AND_ASSIGN XOR_ASSIGN OR_ASSIGN
SUB_ASSIGN

LEFT_PAREN RIGHT_PAREN LEFT_BRACKET RIGHT_BRACKET
LEFT_BRACE RIGHT_BRACE DOT
COMMA COLON EQUAL SEMICOLON BANG DASH TILDA PLUS STAR SLASH PERCENT
LEFT_ANGLE RIGHT_ANGLE VERTICAL_BAR CARET AMPERSAND QUESTION
```

The following describes the grammar for the OpenGL Shading Language in terms of the preceding tokens.

> *variable_identifier:*
>> *IDENTIFIER*

primary_expression:

    variable_identifier

    INTCONSTANT

    FLOATCONSTANT

    BOOLCONSTANT

    LEFT_PAREN expression RIGHT_PAREN

postfix_expression:

    primary_expression

    postfix_expression LEFT_BRACKET integer_expression RIGHT_BRACKET

    function_call

    postfix_expression DOT FIELD_SELECTION

    postfix_expression INC_OP

    postfix_expression DEC_OP

integer_expression:

    expression

function_call:

    function_call_generic

function_call_generic:

    function_call_header_with_parameters RIGHT_PAREN

    function_call_header_no_parameters RIGHT_PAREN

function_call_header_no_parameters:

    function_call_header VOID

    function_call_header

function_call_header_with_parameters:

    function_call_header assignment_expression

    function_call_header_with_parameters COMMA assignment_ expression

function_call_header:

    function_identifier LEFT_PAREN

function_identifier:

    constructor_identifier

    IDENTIFIER

// Grammar Note: Constructors look like functions, but lexical anaylsis recognized most of them as keywords.

constructor_identifier:

    FLOAT

    INT

    BOOL

    VEC2

    VEC3

    VEC4

    BVEC2

    BVEC3

    BVEC4

    IVEC2

    IVEC3

    IVEC4

    MAT2

    MAT3

    MAT4

unary_expression:

    postfix_expression

    INC_OP unary_expression

    DEC_OP unary_expression

    unary_operator unary_expression

// Grammar Note: No traditional style type casts.

unary_operator:

    PLUS

    DASH

    BANG

    TILDA   // reserved

// Grammar Note: No '' or '&' unary ops. Pointers are not supported.*

multiplicative_expression:

    unary_expression

    multiplicative_expression STAR unary_expression

    multiplicative_expression SLASH unary_expression

    multiplicative_expression PERCENT unary_expression   //
    reserved

additive_expression:

    multiplicative_expression

    additive_expression PLUS multiplicative_expression

    additive_expression DASH multiplicative_expression

shift_expression:

    additive_expression

    shift_expression LEFT_OP additive_expression   // reserved

    shift_expression RIGHT_OP additive_expression   // reserved

relational_expression:

    shift_expression

    relational_expression LEFT_ANGLE shift_expression

    relational_expression RIGHT_ANGLE shift_expression

    relational_expression LE_OP shift_expression

    relational_expression GE_OP shift_expression

equality_expression:

    relational_expression

    equality_expression EQ_OP relational_expression

    equality_expression NE_OP relational_expression

and_expression:

    equality_expression

    and_expression AMPERSAND equality_expression   // reserved

exclusive_or_expression:

    and_expression

    exclusive_or_expression CARET and_expression   // reserved

inclusive_or_expression:

    exclusive_or_expression

    inclusive_or_expression VERTICAL_BAR exclusive_or_expression
    // reserved

logical_and_expression:

    inclusive_or_expression

    logical_and_expression AND_OP inclusive_or_expression

logical_xor_expression:

    logical_and_expression

    logical_xor_expression XOR_OP logical_and_expression

logical_or_expression:

    logical_xor_expression

    logical_or_expression OR_OP logical_xor_expression

conditional_expression:

    logical_or_expression

    logical_or_expression QUESTION expression COLON
    conditional_expression

assignment_expression:

    conditional_expression

    unary_expression assignment_operator assignment_expression

assignment_operator:

    EQUAL

    MUL_ASSIGN

    DIV_ASSIGN

    MOD_ASSIGN

    ADD_ASSIGN

    SUB_ASSIGN

    LEFT_ASSIGN // reserved

    RIGHT_ASSIGN // reserved

    AND_ASSIGN // reserved

    XOR_ASSIGN // reserved

    OR_ASSIGN // reserved

expression:

    assignment_expression

    expression COMMA assignment_expression

constant_expression:

    conditional_expression

declaration:

> *function_prototype SEMICOLON*
>
> *init_declarator_list SEMICOLON*

function_prototype:

> *function_declarator RIGHT_PAREN*

function_declarator:

> *function_header*
>
> *function_header_with_parameters*

function_header_with_parameters:

> *function_header parameter_declaration*
>
> *function_header_with_parameters COMMA parameter_declaration*

function_header:

> *fully_specified_type IDENTIFIER LEFT_PAREN*

parameter_declarator:

> *type_specifier IDENTIFIER*
>
> *type_specifier IDENTIFIER LEFT_BRACKET RIGHT_BRACKET*

parameter_declaration:

> *type_qualifier parameter_qualifier parameter_declarator*
>
> *parameter_qualifier parameter_declarator*
>
> *type_qualifier parameter_qualifier parameter_type_specifier*
>
> *parameter_qualifier parameter_type_specifier*

parameter_qualifier:

> */* empty */*

> *IN*

> *OUT*

> *INOUT*

parameter_type_specifier:

> *type_specifier*

> *type_specifier LEFT_BRACKET RIGHT_BRACKET*

init_declarator_list:

> *single_declaration*

> *init_declarator_list COMMA IDENTIFIER*

> *init_declarator_list COMMA IDENTIFIER LEFT_BRACKET*
> *RIGHT_BRACKET*

> *init_declarator_list COMMA IDENTIFIER LEFT_BRACKET*
> *constant_expression RIGHT_BRACKET*

> *init_declarator_list COMMA IDENTIFIER EQUAL initializer*

single_declaration:

> *fully_specified_type*

> *fully_specified_type IDENTIFIER*

> *fully_specified_type IDENTIFIER LEFT_BRACKET RIGHT_*
> *BRACKET*

> *fully_specified_type IDENTIFIER LEFT_BRACKET constant_*
> *expression*
> *RIGHT_BRACKET*

> *fully_specified_type IDENTIFIER EQUAL initializer*

// Grammar Note: No 'enum' or 'typedef'.

fully_specified_type:

> *type_specifier*

> *type_qualifier type_specifier*

type_qualifier:
    CONST
    ATTRIBUTE   *// Vertex only.*
    VARYING
    UNIFORM

type_specifier:
    VOID
    FLOAT
    INT
    BOOL
    VEC2
    VEC3
    VEC4
    BVEC2
    BVEC3
    BVEC4
    IVEC2
    IVEC3
    IVEC4
    MAT2
    MAT3
    MAT4
    SAMPLER1D
    SAMPLER2D
    SAMPLER3D
    SAMPLERCUBE
    SAMPLER1DSHADOW
    SAMPLER2DSHADOW
    struct_specifier
    TYPE_NAME

struct_specifier:

   STRUCT IDENTIFIER LEFT_BRACE struct_declaration_list
      RIGHT_BRACE

   STRUCT LEFT_BRACE struct_declaration_list RIGHT_BRACE

struct_declaration_list:

   struct_declaration

   struct_declaration_list struct_declaration

struct_declaration:

   type_specifier struct_declarator_list SEMICOLON

struct_declarator_list:

   struct_declarator

   struct_declarator_list COMMA struct_declarator

struct_declarator:

   IDENTIFIER

   IDENTIFIER LEFT_BRACKET constant_expression RIGHT_
   BRACKET

initializer:

   assignment_expression

declaration_statement:

   declaration

statement:

   compound_statement

   simple_statement

// Grammar Note: No labeled statements; 'goto' is not supported.

simple_statement:
> *declaration_statement*
> *expression_statement*
> *selection_statement*
> *iteration_statement*
> *jump_statement*

compound_statement:
> LEFT_BRACE RIGHT_BRACE
> LEFT_BRACE *statement_list* RIGHT_BRACE

statement_no_new_scope:
> *compound_statement_no_new_scope*
> *simple_statement*

compound_statement_no_new_scope:
> LEFT_BRACE RIGHT_BRACE
> LEFT_BRACE *statement_list* RIGHT_BRACE

statement_list:
> *statement*
> *statement_list statement*

expression_statement:
> SEMICOLON
> *expression* SEMICOLON

selection_statement:
> IF LEFT_PAREN *expression* RIGHT_PAREN *selection_rest_statement*

selection_rest_statement:

    statement ELSE statement

    statement

// Grammar Note: No 'switch'. Switch statements not supported.

condition:

    expression

    fully_specified_type IDENTIFIER EQUAL initializer

iteration_statement:

    WHILE LEFT_PAREN condition RIGHT_PAREN statement_no_ new_scope

    DO statement WHILE LEFT_PAREN expression RIGHT_PAREN SEMICOLON

    FOR LEFT_PAREN for_init_statement for_rest_statement RIGHT_PAREN
        statement_no_new_scope

for_init_statement:

    expression_statement

    declaration_statement

conditionopt:

    condition

    / empty */*

for_rest_statement:

    conditionopt SEMICOLON

    conditionopt SEMICOLON expression

jump_statement:

    CONTINUE SEMICOLON

    BREAK SEMICOLON

    RETURN SEMICOLON

    RETURN expression SEMICOLON

    DISCARD SEMICOLON   // Fragment shader only.

// Grammar Note: No 'goto'. Gotos are not supported.

translation_unit:

    external_declaration

    translation_unit external_declaration

external_declaration:

    function_definition

    declaration

function_definition:

    function_prototype compound_statement_no_new_scope

API Function Reference

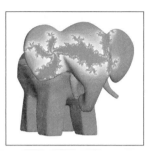

This section contains detailed information on the OpenGL commands that support the creation, compilation, linking, and usage of shaders written in the OpenGL Shading Language, as well as the OpenGL commands added to provide generic vertex attributes and user-defined uniform variables to such shaders.

The reference pages in this section are copyrighted by 3Dlabs Inc., Ltd. © 2003 and are reprinted with permission.

glAttachObjectARB

NAME

glAttachObjectARB—Attaches a shader object to a program object

C SPECIFICATION

```
void glAttachObjectARB(GLhandleARB program,
                       GLhandleARB shader)
```

PARAMETERS

program   Specifies the handle of the program object to which a shader object will be attached.

shader   Specifies the handle of the shader object that is to be attached.

DESCRIPTION

A program object provides the mechanism for specifying all the shader objects that will be used to create a program. **glAttachObjectARB** attaches the shader object specified by *shader* to the program object specified by *program*. This indicates that *shader* will be included in link operations that will be performed on *program*.

All operations that can be performed on a shader object are valid whether or not the shader object is attached to a program object. It is permissible to attach a shader object to a program object before source code has been loaded into the shader object or before the shader object has been compiled. It is permissible to attach multiple shader objects of the same type because each may contain a portion of the complete shader. It is also permissible to attach a shader object to more than one program object. If a shader object is deleted while it is attached to a program object, it will be flagged for deletion, and deletion will not occur until **glDetachObjectARB** is called to detach it from all program objects to which it is attached.

ERRORS

GL_INVALID_VALUE is generated if either *program* or *shader* is not an object handle generated by OpenGL.

GL_INVALID_OPERATION is generated if *program* is not of type GL_PROGRAM_OBJECT_ARB.

GL_INVALID_OPERATION is generated if *shader* is not of type GL_SHADER_OBJECT_ARB.

GL_INVALID_OPERATION is generated if *shader* is already attached to *program*.

GL_INVALID_OPERATION is generated if **glAttachObjectARB** is executed between the execution of **glBegin** and the corresponding execution of **glEnd**.

ASSOCIATED GETS

glGetAttachedObjectsARB with the handle of a valid program object

SEE ALSO

glCompileShaderARB, **glDetachObjectARB**, **glLinkProgramARB**, **glShaderSourceARB**

glBindAttribLocationARB

NAME

glBindAttribLocationARB—Associates a generic vertex attribute index with a named attribute variable

C SPECIFICATION

```
void glBindAttribLocationARB(GLhandleARB program,
                             GLuint index,
                             const GLcharARB *name)
```

PARAMETERS

program   Specifies the handle of the program object in which the generic vertex attribute-to-named-attribute variable association is to be made.

index   Specifies the index of the generic vertex attribute to be bound.

name   Specifies a null terminated string containing the name of the vertex shader attribute variable to which *index* is to be bound.

DESCRIPTION

glBindAttribLocationARB is used to associate a user-defined attribute variable in the program object specified by *program* with a generic vertex attribute index. The name of the user-defined attribute variable is passed as a null terminated string in *name*. The generic vertex attribute index to be bound to this variable is specified by *index*. When *program* is made part of current state, values provided via the generic vertex attribute *index* will modify the value of the user-defined attribute variable specified by *name*.

If *name* refers to a matrix attribute variable, *index* refers to the first column of the matrix. Other matrix columns are then automatically bound to locations *index+1* for a matrix of type **mat2**; *index+1* and *index+2* for a matrix of type **mat3**; and *index+1*, *index+2*, and *index+3* for a matrix of type **mat4**.

This command makes it possible for vertex shaders to use descriptive names for attribute variables rather than generic variables that are numbered from

0 to GL_MAX_VERTEX_ATTRIBS–1. The values sent to each generic attribute index are part of current state, just like standard vertex attributes such as color, normal, and vertex position. If a different program object is made current by calling **glUseProgramObjectARB**, the generic vertex attributes are tracked in such a way that the same values will be observed by attributes in the new program object that are also bound to *index*.

Attribute variable name-to-generic attribute index bindings can be specified at any time by calling **glBindAttribLocationARB**. Attribute bindings do not go into effect until **glLinkProgramARB** is called. After a program object has been linked successfully, the index values for generic attributes remain fixed (and their values can be queried) until the next link command occurs.

Applications are not allowed to bind any of the standard OpenGL vertex attributes using this command, as they are bound automatically when needed. Any attribute binding that occurs after the program object has been linked will not take effect until the next time the program object is linked.

NOTES

glBindAttribLocationARB can be called before any vertex shader objects are bound to the specified program object. It is also permissible to bind a generic attribute index to an attribute variable name that is never used in a vertex shader.

If *name* was bound previously, that information is lost. Thus you cannot bind one user-defined attribute variable to multiple indices, but you can bind multiple user-defined attribute variables to the same index.

Applications are allowed to bind more than one user-defined attribute variable to the same generic vertex attribute index. This is called *aliasing*, and it is allowed only if just one of the aliased attributes is active in the executable program, or if no path through the shader consumes more than one attribute of a set of attributes aliased to the same location. The compiler and linker are allowed to assume that no aliasing is done and are free to employ optimizations that work only in the absence of aliasing. OpenGL implementations are not required to do error checking to detect aliasing. Because there is no way to bind standard attributes, it is not possible to alias generic attributes with conventional ones (except for generic attribute 0).

Active attributes that are not explicitly bound will be bound by the linker when **glLinkProgramARB** is called. The locations assigned can be queried by calling **glGetAttribLocationARB**.

OpenGL copies the *name* string when **glBindAttribLocationARB** is called, so an application may free its copy of the *name* string immediately after the function returns.

ERRORS

GL_INVALID_VALUE is generated if *index* is greater than or equal to GL_MAX_VERTEX_ATTRIBS_ARB.

GL_INVALID_OPERATION is generated if *name* starts with the reserved prefix "gl_".

GL_INVALID_VALUE is generated if *program* is not an object handle generated by OpenGL.

GL_INVALID_OPERATION is generated if *program* is not of type GL_PROGRAM_OBJECT_ARB.

GL_INVALID_OPERATION is generated if **glBindAttribLocationARB** is executed between the execution of **glBegin** and the corresponding execution of **glEnd**.

ASSOCIATED GETS

glGetActiveAttribARB with argument *program*

glGetAttribLocationARB with arguments *program* and *name*

glGet with argument GL_MAX_VERTEX_ATTRIBS_ARB

SEE ALSO

glDisableVertexAttribArrayARB, glEnableVertexAttribArrayARB, glUseProgramObjectARB, glVertexAttribARB, glVertexAttribPointerARB

glCompileShaderARB

NAME

glCompileShaderARB—Compiles a shader object

C SPECIFICATION

```
void glCompileShaderARB(GLhandleARB shader)
```

PARAMETERS

shader   Specifies the handle of the shader object to be compiled.

DESCRIPTION

glCompileShaderARB compiles the source code strings that have been stored in the shader object specified by *shader.*

The compilation status will be stored as part of the shader object's state. This value will be set to GL_TRUE if the shader was compiled without errors and is ready for use, and GL_FALSE otherwise. It can be queried by calling **glGetObjectParameterARB** with arguments *shader* and GL_OBJECT_ COMPILE_STATUS_ARB.

Compilation of a shader can fail for a number of reasons as specified by the *OpenGL Shading Language Specification.* Whether or not the compilation was successful, information about the compilation can be obtained from the shader object's information log by calling **glGetInfoLogARB.**

NOTES

glCompileShaderARB is not required to wait until the compilation operation is completed before returning control back to the application. Any subsequent command that depends on the completion of the compilation (e.g., **glLinkProgramARB**) will block until the compilation is completed. If you need to ensure that the compilation has completed successfully before continuing, you should call **glGetObjectParameterARB** to query for successsful compilation. This query will block until the compilation is complete and the status is available.

ERRORS

GL_INVALID_VALUE is generated if *shader* is not an object handle generated by OpenGL.

GL_INVALID_OPERATION is generated if *shader* is not of type GL_SHADER_OBJECT_ARB.

GL_INVALID_OPERATION is generated if **glCompileShaderARB** is executed between the execution of **glBegin** and the corresponding execution of **glEnd**.

ASSOCIATED GETS

glGetInfoLogARB with argument *shader*

glGetObjectParameterARB with arguments *shader* and GL_OBJECT_COMPILE_STATUS_ARB

SEE ALSO

glCreateShaderObjectARB, glLinkProgramARB, glShaderSourceARB

glCreateProgramObjectARB

NAME

glCreateProgramObjectARB—Creates a program object

C SPECIFICATION

```
GLhandleARB glCreateProgramObjectARB(void)
```

DESCRIPTION

glCreateProgramObjectARB creates an empty program object and returns its handle. A program object is an object to which shader objects can be attached. This provides a way to specify the shader objects that will be linked to create a program. It also provides a means for checking between shaders the compatibilty that will be used to create a program (for instance, checking the compatibility between a vertex shader and a fragment shader). When no longer needed as part of a program object, shader objects can be detached. A program is created by linking the program object. This program is made part of current state when **glUseProgramObjectARB** is called. Program objects can be deleted by calling **glDeleteObjectARB**. The memory associated with the program object will be deleted when it is no longer part of current rendering state for any context.

NOTES

Like display lists and texture objects, the name space for handles for all objects may be shared across a set of contexts, as long as the server sides of the contexts share the same address space.

Changes to a program object made by one rendering context are not guaranteed to take effect in another rendering context until **glUseProgramObjectARB** is called in the second rendering context.

ERRORS

GL_INVALID_OPERATION is generated if **glCreateProgramObjectARB** is executed between the execution of **glBegin** and the corresponding execution of **glEnd**.

ASSOCIATED GETS

glGetHandleARB with the argument GL_PROGRAM_OBJECT_ARB

glGetAttachedObjectsARB with the handle of a valid program object.

glGetInfoLogARB with the handle of a valid program object

glGetObjectParameterARB with the handle of a valid program object

SEE ALSO

glAttachObjectARB, **glCreateShaderObjectARB**, **glDeleteObjectARB**, **glDetachObjectARB**, **glLinkProgramARB**, **glUseProgramObjectARB**, **glValidateProgramARB**

glCreateShaderObjectARB

NAME

glCreateShaderObjectARB—Creates a shader object

C SPECIFICATION

```
GLhandleARB glCreateShaderObjectARB(GLenum shaderType)
```

PARAMETERS

shaderType   Specifies the type of shader to be created. Must be either GL_VERTEX_SHADER_ARB or GL_FRAGMENT_SHADER_ARB.

DESCRIPTION

glCreateShaderObjectARB creates an empty shader object and returns its handle. A shader object is used to maintain the source code strings that define a shader. *shaderType* indicates the type of shader to be created. Two types of shaders are supported. A shader of type GL_VERTEX_SHADER_ARB is a shader that is intended to run on the programmable vertex processor and replace the fixed functionality vertex processing in OpenGL. A shader of type GL_FRAGMENT_SHADER_ARB is a shader that is intended to run on the programmable fragment processor and replace the fixed functionality fragment processing in OpenGL.

When created, a shader object's GL_OBJECT_TYPE_ARB parameter is set to GL_SHADER_OBJECT_ARB and its GL_OBJECT_SUBTYPE_ARB parameter is set to either GL_VERTEX_SHADER_ARB or GL_FRAGMENT_SHADER_ARB, depending on the value of *shaderType*.

NOTES

Like display lists and texture objects, the name space for handles for all objects may be shared across a set of contexts, as long as the server sides of the contexts share the same address space. If handles are shared across contexts, any attached objects and the data associated with those attached objects are shared as well.

Changes to a shader object made by one rendering context are not guaranteed to take effect in another rendering context until **glUseProgramObjectARB** is called in the second rendering context.

ERRORS

GL_INVALID_ENUM is generated if *shaderType* is not an accepted value.

GL_INVALID_OPERATION is generated if **glCreateShaderObjectARB** is executed between the execution of **glBegin** and the corresponding execution of **glEnd**.

ASSOCIATED GETS

glGetInfoLogARB with the handle of a valid shader object

glGetObjectParameterARB with the handle of a valid shader object and the argument GL_OBJECT_TYPE_ARB or GL_OBJECT_SUBTYPE_ARB

glGetShaderSourceARB with the handle of a valid shader object

SEE ALSO

glAttachObjectARB, glCompileShaderARB, glCreateProgramObjectARB, glDeleteObjectARB, glDetachObjectARB, glShaderSourceARB

glDeleteObjectARB

NAME

glDeleteObjectARB—Deletes an OpenGL-managed object

C SPECIFICATION

```
void glDeleteObjectARB(GLhandleARB object)
```

PARAMETERS

object   Specifies the handle of the OpenGL-managed object
                    to be deleted.

DESCRIPTION

glDeleteObjectARB frees the memory and invalidates the handle associated with the OpenGL-managed object specified by *object*. This command effectively undoes the effects of a call to **glCreateShaderObjectARB** or **glCreateProgramObjectARB**.

If a shader object to be deleted is attached to a program object, it will be flagged for deletion, but it will not be deleted until it is no longer attached to any program object, for any rendering context (i.e., it must be detached from wherever it was attached before it will be deleted). If a program object is in use as part of current rendering state, it will be flagged for deletion, but it will not be deleted until it is no longer part of current state for any rendering context. If a program object to be deleted has shader objects attached to it, those shader objects will be automatically detached but not deleted unless they have already been flagged for deletion by a previous call to **glDeleteObjectARB**.

To determine whether an object has been flagged for deletion, call **glGetObjectParameterARB** with arguments *object* and GL_OBJECT_DELETE_STATUS_ARB.

ERRORS

GL_INVALID_VALUE is generated if *object* is not an object handle generated by OpenGL.

GL_INVALID_OPERATION is generated if **glDeleteObjectARB** is executed between the execution of **glBegin** and the corresponding execution of **glEnd**.

ASSOCIATED GETS

glGetHandleARB with argument GL_PROGRAM_OBJECT_ARB

glGetObjectParameterARB with arguments *object* and GL_OBJECT_DELETE_STATUS_ARB

SEE ALSO

glCreateProgramObjectARB, **glCreateShaderObjectARB**, **glDetachObjectARB**, **glUseProgramObjectARB**

glDetachObjectARB

NAME

glDetachObjectARB—Detaches a shader object from the program object to which it is attached

C SPECIFICATION

```
void glDetachObjectARB(GLhandleARB program,
                       GLhandleARB shader)
```

PARAMETERS

program   Specifies the handle of the program object.

shader   Specifies the handle of the shader object.

DESCRIPTION

glDetachObjectARB detaches the shader object specified by *shader* from the program object specified by *program*. This command can be used to undo the effect of the command **glAttachObjectARB**.

ERRORS

GL_INVALID_VALUE is generated if either *program* or *shader* is not an object handle generated by OpenGL.

GL_INVALID_OPERATION is generated if *program* is not of type GL_PROGRAM_OBJECT_ARB.

GL_INVALID_OPERATION is generated if *shader* is not attached to *program*.

GL_INVALID_OPERATION is generated if **glDetachObjectARB** is executed between the execution of **glBegin** and the corresponding execution of **glEnd**.

ASSOCIATED GETS

glGetAttachedObjectsARB with the handle of a valid program object.

SEE ALSO

glAttachObjectARB

glEnableVertexAttribArrayARB

NAME

glEnableVertexAttribArrayARB, glDisableVertexAttribArrayARB—Enable or disable a generic vertex attribute array

C SPECIFICATION

```
void glEnableVertexAttribArrayARB(GLuint index)
void glDisableVertexAttribArrayARB(GLuint index)
```

PARAMETERS

index   Specifies the index of the generic vertex attribute to be enabled or disabled.

DESCRIPTION

glEnableVertexAttribArrayARB and **glDisableVertexAttribArrayARB** enable or disable the generic vertex attribute array specified by *index*. By default, all client-side capabilities are disabled, including all generic vertex attribute arrays. If enabled, the values in the generic vertex attribute array will be accessed and used for rendering when calls are made to vertex array commands such as **glDrawArrays**, **glDrawElements**, **glDrawRangeElements**, **glArrayElement**, **glMultiDrawElements**, or **glMultiDrawArrays**.

ERRORS

GL_INVALID_VALUE is generated if *index* is greater than or equal to GL_MAX_VERTEX_ATTRIBS_ARB.

ASSOCIATED GETS

glGetVertexAttribARB with argument *index*

glGetVertexAttribPointerARB with argument *index*

glGet with argument GL_MAX_VERTEX_ATTRIBS_ARB

SEE ALSO

glArrayElement, **glBindAttribLocationARB**, **glDrawArrays**, **glDrawElements**, **glDrawRangeElements**, **glMultiDrawArrays**, **glMultiDrawElements**, **glPopClientAttrib**, **glPushClientAttrib**, **glVertexAttribARB**, **glVertexAttribPointerARB**

glGetActiveAttribARB

NAME

glGetActiveAttribARB—Returns information about an active attribute variable for the specified program object

C SPECIFICATION

```
void glGetActiveAttribARB(GLhandleARB program,
                          GLuint index,
                          GLsizei maxLength,
                          GLsizei *length,
                          GLint *size,
                          GLenum *type,
                          GLcharARB *name)
```

PARAMETERS

program	Specifies the program object to be queried.
index	Specifies the index of the attribute variable to be queried.
maxLength	Specifies the maximum number of characters OpenGL is allowed to write in the character buffer indicated by *name*.
length	Returns the number of characters actually written by OpenGL in the string indicated by *name* (excluding the null terminator) if a value other than NULL is passed.
size	Returns the size of the attribute variable.
type	Returns the data type of the attribute variable.
name	Returns a null terminated string containing the name of the attribute variable.

DESCRIPTION

glGetActiveAttribARB returns information about an active attribute variable in the program object specified by *program*. The size of a character buffer allocated by the application is specified by *maxLength*, and a pointer to this character buffer is passed in *name*. An attribute variable (either built-in or user-defined) is considered active if it is determined during the link operation that it may be accessed during program execution. Therefore, *program* should have previously been the target of a call to **glLinkProgramARB**, but it is not necessary for it to have been linked successfully.

glGetActiveAttribARB returns the name of the attribute variable indicated by *index*, storing it in the character buffer specified by *name*. The string returned will be null terminated. The actual number of characters written into this buffer is returned in *length*, and this count does not include the null termination character. If the length of the returned string is not required, a value of NULL can be passed in the *length* argument.

The number of active attributes can be obtained by calling **glGetObjectParameterARB** with the value GL_OBJECT_ACTIVE_ATTRIBUTES_ARB. A value of 0 for *index* will cause information about the first active attribute variable to be returned, and a value of GL_OBJECT_ACTIVE_ATTRIBUTES_ARB – 1 for *index* will cause information about the last active attribute variable to be returned. The length of the character buffer required to store the longest attribute variable name in *program* can be obtained by calling **glGetObjectParameterARB** with the value GL_OBJECT_ACTIVE_ATTRIBUTE_MAX_LENGTH_ARB.

The *type* argument will return a pointer to the attribute variable's data type. The symbolic constants GL_FLOAT, GL_FLOAT_VEC2_ARB, GL_FLOAT_VEC3_ARB, GL_FLOAT_VEC4_ARB, GL_FLOAT_MAT2_ARB, GL_FLOAT_MAT3_ARB, GL_FLOAT_MAT4_ARB may be returned. The *size* argument will return the size of the attribute, in units of the type returned in *type*.

This function will return as much information as it can about the specified active attribute variable. If no information is available, *length* will be 0, and *name* will be an empty string. This situation could occur if this function is called after a link operation that failed.

ERRORS

GL_INVALID_VALUE is generated if *program* is not an object handle generated by OpenGL.

GL_INVALID_OPERATION is generated if *program* is not of type GL_PROGRAM_OBJECT_ARB.

GL_INVALID_VALUE is generated if *index* is greater than or equal to GL_OBJECT_ACTIVE_ATTRIBUTES_ARB.

GL_INVALID_OPERATION is generated if **glGetActiveAttribARB** is executed between the execution of **glBegin** and the corresponding execution of **glEnd**.

GL_INVALID_VALUE is generated if *maxLength* is less than 0.

SEE ALSO

glBindAttribLocationARB, **glLinkProgramARB**, **glVertexAttribARB**, **glVertexAttribPointerARB**

glGetActiveUniformARB

NAME

glGetActiveUniformARB—Returns information about an active uniform variable for the specified program object

C SPECIFICATION

```
void glGetActiveUniformARB(GLhandleARB program,
                           GLuint index,
                           GLsizei maxLength,
                           GLsizei *length,
                           GLint *size,
                           GLenum *type,
                           GLcharARB *name)
```

PARAMETERS

program	Specifies the program object to be queried.
index	Specifies the index of the uniform variable to be queried.
maxLength	Specifies the maximum number of characters OpenGL is allowed to write in the character buffer indicated by *name*.
length	Returns the number of characters actually written by OpenGL in the string indicated by *name* (excluding the null terminator) if a value other than NULL is passed.
size	Returns the size of the uniform variable.
type	Returns the data type of the uniform variable.
name	Returns a null terminated string containing the name of the uniform variable.

DESCRIPTION

glGetActiveUniformARB returns information about an active uniform variable in the program object specified by *program*. The size of a character buffer allocated by the application is specified by *maxLength*, and a pointer to this character buffer is passed in *name*. A uniform variable (either built-in or user-defined) is considered active if it is determined during the link operation that it may be accessed during program execution. Therefore, *program* should have previously been the target of a call to **glLinkProgramARB**, but it is not necessary for it to have been linked successfully.

glGetActiveUniformARB returns the name of the uniform variable indicated by *index*, storing it in the character buffer specified by *name*. The string returned will be null terminated. The actual number of characters written into this buffer is returned in *length*, and this count does not include the null termination character. If the length of the returned string is not required, a value of NULL can be passed in the *length* argument.

The number of active uniform variables can be obtained by calling **glGetObjectParameterARB** with the value GL_OBJECT_ACTIVE_UNIFORMS_ARB. A value of 0 for *index* will cause information about the first active uniform variable to be returned, and a value of GL_OBJECT_ACTIVE_UNIFORMS_ARB – 1 for *index* will cause information about the last active uniform variable to be returned. The size of the character buffer required to store the longest uniform variable name in *program* can be obtained by calling **glGetObjectParameterARB** with the value GL_OBJECT_ACTIVE_UNIFORM_MAX_LENGTH_ARB.

The *type* argument will return a pointer to the uniform variable's data type. The symbolic constants GL_FLOAT, GL_FLOAT_VEC2_ARB, GL_FLOAT_VEC3_ARB, GL_FLOAT_VEC4_ARB, GL_INT, GL_INT_VEC2_ARB, GL_INT_VEC3_ARB, GL_INT_VEC4_ARB, GL_BOOL_ARB, GL_BOOL_VEC2_ARB, GL_BOOL_VEC3_ARB, GL_BOOL_VEC4_ARB, GL_FLOAT_MAT2_ARB, GL_FLOAT_MAT3_ARB, or GL_FLOAT_MAT4_ARB may be returned.

Uniform variables that are declared as structures or arrays of structures will not be returned directly by this function. Instead, each of these uniform variables will be reduced to its fundamental components containing the "." and "[]" operators such that each of the names is valid as an argument to **glGetUniformLocationARB**. A valid name cannot be a structure, an array of structures, or a subcomponent of a vector or matrix. Each of these reduced uniform variables is counted as one active uniform variable and is assigned an index. If an active uniform variable reduces to an element of an array, all elements in the array are considered to be active.

The size of the uniform variable will be returned in *size*. Uniform variables other than arrays will have a size of 1, and uniform variable arrays will return the size of the array. Structures and arrays of structures will be reduced as described earlier, such that each of the names returned will be a data type in the earlier list. If this reduction results in an array, the size returned will be the size of this array; otherwise, the size returned will be 1.

It is not necessary for *program* to have already been linked successfully, but it should have previously been the target of a call to **glLinkProgramARB**. A uniform variable (either built-in or user-defined) is considered "active" in a program object if it is determined that it may be accessed during program execution.

The list of active uniform variables may include both built-in uniform variables (which begin with the prefix "gl_") as well as user-defined uniform variable names.

This function will return as much information as it can about the specified active uniform variable. If no information is available, *length* will be 0, and *name* will be an empty string. This situation could occur if this function is called after a link operation that failed.

ERRORS

GL_INVALID_VALUE is generated if *program* is not an object handle generated by OpenGL.

GL_INVALID_OPERATION is generated if *program* is not of type GL_PROGRAM_OBJECT_ARB.

GL_INVALID_VALUE is generated if *index* is greater than or equal to GL_OBJECT_ACTIVE_UNIFORMS_ARB.

GL_INVALID_OPERATION is generated if **glGetActiveUniformARB** is executed between the execution of **glBegin** and the corresponding execution of **glEnd**.

GL_INVALID_VALUE is generated if *maxLength* is less than 0.

ASSOCIATED GETS

glGetObjectParameterARB with argument GL_OBJECT_ACTIVE_UNIFORMS_ARB or GL_OBJECT_ACTIVE_UNIFORM_MAX_LENGTH_ARB.

SEE ALSO

glGetUniformARB, **glGetUniformLocationARB**, **glLinkProgramARB**, **glUniformARB**, **glUseProgramObjectARB**

glGetAttachedObjectsARB

NAME

glGetAttachedObjectsARB—Returns the handles of the shader objects attached to a program object

C SPECIFICATION

```
void glGetAttachedObjectsARB(GLhandleARB program,
                            GLsizei maxCount,
                            GLsizei *count,
                            GLhandleARB *objects)
```

PARAMETERS

program	Specifies the program object to be queried.
maxCount	Specifies the size of the array for storing the returned object handles.
count	Returns the number of handles actually returned in *objects*.
objects	Specifies an array of object handles that is used to return the handles of attached shader objects.

DESCRIPTION

glGetAttachedObjectsARB returns the handles of the shader objects attached to *program*. It returns in *objects* as many of the handles of these shader objects as it can, up to a maximum of *maxCount*. The number of handles actually returned is specified by *count*. If the number of handles actually returned is not required (for instance, if it has just been obtained by calling **glGetObjectParameterARB**), a value of NULL may be passed for *count*. If no shader objects are attached to *program*, a value of 0 will be returned in *count*. The actual number of attached shaders can be obtained by calling **glGetObjectParameterARB** with the value GL_OBJECT_ATTACHED_OBJECTS_ARB.

ERRORS

GL_INVALID_VALUE is generated if *program* is not an object handle generated by OpenGL.

GL_INVALID_OPERATION is generated if *program* is not of type GL_PROGRAM_OBJECT_ARB.

GL_INVALID_VALUE is generated if *maxCount* is less than 0.

GL_INVALID_OPERATION is generated if **glGetAttachedObjectsARB** is executed between the execution of **glBegin** and the corresponding execution of **glEnd**.

ASSOCIATED GETS

glGetObjectParameterARB with argument GL_OBJECT_ATTACHED_OBJECTS_ARB

SEE ALSO

glAttachObjectARB, glDetachObjectARB

glGetAttribLocationARB

NAME

glGetAttribLocationARB—Returns the location of an attribute variable

C SPECIFICATION

```
GLint glGetAttribLocationARB(GLhandleARB program,
                            const GLcharARB *name)
```

PARAMETERS

program
: Specifies the handle of the program object to be queried.

name
: Points to a null terminated string containing the name of the attribute variable whose location is to be queried.

DESCRIPTION

glGetAttribLocationARB queries the previously linked program object specified by *program* for the attribute variable specified by *name* and returns the index of the generic vertex attribute that is bound to that attribute variable. If *name* is a matrix attribute variable, the index of the first column of the matrix is returned. If the named attribute variable is not an active attribute in the specified program object or if *name* starts with the reserved prefix "gl_", a value of –1 is returned.

Attribute variable name-to-generic attribute index bindings can be specified at any time by calling **glBindAttribLocationARB**. Attribute bindings do not go into effect until **glLinkProgramARB** is called. After a program object has been linked successfully, the index values for attribute variables remain fixed (and their values can be queried) until the next link command occurs. **glGetAttribLocationARB** returns the binding that actually went into effect the last time **glLinkProgramARB** was called for the specified program object. Attribute bindings that have been specified since the last link operation are not returned by **glGetAttribLocationARB**.

ERRORS

GL_INVALID_OPERATION is generated if *program* is not of type GL_
PROGRAM_OBJECT_ARB.

GL_INVALID_OPERATION is generated if *program* has not been successfully
linked.

GL_INVALID_OPERATION is generated if **glGetAttribLocationARB** is executed
between the execution of **glBegin** and the corresponding execution of **glEnd**.

SEE ALSO

glBindAttribLocationARB, **glLinkProgramARB**, **glVertexAttribARB**,
glVertexAttribPointerARB

glGetHandleARB

NAME

glGetHandleARB—Returns the handle to an object that is in use as part of current state

C SPECIFICATION

`GLhandleARB glGetHandleARB(GLenum pname)`

PARAMETERS

pname   Specifies the parameter to be queried. Must be GL_PROGRAM_OBJECT_ARB.

DESCRIPTION

glGetHandleARB returns the handle to an object that is in use as part of current state. The argument *pname* specifies the state value to be queried. The value GL_PROGRAM_OBJECT_ARB is passed to obtain the handle of the program object that is currently in use as part of current state.

ERRORS

GL_INVALID_ENUM is generated if *pname* is not an accepted value.

GL_INVALID_OPERATION is generated if **glGetHandleARB** is executed between the execution of **glBegin** and the corresponding execution of **glEnd**.

SEE ALSO

glUseProgramObjectARB

glGetInfoLogARB

NAME

glGetInfoLogARB—Returns the information log for an object

C SPECIFICATION

```
void glGetInfoLogARB(GLhandleARB object,
                     GLsizei maxLength,
                     GLsizei *length,
                     GLcharARB *infoLog)
```

PARAMETERS

object	Specifies the handle of the object whose information log is to be queried.
maxLength	Specifies the size of the character buffer for storing the returned information log.
length	Returns the length of the string returned in *infoLog* (excluding the null terminator).
infoLog	Specifies an array of characters that is used to return the information log.

DESCRIPTION

glGetInfoLogARB returns the information log for the specified OpenGL-managed object. The information log for a shader object is modified when the shader is compiled, and the information log for a program object is modified when the program object is linked or validated. The string that is returned will be null terminated.

glGetInfoLogARB returns in *infoLog* as much of the information log as it can, up to a maximum of *maxLength* characters. The number of characters actually returned, excluding the null termination character, is specified by *length*. If the length of the returned string is not required, a value of NULL can be passed in the *length* argument. The size of the buffer required to store the returned information log can be obtained by calling **glGetObjectParameterARB** with the value GL_OBJECT_INFO_LOG_LENGTH_ARB.

The information log is a string that may contain diagnostic messages, warning messages, and other information about the last compile operation (for shader objects) or the last link or validate operation (for program objects). When a shader object or a program object is created, its information log will be a string of length 0.

NOTES

The information log is the OpenGL implementor's only mechanism for conveying information about compiling, linking, and validating, so the information log can be helpful to application developers during the development process, even when compiling and linking operations are successful. Application developers should not expect different OpenGL implementations to produce identical information logs.

ERRORS

GL_INVALID_VALUE is generated if *object* is not an object handle generated by OpenGL.

GL_INVALID_OPERATION is generated if *object* is not of type GL_PROGRAM_OBJECT_ARB or GL_SHADER_OBJECT_ARB.

GL_INVALID_VALUE is generated if *maxLength* is less than 0.

GL_INVALID_OPERATION is generated if **glGetInfoLogARB** is executed between the execution of **glBegin** and the corresponding execution of **glEnd**.

ASSOCIATED GETS

glGetObjectParameterARB with argument GL_OBJECT_INFO_LOG_LENGTH_ARB.

SEE ALSO

glCompileShaderARB, **glLinkProgramARB**, **glValidateProgramARB**

glGetObjectParameterARB

NAME

glGetObjectParameterfvARB, glGetObjectParameterivARB—Returns a parameter from the specified object

C SPECIFICATION

```
void glGetObjectParameterfvARB(GLhandleARB object,
                               GLenum pname,
                               GLfloat *params)

void glGetObjectParameterivARB(GLhandleARB object,
                               GLenum pname,
                               GLint *params)
```

PARAMETERS

object	Specifies the handle of the object to be queried.
pname	Specifies the object parameter. Accepted symbolic names are GL_OBJECT_TYPE_ARB, GL_OBJECT_SUBTYPE_ARB, GL_OBJECT_DELETE_STATUS_ARB, GL_OBJECT_LINK_STATUS_ARB, GL_OBJECT_VALIDATE_STATUS_ARB, GL_OBJECT_COMPILE_STATUS_ARB, GL_OBJECT_INFO_LOG_LENGTH_ARB, GL_OBJECT_ATTACHED_OBJECTS_ARB, GL_OBJECT_ACTIVE_ATTRIBUTES_ARB, GL_OBJECT_ACTIVE_ATTRIBUTE_MAX_LENGTH_ARB, GL_OBJECT_ACTIVE_UNIFORMS_ARB, GL_OBJECT_ACTIVE_UNIFORM_MAX_LENGTH_ARB, GL_OBJECT_SHADER_SOURCE_LENGTH_ARB.
params	Returns the requested object parameter.

DESCRIPTION

glGetObjectParameterARB returns in *params* the value of an object parameter. This function can be used to return information about an object. The following parameters are defined:

GL_OBJECT_TYPE_ARB

> *params* returns a value of either GL_PROGRAM_OBJECT_ARB or
> GL_SHADER_OBJECT_ARB, depending on whether *object* is the
> handle of a program object or a shader object.

GL_OBJECT_SUBTYPE_ARB

> *params* returns a value of either GL_VERTEX_SHADER_ARB or
> GL_FRAGMENT_SHADER_ARB, depending on whether *object* is
> the handle of a vertex shader object or a fragment shader object.

GL_OBJECT_DELETE_STATUS_ARB

> *params* returns 1 or 1.0f if the object is currently flagged for
> deletion, and 0 or 0.0f otherwise.

GL_OBJECT_COMPILE_STATUS_ARB

> *params* returns 1 or 1.0f if the last compile operation on the
> specified shader object was successful, and 0 or 0.0f otherwise.

GL_OBJECT_LINK_STATUS_ARB

> *params* returns 1 or 1.0f if the last link operation on the specified
> program object was successful, and 0 or 0.0f otherwise.

GL_OBJECT_VALIDATE_STATUS_ARB

> *params* returns 1 or 1.0f if the last validation operation on the
> specified program object was successful, and 0 or 0.0f otherwise.

GL_OBJECT_INFO_LOG_LENGTH_ARB

> *params* returns the number of characters in the information log for
> the specified object, including the null termination character (i.e.,
> the size of the character buffer required to store the information
> log). If the object has no information log, a value of 0 or 0.0f is
> returned.

GL_OBJECT_ATTACHED_OBJECTS_ARB

> *params* returns the number of objects attached to the specified
> program object.

GL_OBJECT_ACTIVE_ATTRIBUTES_ARB

> *params* returns the number of active attributes for the specified
> program object.

GL_OBJECT_ACTIVE_ATTRIBUTE_MAX_LENGTH_ARB

> *params* returns the length of the longest active attribute name for
> the specified program object, including the null termination
> character (i.e., the size of the character buffer required to store the
> longest attribute name). If no active attributes exist, 0 or 0.0f is
> returned.

GL_OBJECT_ACTIVE_UNIFORMS_ARB

params returns the number of active uniform variables for the specified program object.

GL_OBJECT_ACTIVE_UNIFORM_MAX_LENGTH_ARB

params returns the length of the longest active uniform name for the specified program object, including the null termination character (i.e., the size of the character buffer required to store the longest uniform name). If no active uniform variables exist, 0 or 0.0f is returned.

GL_OBJECT_SHADER_SOURCE_LENGTH_ARB

params returns the length of the concatenation of the source strings that make up the shader source for the specified shader object, including the null termination character. (i.e., the size of the character buffer required to store the shader source). If no source code exists, 0 or 0.0f is returned.

NOTES

If an error is generated, no change is made to the contents of *params*.

ERRORS

GL_INVALID_VALUE is generated if *object* is not an object handle generated by OpenGL.

GL_INVALID_OPERATION is generated if *pname* is GL_OBJECT_TYPE_ ARB, GL_OBJECT_DELETE_STATUS_ARB, or GL_OBJECT_INFO_LOG_ LENGTH_ARB, and *object* does not refer to an object of type GL_ PROGRAM_OBJECT_ARB or GL_SHADER_OBJECT_ARB.

GL_INVALID_OPERATION is generated if *pname* is GL_OBJECT_SUBTYPE_ ARB, GL_OBJECT_COMPILE_STATUS_ARB, or GL_OBJECT_SHADER_ SOURCE_LENGTH_ARB, and *object* does not refer to an object of type GL_ SHADER_OBJECT_ARB.

GL_INVALID_OPERATION is generated if *pname* is GL_OBJECT_LINK_ STATUS_ARB, GL_OBJECT_VALIDATE_STATUS_ARB, GL_OBJECT_ ATTACHED_OBJECTS_ARB, GL_OBJECT_ACTIVE_ATTRIBUTES_ARB, GL_OBJECT_ACTIVE_ATTRIBUTE_MAX_LENGTH_ARB, GL_OBJECT_ ACTIVE_UNIFORMS_ARB, or GL_OBJECT_ACTIVE_UNIFORM_MAX_ LENGTH_ARB, and *object* does not refer to an object of type GL_ PROGRAM_OBJECT_ARB.

GL_INVALID_ENUM is generated if *pname* is not an accepted value.

GL_INVALID_OPERATION is generated if **glGetObjectParameterARB** is executed between the execution of **glBegin** and the corresponding execution of **glEnd**.

ASSOCIATED GETS

glGetActiveAttribARB with argument *object*

glGetActiveUniformARB with argument *object*

glGetAttachedObjectsARB with argument *object*

glGetInfoLogARB with argument *object*

glGetShaderSourceARB with argument *object*

SEE ALSO

glAttachObjectARB, **glCompileShaderARB**, **glCreateProgramObjectARB**, **glCreateShaderObjectARB**, **glDeleteObjectARB**, **glLinkProgramARB**, **glShaderSourceARB**, **glValidateProgramARB**

glGetShaderSourceARB

NAME

glGetShaderSourceARB—Returns the source code string from a shader object

C SPECIFICATION

```
void glGetShaderSourceARB(GLhandleARB shader,
                          GLsizei maxLength,
                          GLsizei *length,
                          GLcharARB *source)
```

PARAMETERS

shader   Specifies the shader object to be queried.

maxLength   Specifies the size of the character buffer for storing the returned source code string.

length   Returns the length of the string returned in *source*.

source   Specifies an array of characters that is used to return the source code string.

DESCRIPTION

glGetShaderSourceARB returns the concatenation of the source code strings from the shader object specified by *shader*. The source code strings for a shader object are the result of a previous call to **glShaderSourceARB**. The string returned by the function will be null terminated.

glGetShaderSourceARB returns in *source* as much of the source code string as it can, up to a maximum of *maxLength* characters. The number of characters actually returned, excluding the null termination character, is specified by *length*. If the length of the returned string is not required, a value of NULL can be passed in the *length* argument. The size of the buffer required to store the returned source code string can be obtained by calling **glGetObjectParameterARB** with the value GL_OBJECT_SHADER_SOURCE_LENGTH_ARB.

ERRORS

GL_INVALID_VALUE is generated if *shader* is not an object handle generated by OpenGL.

GL_INVALID_OPERATION is generated if *shader* is not of type GL_SHADER_OBJECT_ARB.

GL_INVALID_VALUE is generated if *maxLength* is less than 0.

GL_INVALID_OPERATION is generated if **glGetShaderSourceARB** is executed between the execution of **glBegin** and the corresponding execution of **glEnd**.

ASSOCIATED GETS

glGetObjectParameterARB with argument GL_OBJECT_SHADER_SOURCE_LENGTH_ARB

SEE ALSO

glCreateShaderObjectARB, **glGetObjectParameterARB**, **glShaderSourceARB**

glGetUniformARB

NAME

glGetUniformfvARB, glGetUniformivARB—Returns the value of a uniform variable

C SPECIFICATION

```
void glGetUniformfvARB(GLhandleARB program,
                       GLint location,
                       GLfloat *params)

void glGetUniformivARB(GLhandleARB program,
                       GLint location,
                       GLint *params)
```

PARAMETERS

program   Specifies the handle of the program object to be queried.

location   Specifies the location of the uniform variable to be queried.

params   Returns the value of the specified uniform variable.

DESCRIPTION

glGetUniformARB returns in *params* the value(s) of the specified uniform variable. The type of the uniform variable specified by *location* determines the number of values returned. If the uniform variable is defined in the shader as a boolean, int, or float, a single value will be returned. If it is defined as a vec2, ivec2, or bvec2, two values will be returned. If it is defined as a vec3, ivec3, or bvec3, three values will be returned, and so on.

The locations assigned to uniform variables are not known until the program object is linked. After linking has occurred, the command **glGetUniformLocationARB** can be used to obtain the location of a uniform variable. This location value can then be passed to **glGetUniformARB** in order to query the current value of the uniform variable. When a program object has been linked successfully, the locations for uniform variables remain fixed (and their values can be queried) until the next link command occurs.

NOTES

If an error is generated, no change is made to the contents of *params*.

ERRORS

GL_INVALID_VALUE is generated if *program* is not an object handle generated by OpenGL.

GL_INVALID_OPERATION is generated if *program* is not of type GL_PROGRAM_OBJECT_ARB.

GL_INVALID_OPERATION is generated if *program* has not been successfully linked.

GL_INVALID_OPERATION is generated if *location* does not correspond to a valid uniform variable location for the specified program object.

GL_INVALID_OPERATION is generated if **glGetUniformARB** is executed between the execution of **glBegin** and the corresponding execution of **glEnd**.

SEE ALSO

glGetActiveUniformARB, **glGetUniformLocationARB**, **glLinkProgramARB**, **glUniformARB**

glGetUniformLocationARB

NAME

glGetUniformLocationARB—Returns the location of a uniform variable

C SPECIFICATION

```
GLint glGetUniformLocationARB(GLhandleARB program,
                             const GLcharARB *name)
```

PARAMETERS

program   Specifies the handle of the program object to be
                   queried.

name   Points to a null terminated string containing the
                   name of the uniform variable whose location is to be
                   queried.

DESCRIPTION

glGetUniformLocationARB returns an integer that represents the location of a specific uniform variable. The array element operator "[]" and the structure field operator "." may be used in *name* in order to select elements within an array or fields within a structure, but no white space is allowed. The location of the first element of an array can be retrieved by using the name of the array, or by using the name appended by "[0]". The result of using these operators is not allowed to be another structure, an array of structures, or a subcomponent of a vector or a matrix. If the named uniform variable is not found in the specified program object, if *name* does not correspond to an active uniform variable, or if *name* starts with the reserved prefix "gl_", a value of –1 is returned.

The actual locations assigned to uniform variables are not known until the program object is linked. After linking has occurred, the command **glGetUniformLocationARB** can be used to obtain the location of a uniform variable. This location value can then be passed to **glUniformARB** to set the value of the uniform variable or to **glGetUniformARB** in order to query the current value of the uniform variable. When a program object has been linked successfully, the locations for uniform variables remain fixed (and their values can be queried) until the next link command occurs.

ERRORS

GL_INVALID_VALUE is generated if *program* is not an object handle generated by OpenGL.

GL_INVALID_OPERATION is generated if *program* is not of type GL_PROGRAM_OBJECT_ARB.

GL_INVALID_OPERATION is generated if *program* has not been successfully linked.

GL_INVALID_OPERATION is generated if **glGetUniformLocationARB** is executed between the execution of **glBegin** and the corresponding execution of **glEnd**.

SEE ALSO

glGetActiveUniformARB, **glGetUniformARB**, **glLinkProgramARB**, **glUniformARB**

glGetVertexAttribARB

NAME

glGetVertexAttribARB—Returns a generic vertex attribute parameter

C SPECIFICATION
```
void glGetVertexAttribfvARB(GLuint index,
                            GLenum pname,
                            GLfloat *params)

void glGetVertexAttribivARB(GLuint index,
                            GLenum pname,
                            GLint *params)

void glGetVertexAttribdvARB(GLuint index,
                            GLenum pname,
                            GLdouble *params)
```

PARAMETERS

index	Specifies the generic vertex attribute parameter to be queried.
pname	Specifies the symbolic name of the vertex attribute parameter to be queried. GL_VERTEX_ATTRIB_ARRAY_ENABLED_ARB, GL_VERTEX_ATTRIB_ARRAY_SIZE_ARB, GL_VERTEX_ATTRIB_ARRAY_STRIDE_ARB, GL_VERTEX_ATTRIB_ARRAY_TYPE_ARB, GL_VERTEX_ATTRIB_ARRAY_NORMALIZED_ARB, GL_CURRENT_VERTEX_ATTRIB_ARB are accepted.
params	Returns the requested data.

DESCRIPTION

glGetVertexAttribARB returns in params the value of a generic vertex attribute parameter. The generic vertex attribute to be queried is specified by *index*, and the parameter to be queried is specified by *pname*.

The accepted parameter names are as follows:

GL_VERTEX_ATTRIB_ARRAY_ENABLED_ARB
> *params* returns a single value that is non-zero (true) if the vertex attribute array for *index* is enabled and 0 (false) if it is disabled. The initial value is GL_FALSE.

GL_VERTEX_ATTRIB_ARRAY_SIZE_ARB
> *params* returns a single value, the size of the vertex attribute array for *index*. The size is the number of values for each element of the vertex attribute array, and it will be 1, 2, 3, or 4. The initial value is 4.

GL_VERTEX_ATTRIB_ARRAY_STRIDE_ARB
> *params* returns a single value, the array stride for (number of bytes between successive elements in) the vertex attribute array for *index*. A value of 0 indicates that the array elements are stored sequentially in memory. The initial value is 0.

GL_VERTEX_ATTRIB_ARRAY_TYPE_ARB
> *params* returns a single value, a symbolic constant indicating the array type for the vertex attribute array for *index*. Possible values are GL_BYTE, GL_UNSIGNED_BYTE, GL_SHORT, GL_UNSIGNED_ SHORT, GL_INT, GL_UNSIGNED_INT, GL_FLOAT, and GL_ DOUBLE. The initial value is GL_FLOAT.

GL_VERTEX_ATTRIB_ARRAY_NORMALIZED_ARB
> *params* returns a single value that is non-zero (true) if fixed-point data types for the vertex attribute array indicated by *index* are normalized when they are converted to floating point, and 0 (false) otherwise. The initial value is GL_FALSE.

GL_CURRENT_VERTEX_ATTRIB_ARB
> *params* returns four values that represent the current value for the generic vertex attribute specified by index. Generic vertex attribute 0 is unique in that it has no current state, so an error will be generated if *index* is 0. The initial value for all other generic vertex attributes is (0,0,0,1).

All of the parameters except GL_CURRENT_VERTEX_ATTRIB_ARB represent client-side state.

NOTES

If an error is generated, no change is made to the contents of *params*.

ERRORS

GL_INVALID_VALUE is generated if *index* is greater than or equal to GL_MAX_VERTEX_ATTRIBS_ARB.

GL_INVALID_ENUM is generated if *pname* is not an accepted value.

GL_INVALID_OPERATION is generated if *index* is 0 and *pname* is GL_CURRENT_VERTEX_ATTRIB_ARB.

SEE ALSO

glBindAttribLocationARB, **glDisableVertexAttribArrayARB**, **glEnableVertexAttribArrayARB**, **glVertexAttribARB**, **glVertexAttribPointerARB**

glGetVertexAttribPointervARB

NAME

glGetVertexAttributePointervARB—Returns the address of the specified pointer

C SPECIFICATION

```
void glGetVertexAttribPointervARB(GLuint index,
                                  GLenum pname,
                                  GLvoid **pointer)
```

PARAMETERS

index   Specifies the generic vertex attribute parameter to be queried.

pname   Specifies the symbolic name of the generic vertex attribute parameter to be queried. Must be GL_VERTEX_ATTRIB_ARRAY_POINTER_ARB.

params   Returns the requested data.

DESCRIPTION

glGetVertexAttribPointervARB returns pointer information. *index* is the generic vertex attribute to be queried, *pname* is a symbolic constant indicating the pointer to be returned, and *params* is a pointer to a location in which to place the returned data. The accepted parameter names are as follows:

GL_VERTEX_ATTRIB_ARRAY_POINTER_ARB
        params returns a single value that is a pointer to the vertex attribute array for the generic vertex attribute specified by *index*.

NOTES

The pointer returned is client-side state.

The initial value for each pointer is 0.

ERRORS

GL_INVALID_VALUE is generated if *index* is greater than or equal to GL_MAX_VERTEX_ATTRIBS_ARB.

GL_INVALID_ENUM is generated if *pname* is not an accepted value.

SEE ALSO

glVertexAttribPointerARB

glLinkProgramARB

NAME

glLinkProgramARB—Links a program object

C SPECIFICATION

```
void glLinkProgramARB(GLhandleARB program)
```

PARAMETERS

program　　　　　　Specifies the handle of the program object to be linked.

DESCRIPTION

glLinkProgramARB links the program object specified by *program*. If any shader objects of subtype GL_VERTEX_SHADER_ARB are attached to *program*, they will be used to create an executable that will run on the programmable vertex processor. If any shader objects of subtype GL_FRAGMENT_SHADER_ARB are attached to *program*, they will be used to create an executable that will run on the programmable fragment processor.

The status of the link operation will be stored as part of the program object's state. This value will be set to GL_TRUE if the program object was linked without errors and is ready for use, and GL_FALSE otherwise. It can be queried by calling **glGetObjectParameterARB** with arguments *program* and GL_OBJECT_LINK_STATUS_ARB.

As a result of a successful link operation, all active user-defined uniform variables belonging to *program* will be initialized to 0, and each of the program object's active uniform variables will be assigned a location that can be queried by calling **glGetUniformLocationARB**. Also, any active user-defined attribute variables that have not been bound to a generic vertex attribute index will be bound to one at this time.

Linking of a program object can fail for a number of reasons as specified in the *OpenGL Shading Language Specification*. The following lists some of the conditions that will cause a link error.

- The number of active attribute variables supported by the implementation has been exceeded.

- The storage limit for uniform variables has been exceeded.

- The number of active uniform variables supported by the implementa-tion has been exceeded.

- The **main** function is missing for the vertex shader or the fragment shader.

- A varying variable actually used in the fragment shader is not declared in the same way (or is not declared at all) in the vertex shader.

- A reference to a function or variable name is unresolved.

- A shared global is declared with two different types or two different initial values.

- One or more of the attached shader objects has not been successfully compiled.

- Binding a generic attribute matrix caused some rows of the matrix to fall outside the allowed maximum of GL_MAX_VERTEX_ATTRIBS_ARB.

- Not enough contiguous vertex attribute slots could be found to bind attribute matrices.

When a program object has been successfully linked, the program object can be made part of current state by calling **glUseProgramObjectARB**. Whether or not the link operation was successful, information about the link operation can be obtained from the program object's information log by calling **glGetInfoLogARB**.

glLinkProgramARB will also install the generated executables as part of the current rendering state if the link operation was successful and the specified program object is already currently in use as a result of a previous call to **glUseProgramObjectARB**.

If *program* contains shader objects of type GL_VERTEX_SHADER_ARB but does not contain shader objects of type GL_FRAGMENT_SHADER_ARB, the vertex shader will be linked against the implicit interface for fixed func-tionality fragment processing. Similarly, if *program* contains shader objects of type GL_FRAGMENT_SHADER_ARB but it does not contain shader objects of type GL_VERTEX_SHADER_ARB, the fragment shader will be linked against the implicit interface for fixed functionality vertex processing.

The program object's information log is updated, and the program is gener-ated at the time of the link operation. After the link operation, applications are free to modify attached shader objects, compile attached shader objects, detach shader objects, delete shader objects, and attach additional shader objects. None of these operations affects the information log or the program that is part of the program object.

NOTES

glLinkProgramARB is not required to wait until the link operation is completed before returning control back to the application. Any subsequent command that depends on the result of linking (e.g., **glUseProgramObjectARB**) will block until the link operation is complete. If you need to ensure that the link operation has completed successfully before continuing, you should call **glGetObjectParameterARB** to query for successful linking. This query will block until the link operation is complete and the status is available.

ERRORS

GL_INVALID_VALUE is generated if *program* is not an object handle generated by OpenGL.

GL_INVALID_OPERATION is generated if *program* is not of type GL_PROGRAM_OBJECT_ARB.

GL_INVALID_OPERATION is generated if **glLinkProgramARB** is executed between the execution of **glBegin** and the corresponding execution of **glEnd**.

ASSOCIATED GETS

glGetActiveAttribARB with argument *program*

glGetActiveUniformARB with argument *program*

glGetInfoLogARB with argument *program*

glGetObjectParameterARB with arguments *program* and GL_OBJECT_LINK_STATUS_ARB

glGetUniformARB with argument *program* and a uniform variable location

glGetUniformLocationARB with argument *program* and a uniform variable name

glGetHandleARB with parameter GL_PROGRAM_OBJECT_ARB

SEE ALSO

glAttachObjectARB, **glCompileShaderARB**, **glDetachObjectARB**, **glUniformARB**, **glUseProgramObjectARB**, **glValidateProgramARB**

glShaderSourceARB

NAME

glShaderSourceARB—Replaces the source code in a shader object

C SPECIFICATION

```
void glShaderSourceARB(GLhandleARB shader,
                       GLsizei nstrings,
                       const GLcharARB **strings,
                       const GLint *lengths)
```

PARAMETERS

shader	Specifies the handle of the shader object whose source code is to be replaced.
nstrings	Specifies the number of elements in the *strings* and *lengths* arrays.
strings	Specifies an array of pointers to strings containing the source code to be loaded into the shader.
lengths	Specifies an array of string lengths.

DESCRIPTION

glShaderSourceARB sets the source code in *shader* to the source code in the array of strings specified by *strings*. Any source code previously stored in the shader object is completely replaced. The number of strings in the array is specified by *nstrings*. If *lengths* is NULL, each string is assumed to be null terminated. If *lengths* is a value other than NULL, it points to an array containing a string length for each of the corresponding elements of *strings*. Each element in the *lengths* array may contain the length of the corresponding string (the null character is not counted as part of the string length) or a value less than 0 to indicate that the string is null terminated. The source code strings are not scanned or parsed at this time; they are simply copied into the specified shader object.

NOTES

OpenGL copies the shader source code strings when **glShaderSourceARB** is called, so an application may free its copy of the source code strings immediately after the function returns.

ERRORS

GL_INVALID_VALUE is generated if *shader* is not an object handle generated by OpenGL.

GL_INVALID_OPERATION is generated if *shader* is not of type GL_SHADER_OBJECT_ARB.

GL_INVALID_VALUE is generated if *nStrings* is less than 0.

GL_INVALID_OPERATION is generated if **glShaderSourceARB** is executed between the execution of **glBegin** and the corresponding execution of **glEnd**.

ASSOCIATED GETS

glGetShaderSourceARB with argument *shader*

SEE ALSO

glCompileShaderARB, **glCreateShaderObjectARB**, **glDeleteObjectARB**

glUniformARB

NAME

glUniformARB—Specifies the value of a uniform variable

C SPECIFICATION

```
void glUniform1fARB(GLint location,
                    GLfloat v0)
void glUniform2fARB(GLint location,
                    GLfloat v0,
                    GLfloat v1)
void glUniform3fARB(GLint location,
                    GLfloat v0,
                    GLfloat v1,
                    GLfloat v2)
void glUniform4fARB(GLint location,
                    GLfloat v0,
                    GLfloat v1,
                    GLfloat v2,
                    GLfloat v3)

void glUniform1iARB(GLint location,
                    GLint v0)
void glUniform2iARB(GLint location,
                    GLint v0,
                    GLint v1)
void glUniform3iARB(GLint location,
                    GLint v0,
                    GLint v1,
                    GLint v2)
void glUniform4iARB(GLint location,
                    GLint v0,
                    GLint v1,
                    GLint v2,
                    GLint v3)
```

PARAMETERS

location   Specifies the location of the uniform variable to be
                    modified.

v0, v1, v2, v3   Specifies the new values to be used for the specified
                    uniform variable.

C SPECIFICATION

```
void glUniform1fvARB(GLint location,
                     GLsizei count,
                     const GLfloat *value)
void glUniform2fvARB(GLint location,
                     GLsizei count,
                     const GLfloat *value)
void glUniform3fvARB(GLint location,
                     GLsizei count,
                     const GLfloat *value)
void glUniform4fvARB(GLint location,
                     GLsizei count,
                     const GLfloat *value)

void glUniform1ivARB(GLint location,
                     GLsizei count,
                     const GLint *value)
void glUniform2ivARB(GLint location,
                     GLsizei count,
                     const GLint *value)
void glUniform3ivARB(GLint location,
                     GLsizei count,
                     const GLint *value)
void glUniform4ivARB(GLint location,
                     GLsizei count,
                     const GLint *value)
```

PARAMETERS

location   Specifies the location of the uniform value to be modified.

count   Specifies the number of elements that are to be modified (this should be 1 if the targeted uniform variable is not an array, 1 or more if it is an array).

value   Specifies a pointer to an array of *count* values that will be used to update the specified uniform variable.

C SPECIFICATION
```
void glUniformMatrix2fvARB(GLint location,
                           GLsizei count,
                           GLboolean transpose,
                           const GLfloat *value)
void glUniformMatrix3fvARB(GLint location,
                           GLsizei count,
                           GLboolean transpose,
                           const GLfloat *value)
void glUniformMatrix4fvARB(GLint location,
                           GLsizei count,
                           GLboolean transpose,
                           const GLfloat *value)
```

PARAMETERS

location   Specifies the location of the uniform value to be modified.

count   Specifies the number of elements that are to be modified (this should be 1 if the targeted uniform variable is not an array, 1 or more if it is an array).

transpose   Specifies whether to transpose the matrix as the values are loaded into the uniform variable.

value   Specifies a pointer to an array of *count* values that will be used to update the specified uniform variable.

DESCRIPTION

glUniformARB modifies the value of a uniform variable or a uniform variable array. The location of the uniform variable to be modified is specified by *location*, which should be a value returned by **glGetUniformLocationARB**. **glUniformARB** operates on the program object that was made part of current state by calling **glUseProgramObjectARB**.

The commands **glUniform{1|2|3|4}{f|i}ARB** are used to change the value of the uniform variable specified by *location* using the values passed as arguments. The number specified in the command should match the number of components in the data type of the specified uniform variable (e.g., **1** for float, int, bool; **2** for vec2, ivec2, bvec2, etc.). The suffix **f** indicates that floating-point values are being passed; the suffix **i** indicates that integer values are being passed, and this type should also match the data type of the specified uniform variable. The **i** variants of this function should be used to provide values for uniform variables defined as int, ivec2, ivec3, ivec4, or arrays of these. The **f** variants should be used to provide values for uniform variables of type float, vec2, vec3, vec4, or arrays of these. Either the **i** or the **f** variants may be used to provide values for uniform variables of type bool, bvec2, bvec3, bvec4, or arrays of these. The uniform variable will be set to false if the input value is 0 or 0.0f, and it will be set to true otherwise.

All active uniform variables defined in a program object are initialized to 0 when the program object is linked successfully. They retain the values assigned to them by a call to **glUniformARB** until the next successful link operation occurs on the program object, when they are once again initialized to 0.

The commands **glUniform{1|2|3|4}{f|i}vARB** can be used to modify a single uniform variable or a uniform variable array. These commands pass a count and a pointer to the values to be loaded into a uniform variable or a uniform variable array. A count of 1 should be used if modifying the value of a single uniform variable, and a count of 1 or greater can be used to modify an entire array or part of an array. The number specified in the name of the command indicates the number of components for each element in *value*, and it should match the number of components in the data type of the specified uniform variable (e.g., **1** for float, int, bool; **2** for vec2, ivec2, bvec2, etc.). The data type specified in the name of the command must match the data type for the specified uniform variable as described previously for **glUniform{1|2|3|4}{f|i}ARB.**

For uniform variable arrays, each element of the array is considered to be of the type indicated in the name of the command (e.g., **glUniform3f** or **glUniform3fv** can be used to load a uniform variable array of type vec3). The number of elements of the uniform variable array to be modified is specified by *count.*

The commands **glUniformFloatMatrix{2|3|4}fvARB** are used to modify a matrix or an array of matrices. The number in the command name is interpreted as the dimensionality of the matrix. The number **2** indicates a 2×2 matrix (i.e., 4 values), the number **3** indicates a 3×3 matrix (i.e., 9 values), and the number **4** indicates a 4×4 matrix (i.e., 16 values). If *transpose* is GL_FALSE, each matrix is assumed to be supplied in column major order. If *transpose* is GL_TRUE, each matrix is assumed to be supplied in row major order. The *count* argument indicates the number of matrices to be passed. A count of 1 should be used if modifying the value of a single matrix, and a count greater than 1 can be used to modify an array of matrices.

NOTES

glUniform1iARB and **glUniform1ivARB** are the only two functions that may be used to load uniform variables defined as sampler types. Loading samplers with any other function will result in a GL_INVALID_OPERATION error.

If the number of values specified by count would exceed the declared extent of the indicated uniform variable, a GL_INVALID_VALUE error is generated, and the specified uniform variable will remain unchanged.

Other than the preceding exceptions, if the type and size of the uniform variable as defined in the shader do not match the type and size specified in the name of the command used to load its value, a GL_INVALID_OPERATION error will be generated, and the specified uniform variable will remain unchanged.

If *location* does not represent a valid uniform variable location in the current program object, an error will be generated, and no changes will be made to the uniform variable storage of the current program object.

ERRORS

GL_INVALID_OPERATION is generated if there is no current program object.

GL_INVALID_OPERATION is generated if the size of the uniform variable declared in the shader does not match the size indicated by the **glUniformARB** command.

GL_INVALID_OPERATION is generated if one of the integer variants of this function is used to load a uniform variable of type float, vec2, vec3, vec4, or an array of these, or if one of the floating-point variants of this function is used to load a uniform variable of type int, ivec2, ivec3, or ivec4, or an array of these.

GL_INVALID_OPERATION is generated if *location* is an invalid uniform location for the current program object.

GL_INVALID_OPERATION is generated if the number of values loaded results in exceeding the declared size of the specified uniform variable.

GL_INVALID_OPERATION is generated if a sampler is loaded using a command other than **glUniform1iARB** and **glUniform1ivARB.**

GL_INVALID_OPERATION is generated if **glUniformARB** is executed between the execution of **glBegin** and the corresponding execution of **glEnd**.

ASSOCIATED GETS

glGetActiveUniformARB with the handle of a program object

glGetUniformLocationARB with the handle of a program object and the name of a uniform variable

glGetUniformARB with the handle of a program object and the location of a uniform variable

SEE ALSO

glDisable, **glEnable**, **glLinkProgramARB**, **glUseProgramObjectARB**

glUseProgramObjectARB

NAME

glUseProgramObjectARB—Installs a program object as part of current rendering state

C SPECIFICATION

```
void glUseProgramObjectARB(GLhandleARB program)
```

PARAMETERS

program   Specifies the handle of the program object whose executables are to be used as part of current rendering state.

DESCRIPTION

glUseProgramObjectARB installs the program object specified by *program* as part of current rendering state. One or more executables are created in a program object by successfully attaching shader objects to it with **glAttachObjectARB**, successfully compiling them with **glCompileShaderARB**, and successfully linking them with **glLinkProgramARB**.

A program object will contain an executable that will run on the vertex processor if it contains one or more shader objects of subtype GL_VERTEX_ SHADER_ARB that have been successfully compiled and linked. Similarly, a program object will contain an executable that will run on the fragment processor if it contains one or more shader objects of subtype GL_ FRAGMENT_SHADER_ARB that have been successfully compiled and linked.

Successfully installing an executable on a programmable processor will cause the corresponding fixed functionality of OpenGL to be disabled. Specifically, if an executable is installed on the vertex processor, the OpenGL fixed functionality will be disabled as follows.

- The modelview matrix is not applied to vertex coordinates.

- The projection matrix is not applied to vertex coordinates.

- The texture matrices are not applied to texture coordinates.

- Normals are not transformed to eye coordinates.

- Normals are not rescaled or normalized.

- Normalization of GL_AUTO_NORMAL evaluated normals is not performed.

- Texture coordinates are not generated automatically.

- Per-vertex lighting is not performed.

- Color material computations are not performed.

- Color index lighting is not performed.

- This list also applies when setting the current raster position.

The executable that is installed on the vertex processor is expected to implement any or all of the desired functionality from the preceding list. Similarly, if an executable is installed on the fragment processor, the OpenGL fixed functionality will be disabled as follows.

- Texture environment and texture functions are not applied.

- Texture application is not applied.

- Color sum is not applied.

- Fog is not applied.

Again, the fragment shader that is installed is expected to implement any or all of the desired functionality from the preceding list.

While a program object is in use, applications are free to modify attached shader objects, compile attached shader objects, attach additional shader objects, and detach or delete shader objects. None of these operations will affect the executables that are part of the current state. However, relinking the program object that is currently in use will install the program object as part of the current rendering state if the link operation was successful (see **glLinkProgramARB**). While a program object is in use, the state that controls the disabled fixed functionality may also be updated using the normal OpenGL calls.

If *program* contains shader objects of type GL_VERTEX_SHADER_ARB but it does not contain shader objects of type GL_FRAGMENT_SHADER_ARB, an executable will be installed on the vertex processor, but fixed functionality will be used for fragment processing. Similarly, if *program* contains shader objects of type GL_FRAGMENT_SHADER_ARB but it does not contain shader objects of type GL_VERTEX_SHADER_ARB, an executable will be installed on the fragment processor, but fixed functionality will be used for vertex processing. If *program* is 0, the programmable processors will be disabled, and fixed functionality will be used for both vertex and fragment processing.

NOTES

Changes to a program object made by one rendering context are not guaranteed to take effect in another rendering context until **glUseProgramObjectARB** is called in the second rendering context.

ERRORS

GL_INVALID_VALUE is generated if *program* is neither 0 nor an object handle generated by OpenGL.

GL_INVALID_OPERATION is generated if *program* is not of type GL_PROGRAM_OBJECT_ARB.

GL_INVALID_OPERATION is generated if *program* could not be made part of current state.

GL_INVALID_OPERATION is generated if **glUseProgramObjectARB** is executed between the execution of **glBegin** and the corresponding execution of **glEnd**.

ASSOCIATED GETS

glGetHandleARB with argument *program*

glGetAttachedObjectsARB with argument *program*

glGetActiveAttribARB with argument *program*

SEE ALSO

glAttachObjectARB, glCompileShaderARB, glDetachObjectARB, glLinkProgramARB, glValidateProgramARB

glValidateProgramARB

NAME

glValidateProgramARB—Validates a program object

C SPECIFICATION

```
void glValidateProgramARB(GLhandleARB program)
```

PARAMETERS

program   Specifies the handle of the program object to be vali-
                          dated.

DESCRIPTION

glValidateProgramARB checks to see whether the executables contained in *program* can execute given the current OpenGL state. The information generated by the validation process will be stored in *program*'s information log. The validation information may consist of an empty string, or it may be a string containing information about how the current program object interacts with the rest of current OpenGL state. This provides a way for OpenGL implementors to convey more information about why the current program is inefficient, suboptimal, failing to execute, and so on.

The status of the validation operation will be stored as part of the program object's state. This value will be set to GL_TRUE if the validation succeeded, and GL_FALSE otherwise. It can be queried by calling **glGetObjectParameterARB** with arguments *program* and GL_OBJECT_VALIDATE_STATUS_ARB.

This function is typically useful only during application development. The informational string stored in the information log is completely implementation dependent; therefore, an application should not expect different OpenGL implementations to produce identical information strings.

ERRORS

GL_INVALID_OPERATION is generated if *program* is not of type GL_PROGRAM_OBJECT_ARB.

GL_INVALID_OPERATION is generated if **glValidateProgramARB** is executed between the execution of **glBegin** and the corresponding execution of **glEnd**.

ASSOCIATED GETS

glGetInfoLogARB with argument *program*

glGetObjectParameterARB with arguments *program* and GL_OBJECT_ VALIDATE_STATUS_ARB

SEE ALSO

glLinkProgramARB, **glUseProgramObjectARB**

glVertexAttribARB

NAME

glVertexAttribARB—Specifies the value of a generic vertex attribute

C SPECIFICATION

```
void glVertexAttrib1fARB(GLuint index,
                         GLfloat v0)
void glVertexAttrib1sARB(GLuint index,
                         GLshort v0)
void glVertexAttrib1dARB(GLuint index,
                         GLdouble v0)

void glVertexAttrib2fARB(GLuint index,
                         GLfloat v0,
                         GLfloat v1)
void glVertexAttrib2sARB(GLuint index,
                         GLshort v0,
                         GLshort v1)
void glVertexAttrib2dARB(GLuint index,
                         GLdouble v0,
                         GLdouble v1)

void glVertexAttrib3fARB(GLuint index,
                         GLfloat v0,
                         GLfloat v1,
                         GLfloat v2)
void glVertexAttrib3sARB(GLuint index,
                         GLshort v0,
                         GLshort v1,
                         GLshort v2)
void glVertexAttrib3dARB(GLuint index,
                         GLdouble v0,
                         GLdouble v1,
                         GLdouble v2)

void glVertexAttrib4fARB(GLuint index,
                         GLfloat v0,
                         GLfloat v1,
                         GLfloat v2,
                         GLfloat v3)
```

```
void glVertexAttrib4sARB(GLuint index,
                         GLshort v0,
                         GLshort v1,
                         GLshort v2,
                         GLshort v3)
void glVertexAttrib4dARB(GLuint index,
                         GLdouble v0,
                         GLdouble v1,
                         GLdouble v2,
                         GLdouble v3)

void glVertexAttrib4NubARB(GLuint index,
                           GLubyte v0,
                           GLubyte v1,
                           GLubyte v2,
                           GLubyte v3)
```

PARAMETERS

index   Specifies the index of the generic vertex attribute to be
                 modified.

v0, v1, v2, v3   Specifies the new values to be used for the specified
                 vertex attribute.

C SPECIFICATION
```
void glVertexAttrib1fvARB(GLuint index, const GLfloat *v)
void glVertexAttrib1svARB(GLuint index, const GLshort *v)
void glVertexAttrib1dvARB(GLuint index, const GLdouble *v)

void glVertexAttrib2fvARB(GLuint index, const GLfloat *v)
void glVertexAttrib2svARB(GLuint index, const GLshort *v)
void glVertexAttrib2dvARB(GLuint index, const GLdouble *v)

void glVertexAttrib3fvARB(GLuint index, const GLfloat *v)
void glVertexAttrib3svARB(GLuint index, const GLshort *v)
void glVertexAttrib3dvARB(GLuint index, const GLdouble *v)

void glVertexAttrib4fvARB(GLuint index, const GLfloat *v)
void glVertexAttrib4svARB(GLuint index, const GLshort *v)
void glVertexAttrib4dvARB(GLuint index, const GLdouble *v)
void glVertexAttrib4ivARB(GLuint index, const GLint *v)
```

```
void glVertexAttrib4bvARB(GLuint index, const GLbyte *v)

void glVertexAttrib4ubvARB(GLuint index, const GLubyte *v)
void glVertexAttrib4usvARB(GLuint index, const GLushort *v)
void glVertexAttrib4uivARB(GLuint index, const GLuint *v)

void glVertexAttrib4NbvARB(GLuint index, const GLbyte *v)
void glVertexAttrib4NsvARB(GLuint index, const GLshort *v)
void glVertexAttrib4NivARB(GLuint index, const GLint *v)
void glVertexAttrib4NubvARB(GLuint index, const GLubyte *v)
void glVertexAttrib4NusvARB(GLuint index, const GLushort *v)
void glVertexAttrib4NuivARB(GLuint index, const GLuint *v)
```

PARAMETERS

index   Specifies the index of the generic vertex attribute to be
                   modified.

v   Specifies a pointer to an array of values to be used for
                   the generic vertex attribute.

DESCRIPTION

OpenGL defines a number of standard vertex attributes that applications can modify with standard API entry points (color, normal, texture coordinates, etc.). The **glVertexAttribARB** family of entry points allows an application to pass generic vertex attributes in numbered locations.

Generic attributes are defined as four-component values that are organized into an array. The first entry of this array is numbered 0, and the size of the array is specified by the implementation-dependent constant GL_MAX_VERTEX_ATTRIBS_ARB. Individual elements of this array can be modified with a **glVertexAttribARB** call that specifies the index of the element to be modified and a value for that element.

These commands can be used to specify one, two, three, or all four components of the generic vertex attribute specified by *index*. A **1** in the name of the command indicates that only one value is passed, and it will be used to modify the first component of the generic vertex attribute. The second and third components will be set to 0, and the fourth component will be set to 1. Similarly, a **2** in the name of the command indicates that values are provided for the first two components, the third component will be set to 0, and the fourth component will be set to 1. A **3** in the name of the command indicates that values are provided for the first three components and the fourth component will be set to 1, whereas a **4** in the name indicates that values are provided for all four components.

The letters **s**, **f**, **i**, **d**, **ub**, **us**, and **ui** indicate whether the arguments are of type short, float, int, double, unsigned byte, unsigned short, or unsigned int. When **v** is appended to the name, the commands can take a pointer to an array of such values. The commands containing **N** indicate that the arguments will be passed as fixed-point values that are scaled to a normalized range according to the component conversion rules defined by the OpenGL specification. Signed values are understood to represent fixed-point values in the range [-1,1], and unsigned values are understood to represent fixed-point values in the range [0,1].

OpenGL Shading Language attribute variables are allowed to be of type mat2, mat3, or mat4. Attributes of these types may be loaded using the **glVertexAttribARB** entry points. Matrices must be loaded into successive generic attribute slots in column major order, with one column of the matrix in each generic attribute slot.

A user-defined attribute variable declared in a vertex shader can be bound to a generic attribute index by calling **glBindAttribLocationARB**. This allows an application to use more appropriate variable names in a vertex shader. A subsequent change to the specified generic vertex attribute will be immediately reflected as a change to the specified attribute variable in the vertex shader.

The binding between a generic vertex attribute index and a user-defined attribute variable in a vertex shader is part of the state of a program object, but the current value of the generic vertex attribute is not. The value of each generic vertex attribute is part of current state, just like standard vertex attributes, and it is maintained even if a different program object is used.

An application may freely modify generic vertex attributes that are not bound to a named vertex shader attribute variable. These values are simply maintained as part of current state and will not be accessed by the vertex shader. If a generic vertex attribute bound to an attribute variable in a vertex shader is not updated while the vertex shader is executing, the vertex shader will repeatedly use the current value for the generic vertex attribute.

The generic vertex attribute with index 0 is the same as the vertex position attribute previously defined by OpenGL. A **glVertex2**, **glVertex3**, or **glVertex4** command is completely equivalent to the corresponding **glVertexAttribARB** command with an index argument of 0. A vertex shader can access generic vertex attribute 0 by using the built-in attribute variable *gl_Vertex*. There are no current values for generic vertex attribute 0. This is the only generic vertex attribute with this property; calls to set other standard vertex attributes can be freely mixed with calls to set any of the other generic vertex attributes.

NOTES

Generic vertex attributes can be updated at any time. In particular, **glVertexAttribARB** can be called between a call to **glBegin** and the corresponding call to **glEnd**.

It is possible for an application to bind more than one attribute name to the same generic vertex attribute index. This is referred to as aliasing, and it is allowed only if just one of the aliased attribute variables is active in the vertex shader, or if no path through the vertex shader consumes more than one of the attributes aliased to the same location. OpenGL implementations are not required to do error checking to detect aliasing, they are allowed to assume that aliasing will not occur, and they are allowed to employ optimizations that work only in the absence of aliasing.

There is no provision for binding standard vertex attributes; therefore, it is not possible to alias generic attributes with standard attributes.

ERRORS

GL_INVALID_VALUE is generated if *index* is greater than or equal to GL_MAX_VERTEX_ATTRIBS_ARB.

ASSOCIATED GETS

glGetVertexAttribARB with arguments GL_CURRENT_VERTEX_ATTRIB_ARB and *index*

glGetAttribLocationARB with arguments *program* and *name*

glGetActiveAttribARB with argument *program*

glGet with argument GL_MAX_VERTEX_ATTRIBS_ARB

SEE ALSO

glBindAttribLocationARB, glVertex, glVertexAttribPointerARB

glVertexAttribPointerARB

NAME

glVertexAttribPointerARB—Defines a generic vertex attribute array

C SPECIFICATION
```
void glVertexAttribPointerARB(GLuint index,
                              GLint size,
                              GLenum type,
                              GLboolean normalized,
                              GLsizei stride,
                              const GLvoid *pointer)
```

PARAMETERS

index	Specifies the index of the generic vertex attribute to be modified.
size	Specifies the number of values for each element of the generic vertex attribute array. Must be 1, 2, 3, or 4.
type	Specifies the data type of each component in the array. Symbolic constants GL_BYTE, GL_UNSIGNED_BYTE, GL_SHORT, GL_UNSIGNED_SHORT, GL_INT, GL_UNSIGNED_INT, GL_FLOAT, and GL_DOUBLE are accepted.
normalized	Specifies whether fixed-point data values should be normalized (GL_TRUE) or converted directly as fixed-point values (GL_FALSE) when they are accessed.
stride	Specifies the byte offset between consecutive attribute values. If *stride* is 0 (the initial value), the attribute values are understood to be tightly packed in the array.
pointer	Specifies a pointer to the first component of the first attribute value in the array.

DESCRIPTION

glVertexAttribPointerARB specifies the location and data format of an array of generic vertex attribute values to use when rendering. *size* specifies the number of components per attribute and must be 1, 2, 3, or 4. *type* specifies the data type of each component, and *stride* specifies the byte stride from one attribute to the next, allowing attribute values to be intermixed with other attribute values or stored in a separate array. If set to GL_TRUE, *normalize* indicates that values stored in an integer format are to be mapped to the range [–1,1] (for signed values) or [0,1] (for unsigned values) when they are accessed and converted to floating point. Otherwise, values will be converted to floats directly without normalization.

When a generic vertex attribute array is specified, *size*, *type*, *normalized*, *stride*, and *pointer* are saved as client-side state.

To enable and disable the generic vertex attribute array, call **glEnableVertexAttribArrayARB** and **glDisableVertexAttribArrayARB** with *index*. If enabled, the generic vertex attribute array is used when **glDrawArrays**, **glDrawElements**, **glDrawRangeElements**, **glArrayElement**, **glMultiDrawElements**, or **glMultiDrawArrays** is called.

NOTES

Each generic vertex attribute array is initially disabled and isn't accessed when **glDrawArrays**, **glDrawElements**, **glDrawRangeElements**, **glArrayElement**, **glMultiDrawElements**, or **glMultiDrawArrays** is called.

Execution of **glVertexAttribPointerARB** is not allowed between the execution of **glBegin** and **glEnd**, but an error may or may not be generated. If no error is generated, the operation is undefined.

glVertexAttribPointerARB is typically implemented on the client side.

Generic vertex attribute array parameters are client-side state and are therefore not saved or restored by **glPushAttrib** and **glPopAttrib**. Use **glPushClientAttrib** and **glPopClientAttrib** instead.

ERRORS

GL_INVALID_VALUE is generated if *index* is greater than or equal to GL_MAX_VERTEX_ATTRIBS_ARB.

GL_INVALID_VALUE is generated if *size* is not 1, 2, 3, or 4.

GL_INVALID_ENUM is generated if *type* is not an accepted value.

GL_INVALID_VALUE is generated if *stride* is negative.

ASSOCIATED GETS

glGetVertexAttribARB with argument *index*

glGetVertexAttribPointerARB with argument *index*

glGet with argument GL_MAX_VERTEX_ATTRIBS_ARB

SEE ALSO

glArrayElement, glBindAttribLocationARB, glDisableVertexAttribArrayARB, glDrawArrays, glDrawElements, glDrawRangeElements, glEnableVertexAttribArrayARB, glMultiDrawArrays, glMultiDrawElements, glPopClientAttrib, glPushClientAttrib, glVertexAttribARB

Afterword

Writing a book requires a lot of time and effort. Sometimes, authors refer to the finished product as "a labor of love." I have to say that for me, writing this book has been "a labor of fun."

I have been fortunate to participate in a major architectural revolution in computer graphics hardware. In the last few years, consumer graphics hardware has undergone a sea of change—from pure fixed functionality to almost complete user programmability. In many ways, this time feels like the late 1970s and early 1980s, when significant advances were being made in computer graphics at places like the University of Utah, NYU, Lucasfilm, JPL, UNC, and Cornell. The difference this time is that graphics hardware is now cheap enough and fast enough that you don't have to work at a research institute or attend an elite graduate school. You can explore the brave new world on your own personal computer.

It is relatively rare to participate in establishing even one industry standard, but I have had the good fortune to play a role in the definition of three important graphics standards. First was PEX in the late 1980s. Next was OpenGL in the early 1990s, and now, the OpenGL Shading Language in the first years of the new millenium. These efforts have been gratifying to me because they provide graphics hardware capabilities to people in an industry standard way. Applications written to a standard are portable, and therefore the technology they are built on is accessible to a wider audience.

It's been a labor of fun because it is a lot of fun and truly remarkable to be one of the first people to implement classic rendering algorithms using a high-level language on low-cost but high-performance graphics hardware.

When our team first got the brick shader running on 3Dlabs Wildcat VP graphics hardware, it was a jaw-dropping "Wow!" moment. A similar feeling occurred when I got a shader I was developing to run successfully for the first time or saw, working for the first time, a shader written by someone else in the group. It seems to me that this feeling must be similar to that felt by the graphics pioneers 20-25 years ago when they got the first successful results from their new algorithms. And it is great fun to hear from end users who experience those same sorts of jaw-dropping "Wow!" moments.

Because of the architectural revolution in consumer graphics hardware, today, people like you and me can quickly and easily write shaders that implement the rendering algorithms devised 20 years ago by the pioneers of computer graphics. In order to implement bump mapping, we looked up Blinn's 1978 paper, and in order to implement particle systems, we looked at Reeves's 1983 paper. I chuckled to myself when I saw the hand-drawn diagrams in Alvy Ray Smith's 1983 memo on digital filtering. Images that took hours to generate then take milliseconds to render today. And shader code that took weeks to develop can now be written in minutes using a high-level shading language developed specifically for this task. It is mind-boggling to think how painstaking it must have been for Mandelbrot to generate images of his famous set in the late 1970s, compared to how easy it is to do today using the OpenGL Shading Language.

And part of the reason that I've so enjoyed writing this book is that I know there are significant new discoveries to be made in the area of computer graphics. If someone like me can simply and easily implement rendering algorithms that previously could run only on software on CPUs, imagine how much more is possible with the programmable graphics hardware that is available today. The availability of low-cost programmable graphics hardware makes it possible for many more people to experiment with new rendering techniques. Algorithms of much higher complexity can be developed. And I know that some of you out there will invent some exciting new rendering techniques using the OpenGL Shading Language.

My mission in writing this book has been to educate you and, perhaps more important, to try and open your eyes to the rendering possibilities that exist beyond the fixed functionality with which we've been shackled for so many years. In my view, there's no longer any reason to continue to use the fixed functionality of OpenGL. Everyone should be writing shaders to render things the way they want instead of the way the fixed functionality graphics hardware has allowed. I encourage you to think outside the box, explore new ways of getting pixels on the screen, and share your discoveries with others. If you want, you can send your discoveries to me at randi@3dshaders.com. I'll include the best ones in the second edition of this book.

Keep on pushing the pixels, and best of luck in all your rendering endeavors!

—Randi Rost,
Fort Collins, CO
June 2003

Glossary

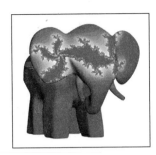

1D TEXTURE—A one-dimensional (width only) array of values stored in texture memory.

2D TEXTURE—A two-dimensional (width and height) array of values stored in texture memory.

3D TEXTURE—A three-dimensional (width, height, and depth) array of values stored in texture memory.

ACCUMULATION BUFFER—An OpenGL offscreen memory buffer that can be used to accumulate the results of multiple rendering operations. This buffer often has more bits per pixel than the other offscreen memory buffers in order to support such accumulation operations.

ACTIVE ATTRIBUTES—Attribute variables that may be accessed when a vertex shader is executed, including built-in attribute variables and user-defined attribute variables. (It is allowed to have attribute variables that are defined but never used within a vertex shader.)

ACTIVE SAMPLERS—Samplers that may be accessed when a program is executed.

ACTIVE UNIFORM VARIABLES—Uniform variables that may be accessed when a shader is executed, including built-in uniform variables and user-defined uniform variables. (It is allowed to have uniform variables that are defined but never used within a shader.)

ALIASING—Artifacts caused by insufficient sampling and/or inadequate representation of high frequency components in a computer graphics image. These artifacts are also commonly referred to as "jaggies."

ALPHA—The fourth component of a color value (after red, green, and blue). Alpha inidicates the opacity of a pixel (1.0 means the pixel is fully opaque; 0.0 means the pixel is fully transparent). Alpha is used in color blending operations.

ALPHA TEST—An OpenGL pipeline stage that discards fragments depending on the outcome of a comparison between the current fragment's alpha value and a constant reference alpha value.

AMPLITUDE—The distance of a maximum or minimum of a function from the mean of the function.

ANISOTROPIC—Something with properties that differ when measured in different directions, such as the property of a material (anisotropic reflection) or a characteristic of an algorithm (anisotropic texture filtering).

ANTIALIASING—The effort to reduce or eliminate artifacts caused by insufficient sampling or inadequate representation of high-frequency components in a computer graphics image.

APPLICATION PROGRAMMING INTERFACE (API)—A source-level interface provided for use by applications.

AREA SAMPLING—An antialiasing technique that considers the area of the primitive being sampled. This method usually produces better results than either point sampling or supersampling, but it can be more expensive to compute.

ATTENUATION—In regards to the lighting computation, this is the effect of light intensity diminishing as a function of distance from the light source.

ATTRIBUTE ALIASING—Binding more than one user-defined attribute variable to the same generic vertex attribute index. This is allowed only if just one of the aliased attributes is active in the executable program or if no path through the shader consumes more than one attribute of a set of attributes aliased to the same location.

ATTRIBUTE VARIABLE—An OpenGL Shading Language variable that is qualified with the **attribute** keyword. These variables contain the values passed by the application through the OpenGL API using generic, numbered vertex attributes. With attribute variables, a vertex shader can obtain unique data at every vertex. They are read-only and can be defined only in vertex shaders. Attribute variables are used to pass frequently changing data to a shader.

BIDIRECTIONAL REFLECTANCE DISTRIBUTION FUNCTION, BRDF—A model for computing the reflection from a surface with anisotropic reflection properties. The elevation and azimuth angles of the incoming and outgoing energy directions are used to compute the relative amount of energy reflected in the outgoing direction. Measurements of real-world materials can be used in this computation to create a more realistic looking surface.

BRDF—See BIDIRECTIONAL REFLECTANCE DISTRIBUTION FUNCTION.

BUMP MAP—A two-dimensional array of normal perturbation values that can be stored in texture memory.

BUMP MAPPING—A rendering technique that simulates the appearance of bumps, wrinkles, or other surface irregularities by perturbing surface normals prior to performing lighting calculations.

CALL-BY-VALUE-RETURN—A subroutine calling convention whereby input parameters are copied into the function at call time, and output parameters are copied back to the caller before the function exits.

CLIP SPACE—See CLIPPING COORDINATE SYSTEM.

CLIPPING—The process of comparing incoming graphics primitives to one or more reference planes and discarding any portion of primitives that are deemed to be outside of those reference planes.

CLIPPING COORDINATE SYSTEM—The coordinate system in which view-volume clipping occurs. Graphics primitives are transformed from the eye coordinate system into the clipping coordinate system by the projection matrix.

COLOR SUM—The OpenGL pipeline stage that adds together the primary color and the secondary color. This stage occurs after texturing in order to allow a specular highlight that is the color of the light source to be applied on top of the textured surface.

COMPILER FRONT END—The part of the compiler that performs lexical, syntactical, and semantic analysis of source code and produces a binary representation of the code that is suitable for consumption by subsequent phases of compilation.

CONSTRUCTOR— A programming language feature for initializing aggregate data types or converting between data types.

CONTROL TEXTURE—A texture map whose primary function is to provide values that are used to determine the behavior of a rendering algorithm rather than provide data for the rendering process.

CONVOLUTION—The weighted average of a function over a specified interval.

CONVOLUTION FILTER—See CONVOLUTION KERNEL.

CONVOLUTION KERNEL—The values that are used to do the weighting in a convolution operation.

CUBE MAP—A texture map comprised of six 2D textures that correspond to faces on a cube. The faces are identified by their axial direction ($\pm x$, $\pm y$, $\pm z$), and the proper face is automatically selected when performing a texture access.

CUBE MAPPING—The process of accessing the proper face of a cube map texture to retrieve the value that will be used in texture application. Cube mapping is one method for performing environment mapping.

CULLING—The act of discarding graphics primitives according to a particular criteria, whether they are back facing with respect to the current viewing position.

DEPENDENT TEXTURE READ—A texture access operation that depends on values obtained from a previous texture access operation.

DEPTH BUFFER—An OpenGL offscreen memory buffer that maintains depth values. This buffer can be used to store the depth of the topmost visible graphics primitive at each pixel. In conjunction with the depth test operation, this can be used to perform hidden surface elimination.

DEPTH-CUING—A graphics rendering technique that alters the appearance of a graphics primitive based on its distance from the viewer. This is often used to make the color of distant primitives fade to the background color in order to make them appear more distant.

DEPTH TEST—An OpenGL pipeline stage that does a comparison between the depth associated with the incoming fragment and the depth value retrieved from the frame buffer. If the test fails, the fragment is discarded.

DISPLAY LIST—A sequence of OpenGL commands are stored in OpenGL-managed memory for later execution.

DISPLAY LIST MODE—A mode of rendering in which OpenGL commands are stored in a display list for execution at a later time, rather than being executed when they are specified.

DISPLAY MEMORY—Frame buffer memory that is allocated to maintaining the image displayed on the computer monitor or LCD. Display memory is read many times per second (the refresh rate) and used to update the visible display surface.

DOUBLE BUFFERING—A graphics rendering technique that involves rendering to a back buffer while displaying a front buffer. When rendering is completed, the two buffers are swapped. In this way, the end user never sees partially complete images, and animation can be smoother and more realistic.

DRIVER—A piece of software that interacts with the native operating system and controls a specific piece of hardware in the system.

ENVIRONMENT MAPPING—A rendering technique that involves saving the scene surrounding an object as one or more specialized texture maps and then accessing these texture maps when rendering the object to compute accurate reflections of that environment.

EXECUTABLE—The machine code intended for execution on the vertex processor or the fragment processor.

EYE COORDINATE SYSTEM—The coordinate system that is defined to have the eye (viewing) position at the origin. Graphics primitives are transformed by the modelview matrix from the modeling (or object) coordinate system into the eye coordinate system.

EYE SPACE—see EYE COORDINATE SYSTEM.

FILTERING—The process of calculating a single value based on the values of multiple samples in the neighborhood of that value.

FIXED FUNCTIONALITY—The term used to describe portions of the OpenGL pipeline that are not programmable. These portions of OpenGL operate in a fixed fashion, and the behavior can only be altered by changing a predefined set of state variables through the OpenGL API.

FLAT SHADING—The term used to describe the application of a single color value to the extent of a primitive (contrast with SMOOTH SHADING).

FOG—A rendering technique that simulates atmospheric effects due to particulates such as those contained in clouds and smog. This is done by attenuating the object color as a function of distance from the viewer.

FRAGMENT—The set of data that is generated by rasterization and represents the information necessary to update a single frame buffer location. A fragment consists of a window coordinate position and associated data such as color, depth, texture coordinates, and the like.

FRAGMENT PROCESSING—An OpenGL pipeline stage that defines the operations that occur to a fragment produced by rasterization prior to the back-end processing stages. For OpenGL fixed functionality, this includes texture access, texture application, fog, and color sum. For the OpenGL programmable fragment processor, any type of per-fragment processing may be performed.

FRAGMENT PROCESSOR—A programmable unit that replaces the traditional fixed functionality fragment processing stage of OpenGL. Fragment shaders are executed on the fragment processor.

FRAGMENT SHADER—A program written in the OpenGL Shading Language that executes on the fragment processor. The fragment shader's **main** function is executed once for each fragment generated by rasterization and can be programmed to perform both traditional operations (texture access, texture application, fog) and nontraditional operations.

FRAME BUFFER—The region of graphics memory that is used to store the results of OpenGL rendering operations. Part of the frame buffer (the front buffer) is visible on the display device, and part of it is not.

FRAME BUFFER OPERATIONS—An OpenGL pipeline stage contaning operations that control or affect the whole frame buffer (e.g., buffer masking operations, buffer clear operations, etc.).

FREQUENCY—The measure of periodicity in a function (i.e., how often the pattern of a function repeats).

FRUSTUM—See VIEW FRUSTUM.

FRUSTUM CLIPPING—An OpenGL pipeline stage that clips primitives to the view frustum.

GEOMETRIC PRIMITIVE—A point, line, or polygon.

GLOSS MAP—A texture map that controls the reflective characteristics of a surface rather than supplying image data for the texturing operation.

GOOCH SHADING—A non-photorealistic rendering technique that attempts to duplicate the look of a technical illustration. This technique is also called a low dynamic range artistic tone algorithm.

GOURAUD SHADING—See SMOOTH SHADING.

GRADIENT—The measure of how rapidly a function is changing in a particular direction. Properly, this is a vector (see GRADIENT VECTOR). More commonly, the magnitude of the gradient vector for the function $f(x,y)$ in a particular direction is referred to as the gradient of the function $f(x,y)$ in that direction.

GRADIENT NOISE—See PERLIN NOISE.

GRADIENT VECTOR—A vector that defines the rate of change of a function in all directions. The gradient vector for the function $f(x,y)$ contains two components: the partial derivative of f with respect to x and the partial derivative of f with respect to y.

GRAPHICS ACCELERATOR—Hardware dedicated to the process of rendering and displaying graphics.

GRAPHICS CONTEXT—The OpenGL data structure that contains the state needed to control the operation of the rendering pipeline.

GRAPHICS PROCESSING PIPELINE—The sequence of operations that occurs when geometry or image data defined by an application is transformed into something that is stored in the frame buffer. This processing is divided into stages that occur in a specific order. Each stage has defined inputs and outputs and can be succintly described.

IMAGING SUBSET—A collection of functionality related to imaging that was added to OpenGL as an optional subset in OpenGL 1.2. The imaging subset contains support for color matrix, convolution, histogram, and various blending operations. Graphics hardware vendors are not required to support this functionality as part of their OpenGL implementation.

IMMEDIATE MODE—A mode of rendering in which graphics commands are executed when they are specified, rather than being stored in a display list to be executed at a later time.

ISOTROPIC—Something with properties that are the same along a pair of orthogonal axes from which they are measured (i.e., rotationally invariant). Contrast with ANISOTROPIC.

KEY-FRAME INTERPOLATION—An animation technique that produces "in-between" results based on interpolation between two key frames. This can save time and effort because the objects in the scene do not need to be painstakingly animated for every frame, only for those frames that provide the key to the overall animation sequence.

L-VALUE—An expression identifying an object in memory that can be written to. For example, variables that are writable are l-values. Array indexing and structure member selection are expressions that can result in l-values.

LEVEL-OF-DETAIL—The value that is used to select a mipmap level from a mipmap texture. Incrementing the level-of-detail by 1 results in selecting a mipmap level that is half the resolution of the previous one. Thus, increasing the value used for level-of-detail will result in the selection of mipmap levels that contain smaller and smaller textures (suitable for use on smaller and smaller objects on the screen).

LEXICAL ANALYSIS—The process of scanning the input text to produce a sequence of tokens (or terminal symbols) for the syntactical analysis phase that follows. Characters or tokens that are not part of the language can be identified as errors during this process. Sometimes this is also referred to as scanning.

LOW-PASS FILTERING—A method of filtering that eliminates high frequencies but leaves low frequencies unmodified. Low-pass filters are sometimes called SMOOTHING FILTERS because high frequencies are blurred (smoothed).

MIPMAP LEVEL—A specific texel array within a mipmap texture.

MIPMAP TEXTURE— An ordered set of texel arrays representing the same image. Typically, each array has a resolution that is half the previous one in each dimension.

MODEL SPACE—See MODELING COORDINATE SYSTEM.

MODEL TRANSFORMATION MATRIX— The matrix that is used to transform coordinates from the modeling coordinate system into the world coordinate system. In OpenGL, this matrix is not available separately; it is always part of the modelview matrix.

MODELING—The process of defining a numerical representation of an object that is to be rendered, for instance, defining the Bezier curves that specify a teapot, or the vertex positions, colors, surface normals, and texture coordinates that define a bowling pin.

MODELING COORDINATE SYSTEM— A coordinate system that is defined in a way that is convenient for the specification and orientation of a single object.

MODELING TRANSFORMATION—The transformation that takes coordinates from the modeling coordinate system into the world coordinate system.

MODELVIEW MATRIX—The matrix that is used to transform coordinates from the modeling coordinate system into the eye coordinate system.

MODELVIEW-PROJECTION MATRIX—The matrix that is used to transform coordinates from the modeling coordinate system into the clipping coordinate system.

MULTISAMPLE BUFFER—A region of offscreen memory that can be used to perform supersampling by maintaining more than one sample per pixel and automatically averaging them to produce the final, antialiased image.

NEIGHBORHOOD AVERAGING—An image processing technique that can be used to low-pass filter (smooth) an image by computing the weighted average of pixels in close proximity to each other.

NOISE—A continuous, irregular function with a defined range that can be used to create complex and interesting patterns.

NON-PHOTOREALISTIC RENDERING (NPR)—A class of rendering techniques whose purpose is to achieve something other than the most realistic result possible. Such techniques may strive to achieve a painterly or hand-drawn appearance, the look of a technical illustration, or a cartoon-like appearance. Hatching and Gooch shading are examples of non-photorealistic rendering (NPR) techniques.

NORMAL MAP—A texture map that contains normals rather than image data.

NORMALIZED DEVICE COORDINATE SPACE—The coordinate space that contains the view volume in an axis-aligned cube with a minimum corner at $(-1,-1,-1)$ and a maximum corner at $(1,1,1)$.

NPR—See NON-PHOTOREALISTIC RENDERING.

OBJECT COORDINATE SYSTEM—See MODELING COORDINATE SYSTEM.

OBJECT SPACE—See MODELING COORDINATE SYSTEM.

OCTAVE—Two frequencies that are related by a ratio of 2:1.

OFFSCREEN MEMORY—Frame buffer memory that is used to store things that are never directly visible on the display screen such as depth buffers and textures (contrast with DISPLAY MEMORY).

OPENGL SHADER—A term applied to a shader written in the OpenGL Shading Language to differentiate from a shader written in another shading language.

OPENGL SHADING LANGUAGE—The high-level programming language defined to allow application writers to write programs that execute on the programmable processors defined within OpenGL.

OPENGL SHADING LANGUAGE API—The set of function calls that have been added to OpenGL in order to allow OpenGL shaders to be created, deleted, queried, compiled, linked, and used.

PARSING—See SYNTACTIC ANALYSIS.

PARTICLE SYSTEM—A rendering primitive that consists of a large number of points or short lines that are suitable for rendering a class of objects with ill-defined boundaries (e.g., fire, sparks, liquid sprays, etc.).

PER-FRAGMENT OPERATIONS—An OpenGL pipeline stage that occurs after fragment processing and before frame buffer operations. It includes a variety of tests aimed at determining whether the fragment should be used to update the frame buffer, such as the stencil, alpha, and depth tests.

PERLIN NOISE—A noise function that is defined to have a value of 0 for integer input values and whose variability is introduced by defining pseudorandom gradient values at each of those points. Also called GRADIENT NOISE.

PHOTOREALISM—The effort to use computer graphics to model, render, and animate a scene in such a way that it is indistinguishable from a photograph or film sequence of the same scene in real life.

PIXEL GROUP—A value that will ultimately be used to update the frame buffer (i.e., a color, depth, or stencil value).

PIXEL OWNERSHIP TEST—An OpenGL pipeline stage that decides whether a fragment can be used to update the frame buffer or whether the targeted frame buffer location belongs to another window or to another OpenGL graphics context.

PIXEL PACKING—An OpenGL pipeline stage that writes pixels retrieved from OpenGL into application-controlled memory.

PIXEL RECTANGLE—A rectangular array of pixels (i.e., an image).

PIXEL TRANSFER—An OpenGL pipeline stage that processes pixel data while it is being transferred within OpenGL. Operations that can occur at this stage include scaling and biasing, lookup table operations, convolution, histogram, color matrix, and so on.

PIXEL UNPACKING—An OpenGL pipeline stage that reads pixels (i.e., image data) from application-controlled memory and sends them on for further processing by OpenGL.

POINT SAMPLING—The process of determining the value at each pixel by sampling the function at just one point. This is the typical behavior of graphics hardware and many graphics algorithms, and it can lead to aliasing artifacts. Contrast with SUPERSAMPLING and AREA SAMPLING.

POLYNOMIAL TEXTURE MAP (PTM)—A light-dependent texture map that can be used to reconstruct the color of a surface under varying lighting conditions.

PRIMITIVE ASSEMBLY—An OpenGL pipeline stage that occurs after vertex processing that assembles individual vertex values into a primitive. The primary function of this stage is to buffer vertex values until there are enough to define the desired primitive. Points require one vertex, lines require two, triangles require three, and so on.

PRIMITIVES—In OpenGL parlance, things that can be rendered: points, lines, polygons, bitmaps, and images.

PROCEDURAL TEXTURE SHADER—A shader that produces its results primarily by synthesis rather than relying heavily on precomputed values.

PROCEDURAL TEXTURING—The process of computing a texture primarily by synthesis rather than relying heavily on precomputed values.

PROGRAM OBJECT—An OpenGL-managed data structure that is used as a container object for one or more shader objects. Program objects are used when linking shaders together. The result of linking a program object is one or more executables that are part of the program object and can be installed as part of current state.

PROJECTION MATRIX—The matrix that is used to transform coordinates from the eye coordinate system to the clipping coordinate system.

PROJECTION TRANSFORMATION—The transformation that takes coordinates from the eye coordinate system into the clipping coordinate system.

PTM—See POLYNOMIAL TEXTURE MAP.

PULSE TRAIN—A periodic function that varies abruptly between two values (i.e., a square wave).

R-VALUE—An expression identifying a declared or temporary object in memory that can be read—for example, a variable name is an r-value, but function names are not. Expressions result in r-values.

RASTER POSITION—A piece of OpenGL state that is used to position bitmap and image write operations.

RASTERIZATION—The process of converting graphics primitives such as points, lines, polygons, bitmaps, and images into fragments.

READ CONTROL—An OpenGL pipeline stage that contains state to define the region of frame buffer memory that is read during pixel read operations.

RENDERING—The process of converting geometry or image data defined by an application into something that is stored in the frame buffer.

RENDERING PIPELINE—See GRAPHICS PROCESSING PIPELINE.

SAMPLER—An opaque data type in the OpenGL Shading Language that is used to store the information needed to access a particular texture from within a shader.

SCANNING—See LEXICAL ANALYSIS.

SCISSOR TEST—An OpenGL pipeline stage that, when enabled, allows drawing operations to occur only within a specific rectangular region that has been defined in window coordinates.

SEMANTIC ANALYSIS—The process of determining whether the input text conforms to the semantic rules defined or implied by a programming language. Semantic errors in the input text can be identified during this phase of compilation.

SHADER—Source code written in the OpenGL Shading Language that is intended for execution on one of OpenGL's programmable processors.

SHADER OBJECT—An OpenGL-managed data structure that is used to store the source code and the compiled code for a shader written in the OpenGL Shading Language. Shader objects can be compiled, and compiled shader objects can be linked together to produce executable code (see PROGRAM OBJECT).

SMOOTH SHADING—The term used to describe the application of linearly interpolated color values across the extent of a primitive (contrast with FLAT SHADING). Also called GOURAUD SHADING.

SMOOTHING FILTERS—See LOW-PASS FILTERING.

SPHERE MAPPING—A method for performing environment mapping that simulates the projection of the environment onto a sphere surrounding the object to be rendered. The mapped environment is treated as a 2D texture map and accessed using the polar coordinates of the reflection vector.

STENCIL BUFFER—An offscreen region of frame buffer memory that can be used together with the stencil test for masking regions. A complex shape can be stored in the stencil buffer, and subsequent drawing operations can use the contents of the stencil buffer to determine whether to update each pixel.

STENCIL TEST—An OpenGL pipeline stage that conditionally eliminates a pixel based on a comparison between the value stored in the stencil buffer and a reference value. Applications can specify the action taken when the stencil test fails, the action taken when the stencil test passes and the depth test fails, and the action to be taken when both the stencil test and the depth test pass.

SUPERSAMPLING—A rendering technique that involves taking two or more point samples per pixel and then filtering these values to determine the value to be used for the pixel. Supersampling does not eliminate aliasing, but it can reduce it to the point it is no longer objectionable.

SURFACE-LOCAL COORDINATE SPACE—A coordinate system that assumes that each point on a surface is at (0,0,0) and that the unperturbed surface normal at each point is (0,0,1).

SWIZZLE—To duplicate or switch around the order of the components of a vector (e.g, to create a value that contains alpha, green, blue, red from one that contains red, green, blue, alpha).

SYNTACTIC ANALYSIS—The process of determining whether the structure of an input text is valid according to the grammar that defines the language. Syntax errors in the input text can be identified during this phase of compilation. Sometimes referred to as parsing.

TANGENT SPACE—A particular surface-local coordinate system that is defined with a tangent vector as one of the basis vectors.

T&L—See TRANSFORMATION AND LIGHTING.

TEMPORAL ALIASING—Aliasing artifacts that are caused by insufficient sampling in the time domain or inadequate representation of objects that are in motion.

TEXEL—A single pixel in a texture map.

TEXTURE ACCESS—The process of reading from a texture map in texture memory, including the filtering that occurs, the level-of-detail calculation for mipmap textures, and so on.

TEXTURE APPLICATION—The process of using the value read from texture memory to compute the color of a fragment. OpenGL's fixed functionality has fixed formulas for this process, but with programmability, this operation has become much more general.

TEXTURE MAPPING—The combination of texture access and texture application. Traditionally, this involves reading image data from a texture map stored in texture memory and using it as the color for the primitive being rendered. With programmability, this operation has become much more general.

TEXTURE MEMORY—A region of memory on the graphics board that is used for storing textures.

TEXTURE OBJECT—The OpenGL-managed data structure that contains information that describes a texture map, including the texels that define the texture, the wrapping behavior, the filtering method, and so on.

TEXTURE UNIT—An OpenGL abstraction for the graphics hardware that performs texture access and texture application. Since version 1.2, OpenGL has allowed the possibility of more than one texture unit, thus allowing access to more than one texture at a time.

TEXTURING—See TEXTURE MAPPING.

TRANSFORMATION AND LIGHTING (T&L)—The process of converting vertex positions from object coordinates into window coordinates, and for converting vertex colors into colors that are displayable on the screen, taking into account the effects of simulated light sources.

TURBULENCE—A variation of Perlin noise that adds together noise functions of different frequencies that include an absolute value function to introduce discontinuities to the function and give the appearance of turbulent flow.

UNIFORM VARIABLE—An OpenGL Shading Language variable that is qualified with the **uniform** keyword. The values for these variables are provided by the application or through OpenGL state. They are read-only from within a shader and may be accessed from either vertex shaders or fragment shaders. They are used to pass data that changes relatively infrequently.

UNSHARP MASKING—A method of sharpening an image by subtracting a blurred version of the image from itself.

USER CLIPPING—An OpenGL operation that compares graphics primitives to user-specified clipping planes in eye space and discards everything that is deemed to be outside the intersection of those clipping planes.

VALUE NOISE—A noise function that is defined by assigning pseudorandom values in a defined range (e.g., [0,1] or [–1,1]) to each integer input value and then smoothly interpolating between those values.

VARYING VARIABLE—An OpenGL Shading Language variable that is qualified with the **varying** keyword. These variables are defined at each vertex and interpolated across a graphics primitive to produce a perspective-correct value at each fragment. They must be declared in both the vertex shader and the fragment shader with the same type. They are the output values from vertex shaders and the input values for fragment shaders.

VERTEX—A point in three-dimensional space.

VERTEX ATTRIBUTES—Values that are associated with a vertex. OpenGL defines both standard and generic vertex attributes. Standard attributes include vertex position, color, normal, and texture coordinates. Generic vertex attributes can be defined to be arbitrary data values that are passed to OpenGL for each vertex.

VERTEX PROCESSING—An OpenGL pipeline stage that defines the operations that occur to each vertex from the time the vertex is provided to OpenGL until the primitive assembly stage. For OpenGL fixed functionality, this includes transformation, lighting, texure coordinate generation, and other operations. For the OpenGL programmable vertex processor, any type of per-vertex processing may be performed.

VERTEX PROCESSOR—A programmable unit that replaces the traditional fixed functionality vertex processing stage of OpenGL. Vertex shaders are executed on the vertex processor.

VERTEX SHADER—A program written in the OpenGL Shading Language that executes on the vertex processor. The vertex shader is executed once for each vertex provided to OpenGL and can be programmed to perform both traditional operations (transformation, lighting) and nontraditional operations.

VIEW FRUSTUM—The view volume after it has been warped by the perspective division calculation.

VIEW VOLUME—The volume in the clipping coordinate system whose coordinates x, y, z, and w all satisfy the conditions that $-w <= x <= w$, $-w <= y <= w$, and $-w <= z <= w$. Any portion of a geometric primitive that extends beyond this volume will be clipped.

VIEWING MATRIX—The matrix that is used to transform coordinates from the world coordinate sytem into the eye coordinate system. In OpenGL, this matrix is not available separately; it is always part of the modelview matrix.

VIEWING TRANSFORMATION—The transformation that takes coordinates from the world coordinate system into the eye coordinate system.

VIEWPORT TRANSFORMATION—The transformation that takes coordinates from the normalized device coordinate system into the window coordinate system.

WINDOW COORDINATES—The coordinate system used to identify pixels within a window on the display device. In this coordinate system, x values range from 0 to the width of the window minus 1, and y values range from 0 the height of the window minus 1. OpenGL defines the pixel with window coordinates (0,0) to be the pixel at the lower-left corner of the window.

WORLD COORDINATE SYSTEM—A coordinate system that is defined in a way that is convenient for the placement and orientation of all of the objects in a scene.

WORLD SPACE—See WORLD COORDINATE SYSTEM.

Further Reading

This section contains references to other useful papers, articles, books, and Web sites. Over the course of time, some Web addresses may change. Please see this book's companion Web site at http://3dshaders.com for an expanded and up-to-date list of references.

3Dlabs developer Web site. http://www.3dlabs.com/support/developer.

Abram, G. D., and T. Whitted, *Building Block Shaders*, Computer Graphics (SIGGRAPH '90 Proceedings), pp. 283–288, August 1990.

Akenine-Möller, Tomas, and E. Haines, *Real-Time Rendering, Second Edition*, A K Peters, Ltd., Natick, Massachusetts, 2002. http://www.realtimerendering.com

Apodaca, Anthony A., and Larry Gritz, *Advanced RenderMan: Creating CGI for Motion Pictures*, Morgan Kaufmann Publishers, San Francisco, 1999. http://www.bmrt.org/arman/materials.html

Arvo, James, ed., *Graphics Gems II*, Academic Press, San Diego, 1991. http://www.acm.org/pubs/tog/GraphicsGems

ATI developer Web site. http://www.ati.com/na/pages/resource_centre/dev_rel/devrel.html

Baldwin, Dave, *OpenGL 2.0 Shading Language White Paper, Version 1.2*, 3Dlabs, February 2002. http://www.3dlabs.com/support/developer/ogl2

Blinn, James, *Models of Light Reflection for Computer Synthesized Pictures*, Computer Graphics (SIGGRAPH '77 Proceedings), pp. 192–198, July 1977.

———, *Simulation of Wrinkled Surfaces*, Computer Graphics (SIGGRAPH '78 Proceedings), pp. 286–292, August 1978.

———, *Light Reflection Functions for Simulation of Clouds and Dusty Surfaces*, Computer Graphics (SIGGRAPH '82 Proceedings), pp. 21–29, July 1982.

Blinn, James, and M.E. Newell, *Texture and Reflection in Computer Generated Images*, Communications of the ACM, vol. 19, no. 10, pp. 542–547, October 1976.

Cabral, B., N., Max, and R. Springmeyer, *Bidirectional Reflection Functions from Surface Bump Maps*, Computer Graphics (SIGGRAPH '87 Proceedings), pp. 273–281, July 1987.

Card, Drew, and Jason L. Mitchell, *Non-Photorealistic Rendering with Pixel and Vertex Shaders*, in Engel, Wolfgang, ed., ShaderX, Wordware, May 2002. http://www.shaderx.com

Cook, Robert L., and Kenneth E. Torrance, *A Reflectance Model for Computer Graphics*, Computer Graphics (SIGGRAPH '81 Proceedings), pp. 307–316, July 1981.

———, *A Reflectance Model for Computer Graphics*, ACM Transactions on Graphics, vol. 1, no. 1, pp. 7–24, January 1982.

Cook, Robert L., *Shade Trees*, Computer Graphics (SIGGRAPH '84 Proceedings), pp. 223–231, July 1984.

———, *Stochastic Sampling in Computer Graphics*, ACM Transactions on Graphics, vol. 5, no. 1, pp. 51–72, January 1986.

Cornell University Program of Computer Graphics Measurement Data. http://www.graphics.cornell.edu/online/measurements

Crow, Franklin C., *The Aliasing Problem in Computer-Generated Shaded Images*, Communications of the ACM, 20(11), pp. 799–805, November 1977.

———, *Summed-Area Tables for Texture Mapping*, Computer Graphics (SIGGRAPH '84 Proceedings), pp. 207–212, July 1984.

Curtis, Cassidy J., Sean E. Anderson, Kurt W. Fleischer, and David H. Salesin, *Computer-Generated Watercolor*, Computer Graphics (SIGGRAPH '97 Proceedings), pp. 421–430, August 1997. http://citeseer.nj.nec.com/curtis97computergenerated.html

Curtis, Cassidy J., *Loose and Sketchy Animation*, SIGGRAPH '98 Technical Sketch, p. 317, 1998. http://www.otherthings.com/uw/loose/sketch.html

Dawson, Bruce, *What Happened to My Colours!?!* Game Developers Conference, pp. 251–268, March 2001. http://www.gdconf.com/archives/proceedings/2001/prog_papers.html

Delphi3D Web site. http://delphi3d.net

DeLoura, Mark, ed., *Game Programming Gems*, Charles River Media, Hingham, Massachusetts, 2000.

———, *Game Programming Gems II*, Charles River Media, Hingham, Massachusetts, 2001.

———, *Game Programming Gems III*, Charles River Media, Hingham, Massachusetts, 2002.

Derbyshire, Paul, *PGD's Quick Guide to the Mandelbrot Set*, personal Web site. http://www.globalserve.net/~derbyshire/manguide.html (defunct)

Dippé, Mark A. Z., and Erling Henry Wold, *Antialiasing Through Stochastic Sampling*, Computer Graphics (SIGGRAPH '85 Proceedings), pp. 69–78, July 1985.

Duff, Tom, *Compositing 3-D Rendered Images*, Computer Graphics (SIGGRAPH '85 Proceedings), pp. 41–44, July 1985.

Ebert, David S., John Hart, Bill Mark, F. Kenton Musgrave, Darwyn Peachey, Ken Perlin, and Steven Worley, *Texturing and Modeling: A Procedural Approach, Third Edition*, Morgan Kaufmann Publishers, San Francisco, 2002. http://www.texturingandmodeling.com

Fernando, Randima, and Mark J. Kilgard, *The Cg Tutorial: The Definitive Guide to Programmable Real-Time Graphics*, Addison-Wesley, Boston, Massachusetts, 2003.

Foley, J.D., A. van Dam, S.K. Feiner, J.F. Hughes, and R.L. Philips, *Introduction to Computer Graphics*, Addison-Wesley, Reading, Massachusetts, 1994.

Foley, J.D., A. van Dam, S.K. Feiner, and J.F. Hughes, *Computer Graphics: Principles and Practice in C, Second Edition*, Addison-Wesley, Reading, Massachusetts, 1996.

Fosner, Ron, *Real-Time Shader Programming, Covering DirectX 9.0*, Morgan Kaufmann Publishers, San Francisco, 2003.

Freudenberg, Bert, Maic Masuch, and Thomas Strothotte, *Walk-Through Illustrations: Frame-Coherent Pen-and-Ink Style in a Game Engine*, Computer Graphics Forum, vol. 20 (2001), no. 3, Manchester, U.K. http://isgwww.cs.uni-magdeburg.de/~bert/publications

———, *Real-Time Halftoning: A Primitive For Non-Photorealistic Shading*, Rendering Techniques 2002, Proceedings 13th Eurographics Workshop, pp. 227–231, 2002. http://isgwww.cs.uni-magdeburg.de/~bert/publications

Freudenberg, Bert and Maic Masuch, *Non-Photorealistic Shading in an Educational Game Engine*, SIGGRAPH and Eurographics Campfire, Snowbird, Utah, June 1–June 4, 2002. http://isgwww.cs.uni-magdeburg.de/~bert/publications

Freudenberg, Bert, *A Non-Photorealistic Fragment Shader in OpenGL 2.0*, Presented at the SIGGRAPH 2002 Exhibition in San Antonio, July 2002. http://isgwww.cs.uni-magdeburg.de/~bert/publications

———, *Stroke-based Real-Time Halftoning Rendering*, Ph.D. thesis, University of Magdeburg, submitted in 2003.

Glassner, Andrew S., ed., *Graphics Gems*, Academic Press, San Diego, 1990. http://www.acm.org/pubs/tog/GraphicsGems

Glassner, Andrew S., *Principles of Digital Image Synthesis*, vol. 1, Morgan Kaufmann Publishers, San Francisco, 1995.

————, *Principles of Digital Image Synthesis*, vol. 2, Morgan Kaufmann Publishers, San Francisco, 1995.

Gonzalez, Rafael C., and Richard E. Woods, *Digital Image Processing, Second Edition*, Prentice Hall, Upper Saddle River, New Jersey, 2002.

Gooch, Amy, *Interactive Non-Photorealistic Technical Illustration*, Master's thesis, University of Utah, December 1998.
http://www.cs.utah.edu/~gooch/publication.html

Gooch, Amy, Bruce Gooch, Peter Shirley, and Elaine Cohen, *A Non-Photorealistic Lighting Model for Automatic Technical Illustration*, Computer Graphics (SIGGRAPH '98 Proceedings), pp. 447–452, July 1998.
http://www.cs.utah.edu/~gooch/publication.html

Gooch, Bruce, Peter-Pike J. Sloan, Amy Gooch, Peter Shirley, and Richard Riesenfeld, *Interactive Technical Illustration*, Proceedings 1999 Symposium on Interactive 3D Graphics, pp. 31–38, April 1999.
http://www.cs.utah.edu/~gooch/publication.html

Gooch, Bruce, and Amy Gooch, *Non-Photorealistic Rendering*, A K Peters Ltd., Natick, Massachusetts, 2001. http://www.cs.utah.edu/~gooch/book.html

Goral, Cindy M., K. Torrance, D. Greenberg, and B. Battaile, *Modeling the Interaction of Light Between Diffuse Surfaces*, Computer Graphics (SIGGRAPH '84 Proceedings), pp. 213–222, July 1984.

Gouraud, H., *Continuous Shading of Curved Surfaces*, IEEE Transactions on Computers, vol. C-20, pp. 623–629, June 1971.

Greene, Ned, *Environment Mapping and Other Applications of World Projections*, IEEE Computer Graphics and Applications, vol. 6, no. 11, pp. 21–29, November 1986.

Gruschel, Jens, *Blend Modes*, Pegtop Software Web site.
http://www.pegtop.net/delphi/blendmodes

Haeberli, Paul, *Paint by Numbers: Abstract Image Representation*, Computer Graphics (SIGGRAPH '90 Proceedings), pp. 207–214, August 1990.

————, *Matrix Operations for Image Processing*, Silicon Graphics Inc., 1993.
http://www.sgi.com/grafica/matrix/index.html

Haeberli, Paul, and Douglas Voorhies, *Image Processing by Interpolation and Extrapolation*, IRIS Universe Magazine, no. 28, Silicon Graphics, August 1994. http://www.sgi.com/grafica/interp/index.html

Haeberli, Paul, and Kurt Akeley, *The Accumulation Buffer: Hardware Support for High-Quality Rendering*, Computer Graphics (SIGGRAPH '90 Proceedings), pp. 289–298, August 1990.

Haeberli, Paul, and Mark Segal, *Texture Mapping as a Fundamental Drawing Primitive*, 4th Eurographics Workshop on Rendering, pp. 259–266, 1993.
http://www.sgi.com/grafica/texmap/index.html

Hall, Roy, *Illumination and Color in Computer Generated Imagery*, Springer-Verlag, New York, 1989.

Hanrahan, Pat, and Wolfgang Krueger, *Reflection From Layered Surfaces Due to Subsurface Scattering*, Computer Graphics (SIGGRAPH '93 Proceedings), pages 165–174, August 1993.
http://www-graphics.stanford.edu/papers/subsurface

Hanrahan, Pat, and J. Lawson, *A Language for Shading and Lighting Calculations*, Computer Graphics (SIGGRAPH '90 Proceedings), pp. 289–298, August 1990.

Hart, Evan, Dave Gosselin, and John Isidoro, *Vertex Shading with Direct3D and OpenGL*, Game Developers Conference, San Jose, March 2001.
http://www.ati.com/na/pages/resource_centre/dev_rel/techpapers.html

Hart, John C., *Perlin Noise Pixel Shaders*, ACM SIGGRAPH/Eurographics Workshop on Graphics Hardware, pp. 87–94, August 2001.
http://graphics.cs.uiuc.edu/~jch/papers/pixelnoise.pdf

Heckbert, Paul S., *Survey of Texture Mapping*, IEEE Computer Graphics and Applications, vol. 6, no. 11, pp. 56–67, November 1986.
http://www.cs.cmu.edu/~ph

———, *Fundamentals of Texture Mapping and Image Warping*, Report No. 516, Computer Science Division, University of California, Berkeley, June 1989.
http://www.cs.cmu.edu/~ph

———, ed., *Graphics Gems IV*, Academic Press, San Diego, 1994.
http://www.acm.org/pubs/tog/GraphicsGems

Heidrich, Wolfgang, and Hans-Peter Seidel, *View-Independent Environment Maps*, ACM SIGGRAPH/Eurographics Workshop on Graphics Hardware, pp. 39–45, August 1998.

———, *Realistic, Hardware-Accelerated Shading and Lighting*, Computer Graphics (SIGGRAPH '99 Proceedings), pp. 171–178, August 1999.
http://www.cs.ubc.ca/~heidrich/Papers

Heidrich, Wolfgang, *Environment Maps and Their Applications*, SIGGRAPH 2000, Course 27, course notes.
http://www.csee.umbc.edu/~olano/s2000c27/envmap.pdf

Hertzmann, Aaron, *Painterly Rendering with Curved Brush Strokes of Multiple Sizes*, Computer Graphics (SIGGRAPH '98 Proceedings), pp. 453–460, 1998.
http://mrl.nyu.edu/publications/painterly98

———, *Introduction to 3D Non-Photorealistic Rendering: Silhouettes and Outlines*, SIGGRAPH '99 Non-Photorealistic Rendering course notes, 1999.
http://www.mrl.nyu.edu/~hertzman/hertzmann-intro3d.pdf

Hewlett-Packard, *Polynomial Texture Mapping*, Web site.
http://www.hpl.hp.com/ptm

Hook, Brian, *Multipass Rendering and the Magic of Alpha Blending*, Game Developer, vol. 4, no. 5, pp. 12–19, August 1997.

Hughes, John F., and Tomas Möller, *Building an Orthonormal Basis from a Unit Vector*, journal of graphics tools, vol. 4, no. 4, pp. 33–35, 1999. http://www.acm.org/jgt/papers/HughesMoller99

International Lighting Vocabulary, Publication CIE No. 17.4, Joint publication IEC (International Electrotechnical Commission) and CIE (Committee Internationale de L'Èclairage), Geneva, 1987. http://www.cie.co.at/framepublications.html

ITU-R Recommendation BT.709, *Basic Parameter Values for the HDTV Standard for the Studio and for International Programme Exchange*, [formerly CCIR Rec. 709], Geneva, ITU, 1990.

Kajiya, James T., *Anisotropic Reflection Models*, Computer Graphics (SIGGRAPH '85 Proceedings), pp. 15–21, July 1985.

———, *The Rendering Equation*, Computer Graphics (SIGGRAPH '86 Proceedings), pp. 143–150, August 1986.

Kaplan, Matthew, Bruce Gooch, and Elaine Cohen, *Interactive Artistic Rendering*, Proceedings of the First International Symposium on Non-Photorealistic Animation and Rendering (NPAR), pp. 67–74, June 2000. http://www.cs.utah.edu/npr/utah_papers.html

Kautz, Jan, and Michael D. McCool, *Interactive Rendering with Arbitrary BRDFs Using Separable Approximations*, 10th Eurographics Workshop on Rendering, pp. 281–292, June 1999. http://www.mpi-sb.mpg.de/~jnkautz/publications

———, *Approximation of Glossy Reflection with Prefiltered Environment Maps*, Graphics Interface 2000, pp. 119–126, May 2000. http://www.mpi-sb.mpg.de/~jnkautz/publications

Kautz, Jan, P.-P. Vázquez, W. Heidrich, and H.-P. Seidel, *A Unified Approach to Prefiltered Environment Maps*, 11th Eurographics Workshop on Rendering, pp. 185–196, June 2000. http://www.mpi-sb.mpg.de/~jnkautz/publications

Kautz, Jan, and Hans-Peter Seidel, *Hardware Accelerated Displacement Mapping for Image Based Rendering*, Graphics Interface 2001, pp. 61–70, May 2001.

———, *Towards Interactive Bump Mapping with Anisotropic Shift-Variant BRDFs*, ACM SIGGRAPH/Eurographics Workshop on Graphics Hardware, pp. 51–58, 2000. http://www.mpi-sb.mpg.de/~jnkautz/projects/anisobumpmaps

Kautz, Jan, Chris Wynn, Jonathan Blow, Chris Blasband, Anis Ahmad, and Michael McCool, *Achieving Real-Time Realistic Reflectance, Part 1*, Game Developer, vol. 8, no. 1, pp. 32–37, January 2001.

———, *Achieving Real-Time Realistic Reflectance, Part 2*, Game Developer, vol. 8, no. 2, pp. 38–44, February 2001. http://www.gdmag.com/code.htm

Kerlow, Isaac V., *The Art of 3-D: Computer Animation and Imaging*, 2nd Edition, John Wiley & Sons, New York, 2000.

Kernighan, Brian, and Dennis Ritchie, *The C Programming Language, Second Edition*, Prentice Hall, Englewood Cliffs, New Jersey, 1988.

Kessenich, John, *OpenGL 2.0 Asynchronous OpenGL White Paper*, 3Dlabs, December 2001. http://www.3dlabs.com/support/developer/ogl2

Kessenich, John, Dave Baldwin, and Randi Rost, *The OpenGL Shading Language, Version 1.051*, 3Dlabs, February 2003. http://www.3dlabs.com/support/developer/ogl2

Kilgard, Mark J., *A Practical and Robust Bump-mapping Technique for Today's GPUs*, Game Developers Conference, NVIDIA White Paper, 2000. http://developer.nvidia.com

Kirk, David, ed., *Graphics Gems III*, Academic Press, San Diego, 1992. http://www.acm.org/pubs/tog/GraphicsGems

Lander, Jeff, *Collision Response: Bouncy, Trouncy, Fun*, Game Developer, vol. 6, no. 3, pp. 15–19, March 1999. http://www.darwin3d.com/gdm1999.htm

———, *The Era of Post-Photorealism*, Game Developer, vol. 8, no. 6, pp. 18–22, June 2001.

———, *Graphics Programming and the Tower of Babel*, Game Developer, vol. 8, no. 3, pp. 13–16, March 2001. http://www.gdmag.com/code.htm

———, *Haunted Trees for Halloween*, Game Developer Magazine, vol. 7, no. 11, pp. 17–21, November 2000. http://www.gdmag.com/code.htm

———, *A Heaping Pile of Pirate Booty*, Game Developer, vol. 8, no. 4, pp. 22–30, April 2001.

———, *Images from Deep in the Programmer's Cave*, Game Developer, vol. 8, no. 5, pp. 23–28, May 2001. http://www.gdmag.com/code.htm

———, *The Ocean Spray in Your Face*, Game Developer, vol. 5, no. 7, pp. 13–19, July 1998. http://www.darwin3d.com/gdm1998.htm

———, *Physics on the Back of a Cocktail Napkin*, Game Developer, vol. 6, no. 9, pp. 17–21, September 1999. http://www.darwin3d.com/gdm1999.htm

———, *Return to Cartoon Central*, Game Developer Magazine, vol. 7, no. 8, pp. 9–14, August 2000. http://www.gdmag.com/code.htm

———, *Shades of Disney: Opaquing a 3D World*, Game Developer Magazine, vol. 7, no. 3, pp. 15–20, March 2000. http://www.darwin3d.com/gdm2000.htm

———, *Skin Them Bones: Game Programming for the Web Generation*, Game Developer, vol. 5, no. 5, pp. 11–16, May 1998. http://www.darwin3d.com/gdm1998.htm

———, *Slashing Through Real-Time Character Animation*, Game Developer, vol. 5, no. 4, pp. 13–15, April 1998. http://www.darwin3d.com/gdm1998.htm

———, *That's a Wrap: Texture Mapping Methods*, Game Developer Magazine, vol. 7, no. 10, pp. 21–26, October 2000. http://www.gdmag.com/code.htm

————, *Under the Shade of the Rendering Tree*, Game Developer Magazine, vol. 7, no. 2, pp. 17–21, February 2000. http://www.darwin3d.com/gdm2000.htm

Lasseter, John, *Principles of Traditional Animation Applied to 3D Computer Animation*, Computer Graphics, (SIGGRAPH '87 Proceedings) pp. 35–44, July 1987.

————, *Tricks to Animating Characters with a Computer*, SIGGRAPH '94, Course 1, course notes. http://www.siggraph.org/education/materials/HyperGraph/animation/character_animation/principles/lasseter_s94.htm

Lichtenbelt, Barthold, *Integrating the OpenGL Shading Language*, 3Dlabs internal white paper, July 2003.

————, *OpenGL 2.0 Minimizing Data Movement and Memory Management in OpenGL*, Version 1.2, 3Dlabs, February 2002. http://www.3dlabs.com/support/developer/ogl2

Lindbloom, Bruce J., *Accurate Color Reproduction for Computer Graphics Applications*, Computer Graphics (SIGGRAPH '89 Proceedings), pp. 117–126, July 1989.

————, personal Web site, 2003. http://www.brucelindbloom.com

Litwinowicz, Peter, *Processing Images and Video for an Impressionist Effect*, Computer Graphics (SIGGRAPH '97 Proceedings), pp. 407–414, August 1997.

Lorensen, William E., and Harvey E. Cline, *Marching Cubes: A High Resolution 3D Surface Construction Algorithm*, Computer Graphics (SIGGRAPH '87 Proceedings), pp. 163–169, July 1987.

Malzbender, Tom, Dan Gelb, and Hans Wolters, *Polynomial Texture Maps*, Computer Graphics (SIGGRAPH 2001 Proceedings), pp. 519–528, August 2001.

Mandelbrot, Benoit B., *The Fractal Geometry of Nature, Updated and Augmented*, W. H. Freeman and Company, New York, 1983.

Mark, William R., *Real-Time Shading: Stanford Real-Time Procedural Shading System*, SIGGRAPH 2001, Course 24, course notes, 2001. http://graphics.stanford.edu/projects/shading/pubs/sigcourse2001.pdf

Mark, William R., R. Steven Glanville, Kurt Akeley, and Mark Kilgard, *Cg: A System for Programming Graphics Hardware in a C-like Language*, Computer Graphics (SIGGRAPH 2003 Proceedings), pp. 896–907, July 2003. http://www.cs.utexas.edu/users/billmark/papers/cg

Markosian, Lee, Michael A. Kowalski, Daniel Goldstein, Samuel J. Trychin, John F. Hughes, and Lubomir D. Bourdev, *Real-time Nonphotorealistic Rendering*, Computer Graphics (SIGGRAPH '97 Proceedings), pp. 415–420, August 1997. http://www.cs.princeton.edu/~lem/pubs

McCool, Michael D., *SMASH: A Next-Generation API for Programmable Graphics Accelerators*, Technical Report CS-2000-14, University of Waterloo, August 2000. http://www.cgl.uwaterloo.ca/Projects/rendering/Papers/smash.pdf

McCool, Michael D., Jason Ang, and Anis Ahmad, *Homomorphic Factorization of BRDFs for High-performance Rendering*, Computer Graphics (SIGGRAPH 2001 Proceedings), pp. 171–178, August 2001. http://www.cgl.uwaterloo.ca/Projects/rendering/Papers

McReynolds, Tom, David Blythe, Brad Grantham, and Scott Nelson, *Advanced Graphics Programming Techniques Using OpenGL*, SIGGRAPH '99 course notes, 1999. http://www.opengl.org/developers/code/sig99/index.html

Meier, Barbara J, *Painterly Rendering for Animation*, Computer Graphics (SIGGRAPH '96 Proceedings), pp. 477–484, August 1996. http://citeseer.nj.nec.com/meier96painterly.html

Microsoft, *Advanced Shading and Lighting*, Meltdown 2001, July 2001. http://www.microsoft.com/mscorp/corpevents/meltdown2001/presentations.asp

——, *DirectX 9.0 SDK*, 2003. http://msdn.microsoft.com/directx

Mitchell, Jason L., *Advanced Vertex and Pixel Shader Techniques*, European Game Developers Conference, London, September 2001. http://www.pixelmaven.com/jason

——, *Image Processing with Pixel Shaders in Direct3D*, in Engel, Wolfgang, ed., ShaderX, Wordware, May 2002. http://www.pixelmaven.com/jason

Muchnick, Steven, *Advanced Compiler Design and Implementation*, Morgan Kaufmann Publishers, San Francisco, 1997.

Myler, Harley R., and Arthur R. Weeks, *The Pocket Handbook of Image Processing Algorithms in C*, Prentice Hall, Upper Saddle River, NJ, 1993.

NASA, *Earth Observatory*, Web site. http://earthobservatory.nasa.gov/Newsroom/BlueMarble

Nishita, Tomoyuki, Takao Sirai, Katsumi Tadamura, and Eihachiro Nakamae, *Display of the Earth Taking into Account Atmospheric Scattering*, Computer Graphics (SIGGRAPH '93 Proceedings), pp. 175–182, August 1993. http://nis-lab.is.s.u-tokyo.ac.jp/~nis/abs_sig.html#sig93

NVIDIA developer Web site. http://developer.nvidia.com

NVIDIA Corporation, Cg Toolkit, Release 1.1, software and documentation. http://developer.nvidia.com/Cg

Olano, Marc, and Anselmo Lastra, *A Shading Language on Graphics Hardware: The PixelFlow Shading System*, Computer Graphics (SIGGRAPH '98 Proceedings), pp. 159–168, July 1998. http://www.csee.umbc.edu/~olano/papers

Olano, Marc, John Hart, Wolfgang Heidrich, and Michael McCool, *Real-Time Shading*, A K Peters, Ltd., Natick, Massachusetts, 2002.

OpenGL Architecture Review Board, J. Neider, T. Davis, and M. Woo, *OpenGL Programming Guide, Third Edition: The Official Guide to Learning OpenGL, Version 1.2,* Addison-Wesley, Reading, Massachusetts, 1999.

OpenGL Architecture Review Board, *ARB_fragment_program Extension Specification,* OpenGL Extension Registry. http://oss.sgi.com/projects/ogl-sample/registry

———, *ARB_fragment_shader Extension Specification,* OpenGL Extension Registry. http://oss.sgi.com/projects/ogl-sample/registry

———, *ARB_shader_objects Extension Specification,* OpenGL Extension Registry. http://oss.sgi.com/projects/ogl-sample/registry

———, *ARB_vertex_program Extension Specification,* OpenGL Extension Registry. http://oss.sgi.com/projects/ogl-sample/registry

———, *ARB_vertex_shader Extension Specification,* OpenGL Extension Registry. http://oss.sgi.com/projects/ogl-sample/registry

———, *OpenGL Reference Manual, Third Edition: The Official Reference Document to OpenGL, Version 1.2,* Addison-Wesley, Reading, Massachusetts, 1999.

OpenGL, official Web site. http://opengl.org

Owen, G. Scott, *Computer Animation,* Web site. http://www.siggraph.org/education/materials/HyperGraph/animation/anim0.htm

Parent, Rick, *Computer Animation: Algorithms and Techniques,* Morgan Kaufmann Publishers, San Francisco, 2001. http://www.cis.ohio-state.edu/~parent/book/outline.html

Peachey, Darwyn, *Solid Texturing of Complex Surfaces,* Computer Graphics (SIGGRAPH '85 Proceedings), pp. 279–286, July 1985.

Peercy, Mark S., Marc Olano, John Airey, and P. Jeffrey Ungar, *Interactive Multi-Pass Programmable Shading,* Computer Graphics (SIGGRAPH 2000 Proceedings), pp. 425–432, July 2000. http://www.csee.umbc.edu/~olano/papers

Peitgen, Heinz-Otto, and P. H. Richter, *The Beauty of Fractals, Images of Complex Dynamical Systems,* Springer Verlag, Berlin Heidelberg, 1986.

Peitgen, Heinz-Otto, D. Saupe, M. F. Barnsley, R. L. Devaney, B. B. Mandelbrot, and R. F. Voss, *The Science of Fractal Images,* Springer Verlag, New York, 1988.

Perlin, Ken, *An Image Synthesizer,* Computer Graphics (SIGGRAPH '85 Proceedings), pp. 287–296, July 1985.

———, *Improving Noise,* Computer Graphics (SIGGRAPH 2002 Proceedings), pp. 681–682, July 2002. http://mrl.nyu.edu/perlin/paper445.pdf

———, personal Web site. http://www.noisemachine.com

———, personal Web site. http://mrl.nyu.edu/~perlin

Phong, Bui Tuong, *Illumination for Computer Generated Pictures*, Communications of the ACM, vol. 18, no. 6, pp. 311–317, June 1975.

Pixar, *The RenderMan Interface Specification*, Version 3.2, Pixar, July 2000. https://renderman.pixar.com/products/rispec/index.htm

Porter, Thomas, and Tom Duff, *Compositing Digital Images*, Computer Graphics (SIGGRAPH '84 Proceedings), pp. 253–259, July 1984.

Poulin, P., and A. Fournier, *A Model for Anisotropic Reflection*, Computer Graphics (SIGGRAPH '90 Proceedings), pp. 273–282, August 1990.

Poynton, Charles A., *Frequently Asked Questions about Color*, 1997. http://www.poynton.com/Poynton-color.html

———, *Frequently Asked Questions about Gamma*, 1997. http://www.poynton.com/Poynton-color.html

———, *A Technical Introduction to Digital Video*, John Wiley & Sons, New York, 1996.

Praun, Emil, Adam Finkelstein, and Hugues Hoppe, *Lapped Textures*, Computer Graphics (SIGGRAPH 2000 Proceedings), pp. 465–470, July 2000. http://www.cs.princeton.edu/gfx/proj/lapped_tex

Praun, Emil, Hugues Hoppe, Matthew Webb, and Adam Finkelstein, *Real-time Hatching*, Computer Graphics (SIGGRAPH 2000 Proceedings), pp. 581–586, August 2001. http://www.cs.princeton.edu/gfx/proj/hatching

Proakis, John G., and Dimitris G. Manolakis, *Digital Signal Processing: Principles, Algorithms, and Applications, Third Edition*, Prentice Hall, Upper Saddle River, New Jersey, 1995.

Proudfoot, Kekoa, *Version 5 Real-Time Shading Language Description*, Game Developers Conference, pp. 131–135, March 2001. http://www.gdconf.com/archives/proceedings/2001/prog_papers.html

Proudfoot, Kekoa, William R. Mark, Svetoslav Tzvetkov, and Pat Hanrahan, *A Real-Time Procedural Shading System for Programmable Graphics Hardware*, Computer Graphics (SIGGRAPH 2001 Proceedings), pp. 159–170, August 2001. http://graphics.stanford.edu/projects/shading/pubs/sig2001

Purcell, Timothy J., Ian Buck, William R. Mark, and Pat Hanrahan, *Ray Tracing on Programmable Graphics Hardware*, Computer Graphics (SIGGRAPH 2002 Proceedings), July 2002. http://www-graphics.stanford.edu/papers/rtongfx

Raskar, Ramesh, and Michael Cohen, *Image Precision Silhouette Edges*, Proceedings 1999 Symposium on Interactive 3D Graphics, pp. 135–140, April 1999. http://www.cs.unc.edu/~raskar/NPR

Raskar, Ramesh, *Hardware Support for Non-photorealistic Rendering*, ACM SIGGRAPH/Eurographics Workshop on Graphics Hardware, pp. 41–46, 2001. http://www.cs.unc.edu/~raskar/HWWS

Reeves, William T., *Particle Systems—A Technique for Modeling a Class of Fuzzy Objects*, ACM Transactions on Graphics, vol. 2, no. 2, pp. 91–108, April 1983.

Reeves, William T., and Ricki Blau, *Approximate and Probabilistic Algorithms for Shading and Rendering Structured Particle Systems*, Computer Graphics (SIGGRAPH '85 Proceedings), pp. 313–322, July 1985.

Reeves, William T., David H. Salesin, and Robert L. Cook, *Rendering Antialiased Shadows with Depth Maps*, Computer Graphics (SIGGRAPH '87 Proceedings), pp. 283–291, July 1987.

Reynolds, Craig, *Stylized Depiction in Computer Graphics*, Web site. http://www.red3d.com/cwr/npr

Rost, Randi, *OpenGL 2.0 Overview, Version 1.2*, 3Dlabs, February 2002. http://www.3dlabs.com/support/developer/ogl2

———, *OpenGL 2.0 Pixel Pipeline, Version 1.2*, 3Dlabs, February 2002. http://www.3dlabs.com/support/developer/ogl2

———, *Using OpenGL for Imaging*, SPIE Medical Imaging '96 Image Display Conference, February 1996. http://3dshaders.com/pubs

Rost, Randi, and Barthold Lichtenbelt, *OpenGL 2.0 Objects*, Version 1.2, February 2002. http://www.3dlabs.com/support/developer/ogl2

Salisbury, Michael, Sean E. Anderson, Ronen Barzel, and David H. Salesin, *Interactive Pen-and-Ink Illustration*, Computer Graphics (SIGGRAPH '94 Proceedings), pp. 101–108, July 1994. http://grail.cs.washington.edu/pub

Salisbury, Michael, *Image-Based Pen-and-Ink Illustration*, Ph.D. thesis, University of Washington, 1997. http://grail.cs.washington.edu/theses

Saito, Takafumi, and Tokiichiro Takahashi, *Comprehensible Rendering of 3-D Shapes*, Computer Graphics (SIGGRAPH '90 Proceedings), pp. 197–206, August 1990.

Schneider, Philip, and David Eberly, *Geometric Tools for Computer Graphics*, Morgan Kaufmann Publishers, San Francisco, 2002.

Segal, Mark, C. Korobkin, R. van Widenfelt, J. Foran, and P. Haeberli, *Fast Shadows and Lighting Effects Using Texture Mapping*, Computer Graphics (SIGGRAPH '92 Proceedings), pp. 249–252, July 1992.

Segal, Mark, and Kurt Akeley, *The Design of the OpenGL Graphics Interface*, Silicon Graphics Inc., 1994. http://www.opengl.org/developers/documentation/papers.html

———, *The OpenGL Graphics System: A Specification (Version 1.5)*, Editor (v1.1): Chris Frazier, Editor (v1.2–1.5): Jon Leech, July 2003. http://opengl.org

SGI OpenGL Web site. http://www.sgi.com/software/opengl

SGI OpenGL Shader Web site. http://www.sgi.com/software/shader

SIGGRAPH Proceedings, Web site of online materials. http://portal.acm.org.

Sillion, François, and Claude Puech, *Radiosity and Global Illumination*, Morgan Kaufmann Publishers, San Francisco, 1994.

Sloup, Jaroslav, *Physically-based simulation: A Survey of the Modelling and Rendering of the Earth's Atmosphere*, Proceedings of the 18th Spring Conference on Computer Graphics, pp. 141–150, April 2002. http://sgi.felk.cvut.cz/~sloup/html/research/project

Smith, Alvy Ray, *Color Gamut Transform Pairs*, Computer Graphics (SIGGRAPH '78 Proceedings), pp. 12–19, August 1978. http://www.alvyray.com

————, *Digital Filtering Tutorial for Computer Graphics*, Lucasfilm Technical Memo 27, revised March 1983. http://www.alvyray.com/Memos/MemosPixar.htm

————, *Digital Filtering Tutorial, Part II*, Lucasfilm Technical Memo 27, revised March 1983. http://www.alvyray.com/Memos/MemosPixar.htm

————, *A Pixel Is Not a Little Square, A Pixel Is Not a Little Square, A Pixel Is Not a Little Square! (And a Voxel is Not a Little Cube)*, Technical Memo 6, Microsoft Research, July 1995. http://www.alvyray.com/Papers/PapersCG.htm

SMPTE RP 177–1993, *Derivation of Basic Television Color Equations*.

Stokes, Michael, Matthew Anderson, Srinivasan Chandrasekar, and Ricardo Motta, *A Standard Default Color Space for the Internet—sRGB*, Version 1.10, November 1996. http://www.color.org/sRGB.html

Stone, Maureen, *A Survey of Color for Computer Graphics*, Course 4 at SIGGRAPH 2001, August 2001. http://www.stonesc.com

Strothotte, Thomas, and S. Schlectweg, *Non-Photorealistic Computer Graphics, Modeling, Rendering, and Animation*, Morgan Kaufmann Publishers, San Francisco, 2002.

Stroustrup, Bjarne, *The C++ Programming Language (Special 3rd Edition)*, Addison-Wesley, Reading, Massachusetts, 2000.

Thomas, Frank, and Ollie Johnston, *Disney Animation—The Illusion of Life*, Abbeville Press, New York, 1981.

————, *The Illusion of Life—Disney Animation, Revised Edition*, Hyperion, 1995.

Torrance, K., and E. Sparrow, *Theory for Off-Specular Reflection from Roughened Surfaces*, J. Optical Society of America, vol. 57, September 1967.

Tufte, Edward, *Visual Explanations*, Graphics Press, Cheshire, Connecticut, 1997.

Upstill, Steve, *The RenderMan Companion: A Programmer's Guide to Realistic Computer Graphics*, Addison-Wesley, Reading, Massachusetts, 1990.

Verbeck, Channing P., and D. Greenberg, *A Comprehensive Light Source Description for Computer Graphics*, IEEE Computer Graphics and Applications 4(7): pp. 66–75.

Ward, Gregory, *Measuring and Modeling Anisotropic Reflection*, Computer Graphics (SIGGRAPH '92 Proceedings), pp. 265–272, July 1992. http://radsite.lbl.gov/radiance/papers/sg92/paper.html

Watt, Alan H., and Mark Watt, *Advanced Animation and Rendering Techniques: Theory and Practice,* Addison-Wesley, Reading, Massachusetts, 1992.

Whitted, Turner, *An Improved Illumination Model for Shaded Display,* Communications of the ACM 23(6): pp. 343–349.

Williams, Lance, *Pyramidal Parametrics*, Computer Graphics (SIGGRAPH '83 Proceedings), pp. 1–11, July 1983.

Winkenbach, Georges, and David Salesin, *Computer-Generated Pen-and-Ink Illustration*, Computer Graphics (SIGGRAPH '94 Proceedings), pp. 91–100, July 1994. http://grail.cs.washington.edu/pub

Winkenbach, Georges, *Computer-Generated Pen-and-Ink Illustration*, Ph.D. Dissertation, University of Washington, 1996. http://grail.cs.washington.edu/theses

Wolberg, George, *Digital Image Warping*, Wiley-IEEE Press, 2002.

Wright, Richard, and Michael Sweet, *OpenGL SuperBible, Second Edition,* Waite Group Press, Corte Madera, California, 1999. http://www.starstonesoftware.com/OpenGL/opengl_superbbile.htm

Wright, Richard, *Understanding and Using OpenGL Texture Objects*, Gamasutra, July 23, 1999. http://www.gamasutra.com/features/19990723/opengl_texture_objects_01.htm

Zwillinger, Dan, *CRC Standard Mathematical Tables and Formulas*, 30th Edition, CRC Press, 1995. http://geom.math.uiuc.edu/docs/reference/CRC-formulas/

Index

informIT

YOUR GUIDE TO IT REFERENCE

Articles

Keep your edge with thousands of free articles, in-depth features, interviews, and IT reference recommendations – all written by experts you know and trust.

Online Books

Answers in an instant from **InformIT Online Book's** 600+ fully searchable on line books. For a limited time, you can get your first 14 days **free**.

POWERED BY

Safari®
TECH BOOKS ONLINE®

Catalog

Review online sample chapters, author biographies and customer rankings and choose exactly the right book from a selection of over 5,000 titles.

Register Your Book

at www.awprofessional.com/register

You may be eligible to receive:

- Advance notice of forthcoming editions of the book
- Related book recommendations
- Chapter excerpts and supplements of forthcoming titles
- Information about special contests and promotions throughout the year
- Notices and reminders about author appearances, tradeshows, and online chats with special guests

Contact us

If you are interested in writing a book or reviewing manuscripts prior to publication, please write to us at:

Editorial Department
Addison-Wesley Professional
75 Arlington Street, Suite 300
Boston, MA 02116 USA
Email: AWPro@aw.com

Addison-Wesley

Visit us on the Web: http://www.awprofessional.com